PROMISE AND PERIL

PROMISE
— AND —
PERIL

America at the Dawn of a Global Age

CHRISTOPHER M^cKNIGHT NICHOLS

HARVARD UNIVERSITY PRESS
Cambridge, Massachusetts, and London, England
2011

Library of Congress Cataloging-in-Publication Data

Nichols, Christopher McKnight.
Promise and peril : America at the dawn of a global age / Christopher McKnight Nichols.
p.   cm.
Includes bibliographical references and index.
ISBN 978-0-674-04984-0 (alk. paper)
1. United States—Foreign relations—1865–1921.   2. United States—Foreign relations—
1921–1923.   3. United States—Foreign relations—1923–1929.   4. United States—Foreign
relations—1929–1933.   5. United States—Foreign relations—1933–1945.   6. Isolationism—United
States—History.   7. Geopolitics—United States—History.   I. Title.
E744.N497   2011
327.73—dc22   2010045000

For Carolyn, Rod, and Lily

CONTENTS

INTRODUCTION: THE OSTRICH AND THE EAGLE

In his 2006 State of the Union address, President George W. Bush repeatedly used the terms "isolation" and "isolationism." He described the dangers of a "retreat within our borders" and ominously depicted isolationists as a group bent on leaving an "assaulted world to fend for itself." "In a complex and challenging time," said the president, "the road of isolationism and protectionism may seem broad and inviting—yet it ends in danger and decline."[1] From his comments a listener might have been led to believe that a battle was raging in American politics between walled-and-bounded isolationists and nation-building internationalists. Was it a case of the ostrich versus the eagle?[2]

One striking aspect of the speech is the power that the word "isolationist" still possesses in our national dialogue. Such a depiction of isolationism was a clever application of a century-old political technique. Like so many others before him, President Bush sought to deploy the dichotomy that pits isolation against international commitment, trading on the negative connotations of the country looking inward. But that formulation misconstrues the rich complexity of the origins of isolationism.

Not all calls for prudence in foreign affairs can be cast in the same light. There always is promise as well as peril when a nation engages internationally or chooses to focus on domestic concerns. Adhering to narrow binaries of "isolation versus internationalism," however, blinds us to the reality of the far more complicated and interesting history of these issues. Intricate blendings of political positions and coalitions have been evolving ever since the United States first aimed to meet the challenges of becoming a world power. Over the past several centuries the "sage advice" about limitations on the nation's role in the world provided by George Washington, Thomas Jefferson, and James Monroe has been construed as leading in different directions. This evidence, in turn, has been mustered to support positions on global involvement and their relation to

1

domestic affairs offered by Americans from across the full spectrum of political persuasions.

In recent years, however, scholars and politicians have emphasized global connections. In so doing, historians, foreign policy thinkers, and political leaders have tended to overlook the significance of ideas about isolation to American history and to the United States' place in the world. A deeper investigation into the tangled elements of isolationism as it became "modern" at the turn of the twentieth century reveals that isolationism did not entail cultural, economic, or complete political separation from the rest of the world. So, although such a separation from the world is the first proposition that comes to mind when discussing those who favored isolationism, it also is the first conception that must be dismissed. In the historical debates about isolation, the very definition of America and the ways in which the nation should interact with the world have been at stake. The inner logic of isolationist arguments turned on the inner life of the nation and on visions of national self-definition, serving to reinforce many, albeit limited, forms of international engagement.

Most prominent Americans at the end of the nineteenth century did not favor complete withdrawal from the world. They knew it was not feasible. Isolationist and interventionist tendencies were not pitted simply against each other in political debates about the nation's encounter with modernity and the world from 1890 to 1940. What sometimes appears to have been a zero-sum conflict between the two approaches emerges upon closer inspection as a more nuanced struggle. Many thinkers and politicians conceived and debated subtle hybrids of these approaches as the nation emerged as a global power. Those with dreams of imperial grandeur combated others advocating domestic reforms; some even made the case that empire was a type of reform. As a result, variant isolationist viewpoints developed and echoed the nation's tempestuous debates as America advanced through the Gilded Age and Progressive Era to World War I and beyond.

"The genius of our institutions," said President Grover Cleveland, "the needs of our people in their home life, and the attention which is demanded for the settlement and development of the resources of our vast territory dictate the scrupulous avoidance of any departure from that foreign policy commended by the history, the traditions, and the prosperity of our Republic." Cleveland went on to define such politics as focused inwardly on domestic economic and political progress. He saw these changes as best supported by a stance of "neutrality, rejecting any share in foreign broils and ambitions upon other continents and repelling their intrusions here." It is, he said, the "policy of Monroe and of Washington and Jefferson—'Peace, commerce, and honest friendship with all nations; entangling alliance with none.'"[3]

These words come from Cleveland's first inaugural address in 1885. That he invoked three iconic Founding Fathers should come as no surprise. He did so—as have many others favoring, opposing, and adapting isolationist arguments—to leverage their authority and to underscore the historical roots of his vision for the nation. Yet Cleveland also realized that the definitions of frontiers and interdependence were changing rapidly in the late nineteenth century. He and other astute observers of the day perceived that the foundational axioms of Washington, Jefferson, and Monroe were important but antiquated. Cleveland and others believed America's "traditional" policy had to be updated to meet the new challenges posed by an industrial society and the nation's burgeoning global commercial and military power.

The final waves of expansion across the continent and the first pushes to annex lands abroad sparked renewed interest in the nature and direction of Manifest Destiny, nearly a half century after the idea was first expressed by the journalist John O'Sullivan in 1845. A series of debates over expansion followed. With new ideas about frontiers and a new commitment to the mission of completing continental expansion came a major shift in how Americans conceived of where and why isolation might begin and end. The flashpoint came with the 1890 American census. Popularized by Frederick Jackson Turner, the census revealed for the first time that the nation finally had filled all of the open spaces within its boundaries. Though population density was paltry in many areas, continental Manifest Destiny appeared to have been fulfilled. That led many Americans to ask, "What now?"

Within the heady dynamism of the 1880s and 1890s the United States was confronted with new questions. As Americans grappled with issues of isolation and international engagement, they debated four related concerns, all of which sound familiar today. What should be the nation's proper relationship to and with the world? How should domestic priorities be weighed against international ones? Were international engagement and domestic improvement at odds, or could they be made compatible?

Could diplomatic and military isolation serve the national interest in an era of dynamically intermingled economies, rising American power, and the potential necessity to intervene abroad to "meet" or "overcome" threats of imperialism, humanitarian concerns, and war?

These questions constitute the focal points of the debates that blended ideas about isolation with new perspectives on internationalism from the 1890s through the 1940s. The various answers offered for these and related questions intersected with new circumstances, new visions of nationhood, and fresh perceptions of the relation between domestic and global imperatives. Amid heated debates about these central issues, modern isolationism developed in tension with emerging views of internationalism and domestic reform.

As Cleveland's comments indicate, there were three main foundational moments, or policy pillars, for American isolationism. These began with George Washington in his oft-referenced Farewell Address of 1796. Yet even before that speech Washington had established the nation's neutrality as a formal policy tradition with the Proclamation of Neutrality (1793) and the Neutrality Act (1794). These neutrality declarations ran contrary to the alliance with France, which had helped win the Revolutionary War. They officially sought to distance the United States from allies and enemies alike and laid out the guiding principle that America would pursue "a conduct friendly and impartial towards the Belligerent powers." Washington's Farewell Address, partly written by Alexander Hamilton along with James Madison and read in Congress almost every year until quite recently, set the explicitly isolationist tone that became the basis for virtually all subsequent invocations of an isolationist "tradition." Washington built on this notion of the new nation as neutral and impartial when he put forward the classic formulation:

> The great rule of conduct for us, in regard to foreign nations, is in extending our commercial relations, to have with them as little political connection as possible. . . . Europe has a set of primary interests, which to us have none, or a very remote relation. Hence she must be engaged in frequent controversies the causes of which are essentially foreign to our concern. . . . Therefore, it must be unwise in us to implicate ourselves, by artificial ties, in the ordinary vicissitudes of her politics, or the ordinary combinations and collisions of her friendships or enmities.[4]

These Washingtonian principles did not turn the nation away from the world but, as many scholars have noted, formed the crux of foreign policy realism and argued for a cautious sense of America's international role and for choosing "war or peace, as our interest, guided by justice, shall counsel."[5] Washington took into account the inherent fragility of American power and the nation's precarious place in the world, emphasizing America's distant geographical position as a key to strategic separation and as a brake on involvement in Europe's hazardous political system. These views were then established as precedent by John Adams and reaffirmed by Thomas Jefferson, who allayed the fears of many Federalists when he underscored a shared set of Washingtonian-Adamsian foreign policy principles in his own inaugural address in 1801.[6] Jefferson asserted this ideal as "peace, commerce, and honest friendship with all nations, entangling alliances with none." Jefferson held a clear belief, reflected in his *Notes on the State of Virginia* (1787) and growing out of his extensive European travels, in American-European foreign policy dualism. His view was grounded on the practicality of a type of isolation, which he defined as having no enduring alliances with the Old World and as steering clear of Europe's petty squabbles. Jefferson's daring and farsighted purchase of the Louisiana Territory in 1803 propelled the great mission of continental expansion and improvement, doubling the nation's territory. And of course the Purchase limited the amount of North American land that European powers could claim or conquer. When regarded in this light, his unilateralist efforts were consistent with the idea of isolation as a guarantee toward maintaining and protecting national sovereignty while avoiding entanglements such as those that Ben Franklin derisively termed Europe's "romantick Continental Connections."[7]

The isolationist torch still burned brightly in 1823, when President James Monroe pronounced his doctrine. An ambitious articulation of American hemispheric power, the Monroe Doctrine evolved as the guiding view for later isolationists who agreed that unilateral involvement across the Americas was perfectly legitimate, but that beyond the Western Hemisphere the nation should avoid foreign wars and the corruptions of particularly Old World political intrigue. As Monroe put it, "In the wars of the European powers, in matters relating to themselves, we have never taken part, nor does it comport with our policy, so to do. It is only when our rights are invaded, or seriously menaced that we resent injuries, or make preparations for our defense." He centered this argument on what he saw as an

5

obvious fact: "With the movements in this hemisphere we are of necessity more immediately connected," and therefore he declared that "we should consider any attempt on their part to extend their system to any portion of this hemisphere as dangerous to our peace and safety."[8]

Thus, in three bold strokes Washington, Jefferson, and Monroe laid out the essential isolationist mode of thinking about their young nation's most advantageous relationship to the world. These arguments became the benchmarks that a broad range of subsequent politicians, thinkers, and citizens later had to confront as they built their own cases for engagement abroad and justified their developing visions of internationalism. One point is clear about interpreting the meaning of their words in their own time. This dedicated triad of America's founders articulated a commerce-first form of unilateralism and a sense of cautious realism, which at its most fundamental level sought to protect their fledgling nation by favoring isolation from almost all entangling alliances as well as conflicts abroad, particularly those involving Europe.[9]

But times change, and so did the nation. A dynamic escalation in the nation's power at the end of the nineteenth century precipitated a major reorientation of its earlier isolationist stance. This transformation affected every level of society and permeated the nation's politics. For the first time in American history the country was capable of taking significant international action as a commercial force and as an imperial power. The United States *could* be like the colonial powers of Europe. It was now a national choice. Industrialization and modernization had radically shifted America's traditional isolationist calculus.

Was the time ripe to openly cast off these archaic values? If so, what should replace them? Should America colonize "available" portions of the Caribbean and South America, the Pacific, Asia, and Africa? Observing sweeping local and global transformations in light of these questions, many Americans recognized that their country should—indeed, had to— play a major international role. But what role should it be? And how would engaging with the world influence society at home?

William James's understanding of personal philosophy—as a way of seeing, understanding, and deriving meaning from the myriad pushes and pulls of society and lived experience—can be used to sort out these roiling political debates as they unfolded and soon gave rise to revised understandings of isolationism. Resembling Jamesian pragmatism, the modern framework for conceiving isolationism represented a new political philosophy and originated in the same fin de siècle era. It was philosophical but also practical in ways that had not been recognized before. Not only did it guide perspectives on how the United States ought to operate in the world, but it also shaped thinking and actions about balancing foreign and domestic priorities. In many ways the developing isolationist worldview represented less an "it" than a "they"—a cluster of related ideas based on a premise of updating, but limiting, U.S. international involvement while hearkening back to specific historical precedents as justification. New refinements of isolationist thought explicitly confronted the challenges of modernity and called for engaging the world economically and often culturally. The concept of isolation also continued to herald avoiding virtually all binding foreign alliances or commitments of military and diplomatic force, except in the nation's "best interest," an idea often vehemently contested because it was clearly open to interpretation. In some ways this was a cosmopolitan isolationism (rather than the more realist isolationism of the early republic), debated and updated to fit the needs of an increasingly powerful and internationally engaged U.S. global position.

In the period after the Civil War and before the Second World War, three pivotal transitions took place during which Americans debated new modes of acting in the world. At stake in all of them were the intense promise and the acute peril of directing American commitment abroad. The first was prompted by the initial convulsions of war and empire in the 1890s. The second featured the debates over eventual American entry into World War I in 1917. The third concerned the attempts after World War I to create idealistic international organizations to make the world safe for democracy. Modern isolationist ideas were central in determining outcomes of these events. The cluster of isolationist ideas—opposing colonialism and entangling alliances, while advocating neutrality and minimizing wars—set the ideological parameters for those on all sides of the debates over America's global involvement.

Isolationist ideas collided with calls for the nation to accept greater internationalism while undertaking extensive domestic reform from the Gilded Age and Progressive Era through the Second World War. Rather than simply negating engagement, the refined isolationist views that developed in the 1890s came to support international commerce and cultural exchanges as well as modest humanitarian intervention abroad with the aim of acting as a moral beacon to the world. Linking nationhood and

ideas about domestic reforms, these roots in the anti-imperialist movement provided a "progressive" cast to later isolationist arguments. The
newer strains of isolationist thought that emerged in the 1890s were vigorously debated, then reshaped in the 1910s, and coalesced by the 1920s and
1930s into a more coherent set of isolationist positions that strengthened
an inclination toward isolation yet combined it with America's new power
to advocate for limited global involvement. Most significant, from the
1890s through the 1930s isolationist ideas operated as a positive view of
adhering to and updating democratic ideals and traditions, blending foreign and domestic perspectives. Yet these ideas also operated as a politico-
intellectual brake that prevented visions of American empire and Wilsonian internationalism from being fully realized.

Tracing the history of isolationist ideas in the 1890s reveals many unexpected connections among the key individuals and groups who developed
hybrid forms of isolationist internationalism. By the 1910s the crucial developing tension was between an emerging transnationalism, a view of
the connections between peoples and groups across (and sometimes regardless of) national boundaries, and American nationalism, which prized
assimilation to American cultural norms and placed the state as paramount. This became most clear during the wartime years from 1914
through 1919, as the dialogue turned into a conflict between these views.
Ideas about isolation generated a vital connection in these debates between internal efforts to direct reform and resources and the external
projection of American power. In the years following World War I isolationist positions regarding nationalism and transnationalism formed a crucial
touchpoint for politicians, thinkers, and reformers in framing their understandings of America's proper global role.[10] As this malleable isolationist
stance gained prominence among proponents and opponents alike, its
many braids provided the basis not just for the significant foreign policy
arguments of the era but also for the vibrancy as well as the negative connotations that the term "isolationism" still possesses today.

Representative figures—ranging from nationalist to radical politicians,
cultural critics to women's suffragists, pacifists and missionaries to racial
reformers—help to illuminate the multiple shades of isolationism. The
group in this book and their wider community of supporters and opponents
includes Massachusetts Republican Senator Henry Cabot Lodge, Harvard
philosopher and psychologist William James, sociologist and racial reformer

W. E. B. Du Bois, YMCA ecumenical leader John Mott, progressive settlement house pioneer and peace activist Jane Addams, cultural critic
Randolph Bourne, socialist leader Eugene Debs, Idaho Republican Senator and staunch isolationist William Borah, and political economist and
international pacifist organizer Emily Balch. Each of these individuals
represents a distinct strain of isolationist thought and provides a window
onto larger groups of people who followed, opposed, or were influenced by
them. Each also spearheaded a wider group with a national—and often an
international—platform, striving to reconcile America's founding isolationist ideals with the realities of America's expanding affluence, rising global
commerce, and multiplying international opportunities for cultural exchange
and the protection of rights. Mostly prominent progressives and progressive-
minded thinkers, largely middle and upper class, they spanned fields as
diverse as mainstream and radical politics, mission and settlement house
work, philosophy, and cultural criticism. Tracing the developing ideas of
these diverse figures reveals that isolationism had progressive origins in the
imperialist/anti-imperialist disputes of the 1890s, a generation earlier than
previous historians have noted.

But why then? The late nineteenth century in which modern isolationist ideas originated provided an environment well suited to reenvisioning
America's place in the world. It was a vibrant era, filled with assertive
nation-states and violently competing nationalisms, all undergoing intensive intellectual and socioeconomic transformation as well as political
disruptions. New financial initiatives in corporate capitalism created, and
were fed by, vertical and horizontal integration in industry on an unprecedented scale. These developments were accompanied by other processes
that shaped modernity: urbanization, a burgeoning popular media, ad-
vances in mass literacy, rapid developments in new technology, and a
growing faith in the "scientific approach."[11]

During this period the sweeping forces of industrialization, globalization, and technological innovation propelled some of the most dynamic
social and economic changes in American history, which in turn led to
new visions of politics. Transatlantic as well as global movements of peoples and ideas, such as those about social democracy and reform, helped
many to find new, public ways to express their private concerns. Evidence
of the nation's social maladjustment was everywhere. Fortunes of capital
and labor increased in vastly inverse proportions in an age popularized
for its "robber barons." The concentrations of corporations and trusts

mushroomed, leading to the country's high internal mobility as well as decreasing independence for workers. Traditionalists lamented the erosion of what they saw as essential religious and community affiliations. All of these factors marked the key characteristics of the new, modern American society. Prices fell; real wages rose; and yet the nation experienced a series of severe economic downturns from 1873 to 1897. The new circumstances—of an urbanizing industrial nation that had recently survived a catastrophic civil war—cast serious doubt on established ideas about politics and progress from across the spectrum. Confronting these economic, social, and intellectual changes, American leaders groped toward new positions about liberty, equality, justice, democracy, and social change.

The result was a growing emphasis on political reform, which flowed from new philosophies seeking to reimpose the norms of personal conscience and responsibility on the chaos of mass society. With industrial modernization driving much of this transformation, new ideas, such as pragmatism and religious freethinking, and an array of new reform movements, such as progressive suffrage and settlement house reforms, developed as ways to solve the pressing problems of labor, race, and gender injustice, social dislocation, immigration, and the apparent moral decay that seemed to be resulting from the modern forces reshaping American life.

Amid the tumultuous fits and starts of modernization, the United States' ascent to commercial and global power produced new calls for America to be more active in the world, to possess a foreign empire, and to increase access to markets abroad. Isolationism was called into question by such claims. The more industrial growth was heralded, and the more international engagement in commerce, ideas, and technology became fundamental to American life, the more pressing were concerns about the costs and benefits of such a transition. Many Americans wondered whether modernity was worth its price. If it was not, they asked: how and what would make modern America better?[12]

In the midst of trying to address these questions and confront new social challenges, modern isolationism originated in the 1890s in the disputes between imperialists and anti-imperialists over American expansionism and the Spanish-American War. Most imperialists claimed that the United States needed to expand abroad to acquire strategic coaling stations and harbors in the Atlantic, Caribbean, and Pacific. They argued this primarily on the basis of political economy and new power. The nation, they declared, required greater access to economic markets in Asia and across South America. In turn, imperialists made the case that this could be accomplished best by acquiring colonial territories and strategic positions, and by building a larger navy, on the model of the European powers.

The ensuing ways of viewing and refining isolationism found many advocates—particularly, of course, among the anti-imperialists—who made their claims against expansion on a more philosophical and abstract basis of democratic ideals, anticolonialism and self-rule, as well as against neo-mercantilist economics, for various sorts of economic rather than imperial internationalism, and for what they deemed a pressing need for domestic reform. Alongside these views developed a barely visible "soft" power form of international engagement. Though it was less outwardly coercive than British or most other European colonial models, and fell far below Theodore Roosevelt's preferred bellicose expansion, there remained an undoubtedly coercive element to nonmilitaristic American imperial economic and cultural engagement. New perspectives on the ability to achieve productive international objectives without direct state applications of power emerged in the same era alongside new nationalist visions of expansionism. Views about the ability to achieve national ends via cooperation, co-optation, and attraction (all soft power approaches) came to enable as well as constrain modern isolationist beliefs, often by making economic rather than diplomatic or military engagement central to U.S. global involvement.[13] Most of the individuals advocating these new positions on the place of the United States in the world at the end of the nineteenth century perceived the inextricable interconnection of diplomatic, military, and economic engagement. They knew such interactions were multilateral as well as reciprocal. However, opponents of imperialism and interventionism generally did not see their aims as obviating trade. In fact, most hoped that limited imperialism would lead to greater trade opportunities at lower costs. They also did not tend to identify themselves as isolationists, or when they did, the reference was infrequent and often in passing. In part the reasons for this are obvious—to be an avowed proponent of "isolationism" in 1900 would not have been possible. It would be anachronistic to say that proto-isolationists at the turn of the century subscribed to an ideology that had not been coined yet.

Nevertheless, the ideas originated in their modern form during the debates over empire in which the word "isolation" figured prominently and the concept of "national isolation" was critical for both expansionists and their opponents. Although the anti-imperialist-isolationist views could not prevent the annexation of several territories after the Spanish-American War and later when the nation contemplated joining World War I, modern isolationist arguments were pivotal to creating the conditions that limited imperialism, inhibited continued territorial annexation, and undermined Wilson's idealistic worldview of collective security via American leadership in the League of Nations. As they gained clarity, isolationist positions increasingly presented a set of alternatives to interventionism.[14]

During World War I, nationalism, the quashing of dissent, and rising patriotic fervor to join the war made many isolationists briefly fall silent. Competing versions of internationalism and a new transnational position that favored connecting cultures and peoples across borders also came under attack during the war years. Any such opposition to the war was subject to persecution by federal, state, and local governments, as well as hypervigilant citizens and so-called patriotic organizations. In the wake of the conflict, though, the ranks of isolationists and those who subscribed to at least some tenets of a broadly isolationist worldview increased dramatically. To these leaders and to many Americans the war seemed not to have been worth the price. Innovative isolationists seized on this belief during the 1920s and 1930s to crystallize their position into a more powerful sociopolitical force. Retreat from international military and diplomatic commitments soon became increasingly popular. In the course of these transformations of society—most evident just before and after the Spanish-American War and World War I—the varied tenets of isolationism and internationalism developed in tandem and sometimes among unlikely allies.

To understand the key origins, debates, and variations on isolationist thought, we should consider the connections between the ideas and actions of such disparate figures as Henry Cabot Lodge and Eugene Debs. Lodge, the reserved Boston Brahmin and emphatically conservative Republican senator, reoriented the iconic Washingtonian-Jeffersonian view of the purposes of national isolation to help justify his aim of international expansion. Yet, surprisingly, he found common ground with the radical socialist labor activist and five-time presidential candidate Debs, who was an international socialist and despised American expansionism. Both men shared an innate understanding of the problems of their time and started from the same basic worldview: they believed their nation had become entangled in what they termed a "global civilization." Lodge and Debs maintained that the benefits of global involvement could be gained only if "traditional" isolationist views and outdated conceptions of the national interest were abandoned or reformulated. Although they agreed on casting off long-standing notions of how America ought to interact with the world, this in no way implied that they concurred about the means or the ends of what a new model of America in the world—or at home—ought to look like.

Lodge diverged radically from Debs when he sought to expand the nation unilaterally in the war with Spain in 1898. Always nationalistic and procapitalist in his rhetoric, Lodge abhorred socialism and most of what Debs stood for. Lodge aimed to update traditional ideas about isolation, such as the Monroe Doctrine's articulation of American hemispheric dominance, in accordance with the nation's newfound ability to access much-needed raw materials, markets, and strategic outposts by force. With strong racist undertones, Lodge pronounced a worldview in which Anglo-Saxon civilizational hierarchy necessitated that the United States rule "lesser" peoples to augment national security, enhance global prestige, and intensify trade and market access, while providing tutelage in a wide array of democratic, moral, and market-based principles. He rejected unrestrained free trade by often advocating major tariffs to protect American industry and shipping. Taken together, Lodge's overall view represented a genuine, but thin and selectively applied unilateral form of isolationism. In large part his worldview of American hemispheric dominance skillfully adapted the Washingtonian ideal of steering clear of foreign entanglements, which he tended to denote in terms of European power politics, and he used this rationale to advance his desired expansionist ends. Lodge thus gave voice to—and helped to provide much of the political philosophy for—a sizeable expansionist group of politicians and thinkers that can be understood as a bloc of isolationist imperialists.

Debs, on the other hand, disagreed vigorously with the territorial expansion abroad and corporate expansion at home that Lodge and his cohort doggedly pursued under the seemingly benign rubric of the "large policy." Debs saw few redeeming qualities in Lodge's pro-business, pro–federal government perspectives. He was an ardent anti-imperialist advocate of the interests of the laboring classes. A charismatic orator and five-time presidential candidate, Debs took every opportunity to rail against expansion as malevolent capitalist aggression and against a return to the evils of colonialism that had been overturned in 1776. He preferred that

America reform from within, gradually becoming socialist and internationalist at the ballot box, while sticking to the old model of avoiding foreign (capitalist) conflicts and alliances.

An ally coming from a different perspective was W. E. B. Du Bois, whose isolationist principles (like Debs's) were entwined with his advocacy for domestic reform. A former student of renowned Harvard psychologist-philosopher William James, Du Bois shared an anticolonial outlook with James. Both men were passionate anti-imperialists. In their attempts to tamp down the bellicose, often nativistic and racist impulses of imperialism in America, they argued for cultural tolerance and a program of fulfilling democratic promises and progress at home. This perspective on reform helped to frame their overall isolationist position to not intervene in wars abroad, to minimize conflicts, and to avoid entanglements.

For James, opposing American expansionism represented the one—and only—major public political commitment of his life. Both James and Du Bois treated American principles of democratic equality as sacred. Accordingly, they believed the nation should adhere wholeheartedly to those beliefs. They had no patience with the expansionist desire to rule foreign peoples, often against their will, or to segregate and disenfranchise citizens at home for a supposed "greater" good defined by increased order and prosperity. In this way their anti-imperialism represented a new way of applying isolationism for an age of American power. However, Du Bois made racial uplift and rights the crucial elements linking his domestic and foreign policy values. Because of this priority, he was inconsistent concerning American military interventions abroad. A vision of the superiority of Anglo-Saxons supported many imperialist presumptions of conquering and ruling others against their will; so, too, racial egalitarianism buttressed the arguments of advocates of empire and opponents of annexations. Anti-imperialists, however, more often than their opponents in the expansionist ranks, invoked racist arguments. They did so to support a widely popular claim that "inferior" peoples should not be incorporated into the American republic and, thus, the United States should not annex the Philippines or Puerto Rico. Of course James and Du Bois, as racial liberals, never advanced racist arguments against empire, though many of their peers did. Du Bois opposed annexation and the war with Spain as antidemocratic and racist. However, he came to reluctantly endorse American entry into World War I. In July 1918, at the peak of U.S. military mobilization, Du Bois embraced the war effort. He called for a "closing of ranks," even permitting segregated military camps as a way of "earning" and displaying the sort of militant patriotism that could help achieve full citizenship for African Americans.

Du Bois and James were not pacifists, which may be regarded as the most extreme form of the isolationist doctrine of neutrality and avoiding foreign conflicts. They shared a broad conviction that the nation should be ready and able to defend itself; however, particularly in the years around 1898, they were antiwar and agreed that cultural exchanges between nations, rather than imperial and military ones, were the best future course to secure progress, achieve peace, and advance democratic values. Later, in the wake of World War I, Du Bois came to regret his position on that conflict and returned to his anti-interventionist, isolationist turn-of-the-century views.

The so-called irreconcilably isolationist, progressive William Borah made a similar transition. A Republican senator from Idaho, whom many contemporaries viewed as the finest speaker of his time and known to his detractors as "the great potate" (as in Idaho potato) or "the great opposer" (for blocking so much legislation, especially regarding foreign policy), Borah initially supported World War I as being forced upon the United States in 1917. Within a year, however, he came to argue against it and in favor of what he deemed vital national goals and reforms (rather than potentially precarious, costly efforts abroad). A fiery orator whose deep, strong voice often brought audiences to their feet in applause, Borah vociferously fought for fencing off the nation from virtually any binding foreign treaties and organizations. He was perhaps the most radical isolationist figure, with a vivid public profile during the 1920s and 1930s. Borah led the effort to reject the Treaty of Versailles and American entry into the League of Nations and the World Court. Yet, in trying to be a genuine "voice of the people," Borah was not inflexible. Even he saw that certain types of international engagement were absolutely imperative to a nation's progress. In fact, during the mid-1920s he softened his rigid views and embraced the limited benefits of acting internationally, albeit in nonbinding ways. He pushed for modest naval arms limitations agreements in 1921–1922 at the Washington Conference while disparaging many of the binding treaties that resulted from the conference. Borah then put these emerging nonbinding internationalist values into practice by spearheading one of the most ambitious and highly symbolic global peace efforts of the twentieth century—the 1928 Kellogg-Briand Pact to outlaw war.

The brilliant cultural critic Randolph Bourne, hunchbacked and deformed from birth, remained resolute in the face of personal and professional adversity. He collaborated with the tenacious settlement house founder Jane Addams and the idealistic settlement and peace activist Emily Balch, to oppose American entry into World War I. All three advocated U.S.-led mediation of the conflict. All three were pacifists and opposed the war without wavering. "Peace," Bourne argued, "could not be forced." A professor of political economy at Wellesley College, Balch lost her job in large part due to her antiwar lobbying and her broader international peace activism. Addams, Bourne, and Balch were part of the American Union Against Militarism (AUAM). The three firmly believed that America's place in the world was just as one of many nations, but that the United States had the global reach to encourage world peace and cultivate global culture. Bourne, who originated the concept of a "trans-national America," articulated a sophisticated case for the importance of a new model of pluralism, embracing all ethnicities, identities, and beliefs, for an increasingly diverse United States. He hoped that this transnational pluralist project, originating in America, might radiate out to the world to destabilize nationalism (and thus national boundaries).

By 1916 Bourne, Addams, and Balch ruefully concluded that given the exigencies brought on by the terrible conflict, peaceful mediation of the war in Europe and international cultural exchanges should come before most progressive reforms. Bourne never saw his ideas through to completion. Although he lived to witness the end of the war, he died from influenza in the epidemic of 1918, just as his career as a cultural critic and writer was taking off. Balch continued her work, emphasizing reform at home and aid abroad, as part of a new model for avoiding war and enhancing peaceful internationalism through her organization—the Women's International League for Peace and Freedom (WILPF). Balch came to collaborate with Borah in several idealistic internationalist initiatives in the 1920s and 1930s, the most significant of which was the movement to outlaw war, and the Kellogg-Briand Pact. Jane Addams's resolution in the face of adversity and bold international peace activism earned her the Nobel Peace Prize in 1931, the first awarded to an American woman. Balch's efforts were more organizational and lesser known than those of Addams. But her influence was significant, her efforts unstinting. Fifteen years later, in 1946, Balch became the second American woman to be awarded the Nobel Peace Prize.

The co-recipient of that prize with Balch was the peripatetic and charming John Mott, who was singled out for his international humanitarianism and the peaceful results of his efforts to enhance global ecumenism. Mott's was a transnational Christian humanism, thoroughly suffused with nationalistic hubris, aiming to spread "the Word" along with American democracy and Anglo-Saxon values. As the leader of the YMCA student volunteer movement for foreign missions, he sought a more robust American effort abroad to realize revivalist Dwight Moody's ambition to "evangelize the world in this generation."[15] He was similar in his internationalism to Balch, but differentiated significantly by his evangelical form of nationalism and willingness to work as part of the Wilson administration and the U.S. government. Mott was much more tied to mainstream politics than were Bourne or Balch. His political philosophy should be understood as a counterpoint to the other models of internationalism emerging during this period. Mott was generally antiwar, ecumenical, and internationally oriented in his mission and student volunteer work. During the war he served as the head of the civilian United War Work Council, and orchestrated the efforts of the Red Cross, the Jewish Welfare Board, the Salvation Army, and many other welfare organizations—all designed to aid prisoners of war and American troops abroad and to minimize civilian suffering across Europe. In that sense, he expressed an American exceptionalism that tied his modern internationalist thought to traditional isolationism. What isolationist politics he aspired to were largely in terms of seeking to oppose and minimize war, remain neutral, and to limit formal government engagement abroad.

Taken together, these core figures animate this book. All were critics of modernization, to various extents, and each turned her or his attentions to politics and the nation's role in the world by the 1890s. Each conceived in her or his own way that the United States had a special duty or mission; at a minimum all believed the United States was historically situated in such a way as to play a unique and different role in the world. Not all were internationalists but each argued for significant forms of U.S. engagement with the world. Of course, with all of these people and their wider communities of thought, what we will be exploring here are snapshots of their ideas and actions to illuminate broader trends related to the development of isolationist thought and its relationship to views about international involvement. The cruxes of their shared concerns were twofold: the effort to recognize the realities of an increasingly interconnected domestic and global world and the development and advocacy of new visions of how to balance private interest and public good.

The term "isolationism" has been inherited rather than invented, as has been amply observed by historians.[16] This inheritance has provided a great wealth of meaning, and yet it also has yielded a host of thorny problems. In many ways the term has been mangled and mistreated. The depth of its meaning has been mostly lost. While almost no one has ever supported unqualified "isolationism" as a complete walling-off of the United States from the rest of the world, by the end of the nineteenth century the word "isolation" was being actively debated, rethought, and applied. By the mid-1930s a distinct isolationist position had crystallized and self-avowed "isolationists" were a powerful force in American political life and policy-making. Recovering what these ideas meant in their own time and how they changed—losing and gaining advocates and new values—is critical to understanding the real historical meanings of "isolationism."

By accepting the term to mean *relative* isolation, historians and political scientists have demonstrated that the American government has never pursued a foreign policy that could be considered purely isolationist.[17] Building on such an observation we must note that before World War I, in the period from roughly the initial debates over U.S. expansion abroad in the 1880s through American entry into the Great War in 1917, growing globalization, interdependence, and an array of international economic factors divided developing isolationist thought into what can be best understood as two distinct strains. The first, *political isolationism*, was often aligned with liberal market-oriented economic views. This concept considered free economic exchanges as independent of politics; economic ties, because they do not entail political entanglements and do not erode American autonomy, were seen as permissible and even essential to national progress. Indeed, one group of political isolationists, today commonly referred to as libertarians, aggressively advocated free trade. But a position of neutral free trade—the commerce-first unilateralism of Washington, Jefferson, and Monroe—in an increasingly globalized economy has been and continues to be problematic. Shipping and trade connect nations in profound ways that can be severely tested in times of war or crisis. Historically the inherent politics of commerce have been most obvious at moments of crisis or conflict. This was acutely demonstrated during the

Spanish-American War, during World War I, in the war's aftermath during the 1920s, and throughout the 1930s in the midst of a cataclysmic world-wide depression and with a second world war becoming increasingly likely.

The second strain has equally long standing. Critics of foreign economic ties, especially those involving processes and policies of globalization, see such forms of commercial exchange as eroding autonomy and self-sufficiency. This often has led them to *protectionist isolationism*. While this viewpoint has been relatively muted in comparison to political isolationism, the camp supporting it has been most heavily criticized because at times its intensely inward focus, for example in seeking such policies as high protective import tariffs, appears naive or antiquated amid expanding, lucrative, and seemingly indispensable international trade. Both political and protectionist isolationism opposed forms of internationalism that would bind the United States to permanent commercial or military alliances.

As they became modern at the end of the nineteenth century, these political and protectionist isolationist arguments had a central point of emphasis in reinterpretations of a tradition that hearkened back to the Washingtonian and Jeffersonian precedent for America's "isolationist" role in the world. Time and again these foundational figures and ideas were cited to justify and avoid most entangling, binding forms of alliances, as well as wars, interventions, and colonial practices. Thus, historical-isolationist claims were the bedrock upon which often-overlapping arguments for their modern, contemporary uses were constructed. Borrowing from and updating the old, these new variations on isolationist political and protectionist points of emphasis included nonentanglement and unilateralism, along with neutrality, self-sufficiency, hemispherism or continentalism, the temporary (ad hoc) nature of alliances and treaties, exceptionalism and specific invocations of America's domestic as well as global mission, shadings of laissez-faire economics, and an aim to minimize war (sometimes pacifist—frequently conditional, rather than absolute—and sometimes antiwar yet hypernationalist). The different strains and variations helped add coherence to the new isolationism, with unilateralism and nonentanglement as central components of these developing views. What is more, these isolationist points of emphasis appeared in vastly different cases, such as for progressive and racial reform at home and evangelical missionary efforts abroad, and not just in more narrowly defined diplomatic terms or specific foreign policy proposals.[18]

By examining the social characteristics and intellectual development of these ideas along with the people who participated in the formation of modern isolationism, we can better understand its developing tensions and compatibilities with internationalism and domestic reform. In so doing, we uncover the crucial first moments when Americans confronted the fact that their nation was capable of meaningful international involvement. The debates over the nation's proper global role that began then persist even to this day. By tracking the developing thought of representative individuals and groups during this formative era, we find that the ensuing debates about the nation's global engagement became intrinsic to broader conversations about what constitutes a "good society" in America. For many of those involved in the debates over isolation, nothing less than the meaning of America was at stake.

This sense of urgency has endured, along with the framework of interrelated intellectual deliberations over isolation, internationalism, and domestic reform. While isolationist views traveled a sinuous route to the current considerations of America's role in the world—among nationalist hawks as well as internationalist doves—these notions still employ symbols, images, and tropes that would be familiar to those who debated U.S. global activities from the 1890s through the 1930s. Indeed, a century later, Americans continue to invoke many of the same isolationist ideas about how best to evaluate domestic and foreign engagement. Some Americans, in keeping with President Bush's remarks in 2006, pit the "ostrich" versus the "eagle." However, the complicated historical development of isolationist thought reveals not a binary "either/or" opposition with internationalist engagement but rather startling levels of combination and flexibility. That is, many American thinkers, politicians, and activists aimed to ascertain and blend the best characteristics of the United States as "ostrich" as well as "eagle" as they struggled to conceive new ways for America to confront both the promise and the peril of international challenges while also addressing pressing domestic concerns.

Now let us turn to see how, in the context of vast social, political, and economic tensions, modern thinking about balancing isolation, internationalism, and domestic social change came to structure American apprehensions of the nation's proper global role. Some Americans clamored for the nation to take its place in international politics. They were adamant that the nation participate in a scramble for new colonies and new markets alongside such nations as England, France, and Germany. Others vigorously objected to the United States' moving abroad as an imperial, interventionist power. One thing, however, was clear: the dawning of a global age required Americans to rethink and reinterpret the United States' long tradition of isolation.

1

NEW WORLD POWER

In the last decades of the nineteenth century American political thought faced new issues about isolationism and broader questions about the nation's relationship to the world. The country was enmeshed in social changes arising from the movement of its people from rural to urban areas and from farm to factory labor. The pace of economic change, international commerce, and political interchange was staggering. A glance at statistics illuminates the essence of this transformation. Total exports grew fourfold over one generation—from $281 million in 1865 to $1.2 billion in 1898—while imports increased almost threefold from $239 million to $616 million. Wheat production rose by 256 percent, corn by 222 percent, sugar by 460 percent, coal by 800 percent, and steel rails by 523 percent. Growth in new enterprises soared, such as crude petroleum production, which rose from three million barrels in 1865 to more than fifty-five million in 1898.[1]

Henry Cabot Lodge, the reserved Boston Brahmin and conservative Republican, became one of the principal actors addressing how the country's growth was reshaping international relations. In the 1890s Lodge reoriented older views of national isolation to help justify international expansion. Ironically, though, Lodge may be best remembered for spearheading the Senate Republican "reservationists" who opposed the Treaty of Versailles and American membership in the League of Nations from 1918 to 1921. Due to his powerful isolationist-nationalist argument that the covenant threatened American sovereignty, opponents in those debates cast him as an inveterate isolationist, a perception that lasted long after his death in 1924.

Lodge's conviction that the nation take an assertive role in the world evolved over time from his battle for expansion in the 1890s to his fight against binding internationalism two decades later. In his 1889 biography of George Washington, for example, Lodge wrote, "Our present relations with foreign nations fill as a rule but a slight place in American politics, and excite generally only a languid interest, not nearly so much as their importance deserves. We have separated ourselves so completely from the affairs of other people that it is difficult to realize how commanding and disproportionate a place they occupied when the government was founded."[2] In this, one of his most quoted early assessments of foreign policy, Lodge exulted in America's invulnerability to European influence and argued for the continued importance of maintaining a distant relationship. Writing to his friend, the author and fellow editor at the *International Review* John Morse Jr., he praised Washington's noble efforts but was measured in applying his foundational policy for the present.[3] Tracing the development of Lodge's expansionist beliefs reveals much about the hazy nature of isolationist ideas in this formative period of the nation's growing global economic and political power.

Lodge's background entitled him to prestige and power, but it was also filled with notions of profound patriotism and a deep sense of propriety. He was born in 1850 into the comfortable Lodge family and the patrician Cabot clan of Massachusetts. A lean, lanky man, he was formal in personal interactions and profoundly interested in U.S. political history. A firm believer in the abolitionist republicanism of his region, Lodge went on to earn a law degree and a PhD in what was then called "history and government" from Harvard University in 1876 (the first such degree awarded). He was a lecturer in history at Harvard for three years and became a prolific writer, treating history and biography as well as contemporary politics. When policy became his principal concern and passion, he secured the Republican nomination as a representative in the Massachusetts legislature, where he remained for seven years. From 1887 until 1893 he served in the U.S. House of Representatives, then from 1893 until his death in 1924 he was a U.S. senator. Nicknamed "The Scholar in Politics," he held views on politics that were informed by his substantial scholarly understanding of American historical precedents and his extensive writing on the subject. He also was well known for holding a grudge, as his later personal attacks and wrangling with Woodrow Wilson would amply illustrate.

From the beginning, Lodge did not endorse a slavish devotion to traditional isolationism. While the above quotation from his biography of Washington is one of the most cited by scholars, a close reading of the book shows an assertive, unilateralist bent to Lodge's conception of Washingtonian isolationism.[4] This assertive element became more pronounced in Lodge's thinking about how America should act internationally, particularly as war with Spain became a reality in 1898. He came to strongly agree with his friend Theodore Roosevelt, who opined, "If we are to be a really great people, we must strive in good faith to play a great part in the world."[5]

Recognizing the emerging economic and military realities of U.S. power, a group of prominent politicians and thinkers—headlined by Lodge and Roosevelt and including naval strategist Alfred Thayer Mahan, Indiana Senator Albert Beveridge, journalist-thinkers Brooks Adams and Josiah Strong, and politicians Elihu Root, Richard Olney, and John Hay—called upon America to become more interventionist. They slowly developed and articulated versions of what Lodge came to term the "large policy," characterized by development of a large navy, the need for a robust ability to project (and defend) American power abroad, and a foreign policy of expansion. Although this group did not always agree, they shared the same basic view that the United States should become more active internationally. National interest, along with a strong sense of American power, providential selection, and a belief in "manifest" as well as Anglo-Saxon racial duty, was crucial to shaping their arguments and policy positions. They also made claims for enforcing international justice by propelling the global advancement of "civilization." In setting up the United States as an ascendant "Anglo-Saxon" power, they established a hierarchical structure that privileged American annexations abroad by implicitly racializing as inferior those who fell outside of the confines of Anglo-Saxonism. Yet simultaneously, to reconcile the logic of expansion with predicted democratic outcomes, many advocates of American imperialism assented that new colonials held the capacity to eventually become citizens; this seemingly simple logical turn thus undermined one-dimensional racist assumptions about the inferiority of neocolonial populations and thereby rejected claims of static incapacity for self-government. However long such a process of democratic tutelage might take was an open question. All of these elements merged in their arguments as expansionists combined to make the case that the nation should break with much of Washington's isolationist injunction against intervention.

These influential individuals produced a novel interpretation that aimed to update isolation in unilateralist, nationalist terms. That is, they argued that the new global power of the United States should be exercised on the nation's own terms, never becoming entangled in foreign alliances, while seeking to enhance national interest and prosperity (broadly defined). In that way isolation and empire would operate in tandem rather than in conflict. This chapter focuses on the development of this "thinly" isolationist rendering of an expansionist political philosophy during the course of a series of signal events: the dire economic consequences of the depression of 1893; the controversy over Venezuela's boundaries and the near war with Great Britain in 1895; the Cuban revolution and its significant successes between 1895 and 1898; the election of William McKinley in 1896 and again in 1900; the rising power of "large policy" proponents in the mid- through late 1890s; the sinking of the USS *Maine*; the formative influence of the yellow press; the war with Spain in 1898; and the subsequent continued conflict in the Philippines. These developments helped to forge the parameters for the debates that ultimately led the nation to war and reshaped how Americans understood the principles of isolation and intervention.[6]

Reconciling Expansionism with the Tradition of Isolation

Advocates of the "large policy" had to tackle a difficult set of intellectual gymnastics to reconcile expansionism with traditional isolation. Lodge epitomized the twin elements of this progression: he developed a coherent new rationale for foreign expansionism as an extension of westward expansion for an age of U.S. global power, and along with a cohort of expansionists he helped turn that argument into practical policy. In his reassessment of isolation in light of modern realities, Lodge worked to lead the nation into war and new territorial expansion, with considerable unexpected consequences.

Throughout the 1880s and into the early 1890s Lodge and other American politicians, thinkers, and citizens often seemed inwardly focused, but this orientation would be forced to change given the rising challenges of modern industrial democracy and increasing international connections. Frequently in this period ideas about American isolation figured in the discussions about both domestic politics as well as foreign affairs. In the "highbrow" periodicals of the era—such as the *Nation, Century, Forum, Harper's, North American Review, Atlantic Monthly, The Independent, Review of Reviews,* and a host of others—a new cultural internationalism suffused policy debates and set the foundations for rethinking the nation's place in the world that was to come.[7]

Grover Cleveland embraced global commerce while embodying anti-imperialist and isolationist positions throughout the 1880s. In opposing Republican plans for creating a protectorate over Nicaragua, Cleveland

announced that such a policy contradicted "the tenets of a line of precedents from Washington's day, which proscribe entangling alliances with
foreign states."[8] In his first inaugural speech in 1885, Cleveland summed
up his isolationist political philosophy as the "genius of our institutions."
His point, though, was more subtle than it might at first appear. In light of
the mounting clamor to join the global colonialism of European powers,
Cleveland intended his remarks to proclaim the sacrosanct legacy of isolationist principles as well as to mount a persuasive claim that such valuable
political concepts ought to continue to guide the balancing of foreign and
domestic commitments. In his words we also see the maturing of a domestically oriented traditionalist view of the benefits of isolation, beginning as early as 1885.[9] Cleveland stressed that domestic progress and national political goals were the keys to ensuring progress and stability.

Yet forces were at work that would drastically reshape the reception of
Cleveland's views. The nation was becoming an industrial giant with
global economic interests in a world made smaller by transoceanic tele-
graphs, advanced steam engines and faster ships, and more exposure to
other cultures, peoples, and ideas. Partly in response to industrialization
and the increase of foreign trade and partly due to major social and economic changes at home, the views Cleveland expressed were increasingly
coming under scrutiny and beginning to be rejected as relics of America's
less modern past.

Alfred Thayer Mahan, author of *The Influence of Sea Power upon History* (1890), was one of the first to reject the cautious, tradition-bound view
of the Cleveland administration. Though by most accounts a mediocre
naval officer, he was a premier exponent of the doctrine of "sea power." In
the mid-1880s he opposed "outlying colonies or interests," but as he studied
the importance of sea power in world history he came to believe that colonies and coaling stations were crucial to national success as part of an expansionist position for building a large, modern navy and attaining global
power status. His view was premised on the unique historical importance
of naval strategy to national greatness, most evident in the title of his provocative book. Great sea power determined national power, he argued;
without it, nations historically failed to attain or hold on to greatness. By
1894, he urged a complete discarding of the older model of isolation. Mahan argued that the United States was now a world power and had to act
accordingly. He implored American leaders to therefore "cast aside the policy of isolation which befitted her infancy." The United States had become

a global leader in industry and commerce, so it must become a naval and colonial power to rival the commercial-colonial powers of Europe, he claimed. Mahan asserted that U.S. leaders should acknowledge these facts and that America had an "inevitable task and appointed lot in the work of upholding the common interest of civilization."[10] Mahan's audacious stand, ahead of Lodge's and Roosevelt's, anticipated that of fellow imperialist advocates of the "large policy," most of whom were not interested in rejecting isolation outright but rather in modifying expansionism and sea power to fit the framework of a refined, new isolationism.[11] Mahan's ideas would reach full bloom in 1897, when he published a new book, *The Interest of America in Sea Power,* arguing that the United States had strategic, naval, and historic reasons to be actively engaged abroad. Mahan argued, "Whether they will or no, Americans must begin to look outward."[12]

For thinkers such as Lodge, an outward view favoring expansion gradually combined with a sense of pressing domestic exigencies. The Panic of 1893 was so punishing that the nation and its leaders had a new imperative: to find new paths to ensure greater stability in the midst of rapid industrialization. Three million wage earners from a labor force of fifteen million were thrown out of work. On the finance and management side, 642 banks, thirty-two iron and steel companies, thousands of small businesses, and more than a third of all railroads closed or went bankrupt. If they were fortunate enough to have a job, children and pregnant women worked side-by-side with healthy young men at assembly lines in factories and sweatshops.

Within a year, America's downturn plummeted to its nadir. According to economists at the time, this recession was a product of industrial overproduction, so-called business cycles, monopolistic trade practices, and financial speculation. These explanations, however, did not immediately lead to solutions. Grand theories meant little to the many Americans who could not find work, who did not know when they would eat their next meal, and whose children seemed to have little future. Nearly one million workers faced their uncertain future by joining picket lines. The result was a series of devastating riots and strikes. In 1894 the bloody and chaotic Pullman strikes brought together railroad workers of various types, with Eugene Debs leading the American Railway Union to battle wage reductions. The strikes paralyzed tens of thousands of miles of railroads across the Midwest, halted the delivery of U.S. mail, and resulted in President Cleveland's federal order to send in U.S. troops to quell the strike, against the wishes of Illinois Governor John Altgeld. That year miners in Alabama, Ohio, and Pennsylvania, and garment workers in New York, also struck as they struggled against the ravages of the recession and the exploitative economic system.

Many believed that these conditions could be alleviated and the economy revived through open access to foreign markets. External outlets for American industrial products appeared to be a miracle cure. New economic data about how important exporting goods was to a vibrant economy made it seem that if U.S. businesses could sell and, in turn, produce more goods, they would thereby create more wealth and more jobs. According to Brooks Adams and other expansionist economists, it also followed that it would help to have permanent colonial or annexed areas to tap for much-needed raw materials as part of the larger political economic project of imperialism. Advocates of the "large policy" framed these economic goals in nationalist language and placed international economic exchange (particularly exports) as the key to national prosperity alongside global strategic interests as the core of their pro-expansionist views. Depression conditions from 1893 to 1897 facilitated such claims. The ravages of yet another and deeper recession encouraged the nation's political and financial elites to look for fresh solutions, and they looked abroad in search of economic stability. Observers like Adams surveyed Latin America and the elusive China market with an eye toward solving the depression by addressing what was then perceived as the "glut thesis" of overproduction. The editor of the *Journal of Commerce*, John Foord, provides a telling example of these connections in domestic and foreign economic political thinking. A Scottish immigrant, he worked for a number of major-circulation papers before becoming editor at the *Journal*, and he was among the most outspoken advocates of an interventionist U.S. presence in Asia. In the 1890s he helped form the American Asiatic Association (AAA) with Clarence Cary, the legal counsel to the American China development company, to lobby Congress for new outposts in Asia, and to advocate what came to be known as the "Open Door" policy designed to expand American interests to equal those of the other great European powers.

Invoking the language of "civilization" against "savagery" and "barbarism," Foord, Clay, and the AAA came together with the large and powerful National Association of Manufacturers (NAM) to call for increased foreign commerce–tinged xenophobia. This business bloc argued the extreme position that the United States must export American goods, or "deport" those who make them. Surplus production and improved productivity, stemming back to the late 1870s, led these pro-expansion business interests to believe that only overseas sales and new markets could rectify the problem. Lodge's broadly pro-tariff, pro-expansion vision of moving abroad to tap new markets built on this rationale and the support of this powerful interest group. As such, the Lodge position might well be considered neo-mercantilist in that it aimed for economic nationalist ends by promoting exports and extractive and strategic relationships with colonial regions while generally limiting imports, though he strongly favored modern industrialization.

A free trader in his youth, Lodge came to reject that position and what he saw as the Democratic Party's "free-trade influences" and argued for protectionism, which he linked firmly to nationalism. In an 1883 biography of Daniel Webster we glean a firm sense that Lodge agreed with Benjamin Disraeli's assertion that free trade was "a mere question of expediency."[13] Indeed, as the Lodge scholar William Widenor has observed, for Lodge the classic free-trade argument that open economic borders, stable currencies, and low tariffs lead to peace made little impact on him as Lodge "already knew where the path to peace would be found."[14]

Many proponents of Lodge's preferred expansionist approach to national prosperity and security worried that war might severely disrupt commerce. In this regard, business interests, such as those involved with the NAM, tended toward a crassly self-serving position: financial as well as industrial leaders hoped force could be a threat to bolster or wedge open access to new markets (across Asia as well as the Americas) and "save" American business, but they preferred that military power be exerted in the form of threats and coercion if possible rather than through a sustained conflict, which would likely disrupt seas lanes and ports essential for increased trade and thereby limit outlets for American goods. As an NAM position paper in the mid-1890s declared, "Our manufacturers have outgrown or are outgrowing the home market"; therefore, their answer was clear: "expansion of our foreign trade is the only promise of relief."[15] Nonetheless, some in the labor community did not see the central problem as one of domestic overproduction *as such*. Labor leaders such as Debs considered such arguments to be specious at best. He viewed the immense profits of robber barons, new trusts, and the emerging vertically and horizontally integrated corporations (all coming at a time of national economic catastrophe) as symptomatic of the oppression of labor and the dangers of unregulated modern industrial capitalism.[16]

Attempting to enhance domestic economic progress pushed Lodge and others to craft more explicitly protectionist policy, largely by using that most favored instrument of the late nineteenth century—the tariff. Fighting to protect local sugar producers predominantly in the American South and to support industry, Lodge, along with a group of Republicans, Northern Democrats, and politicians from Louisiana (who represented sugar planters and refiners) and from West Virginia and Maryland (who protected coal and iron interests), helped to persuade Congress to raise tariffs and protect American farmers and industry. However, after an effort to lower import taxation levels, the Senate amended the House bill; the new bill included the first national income tax (2 percent) but added provisions to raise tariffs. The resulting Wilson-Gorman Tariff of 1894 exacerbated dire farm-labor conditions in Cuba. Pro-tariff interests, among them Lodge but mostly composed of Southern and mid-Atlantic congressmen (members of the oddly aligned "sugar and coal lobby"), may well have intended the effort as a means of destabilizing the agricultural sector in Cuba, helping foment rebellion, and also undermining Democratic anti-interventionist, anti-tariff politicians. Thus, the bill represented a serious defeat for the Democrats and particularly for President Cleveland, who had campaigned on a platform of tariff reform and reduction. Cleveland's defeat was widely heralded in the press as a victory for Lodge and other pro-tariff, pro-industry Republicans. In terms of isolation, the heightened American import tariffs served to keep in place and even raise economic barriers around the nation to protect domestic agriculture and industry at the expense of American consumers.[17]

Amid the conditions of the recession and partisan politicking on the tariff, long-standing processes and dizzying economic changes intersected with political and intellectual transitions. Taken together, multiple layers of this transformation have led many historians to conclude the time was ripe for the nation to shift from an "old" to a "new" foreign policy.[18] The changing ideology of the time as it impacted new visions of America's place in the world is reflected in the prescriptive introduction to Roosevelt and Lodge's co-authored 1895 book, *Hero Tales from American History*. They wrote, "As a civilized people we desire peace, but the only peace worth having is obtained by instant readiness to fight when wronged—not by unwillingness or inability to fight at all. Intelligent foresight in preparation and known capacity to stand well in battle are the surest safeguards against war."[19]

Allied with his friend and confidant Roosevelt, Lodge chose a measured approach in seeking to enhance the nation's global role by emphasizing "readiness to fight."[20] Yet, while building their case carefully, both men became increasingly ambitious for themselves and for their nation. Much of their persuasiveness stemmed from the sheer scope and audacity of their vision and from the dexterity with which they combined a sense of confidence in national progress with grandiose projections of American power in both foreign and domestic arenas. For Lodge, the local and the global were interrelated parts in his nationalist-expansionist scheme, a point that biographers have noted only rarely. Taking a page from Frederick Jackson Turner's "frontier thesis" and blending it with the realist militarism of Mahan and Roosevelt's more unabashed sense of idealistic, even messianic nationalism, Lodge explained in November 1895:

> The continent has been conquered, and now the people's mind is turning to the fact that while we were engaged in this great work other things have been neglected—that we have heeded too little the importance of preserving in every way our institutions, of standing by American principles everywhere, at home and abroad, of putting the United States in the place where they belong in the great family of nations. . . . The American spirit is reviving throughout the country in the last ten years. It means not only the preservation of every institution, the upholding of every American principle—it means Americanism, true Americanism, true patriotism here at home and wherever the flag floats in the most distant area.[21]

This rousing rhetoric embodied Lodge's view that in the new global era American nationalism and national prosperity would be premised on willingness to take unilateral, expansionistic action abroad. These comments also underscore his belief that "materialist complacency" was the internal enemy that had to be defeated. Lodge felt that the renewed vigor of Americanism in an age of growing affluence, despite the economic downturn of 1893 and subsequent labor unrest, would prove that the "flag is a great deal more than the sign of a successful national shop."[22] He began to introduce Mahanian notions of the importance of the navy and preparedness into his addresses on the Senate floor to "put the flag first" (to paraphrase fellow expansionist Albert Beveridge). As a historian and as an exceptionalist, with an Anglo-Saxon sense of superiority and a natural inclination to a Federalist worldview, Lodge assessed that the United States had "carried civilization to the highest point it had ever touched." According to his imperialist mind-set, the English-speaking races had a particular "talent . . . for founding new states and governing distant provinces."[23] Such a vision, of course, missed at least one obvious and crucial element of the story of American continental expansion: namely, Native Americans.

Between 1876 and 1890 not a single year passed without a major bloody confrontation between federal troops and Native Americans—and several years witnessed more than one such encounter. The era's emerging American attitudes about expansion and foreign "adventuring" necessarily assumed some of their content, tone, and texture from those experiences. Indeed, conceptions of "manifest destiny" served to link views about continental settlement and overseas expansion. The question "what comes next?"—which followed from the 1890 census and its declaration that the frontier had closed, and the final major battle of the "Indian wars" at Wounded Knee in 1890—was deeply rooted in understandings of the past and the question "what came before?" Thus, as Lodge, Roosevelt, Mahan, Beveridge, Hay, Root, McKinley, and others in the late nineteenth century concluded that the United States could and should be like the colonial powers of Europe, they were befogging their own history by making what they thought was a clear distinction between continental and foreign expansion. In fact, in many important ways, Americans had already been behaving like those European colonial powers for decades and generations. Though in the early republic negotiations with Native Americans were seen as between "nations," over the course of the century that shifted radically. By the 1890s most Americans no longer conceived of U.S. continental expansion as "foreign policy"; the division between continental expansion (and inherent questions about the treatment of Native Americans), engagement, and incursions "abroad" only widened as debates over American imperialism became more heated at the end of the century.[24]

The Monroe Doctrine Put to the Test

In 1895 a geopolitical crisis impelled Lodge to be more forceful in his advocacy of expansionism in the Western Hemisphere. This event centered on a conflict that reached a crescendo in 1895 and 1896, when America almost went to war against England because of a boundary dispute between Britain and Venezuela. That seemingly petty and remote dispute had an inordinate impact on the United States. It changed the perspectives of many citizens and modified the course of American political philosophy and foreign policy.

American relations abroad recently had come unhinged by crises involving other places previously considered distant and insignificant—Hawaii, Samoa, Nicaragua.[25] Then the back-burner conflict between Britain and Venezuela flared. The fundamental dispute had its origins in the 1840s, when a British explorer and engineer drew up a map of a border between British Guiana and Venezuela that gave much of the Orinoco River to Guiana. Venezuela refused to accept the loss of territory, however. The rejection did not matter much until the 1880s when significant amounts of gold were discovered in the area. Officials in the Venezuelan government seized their chance to hold the region. They formally cut off ties with Britain and called for international arbitration of the dispute, asking specifically for the United States to lead the mediation effort. William Scruggs, the former U.S. ambassador to Venezuela, working as legal counsel for that country, published a pamphlet in 1894 titled "British Aggressions in Venezuela, or the Monroe Doctrine on Trial." He warned that British victory on the boundary issue would provide control over a key waterway and signal a transgression of Monroe's principles. The propagandistic pamphlet triggered a public furor, which in turn instigated a major political controversy. The boundary crisis drew significant attention from politicians, intellectuals, and journalists across South America, the United States, and England.[26]

In America a diverse group of citizens hotly debated the issues surrounding this seminal event. The new challenges of commercial, military, and imperial power clashed head-on with the nation's century-long policy of isolation. The answers to questions raised in the resulting debates would alter the meaning of the Monroe Doctrine and reinvigorate hemispherism, causing a wave of expansionist zeal to sweep the country. The "new" Republican expansionists, headed by Lodge and Roosevelt, were joined by a large number of intellectuals, seminarians, and economists. They confronted old-guard Republican "isolationists," whose allies included Bryan Democrats, new anti-imperialists, and domestically oriented progressive and other, more radical activists.

The issue of Venezuela pushed Lodge in new directions too. He began for the first time to link his ideas about domestic politics, national progress, and the urgent need for economic growth to a broader view of the nation's role in the world. As he noted toward the end of the controversy, there was no avoiding the fact that "these South American countries are waiting, eager to open their markets, to draw closer relations with us."[27] The memories of traumatic cycles of economic booms and busts from the 1870s through the 1890s were evident in the arguments of Lodge and his "large policy" advocates. If foreign markets could be "opened," Lodge, too, came to see that commercial and financial initiatives called for a new political calculus and sophisticated efforts to reorient and strictly enforce the Monroe Doctrine throughout the Western Hemisphere.

In rethinking the political economics involved, Lodge struggled with a characteristic quandary of Americans grappling with the nation's role in the world: a simultaneous desire to engage actively in world affairs and to focus primarily on the needs of American citizens and society. He also worried about avoiding the corruptions of Old Europe and entangling power politics. Lodge was keenly interested in the discussion of how to achieve "progress" both at home *and* abroad. Embarking on an imperial adventure would have far-reaching effects on domestic affairs. In the mid-1890s, he knew the consequences would be shifting resources to naval and military spending rather than investing in domestic infrastructure, in setting industrial regulations, in the burgeoning movement for reforms such as in the meatpacking industry, in alleviating tenement-house conditions, and in resolving questions about immigrant "fitness" and immigration restriction, not to speak of the crying need to respect African American rights and the rising clamor to consider such issues as women's suffrage and the prohibition of alcohol.[28]

Proponents of the "large policy" were never much inhibited by or concerned with those sorts of domestic social concerns, however. They believed the opportunities far outweighed the drawbacks of the country's new global status. Indeed, some scoffed at the citizenry's apparent inward focus and lack of enthusiasm for tackling the international challenges offered to them. "The trouble with our nation," Roosevelt declared, "is that we incline to fall into mere animal sloth and ease."[29] Americans lacked the will to plunge into the bracing currents of world politics, to court great dangers, and to do great deeds, he argued. Instead, they were mired in their own parochial affairs—their families, work, communities, churches, and schools. Lodge and Roosevelt were characteristic of the expansionists in their shared belief that the American people would have to be dragged to greatness by their leaders.

For Lodge and many of his expansionist colleagues, the Venezuelan crisis was pivotal. Much the same was true for William James, *Nation* editor E. L. Godkin, former Missouri Senator Carl Schurz, and many other soon-to-be-anti-imperialists, who are assessed in detail in the next chapter.[30] In the political debates over the Venezuelan boundary controversy, Lodge challenged the strict traditional-isolationist views of the Cleveland administration and instead offered the view that America ought to assert the "supremacy of the Monroe Doctrine . . . peaceably if we can, forcibly if we must."[31] One of his most illuminating articles on the topic, "England, Venezuela, and the Monroe Doctrine," appeared in the June 1895 *North American Review*. It explained Lodge's interpretation of the doctrine as a response to the Venezuelan crisis, setting the framework for what would become the "large policy." He observed:

> The proposition laid down by Mr. Monroe . . . is not complicated. It is merely the corollary of Washington's neutrality policy, which declared that the United States would not meddle with or take part in the affairs of Europe. The Monroe doctrine announced it to be the settled policy of the United States to regard any attempt on the part of any European power to conquer an American state, to seize territory, other than what they then held, or to make any new establishment in either North or South America, as an act of hostility toward the United States, and not to be permitted.[32]

Based on these premises, Lodge argued that the American people "are not now, and never will be willing to have South America, and the islands adjacent to the United States, seized by European powers." He further made the case that a trans-Isthmian canal should be built in Nicaragua, "absolutely controlled by the United States." Thus, Lodge concluded that the policy of Washington and Adams should be maintained "to enforce the Monroe doctrine so that no other power will be disposed to infringe upon it."[33]

In addressing "our blundering foreign policy," Lodge attacked Cleveland and recent administrations for not recognizing America's new place in the world order. During the earlier failed debate on annexing Hawaii in

1893, he lambasted Cleveland for how "easy [it is] to give away something valuable [i.e., Hawaii], especially to England" and for having "a profound contempt for the doctrine that . . . continuity in foreign policy of a great nation is desirable."[34] He then argued in the Senate that the American people must embrace expansion by voting to annex and control Hawaii "as soon as they have an Administration which will not thwart their desires in that respect."[35]

Lodge staked out a robust interpretation of the Monroe Doctrine according to which the United States would not have to defer to England, Germany, or any other Old World power—especially over issues broadly within the American hemisphere of influence, which for him included Hawaii along with virtually all of South and Central America and the Caribbean. Lodge claimed the United States had to annex Hawaii or risk becoming entangled in a major political, and possibly military, confrontation with England or Japan. Not to do so showed weakness, Lodge averred. The nation needed a "great" navy, he said—but he hedged that "a widely extended system of colonization . . . [was] not our line." Instead, the nation needed to "take and hold the outworks as we now hold the citadel of American power."[36]

Secretary of State Richard Olney sent a diplomatic note to England reinforcing a similarly aggressive defense of the Monroe Doctrine and insisting that the British accept arbitration. The Olney missive twisted the doctrine to mean that America could force arbitration or simply intervene as it saw fit in the hemisphere. To reinforce that claim, Olney stated that America was "practically sovereign on this continent, and its fiat is law." President Cleveland referred to the Olney note as a "twenty-inch gun" shooting a warning shot over the bow of the English ship of state.[37]

Developing the "Large Policy"

Rising popular jingoism and increasing international industrial power together created forces that empowered Roosevelt, Lodge, and Mahan. They made an odd team: a sub-cabinet official, a senator yet to ascend to a committee chairmanship, and a naval-military intellectual. Yet they and their allies were able to persuade senior officials, the president, and a wide swath of the public that expansion and war were not only possible but desirable. Lodge and Roosevelt, of course, were among the most unabashed of expansionists by the time of the Venezuelan crisis. However, both rejected the term "imperialism" as a definition of their views. Writing in

1900 to historian James Ford Rhodes, Lodge said, "I do not think that there is any such thing as 'imperialism,' but I am very clearly of the opinion that there is such a thing as 'expansion' and that the United States must control some distant dependencies."[38] Roosevelt preferred "Americanism." Lodge opted for "large policy." Neither liked the term "expansion" but they did accept it.

Though many histories note this political discussion and the new terms for it, few have analyzed its origins in the letters of Lodge and Roosevelt. Replying to Roosevelt on May 24, 1898, Lodge wrote, "The one point where haste is needed is the Philippines, and I think I can say to you, in confidence but in absolute certainty, that the administration is grasping the whole policy at last." Significantly, Lodge went on to elaborate his first use of the concept, saying, "Unless I am utterly and profoundly mistaken, the Administration is now fully committed to the large policy that we both desire."[39] Roosevelt, who at the time was training with his Rough Rider regiment in Florida, quickly responded on May 31, 1898. He hoped his friend's predictions were right but accepted delay.

Clearly both men had an intense resolve and a sense that political craft and patience would be necessary for the success of the "large policy." "For various reasons I am in no hurry to see the war jammed through," said Roosevelt to Lodge. "We shall come out better if we take our time. Moreover, the Administration are continuing very earnestly and I believe will soon undertake an expedition to Porto [sic] Rico, which I believe is useful." He then explained how events should unfold as a whole, noting his view from the field with Troop A of the First U.S. Volunteer Cavalry: "We ought to take Porto [sic] Rico as we have taken the Philippines and then close in on Cuba. Let us get the outlying things first. The Administration I believe to be doing very well and to be following out a large policy." Roosevelt had "strong hopes that the President will act without Congress," but found the actions of Lodge's friend Thomas Reed, the noninterventionist Republican congressman from Maine and Speaker of the House, against the annexation of Hawaii and against "military measure[s]" to be "in the highest degree discreditable."[40]

Lodge and Roosevelt, along with McKinley, agreed that the nation should go abroad to acquire what naval strategist Mahan termed "outlets for the home products and as a nursery for commerce and shipping."[41] Mahan had defined those outlets in military and economic terms, as a means to dual ends: the Asian and Latin American markets.[42] Building on the latest economic insights of the era, the expansionists did not propose the older European model of colonialism or a facile neo-mercantilist outlook, but rather aimed to articulate a new laissez-faire, expansionist, and nationalist view of America's place in global commerce. Access to markets, in short, was regarded by virtually every expansionist as the sine qua non for prosperity at home.

Lodge and his fellow "large policy" proponents did not particularly care how access was achieved. They aimed to secure strategic bases to assist with diplomatic and commercial entrance into previously less accessible areas of Asia and the Americas, to open up and protect shipping lanes, to outgun and outcompete European commercial-colonial powers, and to spread the supposed benefits of Anglo-Saxon Protestant civilization.[43] Such largely market-based arguments were among the most prevalent for—and persuasive to—expansionists, although a host of historians have found that business leaders generally were skeptical about engaging in war (but not new markets or colonies) and thus tended to follow, rather than lead, the expansionist movement of the 1890s. Brooks Adams, whose ideas about the relationship between economics and foreign policy were widely influential, encapsulated the logic of these arguments precisely: "The time has now come when that surplus must be sold abroad, or a glut must be risked." Those nations that did not recognize this essential commercial fact and failed to expand, he declared, were "devoured by the gangrene which attacks every stagnant society and from which no patient recovers." Therefore, Adams wrote, "Eastern Asia now appears to be the only district likely soon to be able to absorb any great increase of manufactures." The United States had no choice, he claimed; the nation had to compete for the "seat of empire."[44]

James Takes Up the Cause

As ideas about American isolation were reinterpreted and the policy of expansion beyond continental borders became more accepted, counterarguments came from a camp of anti-imperialists that had emerged during the Hawaiian annexation debates of 1893. Their opposition arguments became more coherent through the end of the century—beginning most emphatically with the Venezuelan crisis, and gaining traction with the crisis provoked by the ongoing local rebellions against Spanish colonizers in Cuba and in the Philippines. The firmer contours of "expansionist" and "anti-imperialist" positions were established at this time.

William James, like Lodge and Roosevelt, was highly politicized by the bellicose nationalism that arose during the Venezuelan border dispute. In 1895–1896 Lodge and Roosevelt condemned what they saw as President Cleveland's "policy of retreat and surrender" in Hawaii and Venezuela, as orchestrated by his two secretaries of state, Walter Quintin Gresham (who died in 1895) and Olney. When the English refused the "Olney-Cleveland ultimatum," Roosevelt, Lodge, and others argued that Cleveland's response—to appoint a commission to set the boundary—was an act of appeasement to England. Such actions revealed Cleveland as an opponent of a Lodge model for a hard-line interpretation of Manifest Destiny. Cleveland chose to try to avoid the forcible protection and global extension of the Monroe Doctrine, and did not agree to annex Hawaii (or condone the American business interests that had orchestrated a coup on the islands). Lodge argued vociferously for building and expanding a modern navy, for not standing down against England on the Venezuela issue, and for annexing Hawaii immediately. Nevertheless, Cleveland's actions relieved the tension between the United States and the English, and helped avert war.[45]

William James and Carl Schurz regarded Cleveland's diplomatic maneuvering—that is, threatening conflict yet intending to steer clear of war and imperial overstretch—as inflammatory and risky, despite purportedly virtuous motives. James wrote to his friend E. L. Godkin, the renowned and irascible editor of *The Nation*, urging him to be as "non-expletive and patiently explanatory as you can" in the paper—and quickly added, "don't curse God and die, dear old fellow. Live and be patient and fight for us a long time yet in this new war. . . . Father forgive them for they know not what they do!" For the first time, James had seen a blinding and dangerous American jingoism at work in the response to the Venezuelan crisis. He learned that "a nation's ideals can be changed in the twinkling of an eye."[46]

Still, James seems to have perceived Cleveland's efforts as generally trending in a positive direction but still being far too belligerent. As Cleveland petitioned Congress to create a committee to examine the border dispute, he simultaneously warned England not to encroach farther into South America. The abiding issue for him was action contrary to the Monroe Doctrine. He also declared to England that they must abide by the American commission's ruling on the matter or again face the possibility of war, and reiterated that since Monroe the United States had dominion over the hemisphere. Denouncing these competing pronouncements, James called the threat of war a "fearful blunder." What Lodge and Roosevelt saw as Cleveland's surrender, James, Schurz, E. L. Godkin, and many emerging anti-imperialists perceived as a wise turning away from conflict that also served as evidence that rash presidential actions might have led to war.

With typically Jamesian psychological insights, he argued that commissions were premised on cold, hard "reason," while wars appealed more strongly to the baser, heated instincts of passion. So, what could be more "cynical" during this moment of nationalist frenzy, James asked his congressman, Samuel McCall, than "to make of an incident where we pretend to urge on others the use of the humaner international methods the pretext and vehicle of a wanton and blustering provocation to war?"[47] For James, the nation's international reputation was being damaged by heedless bellicosity and the public's warlike response. Recalling isolationist values, James reminded McCall that the United States had been viewed as a beacon of "humanity and civilization." Yet this incident diminished that reputation, he said, because a mere "three days of delirium" proved the American people and state to be a nationalistic danger to world peace as well as to democracy itself. Even worse, James wrote that this crisis pushed back prospects for a "new and more civilized international order."[48]

What is most illuminating about James's response to the Venezuela–British Guiana border crisis is that he was almost as unnerved and shocked by the speed with which America abandoned its principles—being an exemplar of peace, justice, and reason—as he was by the act of abandonment itself. These were exactly the traditional principles that Lodge worked so hard to mesh with his expansionist rhetoric. James argued the nuanced position that responsible reason could lead to action, even possibly a well-thought-out war, but acting on passion, divorced from reason, could cause a minor problem to mushroom into a much larger one. It might instigate actions that were impulsive, uninformed by principle, ignorant of tradition, lacked prudence, or blocked cogent direction for the future. The psycho-philosophical reason for the resort to passion in this case, James thought, was that Americans had a surplus of energy to exert and thus they moved so passionately to support the war.[49]

The uproar over Cleveland's address on the Venezuelan crisis did "not necessarily show savagery, but only ignorance," wrote James to Godkin. His point was that if people recognized the nation's acute lack of knowledge, and acknowledged the enticements of raw emotion, there was still hope. "We are all ready to be savage in *some* cause," he noted. "The difference between a good man and bad one is the choice of the cause."[50] In distinguishing between good and bad casus belli, James was also differentiating himself from prowar expansionist-minded politicians, such as Roosevelt. However, by early 1897 the British were becoming embroiled in South Africa—the embryonic second Boer War—and gradually realized that courting war over an obscure boundary in South America was not worth it. Venezuela and England signed a preliminary treaty in January 1897 and a follow-up in the next month. This became the Olney-Pauncefote Treaty, signed under great pressure from Olney; it was not until October 1899 that final boundaries between Venezuela and British Guiana were set.

Partisanship at the Water's Edge

Lodge drew two broad conclusions from Venezuela and the party politics involved: Republicans had to lead the nation to be more resolute internationally, in part by definitively redefining the meaning of the Monroe Doctrine, and the country had to be powerful enough to enforce its proclamations. "There is nothing which so weakens our position," he wrote, "as the lack of knowledge of just what we mean when we speak of the Monroe doctrine." The situation with Venezuela had improved "by defining our position because that does away with restlessness and uncertainty."[51] He also emphasized that domestic unity was essential to resolute foreign policy, often voicing his hope in the halls of Congress that partisanship would "stop at the water's edge." Lodge was, however, too practical and too savvy a politician to have been optimistic about ever reaching that result.

In early 1895 Lodge was a freshman senator, just beginning to make a name for himself in national politics. His senior colleague in the Senate from Massachusetts, fellow Republican George Frisbie Hoar (soon to be a staunch anti-imperialist foe of Lodge's), tutored Lodge, who in turn saw the party as in need of deep reorientation because it was no longer a party of "human rights statesmen like Sumner and Hoar."[52] Lodge aimed to adhere to the party's consistent progressive image, though he was uncomfortable with some of the self-consciously progressive reformers of the era. Rather, Lodge hoped that his was the "party of progress that fought slavery across the pathway of modern civilization" and that it had a duty to find new directions to advance such an exceptionalist agenda.[53] Lodge argued that by dint of America's distinctive democratic ideals and institutions, resources and resourcefulness, the nation had an obligation to extend and deepen those values and influences at home and beyond the national boundaries as well.[54] Indeed, looking abroad in 1895, Lodge thought that Cuba was a "necessity," but not one requiring war, much less territorial annexation. After insurrection broke out and the Cuban revolutionaries asked for independence that year, he quickly changed course and ratcheted up his interventionist rhetoric, cloaking it in humanitarian language and some seemingly genuine concerns for the oppressed colonials on the island. In an article in the May 1896 *Forum* titled "Our Duty to Cuba," he argued that the revolutionaries needed help rather than annexation.[55] Combining his view of the Monroe Doctrine and his notion of forcibly extending that principle abroad based on humanitarian aims, Lodge reminded his friend Henry Higginson of "the responsibility which we assumed when we announced to the world that no one should be allowed to interfere in the island; the proposition that it is none of our business is precisely what the South said about slavery."[56]

Stemming from the twin forces of duty and destiny, perhaps the best synopsis of the goals of the "large policy" came in the form of what one scholar termed Roosevelt's "rhetoric of militant decency."[57] Roosevelt wrote, "I wish we had a perfectly consistent foreign policy," before the conflict with Spain, the goal of which would be that "ultimately every European power should be driven out of America, and every foot of American soil, including the nearest islands in both the Pacific and the Atlantic, should be in the hands of independent American states, and so far as possible in the possession of the United States or under its protection." Still, he saw the acute need to drum up support for such a policy. "Now, our people are not up as yet to following out this line of policy in its entirety," Roosevelt observed, "and the thing to be done is to get whatever portion of it is possible at the moment."[58]

A didactic series of letters between Lodge and his friend Tom Reed, the powerful Speaker of the House from Maine, in the summer of 1897 reveal Lodge's subtle, complex expansionist logic and how it incorporated pieces of traditional isolationism by updating them for newfound naval and commercial global power. The letters also show that events in Cuba weighed heavily on Lodge. The correspondence demonstrates another significant and almost constant element in Lodge's political thought: his close association of domestic policy-making with foreign affairs.[59] According to

Lodge, capital spent on the navy and army for defense amounted to national insurance. "We ought to continue a modest building of the navy and the forts of our coast cities and something every year. It is madness to economise by cutting off your police and fire departments."[60] Reed retorted, "Insurance is a good thing but over insurance creates what the insurance men call Moral Hazard; meaning the hazard . . . that an over insured man will set fire to his house." Sharp-witted, Lodge showed how deep his view went, saying that the nation was in dire need of any insurance and was playing catch-up. Lodge tried hard to convert Reed to his "large policy" mind-set but to little avail.[61]

Reed saw no real stake in the Cuban revolution. He observed to Lodge that there was a greater need for using resources within the nation rather than on naval fortifications, torpedo boats, or a costly intervention. This inward-focusing aspect shared elements of a traditional isolationist impulse and led him to sarcastically undermine both expansionist and humanitarian rationales for involvement in Cuba, saying "until the federation of the world comes let each nation look out for itself."[62]

Lodge seized on this dismissively unilateralist remark. He explained to Reed that "looking out for ourselves" was exactly what he proposed to accomplish. Self-interested defense against European encroachment, building the navy and coastal fortifications, and asserting the Monroe Doctrine strictly were routes to that end. "My desire," Lodge emphasized, "is to get Europe out of America." And by this he meant the whole hemisphere. Lodge pushed the inevitability of this expansionist process to persuade Reed, whom he felt to have "set himself against the evolution of the country & of the forces of the time."[63] Still, he wrote, "I believe entirely that Canada ought to become part of the United States. I should not think we should go to war for it, but I believe that it ought to come and that it will come and that nothing would conduce so much as that to our permanent peace and welfare. All our troubles with England, except during the Civil War . . . have grown out of the fact that she has colonial possessions on this continent." Reed apparently perceived that there were merits to eventually assuming control over Canada but not Cuba, nor islands in the Pacific. He saw expansion on the continent itself as valid but not beyond the bounds of those "natural" limits. Later in 1898 Lodge related to Roosevelt the demise of his friendship with Reed over their lack of common ground on expansionism and its relationship to domestic political concerns. Lodge said, "I keep out of his way, for I am fond of him, and I confess that his attitude is painful and disappointing to me beyond words."[64]

In their public addresses and private writing Lodge and the group of "large policy" framers expressed a shared similar vision for the future of the United States: it should play a larger role in world affairs and possess "distant dependencies."[65] Significantly, only the nonpolitician of the lot, Mahan, gladly assumed the label "imperialist," and tried to define the term, calling imperialism the "extension of national authority over alien communities."[66] Lodge and Roosevelt, however, helped shepherd the United States through its most unabashed expansion at the turn of the twentieth century, while disavowing the term "imperial" and quashing the notion of American colonization of newly acquired territories.

War on the Horizon

Roosevelt and Lodge outlined a "just war" doctrine that fused domestic natural rights, a humanitarian mission, and an imperialist agenda to resist the foreign "levy" of Spain and to avert continued colonial injustices. "No citizen of a free state should wrong any man," they maintained, ". . . but it is not enough merely to refrain from infringing on the rights of others; he must also be able and willing to stand up for his own rights and those of his country against all comers, and he must be ready at any time to do his full share in resisting either malice domestic or foreign levy."[67] Roosevelt and Lodge's developing ideas about America's international obligations help to explain why ideas about imperial action emerged in the mid-1890s.

As it became dramatically obvious in 1898 that the process of "modernization" had transformed domestic social and economic life, so, too, had these processes irrevocably altered America's international calculus. Americans debating their nation's proper role in the world built on the precedents of continental expansion, of course, but overseas expansionism and the possibility of conflict with an Old World power seemed somehow fundamentally new to many Americans living in the last decade of the nineteenth century. The looming war with Spain, an existing European colonial power, itself represented a significant break from the traditional orientation of limiting engagements, much less conflicts, with the great powers of the Old World.

When William McKinley succeeded Grover Cleveland as president in 1897, the uproar over Cuba persisted and the drumbeat for war accelerated. By June 1897, McKinley issued an ultimatum to the Spanish government "in the name of the American people and . . . common humanity" to immediately end "uncivilized and inhumane conduct."[68] A new administration in Madrid offered a few concessions and recalled controversial General Valeriano "the Butcher" Weyler back to Spain from Cuba. It also issued a relaxation of the *reconcentrado* camp policy of placing Cubans in concentration camps, and outlined possible steps toward Cuban autonomy. While these reluctant diplomatic moves brought about a brief hiatus in the tension, several unpredicted events escalated the pressures that precipitated the waging of the first war between the United States and a European power since the early nineteenth century.

More than a generation had passed since the nation's last major conflict. National expansion was at hand, yet as America moved reluctantly at first, and then more forcefully toward war with Spain in 1897 and 1898, Mahan's injunction "to look outward" prompted intense public scrutiny. Culminating in the Spanish-American War, ideas such as Mahan's and Lodge's fueled the flames of rising expansionist and war fervor.[69] The coming war with Spain intersected with major developments of the new "large policy." The nation's first major intervention abroad to oppose a European power in both the Caribbean and Pacific, and ultimately its acquisition of territorial possessions spanning ten thousand miles, would have vast ramifications on society as well as on political thought.

The popular historian John Fiske provided a wider historical grounding and justification for the new expansionism. A friend to Lodge and Roosevelt, fellow advocate of sea power and expansion, Fiske was a prolific lecturer across the United States, his talks including the oft-requested and aptly titled "Manifest Destiny." It encapsulated his expansionist connection between American history, destiny, and empire. Published in *Harper's New Monthly Magazine* and later appearing as a book at the end of 1885, Fiske's lecture laid out an evolutionary and racial basis for the expansionists, making their desired course seem grounded in historical and scientific inevitability. Like that of Lodge, Fiske's expansionism was "determined by" what he termed "historical or philosophical rather than by patriotic interest."[70] He cited Charles Darwin and Herbert Spencer, asserting that evolutionary theory reinforced an impending fact: the United States and, more broadly, Anglo-Saxon civilization would achieve massive territorial expansion in the coming years. America, Fiske argued, was destined to obtain "a political aggregation immeasurably surpassing in power and dimensions any empire which has yet existed." He further predicted a more peaceful future when "the time will come" that there would or could be one "huge federation," with localities managing their own affairs but with a central tribunal organizing international relations. It would be a time, he prophesied, when we will "speak of the United States as stretching from pole to pole."[71] This perspective posited the triumphs of "Anglo-Saxonism" as evidenced by the imperial sway of Great Britain and the territorial growth of the United States, which he viewed as dual racial and civilizational bases for global hierarchy and for a peaceful future world order.

On its face this view directly contradicted a long-standing American aversion to foreign entanglements. Expansionists, however, did not see it that way. First, they did not seek any permanent alliances with European nations. Second, not being coerced by Great Britain or other powers was a goal of even the limited vision for foreign policy that preceded that of the 1890s. Not provoking those powers was also an objective, but projecting power so as not to be pushed around on the geopolitical stage was now a firm national goal. Third, they believed that the United States held distinctly different and more righteous (because of the nation's democratic origins) perspectives from Old Europe vis-à-vis the New World. Guided by a reinvigorated view of simultaneously protecting the rights established by the Monroe Doctrine, while adding the teeth of an emerging navy to reinforce their ascendant industry, such a vision assumed America was the hegemonic protector of the Western Hemisphere.

According to many social Darwinists, South and Central America and the Caribbean were composed primarily of inferior "dark" peoples, suitable and appropriate for subjugation or tutelage. American anti-imperialists invoked this same racist perspective for opposite ends: to avoid annexation of potentially inferior citizens or subjects. Similarly, anti-imperialists did not want to be corrupted by the inferiority of colonialism itself or the notion that "the United States was never a great nation until [vanquishing] . . . a bankrupt old state like Spain." The latter perspective is suggested by the title of social Darwinist sociologist William Graham Sumner's postwar book, *The Conquest of the United States by Spain*.[72] In the main, however, ideas mixing notions of race with expansion and a hierarchy of civilizations created an environment conducive to expansion. Possession of Cuba became "humanitarian" and "democratic," as well as a self-interested imperative for an emerging global power. William Burgess, one of the most prominent political scientists in the nation and an architect of the doctrine of Teutonic national dominance, turned against imperialism on exactly the grounds of democracy rather than race. He argued forcefully that the United States as a "cosmopolitan state" should do no more than act as an exemplar.[73]

Still, in a democracy the key to making war and engaging in expansion lies with public support. Lodge and Roosevelt disdained the lowbrow nature of pulp journalism and the so-called penny press but found them to be valuable if sometimes unsavory allies in pushing for intervention and expansion. Support for Cuba and war against Spain arose largely from the growing popularity and sensational accounts supplied by William Randolph Hearst's *New York Journal*, Joseph Pulitzer's *New York World*, and their affiliated newspapers across the nation. These papers redefined how Americans came to perceive foreign affairs. The appeal of "yellow journalism"—given this title because of a character in one of the *World*'s comic strips, the Yellow Kid—was widespread and made usually boring foreign policy issues riveting by focusing on lurid accounts from abroad.

Even America's barely literate masses, accounting for almost one-ninth of the American public in 1900 by some estimates, could easily understand the cartoons and graphic pictures of major events. Lavishly colored and detailed, many of the popular political cartoons of the era reveal underlying American racist impressions of Latin Americans as "dark," emasculated or feminized, and in need of liberation. One such potent image appeared in William Allan Rogers's cartoon depicting a young, disheveled Cuban woman, wrapped in the American flag and with arms free from chains and held aloft exclaiming in "Cuba Libre!"[74] With the advent of undersea telegraph lines, "breaking news"—about daring revolutionaries, debauched innocents, terrible atrocities, and dishonorable Spanish oppressors—brought persuasive stories and images to bear on public opinion.[75] However, scholarship on the jingoistic press shows that the American public was stirred up by an array of influences. "Had there been no sensational press," the historian John Offner notes, "the American public nevertheless would have learned about the terrible conditions in Cuba . . . [and] would have wanted Spain to leave." Nevertheless, the yellow presses, led by New York papers and their syndicates, popularized ideas about the absolute need for humanitarian intervention. They argued vehemently that the Spanish empire in the Americas had to end.[76]

1898: *Expansion and the Control of Distant Dependencies*

It is remarkable how many populists and progressives supported the war, at least at first. William Jennings Bryan was enthusiastically bellicose and patriotic. Suffragist Elizabeth Cady Stanton was a vigorous supporter of the war, citing mostly humanitarian reasons, even though fellow suffrage proponent and settlement house pioneers Jane Addams and Emily Balch did not agree with her. "Though I hate war *per se*," wrote Stanton, "I am glad that it has come in this instance. I would like to see Spain . . . swept from the face of the earth."[77] There were some significant exceptions, notably among the social reformers most interested in issues of racial liberalism and populist measures of direct democracy, old-guard abolitionists and staunch protectionist isolationists, and ardent socialists, along with limited numbers among the labor ranks. That said, the closer war with Spain came, the more this group splintered.

Events moved swiftly, then accelerated toward confrontation. On February 15, 1898, the USS *Maine*, sent by McKinley to protect U.S. citizens and interests, mysteriously blew up in Havana's harbor, killing 266 sailors and officers out of a crew of 354. Roosevelt and a cast of expansionist hawks immediately saw their opportunity. Until the explosion of the *Maine*, this group had been a minority and certainly had not been focused on war with Spain but rather had hoped for expansion and war in the abstract. As Roosevelt commented in a private letter before the sinking, "I wish there was a chance that the Maine was going to be used against some foreign power; by preference Germany—but I am not particular, and I'd take even Spain if nothing better offered."[78] Conflict with Germany apparently would have been "preferable" not so much for expansion but as a means of invigorating the nation by presumably confronting and defeating a foremost potential European military and economic rival.[79] A mere day after the *Maine* sank, Roosevelt noted to Secretary Long the improbability of the coincidence in timing the ship's arrival in Havana and its destruction, "by an accident such as had never happened."[80] Writing to a friend, Roosevelt leapt to the conclusion that "the Maine was sunk by an act of dirty treachery on the part of the Spaniards I believe."[81]

Lodge's reaction after the *Maine* exploded can be aptly described as cautious about war but "not too prudent to prepare for it."[82] From the first instant they heard of the sinking of the *Maine*, both Lodge and Roosevelt suspected an external attack in the form of a mine or other explosive. Indeed, as historian William Widenor revealed, expansionists like Lodge and Roosevelt also hoped it would precipitate some sort of conflict. Lodge supported a joint congressional resolution for war, pushing McKinley as much as he could to rush the matter forward because it was an issue of honor as well as policy. Still a "cautious firebrand," Lodge explained the impetus to rush to war in a letter to his mother in these terms, saying war was "as inevitable as the contest between slavery and freedom. The United States and Spain cannot live side by side—one must go and it must be Spain."[83] President McKinley, however, was operating on parallel tracks: making ready for war while continuing to seek compromise with Spain through diplomatic channels even after the explosion of the *Maine*.[84]

But these efforts were short-lived. Arguing for a unilateralist interpretation of the Monroe Doctrine along the lines of Lodge and Roosevelt's, on April 11, 1898, President McKinley sent his war address to Congress. Listing the litany of diplomatic efforts to reach a peaceful solution and the Spanish affronts to the Cuban people, McKinley's address was a case study in invoking the values of neutrality and nonentanglement until the nation could stand no more provocations. To this he did not add a claim of self-defense at this point but rather deployed fresh humanitarian arguments to support immediate intervention and a formal declaration of war against Spain. In this modern understanding America was a hemispheric force for democracy and a defender of a universal vision of justice. McKinley called for an end to the revolutionary war in Cuba, "in the name of humanity, in the name of civilization, in behalf of endangered American interests which give us the right and the duty to speak and to act." Spanish rule in Cuba, he alleged, was too terrible to be allowed to continue.[85]

Thereafter the *New York Journal* reported, "The whole country thrills with the war fever."[86] McKinley's message was laced with more modest humanitarian and reluctantly interventionist ideas, but the bellicose Congress and nation had no doubt about the real meaning of the war. Political debates about entering the conflict immediately centered on when, how, or whether to formally recognize the rebels, whom many Americans did not necessarily view as potential allies. To justify the war most effectively, Lodge and the "large policy" cohort realized that the proper grounds were defending Cuban "freedom" from colonial abuse and ending the horrible system and conditions at the *reconcentrado* concentration camps. On April 19, by a close vote of 42–35 in the Senate and a decisive margin of 311–6 in the House, Congress passed the joint resolution recognizing the

Cuban people and their mistreatment and need for freedom, and demanded Spanish political and military withdrawal from the island. At this time, Lodge was becoming one of the most prominent Republican voices in the Senate. In 1896 he had been appointed to the Senate Foreign Relations Committee and was advancing positions for the gold standard, immigration restriction, and a law opposing the direct election of senators. Though still the junior senator from Massachusetts, Lodge assumed a powerful position as a conservative and hawkish advocate not just of these resolutions but also of Hawaiian annexation and of building a larger, modern navy.

In less than a week, by April 25, Spain and America declared war. It was to be the shortest declared war in American history. Yet to assure the world (and some dissenting anti-imperialists at home) that the United States was fighting only for the good of Cuba and not for colonial gain, Congress passed the Teller Amendment, which restricted America's ability to acquire the island by promising to make Cuba independent after the war was over.

Unilateralist Isolationism

Calling this a "just war" is part cliché, part oxymoron. Justice is and always has been a principal rationalization for conflict between nations, peoples, and faiths. So, too, some combatants describe virtually all wars (not just America's) as "defensive" in nature. In 1898, casting the conflict as a "just" war, in "defense" of the Cuban people, reinforced McKinley's war declaration. While the argument for an increasingly strong economic country in need of markets and mettle-testing going abroad for economic gain was a potent one, for most expansionists, at least at the level of rhetorical justifications, more was in play. They defined their mission, based on a belief in the universality of American ideals and institutions, as one to make the world a better place. This emerging view of promulgating war couched in terms of justice and uplift laid the foundations for the twentieth-century mission-oriented foreign policy vision that historian Walter McDougall aptly termed "global meliorism."[87]

In one year—after only three months of direct conflict in 1898—the United States acquired Puerto Rico, the Philippines, and part of the Samoan archipelago, annexed the Hawaiian Islands, and sustained authority over the island of Cuba. Many, from Andrew Carnegie to Mark Twain, perceived these events as heralding the nadir of American democratic principles. They asked: Was the nation imposing dominion on alien peoples without their consent? Roosevelt and Lodge rejected the premise of such a question. They saw limited American hegemony over these regions as beneficial to the areas themselves. More important to Lodge (whose own political rise to the top of the Republican ranks, along with Roosevelt's, mirrored the ascent of the "large policy" and U.S. gains in the war), the war extended American political and military might to advance economic interests around the globe. Though at first these economic advantages were likely to be modest, Lodge supposed they would gradually increase over time to great profit for U.S. businesses and citizens. Surprisingly, many advocates of progressive reform—particularly of federal-level reform measures (rather than state or local), such as the American Association for Labor Legislation—supported a revised vision of a unilateral, exceptionalist approach to expansion as an extension of the tradition of isolation on the grounds that it would likely enhance national economic prosperity.[88]

Exploring these justifications grounding the Spanish-American War sheds new light on how ideas about isolation influenced expansion and the control of foreign dependencies. The reoriented "large policy" of the 1890s and early 1900s represented a massive change in this regard. Roosevelt, along with Lodge and their "large policy" proponents, subscribed to a belief that war could be good for the nation. At the heart of American thinking at the turn of the twentieth century was a conflicted understanding of barbarism, virtue, and progress.[89] The war was to be an intervention against colonial barbarism. Self-doubt plagued the nation. American "civilization," a progressive force for good, required an embrace of what Roosevelt termed "barbarian virtues" to avoid the "over-sentimentality, over-softness, in fact washiness and mushiness [that] are the great dangers of this age and of this people."[90]

In May and June 1898, Lodge displayed some of his most cogent thinking about the relationship between commerce, expansion, isolation, and how best to justify the war. Writing to his friend Elihu Hayes, Lodge argued that keeping the Philippine Islands was essential because they "furnish a great market." But striking a rousing note and sounding much like Fiske and Brooks Adams, Lodge asserted, "We cannot avoid our destiny. We are too great to be any longer an isolated power. If we should not find an outlet for our products and room for expansion in the east and west Indies our ability to feed ourselves will be but little protection against a great social revolution." He concluded his letter on a decidedly insular point of policy. Blending new international commitments with xenophobia, Lodge reassured Hayes that he would press for a stringent anti-immigration bill in the next session of Congress.[91]

Lodge wrote along these lines in a later personal letter in May 1898, "We have come indeed to the parting of the ways, and I believe we can no longer remain isolated. A nation of seventy millions, with an extending commerce must be a world power. That is one reason why [the annexation of] Hawaii is now being fought so bitterly [in Congress]."[92] He firmly believed—and could see no clear counterargument against the logic—that if the United States did not "take" Hawaii, then the nation might well become embattled in a conflict with Germany or Japan over the islands in the very near future.

From May through June 1898, Lodge's writings made just such a point, but two letters stand out for the clarity of his thought on the matter. First, explaining to a friend, Lodge noted that he and Olney disagreed only in minor ways in terms of how high the tariff should be raised on imported goods. As he put it, the two agreed wholeheartedly that "in the process of development the United States has now reached a time when she must become a world power. This involves no entangling alliances but it does involve leaving our isolation, and in my judgment we cannot help ourself, and the only question is whether we shall do it intelligently or clumsily."[93]

Not long thereafter, writing to George Lyman, Lodge argued "a foothold in the east would be of immense importance to us commercially and industrially. It would be infamy to turn those insurgents back to Spain after they have helped [u]s, therefore we must, at least, hold Manila and Luzon at the peace." He went further, saying, "We have a right to take them as an indemnity any way. England wants us to have them and so does Japan. The rest of Europe will grumble but would rather have us have them than anyone else." Without committing entirely to full annexation or independence, Lodge asserted that expansion and the war would overshadow domestic concerns for the Republican Party. "After [the new territories] have been ceded to us we can decide what we will do with them and we will cross that bridge when we come to it," Lodge summarized. "This extension will help us industrially, and this new foreign policy will knock on the head . . . the matters which have embarrassed us [the Republican Party] so much at home."[94]

Victory and Questions of Citizenship, Masculinity, and Race

On December 10, 1898, the Treaty of Paris was signed. After discussions held since the first peace protocol had been signed on August 12, a formal cessation of hostilities occurred on October 1; the war was officially over. In the end, American troops helped to liberate Cuba and acquired Puerto Rico, Guam, and the Philippines.[95] Reflecting on his decision to claim the Philippine Islands as part of the United States, McKinley stated, "There was nothing left for us to do but to take them all, and to educate the Filipinos, and uplift and civilize and Christianize them, and by God's grace do the very best we could for them, as our fellowmen for whom Christ died."[96]

Guam, Puerto Rico, and the Philippines all became American protectorates. Questions of nationalism and who qualified as an American citizen were thus next on the agenda but were slow to be worked out in detail. The people of these protectorates, as a series of rulings from 1901 through 1922 on the legal status and congressional authority over the flag territories, known collectively as the Insular Cases, made clear, did not have full rights as American citizens. Significant judicial scrutiny on the issue initiated a reckoning with a new political status for those within an American territorial "orbit," who were not enslaved or imprisoned, yet could not share full citizenship. Congress questioned the Puerto Ricans' "fitness for government" and opted for the vague wording of the Paris Peace Treaty, namely that the "civil rights and political status of the territories [was] hereby ceded . . . shall be determined by the Congress."[97] Under the Foraker Act of 1900, a new middle-citizenship status was created, that of "citizen of Puerto Rico."[98]

These were but minor deliberations for those within the expansionist camp, who shared an exceptionalist sense of American mission that was so evident in the expressions of Lodge and Roosevelt. Lodge agreed with fellow imperialist-minded editors Whitelaw Reid, editor of the *New York Herald Tribune*, Albert Shaw, editor of the *Review of Reviews*, and Walter Hines Page, editor of the *Atlantic Monthly*, that these new people could not be fully part of the nation at that time, or quickly. But eventually these "highbrow" advocates of annexation also believed America's colonial subjects would become citizens or might eventually be granted independence. Albert Beveridge, for example, took just such a position in several Senate debates. He hearkened back to Puritan New England and John

Winthrop's idealistic and messianic vision of a "city on a hill" first across the continent, with the "eyes of the people upon us," and eventually spreading back to the Old World and around the world. Beveridge argued to the Senate in 1900 that God "had marked the American people as His chosen nation to finally lead in the regeneration of the world. This is the divine mission of America."[99] Of course, while Beveridge called out for commercial profits along with Christian mission, Mahan, Lodge, and Roosevelt also displayed fiercely nationalistic aims for an increase in America's global power and prestige by dint of following a program of naval and military building and expansion abroad.

By the end of 1899 the McKinley administration also acquired the Pacific islands of Guam, Wake Island, and Tutuila (American Samoa). But events in the Philippines galvanized anti-imperialists. Military and naval successes on land and at sea, along with rapid annexation, did not necessarily lead to either swift or democratic outcomes. When the United States annexed the Philippine Islands on February 6, 1899, as part of the ratification of the Treaty of Paris, peace did not come as expected by the Filipino revolutionaries and citizens. Filipino nationalists declared independence, turned against their former allies, and instigated a campaign against American forces, which they perceived as occupiers, not liberators. From 1899 until 1902, when the insurgency ended, almost five thousand Americans died in the Philippines, about twice the losses during the entire Spanish-American War.[100]

On July 4, 1902, President Theodore Roosevelt issued a Peace Proclamation and Amnesty Grant in which he stated that the islands had been pacified. Roosevelt thereby officially concluded America's first significant undeclared war abroad. The "insurrection" had been quashed (though sporadic fighting continued for several more years), and the beleaguered Philippines were added as an "unincorporated" territory to the list of relatively stable American protectorates overseas.[101] This act in the Pacific signaled to domestic and foreign observers that Lodge, Roosevelt, and their "large policy" cohort had moved beyond their own tenuous extension of the Monroe Doctrine. Hemispheric isolationist principles were no longer being practiced.

Underpinning the rhetoric of the "large policy" was a set of masculinist and social Darwinist ideas that framed how advocates conceived of the hierarchies among nations and races, and reinforced the ways in which a tradition of isolation could be made compatible with the new realities of expansion abroad. Historians of the role of gender on empire, such as Gail Bederman and Kristin Hoganson, have made clear that Lodge and Roosevelt's ideas about manhood were critical to their ideas about empire.[102] In the mid-1890s, Lodge and Roosevelt used language calling for "vigorous" foreign policy, and policies that were "strenuous," "warlike," "strong," "bold," "firm," and even "dignified," which embodied the masculine and aggressive core of their desired assertive vision for expansion and national greatness.[103]

Ideas and language about masculine virtues dovetailed with newly popularized scientific findings about race, intelligence, and social development. Lodge was informed by this cutting-edge popular science; he often quoted the work of Herbert Spencer with regard to his social Darwinist view that American Anglo-Saxon racial advancement toward a higher civilization was just and inevitable. This view went hand in hand with the practical need to maintain and enhance manly Americanism. Racial decay was possible and ongoing, argued Spencer, therefore it followed for politicians like Lodge and Roosevelt to encourage the strengthening of race through the "strengthening" of manhood by taking assertive domestic and international actions. In his lengthy assessment of the role of "Colonialism in the United States," Lodge argued directly from Spencer saying to those who "grumble and sigh over the inferiority of America we may commend the opinion of a distinguished Englishman, as they prefer such an authority. Mr. Herbert Spencer said recently, 'I think that whatever difficulties they may have to surmount . . . the Americans may reasonably look forward to a time when they will have produced a civilization grander than any the world has known.'"[104] Spencer's assessment thus supported Lodge's global line of reasoning that America only needed to be impelled by the force of visionaries to advance toward greater civilization.[105] Interestingly, this was a clear misreading of Spencer's politics. He supported a form of British laissez-faire liberalism that was broadly anti-imperialist and he vehemently opposed the British colonial project during the Boer War.[106]

To counter any possible backsliding, Lodge worked with Roosevelt to encourage what they referred to as "strenuous" activities and to invigorate national assertiveness. What was to become Roosevelt's renowned "strenuous life" concept clearly was evident in Lodge and Roosevelt's co-authored book, *Hero Tales from American History*. In the preface they argued for the U.S. value of "readiness to fight when wronged."[107] In 1899

Roosevelt built on this notion when he coined the phrase "strenuous life," explicitly calling for greater "readiness," which included military prepared-ness, a stronger navy, and imperialist control over Cuba, Puerto Rico, and the Philippines. This nascent idea, however, did not necessarily require expansion at all. Central to this notion, then, was the theme of *Hero Tales*, that the American people must embrace their national "character," their "nature," and work to inspire "heroic virtues" in their race, their govern-ment, and their law.[108]

In articulating a connection between domestic freedoms and the pro-motion of democracy as a foreign policy ideology, Lodge and Roosevelt foreshadowed elements of the liberal internationalism that was associated with Woodrow Wilson two decades later. They declared that "no citizen of a free state should wrong any man; but it is not enough merely to re-frain from infringing on the rights of others; he must also be able and willing to stand up for his own rights and those of his country against all comers, and he must be ready at any time to do his full share in resisting either malice domestic or foreign levy."[109] Taken together, these ideas re-garding American democracy, preparedness, and a globalizing defense and for advancing peace, prosperity, and democracy formed the crux of the Lodge-Roosevelt vision for the necessary updating of the Washingtonian model for American isolationism.

Lodge relied on far more than raw power and hierarchies among peo-ples and countries to make this case. The advancement of American vir-tues was a potent aspect of Lodge and Roosevelt's understanding that "uplifting" foreign people and "tutoring" them in the ways of democracy would be a means of making Americans better, while improving national prosperity in the process. Roosevelt's use of the term "strenuous life" con-noted a "virile, hard-driving manhood, which might or might not involve foreign relations, at all."[110] While expansion of domestic and international markets through building infrastructure and annexing lands was one such measure of progress, as we have seen, far more abstract and far less imperi-alistic notions of national and racial advancement were the foundation of Roosevelt's ideas.

These abstract beliefs buttressed American expansion. So, too, the "large policy" was built on an implicit racist rationale for imposing Ameri-can power over foreign, inferior peoples. In short, to conquer "colored" peoples and rule them against their will, even when justified for their own "benefit" and with an explicit aim of eventual independence, was an undeniable product of a racialized worldview.[111] Interestingly, however, in the public debates over annexing the Philippines, for example, it was anti-imperialists who most often wielded racist arguments to reject the extension of American power over disparate and "inferior" peoples "incapable of being assimilated to the Anglo-Saxon" in the Pacific and the Caribbean.[112] Progressive journalist William Allen White wrote late in March 1899 that his paper, the *Emporia Gazette*, supported the ongoing war in the Philippines. The paper backed the war with Spain along the characteristic lines as much of the American populace. White editorialized, "Only Anglo-Saxons can govern themselves. . . . It is the Anglo-Saxon's manifest destiny to go forth as a world conqueror."[113]

By the late 1890s Lodge and Roosevelt espoused what can be seen as a "conflicted" doctrine when it came to the intersection of race and empire. It should come as no shock that they expressed a characteristic America-centric worldview and racist perception of a hierarchy among peoples. They struggled to racialize both the American population and that of the Philippines, Puerto Rico, and elsewhere in defense of incorporating those peoples and regions under the auspices of American governance. Such foreign policy notions were complicated, blending as they did concepts of Kiplingesque "white man's burden" with views of the democratic tutelage of alien peoples. So, too, they had profound implications for domestic policy as well. Lodge, for example, argued that there was a clear domestic corollary to cordoning off some peoples while including others in the greater American national and colonial sphere. There was an overriding need to set limits and reject "unfit" foreign peoples from joining the nation. Thus, he said, early in the 1890s and certainly after the war concluded in 1898 there was a pressing need for immigration restriction.[114]

Justifying Protectionist Isolation at Home and Abroad

Lodge was a proponent of a form of protectionist isolationism that was grounded culturally on a homogenizing vision of nationalistic Americanization and assimilation of immigrants. This position placed him in opposition to the pluralistic philosophy then emerging and against any embrace of so-called hyphenated Americans, a vision later social critics and pluralist antiwar activists on the Left, like Randolph Bourne, began to reject in the mid-1910s. As Lodge explained in a "Forefathers' Day" address as early as 1888, "Let us have done with British-Americans and Irish-Americans and German-Americans, and so on, and all be Americans. . . .

If a man is going to be an American at all let him be so without any quali-fying adjectives; and if he is going to be something else, let him drop the word American from his personal description."[115] So, too, he saw the war as humanitarian and therefore just. "The final expulsion of Spain from the Americas and from the Philippines is the fit conclusion," he declared, "of the long strife between the people who stood for civil and religious freedom, and those who stood for bigotry and tyranny as hideous in their action as which have ever cursed humanity."[116]

It was Lodge's realist concern with the acquisition and the stability of foreign markets for American goods, and the protection of U.S.-based in-dustry that most influenced Roosevelt's rhetoric. Roosevelt's invocation of manhood and strenuous "tests" for Anglo-Americans in turn informed some of Lodge's masculinized and racialized language.[117] Though Lodge considered racial "progress," the advancement of U.S. manhood, and a providential national mission to be important, he continued to argue, as in the case of the Hawaiian Islands, for instance, that economics and mar-ket expansion "outweighed all other considerations."[118] Using similar logic, Lodge later pushed for long-term American control of the Panama Canal, and port and infrastructure facilities in Mexico and the Caribbean.

Lodge agreed with Roosevelt that this mission against tyrannical pow-ers was elemental to an American foreign policy of "vigorous masculin-ity." Interestingly, both Lodge and Roosevelt applied these ideals not only to diplomacy, but also to domestic reform and local politics. During the Venezuelan crisis in 1895, Lodge acted as a representative of New En-gland industries and helped open Latin American markets "to draw closer relations with us."[119] In turn, at home, Lodge supported limited domestic trust-busting and endorsed high protective tariffs. Always looking out for his constituents, Lodge repeatedly found ways to protect American busi-ness and appropriate funds to the Charlestown naval yard. In his speeches and writings he took every opportunity to reify the Gloucester fisherman as an ideal American and to urge the protection of fishermen from foreign intimidation on the seas. Elihu Root once flippantly remarked that Lodge was "the senior Senator from the fishing grounds" because of the fre-quency of these statements.[120]

Neither Splendid Nor Little

"It has been a splendid little war, begun with the highest motives, carried on with magnificent intelligence and spirit, favored by that fortune which loves the brave," remarked U.S. Ambassador to London (and about-to-be Secretary of State) John Hay in 1898.[121] In his letter to his friend Roosevelt, Hay's gallant depiction of the war is profoundly misleading.

Nothing about the war had been "little" except its duration, from the declaration on April 25, 1898, to the peace on December 10, 1898. The conflict was a massive undertaking for a nation that had never mustered the army and navy for overseas war and territorial conquest. A vast ensemble of people had to be deployed to make war and attain subsequent territorial control. All of these developments, in turn, radically reoriented how politicians, activists, and thinkers grappled with older values for anticolonialism, neutrality, and nonentanglement.[122]

As early as 1899, Lodge looked back and saw that the 1895 Venezuelan crisis and the Spanish-American War were harbingers of a new American worldview and role. He wrote the first history of the Spanish-American War, published in that same year. A sea change had occurred in public consciousness, he said, at the very moment when the "war note [against Spain] rang through the land." Lodge's explanation for this transition continued with the claim that "with dazzled eyes at first, and then with ever clearer and steadier gaze, [the American people] saw that in the years of isolation and self-absorption they had built up a great world power, that they must return to the ocean which they had temporarily abandoned, and have their share in the trade of every country and the commerce of every sea."[123] Indeed, in 1902 another controversy with Venezuela forced Lodge and Roosevelt to take action. These events help to reframe how much American power had changed in the years since the previous crisis. Great Britain, Germany, and Italy sent battleships to blockade Venezuelan ports to coerce the nation to begin repaying debts as had been agreed earlier. Firmly committed to an American Isthmian canal and troubled both by the use of force by European powers in the hemisphere and at the prospect of German incursions in the Caribbean and South America, in a complicated series of maneuvers Roosevelt threatened the use of American naval power while working behind the scenes to end the blockade so that the matter would be submitted for international arbitration, and payment on Venezuela's foreign debts would resume.

Taking a longer view of the evolution of Lodge's views on isolationism, internationalism, and intervention after this point early in the century, it is instructive to look ahead to the decisive role he would play in 1919, as he neared the end of his political career. For some observers his politics appeared to veer wildly from imperialism to isolationism. However, if one bookends Lodge's involvement in articulating the "large policy" of expansion and his push for the Spanish-American War with his high-profile fight against the Treaty of Versailles and the League of Nations, as is common, one misses the continuity in his thought from the 1890s through the 1920s. This was the time when not only Lodge's isolationist positions and principles developed, but also isolationist ideas became increasingly appealing and subject to debate among prominent politicians, thinkers, and citizens.[124]

Just as for many flexible thinkers whose ideas and work spanned a lengthy and active life of work, we can say that there was a "young" Lodge and an "old" Lodge. Still, certain unifying views were evident throughout his lifetime. The belief in America's exceptionalism, that the nation stood apart from the corruptions of Old European politics and culture, was among the most consistent aspects of Lodge's personal and political writings and speeches during the course of his almost half century in politics. Also paramount and unswerving was Lodge's firm desire to preserve and enhance national autonomy, and to avoid being bound by the whims of other countries or alliances. Thus, Lodge's unilateral perspective on how America ought to operate in the world, which guided his expansionist interpretation of traditional foreign policy in his early career, can be seen as guiding his late career efforts to reject the Treaty of Versailles and the League of Nations.

Lodge adamantly opposed any binding alliances that would have forced America to commit military forces abroad to support or defend foreign nations. Such policy actions were anathema to his understanding of the best international pursuits for the United States. Here the idea of mission intersected loosely with views about global engagement and American traditions. To join such a league, for example, would abrogate the Senate's treaty-making and war-declaration functions in the Constitution. These were powers Lodge held sacrosanct. So, too, Lodge in no way rejected the traditional Washingtonian vision of isolation; he endorsed the Monroevian view of that precedent and argued for unilateral rather than multilateral foreign policy initiatives.

Starting in the 1890s, Lodge adapted traditional views of isolation as expressed in the early republic to modern conditions and proposed that America's new power dictated new directions for a nation with a "manifest destiny." However, he argued that his new direction of a "large policy" did not constitute a new ordering of priorities; rather, it emphasized the most fundamental democratic values as enshrined in the Declaration and Constitution. In short, Lodge sought expansion to ensure freedom, prosperity, and protection. He maintained that the long-standing admonition to avoid foreign politics was wise, but as the nation ascended in commercial and military power and moved outward in the 1890s, this tradition had "no bearing on the extension of the United States."[125]

His rationale was simple: expanding on the nation's own terms adhered to the spirit of the isolationist precedents laid out by Washington and reified by Monroe. Unifying Lodge's expansionism in the 1890s and his later isolationist stand against the League was his unilateral interpretation of Washington's Farewell Address as to why and how America should steer clear of binding entanglements yet could take action abroad whenever and however it was in the nation's own best interests. Moreover, all of these views were informed by his belief in the need to encourage domestic industrial productivity and economic growth, especially in light of the recession of 1893.

In February 1899 the Senate passed the Paris Peace Treaty 57–27—with only one more vote than the required two-thirds majority. During the debates Lodge argued on the Senate floor that to reject the treaty would mean being "branded as a people incapable of taking rank . . . as one of the great world powers!"[126] So, too, Roosevelt objected that rejecting the treaty would make the nation "unwarlike and isolated." As he put it, "We cannot, if we would, play the part of China, and be content to rot by inches in our ignoble ease within our borders."[127] Publicly Lodge exulted; privately he disclosed to Roosevelt that the vote had been one of the hardest fights of his time in Congress. There was a strong push back against acquiring the Philippines, Puerto Rico, Guam, and authority over Cuba. On the whole, however, the American population echoed Lodge's public assessments and appeared ebullient about the wartime triumphs. Novelist Henry Adams surveyed the national press and the temper of the man on the street at the time with a dour comment: "I find America so cheerful, and so full of swagger and self-satisfaction, that I hardly know it." He believed the immense levels of hubris were attributable to the rapid, seemingly glorious victory and to "McKinley's prosperity."[128]

Across the Atlantic, the Spanish referred to their loss as *el desastre* (the disaster). More than two hundred thousand troops had failed to subdue the Cuban revolutionaries. Three years of fighting cost roughly fifty thousand

Spanish soldiers and sailors their lives, bankrupting the state treasury, and all but destroying the nation's waning international status. In contrast, the United States lost only 345 in combat and 2,900 in total casualties. After the Paris Peace Conference concluded, the London *Times* dismissed Spain as a world power, opining on December 12, 1898, that Spain's "prestige as a fighting-power, by land or seas, has disappeared."[129]

The war was replete with symbolic power and consequences that Hay and Lodge could not foresee in 1898. Acquiring widespread and long-standing access to overseas territories took on an internal logic of its own. Over time these areas were far from temporary extensions of influence but became integral to both informal and formal American internationalist activities in the region. Together, the state of Hawaii (annexed during the imperial war fever of 1898) and the territory of Puerto Rico (acquired rapidly by U.S. forces that fought a small Spanish garrison) stand as a legacy of the permanence of this "aberration" of American territorial expansion. The war had changed everything, observed Judge H. H. Powers enthusiastically. "A year ago, we wanted no colonies, no alliances, no European neighbors, no army and not much navy. . . . Our role in the world was to be nil. . . . The Monroe Doctrine was construed as requiring no constructive action on our part toward the civilized world. The Washington Doctrine was frankly interpreted to mean national isolation. Our position on these points might be questionable, but it was not equivocal. We at least knew our own minds. Today every one of these principles is challenged, if not definitely rejected."[130] Hay and Powers were contented with the ease of victory and outcome of the conflict. By 1900 the nation had acquired significant lands and could exert new degrees of military and commercial control in the Caribbean and Pacific. Preparedness, as well as the "large policy," seemed to have been vindicated.

Consistency and the "Large Policy"

Very little of what policy-makers, presidents, or nations want remains after more than a century. Certain consistent patterns, and ways of talking about national values, however reinterpreted given contemporary conditions, do endure. Value-laden political formulations underlie the logic of intervention today in much the same fashion as they shaped the thinking that led to war in 1898. At the intersection of ideas, historical circumstance, and action is the gray zone where implicit conceptions of tradition and meaning shape concrete policy.

Historians may err by looking for direct sequences of events that illustrate how meanings reinforce or become reformulated into actions. That is, in the case of the Spanish-American War, historians have often singled out the formative role of yellow journalism, the development of critical ideas about race, naval power, neo-mercantilist economic policy, or imperial outreach as the causal influences most responsible for the conflict. This viewpoint, however, tends to miss or minimize the fact that for those Americans like Lodge, the view that isolation was important could not be fully rejected; it had to be refashioned to support the new world order of American power. This same hybrid mixture of isolation with international involvement, which was itself subject to changing conditions and always under pressure, found resonance among citizens and politicians alike, which in part served to block the path for future empire at the turn of the twentieth century.[131]

Michael Ignatieff, a human rights scholar and politician, has critiqued what he argues are long-standing consistencies in the unilateralist and self-serving nature marking American intervention abroad, while historian Robert Kagan has put forward a positive case for many of the same patterns. In the context of the recent American presence in Iraq, Afghanistan, and Liberia, for example, Ignatieff declared, "Whatever the ostensible rationales—saving lives, repelling aggressors, establishing democracy—increased American power and influence are the most important reasons why interventions happen."[132] With respect to the Spanish-American War, Ignatieff is partly right. The arguments of Lodge and the architects of the "large policy" make clear that humanitarian and democratic rationales were not trivial. Serious humanitarian elements were evident throughout Lodge's model of "large policy" imperialism.

In the case of the war with Spain and in the ongoing war and occupation of the Philippines, the United States embarked simultaneously on a dual project of humanitarian-democratic intervention and an imperial project of expansion. Conflict was spurred by chance events and by the ways in which sensational occurrences, such as the sinking of the *Maine* and how America's jingoistic press interpreted various inflammatory acts of Spanish oppression, reinforced bellicose passions and imperialist judgments. Yet intervention was also an act of will by American politicians, supported by the majority of citizens. And it was crassly imperialist and paternalistic in important ways. Cuban revolutionaries, as historian Louis Perez demonstrated, posed a significant threat to those in the

United States who wanted to keep Cuba on a short leash.[133] Intervention and the resulting American role in Cuban politics served to prevent the installation of a truly revolutionary or independent government in Cuba or Puerto Rico, another realpolitik goal of the "large policy" advocates; and intervention halted any autonomy that might have been possible for an independent revolutionary regime in the Philippines. Nevertheless, the very language of U.S. proprietary relationships over foreign dependencies was and continued to be contested. American democratic ideals coexisted uneasily with empire. Fundamentally unlike the pre-statehood territories during continental expansion, U.S. "colonies" could not be referred to as such. This reticence may appear largely symbolic, but it had real consequences. It prevented the establishment of explicitly "colonial offices" (à la Britain, France, or Germany). The underlying isolationist values reinforced democratic principles that warded off imperial rhetoric in the management of the new acquisitions, which officially became the domain of "insular affairs." So, too, as we shall see, similar concepts inflected the language and practical policy of U.S. entry into World War I as an "associated power" rather than an explicit ally.

From the conclusion of the Spanish-American War until the coming of the Depression, the United States sent troops to Latin American countries roughly thirty-two times, once a year on average.[134] When measured this way, international engagement was the prime foreign policy paradigm. To supplement the Monroe Doctrine, a large bloc of Republican policy-makers deployed the Roosevelt Corollary in 1904 (heavily endorsed by Lodge and in part a result of the second Venezuela incident in 1902–1903) and thereafter used it as a policy instrument to justify intervention on the basis that the United States, acting as a "civilized nation," had the right to stop "chronic wrongdoing" and "exercise an international police power" throughout the Western Hemisphere. Yet for Lodge and the "large policy" advocates, it was critically important that they retain some of the values and particularly the rhetoric of an isolationist tradition. Their new interpretation of Monroe continued, but their further aims of obtaining foreign dependencies simply could not be reconciled to past isolationist precedents.

These ideals of combining nationalism, interventionist unilateralism, and elements of isolation faded briefly as the war in the Philippines dragged on. The excess costs of empire did not appear worthwhile to most Americans. Such ideas, however, continued to motivate Lodge, Roosevelt, and their expansionist colleagues in debates with the anti-imperialists. A decade later, they still aimed to extend and further codify unilateral, hypernationalistic hemispheric dominance. In a major push, Lodge persuaded the Senate to pass what came to be known as the Lodge Corollary to the Monroe Doctrine to pursue these ends. This 1912 resolution stated that "by the word 'colonization' we also cover the action by companies or corporations or by citizens or subjects of a foreign State which might do . . . what the Monroe doctrine was intended to prevent."[135] Here, Lodge further broadened his definitions to protect American interests and to hinder Japanese firms then setting up in Mexico and to compete with European individuals and companies that were expanding their networks across Latin America, as well as in the Pacific.

In contrast, recall that McKinley, speaking to the Home Market Club in Boston in 1899, forcefully stated that the "large policy" aims of American involvement abroad were in keeping with a long view of acting as an anticolonial, nonentangled nation. "No imperial designs lurk in the American mind. They are alien to American sentiment, thought, and purpose. Our priceless principles undergo no change under a tropic sun. They go with the flag." McKinley, like Lodge, wanted to make America's "tradition" work toward his desired ends. He continued by asking his audience a series of rhetorical questions that parallel present-day concerns in which isolationist values play a part in humanitarian arguments for intervention abroad. His was an intensely paternalistic and hierarchical view. "If we can benefit these remote peoples, who will object? If in the years of the future, they are established in government under law and liberty, who will regret our perils and sacrifices?" He concluded, "Always cost and sacrifice, but always after them the fruition of liberty, education, and civilization."[136]

The Backlash Begins

The outspoken anti-imperialist Carl Schurz, a founding member of the Boston Anti-Imperialist League, believed this "cost and sacrifice" was too much to bear. He disagreed with McKinley's logic and assumptions on every count. Schurz rejuvenated a pro-isolation position he had taken in an 1893 *Harper's* article on Manifest Destiny. Unlike McKinley, Schurz had fixed his horizons firmly on the domestic scene and was centrally concerned with protecting individual rights. Schurz unveiled this vision early on, emphasizing the needs of American citizens at home and the principles of democracy and self-determination abroad. "I deny that our duties we owe to the Cubans and the Porto [*sic*] Ricans, and the Filipinos, and the Tagals of the Asiatic islands absolve us from the duties to the seventy-five millions of our own people, and to their posterity," declared Schurz at the University of Chicago convocation in 1899. "I deny that they oblige us to destroy the moral credit of our own republic by turning this loudly heralded war of liberation and humanity into a land-grabbing game and an act of criminal aggression. . . . Their independence, therefore, would be the natural and rightful outcome."[137]

Lodge, Roosevelt, and their expansionist cohort would soon struggle to control the imperialist machine they had helped to engineer. Their political philosophy—expanding and annexing new areas outside the continent, while purporting to remain true to isolationist precedents—did not appear to most American observers to incur great benefits back home. By 1902, Woodrow Wilson was writing about America's new global role as a "revolution." A friend of Roosevelt's, Charles J. Bonaparte, remarked that only a small group still wanted to continue with an activist "large policy" to expand the revolution. He observed that the Philippines had "cost us a great deal of money; and any benefits which have resulted from it to this country, are, as yet, imperceptible to the naked eye."[138] Bonaparte succinctly expressed the general mood of the moment, although the proponents of the "large policy" continued to beat the drum of expansion.

The reoriented "large policy" of the 1890s and early 1900s, and the war with Spain and ongoing counterinsurgency and occupation of the Philippines, represented a massive shift in American political thought and international activities. As McKinley's Assistant Secretary of State John Bassett Moore reflected, the United States had moved "from a position of comparative freedom from entanglements into the position of what is commonly called a world power." Moore identified the kernel of the change: "Where formerly we had only commercial interests, we now have territorial and political interests as well."[139] What is most significant is the radical way in which Lodge and his cohort refashioned the meaning of isolationism to encompass overseas territorial expansion. In late 1898 Lodge reflected on the history of Washington, Jefferson, and Monroe. He explained exactly how he saw the nation's world role connecting to its foreign policy and long-standing traditions. "Isolation in the United States," he wrote, "has been a habit, not a policy. It has been bred by circumstances and by them justified. When the circumstances change, the habit perforce changes too, and new policies are born to suit new conditions."[140]

Developing and applying the "large policy" under the new circumstances of the 1890s had unintended consequences. It aligned expansion and military strength with national progress in problematic ways. And it was particularly difficult to retain as a coherent doctrine because intervention abroad, and particularly the annexation of territories, entangled the nation outside the continent—and beyond the hemisphere—in a dramatically new manner. This generated a swift counterresponse by those who saw through the rationalizations of imperialists like Lodge. The resulting backlash formed the centralizing force for the anti-imperialist movement. From it would emerge new strains and emphases of isolationist thought and one of America's most dedicated, eclectic, and democratic—if ultimately not most effective—political opposition organizations.

2

A BETTER NATION MORALLY

In the mid-1890s William James encountered a cause that would absorb him and lead to his slow, steady politicization. The issue was the obscure yet inflammatory boundary dispute with England over Venezuela's national borders, which also had spurred Henry Cabot Lodge's nationalist sensibilities. In James's case, his political activism on that issue and subsequent spirited advocacy for the anti-imperialist cause arose directly and organically from his philosophical and psychological studies.[1]

James had addressed other political questions of the day—anti-lynching laws, conservation, temperance, women's suffrage, and the status of African Americans—but never before had he taken a prolonged public stance on any political issue as he did with anti-imperialism. Recognizing the consequences of zealous patriotism (that is, a near war with England as well as a public clamoring for international conflict) he was transformed. James began to develop and act upon his views concerning America's role in the world.

He became most politically active in his mid-fifties when he was a widely esteemed psychologist and philosopher teaching at Harvard University. In the fall of 1898, at the height of his enormous analytical talents, James joined the Boston-based anti-imperialist movement. While continuing his life's work on psychology, philosophy, and religious experience, he conceived and articulated a distinctive view of America's burgeoning role in the world. James vigorously explored traditional ideas of how the nation might remain generally isolationist in military and colonial terms, while it also engaged with the world, particularly in regard to culture and ideas.

Before America's war with Spain formally ended, James embraced a public profile as an anti-imperialist leader advocating a more "moral" course in the world and at home, while opposing bellicosity in all spheres of life. James moved quickly. He served as the vice president of the first major anti-imperialist mass meeting held in Cambridge, Massachusetts, on May 17, 1899. His letters and speeches show that he took this role seriously. He attended numerous small meetings in the Boston area and addressed audiences on the dangers of imperialism, particularly from 1899 to 1903. James signed petitions for the Anti-Imperialist League (AIL) in 1902 and 1903, and he gave one of his most memorable addresses at the New England AIL's annual meeting in 1903. In 1904 he became a member of the Philippine Independence Committee and from 1905 to 1907 he was a vice president of the Filipino Progress Association. From 1904 until his death in 1910, he served and was listed as a vice president of the reorganized national Anti-Imperialist League. In 1907 he acted as a vice president of a meeting on the neutralization of the Philippines organized by the AIL in Boston. In 1910, though in ill health and bedridden, James remained resolute. His writings reveal that he continued thinking deeply about militarism and signed an AIL public petition calling for immediate Philippine independence.[2] Most notable, James wrestled with the pugnacity as elemental to human nature and politics in the essay "On a Certain Blindness" (1898), a letter to the *Boston Transcript* (1899), a speech to the New England AIL (1903), an address to the Peace Banquet (1904), and his essay "The Moral Equivalent of War" (1906). Leading up to the Spanish-American War, James thought that Americans "had supposed overselves . . . a better nation morally than the rest, safe at home, and without the old savage ambition, destined to exert great international influence by throwing in our 'moral weight.'" While bellicosity and acquisitiveness are natural instincts, he observed, they can be contained. He argued this was done best when "aggressive" humans sublimated their inner drives toward "moral weight" rather than into "savage ambition."[3] In that way they could refine and conquer nature rather than battle or subjugate each other.

In his activism James argued powerfully for adherence to the "foundational principles" of democracy, anticolonialism, and nonentanglement. He also tried to counter the visceral appeal of imperial conquest with his own compelling language, calling for the renewal of America's "ancient soul" and egalitarian ethics. James and his cohort thought the nation should be guided by goals of expanding rights, reforms, and prosperity domestically, and promoting self-determination for others, rather than intervening abroad. They agreed that international commercial and cultural engagements were worthy. But colonial acquisitions were not.

Examining the tenets of James's political philosophy from when he first rejected warlike efforts for expansion and the "large policy" in the 1890s through 1910 shows that he advanced sophisticated anti-imperialist arguments and that these views often built on isolationist principles. James's thought represents many of the ideas that united a broad, heterogeneous group of Americans against U.S. expansionism at the turn of the twentieth century. These anti-imperialists included James and his former student, the racial reformer W. E. B. Du Bois, industrialist Andrew Carnegie, *Nation* editor E. L. Godkin, former Missouri Republican Senator Carl Schurz, settlement house activist Jane Addams, former president Grover Cleveland, Massachusetts Senator George Hoar, AIL presidents George Boutwell (1898–1905) and Moorfield Storey (1905–1921), businessman Edward Atkinson, writer Mark Twain, labor leader Samuel Gompers, Yale social scientist William Graham Sumner, liberal reformer Thomas Wentworth Higginson, and university presidents such as David Starr Jordan (Stanford) and Charles Elliot (Harvard). In this collection of strange bedfellows, one thing these anti-imperialists could agree on was that the primary U.S. aim should not be imperialism but, rather, solving domestic problems such as moral decay, poverty, housing, and the excesses of monopolies and corporate capitalism brought on by industrialization. Thus, the anti-imperialists developed a modern way of evaluating America's isolationist and internationalist inclinations, given the pressing challenges of industrial society and new status as a global power rising into the twentieth century.

What unified the outlooks of many of these thinkers and politicians was the growing sense that theirs was a period of transition in which the social revolution propelled by industrialization had fundamentally altered the framework of society. James and most of the anti-imperialists resisted this change but saw modernization itself as inevitable, even beneficial. New circumstances, these anti-imperialists said, demanded a modern view of the nation's complex relations with the rest of the world. Yet opponents of empire wanted to preserve long-standing investments in steering clear of foreign entanglements. In many ways their critique was a thorough modernization of old concepts, a transition in ideals that paralleled the "large policy" unilateralist interpretation of America's isolationist traditions.

Overcoming the formalism of the era entailed an active engagement with reality and a modernizing of traditional American values about isolation and international engagement.[4] Moreover, James and like-minded anti-imperialists fused those developing concepts to a domestic reform vision. Theirs was an intellectual "revolt," as one scholar termed it. Thinkers like James sought to dispense with rigid categories of thought while remaining flexible by using the scientific method as just one of many tools of social analysis to argue for democratic ideals and against their abridgement through the pursuit of war and empire.[5] Washington, Jefferson, Monroe, and Lincoln had laid out America's "ancient soul" by establishing the foundational bedrock of America as an anti-imperial and anticolonial democracy, they said. They refined a peculiar vision of isolationism to promote what they interpreted as "traditional" American democratic anticolonial aims, including fighting expansion and annexation, most forms of nationalistic bellicosity, and especially aiming to counter alliances or wars with Old World powers. According to proto-isolationist anti-imperialists, including James, these fundamental ideas continued to pass the pragmatic test of being beneficial concepts that continued to achieve desired ends.[6] As we shall see, while "large policy" advocates attempted to explain their expansionist turn outward as a solution to internal problems and a means of advancing the nation's international power, anti-imperialists agreed that commercial and cultural exchange abroad was beneficial, but sought to turn inward to find solutions to pressing domestic concerns rather than attempt costly imperial incursions that they deemed to be undemocratic.

Anti-Imperialism: A Jamesian Movement

The anti-imperialist movement can be seen as essentially Jamesian in one important sense: it was based almost exclusively on the grounds of abstract principle and then sought to lay out how these principles could be meshed to accord with current events and policies. James's pragmatic axiom that the truth of an idea should be measured "by the conduct it dictates"—along with his belief in broadly democratic values and core individualism—cogently connects his political philosophy to his vision of adhering to American ideals and helps us understand the larger anti-imperial cause.[7]

In short, most opponents of expansionism, like James, did not resist imperial acquisitions for commercial, religious, or humanitarian reasons, although a few did. Instead, with James's arguments among the vanguard, anti-imperialists tended to oppose the "large policy" because it ran directly counter to the bedrock doctrines that they themselves often cited:

Washington's Farewell Address, Jefferson's first inaugural address, the Monroe Doctrine, and Lincoln's Gettysburg Address. In James's arguments, we can see the shape of most of the foremost anti-imperialists' positions. Throughout his political activism, his political philosophy opposed all hints of militarism, arguing that "the only permanent safeguard against irrational explosions of the fighting instinct" would be the permanent separation of "armament and opportunity."[8] He advocated that the nation instead turn inward and devote resources and efforts to domestic improvement, such as to enhance education and intellectual life, civil rights, civic spirit, and other reforms that fell under the broad rubric "progressive" (though anti-imperialists often did not agree on the specifics).

James himself turned inward. His anti-imperialism was part of a broader project he later described as enhancing "the civic genius of the people" to take aim at "internal enemies" of civilization.[9] In this he shared with his anti-imperialist colleagues a collective nostalgia and sanctified sense of the need to avoid large standing armies and overseas adventures to buttress principles of nonentanglement, and most important, as a way to empower reason and reject corruption rather than constrain individuals within a democracy. They asserted that these freedoms were essentially "American" and called for what James termed a "choice of cause."[10] So, too, James and most anti-imperialists urged that the nation should not share the bellicose imperialism that tainted Great Britain, Spain, and many other monarchical European powers. After all, the United States had revolted against such imperialist oppression.[11]

Along these same rhetorical lines lies one of James's most eviscerating anti-imperial arguments: his critique of specious abstractions. Calling for his audiences to note the unfounded and inane qualities of ideas such as Manifest Destiny, the "white man's burden," and "modern civilization," James repeatedly and harshly derided the hubris of the absolute scientific "truth" propounded by thinkers like social Darwinist Herbert Spencer, as well as physicist John Tyndall and biologist Thomas Huxley, which James saw as inherent to imperialist thought. He thought their abstract and absolute nostrums created a "big, hollow, resounding, corrupting, sophisticating torrent of mere brutal momentum and irrationality." These views went hand in hand with James's notion of the value of public philosophers, who illuminate the problems of "aesthetic abstractness" and help to steer clear of the "blindness" of abstraction so often "prattled by" politicians, businessmen, and thinkers.[12]

The assemblage of anti-imperialists fighting imperial expansion ranged across a vast intellectual and political terrain. The most prominent and dedicated anti-imperialists, though, were more alike than dissimilar. Most (unlike James) had long struggled for an array of social and political reforms. In their words and deeds emerge a clear set of insights about how reform at home shaped the way many Americans weighed the purpose and values of the nation's commitments abroad.

The key to understanding the diverse positions of the anti-imperialists is that they argued from the principle that a nation conceived as an instrument of and for its own people should focus on the demos via reform to promote civic values and prosperity domestically. Further, anti-imperialists agreed that America should never emulate the colonial practices or join in corrupting alliances that would bind the nation to the monarchical excesses of Old Europe. Virtually every man and woman who espoused the anti-imperial cause reflected these guiding beliefs in their speeches and writings.[13]

James's social psychological views, however, represented an element in his thought that differentiated him from many anti-imperialists. His scholarly discipline and wide-ranging interests impressed upon him the power of emotion and the visceral attraction of patriotic bellicosity. He saw these twin forces as among the most daunting obstacles the anti-imperialist cause had to overcome. In his writings from the mid-1890s through his death in 1910, James struggled with how tempting it was to buy into the instinctive appeal of personal and national destiny and aggrandizement— to expand outward with martial vigor, seeking honor as well as material gain—yet he also perceived heightened danger and attendant intellectual problems when such emotions laced with patriotic and materialist incentives were infused into the rational processes of generating an interventionist foreign policy.

While the contours of James's political philosophy grew organically from his philosophical and psychological studies, his very modernist position in philosophy and psychology was in tension with his far more traditional views against "bigness" as manifested in any part of American life. This was a tension James never quite resolved and yet one that animated his efforts to reconcile his philosophy and psychology with his political activism. The Venezuelan dispute in the mid-1890s was followed rapidly by America's war with Spain, and this succession revealed to James how a nation could be consumed by war fever in a "twinkling of an eye," as he put it.[14] So when James served as vice president of the New England AIL at the height of his political activities, he built on insights derived from witnessing the rise of American bellicosity and expansionist fervor in the 1890s. In turn, James's well-known pragmatic assessment of ideas was integral to his belief that egalitarian democratic ideals and reform sensibilities ought to inform how Americans see themselves, their country, and their country's behavior toward other peoples and nations.

The Debates Sharpen

James and the anti-imperialist assault on expansionism inverted the developing ideas about expansion seen in Lodge's thought and actions during this period. Lodge and his colleagues claimed the old isolationist principles were outdated but not outmoded; they averred that old isolationism should be modified so that a newly powerful United States could interact with the world unilaterally and forcibly extend national commercial and military power abroad. These arguments amounted to a unilateralist and greatly expanded version of the Monroe Doctrine.

Yet a similarly refined isolationist vision, which blended peaceful internationalism and an antipathy to all elements of colonialism, lies at the heart of the anti-imperial case. Imperialism, James and the anti-imperialists declared, was clearly anathema to America, a nation born out of an anti-colonial revolution to throw off oppressive monarchical rule. Instead, the nation's goal, the anti-imperialists maintained, should be to harness the nation's moral, political, and industrial might at home to fulfill America's true core principles. Eschewing conquest and rule abroad, the nation should widen prosperity and improve social harmony at home, according to James, by rejecting what he termed "bigness." James's position flew in the face of the expansionists' formula. They generally urged the development of large industrial combinations, trusts, and even monopolies, operating around the clock and around the world. They favored heavy and light industry and other primarily export-oriented businesses that would profit from access to the new markets and goods provided by colonies and global trade; rarely did they think in terms of social harmony. Expansionists such as Brooks Adams argued that the nation's economy would atrophy without extension of American power and the founding of a "seat of empire."[15]

While James's essay "On a Certain Blindness" never explicitly referenced American policy toward the Philippines, the allegorical structure for the piece emphasized a sharp contrast to Adams: the flawed "blindness" and "bigness" born of imperialism, the abstractions undergirding this logic, and the need for tolerance and openness about other peoples, places, and experiences.[16] James's views were characteristic of the broader anti-imperialist position, which abhorred the imperialist antidemocratic ruling of alien peoples against their will. But while he was in the mainstream of the movement in this regard, he was not as neatly aligned on the issue of economic interest or racial egalitarianism. James was not much concerned with commerce per se, except in rejecting the greed-based "bigness" of neo-mercantilist arguments for expansion. Many of the business figures working for the anti-imperialist cause—such as Edward A. Atkinson, insurance leader and former cotton mills executive, as well as a cofounder of the Anti-Imperialist League—were more nuanced in their approach to this subject. Inspired by the ideas of Adam Smith, among others, Atkinson often argued in his tracts that colonialism was antithetical to free trade, and colonial wars were unnecessarily injurious to domestic business.[17] James, though, tended to link questions about the economic interests involved in expansion abroad to a primal emotional impulse for acquisition rather than a cold, hardheaded economic analysis. In James's analysis, the effort to achieve colonial rule exulted in the warrior-conqueror-savior hubris. This form of "heroism," he concluded in "On a Certain Blindness," is the sort that "each of us" should oppose because it "presum[es] to regulate the rest of the vast field," by conquest or by solidifying generalizations about races or civilizations, rather than nurturing the individual journeys and the plurality of experience that he so much admired and celebrated.[18]

Against Blind Abstractions and "Bigness"

In condemning the "blind" abstractions of most imperialists, James seems to have developed some of the most important elements of his famous position against "bigness" as well. Just after he composed "On a Certain Blindness" and at the height of the debates over colonial policy in the Philippines during the summer of 1899, a private letter reveals perhaps the best encapsulation of James's anticolonial, anti-bigness connection. "I am against bigness and greatness in all their forms," he wrote. "The bigger the unit you deal with . . . the more mendacious is the life displayed. So I am against all big organizations as such, national ones first and foremost; against all big successes and big results; and in favor of the eternal forces of truth which always work in the individual."[19]

Anti-imperialist old guard Republicans and mugwumps like Senator George Hoar, businessman Atkinson, intellectual Godkin, and Senator Schurz could agree with younger reformers and intellectuals such as Stanford University president Jordan, and reformers Mary Livermore and George McNeil, all of whom assented to most of James's ideas about the blinding corruptions of "the big." Most mugwumps had been abolitionist Republicans who switched parties during the election of 1884. The term "mugwump" was used derisively and derived from the Algonquian word "mugquomp," meaning important (perhaps self-righteous) person of "high and mighty" status. Others in the movement also adhered to Jamesian anti-bigness, seeing enlarged government, corporations, or other entities as generally tending toward greater hubris, avarice, immorality, and sociopolitical repression. This group included such reformers as W. E. B. Du Bois and Jane Addams, and religious and missionary figures, such as Charles Parkhurst, Edward Everett Hale, Charles Ames, and the young evangelical nationalist John Mott. They saw numerous benefits in Jamesian "openness" coupled with the avoidance of "bigness." Of course, these positions contrasted with the goals of expansionism, which was pivotal to the "closed" logic preached by Lodge, Roosevelt, Mahan, and Brooks Adams.[20] Theirs was the type of collective heroism repugnant to James and those allies who shared his individualistic philosophy.[21]

In the most notable of its early publications in 1898, titled "Broadsides," the Anti-Imperialist League introduced its major "Arguments against the Adoption of a So-Called Imperial Policy." For the benefit of fellow citizens, the AIL compiled a description of what "thinking men" from George Washington onward had argued were the best policies.[22] A broad swath of anti-imperialists agreed that no strict and aggressive interpretation of the Monroe Doctrine should be allowed.[23] James approved of David Starr Jordan's position when he said in May 1898 that for the United States to acquire and hold Cuba, the Philippines, or other foreign lands as colonies, "our democracy must necessarily depart from its best principles and traditions."[24] Along strikingly similar lines and on similar grounds in July 1898, Vermont's anti-imperialist Democrats gathered at the state convention to oppose the "imperial policy of the Republican party," to reject the "admission of the Hawaiian Islands to Statehood," and to support William Jennings Bryan. Further, they drew explicitly on a positive view of isolation and argued against "abandoning the Monroe Doctrine, depriving us of the advantages we have enjoyed from our isolated situation."[25]

By the time James published the final version of "The Moral Equivalent of War" in 1910, he had long struggled to mediate between, on the one hand, what he thought was redeeming in the Rooseveltian philosophy of robust action and masculine "strenuousity" and, on the other hand, the anti-imperialist, peace-seeking aims, with his own goal for a pluralist nation that encouraged tolerance and "smallness" over the intolerant homogenizing influence of "bigness." The "moral equivalent" represents his best, and final, effort at such reconciliation. While James lacked specificity in what he argued should be the "conquest of nature" rather than of "fellow man," or precisely what such a conquest would look like, James achieved a great insight in combining psychology, politics, and social philosophy when he argued that military conflict and domination did not need to be considered elemental to human instincts. They could be separated, he said, from the useful aspects of heroism, endurance, and discipline, which might be redirected toward personal responsibility and a heroic form of civic passion. He argued for a "moral equivalent of war" to be waged at home and to serve as a secular doctrine of works designed to bolster individual as well as national values. Thus, James laid the conceptual groundwork for what later became the New Deal's Works Progress Administration and the transnational humanistic U.S. Peace Corps, and was more recently evident in the "soft power" efforts and varied humanitarian projects of the domestic and international outreach of the Teacher Corps and other international nongovernmental organizations.

Anti-Imperialist Principles

Once James had resolved that education would be one of the chief weapons in what he termed "this new war" against imperial impulses, he was astonished that Theodore Roosevelt, his former student, explicitly bashed him by name on the pages of the *Harvard Crimson* for his stance against the Cleveland speech in 1895. Addressing his letter to the future citizens of the United States, Roosevelt equated loyalty with political obedience. James found this conflation untenable. Responding in the *Crimson*, he chastised Roosevelt, saying at least at Harvard, "if nowhere else on the planet," citizens should "be patriotic enough *not* to remain passive whilst the destinies of our country are being settled by surprise." James went on to warn readers they should not be cowed into submission by having their patriotism or masculinity challenged and by being attacked for speaking their minds. Rather, he exhorted them, "Let us consult our reason as to what is best, and then exert ourselves as citizens with all our might."[26]

Carl Schurz eloquently delineated a similar set of pragmatic propositions to James's stand, yet this came at a time when most anti-imperialists had not yet gathered together as a movement to oppose the American expansion. Writing privately, Schurz said, "I believe that this Republic, in that sense, can endure so long as it remains true to the principles upon which it was founded, but that it will morally decay if it abandons them." He continued, "I believe that this democracy, the government of, by, and for the people, is not fitted for a colonial policy . . . and arbitrary rule over alien peoples."[27]

Recall that it was not until the 1890s, marked by the Venezuela incident, that James became increasingly opposed to American interventionism abroad. The same was true for virtually every other anti-imperialist. Whereas James saw the boundary dispute as a lesson in how a nation could be consumed by war fever in a "twinkling of an eye," Andrew Carnegie saw the United States as "sovereign upon the American continent," with the root of the problem lying with England's reluctance to have America mediate the conflict. Carnegie's aim, though, was for a tacit alliance of England and America to be protective but not "domineering."[28] Charles Eliot Norton was more pessimistic and elitist in enumerating what he said were "lessons learned," arguing that the Venezuela controversy proved that America was so controlled by mob instincts and fired by economic and military power that the crisis heralded a "miserable end for this century." "Large policy" advocates (even Cleveland) combined to manipulate what Godkin called a "mad appeal to the basest passions of the mob," and their efforts proved to Norton that the nation had turned toward a future of "error and of wrong." The "rise of democracy to power in America and in Europe," Norton wrote, aghast, "is not, as had been hoped, to be a safeguard of peace and civilization."[29]

By 1898 the force of the nation's underlying bellicosity and desire for conquest forced James out of his somewhat naive sense of American righteousness and exceptionalism. Moving closer to a position combining those of Godkin and Norton, James was motivated by an almost existential understanding of the potential threat imperialism posed. The Republic's democratic ideals, he believed, hung in the balance.

James shared many fundamental assumptions and agreed with most of the prescriptions advocated by the growing ranks of anti-imperialists. Many were mildly pacifist, seeing war as James did, as an expression of bellicose human nature. They vociferously defended America's traditional policy that avoided international entanglements and preserved national autonomy.

Yet many on both sides also made social Darwinist and racist arguments against incorporating alien and "inferior" people into the United States. Imperialists and anti-imperialists often shared such views and even worked together—such as Lodge, Hoar, and Jordan. Seeking to limit the influx of inferior peoples into the continental United States, these erstwhile foes came together in the 1890s to significantly restrict immigration and place stringent merit tests on applicants wishing to enter the country.

Before exploring more of James's views and those of the anti-imperialists on this point, it is necessary to set the context in brief. For instance, in 1892 Professor Theodore Woolsey, a specialist on American foreign policy and international law at Yale, had written that the driving logic of modernizing the navy, expanding coastal defenses, and augmenting the army would build on itself and push the nation further from the foundational values of nonentanglement and a limited anticolonial view of the Monroe Doctrine, especially to counter European countries. "The tendency is not one which will stand still. It must be checked at once or grow greater," observed Woolsey.[30] Presciently, in 1895 these fears were realized, and more fully by 1898.

According to Woolsey, a "sea of adventure" would likely imperil genuinely isolationist principles. "A doctrine of non-interference on the part of European states in this continent, would be changed into a license to interfere on our part." The problem, according to the anti-imperialists and Woolsey, was that such license might come at the expense of domestic progress and could court international dangers by assuming a "burden of responsibilities, heavy cost, and empty glory."[31]

"In our present condition, we have over all the great nations of the world one advantage of incalculable value," explained the anti-imperialist liberal Republican senator from Missouri, Carl Schurz, as early as 1893. "We are the only ones not under any necessity of keeping up a large armament either on land or water for the security of its possessions, the only one that can turn all the energies of its population to productive employment, and the only one that has an entirely free hand." In a *Harper's New Monthly Magazine* article, "Manifest Destiny," Schurz urged the nation to turn against any imperialist impulses. He was aware of the United States' potential power but wanted to maintain the country's long-standing tradition of military and diplomatic isolation. Private and public resources, Schurz said, should be directed toward internal economic and political development rather than to arms or colonies. "This [advantage] is a blessing for which the American people can never be too thankful," he concluded. "It should not lightly be jeopardized."[32]

Domestic progress certainly concerned W. E. B. Du Bois and Samuel Gompers. With the rising labor and civil rights movements of the 1890s, their highest priorities were issues of race and labor, respectively—and they were not centrally concerned with issues of people in distant lands. That is not to say that either was disinterested in foreign issues and both shared a fervent anti-imperialism. From the 1890s through the 1930s, many labor leaders like Gompers supported efforts to restrict the numbers of new immigrants entering the country, often based on the grounds of racial inferiority, and thereby supported the wages and bargaining positions of domestic labor. Similarly, though Du Bois did support stringent quotas on new immigrants, his loyalty to people of color at home coexisted with disquiet about white immigrants and those who competed with African Americans for jobs. In the first edition of *Souls of Black Folk*, for example, immigrants in general and Jews in particular served as targets in several of Du Bois's comments regarding the interaction between America and the world. "The Jew," Du Bois wrote, "is the heir of the slave baron."[33] At another moment in the book Du Bois commented that the "rod" of the Southern empire had passed into the hands of "avaricious Yankees," and "shrewd and unscrupulous Jews."[34] In this way both Du Bois and Gompers honed racial and labor activism within an isolationist, anti-imperialist framework that was far from purely altruistic and often invoked racist justifications.

Progressive reformers did appear in both the expansionist and the anti-imperialist camps, but they were among the most outspoken anti-imperialists, with Jane Addams and Charles Francis Adams in the forefront. And many of the most prominent former abolitionists as well were among the vanguard of the anti-imperialists. Those at the top of the reform hierarchy and on the front lines of the progressive movement also tended to be anti-imperialist. As historian William Leuchtenburg showed, those who were in the middle management of reform or rhetorically reformist in their political outlook, being progressive in limited ways, generally were not anti-imperialist. Theodore Roosevelt is but one high-profile example of the latter position. A person's views on domestic policy and their activities for or against reform thus help identify his or her views on imperialism, isolation, and internationalism but do not singularly help distinguish them.[35]

Along these lines, the Reverend Charles Ames, an avowed anti-imperialist and reform advocate, surveyed the wartime passions of the nation in the summer of 1898. He asked rhetorically, "What will be the effect on our domestic policy? How can we undertake to rule subject provinces in distant parts of the globe without trampling on the principles of free government? Once accepting this way of dealing with other people, how long will it be before some occasion will arise for applying it at home?" Ames's answer, of course, was that the nation should not undertake continued occupation or annexation of foreign nations. He feared that war and imperialism would undercut important social changes at home or might even curtail democratic rights. As Ames saw it, ruling peoples against their will abroad and devoting the resources to do so would be a costly precedent. "The imperial scheme requires us to go very deeply into military and naval expenditure, that we may be ever on fighting footing." At what cost? He remarked, "None will suffer for the folly so much as our own toiling millions." Ames went on to say, "Some of us who have shared the fortunes of our country through two wars are not happy witnesses of the levity with which many of our journalists and some of our statesmen treat of war, as it were in itself more honorable than peace."[36]

Messianism and Mission

Just as it is a mistake to regard all the individuals in this study as purely isolationist, so too is it incorrect to see the religious community or religious motivations as monolithic. Arguments for Manifest Destiny, often couched in providential language, guided most expansionists; so, too, religious impulses often informed the arguments of anti-imperialists. Nevertheless, "manifest" rationales were some of the most prominent and powerful rhetorical devices employed by Lodge and Roosevelt, for example, and by expansion-minded evangelizers. In the 1880s and 1890s progressive Christians were working hard to pursue a distinctive, often expansionistic version of internationalism; however, it was expressed as a largely humanitarian, often nongovernmental impulse. Americans had historical and cultural reasons for viewing religious missions in terms of extension and expansion, whether as pioneers in an essentially hostile environment to be conquered, or as believers in the Calvinistic view of a progression toward

the kingdom of God, or in sharing the general nineteenth-century Western Christian expansionist zeal. Many among the Christian mission
movement saw voluntary groups—particularly religious ones—as the key
to squaring the circle in terms of James's critique of "bigness." That is,
those private groups, often better than government, seemed to preserve
room for individual action and were more appropriate for the work of
spreading ideas and even democracy through faith than were armed agents
overtly bearing the American flag.[37]

Concerned with laissez-faire global capitalism and national competition, expansion-minded evangelizers tended to favor international engagement primarily on the private level, through mission workers. But
when we analyze their rhetoric, they often sounded much like the expansionists. After all, they were guided by abstract notions of universalism
(American democracy) and by Christian civilization's Manifest Destiny
and duty toward creating a new world order (led and dominated by a benevolent, Protestant United States), in this respect similar to Lodge. Let
us take for example one of the most notable advocates of this position,
Josiah Strong.

Even the titles of his works—*Our Country, The New Era*, and *Expansion*—
present Strong's eponymously stringent form of nationalism, brightly aware
of a new world order. His internationalist arguments, Strong argued, were
the logical application of the principles of the reform social gospel from
home. The social gospel attempted to apply Christian ethics to ameliorate
social problems. Strong even considered that service to the world in some
ways might be more important than service to the nation. As historian
Dorothea Muller pointed out, Strong was well known as a fierce patriot,
but his writing indicates that he was much more of a burgeoning internationalist than some have recognized, given his ardor for Americanism and
expansion. In 1900 Strong wrote, "This world life is something greater
than national life, and world good, therefore, is something higher than
national good, and must take precedence of it if they conflict. Local, and
even national, interests must be sacrificed, if need be, to universal interests."[38] Strong thought private missionaries and religious groups were essential to this project, but he prophesied that the twentieth century would
bring unprecedented opportunity to the United States. Internationalism,
scientific progress, and aggressive missionary work all indicated that the
world was "about to enter a new era, for which the nineteenth century has
been the John the Baptist."[39]

Other social gospel leaders held different views about the course of action, but the majority backed Strong's position. From Shailer Mathews to Walter Rauschenbusch and Washington Gladden, social gospelers endorsed the expansionist sentiment as a way to bring about God's kingdom on earth. Mission was not just for going abroad, though; this was a thorough blending of domestic and international. Social gospel advocates in particular were known for their quasi-socialist efforts to save souls while enhancing quality of life and decreasing inequality and suffering within the United States.[40]

While missionaries and social gospel advocates generally were committed to promoting international peace in the final decades of the nineteenth century, they tended to express this in qualified terms, as conditional pacifists. Washington Gladden, for example, presented a characteristic example of this perspective when he claimed in October 1891 that Great Britain and America should cease hostilities and stand shoulder to shoulder "in the coming days, for the defense and extension of Christian civilization."[41] Gladden supported the "large policy" of Lodge, Roosevelt, Hay, and McKinley. He agreed with the U.S. intervention in Cuba and backed acquisition of the Philippines, for example, as humanitarian, moral, and missionary efforts. Later he summed up his perspective, saying that the Christian mission was the key to America's expansionist, exceptionalist destiny. He perceived that in the years after the Spanish-American conflict the United States had "drawn back," but he said this was a mistake that only delayed "the inevitable." According to Gladden, "The well-being of the world is to be settled, more and more, by consultation and cooperation among the world-powers, and this nation must take her share of responsibility." By 1909 Gladden was confirmed in seeing that the U.S. role in the world was essentially an extension of "the Golden Rule," the social gospel writ large.[42]

Scores of other Christian thinkers and activists were working along these same lines. A confidant of Roosevelt, pastor Lyman Abbott, professed as the editor of the *Outlook* (formerly the *Christian Union* paper) that war was appropriate in certain cases. The Spanish-American conflict, Abbott remarked, was such a case; it represented a noble "crusade of blood."[43]

One of the first historians to do groundbreaking work on this subject, Julius Pratt, established that particularly after Admiral George Dewey's resounding victory at Manila Bay, major ecclesiastical figures and prominent religious journals across a range of denominations came out more strongly in favor of continued expansionism and annexation. The Baptist *Standard*, the Presbyterian *Interior* and *Evangelist*, the Congregationalist *Advance*, and the Catholic *World*, among many others, all began to speak of American rule over the Philippines as a mission. Christian duty required a U.S. presence in the former Spanish colonies, they said flatly. Only the peace churches, as evidenced in the Quaker and Unitarian publications, remained absolute pacifists striking an anti-imperial and non-interventionist stance.[44]

The Dangerous Appeal of Imperialism

In the 1898 "Broadsides," the Anti-Imperialist League introduced its major "Arguments against the Adoption of a So-Called Imperial Policy."[45] The pamphlet repeatedly mocked William McKinley's proclamation when he said, "I speak not of forcible annexation, for that cannot be thought of. That, by our code of morality, would be criminal aggression." "Broadsides" claimed his words were hypocritical, un-Christian, and outright lies. Charles Francis Adams Jr., among other anti-imperialists, regarded coercive annexation in noncontiguous areas to the United States as antithetical to George Washington's intent and adverse to the national interest as protected by Monroe in 1823. Adams Jr. declared that the "large policy" was a slap in the face of the most essential values of the Republic and argued for a return to the "tracks of our forefathers."[46] Thus, in combating imperialism, the anti-imperialist again and again asserted that no strict and aggressive interpretation of the Monroe Doctrine and others should be allowed. Adams Jr. was joined by other practical-minded thinkers, such as James, who admitted that the nation confronted a new set of challenges in a modern era but thought one of those challenges was to stay true to principle, as paladins of the best elements of the American tradition.

David Starr Jordan, then president of Stanford University and one of the foremost intellectuals in the anti-imperialist movement, argued the classic anti-imperialist position in San Francisco on May 2, 1898. To acquire and hold Cuba, the Philippines, or other foreign lands as colonies, he said, "our democracy must necessarily depart from its best principles and traditions." The problem was obvious. "There was great danger," Jordan argued, ". . . that in easy victory we might lose sight of the basal principles of the Republic, a cooperative association in which 'all just government is derived from the consent of the governed.'"[47] Later that fall, an article in the *St. Louis Globe* noted that McKinley's movement toward annexation was "what the isolationists call 'yielding to pressure.'" However, the *Globe* argued that the pro-annexation spirit and McKinley's policies amounted to "deferring to popular pressure."[48]

These anti-imperialists represented every major reform type of the late nineteenth century. This was truly a "cooperative association," which included liberal Republicans, mugwumps, civil service reformers, municipal reformers, social welfare workers, pacifists, single taxers, labor reformers and union activists, prohibitionists, Indian rights advocates, laissez-faire advocates, silverites, the remnants of the old abolitionists and the new racial reformers, women's suffragists, and a broad set of social gospelers and other members of the liberal clergy. By 1898, the majority of this group, however, was older, with an average age in the sixties. They were vital, tended to be somewhat conservative, and were often New England mugwump types. Mugwumps largely had been Republican abolitionists in the 1850s who thirty years later switched parties from Republican to independent-Democrat in 1884 to support Grover Cleveland over James Blaine; they did so based on principle, because of the financial corruption and crass machine politics associated with Blaine. Interestingly, Theodore Roosevelt briefly joined this group, supporting Cleveland over Blaine for reasons similar to those of the other mugwumps.[49]

This diverse group conforms loosely to what might be sketched best as a typical mugwump. In *The American Mind*, historian Henry Steele Commager profiled the intellectual type of mugwump in a description that fits the majority of the anti-imperialists, including James. They had, he wrote, "gone to the best schools—one sometimes feels that a college degree was a prerequisite to admission to their club—associated with the best people, belonged to the Century or Harvard Club, read *The Nation* and *The Independent*, and knew politics, for the most part, at second hand."[50] This is significant because while some scholars have depicted the mugwump anti-imperialists as insecure conservative elites, others have argued that they embodied the civic morality of American liberalism. We see elements of both in the positions against expansion expressed by George Hoar, and to a lesser extent in the activism of James.[51]

But James defies clear categorization. He fits inexactly into the mold of a mugwump against empire. Not temperamentally inclined to political activism in the period that the mugwumps earned their label, James was largely apolitical until the mid-1890s. He seems to have taken his politics from only a few trusted sources and did not dwell on them in the way that he surely did after the Venezuelan crisis pushed him into the urgency of politics. Writing in 1889, for example, James credited Godkin's the *Nation* as his major source of political news and views, his "whole political education." Nonetheless, he frequently objected to the testy mugwumpian Godkin's apocalyptic political critiques and often-hyperbolic editorials.[52]

Drawing the Line at the Philippines

The ongoing U.S. counterinsurgency united the anti-imperialists more than any other single foreign or domestic policy question. In late February 1899 James wrote a long letter to the editor at the *Boston Evening Transcript* that was published on March 1 and concisely rendered his views on the movement and on why the line had to be drawn at suppressing Filipino independence. He began the letter, "An observer who should judge solely by the sort of evidence which the newspapers present might easily suppose that the American people felt little concern about the performances of our Government in the Philippine Islands, and were practically indifferent to their moral aspects. The cannon of our gunboats at Manila and the ratification of the treaty have sent even the most vehement anti-imperialist journals temporarily to cover, and the bugbear of copperheadism has reduced the freest tongues for a while to silence. The excitement of battle, this time as always, has produced its cowing and disorganizing effect upon the opposition."[53]

He concluded this portion of the February 26 letter, "It would be dangerous for the Administration to trust to these impressions. I will not say that I have been amazed, for I fully expected it; but I have been cheered and encouraged at the almost unanimous dismay and horror which I find individuals express in private conversation over the turn which things are taking." So what then did James see as the common reaction to the expansionists in his midst? "'A national infamy' is the comment on the case which I hear most commonly uttered," he said. "The fires of indignation are momentarily 'banked,' but they are anything but 'out.'"[54]

Blending his broadly philosophical belief in the dangers of "bigness" with his view that the bellicose acquisitiveness of imperialism itself was a specifically dangerous type of bigness, James's letter went on to express concern that Lodge and his fellow imperialists "seem merely to be awaiting the properly concerted and organized signal to burst forth with far more vehemence than ever, as imperialism and the idol of a national destiny, based on martial excitement and mere 'bigness,' keep revealing their corrupting inwardness more and more unmistakably."[55] Remarkably, James presaged his later elaboration of how bellicose feelings might best be channeled not into war but instead toward the "mastery" of nature. Training toward that end would be key to realizing what he later termed a "moral equivalent" to war.

The "process of education has been too short for the older American nature not to feel the shock," argued James. "We gave the fighting instinct and the passion of mastery their outing; we let them have the day to themselves, and temporarily committed our fortunes to their leading last spring [1898], because we thought that, being harnessed in a cause which promised to be that of freedom, the results were fairly safe, and we could resume our permanent ideals and character when the fighting fit was done." Even more forcefully, James mounted the argument that Americans should now "see by the vividest of examples what an absolute savage and pirate the passion of military conquest always is, and how the only safeguard against the crimes to which it will infallibly drag the nation that gives way to it is to keep it chained for ever, is never to let it get its start."[56]

Taking up and expanding on the dualism between the Old and New Worlds, James asserted "in the European nations it is kept chained by a greater mutual fear than they have ever before felt for one another. Here it should have been kept chained by a native wisdom nourished assiduously for a century on opposite ideals. And we can appreciate now that wisdom in those of us who, with our national Executive at their head, worked so desperately to keep it chained last spring."[57]

In short, James's letters reveal that he was ashamed of his nation for not supporting the Philippine revolution against a colonial power through to full independence. McKinley's "lip service" notwithstanding, no such support of real revolution or the building of a genuine democracy was ongoing. Worse, the revolutionaries were now cast as anti-American enemies. Was it because of greed? Power? Racism? James was sure all were involved, and more. As the scales fell from his eyes, he could no longer think the best of his nation. "Our treatment of the Aguinaldo movement at Manila and at Iloilo is piracy positive and absolute, and the American people appear as pirates pure and simple, as day by day the real facts of the situation are coming to the light." In one of the linguistic flourishes he used throughout this important letter, James explained that not only had he felt the flutter of the war fever making his heart pound, but that he also had come to recognize how dangerous the palpitations really were. "What was only vaguely apprehended is now clear with a definiteness that is startling indeed. Here was a people towards whom we felt no ill-will, against whom we had not even a slanderous rumor to bring; a people for whose tenacious struggle against their Spanish oppressors we have for years past spoken (so far as we spoke of them at all) with nothing but admiration and sympathy."[58]

About General Emilio Aguinaldo, James wrote, "Here was a leader who, as the Spanish lies about him, on which we were fed so long, drop off, and as the truth gets more and more known, appears as an exceptionally fine specimen of the patriot and national hero; not only daring, but honest; not only a fighter, but a governor and organizer of extraordinary power. Here were the precious beginnings of an indigenous national life, with which, if we had any responsibilities to these islands at all, it was our first duty to have squared ourselves."[59]

James's letter perfectly fits with the varied intellectual positions being advocated by the national Anti-Imperialist League in early 1899. Arguments like his dominated the pamphlets and speeches of most anti-imperialists. The AIL's political and publicity goals were simple: to make the next election revolve around the issue of expansion. They asserted that the administration, urged on by an astoundingly war-hungry American public, had pushed the fight to annex Hawaii and Puerto Rico, to keep a base on Cuba, and to buy and administer the Philippine Islands despite its revolutionary government.

This shocked the anti-imperialists. And, James hoped, it shocked his fellow citizens. McKinley had ordered the "commanders on the ground" to "freeze" out Aguinaldo "as a dangerous rival with whom all compromising entanglement was sedulously to be avoided by the great Yankee business concern."[60] James, finally, had recognized the inherent hypocrisy of squelching a popular movement, and, according to James, so did the American public. "Our own people meanwhile were vaguely uneasy," he said. However, while implying that the administration was probably doing its "moral" best, James exhorted that "on its face [the anti-democratic quashing of Aguinaldo and conquest of the Philippines] reeked of the infernal adroitness of the great department store, which has reached perfect expertness in the art of killing silently and with no public squealing or commotion the neighboring small concern."[61]

As the revolution in the Philippines was slowly being cut down by American troops, forcing Aguinaldo to give up his capital and go into hiding, James argued that at last "the Administration had to show its hand without disguise. . . . We are now openly engaged in crushing out the sacredest thing in this great human world—the attempt of a people long enslaved to attain to the possession of itself, to organize its laws and government, to be free to follow its internal destinies according to its own ideals."[62]

Thus, James's belief in the compatibility of liberalism and nationalism was challenged. The terms of this confrontation had been firmly established: it would be the traditional values of American democratic government and self-determination pitted against national Manifest Destiny and "civilization."

James's Analysis of the Stakes

"Why, then, do we go on?" asked James toward the end of this February–March 1899 letter that so brilliantly presented the anti-imperialist philosophy. "First, the war fever," he said, was a prime cause, "and then the pride which always refuses to back down when under fire. But these are passions that interfere with the reasonable settlement of any affair; and in this affair we have to deal with a factor altogether peculiar with our belief, namely, in a national destiny which must be 'big' at any cost, and which for some inscrutable reason it has become infamous for us to disbelieve in or refuse." Eviscerating both Christianization and democratization as rationales for national expansion, James sarcastically noted, "We are to be missionaries of civilization, and to bear the white man's burden, painful as it often is. We must sow our ideals, plant our order, impose our God. The individual lives are nothing. Our duty and our destiny call, and civilization must go on."[63]

James went on to attack the role of the American army in bringing anything good to the Philippine Islands. He argued that missionaries, despite all their own prejudices, would be far better than soldiers in administering the islands. "It is by their moral fruits exclusively that these benighted brown people, 'half-devil and half-child' as they are, are condemned to judge a civilization," he wrote. "Ours is already execrated by them forever for its hideous fruits."[64] James would soon come to reverse this position.

At the intersection of James's analysis of the state of American imperialism and his essentially isolationist views about avoiding the corruptions of entanglement abroad, he remarked that the "impotence of the private individual, with imperialism under full headway as it is, is deplorable indeed." In this we see an interesting parallel to the mission leaders who also extolled the virtues of the individual and voluntary action. U.S. aggressiveness in securing new territories, James assessed, had much tragically in common with the ways in which modern corporations and institutions were usurping what should be sacrosanct American democratic individualism. "One by one we shall creep from cover, and the opposition will organize itself," wrote James. "If the Filipinos hold out long enough, there is a good chance (the canting game being already pretty well played out, and the piracy having to show itself henceforward naked) of the older American beliefs and sentiments coming to their rights again, and of the Administration being terrified into a conciliatory policy towards the native government."[65]

Accordingly, what to do in 1899? For James, "until the opposition newspapers seriously begin, and the mass meetings are held, let every American who still wishes his country to possess its ancient soul—soul a thousand times more dear than ever, now that it seems in danger of perdition—do what little he can in the way of open speech and writing, and above all let him give his representatives and senators in Washington a positive piece of his mind."[66] This was a call to a reenergized isolationism in the form of a radical anti-imperialist movement. It was also a call that underscored an essential difference between James and the mugwump anti-imperialists and Lodge, Roosevelt, and the "large policy" advocates. Recalling the long-standing dispute between Jeffersonian Republicans and Federalists, here again was an instance of the transatlantic enlightenment debate over the proper foundations for civil society and the best sources for republican human inspiration. In this case, James's argument reveals how philosophical temperament seems to have mattered more than social position in terms of recasting the debate in terms of imperialism. Those who believed that the constraints of hierarchy and privilege should be tempered by reason and established by merit, such as James, were pitted against those like Lodge, who was essentially Federalist in viewing challenges to the status quo as negative and in seeking to expand the base of the domestic hierarchy without overturning it.

James followed up these cogent arguments with more public letter-writing. First, he wrote to the *New York Evening Post*, on the failures of America's supposed benevolence in the Philippines (March 10, 1899). Then, heightening his public profile yet further, he wrote to the *Transcript* again, on "Governor Roosevelt's Oration," decrying the speciousness of the strenuous life concept in the pages of the *Boston Evening Transcript* on April 15, 1899.[67]

In the spring of 1899 a group of anti-imperialists in Boston and around the nation used similar tactics. In keeping with James's letter-writing campaign, they aimed to press the anti-imperial cause to the front pages of the popular press and onto the public imagination. Edward Atkinson, the retired textile manufacturer (and the inventor of an early pressure cooker), was an ardent champion of a variety of reform causes as well as one of the most prominent anti-imperialists. Like James, Atkinson was an honorary vice president of the AIL and his name was emblazoned on the organization's letterhead. He took up this publicity cause with almost reckless abandon in early 1899, channeling his considerable resources into the effort and mailing anti-imperialist pamphlets to virtually every national politician and major newspaper he could find.

On April 22, 1899, Atkinson tested his right to free speech and freedom to disseminate political dissent by writing to the War Department. In his letter he requested the names and addresses of several hundred officers and soldiers stationed in the Philippines with the explicit purpose of sending them his anti-imperialism pamphlets. He reportedly received no response from War Department officials. So he took the initiative. Atkinson mailed apparently several hundred of his latest anti-imperial tracts—with titles such as "Hell of War and Its Penalties" and "The Cost of a National Crime"—to American generals, to naval officials such as Admiral Dewey, and to members of the U.S. Philippine Commission. He also sent copies to *Harper's Weekly* and other press outlets, and then mailed them more widely to vague postal addresses for "citizens and soldiers" stationed or living in the Philippines.

The McKinley administration immediately reacted. Postmaster General Charles Emory Smith ordered the seizure of the Atkinson pamphlets from Manila-bound mail sacks in San Francisco. These results proved Atkinson's point—and one of James's worst fears—that imperialist actions abroad were likely to lead to the abridgement of rights at home. Atkinson explained his point. It was un-American, he said, "to suppress free speech and forbid free mails to the people of the United States in their correspondence with the citizens of the United States who are now in the Philippines."[68]

Though Atkinson's case was never prosecuted, the seizure of the mail in San Francisco and a series of rulings by the attorney general and post-

master general made Atkinson a national figure. He vaulted to prominence, as did his and other high-profile writings and AIL efforts to make
the election of 1900 a referendum on imperialism. The pamphlets were
widely distributed in the hundreds of thousands, and Atkinson's own bulletin, the *AntiImperialist*, found a vast readership. As Atkinson wrote to
Carnegie, McKinley's crackdown on anti-imperialist pamphleteering via
Emory's oversight amounted to a "gigantic joke, that such feeble minded
persons as those in the cabinet" had unwittingly stimulated the demand
for the pamphlets and interest in their cause.[69]

By the end of May 1899 the original Anti-Imperialist League had more
than thirty thousand members on its rolls. The national league opened
satellite offices across the country in Boston; New York; Springfield, Massachusetts; Philadelphia; Washington; Baltimore; Cincinnati; Chicago;
Cleveland; Detroit; St. Louis; Portland, Oregon; and Los Angeles. The
organization claimed in its first annual report that "over half a million
contributors" had donated to assist the organization.[70]

Electioneering Argument

As the election of 1900 approached, James's anti-imperialism grew more
strident. So, too, did matters clarify on the national political scene. Former populist Democrat William Jennings Bryan held a complicated series
of positions on anti-imperialism from 1896 to 1900. As Bryan said, "This
nation cannot endure half republic and half colony—half free and half
vassal." However, he has been described accurately as a "missionary isolationist" who courted the anti-imperialists while arguing for a practical solution to the question of how to resolve America's territorial holdings after
the victory against Spain. He agreed to the Paris Peace Treaty, saying that
it would be "easier . . . to end the war at once by ratifying the treaty and
then deal with the subject in our own way."[71] "Isolation" figured prominently in the electioneering debates over American empire, usually cast
negatively and hurled as epithet. "Isolation or Expansion?" ran one banner headline.[72] "Isolation Past, Says Senator Cushing Davis," ran another
headline.[73] Indeed, expansionists rapidly turned elements of the venerable
Washingtonian model for unentangled isolation on its head, as Yale President Arthur Hadley did, when he asserted that practical power for a "new
era" dictated expansion as inevitable. Hadley cast his opponents as not
thinking clearly; there was no alternative to annexation and empire, he
argued, because the nation "has grown far beyond that point where it is

possible to shut ourselves in a shell like a turtle and live in seclusion."[74] Bryan, of course, explicitly ran and lost on an anti-imperial platform in 1900 and a pledge to give the Philippines their independence. To some observers, the isolationist position had lost.

If before the war James had opined favorably on some ends the conflict might bring, saying, "The great thing will be the driving out of Spain," his mild war fever had long since passed by 1900. In its place came despair and activism. He worried that "militarism would replace democratic, rational attempts at negotiations." What came to be called the ongoing Philippine Question revealed to James a new, frightening truth about America. The war was a "mission of impregnating the Philippines with American ideals and educating them for freedom," he argued. "You may depend on it that it is sheer illusion, and can only mean rottenness and ruin for them." For him, McKinley's victory in the election answered the Philippine Question, as a harbinger of the "death of the old American soul."[75]

While McKinley and most Republican backers of the war and expansionism were centrally concerned with the economic implications of solving the so-called glut in domestic overproduction by tapping new Latin American and Asian markets, James was not. Hearkening to French psychologist Gustave Le Bon's work on the psychology of the crowd, James derided the reactions of the American public as an example of group hysteria. He analyzed imperialist arguments for war as a cover for underlying mass passions for acquisition and conquest. "There are worse things than financial trouble in a nation's career. To puke up its ancient soul . . . in five minutes without a wink of squeamishness, is worse; and that is what the Republicans commit us to in the Philippines."[76] While many imperialists and anti-imperialists alike were similar to James in expressing exceptionalist visions for their nation, James's eloquent expressions of his burgeoning disillusionment were characteristically anti-imperialist.

Mark Twain and William Dean Howells were among those who shared his discouragement. Twain, for example, wrote a satire in the *North American Review*, "To the Person Sitting in Darkness."[77] In that piece he derided virtually everyone and every organization involved in American work abroad and in particular attacked religiously motivated expansionist profiteers. "And as for a flag of the Philippine Province," wrote Twain at the end of the piece, "it is easily managed. We can have a special one—our States do it: we can have just our usual flag, with the white stripes painted black and the stars replaced by the skull and cross-bones." He acerbically concluded, "Progress and civilization in that country can still have a boom, and it will take in the Persons who are Sitting in Darkness, and we can resume Business at the old stand."[78]

The article produced a vicious response, most particularly the American Board of Foreign Missions, which strongly objected to having missionaries compared to soldiers and avaricious swindlers. In a sharp indirect retort, for example, YMCA youth mission leader John Mott said, "The [broad evangelical mission] Movement stands pre-eminently for the emphasis of the belief that by a great enlargement of all agencies employed by the missionary societies, the gospel can and should be brought within the reach of every creature within this generation."[79]

Once the war was over, Mott continued to make his case in speeches and in works such as his widely distributed and popular book published in 1900, *The Evangelization of the World in This Generation*. "In several countries, notably in the United States, Canada, Great Britain and Ireland, the members of the [Missionary] Movement have adopted as their watchword, The Evangelization of the World in this Generation. . . . All non-Christian nations are being brought under the influences of the material civilization of the West, and these may easily work their injury unless controlled by the power of pure Religion." Mott continued, "The evangelization of the world in this generation is not, therefore, merely a matter of buying up the opportunity, but of helping to neutralize and supplant the effects of the sins of our own people."[80] This cause was Mott's analog to James's concept of "civic passion." Mott's answer was that the YMCA and other private religious and mission organizations ought to work with the U.S. government to achieve his desired ends of absolving the nation of the sins of its own people. (James, with tongue in cheek, had supported such a notion.) In an interesting blending of the foreign with the domestic, this position was even cast in terms of racial improvement at home. In the *Savannah Tribune* on March 7, 1900, an African American army captain named F. H. Crumbley, serving in the Philippines, was quoted approvingly when he endorsed the war and expansion. "The young colored men and women of Christian education [in America]," said Crumbley, would find opportunities for mission work as well as "every opening for the Negro in business."[81]

Twain completely disagreed with such a view. He continued his assault against America's imperialist and evangelizing forces. He was quoted in the *Chicago Tribune* on October 10, 1900, about his homecoming from

Europe and his dislike for the anti-Filipino administration. He proclaimed himself to be in favor of the ideals of "Washington" and "the flag," saying, "I am opposed to having the eagle put its talons on any other land." Twain sent a mocking "greeting from the nineteenth century to the twentieth century," published in the *New York Herald* on December 30, 1900. In it he wrote, "I bring you the stately nation named Christendom, returning, bedraggled, besmirched, and dishonored, from pirate raids in Kiao-Chou, Manchuria, South Africa, and the Philippines, with her soul full of meanness, her pockets full of boodle, and her mouth full of hypocrisies. Give her soap and towel, but hide the looking glass."[82]

After the turn of the twentieth century, many Americans, still coping with their aborning global power, saw the need for new ideas: what could reconcile the relationship of Washingtonian-Jeffersonian isolationism and principles of self-rule with expansionist argument for strategic, economic, and even humanitarian notions of how the nation ought to operate in the world? These were the pivotal intellectual tensions that James, his fellow anti-imperialists, reformers, and their opponents in the ranks of the expansionists faced.

Some scholars have observed that James did not hold his fellow anti-imperialists in high regard. This is accurate in that at times he expressed dissatisfaction with the movement, but overall the characterization can be misleading. The problem with the anti-imperialist movement as far as James was concerned was twofold. It was overly idea-driven, and thus ineffectual; and it had to "blow cold air" on the hot flames of bellicose imperial nationalism—no mean task.[83]

The anti-imperialists in Boston, according to James, were largely a group of "pure idealists" talking to "themselves." Reflecting privately on some meetings, he labeled them a "pathetic affair."[84] He recognized that "pure" talk, ideas, and even efforts to invoke sacred national principles of the Declaration and Constitution would not greatly diminish the psychological appeal of jingoism. From his earliest letters on the Venezuela incident, James perceived that the "will to dominate" and passion for conquest had deeper, instinctual roots. As he wrote to a socialist friend, Ernest Crosby, "Man's instincts are rapacious, and under any social arrangement, the *rapatores* will find a way to prey."[85]

Later building on this core insight into instinctual bellicose behavior, and in trying to find an alternative to it, James wrote "The Moral Equivalent of War," which appeared in the *Popular Science Monthly, McClure's,* and *Atlantic Readings*, among other places, between 1906 and 1910. In the essay, first given as a speech at Stanford, James called for a quest to control nature to supplant the "big and hollow" domination of individuals and nations. That would harness the instinct for heroism, sacrifice, and strenuous work, which he called a "civic passion." Noting that the modern world offered few such outlets, James exclaimed, "the reflective apologists for war," and its inherent "'horrors' are a cheap price to pay for escape from the only alternative supposed, of a world of clerks and teachers, of co-education and zoophily, of 'consumers' leagues' and 'associated charities,' of industrialism unlimited, and feminism unabashed. No scorn, no hardness, no valor any more!" His response seems naive and dilute compared to the rousing zeal that inspired Roosevelt's vision of a strenuous, warlike life. What is most important is that James argued that "heroism, endurance, duty, and discipline" could be realized in efforts such as clearing forests or working in iron mines, on freight trains, on fishing fleets, even in dishwashing, as part of a larger effort to combat and tame man's "immemorial enemy": Nature.[86]

Urgency about Race and Internal Reform

Many arguments against empire—and some for it—were based on racial hierarchies that tended to depict America as a white, Anglo-Saxon, superior nation, obscuring or trying to ignore the sizeable populations of African Americans and others who did not conform to such racio-national generalizations. The rhetorical-political battle over conquering inferior races abroad mirrored conflicts over racist attitudes at home. It also reflected a deep concern with reconciling amorphous late nineteenth-century scientific definitions of race with facts on the ground and presuppositions about the possibility of change. That is, in reading the texts of both imperialists and anti-imperialists, one finds a sense of the malleability of culture evidenced by the interchangeability of the terms "race" and "society," and even "civilization."[87] So, too, anti-imperialists most often claimed racism as an instrument to help make claims against annexing new areas so as to prevent the incorporation of waves of "inferior" peoples into the Republic. As Samuel Gompers put it in terms of the Philippines, "If the Philippines are annexed, what is to prevent the Chinese, the Negritos and the Malays," along with other "semi-savage races" from "going to the Philippines and from there swarming into the United States engulfing our people and our civilization?" Echoing Lodge's answer to a similar question about immigration and new "nationals" but tackling it from a distinctly anti-imperialist approach, Gompers explained his view by rejecting annexing other lands. As president of the American Federation of Labor, Gompers believed that keeping domestic wages up and not bringing in large numbers of new, poor immigrants was crucial to national progress and to the working American. By barring further annexations he aimed to "close the flood gates" against unfit immigrants "coming from what [would] then be part of our own country."[88]

Concerns about racial egalitarianism and the impermanence of race as a deterministic biological fact, along with the rising legal culture of segregation at home and colonialism abroad, spurred debates over race and motivated James's opposition. A self-proclaimed radical empiricist, James believed firmly in judging each individual by his or her own skills and attributes rather than using abstractions, such as race or class, to make generalizations. Such a view underpinned the moral imperatives of the domestic reformers who argued against expansionism, and provided an argument for greater isolation. Although quite a few anti-imperialists opposed new colonies because they did not seek to integrate more "inferior" peoples into the nation, quite a few anti-imperialists were racial liberals or reformers in the vanguard of domestic race reform like W. E. B. Du Bois and James, immigrant advocates like Jane Addams, or former abolitionists, such as Senator George Hoar, and the sons of prominent abolitionists, such as William Lloyd Garrison Jr.

Du Bois provides insight into how ideas about internal reform on issues of race and fulfilling democratic principles dovetailed with activities against imperialism. At the fourth Conference for the Study of the Negro Problems, in May 1899, Du Bois strode to the podium in Ware Memorial Chapel, Atlanta, and "lectured" the man presiding over the conference, Georgia Governor Allen Candler. Candler had told the crowd that there were as many "God-serving and God-loving" blacks as whites in Georgia. Du Bois agreed, of course, but he quickly corrected the governor's simple observation by underscoring the hard, bitter facts about the scant opportunities available to those God-loving African Americans. "The nation which had robbed them of the fruits of their labor for two and a half centuries, finally set them adrift penniless," said Du Bois. Most were "still serfs bound to the soil or house servants." In fact, in a nation of more than seventy-six million people, according to the latest census, a mere five thousand were African American businessmen. Du Bois cited his own groundbreaking study, "The Negro in Business," to point out that their occupations were as disparate (e.g., plumbers, grocers, and real estate agents) as their number was small.[89]

One year later, at the same conference, the fifth Atlanta Study, Du Bois turned his keen analytical eye to education and reported the results, which were worse than expected. In "The Negro Common School," Du Bois chronicled the ever-widening educational divide between black and white schoolchildren in the South. His study carefully documented three decades of segregated school conditions, with scores of tables noting years of enrollment, grades and aptitude attainment levels, material resources available, graduation statistics, and even college attendance where data were available. Industrial schooling of the sort advocated by Booker T. Washington did not appear to be a good answer because African American children were thwarted at the institutional level by teachers and bureaucracies, or had their educations circumscribed early in life by the need to work. The study led Du Bois to conclusions that confirmed his earlier arguments about how to best achieve reform and racial uplift.

"Race antagonism," said Du Bois, "can only be stopped by intelligence. It is dangerous to wait, it is foolish to hesitate. Let the nation immediately give generous aid to Southern common School education."[90] The point of his studies, public comments, and reform perspective was obvious to any observer at the time. Du Bois and many of his colleagues believed that a massive social commitment to African Americans in the South, as well as across the nation, in order to achieve real equality of opportunity should be a national priority. The prescriptions for how to use new funds varied. Proposed initiatives included better teachers; increased levels of educational material (i.e., textbooks, in-school tools, writing implements); smaller class sizes; and more attention to keeping children in school and minimizing time in the fields or doing other agricultural work during the school year.

He aimed to cultivate what he famously termed the "talented tenth" of the race. By uplifting that fraction, the entire group would understand their potential for excellence not only with respect to other students and citizens, but also in the eyes of the whole society. Equality of ability, he thought, could be best demonstrated first by the exceptional, and this also fit what he termed a "sociological imagination." Toward the goal of combining analysis of the unique orientation of modern reality with the history of American inequality and the duties of intellectuals for producing a practical politics, Du Bois helped to found the Niagara Movement for the advancement of the Negro race (1905), which then led him to assist in founding the National Association for the Advancement of Colored People (NAACP, 1909).[91]

Looking abroad, Du Bois saw the problems of his nation writ large around the world. Western civilizations tended to treat other races and societies with the contempt of the colonizer—turning to abstractions about inferior races and primitive development, rather than seeing the panoply of individuals of various attributes within and across societies, and in terms of the developmental stages of social groups. Along the same lines, Du Bois observed that was not enough of a public intelligence apparatus to oppose such a status quo at home, or abroad.

Du Bois's survey of the American occupation of the Philippines confirmed these views. Policies of segregation and unequal treatment at home seemed to him to mirror malignant imperialism abroad. Both were a cancer on his nation otherwise so blessed with democratic potential. In short, he said, "armies and navies are at bottom the tinsel and braggadocio of oppression and wrong." His "Credo," issued as an article in the *Independent* in 1904, renounced war and affirmed reform at home. Such reforms, Du Bois insisted, had to precede major efforts abroad. It was hypocritical to talk of spreading democratic values to faraway lands, he proclaimed, when they were far from achieved at home. Further, he argued from a modified imperialist line of reasoning that American exceptionalism itself made a potent conceptual case for eliminating the color line for, as Du Bois put it, "Negro and Filipino, Indian and Porto [sic] Rican, Cuban and Hawaiian, all must stand united under the stars and stripes for an American that knows no color line in the freedom of its opportunities."[92]

The African American press provides examples of editors and their papers who espoused racial identifications with the "colored peoples of the Philippines." Some fit neatly with Du Bois's view, while others regarded the Filipinos as inferior foreigners with no claims on the sympathy of Americans, much less black Americans. However, the majority of the African American press appears to have been both anti-imperialist and sympathetic on the grounds of racial injustice in both tone and advocacy. Indeed, as historian Paul Kramer has found, "Many critical editors made equivalences between imperialism and Jim Crow, urging their readers to break with traditional Republican allegiances and encouraging black men to refuse Philippine military service."[93] H. C. Astwood, editor of the

Philadelphia Defender, for example, saw the slaughter and war in the Philippines as "one of the most unrighteous acts ever perpetrated by any government." Indeed, the conflict in the Philippines gave rise to the racist epithet "gu-gu" for Filipinos, a term that was sometimes used interchangeably with the word "nigger" in the new colonial context, a point many African American soldiers remarked on with great scorn for the racist views of their comrades in arms. Much of the anti-imperialist press and pamphleteers, both black and white, highlighted the extension of Jim Crow abroad. They mustered their anti-imperial case on the grounds of neglecting domestic needs and the evils of exporting domestic race hatreds (or, in other cases, seeking to include inferior races within America's already tumultuous racial political landscape). Editors argued that imperialist adventures abroad drained resources and lives—as a dangerous distraction—from the correction of domestic injustices and requisite sociopolitical reforms for America's own "dark skinned peoples." The editor at the *Broad Ax* put the war in the following context. It was designed, he said, to divert local attention and "to satisfy the robbers, murderers, and unscrupulous monopolists, who are ever crying for more blood."[94]

Reforms at Home and Missionaries Abroad

Evangelicals in, and preaching at, America's seminaries and colleges had a different view from that of Du Bois and James about where and how national resources should be allocated. Most evangelicals looked inward at the masses of God-fearing and God-loving Americans—the majority of them white—as a resource to be tapped for mission work abroad. Some of them did see the pressing needs for racial and democratic reforms needed at home, such as Washington Gladden and Walter Rauschenbusch. This was isolationism of a sort. They turned inward toward fulfilling those same principles and beliefs at home through liberal Christian progressive reforms. But most argued that the necessity of winning souls for Christ was urgent. The mission, they said, was the most significant challenge of the day because a modern, immoral world was teetering on the brink of a fall into the chasm of irreligion.[95]

Among the vanguard of those who advocated efforts abroad without significant military or diplomatic connections was John Mott, the passionate leader of the Student Volunteer Missionary movement (SVM) and a director of the YMCA, both of which were aggressively evangelistic in their outreach throughout the end of the nineteenth century and the first half of the twentieth. Mott, a Methodist, along with like-minded others such as Dwight Moody, aimed to add religious, philosophical, and institutional components to support the projects of Americans moving to other countries.

For Mott the missionary office was like the arm of government, "a miniature of a foreign office," as one editorial put it, but not directly linked to the state.[96] After 1901 Mott became responsible for directing the foreign expansion of the North American YMCA as well as the SVM. Interestingly, while Mott coordinated with high-ranking U.S. and foreign politicians, he advocated independent, "indigenous" YMCAs in other nations. Christian principles, he said, might help to counteract the ill effects of imperialism. For him, America was not an imperial power. He did argue, though, that American technology and democratic expertise could be instrumental to spreading Christianity across the globe.

On behalf of the YMCA, the SVM, and the World Student Christian Federation (WSCF), founded in 1895, Mott traveled around the world for a second time in 1901–1902, to Australia and across much of Asia in 1903, to South Africa and South America in 1906, to the far reaches of China and across Japan in 1907 for the WSCF conference in Tokyo (the first international meeting in Japan), and to Europe at least once annually. These Americans looked outward to export the principles of the so-called social gospel along with democratic ideals.[97] Sparked by the central concern of the anti-imperialists—the controversial occupation of the Philippines—large numbers of Americans looked away from the nation's shores and aimed to evangelize or colonize; others, however, including many in the anti-imperialist camp, set these priorities in reverse and looked inward at reform to moralize or democratize. The latter worldview could hold more of the former (minus the colonialism, of course). It aimed to foster an Americanizing evangelical internationalism alongside a set of predominantly Christian appeals for progressive domestic change along isolationist lines.

Since early in the nineteenth century, American Christians had been building the infrastructure and opening channels for missionary work in Africa, across Asia and Latin America, and in Europe. Increasingly influential after 1900, young college-age groups composed the bulk of the evangelical Protestant Americans and Canadians involved in the international youth mission movement. Americans had conducted mission work for many years, exporting an array of American beliefs, ideals, and interests, as well as commercial goods. As the nation took a more significant commercial, military, and colonial place on the global stage, imperial outreach and evangelical outreach appeared to be intertwined—yet this left the thorny puzzle about how they ought to interact.[98]

For Mott, Dwight L. Moody, and other evangelical mission leaders, an expansive understanding of what they termed the "watchword" objective for the "evangelization of the world in this generation" can be seen as akin to an extension of American (and Anglo-American/Christian) power across the world. Promulgated by American yellow journalism and many Christian philosophers, the American-centric, thoroughly exceptionalist visions for global Manifest Destiny went hand in hand with Mott and Moody's goals for global evangelization. So, too, did it sometimes coincide with ideas, implicit or explicit, about the racial inferiority of those peoples and nations receiving missionaries.[99]

Yet for missionaries and their advocates, this outward spread did not entail an endorsement of most types of entangling alliances for the United States. Mott often spoke about the coming of war in early 1898 as a loss no matter the outcome, because the real "war" was one for saving souls by bringing them to Christ. Later, Mott came to view American power and the victory in 1898 as part of what he termed the "larger evangelism." In talking about the important applications of the principles of the social gospel at home and abroad, Mott aimed to revitalize American morality. He hoped to shake up the status quo by incorporating egalitarian Christian principles into such aspects of modern life as "finance, commerce, industry, labor, the movies, the press, learning, and all society." In so doing he perceived a clear hierarchy in that "[Jesus Christ] only has authority to rule social practices."[100]

Religious considerations ran through the new isolationist ideas that embraced largely private forms of international involvement. Within this original and distinct isolationist perspective, political alliances were secondary to the goals of uniting people and nations through mission work. Alleviating poverty and saving souls, international organizing of the first nongovernmental organizations (NGOs), and the binding power of salvific faith were paramount. Unifying the various strands of missionary, evangelical thinking gave birth to a new movement for the early twentieth century: transnational Christian humanism.[101]

This trend found its best expression in the well-reasoned evangelism, idealism, and actions of Mott and the YMCA. Their efforts amounted to what historian Robert Crunden called an attempt by certain progressives to enact a "Presbyterian foreign policy," later embodied in some of the idealistic and moralizing religious rhetoric employed by Woodrow Wilson as the nation again debated and then fought a war with European powers, and subsequently sought to restructure a more peaceful world order thereafter.

Domestic Priorities First

Examining the thought of progressive reformers yields a precise sense of their views about isolation and internationalism. In particular, those reformers for whom issues of racial injustice were paramount, such as Du Bois, held reform ideals that provide a unique window into how they constructed their broader worldviews. Du Bois's views of civil society's best course of action through the prewar years (until 1913) were framed by a more global sense of what was at stake. "Belting the world" implied to him an international need for overcoming the color line—first at home, then abroad.[102]

In the 1905 Declaration of Principles at Niagara, Du Bois stated his case that the nation needed to look inward to reform at home before devoting any significant resources abroad. He said, "The Negro race in America stolen, ravished and degraded, struggling up through difficulties and oppression, needs sympathy and receives criticism; needs help and is given hindrance, needs protection and is given charity, needs leadership and is given cowardice and apology, needs bread and is given a stone. This nation will never stand justified before God until these things are changed."[103]

For Du Bois and a fascinatingly diverse group of others, from accommodationists such as Booker T. Washington to social Darwinists such as William Graham Sumner, the "best" domestic course of action for the United States was to take care of reform at home before becoming engaged in international affairs. Still, Du Bois, for example, continued to cast domestic racial discord as simultaneously a national and an international challenge. While many reformers from almost every reform perspective opposed American imperialism, the majority of self-identified progressives supported the war against Spain in 1898, if not the continued occupation of the Philippines and the annexation of lands outside continental North America. Within moments of the Paris Peace Treaty, a backlash developed first among members of the anti-imperialists but also progressive-minded reformers on a parallel track. This formula for international engagement—to seek reform first at home and set an example by adhering and striving to fully realize American ideals within domestic society— became paradigmatic within much of the twentieth-century debates among liberals. This is not to say that progressives cast aside international reform or engagement but, rather, sought to prioritize, as the anti-imperialists did, by emphasizing certain domestic problems as paramount and specific foreign policies, such as expansionism, not just as contradictory to American ideals but also as countering domestic reform by wasting much-needed resources and energies abroad.

As many Americans shifted their attentions toward domestic reform in the years after the Spanish-American War and the eventual quashing of the military wing of the Philippine independence movement, even Lodge and Roosevelt had to shift gears. As the popular zeal for empire waned, in early 1904 Lodge wrote an article for *Century* magazine on the topic and a new path for his domestic policies that had a direct bearing on foreign policy. "There are many public questions which affect the welfare of the United States," he declared, "but there is none which goes so deep or is so much involved at it is in this"—no, he was not talking about expansion. He referred to another core isolationist reform issue that was of deep personal concern to Lodge: immigration restriction.[104]

Du Bois embodied this shift toward the domestic as well, though he never relinquished an aim to pursue global racial justice as well as domestic egalitarianism. In the years after 1898 he increasingly made the case that expansionist policies had to be rejected because they were based on an inherent racialist worldview. Practically, this racial liberal view also made the important anti-imperial case that expansionism diverted resources, focus, and moral force from pressing issues within the United States. In this regard there came a convergence between Mott's changing goal (after roughly 1908) for social gospel at home and aggressive missionary activities abroad with Du Bois's aim for major reform at home, so that the nation could then serve as a beacon to the world. The settlement house reform movement, epitomized by Jane Addams at Hull House in Chicago and Emily Balch at Denison House in Boston, provides insight into this inward-outward fusion, with progressive settlement workers focusing inward yet on problems with international implications.

He could not have stated a "turn inward" set of reform priorities any better than he did at Niagara. However, by the time war came in 1914, Du Bois's ideas were challenged as the nation contemplated joining the conflict. He began to think that perhaps turning outward would provide a vital opening for enhancing African American citizenship rights. Emily Balch and Jane Addams, however, remained resolutely against intervention. In the interest of advancing the claims of African Americans to full citizenship, though, Du Bois made a Faustian bargain in the pages of the NAACP's official organ, the *Crisis*, which he edited, and in several national editorials and speeches. To fulfill a nationalistic "greater good," Du Bois along with an array of other liberal intellectuals and reformers reluctantly endorsed the war effort and the Wilson administration.

For individuals like Mott, who advocated limited governmental involvement (preferring what might be seen as a visceral attraction to isolation in the abstract), spreading evangelization and Americanization abroad also required intense thinking and planning to reform the nation at home. While Mott represented the outward-looking reformer, Du Bois represented the inward-looking reformer—a host of reformers also struck a similar balance in their views about partial isolation from foreign wars and colonialism as enhancing attention to issues of social justice and reform, ranging from Jacob Riis to Jane Addams.

Losing the Battle, Winning the Fight?

Like his student Du Bois, William James viscerally felt the challenges to social justice imposed by onrushing modernity. By the time James stepped to the podium of the Twentieth Century Club to address the annual meeting of the New England Anti-Imperialist League in 1903, the country had been engaged for three long years in a bloody counterinsurgency struggle in the Philippines. To James, this was, quite starkly, the preeminent issue of the day. But on that afternoon, with the Philippine insurrection almost completely quashed, James had to admit to his fellow anti-imperialists that they were losing the battle. "I think we have candidly to admit," James remarked, "that in the matter of the Philippine conquest we here and our friends outside have failed to produce much immediate effect."[105]

Their attempts to field and endorse anti-imperialist candidates in the political process, most notably the unsuccessful Bryan campaign in 1900, had fallen flat. Dedicated as he was to rational paths of a newly activist politics, James's speech exposed his intense emotional efforts to find "useful" national ideals, to build on natural human instincts for power and strenuous effort, and to revivify free speech—all by returning to the nation's original revolutionary anticolonialism and core values of individual self-determination.

" 'Duty and Destiny' have rolled over us like a Juggernaut car," James ruefully confessed. As he saw it, the "unwieldy bulk [of abstractions like duty and destiny] the majority of our countrymen were pushing and pulling forward, and our outcries and attempts to scotch the wheels with our persons haven't acted in the least degree as a brake."[106] Among his most evocative turns of phrase, these words strike not so much an intellectual blow as an emotional one. James's argument against specious abstractions fused his psychological insights with his anti-imperial political philosophy. Reflecting a view he expressed earlier in *Principles of Psychology* (1890), James argued that the human mind is inherently "selective and yet also positive," while being driven by primal urges. Blending this personal psychological understanding with a view of the "selective" manner of reasoning, he designed his anti-imperial critiques to appeal to listeners' reason and emotion. His continued activism aimed to reach the conscience of his audience and to evoke being swayed (as he had been once) by war fever. Despite the difficulty of the moment, as a radical empiricist James thought the present was never static. He hoped to prevent un-American intervention and rule abroad by reforming democratic values at home.[107] James also maintained that innate bellicose motivations were at work in the human psyche. This helped explain, he said, the wide appeal of imperialist abstractions and expansionist adventures for the American public. It also served to reinforce the near Sisyphean battle ahead for the anti-imperialists.

Others in the progressive reform movement held similar beliefs. For example, Jane Addams's *Newer Ideals of Peace* (1907), her second book, combined ideas from her first book, *Democracy and Social Ethics*, published in 1902, with a vision she first articulated in essays and lectures during 1899, as part of the anti-imperialist movement. In *Newer Ideals*, Addams tried to bridge two heretofore distinct discourses: those related to peace, arbitration, and antimilitarism and those related to democracy, social ethics, and government. Addams had been addressing antiwar meetings since the Spanish-American War. In 1902 at Chautauqua she gave a series of lectures on Leo Tolstoy and the ideas underlying *War and Peace*. In the spring of 1903 she addressed the Ethical Culture Society of Chicago on "A Moral Substitute for War" (which later became part of the conceptual base for James's 1906 address and essay titled "The Moral

Equivalent of War"), and in 1904 in Boston she shared the platform with James at the thirteenth Universal Peace Conference.[108] James and Addams argued that there were viable alternatives to war. When instincts for war combined with overzealous jingoism and specious arguments, they said, every single one of the imperialist decisions of politicians became rash.[109] According to James, abstractly justified decisions to engage in war and empire—such as those of his former student Theodore Roosevelt—had the potential to irrevocably undermine national ideals.[110]

Changing Conditions Yield Optimism

As the war receded, James became more hopeful. His 1903 speech made it explicit: all did not seem lost to him. At the end of his first salvo of comments James declared this optimism, saying, "if we look round us today we see a great change from the conditions that prevailed when the outbreak of hostilities first called us into being. Religious emotion and martial hysterics are both over with the public, and the sober fit is on." In one of the most provocative assessments of the dim present but brighter future for the anti-imperialist cause, James concluded, "The consciousness which the experience has cultivated is a consciousness that all the anti-imperialistic prophecies were right. One by one we have seen them punctually fulfilled." According to James, these unfortunate foretellings were numerous and included

> the material ruin of the Islands; the transformation of native friendliness to execration; the demoralization of our army, from the war office down—forgery decorated, torture whitewashed, massacre condoned; the creation of a chronic anarchy in the Islands, with ladronism still smouldering, and the lives of American travelers and American sympathizers unsafe in the country out of sight of army posts; the deliberate reinflaming on our part of ancient tribal animosities, the arming of Igorrote savages and Macabebe semi-savages, too low to have a national consciousness, to help us hunt the highest portions of the population down; the inoculation of Manila with a floating Yankee scum; these things, I say, or things like them, were things which everyone with any breadth of understanding clearly foretold; while the incapacity of our public for taking the slightest interest in anything so far away was from the outset a foregone conclusion.[111]

James's comments thus invoked and updated the traditional intellectual model of Washingtonian-Jeffersonian nationalist isolation. As he remarked, "It is only fair to President McKinley and his coadjutors and successor to say that their better angels also had a finger in the pie, and that the institution of our civil commission has gone far toward redeeming our national reputation for good sense." The key for James, it seemed, was that these good ideas had "come too late for any solid success." The tragic point for him was that the United States was finally "trying to do with our right hand what with our left hand, the army, we had made impossible in advance. When we landed at Manila," said James, "we found a passionate native cordiality, which would have met us half way in almost any scheme of protectorate and co-operation which we might have proposed." The moment had been lost, and thus, he claimed, "'like the base Indian,' we threw that pearl of a psychological moment away, and embarked, callous and cold, and business-like, as we flattered ourselves, upon our sinister plan of a preliminary military deglutition of them, just to show them what 'Old Glory' meant."[112]

James, of course, vehemently opposed the "big" and businesslike military government of the Philippines in keeping with his goal to keep armament and opportunity apart. He wrote, "Let our civil commission do what it will now, the hands will not move backward on the dial, the day of genuine co-operation with the Filipinos is forever past. We cannot even be certain that the well-meaning commission will be anything but what the army thinks it, a sop to sentimentalists at home, and in the Islands a safe cover for the treacherous natives to hatch a new rebellion out."[113] In this sense, James clearly was no realist; he prized ideals over straightforward views of national interest as defined by strategic outposts, new markets, and new territories. He then summed up the present state of the anti-imperialist cause. James concluded that the "first act is over, and what is done can't be undone." More problematic, according to James, was what would come in a second act. "Difficult as it is to keep hot words of accusation from rising to our lips whenever we think of the men who threw away so splendid an American opportunity—threw it away with our own action in the Cuba case before us as the only precedent we had to follow—nevertheless it is bad politics to dwell too long upon events of yesterday," he declared. "We opponents of an imperialist policy must simply hand over our brief for the past to the historians' keeping."[114]

Ultimately, James maintained, "Let us drop yesterday and its sins, then, and forget them. The attitude of 'I told you so' is sterile, and wise men know when to change their tune. To the ordinary citizen the word anti-imperialist suggests a thin-haired being just waked up from the day before yesterday, brandishing the Declaration of Independence excitedly, and shrieking after a railroad train thundering toward its destination to turn upon its tracks and come back. Anti-imperialism, people think, is something petrified, a religion, a thing that results in martyrdom, for which to 'discuss' means only to prophesy and denounce. If, so far, some of us have struck a slightly monotonous attitude, we have our good excuse." This was key to James. So too was Aristotle's notion that all men are political, though James did not follow Aristotle that war was a way of life.[115] Anti-imperialists in their antiformalism had to be flexible, alive to changing circumstances, and guardedly emotional. James believed, rather, that the "wounds which our love of country received in those days of February, 1899, are of a kind that do not quickly heal. They ache too persistently to allow us easily to forget. Forget we must, however, we must attend to the practical possibilities of today."[116] In this peroration, he promulgated a modernized isolationist anticolonial view. It stands as a psychological analysis as much as a piece of political philosophy.

Recurring Themes

These heated debates over expansion and the terms of annexation abroad pushed the anti-imperialists to fathom deeply the ramifications of any major American international engagement. In most cases, the result was that they favored commercial and cultural ties. However, most political and all military imperial experiments, they asserted, represented an existential threat to the nation. Anti-imperialists nonetheless tended to adhere to a fairly traditionalist orientation, which undergirded their positions and broader outlooks on America's proper relationship to and with the world. Like James, they struggled to reconcile and reevaluate the merits of traditional roles and views, while updating them for a new era. Thus, anti-imperialists diverged often on which domestic reforms were of paramount importance, thereby fracturing the unanimity that might have helped them achieve a more cohesive foreign policy position and political effectiveness. They frequently agreed only on mutual opposition to "imperial" policy and on a broad commitment to internal development. Still, many agreed on "progressive" and activist politics, as James became politicized in the mid-1890s and as the sweeping reform agendas of Du Bois and Addams throughout the period demonstrate.

Adapting older ideas about isolation, James was in the vanguard of this anti-imperialist group. When he was specific about the form international politics should take, he emphasized a belief in neither entangling alliances nor voluntary conflicts. He also added his own social psychological understanding for the need to channel natural instincts to overcome the stultifying effects of modernity and encourage a more peaceful and fulfilling future rather than one full of animus, war, and base nationalism.

Many of the reforms he favored—and views on racial injustice, cultural tolerance, progressive education, immigration, and the role of "big" business in American life—all were points in partial dispute among anti-imperialists at various times, and this undermined the effectiveness of the movement as a whole. Yet, taken together, the wide-ranging ideas of anti-imperialists reveal striking consistencies. The anti-imperialists laid out many crucial arguments (for the next century) for opposing American wars. They confronted the realities of a nation easily prompted to war fever—having just won its first conflict with a European power (other than England) and gaining a toehold in the Pacific and the Caribbean as a colonial power. In so doing they presented a much more limited and internally oriented vision for the nation: act in the world primarily as an exemplar, perhaps as mediator, certainly as a commercial and cultural presence, but not as a conqueror or colonizer. These ideas were a resource for many of the key political dissents and movements (e.g., antiwar and civil rights) of the twentieth century. Seen in this light, the legacy of anti-imperialist political thought appears to have been underestimated.

At the apex of the era of progressive reform, many reformers focused on the same issues that concerned James. Sadly, James died from heart failure not long after "The Moral Equivalent of War" began circulating widely in 1910. Rather than endorsing America's going aggressively abroad, many progressives, such as James's friend and former student Du Bois, sought racial reform at home while seeing the problems of race-based imperialism as an international challenge. James, too, cried out for what he called "civic passion" as part of a larger effort to refine policy while adhering to the ideals at the heart of America's "ancient soul." Like James, the anti-imperialists were united by their unflinching desire to avoid imperial excesses.

James and the Legacy of Anti-Imperialism

By the time James's 1906 "Moral Equivalent of War" address found a wide audience, around the end of the decade, his efforts to mediate between the two most dominant strands of possible U.S. policy had reached their apex in his thought. He aimed to build on what he considered the few redeeming elements in the Rooseveltian philosophy of robust action and masculine "strenuousity," while also rejecting both war and empire. To those strands he added an additional objective, to move toward a pluralist nation in which individuals would be judged and could rise or fall only by their effort and by cultivating innate attributes. The "moral equivalent" thus brought these bold goals together. It represented James's best and last effort at such a reconciliation.

While James lacked specificity in his conception of how the "conquest of nature" could practically replace the conquest of "fellow men," he combined psychology, politics, and social philosophy to make the insightful argument that military conflict and domination need not be considered elemental to human instincts. They could be separated, he claimed, from the useful aspects of heroism, endurance, and discipline, which might be redirected into personal responsibility and a heroic form of civic passion (his "moral equivalent of war," waged at home). As Jon Roland has pointed out, James's activist politics on the eradication of war helped to lay the conceptual groundwork for programs such as the Works Progress Administration, the U.S. Peace Corps, AmeriCorps's Volunteers In Service to America, and recently the domestic outreach of the Teacher Corps.[117]

Revising older ideas about isolationism, James's political philosophy also presented a fresh interpretation of traditional values about America's proper role in the world that put him at the forefront of the anti-imperialists and of the political thinkers of the early twentieth century. As a psychologist and philosopher, James analyzed the degree to which instinctive bellicosity could be civilized; as a political activist, he argued that the United States should be the first nation to prove that warlike aggressive urges could be rechanneled toward the social good.

As most historians rightly note, America acquired no more significant colonial possessions, declined to establish a central agency or system for administering its colonies, and failed to expand or reorganize the nation's army and navy to sufficiently defend the territories it had acquired. Indeed, during the first decade of the twentieth century the American public was not very supportive or concerned by the Roosevelt and Taft administrations' sending delegates abroad, mediating the Russo-Japanese War, or undertaking small-scale interventionist actions. Even if the anti-imperialist movement itself was not a viable organization in the long term, its activities seem to have had a compelling, subtle ideological impact on established isolationist-modeled views of how the nation ought to act in the world. This vision appeared to offer a reliable guide for the nation as it moved forward as a postcolonial world power.[118]

Though James wanted the United States to be strong enough for self-protection, he qualified that requirement by seeking robust commercial, cultural, and intellectual engagement (in his vaunted "marketplace of ideas") through peaceful internationalism (a "soft power" of sorts). The turn of the twentieth century witnessed changes in the nationalism of many domestic observers of the American scene, and James belonged to this generation that found itself caught between diversity and unity. He, like many of his friends, allies, and others in roughly his age cohort, embraced the burgeoning plurality of modernity but not its excesses. He was ambivalent in his hopes to maintain and expand America's democratic ideals along with certain tenets of Victorian morality while rejecting absolutist beliefs and practices.[119] His pragmatic framework for a refined isolationist anti-imperialism and partial internationalism came to be embraced by progressive liberal intellectuals like John Dewey, Walter Lippmann, and Walter Weyl before World War I. But James added his own social psychological and moral understandings to this forceful hybrid politics.[120] By confronting the realities of the globalizing world at the turn of the twentieth century and America's new military power, the anti-imperialist movement laid out the rhetorical parameters that would shape many of the most powerful antiwar arguments over the next century.

3

TOWARD A TRANSNATIONAL AMERICA

On Friday afternoon, July 28, 1914, Randolph Bourne and his Columbia college friend Arthur Macmahon arrived in Dresden, Germany. The day was warm, with clear skies and sunshine. But the good weather masked the fact that the summer would grow ever darker for Dresden and for the world. Bourne and Macmahon watched throngs of patriots singing the nationalistic anthem "Die Wacht am Rhein" (Watch on the Rhine) before they pressed on to Berlin. Three days later crowds rallied behind the kaiser and the crown princes of Germany as their royal entourage arrived in Berlin from Potsdam. Stunning news came with them: Germany's ally Austria had declared war.

In an instant the atmosphere changed. "If ever there was a tense and tragic moment," Bourne observed later, it occurred as he first heard the declaration of war, "when destiny seemed concentrated into a few seconds."[1] Days afterward, watching the first columns of German reservists parade down Berlin's tree-lined Unter den Linden and Friedrichstrasse, Bourne rued how rapidly the war fever eroded civility and cultural tolerance. Seeing an entire nation galvanizing itself for war shattered his illusions. "No one," he said, "was more innocent than I of the impending horror."[2] The war would change Bourne's thought as much as it did for many Europeans, transforming him from a progressive dreamer into an increasingly lone voice advocating a bold, new concept—a "transnational America" that could become a leading light for the world.

Though his visit was cut short—to just two weeks—because of the impending conflict, the twenty-eight-year-old Bourne revealed his keen eye for observing people and politics. He still saw fit to explore some of the deeper nationalistic and political truths behind the brewing war, finding the German government to be far more complex than it had appeared from the United States. "Undemocratic in political form, yet ultra-democratic in policy, and spirit," Bourne wrote publicly, for Germany "ordinary neat categories of political thought simply didn't apply." No one seemed to be "groaning under 'autocracy' and 'paternalism,'" as far as he could tell. "One found oneself," he assessed, "for the first time in the presence of a government between whom and the people there seemed to exist some profound and subtle sympathy, a harmony of spirit and ends."[3]

Bourne's private reflections were more critical. "The whole German atmosphere is more unsympathetic to me, and while I am glad to have seen this part of the world," he opined in a letter to his mother, "I doubt if I should ever be tempted to come here again."[4] While leaving Berlin, Bourne and Macmahon were surrounded by frightening crowds, "hysterical from both fervor and anxiety." After departing Germany en route to Sweden, the men again encountered trains and streets filled with exuberant soldiers. Inflamed with passion and singing hotly patriotic songs, these intensely nationalistic Germans were alien to Bourne. "The whole world seemed in flight before some invasion of Vandals." The warm summer weather had turned, as if mirroring the turbulent mood and apprehensive expressions of those awaiting the coming war.[5]

Bourne longed for sun when he arrived in unrelenting rain at the usually quiet city of Malmo, Sweden. The city was overrun by regiments of young "flaxen-haired" army recruits along with an array of refugees. Society had become "nothing but war" in the blink of an eye, Bourne said. Soaked while moving from hotel to hotel in search of lodging, Bourne and Macmahon came face to face with a group of proud peasant recruits buoyed by their new status and brandishing bayonets. Pressed against a wall, Bourne escaped unharmed, but a bayonet ripped his umbrella and came dangerously close to cutting him. "It seemed the breaking point," Macmahon commented about their narrow escape, "the final indignity."[6]

Return and Commitments at Home

Back in the United States by the end of 1914, Bourne watched his own nation slowly enter the same state of "fervor and anxiety" he had witnessed in Germany. He came to argue against joining the war, against an assimilationist strand of strident "Americanism," and against wartime repression. He urged the nation to serve as a mediating "neutral" for global peace. His domestic agenda remained largely unchanged and his commitments to several progressive causes became more vociferous: he called for sweeping liberal reform of education, encouragement of the arts broadly defined, and greater cultural tolerance through a campaign to inculcate an authentically pluralistic understanding of citizenship and ethnicity.[7]

One of the most influential intellectuals of the early twentieth century, Bourne was both admired and pitied. Disfigured and hunchbacked from birth, Bourne was a brilliant and widely read essayist who became a bristling opponent of American entry into World War I. Less than two years after he returned from visiting the Old World, Bourne seemed to have fully absorbed his experience and wrote about its significance in his formal "impressions" for Columbia regarding his Gilder travel fellowship (later published), in his private letters, and in his personal notes. Bourne argued that competing parochialisms had undermined European harmony, while commenting on similar nativistic and nationalist "Americanization" efforts being put forward by prominent Americans both inside and outside of the government. The paths, he underlined, were ominously similar.

To avoid the nationalistic path to war he had observed in Europe, Bourne advocated that America "reject" the "melting pot" concept, which he regarded as an illusion. It was wrongheaded and futile, he argued, to promote homogenizing identities that inevitably would stifle individuals and groups. In place of this effort, he said, the country should embrace a more inclusive and tolerant vision for society, a vision he termed a "transnational America." "No reverberatory effect of the great war has caused American public opinion more solicitude than the failure of the 'melting pot,'" he wrote. "The discovery of diverse nationalistic feelings among our great alien population has come to most people as an intense shock." The country, Bourne declared, needed a new framework for social relations to avoid violence.[8]

Most historians are familiar with Bourne's phrase "transnational America." It is one of the hallmarks in the history of American pluralism and social thought, yet its meaning remains elusive. The definition for Bourne was multifaceted, implying more than a mere blurring of national boundaries. Lately, as international and global history have become increasingly en vogue—and with the popularity of ideas such as Thomas Friedman's "flat world"—the term "transnational" has been bandied about without much attention to its origins. Bourne himself saw it as a "higher ideal," or a "cooperative Americanism," modeled in part on Zionism. Comprised of "a freely mingling society of peoples of very different racial and cultural antecedents," Bourne's transnationals would share "a common political allegiance and common social ends but with free and distinctive cultural allegiances which may be placed anywhere in the world they like."[9] While most scholars realize that Bourne's "transnational America" concept was original and represented a halfway point between strict forms of parochialism and the assimilationism implicit in the Americanization campaigns during World War I—few have explored its wider genesis or immediate legacy. In addition, many scholars have missed the significance of transnationalism to explain a complex element in Bourne's intellectual biography: transnationalism helps in bridging Bourne's thinking about domestic reform and foreign policy. This crucial concept united three major drives in his thinking: fierce pluralistic and progressive reform at home, avid pacifistic internationalism abroad, and passionate advocacy for a noninterventionist American role in the world.[10]

One reason that the significance of transnationalism has remained unclear is the difficulty of relating Bourne's ideas about internationalism, peace, and foreign policy with the rest of his vast array of writings. Here was a thinker whose concerns were dizzying: they ranged from pragmatism to progressive education, from issues of citizenship, pluralism, and ethnicity to youth culture, from art and literary criticism to antiwar activism. His quasi-spiritual, idealistic notion of a "beloved community," the subject of much historical scholarship, often has played a central role in explaining his cultural criticism, of which transnationalism was a part.

Bruce Clayton's excellent biographical account, for example, and Casey Blake's intellectual genealogy of the "beloved community" cast his politics as a form of romantic defeatism. Most scholars have emphasized Bourne's idealistic literary criticism and position as a cofounder of modern American cultural radicalism—in the matrix of "Young American" social critics of the age—to examine his burgeoning political activism and writing.[11] James Vitelli described the cultural politics of transnationality in his biography of Bourne, saying, "What is of interest here is the way Bourne pulled back from his call for a purely 'national' culture and proposed a quest for 'a new and more adventurous ideal.'"[12] Yet Vitelli and others have argued that Bourne's transnational vision was "suspended" for the "duration of the war." Leslie Vaughan asserted along similar lines that Bourne's self-described "below the battle" politics were neither a retreat nor a position taken outside the fray, but rather a "third way" formula for creating an alternative politics.[13]

Building on these insights, we can see that Bourne developed transnationalism as an alternative to wartime Americanization. What is missing from most historical accounts, however, is that Bourne's thought was far from suspended in wartime. Rather, the argument here is that in most respects it was the product of the war, when Bourne fused a soft type of isolationism to his transnational ideal. His firsthand experiences as the war began in Europe deeply informed Bourne's later antiwar activism. Thus, the most intense focus here is on a theme that many scholars have not explored: Bourne's development and advocacy of a type of isolationist pluralism.

During the war Bourne and his close friend and ally, the author and fellow "Young American" Van Wyck Brooks, sought to create what Bourne called a "focal centre" to channel "impelling, integrating forces" for society in America and abroad. Transnationalism was, in short, Bourne's attempt to imagine a cosmopolitan and peaceful new society for America whose model of social relations might then be extended around the world. It was both a domestic and a foreign policy ideal. As such, the concept creatively incorporated his views about cultural pluralism into the longer intellectual tradition of the United States' "steering clear" of foreign entanglements in the form of European-style power politics or wars. In this way, he conceived a generally anti-interventionist, antiwar isolationism built on a particular vision of the nation's foundational democratic principle to seek peace and avoid binding permanent diplomatic alliances, which he often described as his favored type of neutrality. Bourne, however, deplored the nativism and Americanism inherent in many versions of isolationism.[14]

Bourne's was what we might now term a soft-power approach to international engagement. He argued for meaningful isolationism that engaged with the world in terms of commerce and especially culture, hearkening to the dictum in Jefferson's 1801 inaugural address, that the United States should seek "peace, commerce, and honest friendship with all nations; entangling alliances with none." Building on his interpretation of these political traditions and America's immigrant past and present, Bourne emphasized cross-cultural individual and group, rather than governmental, commitments abroad. Thus, Bourne developed his new perspective as an outgrowth of what can be seen as a broadly nineteenth-century vision of America's proper role in the world—one largely, but not always, premised on the nation being free from committing military forces or significant diplomatic energies to European entanglements and permanent alliances. He then combined and updated this orientation with a characteristically non-statist community-oriented modern vision for a tolerant mixing of multiple ethnic cultures both at home and abroad.

Although Bourne often called himself a pacifist, he was willing to admit that there could be pragmatic arguments for a particular war. His main point, however, was that the bar for such arguments should be high because of the great cost of war—not only to combatants, but to noncombatants in belligerent nations, to nominally neutral people, to domestic progress (broadly defined), and to the sorts of democratic ideals and practices (e.g., free speech) often strained or curtailed in wartime. For Bourne, his isolationist stance meant avoiding aggressive wars and interventions, colonialism in all forms, and binding permanent diplomatic alliances that would force the commitment of American forces abroad, and combined those views with a firm support for cooperative international processes such as arbitration, mediation, cultural exchanges, and other forms of peaceful relations with all nations.

Tapping into deep-rooted American traditions about how the nation ought to engage with the world, Bourne fused a cosmopolitan view of global engagement, tempered by a broadly Jamesian opposition to "bigness," specious abstractions, and colonialism, with a vision for a tolerant mixing of multiple ethnic cultures at home and abroad. Here Bourne applied pragmatism and social psychology in his argument that overlapping "citizenships" of members within society could be interconnected into a mollifying, cosmopolitan whole that rejected nationalistic militarism. He argued that when combined in this way a "trans-national America" would be incapable of being a military or diplomatic aggressor in the world.

This intrinsically "positive" cast to Bourne's foreign policy–domestic politics hybrid is conspicuously absent in most scholarly evaluations of his broader political thought. For instance, Christopher Lasch once commented that Bourne's opposition to the war was "a politically negative act (however appropriate or correct) signifying his continuing preoccupation with the personal as opposed to the public." This view is incomplete. Transnationalism was radically "public" as a cultural proposition and in its idealistic isolationist thought, guided by Bourne's aim for peaceful cultural engagement across borders and peoples.[15] So too, it was far from politically negative as an affirmative politics based on authentic tolerance and fully realized social justice—for a multicultural society. Such a view, according to Bourne, could only be characterized by a decentralized domestic pluralism that explicitly opposed the conformity promoted by wartime Americanizers, such as the hyperpatriotic National Security League (NSL) and the Committee on Public Information (CPI).

Still, the question remains: What precisely was "transnationalism"? Based on the perceived failure of melting-pot assimilation and the rival ethnic views appearing at home, transnationalism was Bourne's attempt to imagine a new America in which multiple cultures of ethnic and personal identifications, or overlapping types of "citizenships," could be interconnected into a domestic political framework. For him, public and private experience should be inseparable as individuals come together to operate in a projected "environment of the Beloved Community." The transnational concept creatively incorporated Bourne's views about cultural pluralism and progressive social change into the longer intellectual tradition of "steering clear" of foreign entanglements in the form of European-style power politics or wars.[16]

Bourne's personal sense of isolation as a man and as a thinker is crucial to understanding him and his unusual hybrid of political isolationism with international engagement. He never fully worked out what he meant by transnationalism, as he died at the height of his intellectual prowess in December 1918. Still, Bourne's unpublished writings and published works, when contextualized alongside the intellectual and political transformations from 1911 to 1918, reveal that, working with a small cohort of liberal critics of Wilson and the progressive prowar position, he developed a potent and influential pluralist, noninterventionist, and cosmopolitan form of isolationism.[17]

Three stages were crucial for Bourne's emerging ideas and their ramifications. First, from 1914 through early 1916, after he joined the staff of the *New Republic*, his increasing personal and political isolation catalyzed his antiwar vision. In these years he gradually found his own voice as an opponent of entering the European war and developed what became his pluralistic ideal for a transnational America, which was first published in July 1916.

In the second stage, best seen in 1916 and 1917, his opposition to the war, conjoined with other progressives and socialists, was essentially noninterventionist. For the first time he generated an explicit foreign policy vision, which aimed at making the United States a force for international peace, while keeping it out of the European war and reforming to build a more open, inclusive, and transnational society at home.

Third, as we will see in more depth in the next chapter, Bourne's pluralist views and his antiwar attacks on the increasingly prowar camp of his fellow intellectuals, most notably John Dewey and those at the *New Republic,* inspired him to revise transnationalism and his antiwar position in light of events on the American home front from 1917 through 1918. Although he had difficulty getting some of his most overtly political observations and articles published because antiwar views were then unpopular and subject to censorship, his many proposals finally were unified by a broadening of his unique form of isolationism into an alternative to wartime Americanization. His long-standing sense of personal isolation facilitated his crafting of a philosophy that was both isolationist and transnational.[18]

During all three stages Bourne's private life and professional reverses influenced his politics of cultural radicalism. His physical disabilities often isolated him in public settings and propelled him toward the written word. He also asserted that his own condition provided him with a peculiar sympathy for minority groups and those discriminated against, leading to his firm belief in the need for thoroughgoing progressive social reform to help alienated individuals and groups. As public opinion moved toward favoring entrance into the European conflict, so, too, did the views of many in Bourne's intellectual community. He was shunted aside or rejected even by many of those he had considered friends. Editors and government oversight curtailed Bourne's ability to publish, particularly in writing the charged political commentary that he so desired to reach a wide readership. As his sense of personal isolation deepened, his arguments against the war and for national politico-military isolation grew more strident.

Bourne advocated an active U.S. role in the world—without the use of force unless America was directly attacked and with strong cultural, commercial, and political programs. This may seem paradoxical, but Bourne saw both as compatible. He divorced governmental international involvement from the use of force except when absolutely necessary, and idealistically affirmed that outside government Americans ought to be otherwise fully engaged with the world.[19]

The maturation of Bourne's transnational ideology is best understood as a form of isolationism created in response to the rising pressures of nationalism everywhere. As such, it formed an organic connection between transnationalism at home and his antiwar position for the nation abroad. Bourne's transnational aims for domestic pluralism and his pacifistic isolationist hopes for global peace were marginalized during World War I, but they later became widely influential for generations of antiwar activists and thinkers, such as Noam Chomsky, Christopher Lasch, and Dwight Macdonald, who have all invoked and deployed Bourne's ideas.[20]

Bourne's Early Years

Born in Bloomfield, New Jersey, in 1886 to an upper-middle-class family, Bourne once termed his birth "terribly messy." A botched forceps delivery and an acute bout of spinal tuberculosis at age four left him shorter than five feet tall, slightly disfigured and hunchbacked. Bourne's mother, though, saw only the best in her son, whom she loved deeply. She encouraged him to persevere with a focus not on body but on mind. He read voraciously. He wrote. He played the piano. Yet his childhood was not easy. His father failed at numerous businesses, did not give Randolph much personal attention, and left the family when Bourne was only ten years old.

After his graduation from high school in 1903, Bourne passed all of the admissions tests and hoped to attend Princeton University. But his uncle, Halsey Barrett, a lawyer and the family benefactor after his father departed, refused to help pay his tuition for Princeton or any other college. Crushed, Bourne carried on, later terming the ensuing year (1904–1905) as a time of a "transvaluation of values" in his life.

Bourne labored for close to six years in mundane jobs in manufacturing positions and as a piano teacher. These experiences from 1904 through 1909 fueled his intense belief in the need for regulation and reform of the workplace to improve the everyday life of the common worker. He gradually developed a quasi-socialist suspicion of capitalism that influenced his lifelong belief in education reform and the power of education to uplift the masses. Many other disaffected young men of the early 1900s shared his progressive, reform-minded, pro-labor views.

At one time he made player-piano rolls by hand for the organist Frederick Hoschke. Working in a home factory, Bourne became skilled at producing rolls more quickly, thereby earning higher total wages. Hoschke countered by reducing the piece price, lowering Bourne's total income. Protests and appeals were met by Hoschke's cool reminder to Bourne that he was "perfectly free" to stay or go. Bourne later reported that he had returned "cravenly to my bench" and that was formative in his understanding of the true nature of unrestrained capitalism.[21]

He was not "free," and fighting this system directly from the bottom up, as an individual worker, was not possible. He needed the work far too much to be able to bargain as an equal. Laissez-faire notions, Bourne perceived, were far removed from the brutal realities of the industrial workforce, and collective bargaining was the only hope for a more positive future for American labor. Later, after 1914, Bourne built on these realizations. He aimed to strengthen the conditions of workers and "hyphenate" Americans (German Americans, Irish Americans, and so forth), broaden access to education and the arts, and embark on an ambitious program to dynamically combine America's diverse national cultures to reject "hyphen stigma" rather than assimilate them into a homogenous whole.[22]

Desperate to escape the cycle of subsistence piecework, while also teaching piano part time, Bourne again applied to college in 1909. His fortunes changed at last. He won a scholarship to attend Columbia College, where he thrived. Within a year he had published his first article and been elected to the editorial board of the *Columbia Monthly*. Reflecting later on his time at college in New York, Bourne considered these years, from 1909 to 1913, the most important ones of his life. He believed that his time at Columbia was formative not just because of the excellent education, but also because the city itself served as an intellectual proving ground. New York intellectuals embraced Bourne quickly because of his flashing wit and willingness to discuss any topic at any time. He met, learned from, and came to revere his eminent professors, such as the historians Charles Beard and James Harvey Robinson and the philosopher-educator John Dewey, while also enjoying the stimulation of peers such as his close friends Van Wyck Brooks and Arthur Macmahon.

He began to publish essays in the *Atlantic Monthly* in 1911, working with editor Ellery Sedgwick. He later published in the *Dial*, under the increasingly liberal editorship of Martyn Johnston. At the *New Republic*, founded in 1914, he was honored to join forces as a contributing member of the staff with editors and writers he admired: Herbert Croly, Walter Lippmann, Walter Weyl, and Dewey. By the time America joined the war, he was also publishing with the upstart cultural magazine *Seven Arts*, on which he collaborated with friends like Van Wyck Brooks and Scofield Thayer.

Enmeshed in this network of thinkers, both liberal and conservative, he participated in New York salon-clubs, such as the Liberal, Heretics, and Socialist, where he could discuss topics related to the club's theme with visiting intellectuals as well as local members. He was rarely fully satisfied by these conversations, as his letters attest. Eric Sandeen, biographer and compiler of Bourne's collected letters, has observed that his subject was at his best when writing. He was "adept at parceling out his personality to his correspondents, and he was particularly generous toward the women with whom he exchanged letters."[23] He befriended a number of women and carried on corresponding relationships that were both flirtatious and highly intellectual, such as with anthropologist Elsie Clews Parsons, the writer-editors Agnes de Lima and Alyse Gregory, more limited exchanges with peace activist–settlement house visionary Jane Addams, as well as a host of feminists, social workers, socialists, and pacifists. Bourne made friends with fellow cultural critic Brooks early on and carried on a vibrant epistolary exchange with him throughout their lives while also collaborating on various publications. Amos Pinchot, the outspoken proponent of neutrality; noted radical Max Eastman; social justice crusader Winthrop Lane; journalist and communist activist John Reed; and Mabel Dodge Luhan, hostess of a salon famed for the brilliance of those who gathered there, were among Bourne's sympathetic allies.[24]

From the middle of the 1910s on, Bourne was a high-profile member of the Greenwich Village renaissance. He sought out exchanges of ideas in the free marketplace of the New York intelligentsia until the momentous events he had observed in Europe impelled America to enter the war. Pressing political conditions at home in the United States spurred him to cultivate what he called his "radical will," a public, forceful voice calling for major liberal progressive reform at home and opposition to war abroad.

In July 1916, Bourne formulated his radical opposition. "No Americanization will fulfill this vision which does not recognize the uniqueness of this trans-nationalism of ours." He spoke about the nation and the pressures he felt impinging on him and his "beloved community" of intellectuals.[25] Yet the war shut down conduits through which Bourne could express his voice as he came into his own. Once the Wilson administration officially endorsed the war effort in 1917, Bourne's opposition made him a pariah in even the liberal intellectual circles that had embraced him.

As the nation inched toward formal entrance into the European war from 1914 through 1917—debating first neutrality, then preparedness, then the draft, and finally entry into the conflict—Bourne perceived matching upsurges of dangerous, nationalistic sentiment and stubbornly clung to the belief that he was part of a larger progressive, transatlantic project to "change the world," as one scholar has termed this movement.[26]

His prediction that participation in the conflict would distort America's society as it had in Germany and elsewhere held true. Not long after war broke out in Europe, Bourne observed, "The wheels of the clock have so completely stopped in Europe, and this civilization that I have been admiring so much seems so palpably about to be torn to shreds that I do not even want to think about Europe until the war is over and life is running again."[27] Persistently optimistic with regard to intolerance and the flawed American melting pot, he hoped that the light might reach his fellow intellectuals, who, in turn, might assist him in persuading ordinary U.S. citizens to turn their backs on the growing blind patriotism and the illusion of melting-pot Americanism. Bourne determined to work toward that end. He strived to "slowly sting people into new ideals and tastes, and meanwhile not let one's soul be poisoned by the hostile environment."[28] Such a belief for a young, relatively unknown intellectual seems particularly naive. Bourne's idealistic stance shifted toward a more stalwart antiwar, isolated form of cultural internationalism. He emphasized the importance of generating a vanguard of "radical youth" to spread these arguments widely and deeply. But he despaired that this was not possible in the current American environment. He also feared that his personal and professional worlds were teetering on the precipice of collapse, just when it seemed that his career was taking off at the *New Republic*.

After he published "Trans-National America" in the summer of 1916 in the *Atlantic Monthly*, through the turn of the year 1917 Bourne attempted to bring order to chaos by using his cultural criticism as a platform for encouraging major social and educational change. He hoped his ideas would change the world. Bourne advocated what he called the "experimental life"—that is, the testing out of ideas in everyday experience. His private letters along with his published writing demonstrate just how deeply his reformist passion combined with his fear of failure and his immanent concern with being abandoned by friends and colleagues. Yet, surprisingly, he remained a resolute and personally tough figure: he abhorred those who patronized him, disdained those who did not give his arguments a fair reading, and despised those who reacted to his physique with disgust.[29]

For subsequent generations of intellectuals and scholars, he was a prophet of radical-willed youth, a mythic figure. His thought and life became a legend—his powerful advocacy of radical intellectualism, his searing attacks on the prowar intelligentsia headed by Dewey, and his untimely death. Made most poignant in the ghostly verse of John Dos Passos's *1919*, Bourne was a David-like character out to slay the many Goliaths of his time.[30]

A Lonely Spectator

On July 14, 1915, Bourne wrote despairingly to his confidant Alyse Gregory, not yet his editor at the *Dial*, "I shall give up clamoring to be 'in' things, 'do' things, and accept my fate as a lonely spectator, reserved from action for contemplation."[31] But shortly afterward he was rejoicing at finding an intellectual home, albeit briefly, at the *New Republic*.[32] The *Atlantic Monthly* editor Ellery Sedgwick and the Columbia historian Charles Beard recommended Bourne to the would-be editor-in-chief of the *New Republic*, Herbert Croly. He had written to Bourne in Europe in June 1914, offering him a position as contributing writer upon his return. Croly, whose work Bourne greatly admired, explained that the new publication would be "radical without being socialistic." It would have a "general tendency" to be "pragmatic rather than doctrinaire." The mission, according to Croly, was to "build up a body of public opinion behind a more thoughtful and radical form of progressivism than that which ordinarily passes under that name."[33] To others, like Justice Learned Hand, Croly emphasized a moderate thematic focus that he started to call a "new liberalism." But Bourne gravitated to the more revolutionary ideas espoused by Croly in their private correspondence. Bourne believed that the new journal would serve as a beacon to like-minded "radical" progressives. The two men agreed that the magazine would function as a conduit for articulating a program for social change.[34]

Bourne was immediately enthusiastic about the opportunity. As a regular contributor to the magazine, he was guaranteed an income of $1,000 a year, a significant amount for a fresh college graduate who had labored in a home factory that paid at most $700 per year. He was overwhelmed by his big break. He would be surrounded by some of the preeminent minds of the day. The talented editorial staff comprised many leading lights of the progressive intelligentsia. By and large they agreed on a collective mission: Croly's "new liberalism" for a "New Republic." What they wanted was largely what inspired Bourne: they hoped to create a planned society through a series of progressive reforms, most in education and in improving democratic institutions, in line with what Walter Lippmann called "mastery."

Croly's *Promise of American Life* (1909) argued precisely this point: namely, American "promise" was not "self-fulfilling" and therefore had to be orchestrated to come into fruition. His *Progressive Democracy* (1914) built on these arguments. The economist Walter Weyl, also an editor, expressed an equally wholehearted progressive social control perspective in *The New Democracy* (1912). Fellow editor Lippmann's renowned *Drift and Mastery* (1914) was inspired in part by Croly's and Weyl's argument. Lippmann said the tension between expansion and consolidation, traditionalism and progressivism, emotion and rationality, could be managed. This sort of radical model for social control, a mastery engineered by well-meaning intellectuals, deeply influenced Bourne. They agreed that "mastery" could be attained through a type of pluralistic embrace of science as the diagnostic instrument. This, they said, would be the primary discipline of democracy.[35]

These ideas similarly influenced others on the staff, including Philip Littell, who wrote a column on "Books and Things," and Francis Hackett, the well-known literary editor of the *Chicago Evening Post*. Hackett was widely regarded as one of the most erudite commentators on the literary scene in America. During the years before the war, the contributors list for the *New Republic* is a who's who of leading social, political, literary, and philosophical lights of the era: John Dewey, John Reed, George Santayana, Charles Beard, James Harvey Robinson, H. G. Wells, Robert Frost, Amy Lowell, Conrad Aiken, Graham Wallas, George Bernard Shaw, and James Bryce.

Considering the mission and prominence of his prospective colleagues, Bourne noted to his confidante Alyse Gregory, "It seems like just the opportunity that I have wanted to get myself expressed, and I am only hoping to be able to be really big enough for the opportunity."[36] Yet he was soon dismayed that national affairs and most literary issues in the fine arts, categories on which he aimed to write, had been allocated to his more celebrated comrades. Croly assigned him progressive education, urban planning, and religion as his "special" topics. Accordingly, the first issue of the *New Republic* featured Bourne's "In a Schoolroom." In this evaluation of his own suburban New Jersey high school he saw a "paradoxical situation": changes in the organization of teachers and curriculum did not tend to result in better-educated students. He studied the exemplary schools of Gary, Indiana, which had applied new Deweyan educational ideas and an efficiency-based organization, finding Bloomfield sad in comparison. His general critique of the public schools was the paradoxical situation in which the "more excellent became its primary methods the poorer became the product at the end of the system."[37] Croly admired Bourne's critique but found it to be, at times, a bit too radical in its implicit calls for change. He responded by advising Bourne to keep in mind the paper's brand of liberalism as paramount in his journalism. He wrote, "I believe . . . that a certain amount of conscious patriotism is necessary." He continued, "We have got to be thoroughly critical, but there must be also a positive impulse behind our criticism. That means, translated into practical terms, that we have got to discover and try to develop the beginnings of sound work whenever they appear in this country."[38] Bourne reluctantly agreed to emphasize "sound work" and "conscious patriotism" in his essays on education and urban planning.

Croly's comments to Bourne on his journalistic style reveal how rapidly the veneer of the *New Republic*'s liberal agenda wore away under domestic pressures, a process that accelerated as the European conflict intensified. The war forced the periodical to take a stand while it was still in its infancy.

In 1913, only a year before the outbreak of the war, and almost two years before the *New Republic* was up and running, Walter Lippmann had posited scientific "mastery" of the tensions in society as the paramount alternative to a "drift" characterized by the new physical and psychological conditions brought about by socioeconomic change. Persuaded, the progressive reformer Bobby Rogers wrote to Mabel Dodge in 1914 that when Lippmann's proposed mastery was "beginning to shake me in my very firm belief in original sin . . . this war has restored it triumphantly." To Rogers, the war exemplified drift. "Bad education" had not been the cause. That much was clear. "Illogical passion," he said," was an awfully hard element to socially control or "teach" out of mankind.[39] The war thus also forced Lippmann and Croly to refine their ideas about progressivism and reform techniques, in the context of international interaction, on the pages of the *New Republic*. They had to determine how European conflict would affect their goals for progressive reform in education and politics. How would the war impact the fate of their desired progressive "mastery" in America?

In much the same way, Woodrow Wilson's dedication to internationalism was based upon the hope that a sound formulation of social control could vanquish the sorts of "illogical passions" that Rogers wrote about.

While Bourne witnessed firsthand hypernationalism run amok in Germany, Wilson regarded America as a nation of many nationalities in need of purpose. At first Wilson advocated an isolationist position. From the 1912 campaign through 1915, Wilson had adhered to the tradition of isolation from European wars. After August 1914, Wilson often argued that Europe had thrown itself into "a war with which we have nothing to do, whose cause cannot touch us." The prescription was to remain neutral in mind as well as in body. While he recognized that sentimental attachments would differ, Wilson asked citizens to restrain themselves as much as possible. He contended that if the nation did not "act" belligerently, America might play a more instrumental role in making a lasting peace.[40]

Bourne, along with the editors and staff of the *New Republic*, agreed with this position. So did most Americans at the time, liberal pacifists and conservative nationalists alike. This agreement encompassed a wide, divergent group: Eugene Debs and Victor Berger, labor organizers such as Samuel Gompers, radicals in the ilk of Max Eastman and his sister Crystal Eastman, pacifist Secretary of State William Jennings Bryan, reformers such as Robert La Follette and Jane Addams, pacifists and feminists such as Emily Balch and Margaret Sanger, scholars such as John Dewey and Charles Beard, racial egalitarians and activists such as W. E. B. Du Bois (at least at first), and missionary internationalists, such as John Mott, who held traditional isolationist beliefs about the importance of noninterventionism. But neutrality for Wilson was not simply what he asserted to be a "petty desire to keep out of trouble."[41] Rather, it was an effort to place the nation in a position above the fray as a mediator for peace and as a power for greater good in the world. As a *New Republic* editorial struggled to make clear in late 1914, "The European war is a challenge to the United States to justify its independence. The nation can not be independent in the sense of being isolated. It can be independent in the sense of being still more completely the master of its own destiny." Not merely a "renunciation of European entanglements," American independence, the editors also argued, called for "the adoption of the positive and necessary policy of making American influence in Europe count in favor of international peace."[42] This stance was simultaneously anti-isolationist in rhetoric and in favor of international mediation in practice. Nevertheless, despite calling for an "end to isolation," it built on the very foundations and appeal of bedrock isolationist concepts such as keeping the nation out of the war, avoiding taking sides in European power politics and conflicts, maintaining autonomy, and (at this point) opposing militarization at home.

In contrast, Theodore Roosevelt, Robert Lansing, Henry Cabot Lodge, and others in a pro-British, prowar camp rejected such a position as fence straddling. They particularly disliked the forms of peaceful and cooperative mediation Wilson and the *New Republic* editors sought to engineer. Instead, they saw preparedness for war as crucial, support for England and America's natural allies as pivotal, and entry into the conflict as inevitable. According to Lodge, the reasons for this were a combination of national honor, economic interest, the exercise of neutral rights, and a sense of the strategic imperative not to permit the forces of the kaiser to win.[43]

When confronted by such arguments, Wilson held course throughout late 1914 and into 1915. He continued to aim for an association that would become a force "so much greater than the force of any nation now engaged, or any alliance hitherto formed or projected, that no nation, no probable combination of nations could face or withstand it."[44] This objective—what became the League of Nations—caused further splintering in and among the groups who opposed entry into the war on isolationist or other grounds and those who argued for preparing to join the war. Just as in the debates between the imperialists and anti-imperialists at the turn of the twentieth century, some variation of international engagement was fundamental to virtually all of those involved. Yet Wilson took strong actions to intervene in Mexico against General Victoriano Huerta; Wilson refused to recognize Huerta's new revolutionary government and sent troops that eventually occupied the port city of Veracruz in 1914. One partial blind spot for Bourne was represented by these events. His strong focus on domestic progressive reform, pluralism, and a foreign policy emphasis on mediation and steering clear of intervention in Europe came at the expense of his engaging more critically with American interventions in Latin America and particularly Wilson's deployment of U.S. forces to fight in Mexico from 1914 through early 1917.[45]

Staying out of the war, however, was of paramount importance to those advocating neutrality, whether they were strictly isolationist or more internationalist seekers of a mediated peace. Thus, by the time of Wilson's campaign for reelection, slogans epitomized by the phrase "he kept us out of war" propelled him to a narrow victory.[46] That sentiment was short-lived.

On May 7, 1915, a German submarine fired torpedoes and sank the British passenger liner the *Lusitania*, causing 1,198 deaths, 128 of whom were

Americans. Despite the fact that those U.S. victims had been traveling on a belligerent ship, many Americans saw their loss as resulting from an unconscionable violation of neutrality. The nation was incensed. The press covered the story relentlessly. Yet, American interests helped prevent any serious breaks with any of the Allied nations. Heavy industry, in particular, continued filling large orders and sending massive amounts of matériel to the Allies. Great Britain, along with France, blockaded Germany, with effective results. American trade, including goods and loans, with Germany was reduced from approximately $345 million in 1914 to a mere $29 million in 1916; during the same period, U.S. trade with the Allied powers rose remarkably fast, from $753 million to nearly $3 billion. In effect the United States was supporting the Allied war effort and all involved knew it. After the *Lusitania* incident, complete neutrality came to seem impossible.[47] It was hard to envision a scenario in which the federal government would prohibit all trade with belligerents and all travel that might bring American citizens or goods into the line of fire. The de facto policy of favoring nonblockaded nations continued. In response, Germany resumed submarine warfare against Allied and "neutral" commercial sea traffic, inspiring provocative comments from the American press and populace.[48]

In his own circles Bourne began to feel marginalized. He considered himself increasingly an outsider among his colleagues at the *New Republic* as he opposed the rising war fervor, and he was rarely invited to their sumptuous editorial staff lunches, which frequently entertained esteemed visiting thinkers. Bourne may have perceived these slights as greater than they were. He was in conflict with Croly on his assignments because he was shunted toward writing book reviews and away from national political pieces. True "usefulness"—his own term and self-assigned progressive rationale for writing—had become problematic. How could one be "useful" when it was hard to write and publish truly meaningful social criticism? Were love of country and love of progressive reform at odds? What was the role of the intellectual in a time of enveloping patriotism? The intellectual community in which Bourne had been at home, for which he had held high hopes of being "big enough," was moving in the opposite direction from him. Confronting this challenge defined the rest of Bourne's life.

One related counterfactual point bears further scrutiny. Throughout 1915 Bourne struggled to hone a precise opinion of the war and the best role for the nation in the world. His letters reveal that he still seemed open to the pragmatic, progressive, and idealistic rationale propagated by Dewey, Croly, Lippmann, and even investigative journalist George Creel. However, Bourne was not offered the opportunity to write feature articles on these subjects for the *New Republic* or for other magazines. Although it is not likely he would have changed his ultimate position against what he later termed the "rudderless" manner in which the nation went to war and then set militaristic and punitive war aims, Bourne might have moderated his perspectives. If he had been more willing to agree with his fellow intellectuals or to help them formulate a more Jamesian pragmatic policy, then those Bourne admired at the *New Republic* and in the greater liberal intelligentsia might have permitted him more latitude. Croly, in particular, might have offered more opportunities for him to write not just reviews but also opinion pieces.[49]

The lack of "useful" outlets, however, turned him increasingly away from compromise with the liberal intellectuals who were gradually moving toward endorsing the war. "It used really to worry me," Bourne wrote privately, "to be filled with so much reforming spirit, and to be so detached from any machinery of change. I felt very useless and treacherous, and envied those who were in the heat of the fray. But after the desperate attempts I have made this year, only to be shouldered out almost before I knew it, I am convinced that some deep destiny presides over it all, that I have unsuspected powers of incompatibility with the real world."[50] This dread of incompatibility and desperate struggle for relevance heightened as the nation debated armed neutrality, then the draft, and finally intervention, all at odds with Bourne's values.[51]

Personal Isolation and Transnationalism

Bourne's personal isolation has not often been discussed as a contributing factor in his antiwar radicalism. Yet to Bourne's contemporaries the dramatic contrast between his physical disfigurement and his intellectual brilliance was striking. One anecdote reveals how powerfully Bourne's appearance impacted his professional and intellectual life.

Long before the debates about the war, in 1911 the well-regarded and well-connected *Atlantic Monthly* editor Ellery Sedgwick, after having read some of Bourne's journalistic writings at Columbia, invited Bourne to lunch at the prestigious Century Club in New York. When Bourne was ushered into the Century, his appearance startled and revolted Sedgwick, who said that he had to leave for another commitment and was sorry to have to miss the luncheon. Sedgwick commented that at the time he found Bourne "a dwarf in stature, without a redeeming feature." Later, the two men became friends, and Sedgwick regretted his callous behavior in their first meeting and became a patron of Bourne's work; the *Atlantic* published most of Bourne's best-known articles from 1911 until 1918. However, this awkward meeting (and others like it) reveals Bourne's dispiriting personal interactions.[52]

Despite his many friendships, he felt deep loneliness, which in turn influenced his politics. In his letters during the war years he appears as a tortured soul, worried that the close companions upon whom he relied for personal and intellectual sustenance would simply depart. "Please don't leave me in the lurch," he wrote to Gregory. "Too many of my friends make me feel that they may, and I have horrible moments of littleness and panic. . . . I need them, but they would light-heartedly never feel the need of me. . . . Yet as a hermit, I should die."[53] At other moments it appeared to Bourne, "friends in quantity seem less attractive than they used to be. I seem always to be pursuing them, and this grows monotonous," he remarked. "I must always expect to be poor and unloved and obscure. I shall probably have enough to be thankful for if I am warm and fed, and may creep into the Public Library now and then to read with other . . . poor, unloved, and obscure."[54]

Bourne's inability to complete a major book-length piece of scholarship along the lines of what he deemed Lippmann's "magisterial" *Drift and Mastery* enhanced his insecurity. He revealed this deep-seated fear when he remarked that his legacy might just be for his promise rather than his oeuvre. "There is nothing at all of permanence," he complained. "I remain . . . 'a promising young author.'"[55] Isolation of both the nation and himself were the fountainheads of how he perceived his world.

To break out of this box, Bourne developed a number of lofty, sometimes naively idealistic, and inclusive visions of cosmopolitanism: these ideas shaped how he understood his own "promise" and the pluralism he articulated in July 1916, when the *Atlantic Monthly* published his "Trans-National America." To provide a context, that same summer Wilson embarked on a national speaking tour, and by midsummer, preparedness policy had become law. Soon the nation's ambitious preparations for possible conflict were well under way. After a tumultuous year trying to work his views into review and opinion pieces for the *New Republic*, Bourne could no longer continue along the magazine's path that Croly had termed "conscious patriotism." Instead, Bourne advanced a threefold set of proposals for a transnational vision—not only for the nation but also, ultimately, for the world.

First, Bourne claimed that the concept of the melting pot was conceptually and practically bankrupt. Second, he called for a "trans-nationality" that embraced the lived "reality" of multiple ethnic, national, racial, and other "citizenships," clearly expressed by the people. Third, he mounted what later became a forceful assault on the war and on every aspect of American jingoism.

For Bourne, universal principles of humanistic solidarity reinforced the bedrock duties of an intellectual—to observe culture and to enact change. Taken further, his transnationalism attempted to find a way to transcend state borders and to nurture authentic pluralism. Bourne assaulted the "gregarious impulse" that drove intellectuals like Dewey, himself a pluralist and pragmatist, eventually to endorse the war effort. Bourne aimed to blend cultures and peoples. He wished to overcome what he saw as the tightening rules for assimilation, which he assumed often encouraged violence and ethno-cultural intolerance, by finding new ways to unite citizens within and across nations.

That was easier said than done. The dependence of national antagonisms upon improbable processes of assimilation within nations—coupled with commercial conflicts between nations—led, perhaps inexorably, to military conflict, according to Bourne; yet nationalistic assimilation had little to no practical benefit. This argument against the ends of both national and commercial conflicts connects his ideas to those of British internationalist Norman Angell, whose work Bourne cited favorably in letters to his friend and former college roommate Simon Pelham Barr, who also succeeded him as editor of the *Columbia Monthly* student literary magazine.

In his best-selling book *The Great Illusion* (1911), Angell attempted to expose and overturn the illusion that war was useful for industrial societies. Few of Bourne's historians and biographers have connected these two thinkers, but Angell's ideas clearly resonated with Bourne. In fact, he solicited Angell to contribute an essay to the pacifistic collection *Towards an Enduring Peace*, edited by Bourne and published in 1916. Two years before, Angell had helped to found the Neutrality League to try to keep Great Britain out of the war. His well-documented and well-received economic arguments against conflict became very influential in the United

States—particularly among pacifists, socialists, and many progressives—even rising to the attention of Woodrow Wilson. Angell traveled widely across America, giving lectures and leading study groups. He spoke several times in New York City's Greenwich Village, where Bourne most likely heard him in person.[56]

Bourne seems to have thought Angell was engaged in a similar, Croly-esque mission to fulfill America's "promise." Bourne agreed that such an outcome might best be understood through the nation's unique possibility to adopt and advance transnationality. The key to fulfilling such a project of "promise," according to both Angell and Bourne, would be for America to help prevent global conflict. In making such a case, Bourne explicitly deployed Angell's social and economic arguments that war was "inadequate" for solving international disputes. If war could not be counted on to advance national interests, then what would?

By 1915 Angell examined the ongoing war and penned a book-length plea with his answer: American leadership. A leader in the British and European pacifist ranks, he recognized that "the power she exercises to this end [international leadership] need not be military"; still, Angell argued, "it is the mission of America in her own interest to devise it; that the circumstances of her isolation, historical and geographic, enable her to do for the older peoples—and herself—a service which by reason of their circumstances, geographical and historical, they cannot do for themselves."[57] Bourne admired the British pacifists and Fabians, and seems to have found solace in this shared view that America's culture and capacity for international mediation were paramount. At the time, American exceptionalism also appealed to Wilson, who both tacitly supported the British war effort and yet, as Robert Tucker has shown, longed to serve as a mediator to end the conflict.[58] Along the same lines, Angell earlier had contended that the "fight for ideals can no longer take the form of a fight between nations, because the lines of division on moral questions are within the nations themselves and intersect the political frontiers."[59] Thus, like Bourne, and unlike Wilson, Angell felt that America should remain distant. In so doing, by dint of being removed from the rival nationalisms of Europe, Angell's and Bourne's America was then best equipped to be the agent of global peace.

"There is no modern State," observed Angell as early as 1911, "which is completely Catholic or Protestant, or liberal or autocratic, or aristocratic or democratic, or socialist or individualist; the moral and spiritual strug-

gles of the modern world go on between citizens of the same State in unconscious intellectual cooperation with corresponding groups in other
states, not between the public powers of rival States."[60] Almost transnational in orientation, Angell took pains to prove a point that Bourne firmly
supported as well. Cultural, ethnic, political, and commercial conflicts
must be made compatible within nations themselves as well as across
them. To this end Bourne's transnationalism was an application of Angell's ideas, and in his last unpublished essay, "The State," Bourne echoed
and revised Angell's words, saying "war is the health of the state." By that
he meant the economic machinery and repressive political instincts of
most states thrive in the hyperpatriotic environment provided by warfare.
The old isolationist axiom that America could have nothing permanent
and political to do with Europe Bourne and Angell agreed was a fallacy.
There could never be complete isolation in a world of international trade
and a large-scale global war, of course. According to Angell, "There is no
such thing as one nation standing out and maintaining indefinitely a social spirit, an attitude towards life and society absolutely distinct and different from that of the surrounding world."[61]

Paradoxically, despite these shared views, they placed different values
on what should be emphasized in politics. Angell preferred a practical
approach. He wanted an "end to American isolation," in which the
United States did not commit military forces but did act as a primary
international leader for the peace associations advocated by Woodrow
Wilson.

Bourne, on the other hand, remained as much an advocate of his trans-
national project as a proponent of international peace programs, and disparaged "leagues to enforce peace." Angell, a future Nobel Peace Prize
winner, was called upon to work with President Wilson in 1917–1918.
He helped Wilson's brain trust develop an internationalist plan to avert
future wars through the League of Nations. The outbreak of World War I
redirected many international evangelizers away from their calling in
missionary work. For example, John Mott moved from the increasingly
difficult task of evangelizing during the conflict to concentrating his
Christian charitable efforts for prisoner-of-war and refugee relief for all
the belligerent nations. In 1915 he became the general secretary of the International Committee of the YMCA. As chairman of the National War
Work Council, Mott came to Wilson and offered the YMCA's resources
for service to fighting men and prisoners (with approximately twenty-six

thousand men and women involved worldwide). In 1916, Mott continued to serve, this time on Wilson's Mexican Commission, and in 1917 as a member of the Root Mission to Russia.[62]

After the war, Mott needed to rebuild relationships in the WSCF, various SCFs and the world YMCA, and missionary movements, as well as to continue with relief, prisoner, and repatriation efforts in the Orthodox lands of Eastern Europe, where Mott laid foundations for what the YMCA later termed "Protestant-Orthodox rapprochements." Mott still supported the war effort as a genuine good. Sounding much like some of the progressives who sided with Wilson, Mott said in a 1917 speech at DePauw University in Greencastle, Indiana, "At the close of the War there will be an unparalleled opportunity for reconstruction, for that will be a time of incalculable plasticity." If none of the techniques employed to prevent the war—leagues, laws, and ideas such as socialism—succeeded, according to Mott, then faith would help reshape a "reborn" postwar world. As he declared, "It is our belief that the principles of Christ are meant to be applied here and now and in every relationship, including the international."[63] Angell, however, turned against Wilson almost immediately after the armistice was declared. He launched a scathing public critique of Wilson and the peace settlement, particularly opposing its punitive economic stipulations, bound to lead to future conflicts.

Angell challenged his audiences to overcome base instincts and to recognize the intense interconnectivity of people, ideas, and nations in the modern world. "Are we in blind obedience to primitive instincts and old prejudices?" he asked. "[Are we] enslaved by the old catchwords and that curious indolence which makes the revision of old ideas unpleasant, to duplicate indefinitely on the political and economic side a condition from which we have liberated ourselves on the religious side? . . . Spilling oceans of blood, wasting mountains of treasure—to achieve what is at bottom a logical absurdity, to accomplish something which, when accomplished, can avail us nothing?"[64]

Bourne emphatically responded to that rhetorical question: no, we need not be subject to those instincts. Adapting William James's concept of a "moral equivalent to war"—originally applied by James to redirect the human instinct of bellicosity so that it could serve mankind—Bourne published "A Moral Equivalent for Universal Military Service" in the *New Republic* in July 1916, just a month after he had published "Trans-National America." Addressing liberal intellectuals such as Dewey, Bourne acknowledged, "The best will in America at present seems to crave some kind of national service. . . . Until we satisfy that craving," he stressed, "we run at half-power, and suffer all the dissatisfaction and self-despising that comes from repressed energy." Building on this thinly Freudian psychological construct, Bourne then outlined what an army of dedicated youth might do if properly educated and possessed of true "talents" and cosmopolitan "energies." He proposed an early version of a VISTA (AmeriCorps' Volunteers In Service to America), yet of an American exceptionalist sort. Such a corps would be "warring against nature and not against men, finding in drudgery and toil and danger the values that war and preparation for war had given." Bourne proposed an alternative to military service. "I have a picture of a host of eager young missionaries, swarming all over the land, spreading knowledge of health, the knowledge of domestic science, of gardening, of tastefulness, that they learned in school."[65]

Fellow peace activist and journalist Oswald Garrison Villard also decried the arguments that only military service would serve to discipline the nation's wayward youth, buttress democratic practices, promote industrial efficiency, or otherwise "furnish America with a soul." Thus, while Dewey refined his arguments in support of preparedness and draft policies in a series of articles, and Croly editorialized about the need for preparedness (both in the *New Republic*), Bourne crafted a new mission for radical youth, which he developed in such later writings as "Twilight of the Idols," when he invoked the spirit of William James to help sort out the proper course of present and future action.[66] Like James's prescription before him, this was much more of an idealistic vision rather than one firmly moored to a plan or policy.

In the meantime, others were engaged in debates over preparedness. It seemed to Croly and the other "pragmatic liberal" editors at the *New Republic* that these debates missed the point. Both sides—those for starting programs to purchase and stockpile war matériel and mobilize troops, as well as those opposing any semblance of building up the army, navy, and surplus military supplies—in the editorial page's words, "identify war and peace with more or less armament." Instead, neither arms nor the lack of them would ensure the future peace of the nation or the world. Thus, they editorialized that the "essence of preparedness is a definition of foreign policy." It was easy for Croly to attack extremist noninterventionists, pacifists, and antipreparedness advocates. For example, the radical Crystal Eastman argued in a letter to the *New Republic* that there was no need to discuss foreign policy. National disputes were "unavoidable," she said, and the only pertinent concern was "by what means" they should be settled. The *New Republic* editors derided these Eastman-type pacifists, rebuking them for naïveté and for missing the essential psychology of sacrifice involved. "Treaties," the editors argued, "will never acquire sanctity until nations are ready to seal them with their blood."[67] Croly and Weyl thus advocated preparedness as a policy because the nation might be forced to enter the conflict and would require the psychological ability (as much or more than arms) to participate in martial treaty "sealing by blood." In contrast, more extreme opponents of preparedness, such as Robert Herrick, called war and "arbitration by arms" an anachronism, "as silly as to speak of a trial by combat or other medieval fantasy."[68]

Yet these increasingly heated debates over preparedness and entering the war in late 1916 and early 1917 continued to manifest strong undercurrents of pro-neutrality sentiments. Such views not only emanated from the antiwar Left in which Bourne felt at home but also came from the more socially conservative circles of American Protestant evangelicals, who numbered approximately twenty-four million, and Catholics, who accounted for nearly sixteen million Americans, in 1917. At least officially, the evangelical, Catholic, and peace church presses campaigned against participating in a secular crusade and militaristic preparedness, much less a bloody war. A typical concern was voiced by the *King's Business*, an evangelical paper, which cautioned against the modernist propensity to "substitute democracy for a divinely appointed plan of REDEMPTION."[69] American Jews also were concerned about with whom the nation would ally if it entered the fray, and they cautioned against entering the conflict on the side of the oppressive Russian czar. Many Americans across faiths preferred neutrality and noninterventionism, often couched in the language of long-standing tradition as a rationale, at least until such time as the nation was directly attacked and conflict became inevitable.

However, it was fast becoming clear that war was an irreducible possibility. Bourne, too, in his role as a cultural and political critic, agreed to the widespread proposition that the current conflict and looming entrance into the war called for a well-reasoned policy. Yet the resulting foreign policy framework advanced by the *New Republic*, as seen in the editorial pages, was not erected on the sturdiest ground. It was limited and dependent, pivoting on abstract ideas about keeping "reason" alive and mediating among belligerents. As Bourne observed, the most crucial question remained: will the nation and its leaders choose war or peace? And the decision was essentially defaulted, left to reside in the interaction of European deeds with the diplomacy of the Wilson administration.

The *New Republic*'s editors borrowed from pacifists like Bourne and Herrick, and used portions of the popular neutrality arguments that appeared in the Christian presses. Croly et al. maintained that America could serve as a true neutral nation and thereby propel the cause of peace. "The American people do not intend to take part in the war," they asserted. The editors argued that the nation could "contribute to the terms of peace [by] . . . keeping alive in the world the light of reason."[70] In such declarations they overlooked that the nation had begun to supply significant amounts of war matériel and loans to back England and its allies by late 1915, while the British navy blockaded American commerce with Germany and its allies.

Then secretary of state under Wilson, William Jennings Bryan held similar views, but they began to change in late spring 1915. Bryan had surveyed Europe with horror and dread in the summer of 1914 but still hoped America would stay clear of the conflagration across the Atlantic. An idealistic near-pacifist, former anti-imperialist, and isolationist who believed in international adjudication of conflicts, Bryan considered America's primary duty to be one of *preventing* hostilities from spreading. Yet he perceived that within mere months of the war's breaking out in Europe that the United States was already responding with neither neutral tones nor deeds. In an effort to stanch American intolerance, Bryan attempted to keep German radio stations on the air. He hoped to permit Americans to hear all points of view on the war despite the predominant national leaning toward the Allies and Great Britain in particular.

A belief that the real issue at stake was American industrial and financial backing of the war effort made strange bedfellows of Andrew Carnegie, Eugene Debs, and William Jennings Bryan. In his role as secretary of state, Bryan was able to persuade a number of banks not to lend money directly to the belligerent nations. But this could not be maintained for long. "Expressions of sympathy are disturbing enough when they do not rest upon pecuniary interests," he wrote to Wilson. "They would be still more disturbing if each group was pecuniarily interested in the success of the nation to whom its members had loaned money."[71] But by summer 1915 Bryan felt he had only one card left to play. He very publicly resigned his position as secretary of state. American economic interests and diplomatic sympathies for the Allies—attitudes he could neither prevent nor weaken—had propelled the nation to the brink of entering an otherwise "unnecessary" conflict. Resignation was Bryan's final, symbolic, and belated gesture. While it garnered significant public attention in America and in Europe, there were few practical or public effects stemming from Bryan's act.[72]

On the other hand, Robert Lansing, the counselor of the Department of State, and Wilson's chief adviser and friend, Edward House, known as "Colonel," though he never earned the rank, argued that the purpose of diplomacy in wartime was not simply to keep peace but to uphold national ideals and to obtain advantages for American business. House also maintained that diplomacy in wartime should enhance national prestige and security. Given the widespread desire for business prosperity and the underlying American affinity for the Allied powers, Bryan's noninterventionist-isolationist stance seemed bound to fail.[73]

A small number of Americans launched international peace initiatives, and Bourne played a significant, if midlevel, role. While he continued to pursue cosmopolitan transnationalism as a primary avenue, he also advocated peace conferences and associations rather than a large-scale league of nations. The two were compatible ideals for Bourne. He shunned high-profile activities such as Henry Ford's peace ship, although he supported its aims, and preferred behind-the-scenes intellectual interchanges.[74]

Bourne had envisioned America's role in prevention even before the outbreak of the conflict in 1914. He penned a pamphlet for the American Association for International Conciliation (AAIC) titled "The Tradition of War." Published during his travels in Europe, his pamphlet argued audaciously that through modernity the world was becoming new in all aspects. The historic change being witnessed around the globe, he wrote, was a transition from "a feudal society based on isolation and force to an industrial creative society based on co-operation and exchange [which] has definitely and for all time relegated war to the dusty limbo of the past." Therefore, the aim, according to Bourne, ought to be to overcome "militarists." These men, like Wilson and his prowar cohort, "befuddle the wits of the masses of people with shibboleths of 'patriotism,' identifying the war ideals with love of country, and representing hatred of militarism as in a way synonymous with disloyalty to country."[75]

The AAIC enjoyed the support of prominent individuals such as Lyman Abbott, Charles Francis Adams, Andrew Carnegie, Nicholas Murray Butler of Columbia, Bryan, James Ford Rhodes, Harvard President Charles

Eliot, and Stanford President David Starr Jordan, among others. After two full years of war in Europe, however, membership in peace organizations became politically dangerous for Americans. Many of the leaders who might have brought much-needed political clout in the past distanced themselves from the AAIC during late 1916 and into 1917.

Bourne persevered, and in October 1916 he worked with the AAIC to organize intellectuals for a symposium on peace. His purpose was "to present a discussion for some of the most hopeful and constructive suggestions for the settlement of the war on terms that would make for a lasting peace."[76] Adding to his opposition to committing forces abroad, he had no patience with any binding overseas military alliances. Culturally, intellectually, and commercially he was for international engagement; diplomatically and militarily, he was an isolationist. Thus, the closer America came to entering the war, the more it reinforced for him that conflict brought out the worst "conscience" and the willful abridgement of rights, as evidenced by Wilson's statements and those of accommodationist liberals like Dewey and Du Bois. According to Bourne, the problem with this Deweyan logic was that it conflated international "association" and "participation" in the conflict abroad with domestic progressive reform. Bourne also saw these as inherently connected but believed that to participate rather than arbitrate abroad obliterated the values of progressivism at home. Many former pacifist and liberal opponents of U.S. entry into the war moved away from such a stance. In once such instance, when Robert Herrick publicly retracted his conviction that war and arbitration by arms were "anachronistic," Bourne was disappointed and disillusioned.

One of the many critiques contained in "Trans-National America" was Bourne's argument against his former reform allies turned accommodationist thinkers. He saw their reasoning as a fallacious connection of two contradictory points. According to Bourne, the nation could serve the world as an exemplar-mediator-democratizer, but not while intervening as a combatant in a fundamentally un-American war. For this reason he focused on how nationalistic conflict fanned the flames of fire below the "melting pot" of coerced assimilation, thus heightening belligerence in both degree and kind.[77]

Bourne believed war itself was the enemy of humankind. Just as James had remarked in his anti-imperialist writings, Bourne also thought along anti-imperialist lines that being warlike was deeply seated instinctually in human nature. To be truly civilized, then, would require restraining these urges as much as possible unless directly threatened. In essence, like James, Bourne saw conquering war to be possible and thus existentially essential. "We need to learn to live," he wrote, "rather than die."[78]

He had rising doubts about another aspect of preparedness: did Woodrow Wilson see that entering the war would preclude the American ability to assist in finding an enduring peace? "I can't make out," Bourne said privately, "whether the President is wobbling innocently towards [entering the war], like a child playing with fire, or is running a high and daring successful course, which will bring us out with prestige."[79]

While Bourne was unsure of Wilson's political acumen and objectives, Jane Addams, Debs, and others had no such doubts. They called for nonviolence from 1915 through 1916, and many of them continued to do so thereafter. These dissenters reasoned that the nation should collectively rethink de novo the relationship between international conciliation and the United States. African Americans, confronted by the challenge of whether to support armed neutrality, mostly took a different perspective. The issue of civil rights was paramount, and American entry into the war seemed to offer opportunities.

By July 1916, as editor of the *Crisis*, Du Bois had compiled and published a sample of generally prowar editorials excerpted from various black presses. While often cautious in their assessments, the opinions Du Bois presented were in accord with the statements of the *Southern Workman*. One writer from that paper proposed that an avalanche of forthcoming African American soldiers would strike a "shattering blow to race prejudice." Indeed, to Du Bois the salient factor was to reconcile bitter realities with realistic goals. He therefore agreed that black conscripts would generate respect for the race and demonstrate the patriotic virtues of African American citizen-soldiers. They would form a wedge toward the granting of full and complete citizenship rights. However, Du Bois observed that this process was likely to be painful.[80]

The African American community, as evidenced by the black press, for example, was deeply divided on the incendiary issue of segregated camps. Du Bois termed this the nation's "Perpetual Dilemma," that is, to "choose between insult and injury." Yet the start of the draft forced him to compromise. He reluctantly shifted toward an accommodationist perspective, the type he had caricatured as Booker T. Washingtonian in *Souls of Black Folk*. Du Bois set aside reservations about segregated military camps and limited any possible role of the nation as an international mediator.

Instead, this former anti-imperialist and anti-interventionist seized the moment as a racial opportunist. Du Bois argued that going to war was a crucible for citizenship, offering unprecedented possibilities for African American equality as a potential result.

Du Bois did not address Bourne's antiwar arguments explicitly, yet his line of reasoning clearly did not embrace a transnationalist means to achieve what both men hoped would be a more inclusive set of social and political relations. At this time Du Bois envisioned full and equal citizenships rights with an emphasis on cultivating African American educated achievers. Such views tended to reinforce nationalism and group parochialism; they did not embrace the personal and collective differences overlapping within Bourne's antiwar transnationalist model for radical national pluralism. Du Bois directly rejected an isolationist stance on America's role in the European war.

In a Dewey-like turn of thought, Du Bois articulated the official NAACP position when he wrote in the *Crisis* that the thorny predicament presented by segregated conscript camps became "entirely academic" once war had been declared. In essence, relying on a pragmatic "plastic juncture" rationale, the Du Bois calculus turned on racial, domestic, and inward-focused criteria, despite ostensibly being concerned with foreign policy and the European war. Rejecting his previous anti-imperialist views against American meddling abroad and regimes of "bigness" at home, Du Bois opined that the central choice was "between conscription and rebellion." "The war is critical. . . . This is our war." Dissent, he asserted, would set back the cause of the NAACP by painting the race as unpatriotic obstructionists, or worse, as rebellious traitors.[81]

In "Trans-National America" Bourne took up a related set of themes about nationalism, identity, and the best path forward. He attempted to reconcile the demands of asking the nation to serve the world as an exemplar and also as a mediator, cultivating and tolerating differences at home, and avoiding intervention in an intolerable war abroad. Hearkening to the "experiential life" he prized so highly, Bourne applied the lessons of rising nationalism he had learned first in wartime Germany and then upon his return to the United States. Times of crisis revealed that to be "American" was to be characterized by interrelated identities, according to Bourne. Instead, the coercive process of assimilating immigrants into American culture and forcing uniformity in the language of patriotism both solidified a "centrifugal, anarchical" social organization, which he saw as tending to divest individuals of their cohesive ethnic traditions; it thus limited their potential contributions to the composite culture of American society. Bourne's answer was to aim for international reconciliation much like his view of how best to moderate domestic ethnic differences. He hoped that even in wartime the United States could adopt a nonbinding cultural internationalism on its own terms and in so doing would radically reverse the ethnocentric, "entangled" form of Wilsonian internationalism. Unlike Du Bois, who allied with Dewey at this time, Bourne sided with socialists like Max Eastman, pacifists such as Emily Balch, and labor leaders such as A. Philip Randolph, who also were unable to condone the war effort on racial, patriotic, economic, or pragmatic grounds. Bourne was pained not to be able to bring himself to join the side of his former liberal progressive colleagues, because he could not countenance what he saw as their Faustian bargain to compromise in the present, on purportedly pragmatic grounds, to achieve possible progressive gains in the future.[82]

4

THE POWERFUL MEDIATING NEUTRAL

From 1914 through 1918, the practical elements and new contours of modern isolationist thought crystalized in ways that would become far more entrenched after the First World War and ultimately would define much of the interwar isolationist position. These were achieving peace and economic progress at home, prohibiting loans and material aid to combatants and nations abroad, attempting a genuine rather than a rhetorical neutrality, keeping citizens and vessels away from belligerent areas, and requiring a popular backing (even a referendum) for the declaration of war.

Randolph Bourne, who would not have identified himself as an isolationist, invoked isolationist principles when he combined American exceptionalism with the stricture against foreign entanglements to argue that the nation had a unique capacity to become transnational. According to Bourne, America was a country composed of democratically oriented, individually driven immigrants. It was a new nation unsullied by the corruption of the Old World and defended in part by the geographic remove provided by the Atlantic and Pacific Oceans. "Only America," Bourne said, "by reason of the unique liberty of opportunity and traditional isolation for which she seems to stand can lead in this cosmopolitan enterprise." Bourne ventured deeper into a political world increasingly disposed against his views. Despite the obstacles, he persevered. In the context of an America thoroughly enmeshed in debating and then entering and fighting in the war, Bourne's long-standing sense of personal isolation helped produce an antiwar philosophy that was both isolationist and transnational, as well as influential for generations of war dissenters to come.[1]

Bourne proposed an alternative to wartime Americanization programs that sought to homogenize the population and to induce what he deemed a bland conformist patriotism. He asserted, "Only the American—and in this category I include the migratory alien who has lived with us and caught the pioneer spirit and a sense of new social vistas—has the chance to become that citizen of the world."[2]

Toward the end of his seminal essay "Trans-National America" Bourne observed, "The war has shown America unable, though isolated geographically and politically from a European world-situation, to remain aloof and irresponsible. She is a wandering star in the sky dominated by two colossal constellations of states." He asked, "Can she not work out some position of her own, some life of being in, yet not quite of, this seething and embroiled European world? This is her only hope and purpose." In answer, Bourne urged the reader to reach two conclusions about the meaning of American society and the nation's proper role in the world: the United States should encourage transnationalism, and it must remain out of direct involvement in foreign wars and power politics.[3]

What would such a politics and society look like? Bourne asserted that if fulfilled, with "a trans-nationality of all the nations, it is spiritually impossible for [America] to pass into the orbit of any one. It will be folly to hurry herself into a premature and sentimental nationalism, or to emulate Europe and play fast and loose with the forces that drag into war." In addition, he embraced America's traditional reluctance to join foreign wars and the recent neutrality debates, saying, "Let us look at our reluctance rather as the first crude beginnings of assertion on the part of certain strands in our nationality that they have a right to a voice in the construction of the American ideal." Uniting these elements of Bourne's cosmopolitan internationalism and his invocation of exceptional geographical and historical isolation was his argument for the uniquely "American" capacities and composition of its people.[4]

It was a provocative ideal, not a programmatic one. He proposed to deploy what he suggestively termed America's "pioneer spirit." This spirit, properly engaged, could facilitate a peace process through conciliation in the global community, while dynamically building cultural connections. In opposition to the Wilson administration and wartime "melting pot" proponents, Bourne aimed to combine ethnic and racial pluralism with a cosmopolitan isolation from entanglement in international conflicts to engage the global cultural community.[5]

George Creel, the famed muckraking progressive journalist and head of the prowar nationalist Committee on Public Information (CPI), who had once expressed an anti-imperial resistance to American intervention abroad, asserted a similar assessment of national "character" but took it in an opposite direction. According to Creel, America instinctively followed two basic traditions. First, the Monroe Doctrine inspired a neutral "gospel of democracy"—and did not permit European interference in American hemispheric affairs. Creel's emphasis, it is important to underscore, built on Monroevian robust hemispherism. His focus, though, was on *them* interfering with *us*, rather than the reverse; thus, his ideas shared the same logical defensive, unilateralist, and interventionist underpinnings as Lodge's "large policy" interpretation of the Monroe Doctrine. Second, Creel argued that the nation maintained a genuine impartiality largely based on geographical distance—which became "advocacy of arbitration as a substitute for war." However, Creel and Bourne came to very different conclusions about this second proposition. Creel further argued that isolation in terms of not committing troops abroad, or sticking only to a policy of arbitration, was an atavistic policy that could only lead to ruin. Americans were sentimentally "isolationist," he said, and this was a weakness. Thus, Creel concluded that while it was no simple process for the nation to join the European war—and, he said, the administration rightly had been reluctant to deviate from these twin pillars of American isolationism—it had become utterly necessary not only to enter the European conflict but also to encourage an homogenizing patriotic form of Americanism at home as well. "It required three and a half years of violated neutrality to tear the bandages of tradition from our eyes," he said, "but when the wrappings were finally removed we saw that America's 'detached and distant situation' had never been more than a vain hope."[6]

No such scales dropped from Bourne's eyes. He could not see Creel's case, which was an exemplar indicative of the views expressed by a large bloc of pro-Wilson liberals who aimed to muster patriotic support for the war and spearheaded an array of domestic nationalist Americanization programs. Beginning with "Trans-National America," Bourne refined his rebuttal to statements such as Creel's. His ambition was to influence intellectuals to help develop a national life that would transcend national borders and be more fulfilling than any individual national culture (e.g., that of Italy or America).

As late as the end of 1915 Bourne had still hoped the nation could be kept out of war. But 1916 was pivotal in hardening Bourne's antiwar thought, writing, and actions. Creel was an outspoken advocate for Wilson throughout his 1916 presidential campaign (Creel had been a vigorous supporter in 1912 too) and by 1917 the CPI formed with Creel at the helm and national military preparedness for the war became policy. Native-born Americans—Bourne's so-called Anglo-American patricians—declared themselves besieged, nationalistic bellicosity was on the rise, immigration had been reduced to a trickle, and nativist sentiments continued to increase. Opposing this "drift," Bourne said immigration should be enlarged and embraced. Diversity of people and opinions formed the spirit of America. Immigrants of the "new" and "old" stock provided a unique possibility: not for any facile assimilation of the melting pot, but for the integration, combination, and cross-fertilization of people, ideas, and cultures. Bourne aspired to be part of a larger process of transition. He ambitiously aimed to help lead a progressive transformation of American national values to move beyond "parochialism" and toward a truly "cosmopolitan spirit."[7]

Throughout 1916, the editors at the New Republic tenuously clung to a pro-Wilson position, delicately balancing diplomacy and belligerency. But late that year they shifted from a spirit of preparedness to one of all-out armament. Bourne could not tolerate such a transition in national policy, much less at the magazine where he primarily worked. But he had little say in the matter. Viewed in this light, Bourne's book reviews take on greater significance. His reviews both served as studies in proper cultural criticism and also operated as conduits to present (and often to smuggle) his political views out to wider audiences.

Bourne's review of sociologist Frances Kellor's pro-assimilation book, Straight America (1916), served as a springboard for clarifying his political philosophy. Bourne carefully distinguished between nativism and Americanism. As he put it, Americanism was and ought to be less rooted in a shared culture than in shared political ideals. Tolerance of various cultures would be essential to a harmonious and dynamic future. In assessing Kellor's book, Bourne seemed genuinely surprised to find the previously staunch liberal progressive, an activist for labor and immigrant rights, calling for a "coercive" model of Americanization. Bourne attacked her view as one descended from a "ruling class which needs democratizing." Instead of her "coercive" form of chauvinistic, blindly homogenizing nationalism, Bourne called for a "cooperative Americanism."

This associational Americanism could not be modeled on Europe, where cooperation clearly failed while base belligerent nationalism triumphed. Bourne derided that Old World framework, as well as America's "melting-pot" notion, calling them "false" models for assimilation. Instead, he argued for a gradual, community-oriented domestic focus, essentially the transnational. "Miss Kellor," Bourne explained, "makes a noble plea for an Americanism which is much broader than the 'nativism' of the Anglo-Saxon, but she yokes it to a program which is almost necessarily nativistic in its implications. It is notorious that the conception of national unity which includes military service, belligerent defense of American rights, is one held largely by the staunchly nativistic element." Bourne went on to explain his essential mission: The "men and women of goodwill who are working for practical Americanization in social reorganization and genuine economic and educational assimilation of the immigrant are mostly in the other camp. They are not content with an 'industrial mobilization' which is a mere war measure." As suspicion of German Americans dovetailed with hypernationalist nativists calling for "100 percent Americanism," Bourne perceived that the time for half measures toward patriotic unity was long gone.[8]

Kellor's relatively muted xenophobia was, nonetheless, a setback. As far as Bourne was concerned, she had succumbed to war fervor. In a speech before the conservative militarist National Security League in 1916, she exclaimed against the looming danger of America being undermined from within by "alien influences." In light of her advocacy, Bourne's review of Kellor's book provides a primer on his views about how to combat the insidious influence of nativist patriotism. He concluded his essay with a rousing argument against "a premature cohesion on a basis of belligerent self-protection [that] would defeat that slow learning to live together which a wide and modern Americanism involves."[9]

By December 1916, Croly and the *New Republic* editors presaged Wilson's words in an editorial accepting a version of his notion of seeking "peace without victory." Within a month, Wilson addressed Congress and laid out a series of resolutions that defined the postwar environment he envisioned: self-determination for all nations, and a permanent "concert of power" including "democratic nations," an initial articulation of the League of Nations concept. As he put it, "Victory would mean peace forced upon the loser, a victor's terms imposed upon the vanquished. It would be accepted in humiliation . . . a bitter memory upon which peace would rest, not permanently but only as upon quicksand." Therefore, Wilson argued that "only a peace between equals can last. Only a peace the very principle of which is equality and a common participation in a common benefit. The right state of mind, the right feeling between nations, is as necessary for a lasting peace as is the just settlement of vexed questions of territory or of racial and national allegiance."[10] By January 1917, when Wilson made this declaration, however, Bourne could no longer accept that Wilson's warlike actions would match his lofty rhetoric. Indeed, there seemed to be no remaining chance for peaceful American mediation. Indeed, by 1917, American loans to the Allies had soared to roughly $2.25 billion, while loans to Germany stood at a trifling $27 million—roughly 83 to 1. Opponents of Wilson's rhetoric of neutrality, such as Bourne, pointed to the startling investment in the Anglo war effort and called hypocrisy, wondering how the United States could possibly keep out of a conflict the nation already appeared to be participating in materially. Thus, by early 1917 Bourne's exceptionalist transnationalism was in "irreconcilable" opposition to the *New Republic*, to Wilson, and to the majority of his fellow citizens.[11]

Only a small group of progressives, socialists, and populists remained prominent opponents of intervention. Working with Amos Pinchot, Winthrop Lane, and socialist Max Eastman, Bourne formed an ad hoc committee, the Committee for Democratic Control, to oppose entry into the war. This group developed from the American Union Against Militarism (AUAM), which had changed its name and shifted its mission in early 1916 to the Anti-Preparedness Committee.[12] The new group opposed a campaign of military buildup and conscription, while favoring a characteristically democratic-progressive measure to seek a national referendum on the war. Under the rubric of the Committee for Democratic Control, the four men cosigned a national advertisement published in newspapers and magazines in March 1917, asking, "Do the American People Want War?" Bourne believed that the people did not want war. As he and the Committee saw it, business and political elites favored the conflict. He hoped that pro-peace women activists, in particular, might be a logical source of allies and a useful means of being heard nationally. But many of the feminists and African American leaders whom Bourne counted as personal friends or whom he believed were allies in a collective progressive peace mission frustrated him when they flooded the ranks of the Wilson administration in 1916 and 1917.[13]

"Peace without victory" and its reliance on according all nations and peoples equal rights had an idealistic appeal for many progressives, and though Wilson was not calling for immediate national self-determination, many observers interpreted these statements and his later Fourteen Points in that light.[14] Others joined the Wilson cause of progressive internationalism. For example, Carrie Chapman Catt, the celebrated suffrage movement leader, eagerly participated in Liberty Loan drives as part of the Women's Advisory Committee of the Council of National Defense. Du Bois expressed a similar sentiment when he wrote that it was time to support the war, to "close our ranks shoulder to shoulder with our own white fellow citizens."[15]

Bourne was also diametrically opposed to any closing of ranks to join with belligerent powers abroad and defend "democracy." He termed this Lippmann-esque "drift" and saw it emanating from fellow progressives and *New Republic* colleagues. He suggested that the alternative to closing ranks in war would be a peaceful mediation abroad and cultural tolerance and dynamic pluralism at home. In "The Jew and Trans-National America," a speech to the Harvard Menorah Society published in December 1916, Bourne made new connections in his views of pluralism, religion, and politics. Bourne, a Protestant from an old Puritan family, expanded the conception of "transnationality" to include the practical "international idealism" of Zionism into a "co-operative Americanism." He proposed a secular, American version of Zionism to unite people of various identities and overlapping "citizenships" under a centralizing ideology, which could substitute for the inflexible forms of nationalism of the day. An "ardent Zionism," argued Bourne, would be one that "involves the responsibility for an equally ardent effort for that progressive democratic reconstruction in America which is the ideal of all true Americans, no matter what their heritage or trans-nationality."[16]

What Role for Religion? And the Intellectuals . . . ?

Surprisingly, Bourne rarely mentioned religion in his works on transnationalism, except the internationalism of Zionism. Yet his pluralistic aims had much in common with religious dialogue. His transnationalism represents a secular jeremiad in the oldest American Puritan tradition.[17] This jeremiad tradition, referring as it does to the archetypal warning of moral declension identified with the ancient Hebrew prophet Jeremiah, described a narrative of social deterioration, and proposed a salvific prescription to reconstitute a better society. His thought was not based on the well-known principles of conscientious objection or strict pacifism, although both appear as rationales in his writings. Instead, he described his method as engaging "from below the battle," not within it, but not fully outside it either. Bourne's antiwar arguments culminated in a haunting assessment of the ethics-eviscerating relationship between the modern nation-state and its social culture when involved in warfare.[18] At bottom, his jeremiad was animated by fear of the destabilizing and stultifying effects on culture of prolonged international conflict and national conformity. Combining ideas about isolation with his transnational hopes for culture and his opposition to war, one of Bourne's final unpublished works, "The State," came closest to summarizing this compelling combination of beliefs, as a critique of what happens when a proto-military-industrial complex develops alongside a domestic politics of rampant patriotism.[19]

"The results of war on the intellectual class are already apparent," Bourne wrote. "Their thought becomes little more than a description and justification of what is going on. They turn upon any rash one who continues idly to speculate. Once the war is on, the conviction spreads that individual thought is helpless, that the only way one can count is as a cog in the great wheel." He rebuked American intellectuals who by the summer of 1917, "in their pre-occupation with reality, seem to have forgotten that the real enemy is War rather than Imperial Germany."[20]

Bourne believed the key to being an intellectual critic was to perform this role naturally and consistently. "The 'irreconcilable' need not be disloyal. He need not even be 'impossibilist.' His apathy toward war should take the form of a heightened energy and enthusiasm for the education, the art, the interpretation that make for life in the midst of a world of death." His isolation wounded Bourne and he struggled to make his voice heard. "The intellectual who retains his animus against war will push out more boldly than ever to make his case solid against it. The old ideals crumble; new ideals must be forged. His mind will continue to roam widely and ceaselessly. The thing he will fear most is premature crystallization. If the American intellectual class rivets itself to a 'liberal' philosophy that perpetuates the old errors, there will then be need for 'democrats' whose task will be to divide, confuse, disturb, keep the intellectual waters constantly in motion to prevent any such ice from ever forming."[21]

Pluralism, Transnationalism, and Doubts about Enforcing Peace

Bourne's proposal for stirring the intellectual waters and fomenting social change formed a distinctly new schema. As he refined his framework for transnationalism, he drew primarily upon the pluralistic philosophy advanced by Horace Kallen in "Democracy vs. the Melting Pot," which appeared in the *Nation* in February 1915. Bourne invoked Kallen's ideas about national identity as a model. Both men said the melting pot's objective of homogenization was deleterious to national culture.[22] Bourne argued for dynamic mixing of diverse groups to encourage an eclectic cosmopolitanism. Kallen, on the other hand, focused on strengthening the protective environment of America's national culture. His goal was for the nation to strive to be hospitable to immigrant groups, to protect and nurture them. Thereby, he believed, these groups would become invigorating, relatively autonomous participants in national life.

These Kallen-Bourne articulations of pluralism resonated with the internationalists who opposed preparedness and entry into the European war. Jane Addams, for one, adhered to just such a vision when she observed the collection of ethnicities every day at the doors to her Chicago Hull House settlement facility. Working with both immigrants and native-born Americans who were indigent and needed support, Addams had an intimate knowledge of the underside of American modern capitalism and immigration policies. Her efforts in the settlement house, and her lobbying to champion its progressive cause, reinforced Addams's belief that dynamic international mixing was possible and, in fact, necessary for a healthy urban America. A transnationality was emerging, she affirmed: "I believed that there was a rising in the cosmopolitan centers of America, a sturdy and unprecedented international understanding which in time would be too profound to lend itself to war." Addams's use of the term "cosmopolitan centers" is significant. She defined these as a locus for what she hoped was a rising international "consciousness" that was practical, and similar in meaning, yet did not fully embrace the transnational application Bourne intended as his pluralist political philosophy.

Addams's colleague on the Women's International League for Peace and Freedom (WILPF) and founder of Denison House in Boston, the intense, thin, dark-haired, pro-immigrant activist Emily Balch, also came to regard a pluralistic America as a peaceful force for international justice. Balch set this principle in opposition to the unrestrained dangers of nationalism. She evoked the metaphor of an orchestra. To Balch, the nation's many "races" and the cacophony of their varied interactions could be harmonized powerfully just as the "wind and string instruments in a symphony." She argued for the continued influence of the American Union Against Militarism to help keep the nation out of war. But more than avoiding the conflict, according to Balch, a larger, more significant collective project must be accomplished. The sum of the nation's "races" would be greater than its parts. If joined together, these powers could be mustered for domestic reform and international peace. The American orchestra might play a tune that the whole world would hear and should follow.[23]

This was an abstract and ideal vision, yet Bourne and others like Addams and Balch hoped it could be tied to practical policies with effective political and institutional outcomes. Bourne believed these diverse groups would perform an additive function for society and politics. As David Hollinger explained, such a cosmopolitan ideal is definite enough to be clearly distinguished from the cultural pluralism that Horace Kallen advocated.[24]

The crucial difference is that cultural pluralism is committed to the survival and flourishing of the ethnic group as such, while most forms of cosmopolitanism are "inherently suspicious of ethnic particularism."[25] Cultural pluralism means a society comprising particular groups, each respecting the others. Bourne, however, promoted an even more intense cross-fertilization of cultures. Here his transnationalism subsumed his view of cosmopolitanism. That is, he argued for a transnational society that would tolerantly encompass a wide variety of cosmopolitan perspectives while permitting all to flourish and overlap heterogeneously within the envelope of transnationalism. Yet however nobly conceived, his was an imprecise and at times not entirely inclusive system. Bourne had little tolerance for his base, fellow Americans, whose moral and political standards were "those of the mob." He occasionally called this group "halfbreeds" and derided them as the "flotsam and jetsam of American life" because of their shared love for "leering cheapness and falseness of taste and spiritual outlook."[26] Culturally and civically elitist critiques of mass culture aside, Bourne held hope that even many of the most base individuals could be redeemed within a transnational America. Bourne aimed for his cultural project to generate an enhanced national life by embracing distinct ethnic groups and protecting them from the homogenizing influence of Anglo-Saxon American intolerance. In this effort Bourne blended Kallen's cultural pluralism with his own cosmopolitan ideal to propose that immigrants and natives ought to work together as "integrating forces."[27]

Those forces would generate an expansive, cumulative transnational culture, which Bourne later connected to foreign policy in his penetrating assessment of "The Collapse of American Strategy" and in "Doubts about Enforcing Peace." Bourne propounded an idealistic as well as a practical politics in "Doubts about Enforcing Peace," a six-page essay intended for publication but never placed in print. He thought the advocates of the League of Nations were "more realistic than the professional pacifists." But he had cautioned that without what he termed the "impelling and integrating forces" of collective tolerance and embrace of difference, their ideas might bring "tremendous possibilities of peril to this country."[28] True, America should facilitate international mediation, he said. Yet the primary focus abroad, Bourne argued, ought to be "international justice" rather than picking favorite allies. The nation should under no circumstances, and particularly not under the auspices of a League providing for "armed enforcement of peace," engage in a "war in which we perhaps ha[ve] no concern whatever."[29] His attitude in this piece, therefore, was clearly isolationist. Bourne saw an integral intersection between domestic and foreign policy autonomy at the locus where pragmatic evaluation of means and ends helped to shape the role the nation ought to take in the world. It was on the grounds of this connection between a pragmatic means-ends emphasis on domestic reform goals and securing a peace that could not precipitate new wars via alliance mechanisms that Bourne's views contrasted with what he deemed the "illogic" of war, ultimately leading him to break with Dewey.[30]

The Conservation of American Promise

America could not always remain outside the fray, as Bourne recognized. Transnationalism might be the answer for the future, but for the present he needed to make the case for an alternative domestic and foreign policy. In the final stage of his wartime intellectual development, Bourne embraced this challenge. In "The Collapse of American Strategy," published in August 1917 in the *Seven Arts*—with the first American troops already on the ground and fighting in Europe—Bourne presented his most penetrating dissection of U.S. foreign policy. War and nationalism were the primary causes of conflict, he said, with ever-heightening costs to these errors in judgment. A series of flawed decisions had brought the nation into World War I, he wrote, and due to the burdens of such poor leadership there was little promise of achieving a world "safe for democracy," at least in 1917.

Public opinion seemed to have forgotten the explicit logic of "definite international ideals," Bourne observed. These ideals, such as defending and reinforcing democracy abroad and at home, treating all nations as

equal in values, and creating a lasting peace under the auspices of a benevolent global league and treaty, were what Wilson articulated to first
inspire the nation to plunge into the war.[31] Where were such principles,
Bourne asked, when punitive measures were being discussed for a postwar settlement? Given the failed initiatives to negotiate a peace settlement, "American liberals who urged the nation to war," Bourne argued,
"are therefore suffering the humiliation of seeing their liberal strategy for
peace transformed into a strategy for prolonged war."[32] Events had proved
him grimly right. "Those Americans who opposed our entrance into the
war believed that this object [peace based on an international covenant]
could best be worked for by a strategy of continued neutrality and the
constant pressure of mediation," Bourne remarked sadly. "They believed
that war would defeat the strategy for a liberal peace."[33] He concluded that
once the nation had entered the war this deeply, it was "rudderless."[34]

By the end of 1916 and into early 1917 the radical Bourne veered into an
almost untenable position in American literary and political circles. He
was influential among only the few remaining outspoken socialist dissenters and antiwar activists. The socialist magazine the *Appeal to Reason* was
first censored, so it could no longer cross state lines or travel through the
public mail. In mid-1917 it became a prowar organ. Another socialist
press, the *Masses*, was censured shortly thereafter. Bourne still placed
book reviews in the *New Republic*, but they were confined to the books
or topics under review and did not permit him much range for cultural
criticism, much less opposition to the war or the policies of the Wilson
administration.

Not destitute, Bourne still found himself far from fulfilling the public
promise heralded by his writings of 1914 and 1915. His letters from early
1917 reveal that Bourne was a man without much hope. He lived mod-
estly, as he always had, but the comfortable lifestyle he had gained with
his position at the *New Republic* slowly ebbed. He moved apartments in
New York several times and said that he struggled to make ends meet. Although he continued to publish throughout 1917, in a private note penned
in November, he admitted his desolation. "I feel very much secluded from
the world," he despondently wrote, "very much out of touch with my
times, except perhaps with the Bolsheviki. The magazines I write for die
violent deaths, and all my thoughts are unprintable. If I start out to write
on public matters I discover that my ideas are seditious, and if I start to
write a novel I discover that my outlook is immoral if not obscene. What

then is a literary man to do if he has to make his living by a pen?"[35] His cerebral ruminations could not compete with the visceral appeal of a Wilsonian call to patriotism, the censoring of the mails, and self-censorship of magazine editors, much less the popular appeal of Theodore Roosevelt's vigorous nationalistic "manhood" of an American military mission.

The war resolution passed on April 6, 1917, and with it came an end to most of what remained of public dissent. In his address to Congress, Wilson called forth American patriots. He romantically invoked truth, justice, and democracy—even a proactive call for tradition-based engagement with the world stemmed from his updated interpretation of the early republic's precedent. "Right is more precious than peace," he said. Giving rise to the first full-fledged articulations of his idealistic internationalism, Wilson boldly proclaimed a new American role in the world: "We shall fight for the things which we have always carried nearest our hearts—for democracy . . . [to] make the world itself at last free."[36] These were potent words. By positing America as a force for global democracy and mobilizing patriotism toward that cause, the administration further marginalized would-be dissenters, casting free-speech advocates, progressive reformers, suffragists, socialists, and others as unpatriotic if they did not support the war.

The archetypal isolationist of the 1920s and 1930s, Idaho Senator William Borah, was a reluctant nationalist supporter of the war. Although he frequently asserted in his speeches, interviews, and private as well as public writing, "It would be one of the greatest calamities that could happen to us to get into this war," Borah could not withstand the firestorm of patriotism that erupted in late March and early April 1917. Borah agreed with Wilson and sought for the United States to enter the war as an "associated" rather than an "allied" power. This is a significant distinction, because for Borah the nation would be taking a unilateral action and could remain relatively "un-entangled." Still, the staunch isolationist Borah still could agree only tentatively to Wilson's terms. He assented to the break with Germany, then the arming of merchant vessels for self-defense in 1916, and finally in the war declaration. Yet Borah remained troubled by America's willingness to embrace a foreign war on a distant continent. His injunctions were indicative of an underlying political calculus. "I join no crusade," he said. "I seek or accept no alliances; I obligate this Government to no other power. I make war alone for my countrymen and their rights, for my country and its honor." He quickly came to regret this vote.

Even at the end of his speech, in Bournian fashion Borah asserted that German Americans had as much claim to patriotic citizenship as any other citizen. Their loyalties and activities, he said, should not be questioned.[37]

Yet the sheer emotional force of nationalism did not go unchecked. It rapidly became hyperpatriotic, with dangerous ramifications. In Congress, there was continued principled opposition to a rapid march to war, although it was limited. The war resolution passed by 82 to 6 in the Senate and 373 to 50 in the House of Representatives. This vote of fifty in opposition represented a strong minority rebuke of Wilson's position. It was the first and last major vote against an American war of the twentieth century. Most senators who spoke against going to war deployed idealistic arguments to support their position that the nation ought to maintain a fully isolationist stance. For example, Mississippi Senator James Vardaman agreed with the idealism of Wilson's view for postwar international peacekeeping but said that "the world will not take his big ideas by force of arms." Instead, Vardaman declared, "Moral reform must come by virtue of inherent merit and not by force of standing armies."[38]

Nebraska's isolationist Senator George Norris trotted out the old "not against our interests" and "no entanglements" positions with his speech against the vote. The real interventionists, Norris said, were "concealed in their palatial offices on Wall Street, sitting behind mahogany desks, covered up with slipped coupons . . . coupons stained with mothers' tears, coupons dyed in the lifeblood of their fellow men." Rather, he said, America should not heed the industrials and warmongers, but "ought to remember the advice of the Father of our Country and keep out of entangling alliances."[39] Along with Norris, other prominent progressive Republican senators opposing the war resolution were North Dakota's Asle Gronna and Robert La Follette. Joining them were Oregon's Joseph Lane, Missouri's William Stone, and Vardaman, Democrats from the reform-oriented Bryan camp.[40] In a nod to traditional notions of not entering into entangling alliances, Congress approved the war provision and joined the Allied Entente not as an ally per se, but rather as an "associated power."

Across the country, nationalistic sentiments flared high, inspired by Wilson's high-minded yet thoroughly patriotic rhetoric. The bellicose cries would have reminded William James of those he first experienced with the Venezuelan crisis and later the war with Spain. The war fervor for World War I , though, was grounded in the perception of having been attacked. Germany's resumption of unrestricted submarine warfare, according to Wilson, Lodge, Roosevelt, and the prowar camp, had forced America reluctantly out of neutrality. The new American Legion exemplified the hypernationalist zeal of the moment. The organization made of veterans and militarists, claiming hundreds of thousands of members by mid-1917, crafted a series of appeals for "100 per cent Americanism," calling citizens to arms and emphasizing the most self-protective, xenophobic aspects of the American creed. As wartime fears intensified, federal officials and judges virtually ignored the First Amendment, permitting vigilantes to force German Americans to prostrate themselves before the flag. The postmaster general was empowered to censor the mails and thus speech itself while trying to stamp out dissent. Within the year the Selective Service Act (SSA) was passed, despite limited if quite vocal resistance and considerable draft dodging in the South as well as in the North and Midwest. Under the SSA the draft brought nearly three million men into the army and an additional two million into other branches of the American Expeditionary Force (AEF). Because of the difficulty mobilizing, significant numbers of American troops did not arrive in Europe until the summer of 1918.[41]

With the nation engulfed in the war, Bourne continued to argue that no "league to enforce peace" could produce "international order founded on universal militarism."[42] Drawing on the pragmatic anti-imperialism of William James and the self-controlled "will to power" philosophy of Friedrich Nietzsche, Bourne argued that bellicose feelings should not be praised. Rather, they were an expression of flawed "will" and ought to be channeled away from brutality and toward the benefit of civilization. Taking a page from Jamesian social psychology, Bourne assessed the negative personal and political implications of the visceral attraction of war. Imperialism, conflict leading to combat, and unfair trade practices, along with nationalistic and ethnic rivalries, formed the collective root cause of virtually all international problems, according to Bourne. Movement forward, therefore, and the "'antidotes to imperialism' must precede the mischievous intellectualisms of a League to Enforce Peace."[43] The nation had fallen victim to insidious "power politics" and unrestrained emotional patriotism, both of which were constituted by the relations "between what States infallibly and calamitously are, huge aggregations of human and industrial forces to be hurled against each other."[44]

As modest numbers of AEF troops first gathered in France in June 1917 and maneuvered near the French front for the first time by October,

Bourne rued such events. He admitted to himself that the opportunity for cultural international engagement and American-led peace initiatives had long since slipped away in the midst of mobilization and calls for America to participate in a decisive war-ending battle. Indeed, a system of postwar reparations appeared to be almost a foregone conclusion. He reluctantly agreed in general with the policy position held by those antiwar internationalists still operating, although under intense state and federal scrutiny. They had organized the People's Council of America and in May 1917 this group, most of whom were socialists, launched its own mock-Wilsonian campaign for "democracy and peace." The group's first event brought together a surprising fifteen thousand people at Madison Square Garden to hear an array of speakers. It is unclear whether Bourne attended this gathering, but he no doubt supported it. The People's Council embraced the so-called Stockholm Plan, whose three parts were no forcible annexations, no punitive indemnities, and self-determination for all nationalities.

Led by the prominent New York socialist Morris Hillquit; Louis Lochner, the Ford peace ship planner; James Maurer, head of the Pennsylvania Federation of Labor; and Emily Balch, peace activist and professor of political economy at Wellesley College, among others, the People's Council pushed for new mediation to end the conflict without a punitive peace process. Many of the same individuals involved in the People's Council with Bourne were also part of the American Union Against Militarism. On the first day of February 1917, just after Germany issued a formal resumption of unrestrained submarine warfare, the AUAM telegraphed the president, arguing that the United States should "refuse to allow herself to be dragooned into war at the very end by acts of desperation committed by any of the belligerents."[45] Signing this telegram, which subsequently appeared in many prominent publications such as the *New York Times* as a paid advertisement, were Bourne, Emily Balch, Lillian Wald, Crystal Eastman, Oswald Garrison Villard, Henry Dana, George Foster Peabody, and John Haynes Holmes, among others. The Woman's Peace Party (WPP), organized in 1915 under the leadership of Addams and Carrie Chapman Catt, heightened its antipreparedness antiwar activities in the New York branch headed by Crystal Eastman. But on the third day of February, Wilson's public reply was also a message to the array of antiwar groups, from stalwart nationalist populists to absolute and conditional pacifists. Wilson announced that in response to the aggressive declaration of uninhibited submarine combat, he had officially severed diplomatic relations with Germany. Bourne continued to be idealistic, but also pessimistic and vague at times in his dissent.[46]

He saw the benefit of a more grounded agenda, however, and assented to what might be termed a broad interpretation of the "Stockholmian" objectives that went far beyond the terms for peace. For Bourne, much more was at stake than mere "policy" and he did not seem to be particularly concerned with any specific details for a future peace treaty. Instead, he pessimistically bemoaned larger losses: the gradual collapse of democratic ideals at home and international cultural interaction. The main practical problem, however, was not this pessimistic idealism but, rather, that the People's Council was maligned in much of the mainstream press before it could advance a realistic set of proposed politics. According to Bourne, it was his association with the People's Council in particular, and other pacifist organizations in general, that hurt him in the public eye and in his attempts to write for mainstream organs like the New Republic and Atlantic Monthly. Indeed, as Bourne's letters reveal, once it was well established that Henry Dana, Columbia University assistant professor of comparative politics and grandson of H. W. Longfellow, was an ardent member of the council, as well as at least ten other prominent peace organizations, he too was branded as "disloyal" in the New York newspapers.

The disparaging coverage inflicted what Bourne called "the gravest damage upon the good name and influence of Columbia University," leading to Dana's dismissal from his teaching position there.[47] So, too, it is likely that the high-profile protests of the People's Council, its paid advertisements and telegrams in particular, and Emily Balch's role as a founder and key adviser to the council led academics to tar her as well. As she later expressed it, her activism for international peace "overstrained the well known liberality of Wellesley College" and terminated her teaching career.[48]

However, Balch voiced private reservations about the People's Council as well. What it had in common with other peace groups was a fiercely noninterventionist agenda characterized by a reliance on American traditions of not entering into foreign wars or alliances, particularly with Europe, and the council's viewpoints were infused with elements of pacifism and socialist internationalism. But the People's Council seemed to its members and to the press as much about protest and antiwar pomp as any practical efforts to find solutions to the European war. Balch, in contrast, struggled long and hard against the war effort in keeping with a personal bent toward the practical and that which could be accomplished. But in a letter to Jane Addams she confessed that by June 1917 she wished for "a fresh perspective after my rather feverish winter ending in the raising of this Djihn or Frankenstein of a People's Council. . . . I want to see the spirit of it more constructive. Protest is such a sterile spirit." Sounding much like her acquaintance and comrade-in-arms Bourne, Balch wrote, "The war people command more sacrificial ardor, at least the best of the idealists do. Boston—old Puritan Boston—is in a white glow of it. I can imagine how I look to them."[49]

The issue of the war and the suppression of its opponents split families and friends, as we have seen. In Balch's case, her own brother, living in Boston, Francis, and her sister, Alice, in New York, wrote her often saying that they disagreed with her activities—they were among the white hot "glow "—although they admired her convictions. Alice wrote to Emily, saying, "I have felt so bitterly part of the time about your activities that I just didn't dare write. . . . It only seemed to me that you assume all the world is as good as yourself and that you are easily deceived." Alice concluded, "I would like you to know that while I do not agree with your propaganda, I do thoroughly admire you for your courage and devotion."[50]

In "A War Diary," published in September 1917, Bourne voiced similar concerns to those that Balch noted and he, too, felt isolated. It was not the reviling and opprobrium that was most difficult for Bourne and Balch, it seemed, but the loneliness. As Jane Addams eloquently remarked in *Peace and Bread in Time of War,* "The misunderstanding encountered by the pacifist with his previous cause in the keeping of those who control the sources of publicity" brought her "very near to self-pity, perhaps the lowest pit into which human nature can sink." And yet for Addams sacrosanct American values, traditions such as free speech and long-standing conceptions of isolation from Europe gave her solace. The pacifist in wartime, said Addams, "finds it possible to travel from the mire of self-pity straight to the barren hills of self-righteousness and to hate himself equally in both places."[51]

Meanwhile, in his "War Diary," Bourne tried not talk about the problems of persecution; rather, he maintained that Americans must attempt to transcend simple Americanization models of nationalism in wartime. Since the nation had joined the European war, Bourne's goal was to help bring the conflict to a speedy resolution, but most important to him was to block the United States from entering all future wars, not just to find an immediate peace. What is more, he implied in his war diary that the emerging transnational sentiment held an exceptional "promise" to be persuasive in the global marketplace, as what he termed a "moving idea." "The conservation of American promise," he said, ought to be a re-orienting of Croly's "Promise of American Life." This conservation, Bourne declared, "is the present task for this generation of malcontents and aloof men and women." But more than just a mission, he saw this as a call for a renewed political and cultural philosophy. "If America has lost its political isolation, it is all the more obligated to retain its spiritual integrity. This does not mean any smug retreat from the world, with a belief that the truth is in us and can only be contaminated by contact."[52] At issue for Bourne was the role the country should have played in 1914 and how to rethink the nation's proper global position moving forward. "The greatest obstacle to peace now," he argued, taking up the mantle of his radical colleagues, is "the lack of the powerful mediating neutral which [America] might have been."[53] Bourne's sophisticated argument for how the United States should benefit from partial isolation can be distilled from this argument as a belief that the nation did not require a "smug retreat" from the world to be advantageously isolated from international conflicts and entanglements, while embracing transnational cultural contacts.

Taking this one step further, Bourne explained that he wanted the nation to focus on improving democratic practices and fulfilling the nation's ideals at home. He argued, "The promise of American life is not yet achieved, perhaps not even seen, and until it is there is nothing for us but stern and intensive cultivation of our garden. Our insulation will not be against any great creative ideas or forms that Europe brings. It will be a turning within in order that we may have something to give without."[54]

This phrase is critical to Bourne's sharp critique and philosophy for how the nation ought to operate intellectually and politically in the world: to focus "within" so that "we may have something to give without." These are provocative and powerful injunctions of the sort that Washington and Jefferson laid out more than one hundred years before Bourne explored similar notions in a radically different global context. Thus, he rebuked the weak Wilson administration's efforts to spread democracy in places like Haiti, the Dominican Republic, Mexico, and elsewhere when he assessed that many of these "old American ideas which are still expected to bring life to the world seem stale and archaic."[55] Bourne argued, "It is grotesque to try to carry democracy to Russia. It is absurd to try to contribute to the world's store of great moving ideas until we have a culture to give." The "inward" concerns were largely cultural and reformist in nature, while his outward perspective was more policy-focused. Finally, Bourne integrated the drives of ideas with his overarching agenda. He challenged his readers: "The war—or American promise: one must choose. One cannot be interested in both."[56]

Bourne's "American Promise"

Bourne's wartime critique centered on what pragmatists argued was an instrumental moment in social reform. To Bourne, Croly had been right about the prewar "promise" but was not forceful enough about it. There was no choice. America must "conserve and fulfill this promise." In this sense, Bourne's isolationism can be seen as an "open" pragmatic philosophy, but he did not provide great specificity in its direct policy applications. In terms of foreign policy, Bourne knew that he had to offer some concrete ideas. He and many others in the antiwar movement shared a simple aspiration to maintain the long-standing American reluctance to be involved in European alliances and conflicts. Even in wartime Bourne approached national culture as "unique." Therefore, his approach to foreign policy built on this exceptionalist model despite the nation's further homogenized hyperpatriotic culture when marshaled for the conflict. Bourne attempted to counter the forces of Americanization by fusing his pluralistic vision for national culture and began from a characteristically "isolationist" premise: America's perspective on the world as being utterly different from the historical outlook in European societies.

Surely the nation should not disengage from the world stage, he often insisted. Rather, Bourne believed that the nation had a moral obligation to contribute "moving ideas" to the global community. Indeed, even immigrants who traveled back to their native lands from the United States, according to Bourne, would have a critical appreciation for "the superiority of American organization." American intellectuals were his choice as purveyors of these ideas and practices, which he argued were the sorts of sweeping concepts that inspired men and built institutions to enact meaningful individual and collective change (e.g., progressivism, socialism). Intellectuals were the vanguard of this process, particularly in America, where he aimed for reform along characteristically progressive lines.[57]

Distilled from his writings are at least six major goals: first, emphasize education; second, encourage social and intellectual pluralism; third, mix cultures; fourth, promote immigration and noncoercive assimilation; fifth, cultivate freedom of thought with fierce debate; and sixth, nourish the life of the mind.[58]

These broad goals and six major points could be agreed upon by much of the American intelligentsia of the 1910s. They were also essential to Bourne's wartime attack on John Dewey, which historian Robert Westbrook notes "is often said to have marked a break with Dewey's philosophical pragmatism, which [Bourne] had once enthusiastically shared."[59] Yes, Bourne broke with much of the mainstream American Left in taking on Dewey. This is true, but it is crucial that his critique of Dewey was neither originally intended as a true break with Dewey nor did it constitute a leap from the ranks of the Left. In fact, for Bourne his critique of entering the European war represented a genuine attempt to persuade his intellectual mentors-turned-adversaries—Dewey, Croly, Lippmann, and Weyl, among others—by engaging them in direct dialogue. As Westbrook rightly observed, Bourne self-consciously cast his own case from "within the framework for ethical deliberation that he had learned from Dewey" and Bourne beseeched his fellow liberals to present compelling evidence showing that war was, in fact and in prospect, an "effective means to the democratic ends" that they shared.[60] Unconvinced by the prowar editorials and "plastic juncture" progressive arguments presented by the editors at the *New Republic* and their allies, Bourne used the applied logic of pragmatic evaluation to mount his evidence for a noninterventionist approach to the war and to mediating the peace.[61] If anything, Bourne wanted to remind Dewey of his teachings about pragmatism and stimulate more progressives to join his cause.

Bourne's pragmatic line of reasoning, however, persuaded few of his friends at the time, however, and none of his enemies. Ideas about isolationism played an important, if minor, role in his proposed vision for how the nation ought to act in the world and in his related critiques of Dewey's prowar stance.[62] Bourne summarized Dewey's positions accurately in disparaging them, saying that Dewey believed that American participation in the war was virtually inevitable, and thus the nation *should* become entangled.[63] Given the inevitability of entering the conflict, the war ought to be intelligently directed so that it could be used to engineer an outcome more worthwhile than simply defeating Germany. In particular,

Bourne objected to Dewey's positions and detailed their points of divergence in his article "Twilight of the Idols." Bourne argued first and foremost that war was an "uncontrollable" phenomenon. According to Bourne, neither could it be directed easily, nor could its result be predicted accurately.

He therefore derided Dewey as being too idealistic and not realistic enough, as the pragmatic method required. "I think of [William] James now because the recent articles of John Dewey's on the war suggest a slackening in his thought for our guidance and stir, and the inadequacy of his pragmatism as a philosophy of life in this emergency." The war risked undermining domestic reform with "education as its national enterprise."[64] In his view James likely would have valued the foreign policy tenets of Bournian transnationalism such as "insistent care for democratic values at home, and unequivocal alliance with democratic elements abroad for a peace that should promise more than a mere union of benevolent imperialisms." He commented that the use of "force" would yield limited international benefits and risked undercutting efforts at domestic reform with "democratic politics" and "education as its national enterprise."[65]

This point bears further scrutiny. For it suggests that Bourne and Dewey disputed where to lay a prime emphasis: would it be at home or abroad? And could the two be separated? As historian Robert Westbrook has shown, "Isolation was not only an illusion but an illusion that foreclosed what Dewey saw as an important American mission."[66] To Bourne, Dewey was wrongheaded in this light because isolation from foreign conflict was compatible with—perhaps essential for—a transnational American project. There could be no separation of the foreign and the domestic for Bourne, but there could be separation of military force from genuine international mediation. Admittedly, this was a difficult distinction to make if one were trying to enact practical policy while making the best progressive choice, as Dewey asserted in his writing. But those were not Bourne's central concerns.

Bourne concluded his article on "The Collapse of American Strategy" by savaging the positions offered by former liberal comrades of his, such as Dewey and Lippmann. He wrote that the "American liberals who urged the nation to war are . . . suffering the humiliation of seeing their liberal strategy for peace transformed into a strategy for a prolonged war."[67] The war would have likely burned itself out more rapidly—and a peace could have been led by a neutral, mediating United States—according to

Bourne, if only America's liberals had not been so misguided as to support Wilson and back a belligerent war effort.[68]

If one had been a "betting" progressive in 1917—as Dewey, Croly, Lippmann, Creel, and a host of others certainly were—one would have sided with the Wilson administration. It is likely that one would have believed Dewey to have been right; to have placed the correct bet; and all that even if Dewey's pragmatic rationale and optimism appeared somewhat unconvincing. Most of the "intelligent pacifists" like Dewey considered it probable that the war could be won only with direct American involvement. More to the point, those allied with self-styled "progressive" Wilson believed that being on the side of the victors would put the nation in a position to help dictate the terms of peace while placing in positions of power those progressive intellectuals who were involved in the war and peacemaking process. Possessing these posts might be useful for enacting meaningful progressive reforms, such as those Dewey and other progressive reformers advocated for education. Thus, Westbrook concluded, "Isolation was not only an illusion but an illusion that foreclosed what Dewey saw as an important American mission."[69] Bourne was genuinely perplexed that his brilliant former intellectual mentors—themselves leading liberal lights in American political life—could have been so wrongheaded. He thought no such pragmatic grounds existed for joining Europe's war. Rather, as he saw it America's mission made isolation from foreign conflict compatible with—perhaps essential for—his transnational American project.

Collapsing American Strategy

Bourne's arguments for combining international peace, isolation from conflict, domestic pluralism, and progressive reform tended to fall on deaf ears in wartime America. But these ideas were powerful nonetheless; he was able to secure at least a modest hearing for his visions because he was a prominent intellectual cultural critic operating in the Croly-Lippmann-Dewey liberal circles, and about the only one who in that cohort who did not side with Wilson and the war effort. Most progressives allied with the war believed there would be a "plastic juncture" for reformers after the conflict. However, Bourne pointed out the catastrophic risks of co-option if intellectuals were integrated into the state's apparatus. His potential allies in the transnational project did, in fact, become his enemies, just as he had feared. The *New Republic's* support of the war and Lippmann's direct participation in its conduct, working as assistant secretary of war and eventually helping to write the Fourteen Points proposal to end the war, all these were what Bourne termed acts of intellectual self-annihilation—a "suicide" of sorts.[70]

A number of small-town liberal editors agreed with Bourne and his antiwar colleagues. The editor of a Canton, Ohio, newspaper urged Bourne to "keep it up" in his work with Amos Pinchot, who said the war was caused by the imperialist competitive system. Both men were active in the AUAM, which Pinchot helped to lead. Not all opponents of militarism were isolationist in their orientation, of course, but a great many bought into the positions of opposing U.S. involvement in the European war and expansionism, seeking to limit American military involvement in the world, and drew upon isolationist and historicist interpretations of American democratic ideals at home and as an exemplar rather than as a global crusader. At the AUAM, some of the most active members were among Bourne's allies: Emily Balch, Roger Nash Baldwin, Crystal Eastman, Oswald Garrison Villard, Paul Kellogg, Henry R. Mussey, Alice Lewisohn, Zona Gale, and Florence Kelley.

The Ohio editor approved of their activities. He urged Bourne to continue "trying to keep a little bit of light alive in the darkness." Pinchot and Bourne also sympathized with the antiwar position of the *Masses*, the socialist anti-intervention paper. Along with others like Addams, Debs, and socialists Floyd Dell and Max Eastman, Pinchot and Bourne pushed the boundaries of accepted free speech in high-profile antiwar speeches, essays, and advertisements throughout the early months of 1917. Pinchot's most prominent AUAM advertisement was published nationally in 1917. It read: "We cannot bring democracy to Europe by going to war. We can preserve democracy in the western hemisphere by staying out." Among the organization's notable achievements at the time was the successful participation in a pacifist campaign to persuade Wilson against a declaration of war against Mexico in 1916.[71]

These activities raised suspicions. Federal agents raided their offices in New York. Postal authorities frequently confiscated AUAM publications. However, through a targeted set of print advertisements, sporadic publications, conferences, and word of mouth, the organization continued unintimidated. Based on such occurrences, the historian John Milton Cooper Jr. concluded accurately, "Though the signs were still sparse, a substantial isolationist position did appear to have formed" in 1916 and 1917.[72]

The government's position hardened, though. In July 1917, federal authorities alleged that articles in the *Masses* by Dell and Eastman, as well as cartoons by Art Young, Boardman Robinson, and H. J. Glintenkamp, violated the Espionage Act. Under the strictures of this act, no material undermining the war effort could be published or sent through the interstate mail. Subsequent litigation forced the *Masses* to close its doors and stop publication. The oppression was hardly helped in April 1918, when after three days of deliberation, a jury failed to agree on the guilt of the men in violating the terms of the Espionage Act.

In a perceptive psychological diagnosis of how and why intellectuals continued to flee to the prowar camp given the increasingly severe repression of free speech, Bourne maintained that it was the intellectuals' desire for immediate influence that was most significant. Acting in concert with the "feeling of being with and supported by the collective herd" was the essence of the intellectual, according to Bourne, with a "will to power, the nourishment of which the organism so constantly demands."[73] Building on the Nietzschean philosophy that he admired, Bourne believed that the ideal stance should be a resolute "willful" intellectual. As Christopher Lasch has explained the logic at work here, Bourne firmly believed that this "type" ought to be isolated from the herd mentality *and* profoundly involved in the world. He or she should be interested in shaping policy and public opinion rather than bending to it. Intellectuals, however, were all too human. They were too tempted to submerge their autonomy in a self-deceptive quest for influence.[74]

Once intellectuals fell prey to the "hysteria of the mob," he argued, they were more willing to set aside the Jamesian pragmatic calculation of judging an idea by the "conduct that it dictates." This logic permitted imperfect and, at worst, even immoral means in the hopes of achieving progressive ends. He considered that it was either naive or irresponsible for thoughtful pragmatists like Dewey to put aside the educational pursuits they knew would make democracy vibrant. Thus, Bourne gathered momentum as he attacked Dewey's arguments and Lippmann's prominent position in the Wilson administration as becoming part of the war effort. Best developed in his final essay, "The State," Bourne's critique emphasized the insidious interconnection of industry, commerce, politics, and the national war machine.[75]

Like Eugene Debs and Jane Addams, Bourne found odd alliances among his antiwar cohort. Each in an individual way perceived the "promise of

American life" not in terms of Croly's state-led regulatory initiatives, social control, or capitalist outcomes.[76] In their place, Bourne drew a distinction between the state and government. His "promise" issued from the combination of private, individual, and intellectually driven voluntary associations inherent in collective, positive democratic "governing." This was a progressive call for reform to energize "para-state" institutions, such as philanthropic organizations, unions, suffrage groups, and other civic associations.[77] But unlike Debs and American antiwar socialists, Bourne never fully developed a blueprint of what this might look like. He believed that under Wilson this sort of course of action had been elbowed out. Instead, the "government [was] coercing into obedience the minority groups and individuals which lack the larger herd sense."[78]

Du Bois, a leader of one of these groups, had been right about the tendency of African Americans to flock to the war cause, partly out of patriotism and partly out of a hope to parlay participation into greater fulfillment of citizenship rights. Despite significant military racism (e.g., the marines would not accept blacks), nearly four hundred thousand African American troops mustered for the conflict, "un-coerced" in Bourne's sense. A series of prominent violent incidents, such as one in Houston in which abused black soldiers killed seventeen whites, ensured that few or no lasting benefits for racial relations emerged from the generally valiant combat of black soldiers in Europe.

Bourne's overarching goal on the issue of ethnicity and citizenship, to repeat, was transnationalism. This was echoed by Jane Addams and Emily Balch, and among settlement house workers, along with many labor and immigrant activists. In Bourne's thought, intellectuals were the vanguard for the transnational process and no patriotic effort by minority groups would achieve what authentic, expansive reform could fulfill. That Du Bois, one of the foremost African American intellectuals in U.S. history, would endorse the war effort and reluctantly assent to segregated military camps and facilities was an issue Bourne did not address, and yet it was a decision that clearly must have rattled his faith in the power of intellectual reformers. Undaunted through 1918, Bourne placed his hope for the future in intellectuals who might embrace the difference of African Americans and other ethnic, or national, identities.[79]

Patriotic Dissent and Wider Intellectual Objectives

At a time when much dissent was cast as sedition, Bourne's point was not to jettison nationalism altogether. Rather, he aimed to "redeem nationalism from nativism by challenging the Anglo-American monopoly on true 'Americanism.'"[80] As the historian Jonathan Hansen has argued, the dissent of Bourne, Du Bois, and Debs, among others, held a consistent tone of "cosmopolitan patriotism." Calling himself a "realistic pacifist," Bourne's advocated prescriptions were largely untenable as a practical policy in America. When those holding the reins of power, notably Woodrow Wilson, previously had expressed beliefs that only "Anglo-Saxons" had a unique capacity for democracy and liberty, Bourne's transnational idealism could not hold a significant portion of elites who tended to share Wilson's views. Invoking "the spirit of William James," Bourne similarly adhered to the older anti-imperialist critiques of big business. He railed against the capitalist structure that left most industrial workers relatively powerless in the face of their size and scope. Bourne hearkened occasionally to the lessons he learned in the piano-roll industry as he took a Jamesian turn in his critique of the intersection of two modes of "bigness"—the state and the war materials industry. In analyzing the relationship between commercial greed and the application of military force, Bourne saw the rise of a proto-military-industrial complex that propelled an inexorable "terrifying logic" of intervention.

In the last two years of life, Bourne found his voice on this subject, as more than one scholar has noted.[81] In his formidable essay "The War and the Intellectuals," his arguments reached a fever pitch. Bourne attacked former allies and current friends alike, whenever their politics supported the war. He shrewdly anticipated the cost in lives, the spiritual impoverishment, and the obstacles to reform that he rightly asserted would occur in the wake of war.[82]

Some liberals edged toward an admission that there was a steep price to pay for having endorsed Wilson's management of the war effort. By December 1917, Croly too backpedaled from his assessments of the domestic environment created by involvement in the war. He pressed for a "Counsel of Humility" for those who talked too glibly about the horrors of war, no matter that it was for democracy and for a league of peace, and particularly if it led to repression of opposing views.

Walter Weyl, now back on the masthead of the *New Republic*, also pushed for a slight moderation in the liberal embrace of the war effort. He published a set of hopes for economic and political international peace in *The End of the War* and found his arguments widely attacked by more militant defenders of the war effort as "Teutonic internationalism" and "New Republic–type of thinking." The British war critic Norman Angell was confronted by a mob in New York in late 1917, roughed up, and asked about his knowledge of "subversives" at the *New Republic*. The magazine itself came under surveillance by federal agents in early 1918 until George Creel came to its defense and identified it as a supporter of the administration.[83]

With all of these crosscurrents swirling about in 1917 and 1918, the tone of disillusionment and despair in Bourne's antiwar essays at this time was attenuated by his natural inclination toward affirmation and optimism.[84] He closed his essay on the war and the intellectuals with words evoking tragic irony, given that he would die within mere months. Bourne appealed for a "heightened energy and enthusiasm for the education, the art," and "the interpretation[s] that make for life in the midst of the world of death."[85] In "Twilight of the Idols," finishing his analysis of where the seeds of American promise lay, Bourne stated that a "more skeptical, malicious, desperate, ironical mood may actually be a sign of more vivid and more stirring life fermenting in America today."[86] In "A War Diary" he ended with the "hope that in the recoil from war we may find the treasures we are looking for."[87] In short, Bourne's belief in the integral role of the intellectual has not often been viewed in terms of ideas about isolation and a new vision of American internationalism. Yet these ideas were central to his belief that the intellectual was vital to enact change.

Bourne's works demonstrate, again and again, a profound, if sometimes overstated, belief in the imperative for a style of distinctive engagement by the intellectual—that is, from without, not from within, mainstream political culture. Although he was being sarcastic when he wrote "a war made deliberately by the intellectuals!" he was not being cynical. Instead, he believed that American intellectual-led international conciliation abroad (e.g., through the American Association for International Conciliation) and a methodical domestic transformation into a transnational United States would concentrate national energies on internal improvement through reform.

Later Bourne wrote to his friend Van Wyck Brooks that future "'leaders' will be simply those articulate souls who can express most convincingly desired values."[88] And Bourne hoped his legacy would rest on these desired values for reform. Given the great resources being devoted to the military, Bourne took a page from the broader antiwar playbook to consistently argue: first, the nation should be an international voice for peace and arbitration, and not be involved in this war; and second, the nation would be better served by a massive federal investment in the types of social programs favored by Dewey and other progressives.[89] A postwar nation, he contended, should move forward with far-reaching reforms. "We must see if the lesson of the war has not been for hundreds of these later Americans a vivid realization of their transnationality, a new consciousness of what America meant to them as a citizenship in the world. It is the vague historic idealisms which have provided the fuel for the European flame. Our American ideal can make no progress until we do away with this romantic gilding of the past."[90] Sanguinely, he rejected a misty nostalgia about the past. Bourne reasoned, "All our idealisms must be those of future social goals in which all can participate, the good life of personality lived in the environment of the Beloved Community."[91] In transnationalism, the ideal would be prospective: "an enterprise of integration into which we can all pour ourselves, of a spiritual welding which should make us, if the final menace ever came, not weaker, but infinitely strong."[92]

Despite the passion in his flowering cultural criticism and his hopes for an "enterprise of integration," Bourne increasingly felt his energies sapped. He was depressed in mood and depleted in health. Bombarded by a series of bad colds, Bourne simply could not muster all of his effort to write as much or as passionately as he wanted. As Eric Sandeen observed when editing Bourne's correspondence, "Aside from the tender letters to Esther Cornell [soon to be his fiancée in 1918], Bourne's letters become much more perfunctory during this period [from 1916 to the end of his life]."[93] Based on a thorough review of Bourne's public and private correspondence, it is clear that pouring forth his emotional and critical energies into his writing as he "rose to intellectual maturity in *The Dial* and the *Seven Arts*" greatly drained what vigor he had left for his correspondence and friendships.[94] Sandeen noted that Bourne's public essays and private letters from this period reveal a marked sophistication and penetrating logic. Virtually all of Bourne's thinking was focused on the fight against the war.

During this period his energies further diminished and he was unable to establish a stable social life. Writing to Brooks while citizens celebrated the coming of peace on the streets of New York in November 1918, Bourne realized how glad he was to be emerging from wartime suppression. "As a pacifist, I rejoice at the innocent uprising of the unconscious desire on the part of the populace for peace, and the throwing off of the repressed reluctance for the war."[95] Echoed emphatically in his description of the previous several years is this sense of a lost and terrifying time. In his final surviving letter to his mother, Bourne revealed how deeply alone he had felt as a man and as a dissenting radical in wartime: "Now that the war is over, people can speak freely again and we can dare to think. It's like coming out of a nightmare."[96]

Almost alone in the ranks of American intellectuals and radical dissenters, Bourne continued actively to denounce involvement throughout World War I. He had foreseen that, beyond the high cost in young lives, the war would bring a level of "spiritual impoverishment" to the nation and disillusionment in the intellectuals and progressives of various stripes that espoused social change. In the end the progressives who sided with Wilson were wrong at least insofar as being able to achieve significant reform in postwar America, as Bourne predicted. Entering the conflict served to stifle change, undermine social tolerance, and exacerbate antiradicalism. As Bourne observed in a book review, "The 'antidotes to imperialism' must precede the mischievous intellectualisms of a League to Enforce Peace."[97] He was always wary that any league created in the wake of a devastating, nationalistic war would mete out unequal international justice.

Bourne's "Vigorous Assertion of Values"

By 1919 the sociologist Frances Kellor, who had called for a "coercive" Americanization in 1916, and been widely rebuked by Bourne, came to see that Bourne had been right about her views, about the war, and about how to begin to seek peace. Kellor publicly recanted the perspective she had expressed in *Straight America*. She recognized that the nationalistic approach she had advocated actually weakened the American "social cohesion" that she desired. In 1920, she published *Immigration and the Future*, which in Bournian language reaffirmed her earlier commitment to embracing immigrants and various national cultures as well as to the sort of local and international conflict resolution and arbitration that Bourne and others such as Debs and Eastman had been calling for before and during the war.

From the time of his travels in Europe during 1913–1914 to his death from influenza at age thirty-three in 1918, Bourne witnessed firsthand on two continents the burgeoning of bellicose nationalism that overwhelmed much of the great potential for progressive reform that had provided him so much hope. Throughout these years Bourne contemplated the psychological and cultural consequences of what it meant for a nation to be at war. His developing notion of an isolationist antiwar pluralism was the product of his wartime experiences. His activism in turn embodied the costs for the small, outspoken group of individuals who opposed American entry and participation in World War I. In conflict with many of his fellow intellectuals who came to favor a Wilsonian vision for the war and later peace, Bourne became even more of an outsider under the conditions of wartime America than he had been as a physically disabled man.

His ideology assumed the status of faith for him when he said, "One keeps healthy in wartime not by a series of religious and political consolations that something good is coming out of it all, but by a vigorous assertion of values in which war has no part."[98] Since his works were repressed and his former friends and allies largely estranged, isolation pushed Bourne further toward advocacy of the isolated-intellectual ideal. Calling himself a pacifist propelled him to refine a new schema of American pluralism: cosmopolitan, noninterventionist, and based on a broadly exceptionalist view of the importance of adhering to the tradition of American military-political isolation.[99]

While his prescriptions for policy were often diffuse, Bourne's idealism, pluralist philosophy, and role as a peace activist acted like beacons to other radical intellectuals who opposed war in his generation and in future years. As the historian Merle Curti concluded, "It seems surprising that friends of peace did not attach more weight than they did to propaganda as a means of enlisting the sympathy of Americans on one side or the other. . . . Randolph Bourne was virtually alone in calling attention to the fact that many who shouted loudly in behalf of the freedom and democracy for which the Allies stood were contemptuous of democratic strivings in our midst; that many well-meaning people who had never been stirred by the horrors of 'capitalist peace at home' had a large fund of idle emotional capital to invest in the oppressed nationalities and ravaged villages of Europe."[100]

Bourne's transnational isolationism formed a foundation for his cultural criticism. If America could not stay out of petty European affairs, then what hope did the nation have for being the ideal location for his pluralist "no-place" after all? To some, an isolated yet transnational United States might be contradictory. For Bourne such goals were thoroughly compatible, and they proved influential. Indeed, the backlash against World War I led to the movement to outlaw war. America was a leading force in this effort, which culminated in the international Kellogg-Briand Pact of 1928, and the symbolic censure of industry by the Nye Commission in 1936. Some of Bourne's transnational arguments are also visible in early elements of multiculturalism in post–World War II America. These developments demonstrate that Bourne's influence was in ascension at the time he died.

For almost a hundred years, and in each national crisis since World War I, Bourne's many admirers have hailed him as a martyr to their diverse causes. Certainly the American forms of pacifism that have been intertwined with a theological mind-set, including the sort of witness-for-peace perspective of later antiwar and pacifist activists—such as David Dellinger, Stephen Carter, George Houser, the Berrigans, and even in some of the antinuclear movements—would have been alien to the quasi-pacifistic radical activist mind-set Bourne espoused. Yet generations of intellectual, reform-minded, and secularly oriented noninterventionist activists and thinkers have hearkened back to the Bournian tradition. Recently the often-darkly Bournian tones emanating from observers of the latest American policy in the Middle East situates them within a line of antiwar pluralist thought, with roots in isolationism, and remarkable resemblance to Bourne's transnationalism. We have heard these faint echoes coming from a wide range of liberal internationalist thinkers, including John Dos Passos and Dwight Macdonald, Noam Chomsky and Christopher Lasch, and most recently the moral critiques of Michael Walzer and the humanitarian internationalism of Michael Ignatieff.[101]

Bourne's ideas and his critique of the wartime state have endured in the rhetoric and behavior of his intellectual descendants. Rethinking Bourne's ideas about transnationalism and antiwar pluralism may tease some modern readers to find continuities with contemporary discussions about the internationalist and noninterventionist options available to America in a troubled and violent world. Drawing out those distinctions is beyond the scope of this book. But what is most important to note is that these ideas have been partly institutionalized. Peace initiatives, para-state organizations, and citizen outreach, ranging from the Red Cross to the Fellowship of Reconciliation to VISTA and the Peace Corps, are potent global forces for peaceful cultural interchanges and philanthropy that work on the transnational principle of connecting peoples and cultures across and sometimes regardless of nationalisms and national boundaries. The Randolph Bourne Institute, for example, a small, contemporary nonprofit American-based organization founded in 2001, directly invokes Bourne's name as well as his isolationist antiwar pluralism to lobby for a Bournian vision of pluralist and pacifist transnationalism. "To honor [Bourne's] memory by promoting a non-interventionist foreign policy for the United States," the institute's mission statement asserts, "[is] the best way of fostering a peaceful, more prosperous world."[102] This message mixes Bourne's ambition for America to be a "mediating neutral" with his domestic notion of transnational pluralism to adapt his ideas for the globalized, flattened world of the twenty-first century.[103]

The World War I context helped produce the conditions that generated Bourne's isolationist form of protest, yet it also severely undermined his ability to reach a wider contemporary audience or to have more practical influence. By being so explicitly oppositional, he limited his ability to be heard and to find allies; his intellectual journey transformed him from rising progressive star to censored and maligned antiwar activist. Yet his legacy means that historians must broaden the all-too-narrow, negativistic understandings of isolationism. Bourne's concept of a transnational America created a soft form of isolationist pluralism—broad, optimistic, and still very much with us today.

Bourne's "vigorous assertion of values" against the wartime state found resonance with fellow high-profile liberal dissenters and even among staunch isolationists. Some of Bourne's predictions seemed prescient not long after his death when so-called Irreconcilable politicians opposed the Versailles Treaty and the League of Nations on isolationist as well as partisan grounds. Led by Senator William Borah, the mostly Republican bloc of isolationists were hardly the types of young radical "malcontents" that Bourne envisioned would take up any aspects of his antiwar, anti-League cause.

When these isolationist positions first emerged coherently during the war, distinct variations appeared in the views of intellectuals like Bourne, socialists such as Debs, feminists and peace activists like Addams and Balch, and progressive politicians such as Robert La Follette and Borah. The countervailing curtailment of free speech by private, local, state, and federal officials, however, tended to treat all such positions monolithically. To begin to make sharp distinctions among these positions of isolationist, ultranationalist, and internationalist opponents, who joined together to defeat ratification of the League of Nations charter, the thought and activism of Eugene Debs is important. Just as Bourne looked inward toward reforming the country and making it transnational, Debs looked outward and hoped that international socialism would reshape American society and obviate the need for war.

Figure 1. Jane Addams (front row, second from left), Emily Greene Balch (third row, standing with hat, first on left), and forty-three other delegates to the First International Congress of Women at The Hague, Netherlands, in 1915. Women's International League for Peace and Freedom Records, Swarthmore College Peace Collection.

Figure 2. Senator Henry Cabot Lodge giving a speech during his reelection campaign in 1922. National Photo Company Collection, LOT 12354-3, courtesy of the Library of Congress Prints and Photographs Division, Washington, D.C.

Figure 3. Senators William Borah, Henry Cabot Lodge, and Reed Smoot after consulting with President Coolidge, May 7, 1924. National Photo Company Collection, LOT 12296, v. 3, p. 5, courtesy of the Library of Congress Prints and Photographs Division, Washington, D.C.

Figure 4. Secretary of War Newton D. Baker presents John R. Mott with the Army Distinguished Service Medal on the steps of the U.S. Capitol in 1919. Harris & Ewing Collection, LC-H261- 30373, courtesy of the Library of Congress Prints and Photographs Division, Washington, D.C.

Figure 5. W. E. B. Du Bois in the NAACP *Crisis* magazine offices, just after World War I, circa 1920–1921. W. E. B. Du Bois Papers, Photo Collection, Special Collections and University Archives, W. E. B. Du Bois Library, University of Massachusetts at Amherst.

Figure 6. Eugene V. Debs addressing a public rally, most likely in Chicago in 1912. This photo often has been mistakenly attributed as Debs's address in Canton, Ohio, in 1918, for which he was jailed. Courtesy of the Debs Collection, Special Collections Department, Cunningham Memorial Library, Indiana State University, Terre Haute.

Figure 7. William James, portrait while reading, circa 1894–1895. MS Am 1092 (1185) #71 (photographer Sarah Carlisle Choate Sears), Houghton Library Collection, Harvard University.

Figure 8. Randolph Silliman Bourne at desk, one of a rare few portraits he permitted to be taken, circa 1913. Randolph Silliman Bourne Papers, Rare Book and Manuscript Library, Columbia University.

Figure 9. Randolph Silliman Bourne (left) with Arthur W. Macmahon. The two friends on the steps of a house, most likely in New York and photographed just before or just after their travels in Europe, circa 1912–1915. Randolph Silliman Bourne Papers, Rare Book and Manuscript Library, Columbia University.

Figure 10. Emily Greene Balch portrait, circa 1915–1920. Emily Greene Balch Papers, Swarthmore College Peace Collection.

Figure 11. Emily Greene Balch (rear right, with hat) at the WILPF Executive Committee, gathering in front of Maison Internationale, Geneva, March 1928. Women's International League for Peace and Freedom Records, Swarthmore College Peace Collection.

Figure 12. Woman's Peace Party Demonstration, circa 1915–1919, Crystal Eastman (second from right). Lella Secor Florence Papers, Swarthmore College Peace Collection.

Figure 13. "Interrupting the Ceremony," McCutcheon, *Chicago Tribune*, 1918. This anti-League cartoon sets up Uncle Sam as marrying "foreign entanglements," with a document marked "peace proceedings" at their feet. Image courtesy of Van Pelt Library, University of Pennsylvania.

Figure 14 (*right, above*). "Civilization Begins at Home," from *New York World*, this version was published in the *Literary Digest*, November 26, 1898. This anti-imperialist political cartoon shows President William McKinley looking avariciously at a map of the Philippine Islands while behind his back Lady Justice draws a curtain to expose a lynched man and injustice and poverty abounding. Image courtesy of Van Pelt Library, University of Pennsylvania.

Figure 15 (*right, below*). "Another Blindfold Test," Carey Orr, *Chicago Tribune*, 1928. This political cartoon is skeptical of new internationalist peace initiatives such as the Kellogg-Briand Pact. Carey Orr Papers, Box 16, "Another Blindfold Test," *Chicago Tribune*, 1928, Special Collections Research Center, Syracuse University Library.

"CIVILIZATION BEGINS AT HOME."

Figure 16. "Try This on Your Phunnygraph," Albert Reid, *Idaho Daily Statesman*, April 22, 1923. This cartoon depicts Senator William Borah as a singer and critiques him for his tendency to play both sides of issues. MG10, William Edgar Borah Collection, Book III-29, Special Collections & Archives, University of Idaho, Moscow.

5

VOICES OF THE PEOPLE

"Let your voice go, go everywhere, in every town and city," socialist and jailed Industrial Workers of the World (IWW) organizer Carlo Tresca urged Eugene Debs.[1] By the autumn of 1916, when Tresca, imprisoned for organizing a mine strike, exhorted Debs to action, America was buffeted by mounting waves of anxiety about joining the European war and by a series of high-profile labor disputes. Tresca's impassioned cry represented the spirit of these trying times.

Like other antiwar activists, the socialist labor leader Debs felt a feverish urge to reach the masses. Creating a socialist presence everywhere, "in every town and city," had always been a major goal of American socialists. Surveying changing social, national, and geopolitical circumstances, Debs, like Randolph Bourne, began to make an important series of rhetorical shifts in how he stressed and expanded such objectives. What united figures like Bourne and Debs, and their loosely arrayed set of allies, was an effort to oppose exporting domestic policy abroad, and instead to cultivate progressive, or socialist, domestic policies that could serve as the basis for nonmilitaristic international engagement. For Debs this meant that he no longer focused solely on issues of industrial unionism, socialist revolution, or antifederal encroachment and anticapitalist ideas. From 1912 to 1920, he widened his definition of the proletariat, appealing to rural constituents, and with the coming of war he expanded his opposition to the government by intertwining a scathing critique of the "plutocracy" with an embrace of free speech and an invocation of the right to dissent as part of a broader socialist movement to fulfill what he believed were America's democratic promises to support and empower its people.[2]

Debs's intellectual and political development during the critical years leading up to and through World War I provides a window into varied antiwar ideologies as they spread through disparate groups, advancing national connections in radical thought while attempting to channel the voices of the people. One region not particularly well known for its anti-war activism or radicalism, the South, was an important part of that national network. In an effort to promote antiwar and socialist activity in that region and across the nation from 1912 to 1920 Debs increasingly oriented his thinking toward typically rural areas, farmers, and a more explicit emphasis on an idealized liberal interpretation of what he saw as the American "common man." Debs's regional activities were thus part of a more sweeping universalist project.[3]

Debs's astonished reaction to parochial socialists in Europe mirrored Bourne's. Both men were surprised by the depth and power of belligerent nationalism. Relating Debs's activities in the South to his socialist worldview, this chapter illuminates another view of how America's seemingly exceptional potential for pluralism could be leveraged for large-scale political activism to reshape democracy and society. The chapter examines tensions among regionalism, nationalism, isolationism, and internationalism. One focus here is on the little-known antiwar activism and draft resistance in the South, which reveals Debs's connections to the national network of radicals opposing American entry and participation in World War I, whose nonconformist internationalist perspectives were increasingly marginalized and then criminalized in wartime.

In Debs's structural analysis of how to reconcile democracy and empower labor, he remained an internationalist vis-à-vis flows of capital and in terms of class-based critiques. However, in terms of the exceptionalist and populist elements that became more pronounced in Debs's arguments during the wartime years, his framework of analysis was also historicist and comparative. That is, Debs deployed American values as a way to mount antiwar arguments that were very much isolationist. He believed there would be an organic succession of historical developments, leading toward a broader socialist movement, and local conditions and traditions in places like the United States would influence this course of world-historical events in a decisive way.

Detaching the narrative of Eugene Debs from the traditional categories of socialist activism, one can see that the ideology of his growing protest against the war was at base a type of isolationism that was paradoxically informed by his belief in the ultimate triumph of international socialism. The former head of the American Railway Union and a stalwart labor activist, Debs considered himself a socialist and a worker foremost—but his antiwar activist arguments have much in common with the principles of isolationism already laid out. Those include Debs's repeated invocation of America's foundational values and icons, his espousal of a policy of neutrality, and his desire to minimize the conflict as a whole by avoiding American military aid to any belligerent nation. Moreover, he emphasized the nation's need for domestic reform (to become socialist) to ensure equal protection under the law and more evenly distribute prosperity across society. By situating Debs's antiwar socialist messages in the wider matrix and political spectrum of opponents of preparedness, the war, and the draft, we can better see the parts of his belief system that were inherently isolationistic and we more fully appreciate how he blended domestic socialist politics with a comprehensive worldview. The most significant isolationist elements of this mix, however, came from Debsian socialism's embrace of traditional U.S. constitutional principles and what he saw as America's foundational values for "steering clear of foreign entanglements" coupled with freedoms of expression and dissent. In turn, Debs combined these democratic commitments with a commitment to global peace by which he was convinced national as well as international bonds of labor brotherhood would eventually prevail over petty nationalisms and capitalist rivalries.

Socialism had its strongest hold in the big cities of the Northeast and Midwest but Debs hoped for more. After the remarkable poll results in 1912 in which the Socialist Party of America (SPA) received nearly one million votes and garnered a host of national, state, and local offices, Debs wanted to build on this achievement. He shifted his efforts in two new ways to better nationalize his socialist party and the movement: first, he placed a neo-Jeffersonian emphasis on a rural workingman's populism, and second, he advocated an anti–big business, anticapitalist, anti–big government stance that blended well with his later championing of the right to speak out against America's entering the European conflict. Thus, he created another type of antiwar thought that was internationalist and yet also isolationist in intriguing ways.

In this effort Debs differed from previous isolationist thought largely based on the global element infused into his core belief in the worldwide socialist revolution. Still, he reinforced Jamesian anti-imperialist and anti-"bigness" arguments. Debs cast big business, big government, and large-scale capitalist wars as antithetical to the values and interests of the working man or woman—in any country. In particular, he made the case that large monopolies and the influence of the "monied power" on politics and across society were anathema to the free, democratic citizens of the United States. Thus, Debs's rhetoric contains a surprising degree of American exceptionalism, according to which he often allied himself explicitly with "comrade" revolutionaries such as Washington, Jefferson, and Lincoln.

After war broke out across Europe in 1914, Debs was shocked—as were most American socialists and progressives, and many observers worldwide—when the majority of socialists in virtually every European country joined their respective nationalist war efforts and turned against each other. Their nationalism trumped their dedication to socialist internationalism, and in response Debs's views changed. He emphasized organization and peaceful internationalism over revolution. In this he built on long-standing isolationist views of American neutral global involvement. Debs declared that American freedoms were sacrosanct and must be protected by the nation's remaining out of the corrupting European war, particularly the power politics of monarchical capitalist governments. Along with bohemian intellectuals, such as Bourne and Max Eastman, and liberal-pacifist/antimilitarists, such as Jane Addams and Crystal Eastman, Debs used his platform as America's preeminent socialist politician to espouse international pacifism, while at the same time encouraging the destruction of Western capitalist and monarchist governments from within (the very same ruling classes, he said, who had caused the war).

Yet Debs, who saw Americans as exceptional with regard to the hierarchical and archaic values that dominated Europe, was even more astonished by how much of organized labor—particularly common socialist union members, the "rank and file" itself—within the United States in 1916 and 1917 became fiercely jingoistic in support of Wilson's war effort. Many socialist and liberal intellectuals who did advocate international peace and related critiques of the status quo—such as thoroughgoing domestic social and economic reform, as well as the opposition of preparedness programs, entry into the war, and the draft—were prosecuted under the new Espionage and Sedition Acts (1917, 1918). These laws, in turn, eventually formed the legal grounds for Debs's high-profile sedition trial, conviction, incarceration, and presidential campaign from jail in 1920.

This shift in Debs's tactics toward more rural and populist audiences, particularly during the wartime years, had reverberations in the arguments of the larger community of war resistance, especially those of antiwar Southern Democrats. Most general histories of the period tend to overemphasize the zealotry of Southern and national militarists for the war, thus obscuring the extent of the opposition to World War I.[4] Debs's attempts to appeal to rural constituents with his antiwar, anticapitalist rhetoric would align him with many in the South who had no interest in socialism.[5]

A fascinating group of socialist allies, spearheaded by Debs, along with a host of populist-oriented racist firebrands, such as Georgia Senator M. Hoke Smith and South Carolina Senator "Pitchfork" Ben Tillman, and a limited number of pacifists fused what was essentially a tactic of antiwar "ruralization" (in some cases "Southernization" and in other cases "internationalization") with a broader national attempt to oppose preparedness, conscription, and the war. Ideas about isolation help us understand that common short-term goals united Debs and other radical opponents of the Wilson administration, such as dissenting Southern and Midwestern Democrats, despite their dissimilar long-term objectives. This was no simple rhetoric of exceptionalism, because for Debs these free-speech, antiwar views had everything to do with the United States' remaining apart from the corruptions of global capitalism and monarchical power politics. Not that he considered America immune—far from it. Debs heightened his activism because he feared the nation might be made all the worse by rejecting the tradition of nonintervention and being infected with the virus of European-style nationalism and politics. He hoped, perhaps naively, that if such engagement were stemmed off, a socialist revolution could be more rapidly and bloodlessly achieved at the ballot box in the United States.

After the Bolshevik Revolution in 1917, Debs began to have more hope for socialism abroad, but at home his opposition to the war was firmly grounded in isolationist calls for American republican traditions of non-entanglement, minimization of conflict, and the desire to become a beacon—in his case, of socialist values—not just for the United States, but to and for the world. This is not to say that there were not significant influences on Debs from the outside in. The period from 1912 to 1920 marks Debs's profound shift to develop and deploy more populist language to enhance his national political appeal. Exogenous influences on Debs, such as the war in Europe, as we shall see, served largely as negative examples of nationalism trumping local and international socialist brotherhood. They also represented the disenchanting influence of capitalism to Debs, as he saw the hypernationalist movement for war and its homogenizing

Americanization campaigns as marking a casting aside of Americans' natural comradeship and diversity, in favor of a form of class stratification that eviscerated the nation's vaunted foundational value of democratic individual rights.

Against the War and in the South

To reach a less urban-industrial audience, Debs promulgated an anti–big business and pro-labor political system based upon the inviolability of individual rights. Italian immigrant Carlo Tresca's cry to "go everywhere" to "every town and city," ignoring as it does the farms, ranches, and villages of rural America, illustrates the ingrained anti-agrarianism of many socialists and members of the Left in the United States at the time.[6] Marxist socialism, of course, was designed to be an ideological organization for wage earners of the working class. Southern and Midwestern farmers, however, whether they were tenants, small farmers, or sharecroppers, could not be strictly defined as wage earners. Even more to the point— and worse for socialists—a goodly number of farmers owned their own land, and therefore were theoretically members of a "landed" middle class, though they were cash poor and often impoverished. Debs wished to eliminate such prejudice. After the 1912 election he increasingly connected agrarians of all types (e.g., farmers, day laborers) with urban industrial labor (e.g., manufacturing line-workers, railroad firemen) into his language, explicitly widening his concept of the American proletariat.[7] What this meant practically was that Debs's antiwar rhetoric sounded like a primer for U.S. foundational values blending the Constitution with Washington's 1796 Farewell Address and echoing the anti-imperialist injunctions against being involved abroad unless absolutely essential for the nation's survival.

Radical socialist groups, such as the IWW, invoked such notions to great effect across the South and Midwest because of their militancy and attraction to laborers who were unruly given the hard conditions in which they worked. But the IWW operations in the rural South faced special challenges unique to the region, specifically the matter of race and the reality of landowning farmers. It was IWW policy under the leadership of "Big" Bill Haywood not to compromise Marxist principles. Thus, the militant labor group would not organize or include even the most sympathetic rural unions if they included landowning farmers. Instead, and despite the common cause, the IWW stuck to ideology in defining such landowners as nonproletariat aliens. Adding further complications were the racial politics of the South that often, but far from always, prevented bi- or triracial organizing efforts from gaining any real traction because unions that included African Americans were difficult to hold together, or to fuse with larger leagues, and often further fragmented when people of various ethnicities appeared as strikebreakers.[8]

Such problems were obvious to Debs in 1912 as he worked to tap a broader cross section of the proletariat and their electoral power in the South, Southwest, West, and Midwest. After the excellent showing by the Socialist Party of America at the polls in 1912 proved the party could make substantial inroads, even in "farm" country, Debs pushed further. The SPA polled more than nine hundred thousand total votes for Debs, roughly 6 percent nationally, and won a host of city and state offices, earning 2–3 percent of the vote on average in the Southern states in 1912. Areas that were politically divided or activated by the rise of the Bull Moose Party, populist outrage, or labor unrest provided greater support for the party (e.g., 8.27 percent of the vote in Texas, 9.45 percent in Florida, 6.64 percent in Louisiana). What are best seen as "ruralization" and "Southernization" thus corresponded with a further "nationalization" of Debs's democratic socialist message at a pivotal point in national politics.

Debs's argument hearkened back to the Civil War era Radical Republicans, and Wendell Phillips after the war, and the pioneers of a worker-farmer alliance with a "producerist" ideology. These ideas had a clear influence on the development of American labor organization and on Debs's potent populist appeal in particular. In a telling front-page article Debs explained the innate appeal of socialism to farmers in the South. Writing in the Hallettsville, Texas-based weekly socialist newspaper, the *Rebel*, edited by Tom Hickey, Debs proposed—as his evocative title indicated—that socialism was "Sweeping the South."[9]

In this article, and in his subsequent efforts over the next decade, Debs faced head-on the classic socialist "Land Question" conundrum. For a ruralizing and nationalizing SPA under Debs's leadership, this task was daunting. How should the party incorporate farmers and those who labored, even sometimes owning land, but were not logically members of the Marxist proletariat? Debs argued that all were workers. All needed socialism. And socialism needed them all. In this article, Debs declared that a sweep of the South was already in progress. Dual concerns about land ownership and race, however, remained critically important and divisive, particularly in the non-urban South.[10]

Debs discovered during speaking engagements and time touring the South that the "unity of workers who cultivate the farms" with those who labor as "industrial workers of the cities" was under way and ought to be encouraged. Debs praised the socialist presses and loyal party organizers, urging them to redouble their activities. He believed that papers and partisans in the South and Midwest were the vanguard for first organizing and then incorporating farmers, both tenant and poor landowner, with urban, industrial workers. To systematize this process, Debs first wanted to build on long-standing, powerful critiques of structural inequality and injustice in American society. He then hoped to generate a national socialist consensus and a democratically elected revolution by bringing the "divided" camps together.[11]

The pages of the socialist presses from the election year of 1912 through 1914, such as the *Rebel, National Rip-Saw, Appeal to Reason,* and *International Socialist Review,* reiterated Debs's concerns. They reveal the importance of farmers to Debs's efforts to sweep the South. He sought to reach large groups of rural and small-town farmers and workers. Debs wrote that this would consolidate the "economic and political unity of workers who cultivate the farms and the industrial workers of the cities."[12]

According to estimates by several historians, these messages were reaching many of those targeted by Debs and others in the SPA. Before 1915 these periodicals were reaching approximately one hundred thousand readers in the South and Southwest alone, and by late 1915 the *Appeal* was reaching more than three hundred thousand people in the South and close to one million nationwide. As historian Arthur Schlesinger Jr. observed regarding the formative period leading up to the 1912 election and immediately thereafter: "Was not socialism in the United States now on the verge of meaning something? By 1912 the Socialist Party had 118,000 dues paying members, of whom over a thousand held public offices—including 56 mayors, over 300 aldermen, some state legislators, and one Congressman. It had five English dailies and 262 English weeklies as well as a large number of foreign-language journals." Yet the issue of how to fuse farmer-labor groups, often in areas where race, labor, and religion were violently at odds, posed major problems for organizers in the South and Midwest. But some did find workable solutions. The agrarian socialists whom historian Jim Bissett analyzed, for example, found effective means to reconcile Southern evangelicalism by mixing "Jesus and Marx." They aimed to naturalize rural landowning and farm-labor realities with elements of New Testament theological notions of justice to fit the organizing tenets of socialists and labor leaders.[13]

In his outreach efforts Debs's "ruralization" was most effective in the Midwest and Southwest, as historians Bissett and James Green have shown. In large part this success can be explained by the fact that these were areas where the remnants of producerist and populist political activism remained strong, providing a ready base to organize for the cause. Debs often bypassed Southern elite spokesmen, and his speeches and writings were largely filtered to constituents on the ground through the radical presses, particularly the Girard, Kansas-based socialist *Appeal to Reason*, which had the widest circulation across the South, and smaller papers, such as that small-town Texas paper, the *Rebel*. These conduits appear to have worked effectively—at least until America joined the European war and most socialist and radical political papers were censored in the summer and fall of 1917.[14] As the best-known symbol of socialism and radical unionism across the nation, Debs's presence could draw a crowd in the smallest speaking stops or at isolated groveside gatherings. His messages also were disseminated via pamphlets passed out by hand and, at times, through reporting in the mainstream media.

Most significant to the dispersal of Debsian socialist principles were vibrant, small socialist party locals. Their summer-to-fall mass meetings, known as "encampments," were among the best communications channels. Modeled after religious revivals and earlier populist gatherings, these encampments were a major source of rural exposure for Debs and other national socialist figures. As historian Stephen Burwood explained, encampments were usually located "just outside small towns and lasting anywhere between two days and a full week, they attracted between 5,000 and 20,000 people from up to 100 miles away and were the highlight of the year for literally hundreds of thousands of embattled farmers and small townsfolk. Socialist songs, choral work, and classical music were interspersed with serious discussions, classes, and set-piece oratory."[15]

Speakers for these occasions were most often national socialists with name recognition, or regional leaders. Debs was extremely popular and effective at these events, according to most accounts. Writing in 1914 Debs extolled these camps and his experiences speaking throughout the South. He found the Texas socialist movement particularly meritorious and honored the tenant farmers he met there for their "class conscious enthusiasm." Proclaiming them to be "real Socialists," Debs argued that these farmers in fact were fully part of the "revolutionary movement of the working class." In his assessment, Texas tenant farmers revealed the radical nature of the encampments. The events also reinforced, to Debs at least, that there was an acute need to tap these radical masses, to organize and better energize rural farmers and laborers. Debs wrote that they were "ready for action, and if the time comes when men are needed at the front to fight and die for the cause the farmers of Texas and Oklahoma will be found there."[16]

A number of Southern farm-labor groups and related cooperative movements worked out of an explicit Debsian ideological framework, but not all.[17] James Green's scholarship has shown this definitively in the Southwest, where Debsian arguments were widely persuasive, particularly at leadership levels. Nigel Sellers also demonstrated the perplexing challenge that confronted socialist organizers aiming for an expansively defined proletariat in the South. Two central problems remained to be surmounted if socialism was to sweep not just the places where it already had a firm hold, in Northeastern cities and in the Midwest, but also across the South and West: how to organize industrial workers alongside rural and agricultural laborers, and how to overcome the challenges of cross-race socialist organizing, particularly in the South. After all, it had been twelve short years since Debs's first major speech-making tour across the South was cited by W. E. Farmer, then president of the Socialist Party of Texas, in a report to the *Social Democratic Herald*. Farmer argued that Debs's bold socialist orations were crucial in persuading the "independent socialist parties of Texas, Tennessee, and Arkansas" to incorporate under the single rubric of Debs's new, national Social Democratic Party (SDP). Yet still the Socialist Party had not made the significant inroads with labor in the South that Debs had hoped for at the turn of the century.[18]

Debs's private correspondence establishes his frequent contact with rural Americans and Southerners of various walks of life. It reveals, too, his personal concern with the farm-labor alliances in the Midwest, Southwest, and his rejection of what he termed the "Bourbon" Southerners, which included such notables as President Wilson, Secretary of the Navy Josephus Daniels, from North Carolina, and later chief presidential adviser "Colonel" E. M. House, a Texan who seemed to dominate the Wilson administration. Debs's judgments about how to organize in these areas drew upon elements that were as characteristically Southern as they were Midwestern, and as traditionally conservative as radical. Furthermore, Southern Democratic war opponents sounded much like Debs, who himself accommodated to their speaking style. Thus, Southern opponents of war and Debsian socialists came to express strikingly similar renderings of a persuasive populist critique of big business and a strong federal government.[19]

During and after the campaign of 1912 Debs's strategic and rhetorical transition comes through quite clearly in his papers and correspondence, as well as his other public work at the time. His changing language evoked the nineteenth-century Knights of Labor concept of a "cooperative commonwealth" in an attempt to unite rural and urban labor. Indeed, in the years leading up to World War I, from 1908 to 1914, with Debs at the SPA's helm, the movement achieved its strongest grassroots support in the Southwest, in Oklahoma and Texas, and in the Southern states of Arkansas and Louisiana. The language used was classically producerist. As James Green demonstrated, socialism linked ideas of populism throughout the South and into the Midwest, to act as an "educational as well as a political force" through the dissemination of local and national radical papers, through speaking tours, and through various organizations.[20]

Debs's broadened rhetoric aimed to be "educational" in just this sense. In Louisiana, for example, Debsian socialists passed out literature about the Debs candidacy widely in rural, wood-industry areas of the state, and helped to organize disaffected farmers and lumberjacks. In response, Debs received one out of every fourteen votes cast in the 1912 presidential election in Louisiana. Debs polled more votes in the state than did incumbent William Howard Taft. One explanation for this unexpected popularity is that the data indicate a strong voter turnout and appeal in the upland hill parish areas. This was the region where poor treatment of workers by lumber industry executives galvanized socialist union activism; this sort of capitalist coercion was exploited by socialist union organizers, especially when it provoked action the IWW could respond to aggressively, often with violent tactics. Nearly 70 percent of the Debs vote in Louisiana came from these areas. For the next four years, from 1912 through 1916, Debs tried to build on grassroots successes in the Southwest, exemplified by the results in Louisiana, so that he might address and organize an expanded proletariat. However, he did this against a steep incline. He faced socialist union-breaking efforts across the region and the rising wartime patriotism that curtailed the publication and presentation of socialist and radical speech in 1917 and 1918.

In his article "Sweeping the South," Debs complimented the work of the socialist presses, such as the *Rebel*, which he deemed the "lustiest" revolutionary paper in the nation. He also praised the "encampments." The "educational propaganda of the *Rebel*," wrote Debs, "and the well directed activity of the industrial union of renters are making for the economic and political unity of workers who cultivate the farms and the industrial workers of the cities." He continued by saying that these efforts were "bringing them all into intelligent, militant and harmonious cooperation for the overthrow of the present despotic system and the establishment of a genuine system of self-government in which the common people will be sovereigns."[21]

Later in that issue of the *Rebel*, several other articles argued for the same project of unification, with an eye to the city first, then bridging the interests of urban, industrial labor and their rural brethren, "cultivators" and "renters." In an article penned by Emil Seidel, the mayor of Milwaukee, for instance, we see another example. Concurring with the ruralizing fusion goals of Debs, Seidel argued that farmers and workers had mutual misconceptions, perpetuated by their capitalist oppressors, and therefore they shared powerful underlying interests. Those cultivating the farms and industrial laborers had a "common enemy," he said, who kept them down. According to Seidel, socialism was the only answer for them to turn the tables.[22]

Southern socialist Covington Hall agreed with Seidel, although he emphasized the rural areas first. Hall saw all too well how hard the Debs challenge of focusing on non-urban, nonindustrial laboring Southerners would be. Hall faced similar challenges in trying to encourage the IWW to incorporate sharecroppers. Hall pushed the organization hard to think more creatively. Oscar Ameringer had influenced Hall, Debs, and prominent socialists when he argued in his 1912 pamphlet "Socialism for the Farmer" and in a host of articles in the smaller socialist presses that every farmer should "vote red." Ameringer, Hall, and Debs employed and expanded on the ideas expressed by Julius Wayland in his organizing efforts especially across the Mississippi Valley area from the late nineteenth century until his death in 1912.[23]

While Ameringer was thinking mostly about the Midwest, Hall's aim was precisely the same in the South, West, and nation as a whole. He wanted the IWW and the SPA to adapt their organizing models to those agrarian regions by rethinking a farm-labor alliance to better incorporate blacks, Latinos, and whites under the banner of a socialist union or party. Nonetheless, from 1917 until his incarceration in 1919, Debs's messages against big business and the war, and for a composite isolationist and socialist internationalist foreign policy, continued to find receptive ears and became increasingly vituperative, culminating in his infamous antiwar speech in Canton, Ohio, which resulted in his conviction under the Espionage Act.[24]

As War Approaches: Solidarity, Ruralization, and Debsian Socialism

In "A Plea for Solidarity" (1914) Debs set the stage for these developments by arguing for a strategy to achieve socialist political success through direct democratic campaigning without betraying core values. His central concern was with inclusivity. He wanted to unify all "those who labor"—in part evoking the older producerist arguments—through greater proletariat, union, and party solidarity. Debs maintained that the future of solidarity necessarily hinged on the continued ascent of an all-encompassing form of industrial unionism. Citing the Webster definition of the proletaire as "a low person," Debs agreed that this was a "sufficiently explicit definition of the *proletaire* by his bourgeois master which at the same time defines his status in a capitalist society, and it applies to the entire working and producing class; hence the *lower class*."[25] Therefore, he worked to popularize such a broadened definition. As he put it, the "proletariat and the working class are synonymous terms. I know of no essential distinction between skilled and unskilled salary and wage-workers."[26]

Speaking against the old model of exclusive craft unions, Debs continued to open up his classification of "industrial labor" to include rural "toilers" as part of his hope for the future of socialist organization in America. In 1914 the *Appeal to Reason* confirmed Debs's expanded notion of the "real" proletariat when it published a broadside that explored the identities and profiles of those who sold subscriptions to the paper, titled "Who's Who in Socialist America." This evidence reveals that only one-fifth of the nearly five hundred people featured were foreign-born and of those who responded, more than half lived in cities of under ten thousand, one-quarter lived in large cities, and one-fifth lived in rural America. Most important, reflecting Debs's aims for nationalizing the party, 69 percent of these top salesmen for the *Appeal* could best be described as workers and 75 percent lived outside of major metropolitan areas. Socialist Party minutes from 1914 also indicate that rural representatives and Southern participants were widely present, and every single Southern state contributed at least one delegate to the annual convention that year.[27] Given these realities, Debs sought a "new alignment" of the "entire working and producing class."[28]

Living in Terre Haute, Indiana, with roots deep in the Midwest, Debs was hardly a native Southerner, but he did have strong small-town and farming ties. Throughout 1914 he worked hard at enacting his rural strategy. He toured the South with a group of speakers and organizers from the *Rip-Saw* that included Kate O'Hare, among others, and was particularly active across Texas. Here Debs found amazement at the "great crowds and intense enthusiasm" that made the gatherings of thousands of farm families in groves outside of small towns "something of a revelation." According to the *Rip-Saw*, "They came in procession and all the highways were filled with their wagons. Every man, woman and child carried a red flag. . . . Far as the eye could reach along the roads there was a stream of farmers' wagons, filled with their families, and all of them waving red flags. It looked as if the march to the Socialist Republic had actually begun." Stopping at scores of small to midsize towns and encampments in Texas, as well as parts of Oklahoma, Louisiana, and Arkansas, from June through August, Debs experienced a revelation. In spite of the heat, humidity, and drought characteristic of summer in Texas and across much of the South, "these farmers," declared Debs, "have the true Socialist spirit." He continued optimistically, writing, "Many of them have scarcely a crop between themselves and destitution and yet they are the most generous, wholehearted people on earth, and for Socialism they would give the last of their scant possessions."[29]

War Limits Socialism's "Inevitable March"

In August 1914 the outbreak of war took Debs, like most Americans, by surprise. Socialist optimists like Debs who had believed in an "inevitable march" toward international socialism were shocked by how rapidly European socialists embraced their various flags and entered the ranks. Debs opposed the war immediately. He supported Wilson in his efforts to mediate the conflict and to steer the nation on his pledged path of neutrality. Debs's speeches of 1914 and 1915 decry the capitalist nature of the conflict, of course, but also strongly denounce war in favor of American isolation, identifying with the ideals of the Founding Fathers and emphasizing neutrality. Presciently, he forcefully pointed out the curtailment of democratic liberties because of war. He proclaimed that he had "no country to fight for; my country is the earth; I am a citizen of the world." In keeping with his view of the class nature of the European war, he stated, "I am not a capitalist soldier; I am a proletarian revolutionist." And he concluded many speeches by asserting, "I am opposed to every war but one; I am for that war with heart and soul, and that is the world-wide war of the social revolution. In that way, I am prepared to fight in any way the ruling class may make necessary, even to the barricades."[30] As it developed over time, this is exactly the sort of rhetoric that kept Debs firmly moored to socialist internationalism while also opposing the war and invoking exceptionalist and democratic arguments for anticapitalism, pro-rights reform at home.

All of his speeches led, in the spring of 1915, to one of his most debilitating physical collapses. He was bedridden, was placed in a sanitarium to recover, and was wracked with "physical exhaustion," apparently "torn leg muscles," and "severe congestion" that he said required "large doses of morphine" just to keep him from being "frantic." Debs was unable to give speeches throughout the fall.

By the end of 1915, after he came to believe that Wilson would acquiesce to the American capitalist plutocracy that had "bet" on the Anglo war effort, he discussed the European war in his article "The Prospect for Peace." Debs struggled to show American workers what he considered to be the true, warmongering nature of the "ruling class robbers." Again, he argued that labor, rural and urban, industrial and farm based, needed to cast off their bellicose capitalist leadership. Later that year he expanded this argument in an article with the self-explanatory title "Ruling Class Robbers."[31]

Appalled that so many socialists in Europe had joined the war efforts of their countries rather than to continue to regard their fellow laborers across national boundaries as comrades, the Socialist Party of America whimpered out of the Second International (a worldwide organization of socialists and labor parties in Paris, lasting from 1889 to 1916) by voting not to continue paying dues for 1915. From that time on the party concerned itself primarily with keeping America out of the war. At this early stage they found many allies. Wilson was still pledging neutrality, and a multitude of small but vocal pressure groups sprang up or found their voice on issues of peace and nonentanglement, such as the American Peace Society, the American Union Against Militarism, the People's Council, the Emergency Peace Federation, the Woman's Peace Party, and the Carnegie Endowment for International Peace, among some of the most prominent.[32]

The year 1915 also marked another advance of Debs's ruralization aims in the founding of the Non-Partisan League (NPL) by North Dakotan Socialist Party organizer A. C. Townley, who espoused a collective agrarian socialist solution to farmers' problems. The NPL, which rapidly gained influence in the Midwest and West, nominated and endorsed candidates such as Lynn Frazier, who won the North Dakota governorship in 1916 (removed by recall vote in 1921). The platform was one that most socialists could support, such as state ownership of grain elevators and flour mills, and the formation of a state-owned collective bank, as well as jointly owned farming facilities. Debs supported these goals, but he did clash with NPL leadership because they were not sufficiently revolutionary in outlook. Debs's primary concern in the pivotal year of 1916 was to expose Wilson's supposed liberal and progressive policies as conservative, anti-worker, and militaristic.

In August 1916 a former senator from South Dakota, Richard Pettigrew, wrote Debs to recommend an activist who would "render you very valuable assistance among the farmers of your district."[33] Henry Loucks had been chairman of the Populist Party convention and had helped author the Populist Platform of 1890, which, Pettigrew reminded Debs, "declared for the public ownership of land and the means of transportation and communication." Further, Loucks had "just written a book," *The Great Conspiracy of the House of Morgan and How to Defeat It* (1916), "on the money question."[34] What is interesting in these letters is that Pettigrew and Debs corresponded cordially, calling each other "dear friend" (although not all of the correspondence remains). Pettigrew had been a staunch anti-imperialist as a Republican in the Senate from 1889 to 1901, as well as a free silverite and single tax advocate. More to the point, by the summer of 1916 he was also well known for speaking out and writing to oppose America's entry into the war. Ultimately, Pettigrew, like Debs, was indicted for felony conspiracy under the Espionage Act, although he was never brought to trial.

The Socialist Party was the only major national party organization to publicly condemn America's participation in the war, and the closer the nation came, the more socialists were open to attack for this view. Yet their position also presented them with a unique opportunity. In the months following the SPA's national convention in St. Louis in April 1917, Socialists were able to rally many antiwar groups under their campaign banner. Five days after the war resolution passed, Debs wrote to the party secretary, Adolph Germer, noting ominously his prediction that "conscription, enforced military service, a rigid censorship, espionage, military training in public schools, the guarding of industrial plants by federal troops, compulsory arbitration, the penalizing of strikes" all lay on the horizon.[35] In many states even in the summer of 1917, one paper noted, socialists were issuing an antiwar clarion call "in evidence almost everywhere."[36] Still, the limitations of the small socialist presses and the autonomy ceded to local parties made efforts at broadening their influence and organizing a wider group of activists, including non-socialists, under a catchall antiwar banner quite difficult.

In addition, the peace organizations and the Socialist Party had some major differences. Many stemmed from the distinction between opposing all wars or just certain wars, as well as socialism's argument that the causes of conflicts between nations was essentially a problem of capitalist oppression. The internationalist socialism of such views underscored these differences, which together prevented the closer collaboration toward shared ends that might have nationalized a joint peace movement and party.

International Socialism and Patriotism

Nor were the socialists united even within their own party. A fascinating turn of events in Milwaukee illuminates some of the tensions between Debsian socialism, internationalism, and the interpretation of patriotism and American pride in wartime, even before entry into World War I. A look at Debs's correspondence reveals that American socialists faced the same dilemma as their European comrades. How could they harmonize their love of country with their ideological mission to bring about a global proletarian revolution and to relinquish parochial nationalism in favor of socialist internationalism? In many ways this was the central dilemma of American Socialist Party members and nonaffiliated believers. In the summer of 1916 Debs wrote to Daniel Hoan, the former attorney of the Wisconsin State Federation of Labor and city attorney who had just been elected as the socialist mayor of Milwaukee, where he served from 1916 through 1940. Debs asked Hoan if he had "headed a military preparedness parade" in the city. Debs had heard this claim and told Hoan he "denounced it at the time as a falsehood" and "simply cannot believe anything of the kind," but since then it had been "repeatedly charged."[37]

The response from Hoan displayed the deep contradiction between native patriotism and socialist internationalism. To Debs, it was an either/or proposition. For Hoan and many others, the two courses apparently could be made compatible. Hoan replied that the event was not labeled as a "Preparedness Parade" but rather as "A Patriotic Demonstration." He noted that Theodore Roosevelt's hyperpatriotic Security League had "at the outset . . . attempted to organize a regular preparedness parade," but "all of us socialists declined to participate, as did the federated trades council." Three weeks before the parade, the organizing citizens' council saw it would likely "fizzle" and so declared that it "would not be a military preparedness parade, or for more munitions, but merely a demonstration of national loyalty." The city socialist caucus as well as the county central committee voted that Hoan should participate, even "while the socialists generally could remain out of the parade." It was the consensus, according to Hoan, that to not have the Socialist Party and its highest official, the mayor of the city, participate would "be to deny any national feeling whatsoever, and probably cripple the party locally for years." Hoan then went on to explain his understanding of the ways in which socialist internationalism, patriotism, and American nationalism intertwined.

"While demonstrations originating from capitalist sources are hypocritical and more or less disgusting," Hoan wrote, "I submit that careful thot [sic] will lead any thinking socialist to the conclusion that every socialist is imbued with a genuine patriotic spirit, and that we are devoting our lives to make this nation a better place in which men who toil may live, as well as displaying an international patriotism." With his reply to Debs, Hoan enclosed an official account of the parade and the socialist participation in it. He concluded his letter by trying to persuade Debs of a much larger point. His aim was to recast American patriotism in socialist antiwar terms. Hoan explained that his community and local party had agreed with his decision. They all thought it would be preferable "rather than scoff at the word patriotism, to seize upon it and make it a word to express our ideas and popularize our thots [sic]."[38]

Debs shot back a stern rebuke in which he noted that he regretted Hoan had been placed in a position to take such action. "I cannot at all agree to the views regarding patriotism expressed in your communication," he responded tersely. "Socialists are not required to demonstrate their patriotism for the benefit of the capitalist class and that class will not only not thank them for it but hold them in greater contempt." Debs chastised Hoan that perhaps "the capitalist politicians were just a little too shrewd for the socialist politicians of Milwaukee." "Their press," he commented, would not "spread the news over the country that the socialist mayor of Milwaukee had marched at the head of a preparedness parade." In turn, Debs reminded Hoan that he would only endorse preparedness for peace. Patriotism based on sheer demonstrations of unity in nationhood left it without the underlying social democratic, revolutionary principles that Debs told Hoan were the core of his political convictions. Even if Milwaukee socialists like Hoan effectively used such a "perversion of principle" as advantageous "vote-catching politics" to get themselves elected, Debs wrote that he could never accept such a compromise. The truest patriotism, Debs claimed, was not national but international—to fellow comrades in the international proletariat. Debs even stated that if he were forced to march as a socialist in a capitalist parade, he would "quit the party."[39]

This exchange was just one example among many of the serious contradictions the war generated for socialist Americans and for pacifists as well. Debs's most heartfelt belief had always been that America's exceptional democratic values were the nation's greatest resource. Given this conviction, Debs often argued those values were American labor's birthright as well as the eventual instrument by which to achieve a socialist revolution through a peaceful transition at the ballot box. But such views seemed in contradiction to his claims to Hoan and other "patriotic socialists" that these very same workers did not have any reason to at least "demonstrate," if not fight for a country that he praised so highly for its principles.

Like Jane Addams, Balch, and Bourne, Debs resolved some of these competing pushes and pulls of patriotism by arguing that his socialism, and their pacifism, did not in any way make them undemocratic. (Addams remained a pacifist but lectured for the Department of Food Administration and the Woman's Peace Party on food conservation in wartime.) All of them came to argue at different moments, as did many Southern populists and other antiwar activists, that it was American and European leaders who were antidemocratic because they put forward the view that war was inevitable, creating propaganda to support such assertions, and then never submitted to a national referendum to measure the will of the people to engage in war.[40]

Running for Congress, Opposing Entry in the War

After these disputes in the summer of 1916, and several bouts of severe health problems, a weary Debs felt that he could not run for president for the fifth time. He said it was time for a new face for the party, such as the prominent socialist writer Allan Benson, to stand for national office. Debs did not run for the presidency in 1916. Instead, at sixty-one years old, he decided to run for the Fifth Congressional District, his home in Indiana. He defeated the local Democrat handily but lost resoundingly to Republican Everett Sanders. Disappointed, he forged ahead. With the campaign in full gear, helping Benson galvanized Debs. He projected dire ramifications of American entry into the European war, noting the likely "outlook of class war," as "world war" loomed. By late 1916 his predictions were widely reprinted in the *Rip-Saw*, the *Appeal to Reason*, and elsewhere, thereby reaching at least modest numbers of the rural constituents across the nation that he aspired to convince. As he continued to write enthusiastically on these topics, Debs's energies were reinvigorated.[41]

In early 1917 he embarked on a short speaking tour in the Midwest and Northeast. His withering criticism of Wilson's pro-Anglo "neutrality" emphasized that the Southern, Southwestern, and Midwestern working farmer, like the working industrial laborer, would pay the price in this conflict. After Congress passed the war resolution on April 6, 1917, Debs continued to assert that entering the conflict signaled a "class war" in which conscription would have dire effects on the families of small farmers and industrial laborers. Debs clung to a sanguine belief that he could speak for all the "men and women and children who toil." As their spokesman, he felt that he had to continue to tour. He hoped to inspire a mass realization of the manifold injustices of the war, inherently linked to fatal flaws in the competitive capitalist system, and thereby expedite the coming "day of the people."[42]

Opposition to Selective Service—more than any other single issue— united Southern Democrats with radical socialists like Debs, as well as with pacifists, progressive antiwar activists, and advocates of the social gospel. Much of Debs's specific reasoning, even some of the radical tenets of his socialist revolutionary critique, were consonant with the attacks of Southerners in Congress, such as Claude Kitchin of North Carolina, majority leader of the House of Representatives, and Senator James Vardaman of Mississippi, the renowned racist firebrand. A cohort of predominantly Southern politicians who opposed Wilson's foreign policy by upholding traditional isolationist, states' rights beliefs supported both Kitchin and Vardaman. Others, such as Georgia's Senator M. Hoke Smith and Tom Watson also from Georgia (the former Populist Party candidate for president in 1904 and 1908), built upon a populist tradition that linked the South and Midwest when they vehemently opposed the imposition of a mandatory national draft. These antiwar, anti–federal government, anti–big business sentiments often developed at the intersection where the radical Right and Left met. Virtually all of these Southern politicians were against entering or participating in the war but also were socially conservative staunch segregationists, which made them unlikely allies for racial liberals in the broader antiwar movement.

Nonetheless, drawing upon Georgia's steadfast resistance to federal intervention, Watson and his colleagues mounted a formidable challenge. They found common ground in arguing from an age-old states' rights logic, in this instance one that made the case that the proposed draft legislation was unconstitutional. They were fighting a patriotic tide, however. Both Watson and Smith tended to be dismissed by the Northern press as German sympathizers or race-baiters. Debs and all antiwar pacifists also opposed conscription, and much of the mainstream press denounced him as an unpatriotic socialist radical. This diverse community of dissent, however, was connected by their attempts to address the same audiences of "common" Southerners and disillusioned rural groups. Watson, Smith, Vardaman, and Kitchin, in combination with Debs and other socialists such as Allan Benson, socialist candidate for president in 1916; Victor Berger, the first socialist elected to Congress (from Milwaukee); Mary Harris "Mother" Jones; and others composed a group with remarkably similar rhetorical advocacy of antiwar, anti-interventionist ends, yet often within contradictory arguments vis-à-vis means. Taken together, this set of people might have been termed "Procrustean Bedfellows" by C. Vann Woodward."[43]

In his most scathing letter regarding Wilson and the South, Debs implied that from actions such as breaking up the women's March for Suffrage on inauguration day in Washington, D.C., in 1913, "we can see what the soldiers, sailors, and marines are really for." These troops were agents of repression, he said flatly. Linking the rights of women to the rights of workingmen, Debs rebuked Wilson for his relationship to elite, atavistic Southern supporters. "He has not dared to offend the Bourbon democracy of the South which [is] a century behind the times and still prates of 'chivalry' to women while it pampers frivolous parasites in 'high life' and exploits the marrow of their puny bones the children of the poor in their infernal cotton mills and other industrial slaves pens." After a group of police disrupted a rally for women's suffrage, Debs remarked in this letter that Wilson was a "Dixie-land" Democratic enabler of a party and a policy built upon a progressive facade with a bulwark of antiwoman, anti–African American, and antiworker sentiment. Debs went on to attack the real culprits, the "'nigger'-hating democratic (?) party of dixie-land [that] determines Wilson's anti-woman policy."[44]

His most pointed and consistent critiques, however, did not target women's rights, race, or the Democratic Party. Debs charged that the Wilson administration was a tool of the "Northeastern plutocracy" and their Southern and Midwestern commercial allies. Here, recalling populist rhetoric, Debs judged Wilson to be "without regard" for the nation's laborers, farmers, and common men. It was this latent populist protest against ruling elites and Big Capital that had the most appeal. Many applauded the essential Jeffersonian message, even in places and for persons where socialism was anathema and Debs's attack on conservative views of race and gender would be poorly received.[45]

Emphasizing this point of agreement should not obscure the ways in which racial tensions in the South accentuated Southern distinctiveness in virtually all political matters, which Debs clearly knew and which limited the abilities of socialists to organize across the Southern states. Quite a few of those in the South who corresponded with Debs, however, tended to ignore his liberal beliefs on race and gender—on which they differed—in favor of the more pressing political objectives they shared. Similarly, Tom Watson set aside much of his anti-Semitic and segregationist language during his battle against Selective Service. Thus, Debs found surprisingly fertile terrain in his efforts to "sweep the South" because of the convergence of selective political opportunism and an array of new and old populist, radical Democratic, and socialist antiwar arguments.

Against Preparedness and War

The development of opposition to preparedness and the war was in part a regional phenomenon located, of course, within the scope of national and international politics. A 1914 poll of national newspaper editors by the *Literary Digest* revealed the depth of Southern antiwar opinion. A higher

percentage of Southern editors preferred a course of strict American neutrality than those of any other section in the nation.[46] In the summer of
1914 Debs had railed against calls for American war preparedness. Calling
such a policy "a monstrous conspiracy . . . against the common people,"
he decried actions that might turn the nation into a military oligarchy.
Debs attacked military-financial elites—calling them "plutocrats" and
"greedy dogs, who can never have enough"—in a series of speeches to
farmers, coal miners, and railroad workers across the Texas panhandle
and Oklahoma.[47]

Writing to the *New York Sun* in 1915, Debs predicted the consequences
a policy of conscription and preparedness might incur for the working
class and the nation as a whole. "A large standing army, a powerful navy,
and a stupendous military armament such as President Wilson proposes,"
he wrote, "means a military autocracy and it can mean nothing else." He
continued in some of his strongest language, "If the American people acquiesce in such an obviously plutocratic program they themselves . . .
[will be] conscripted and fight and die to maintain plutocratic supremacy
in the United States."[48] Others, though, more unilateralist and pro-British
in orientation, strongly disagreed.

Just as Henry Cabot Lodge had advocated preparedness programs and
an expanded navy in the mid-1890s, so too did Lodge again urge preparedness as world war flared in the mid-1910s. Lodge's views provide a
lens on the preparedness mind-set that Debs so vigorously opposed. "The
first service which the United States can render to the cause of peace is to
preserve its own," Lodge asserted in 1917 when his thoughts on the matter
had been fully formed. By this, Lodge explained, he meant the guiding
policy of the United States should be "the most absolute and scrupulous
observance of every treaty we enter into; by the termination of all treaties
for arbitration, which we know well we should not under certain conditions and in time of stress regard, for no such war-breeding treaties ought
to cumber the ground." He continued, "Lastly, by the establishment of
such national defences, both by land and sea, as to insure our country, so
far as it can be done, from wanton attack."[49]

Lodge's prescription for the nation, in short, was an amalgam of previous expansionist, nationalist, and isolationist beliefs. He firmly believed, for
example, that the nation should present an official pronouncement that it
was U.S. policy to protect and oversee all shipping in the Panama Canal.[50]
As he built toward this position, in December 1914 Lodge's correspondence

with Roosevelt showed him to be increasingly despondent about Wilson's actions. Citing the president's inability to administer an appropriately vigorous course of action, Lodge wrote that he was disgusted with Wilsonian efforts at mediation and resistance to building up U.S. military strength. Roosevelt sadly agreed, saying, "I see that Wilson is against any investigation into our un-preparedness. Upon my word, Wilson and Bryan are the very worst men we have had in their positions."[51] Lodge was more measured, saying, "Yes, they are against our investigation with a view to showing the condition of national defenses . . . a very serious thing for the country. Wilson and Bryan go beyond anything we have ever had, and there are certain persons who I think were pretty inefficient in the past."[52]

Not long thereafter, discussing Wilson's actions to cut off loans to France, export submarines, and not respond to the violation of Belgian and Chinese neutrality, Lodge wrote to Roosevelt. He praised Roosevelt's description of Wilson's policies—as "furtive meddling"—and went on to describe all of the transgressions against American shipping and finance.[53] In August, Lodge argued that the United States should head a "league of neutrals."[54]

Lodge gave an illuminating speech at the common in Lynn, Massachusetts, for the city's Flag Day celebration on Sunday, June 14, 1915, which is characteristic of the ultranationalist perspective that Debs despised. Lodge said, "We *cannot* suffer American lives to be taken illegally and wantonly without seeking redress. . . . We cannot afford, as a nation, to allow the humblest citizen among us to suffer in any way by wrong or by injustice." He presented a new version of an older argument espoused in his days as an expansionist, regarding Beveridge's concern about whether the flag follows commerce or commerce follows the flag. Still, Lodge saw this as nationalism and no grounds for idealistic peacemaking or spreading of democracy. For Lodge, the flag symbolized American protection, which seemingly extended to all citizens, no matter where they went, even aboard belligerent vessels, as long as they were not involved directly as combatants or were not committing criminal acts. Lodge explained, "Wherever any American citizen goes lawfully and legally there the flag goes with him, and there it ever must go, for if the flag does not protect the citizen, the citizens in time to come will not protect the flag. We must protect the flag and in so doing protect each one of us."[55]

By the end of 1915, though, such views were still in the minority. Anti-British opinion among farmers and their representatives throughout the

South had reached a relatively high pitch, due to the negative consequences of the British naval blockade; some called for reciprocally harsh sanctions. In Texas, where the Socialist Party and Farmers Union achieved a substantial following, anti-British feeling flared significantly. This was echoed throughout other predominantly agricultural areas of the South. One of the few avowedly pro-British senators from the South, John Sharp Williams of Mississippi, noted the power of Southern Anglophobia in a letter to Wilson with the remark that "every politician in the South had to be anti-British."[56]

Inconsistent agricultural policies and the lack of wartime markets for cotton and wheat further fed the economic basis for anti-British sentiment. Debs and Southern Democrats who opposed preparedness programs also gained support because Wilson had seemed to neglect his agrarian and labor bases early in his first administration in favor of working on national progressive causes. The so-called cotton crisis in the summer of 1914, with plummeting prices and lack of federal intervention, called Wilson's position into question. Even in his initial address to Congress in 1913, Wilson alienated many of his supporters among Southern and Midwestern agrarian interests, saying, "The farmers, of course, ask and should be given no special privilege, such as extending to them the credit of the Government itself."[57]

While he vacillated on the question of whether farmers were not like other members of the "ordinary money market," Wilson did not see fit to endorse pro-farm, pro-cotton, or pro-tobacco credit. "Cotton" Tom Heflin of Alabama and other politicians with heavily rural and agrarian interests argued for emergency legislation once the European conflict began to close off markets and cut demand. Debs called for crop credits to protect small farmers and industrial labor. Anti-British beliefs often corresponded with anti-Northern and anticapitalist sentiments. Perceiving this, Wilson eventually capitulated to proponents of farm and crop credits when he signed the rural credits bill in January 1916, after he let it languish in Congress for almost two years without his endorsement.[58] Kitchin saw alliance on the credits bill as mere subterfuge to placate Southern and Midwestern farming interests. "I fear that the President is going to watch for the first opportunity to strike at Germany," he wrote privately.[59]

Debs ominously agreed with such predictions. He revised his famous remark, saying, "Years ago I declared that there was only one war in which I would enlist and that was the war of the workers of the world against the exploiters of the world." In dissecting the causes of war, he continued, "The working class had no interest in the wars declared and waged by the ruling classes."[60] In a 1916 essay in the *International Socialist Review*, which was reprinted in local socialist papers such as the *Rip-Saw*, Debs situated domestic events in an international context. He discussed the major mine strikes on the Mesabi range in Minnesota, for which Carlo Tresca and hundreds of other mine labor activists were later imprisoned. Contemplating these strikes, the true working-class meaning of Labor Day, and "the state of the class war and its outlook," somehow Debs remained cautiously optimistic in his writing.[61]

There was an undeniable isolationism in his arguments against American entry into the war and against policies of preparing for conflict. Debs again pressed his claim. He advocated that America stay aloof from the war for two reasons. First, the working classes were the cannon fodder for capitalist wars. Second, Debs still hoped to avoid the fractures brought on in Europe by the war and to proselytize, so that when they were ready, they could start the domestic revolt (by ballot or arms) that would lead to the socialist revolution. But finding better ways to organize the masses of untapped workers was essential to such a process. Debs therefore asserted that narrow union strategies and a focus on skilled, purely industrial or artisan labor were worthless in organizing for the coming domestic socialist revolution. Still, he perceived problems at the base. "The fatal tactics of craft unionism are in evidence in all preliminary stages of this struggle." How then to organize? Debs's response was unequivocal. "These unions in the past have had no connection and little or no sympathy with other unions and other workers. . . . The time for craft union aristocracy has gone by. The industrial union embracing all and fighting and winning for all is the demand and the lesson of the years." The land issue, though, seemed to divide Midwestern, Southwestern, and Southern socialists from the mainstream, and Debs struggled to unite these largely rural farmers and laborers with urban workers in concept and in practice.[62]

A shared basic belief in national, sectional, or class-based "opposition" to joining a European conflict connected many of these arguments. Advocating varied levels of their disinterest in the European conflict, those who resisted resolutions that might lead to war concurred that they had little incentive to participate in the conflict and that preparation represented a slippery slope to war regardless of national "interest." Like Debs, Kitchin in the House and Vardaman in the Senate argued for a traditional

American approach to foreign affairs. They all perceived preparedness as a route to war. Kitchin and Vardaman united to lead the opposition to the preparedness program within the Democratic Party, seeking some ties to former populists, but not socialists, to help them rally voters and other politicians to the cause.

Kitchin, a North Carolinian, and Vardaman, a Mississippian, represented a different "solid" South, which included M. Hoke Smith (Georgia), A. Jeff McLemore (Texas), Ben Tillman (South Carolina), and William Kirby (Arkansas), among others. In direct defiance of Wilson, Jeff McLemore attempted to chart a path clear of the war. He proposed a resolution to urge Americans to stay entirely out of the conflict by not taking passage on armed ships of belligerent nations. Indeed, these influential men could have steered to passage what came to be known as the McLemore Resolution if Wilson had not urged fellow Democrats in Congress to table it in early 1916. The appearance of a robust opposition from the generally party-oriented Southern Democrats toward one of their own, Wilson, and toward a largely Southern cabinet in full control for the first time since Reconstruction, indicated the true intensity of this disagreement.[63]

From the former slave states, Southern Democrats in the House voiced significant if ultimately inconsequential opposition to Wilson's initial drive for "armed neutrality." The vote on the first bill for a neutral preparedness policy was 108 to 24.[64] Meanwhile, Debs, slowed by sickness and headaches, continued to rail against a drive for armed neutrality, calling it contrary to the interest of the "common man." Farm communities and urban working-class neighborhoods displayed opposition to armed neutrality in early 1917. Wilson quickly recognized the problem this posed and asked Congress for the initial funding necessary for Samuel Gompers to attempt to sway the working-class and rural opinion on the subject by forming the prowar Alliance for Labor and Democracy. Despite the effort, on a tour of the upper Midwest, Debs related to Frank O'Hare how united his rural and urban constituents had become. "Farmers and their families have come from a hundred miles around" to attend his antiwar speech.[65]

This degree of formal opposition from Southern politicians, nearly one-quarter in Congress voting against an armed neutrality statement, continued to demonstrate the depth of opposition to *any* intervention in the European war.[66] As time passed and military action became increasingly likely, many politicians who at first did not agree eventually were persuaded to sign on to preparedness measures or the war resolution itself.

Nonetheless, visible Southern resistance, like that of the Midwest, came from many directions. Some of this popular sentiment forced its way upward from farmers and laborers in powerful moments of opposition, and some of it issued forth from a group of vocal, well-respected members of Congress. As war policy became defined, clear opposition continued to spread on the ground.[67]

When the issue of the war resolution was close to coming before the Senate, a small group of Massachusetts pacifists arrived in Washington, D.C., and made front-page headlines around the country. The pacifists stormed into Lodge's office at the Capitol in the late morning of April 2, demanding that he vote against joining the European war. Three of the group's leaders, Alexander Bannwart, Reverend Harris Drake, pastor of Christ Church in Dorchester, Massachusetts, and Anna May Peabody, presented Lodge with their calling cards in the corridor beyond his office. According to several press accounts, they asked if he would approve a war resolution, and when he replied yes, the pacifist group "remonstrated him on his position and declared that war was cowardly." The situation escalated quickly. Reportedly Lodge retorted, "National degeneracy and cowardice are worse than war," adding "I regret that I cannot agree with your position, but I must do my duty as I see it."[68]

This statement inflamed Bannwart, apparently a man of a "powerful build," who threatened Lodge and called him a coward. Incensed, the senator turned his back on Bannwart, saying, "If you say I am a coward you are a liar." According to Lodge's official statement at the time, Bannwart then replied angrily, "You are a damn liar," to which an infuriated Lodge responded, "No, you are a liar."[69]

Some pushing ensued. The irate Bannwart then reportedly punched Lodge in the face. According to the *Boston Evening Transcript*, a surprising event followed. The lanky, "ninety pound," sixty-seven-year-old Lodge then punched the younger, stocky man, causing blood to spill from Bannwart's nose, and knocking him to the ground. The group of pacifists closed in, but Lodge was able to escape with the help of aides and passersby. Bannwart was subsequently charged with assault.[70]

That night and the next morning headlines around the country blared "Weighs Only 90 Pounds—But Oh My!" "Senator Lodge Fells Pacifist Who Called Him Liar and Coward," "Senator Lodge's Well-Aimed Blow," and "Pacifists Pushed Aside."[71]

This interlude may have garnered a modicum of sympathy and support for the pro-British, prowar Lodge, but the correspondence of Claude Kitchin demonstrates the wide array of constituents who agreed with his impassioned speech on the floor of the House preceding his vote against the war resolution on April 6, 1917. Even into April 1917, many Americans still could not see why the nation should break with the policy of nonentanglement to join a foreign war. Lodge, Roosevelt, and even Wilson's pro-British stance were widely powerful and had swayed many citizens, but the view was not yet in full ascendance. The mayor of Winston-Salem, North Carolina, for example, wrote to Kitchin that the no vote to the war resolution was "the greatest act of your life"; a clergyman echoed these sentiments, lamenting, "Would that we had more like you."[72] The president of Concordia College (Conover, North Carolina) said that Kitchin had given a "great address" that would "stand in history."[73] Even such a small sample shows how Kitchin's support originated from various professions and was not limited to the North Carolina rural citizens who later became the majority of draft resisters in his state.[74]

Ideological connections, however, do not necessarily make for allies. Many dissenters, such as those of the non-socialist-affiliated farmers' alliances in the South, and in addition sympathetic politicians Robert La Follette in Wisconsin, Tillman in South Carolina, and Watson in Georgia, did not agree with Debs's opposition to war as an extension of his logic of a socialist revolution. Kitchin and Vardaman, of course, did not approve of democratic socialism either. Yet an essential continuity undergirded the logic of those who opposed the war. Debs's analysis of the Spanish-American War, American involvement in the Philippines, as well as the European conflict—all demonstrated this shared perception. The underlying cause of violent conflict between nations and within nations, they all agreed, derived most directly from the unrestrained influence of commercial conquest, broadly defined.[75]

Most opponents of World War I across the nation did not consider such abstract concepts in great detail. They were not intellectuals, politicians, or radicals. Most opponents of the war were farmers. From their perspective, commercial profiteers, especially above the Mason-Dixon Line, had the most to gain in the war. The notion that farmers were being abused by both major parties and exploited by business was not new. In the Gilded Age, widespread resentment gave rise to the Grange, Agricultural Wheel, farmers' alliances, and a host of similar organizations.[76] This was the historical-ideological milieu out of which many Southern Democrats sprang, most notably Watson and Kitchin, who frequently asserted that financial interests above the Mason-Dixon Line were pressing for commercial advantage in the European war at the expense of the Southern farmer.[77]

To this long-standing populist critique of big business Debs added socialist language. Writing to Debs from Salt Lake City, Murray King, a leader of the Farmer-Labor Party after World War I in Minnesota, remarked, "We are praying, as only free thinking Socialists can pray, for your election to congress [sic], because we recognize in you the typical voice of the toiler."[78] Debs mirrored these populist sentiments of the toiler of land and machine. "No war," he asserted, "was ever caused by the working class but always and everywhere by the exploiting class. But the exploiting class never fights."[79]

One of the most forceful of the farmers' advocates, Hugh Q. Alexander, president of the North Carolina Farmers Union, demonstrated many of these same Debsian anticapitalist strains. "We are driven to war," he argued, "by the munitions mongers, the bankers, speculators, the jingo press and the devil, and all for their profit, while all that is expected of the farmers is that they furnish the men to the fighting and then bear the great bulk of the war taxes."[80] Like Alexander, Debs appealed to the "common man" when he deployed remarkably similar phrasing later in his legendary address at Canton, Ohio, in 1918. In that speech Debs propounded an extreme version of Jamesian anti-"bigness." He blasted the "Junkers" and "barons of Wall Street," who as prowar patriots supported the conflict and conscription, while the "working class make the supreme sacrifices."[81]

In the Matrix of Antiwar Radicals

Within a day of the passage of the war resolution, the SPA held a national emergency convention in St. Louis on April 7, 1917, and declared that Wilson's resolution was "a crime against the people of the United States." In the Midwest, the Akron *Beacon-Journal* remarked that the country had "never embarked on a more unpopular war."[82] Resistance quickly spread to farmers and workingmen in the region. The conservative *Beacon-Journal* went on to assert that there was "scarcely a political observer . . . but what will admit that were an election to come now a mighty tide of socialism would inundate the Middle West."[83] In rural parts of the region, as in the South, war opposition tended to spread upward from a grassroots level.

On the ground, opposition was generally more active and less discursive. Remaining out of foreign wars, the oldest of isolationist ideas was clearly at work, although as labor historian David Montgomery argues, it is hard to find evidence of such matters because of the poor written record of the many average laboring Americans. Thus, it is difficult to ascertain the exact rationale behind the actions of most individual workers, particularly in industrial labor. Still, Montgomery has shown that workers' day-to-day conduct neither conformed to American Patriotic League (APL) expectations nor displayed fierce dissent in the face of wartime oversight, patriotic furor, and propaganda.[84] The possibility of energizing a united labor community propelled Debs and was echoed by the SPA's efforts to assemble a powerful farm-labor, urban-rural alliance and promote a "campaign of education among the workers to organize them in strong, class-conscious, and closely unified political and industrial organizations."[85]

Yet the Socialist Party was embroiled in furious debates. The March 1917 minutes of the national committee record that Southern delegates were evenly split on whether to call, or delay, an emergency convention in 1917 on the issue of American entry into the war. Many like G. J. Braun of Tennessee argued, "Before convention will be called, all indications point that we will already be at war, and as American socialists are hopelessly divided, running from one extreme to the other, from non-resistance to jingoism, I believe that party unity can best be served by delaying convention."[86]

Throughout the South a widespread rural-progressive opposition appeared predominantly in areas where the Farmers Union was strong.[87] Protests to federal encroachment—through conscription and additional excise taxes—flared into vocal dissent, and active and violent opposition, as well as passive draft-dodging across the nation. Just after the Selective Service Act took effect in 1917, Senator Thomas Hardwick of Georgia wrote that there was "undoubtedly general and widespread opposition on the part of many thousands" to the draft in his state. He went on to note that "numerous and largely attended mass meetings held in every part of the State protested against it."[88]

This pattern, echoed throughout the nation, is well represented by the events of the Green Corn Rebellion in Oklahoma. In July and August

1917, the rebellion began in the south-central part of the state when more than four hundred debt-ridden sharecroppers and tenant farmers, some of whom were members of radical movements such as the Working Class Union and the socialist "Jones Family," many of whom were of Creek, Seminole, or African American ancestry, banded together against local and state power in defiance of the new federal conscription law. They cut telephone and telegraph lines, knocked down water towers, and attempted to burn bridges to isolate themselves and destroy symbols of capitalist and state power. The Green Corn rebels, so named because of a Creek harvest festival of the ripening of the corn, intended to march to Washington, eating green corn along the way, and join forces with like-minded farmers and workers to ultimately overthrow the government, prevent the war, and reform the domestic economy to "restore to the working classes the full product of their labor."[89] Within a short time the well-armed forces of the local APL and state marshals crushed the rebellion and jailed its leaders. The swiftness of their defeat meant that many of the Green Corn rebels never even left the central farm on which they began organizing. Some scholars argue that the efforts of the Green Corn rebels were less the deeds of an armed insurrection and more the actions of an aggressive political protest akin to the march of Coxey's army on Washington in 1894.[90] Nonetheless, like Coxey's army, the Green Corn rebels were cast by the mainstream press as symbolic of the dangers of rural political (especially socialist) activism. Media coverage of these events was sensational and stoked the fires of fear of an insurrection of the unemployed.[91]

A similar outcome befell the Farmer's and Laborer's Protective Association (FLPA) in Texas, a multiracial anti-draft, working-class organization. When some members of the FLPA attempted to purchase weapons for self-protection against federal power and draft enforcement, local authorities were tipped off by federal agents within the group. The agents moved in and raided the association's meetinghouse as well as the homes of the majority of its members. The policing efforts culminated in more than fifty arrests and the evisceration of the FLPA movement. Despite a lack of solid evidence to convict or even produce indictments for many of the members, these well-publicized actions served to undermine efforts to organize working-class (particularly multiracial) opposition to the war across Texas.[92]

Socialists were far from alone in their efforts to oppose the war nationally, but they were the most prominent group to do so, and became the target of the greatest number of attacks, many of which were violent. Collaboration between socialists and pacifist organizations continued to occur, at least in high-profile settings, during the middle months of 1917. In Chicago a quiet gathering of three thousand pacifists came together to hear Congressman William Mason and at least six prominent socialists speak. The group concluded the peace rally with a series of demands based on a shared socialist position to end the war: "No Annexations, No Indemnities."[93] Similar gatherings caused greater concern. At a parade in Boston on July 1, 1917, depending on which account is more credible, between eight thousand and thirty thousand socialists, trade unionists, labor activists, and their allies marched. They carried anti-annexation signs and placards and flags demanding peace. Accounts of the protest differ, but clearly some soldiers and sailors confronted the protestors. There were reports of widespread fighting, including several deaths, and the Socialist Party headquarters for Massachusetts was ransacked and burned, apparently while police stood by watching.[94] Scores of other such examples from cities both large and small flared up during the summer of 1917. As socialist Max Eastman, editor of the *Masses*, remarked about such outbursts, "In nations as well as individuals, hysteria is caused by inner conflict." As he noted those who opposed the drift into hysterical conflict, Eastman did a good job of cataloguing the diverse antiwar community. "We had the whole Socialist Party and the IWW with us, the pacifists, many of the humanitarian uplifters, most of the Quakers and deep-feeling Christian ministers, the Irish, the 'hyphenated-Americans,' the old-fashioned patriots faithful to George Washington's Farewell Address, and millions of plain folks."[95] Hardly a cohesive group, nonetheless they shared many convictions.

Across the Midwest antiwar socialists found the most overt allies from other causes, such as progressives in the settlement house movement, from populists opposing an arbitrary draft, and from other pacifist organizations. In Minneapolis, Mayor Thomas Van Lear vigorously denounced conscription policies and derided the "wall street interests" that had brought the nation into the war. He toured the state, speaking to 7,500 farmers at one rally alone at the small college of New Ulm.[96]

After the Selective Service Administration was created in May 1917 and took bureaucratic shape over the next several months, county-level draft board reports in the South demonstrate widespread draft resistance. Historian Jeanette Keith's intensive research in Selective Service files reveals that from a total of 557 rural county draft boards in the South, 214 counties (38.4 percent) stated that leaders of their communities tried to institutionalize practices of resistance and "encouraged young men to file for exemptions from service."[97] Class, regional, and federal jurisdiction collided on this issue of exemption status, as Debs had predicted. The provost marshal general's rules corralled an inordinate percentage of Southern married sharecroppers, rural day laborers, and small farmers into the ranks of those who were not exempt on the grounds that they *could* support their families with the $30 monthly army salary. The lower the earnings, the higher the probability of being a soldier—a formula for catalyzing political resistance.[98]

Despite Wilson's assurances that farmers would receive exemptions, this did not tend to happen in the poorer regions of the South and Midwest, thereby exacerbating political resistance and draft-dodging.[99] The Green Corn rebels provide one high-profile example of collective opposition, but individual draft evasion was far more common, and often far more effective. Federal statistics on prosecutions for avoiding the draft are useful for documenting the effects of this policy in relation to regional dissent patterns. In Georgia "men were prosecuted under the draft laws at a rate of 0.146 per thousand" eligible draftees, while in North Carolina the rate was 0.073. Keith's comparative analysis of this data showed that Georgia's rate was significantly elevated over states such as Iowa (0.054) or Indiana (0.044), although it was less than New York, where draft resistance and vigorous prosecution by attorneys general were also particularly high (0.256).[100] In the first six weeks after the patriotic call for one million troops went out, a mere seventy-five thousand volunteered.[101] "Many Southern white men in both [the Civil and First World] wars," observed historian Jacqueline Jones, "saw the defense of their own communities as the only cause worth fighting for. They resented the order to leave their homes and fight elsewhere—for New Orleans planters in 1862 or Belgians and French in 1917."[102]

In an editorial on March 11, 1917, the *Greensboro Daily News* discussed conscription and asserted that wealth and corporations were the overriding impetus for war, not the great "silent" masses. "The masses of people of this section," the paper continued, "have little desire to take a hand in Europe's slaughter and confusion."[103] Such sentiments did not change after conscription began. They became more fervent across the Carolinas. After the war resolution passed, the *Farmer's Tribune*, a South Carolina agricultural journal that frequently praised the politics of "Pitchfork" Ben Tillman and the antiwar stance of North Carolina neighbor Claude Kitchin, rhetorically asked, "Why should we fight England's war?" The *Tribune* reminded its readers of the British actions against their crops in 1914–1915, asking again, "What about our cotton?"[104] Former populist Tom Watson echoed this argument in language almost identical to that of Debs, placing antidemocratic actions and the unconstitutional nature of conscription as his two central issues. Watson scheduled several major anti-draft rallies, including one large gathering in Macon, which was called off under threat of violence. He also appealed to fellow Georgians and Southerners in general to challenge the constitutionality of Selective Service and reportedly collected $100,000 for a campaign on this issue.[105] In contrast to the perception of ardent militarism in the South, significant and pervasive draft resistance was evident particularly among poor, generally rural men in the South and in the same demographic configuration across the nation.

A similar pattern emerges in the words and votes of Southern-state delegates to the national meetings of the Socialist Party. Southerners opposed the war in surprising numbers. At the party's St. Louis convention of 1917, two hundred total delegates, allocated on a representative basis according to 1916 membership rolls, included one each from Alabama, Georgia, the District of Columbia, Mississippi, Virginia, South Carolina, North Carolina, and Louisiana; two each from Florida, Arkansas, and Tennessee; four from Texas; and a host from the Southwest and southern Midwest, including eighteen from Oklahoma (second only to nineteen from New York). All of these members signed the antiwar proclamation, and many, such as those from Tennessee, Georgia, and Virginia, affirmed a critical minority report, which further condemned the war and conscription, while seeking nationalization of vacant land and all utilities.[106]

Many of the rural Americans who had been exposed to these ideas by socialists, populists, and progressive labor activists before the war apparently were persuaded to view the war in Europe in class terms. As Keith concluded, "Far from being ignorant, many rural Southerners exhibited a sophisticated understanding of events and motives. . . . These were people who took their politics seriously."[107] And they did. In the nation as a whole, as well as in the South, the best estimates indicate that more than 330,000 men directly evaded the draft as "deserters" by not responding to induction.[108] This point supports anecdotal evidence of local draft resistance, particularly in the rural South, and demonstrates this remarkable but largely unrecognized opposition. In North Carolina, for instance, the rate of those evading the draft or deserting after induction was 6.5 percent. This figure does not measure those who eluded registration rolls entirely during three successive registration roll calls.[109]

At the national level, John Chambers ascertained from Provost Marshall General Enoch Crowder's reports and working estimates that between 2.4 million and 3.6 million men may have avoided either the draft or registration outright. Incredibly, the number of evaders is roughly the same as the total number of troops mustered for the war. Further, most of these deserters were never pursued and prosecuted.[110] Judging from Selective Service Administration internal reports and arrests, according to Chambers, "dodgers" tended to be "poorer men: agricultural or industrial laborers, isolated and alienated from the large society or the national war effort because of geographical location or their economic, ethnic, or racial status."[111] The numbers bear out this conclusion. From the first six thousand arrests for failure to register in the summer of 1917, most were in the Appalachian Mountain regions of Virginia, the Carolinas, and Mississippi; in the rural areas of Oklahoma, Texas, Louisiana, Missouri, and southern Illinois; as well as in farming, timber, and mining sections of Minnesota and Colorado.[112]

Toward a Class War?

While it is difficult to quantify the exact numbers of dissenters in the South, the resistance of deserters was violent enough to force large-scale federal military action. Armed bands of white deserters were reported throughout a number of remote locations in the South, and these groups eventually became unmanageable. Dangerous activities of deserters reached a pinnacle by the end of 1918, when the governors of Georgia, Mississippi, and Tennessee were actually forced to request federal troops to find and disarm bands of deserters. The National Guard was called out in Arkansas to put down rural draft resisters who were attacking law enforcement officers when they came to induct or arrest the draft evaders. While Debs was not likely to have been aware of all of these events, the heightening violence in wartime America prompted him to forecast the imminence of class war.[113]

New patriotic leagues and organizers found myriad outlets for enforcing conformity through violence from the summer of 1917 through 1921, sparking a period of intense race and labor conflict. On June 9, 1917, Justice Department officials seized Lawrence Pearson, a socialist organizer from Roanoke, Virginia, for seditious distribution of the socialist tract "A Rich Man's War and a Poor Man's Fight."[114]

Nowhere did this rich-poor discrimination apply more than in cases of repression of dissenting agrarians and the poor, particularly African Americans. Federal conscription policies were often enacted by state and local concerns. This effort was accompanied by the migration of close to a half million African Americans from rural and Southern areas into Northern and Western cities, mostly seeking industrial work. Not just socialists like Debs and Kate Richards O'Hare, but laborers accused of working with the IWW, and minority groups and religious groups (from African American migrants to members of the peace churches, such as the Quakers) felt the harsh reprisals of patriotic organizations such as the National Security League and what became a vigilante wing of the Justice Department, the APL. The crescendo of repressive actions culminated in 1917 when the first wartime race riots broke out in East St. Louis, Illinois. Nine whites and at least thirty-nine African Americans were killed.[115] At this beginning of significant race and labor strife, Debs was so ill with severe pain and depressed by the events swirling around him that he could "barely . . . stand on [his] feet."[116] This hyperpatriotic repression and labor conflict only heightened after the easing of wartime strictures on industrial production with the coming of the Red Scare in 1919. These events served to confirm Debs's increasingly grim outlook on the ways in which the war was likely to stifle American socialist and radical politics.

Higher in the social stratum, and especially on the left, Debs found less support. Mobilization and conscription after the formal declaration of war, of course, changed the calculus for many liberal dissenters, socialists, and outright pacifists. Most liberal pacifists responded to pragmatic arguments for war. As we have seen, John Dewey, Herbert Croly, and Walter Weyl—the progressive hierarchy of the New Republic—argued that once war had been declared it was pointless to resist. The pragmatic thing to do, they believed, was to participate in rapidly ending the war and to await the "plastic juncture" when correction through progressive-minded reform might be made during the peace process.[117] Similarly, in the midst of a rising tide of wartime patriotism from 1915 to early 1917, and after a series of debates over inserting an antiwar "disarmament and world peace" manifesto into the proceedings of the Socialist Party, a significant number of SPA members who were friends with Debs, such as William English Walling, Charles Edward Russell, Algie M. Simons, and J. Phelps Stokes, publicly resigned from the party to support the war effort.[118]

The acceptance of the war affected another group as well. From 1914 until the United States became a belligerent in 1917, many in the religious community, particularly missionaries, were aghast at the horrors of the war and actively supported peaceful mediation to end the conflict rapidly. One of the most powerful of the organizations designed to seek these ends was the Church Peace Union. John Mott was a trustee of the union, and he played a prominent role in trying to find compromises in the disputes that divided the group. He had just arrived back home after his first trip to the war zones in the late fall of 1914 when the union split, and he was asked to become president of the newly formed American League to Limit Armaments, a precursor of the antipreparedness movement. Mott refused the offer.[119] His assessment of the great opportunity that the period after the war would likely bring sounded a lot like progressives who sided with Wilson, making the "plastic juncture" bargain (though Mott envisioned a postwar evangelization of the world).

By 1916, many of the Church Peace Union trustees, Mott included, found the union becoming "political" in opposing preparedness during the presidential campaign, and he took a much less active role thereafter. His position, in fact, was quite the opposite. He supported Wilson, and once the United States had entered the conflict, Mott took a series of charitable management positions, working closely with the administration as a leader of the National War Work Council of the YMCA.

Mott called for victory, but in his public statements he was careful to not make any critical remarks about any of the belligerent nations. As Mott's biographer C. Howard Hopkins noted about his deliberate neutrality in 1917 through 1918, "One is conscious of the tension between the American and the internationalist in him."[120] His was a conflicted refusal to take sides. While Mott formally prepared to have the YMCA and his missionaries work with the League of Nations in the postwar period, there is no evidence that he supported the League concept or treaty itself; and despite his support for Wilson, it does not seem that Mott ever lobbied on the fractious issue of congressional ratification and American entry into the League (or the World Court).

He served as general secretary of the United War Work Council, which primarily helped provide services to military personnel. His charitable interests went beyond this task and so he hoped to expand the effort by bringing together a host of American and international nonprofit groups for an expansive relief mission. The culmination of this vision was the November 1918 United War Work Campaign, led by Mott, initiated by Harry Fosdick of the Rockefeller Foundation (at the request of President Wilson), and spearheaded by Secretary of War Newton D. Baker. Mott's YMCA centralized and conducted the major fund-raising campaign along with six other welfare organizations: the YWCA, the Jewish Welfare Board, the Knights of Columbus, the Salvation Army, the American Library Association, and War Camp Community Service. The effort resulted in an astonishing $200 million in donations to aid prisoners of war and American troops abroad and to minimize civilian suffering where possible.[121]

Under Mott's able leadership this American-led international charitable movement gained such momentum that it continued well past the armistice. When the war ended on November 11, 1918—the day the drive was scheduled to open—Mott immediately redirected the purpose of the campaign to peace readjustment. In a famous telegram, he instructed all campaign workers to continue as if nothing significant had altered their mission of relief and service "to prevent period of demobilization becoming period of demoralization." For his tireless efforts in organizing wartime philanthropy, Mott received the Army Distinguished Service Medal in 1919.[122]

Like Mott, many Southern politicians sought at least compromise or appeasement with the Wilson administration. In areas of greater evangelical faith, particularly across the South, too, local politicians reluctantly came out in favor of entering the war to achieve reelection or to try to create meaningful change after the war ended. Others, however, stuck to their oppositional guns. James Vardaman, who was targeted for removal from the Senate by Woodrow Wilson, and Claude Kitchin remained largely true to their antiwar convictions, even campaigning on their own "loyalty," as evidenced by their vehement protests against conscription and war. Yet the two men met different fates at the polls. Vardaman lost in the primaries of his reelection campaign in Mississippi in 1918, in a well-engineered campaign by Pat Harrison, who was supported and funded in part by John Sharp Williams and the Wilson administration. Claude Kitchin, in contrast, was reelected with large pluralities of the vote in his next three campaigns in North Carolina. While it has not been shown definitively that their views against the war determined these contrasting election results, it is probable that Kitchin's more rural constituents supported him because they continued to oppose the war and conscription.

Vardaman, on the other hand, who was hailed with cries of "Kaiser von Vardaman" at many rallies in Mississippi, had an uphill battle to fight and is rightly portrayed as having lost his seat in the Senate because his antiwar and pro-labor views were not shared by a majority of Mississippians. Interestingly, the polarizing Tom Watson decided to run for Congress in Georgia in 1918 and attained surprisingly good results despite losing. A number of other Southern congressmen who opposed Wilson's war policies in some form were reelected. John Burnet, who defended Claude Kitchin's opposition to the war, was reelected in Alabama. So was George Huddleston of Alabama, who Woodrow Wilson exclaimed is "in every way an opponent of the Administration."[123] Mississippi's Thomas Sisson, who had fought the conscription act, was also reelected, along with other opponents of Wilson or war.

By May 1918, Debs issued a statement calling for a new convention to revise the planks of the 1917 St. Louis platform, given ongoing American participation in the war. Some in the non-socialist press, such as the *New York Daily News*, took this to mean that Debs had gone over to the prowar socialist side. This was hardly the case. Debs immediately responded with a heated denunciation of the capitalist war. Voters on the ground echoed his sentiment, at least in major cities in the Midwest and the Northeast. In Buffalo the socialist vote climbed from 2.6 percent to 30.2 percent. In Chicago the vote in 1915 polled 3.6 percent and only two years later the Socialist Party polled an astonishing 34.7 percent.[124] No such startling polling results occurred in the South, where socialist candidates had a difficult time simply getting onto the ballot, yet overall these municipal election results surprised many, including some subsequent scholars.[125]

In the municipal elections during 1917—under the heightened tensions of aggressive nationalism, former progressive journalist George Creel's Committee on Public Information advanced the public relations propaganda machine, and the intensifying range of the APL—the Socialist Party made major gains. While Debs did not run for office in 1918, in the New York mayoral campaign he endorsed Morris Hillquit, the socialist candidate. Hillquit received a remarkable 22 percent of the vote (five times the registered socialist vote in the city). Overall, ten socialists were elected to the New York State legislature.[126]

Such events were unremarkable to Debs's correspondents, even in the South. Although the socialist vote in Dixie was depressed by Democratic efforts for two-party ballots and other measures, Debs remarked that there were signs of positive change and yet still much to do. In a letter he noted the ongoing legal challenges that he and others faced. "But I must be frank enough to say in this connection that I have no time for bickering, unraveling misunderstandings or settling of personal differences between comrades." He went on to detail a number of transgressions and priorities. One example, from the South, stood out to Debs. He noted, "There are still in jail and under indictment hundreds of our comrades unable to furnish the exorbitant bail bonds demanded. . . . Among the heaps of unanswered letters on my desk is one from a young woman comrade, a school teacher, tubercular, who has been in a filthy Texas jail for months, for weeks held incommunicado, saw no living person but the white-livered brute that threw a hunk of sour breads, a dish of tainted beans and a little water, with a ten year sentence upon her head, as noble a soul as ever lived in this world." Rising to a characteristic crescendo, Debs declared, "To these comrades we owe everything."[127]

Months later Debs tried to find "every atom of strength" to help his comrades. Again, he received a letter, this time from Dallas, Texas. Covington Hall was writing with optimism. With the end of the war a movement toward socialism and freedom for Debs seemed in sight to Hall. He noted that a number of his state senators were sympathetic to him, his socialist ideas, and his cause to free Debs. He told Debs of his many attempts to get him released from prison and, interestingly, singled out that Tom Watson was a strong advocate of clemency. Further, Hall noted—à la the best-selling author of *Looking Backward*, socialist Edward Bellamy—that capitalism, therefore, must be in its final days given the violent ongoing repression of socialists that could "only" serve to stir up the revolution. Hall went on to cite recent election results and boldly declared that Debs's "imprisonment has done more than all else combined to destroy the Democratic party."[128]

Unfortunately for Debs, Hall and clemency advocates like Watson were wrong. Debs's antiwar ideology and position as a figurehead for radical politics, as Murray Kaufman astutely discerned, led during 1917–1918 in the other direction. "A dual image of Debs began to emerge in the media: to the majority of newspapers and magazines, Debs became a 'traitor'; to those few publications in opposition to the war, Debs became a heroic giant."[129] Even in his hometown of Terre Haute, Debs was shunned by many of his neighbors late in 1917, while a year before the local newspapers had reported that he was a beloved citizen even to those not sharing his beliefs.[130]

Government legitimation of prowar orthodox points of view came first and most powerfully in the form of the Espionage Act passed on June 15, 1917, which provided harsh penalties for any person who willfully attempted to obstruct the war effort or induced others to do so. As legal scholar Geoffrey Stone has argued, "Wilson understood that, if allowed to fester, antiwar dissent could undermine morale and make it more difficult for the nation to prosecute the war successfully."[131] Wilson explained that the Espionage Act was needed because there would always be those elements in society who "cannot be relied upon and whose interest or desires will lead to actions on their part highly dangerous to the Nation in the midst of war."[132] These provisions were later reinforced by the sweeping Sedition Act of 1918, which itself was eventually repealed by Congress in 1920. Debs proclaimed that these acts were antithetical to the natural rights of citizens in the United States.[133]

Indeed, as the lead attorney for the American Union Against Militarism accurately observed, "Any Post Office official, under this [Espionage Act censorship] provision, may forbid the use of the mails to any matter that he deems nonmailable. Before the question of the mailability of the matter can be determined by the courts the work desired will be done and [the] publisher ruined."[134] While such capricious censorship meant the virtual end of the radical press as 1917 drew to a close, Debs continued his antiwar campaign across the nation despite the ongoing war on socialists that gutted the already fragmenting SPA. In late 1917 the organization's main paper, the *Appeal to Reason,* changed editors, from antiwar Fred Warren to prowar Louis Kopelin. The paper then officially sided with Wilson. Utilizing the postmaster general's powers, the government suppressed Tom Hickey's *Rebel* in 1917 under the Espionage Act. In 1918, under increasing pressure from patriotic groups, the Non-Partisan League fired Hickey as an organizer explicitly because of his outspoken radical socialist calls for revolution.[135]

Additional assaults on antiwar, anticonscription populists like Watson, whose rallies were thwarted by violence (Watson was dubbed "pro-German" by much of the national press), further undermined what might have been a more cohesive community of dissent, at least one minimally defined by opposition to the war and to the excesses of big business. Given their similar arguments against the draft, the war, and the capitalist wealth structure that each made, the fact that Watson and Debs do not appear to have corresponded during this period—or noted each other's plight—provides an insight. Both in ideology and in practical politics, radical Southerners could never embrace a socialist with the liberal social beliefs that Debs held.[136] This peculiarity provides a new lens with which to view the intersection of dissent ideologies and the possibilities for political alliance in the South. Antiwar arguments tended to be aimed toward constituents on the ground, or directed at the Wilson administration and the halls of Congress. There was surprisingly little "horizontal" ideological contact. Because segregationism and socialism were often diametrically opposed, Debs, Watson, Kitchin, and others bypassed virtually all of those outside of their own narrowly defined political perspectives. Particularly on issues of race, but also on issues of practical policy, they could not find a middle ground that held the potential for creating a more unified community of dissent.

Virtually all antiwar thinkers also agreed upon anti–big business sentiments, as well as many arguments for regulation of capitalism. In this vein, Watson, Kitchin, and Covington Hall could all nod in approval when Debs asserted that the Supreme Court sought to "continue to grind the flesh and blood and bones of puny little children into profits for the Junkers of Wall Street."[137] In much the same way, socialist-type critiques of capitalism, often termed "populist" by Southerners suspicious of socialism itself, were central to Watson's editorials on economics. In an analogous assessment, Watson argued that the barons of Wall Street were coercing "our boys" to fight a war not in the national interest. Historian C. Vann Woodward rightly noted that in this editorial Watson again omitted much of his racist and anti-Semitic language in order to fashion a more appealing critique of the draft policy and the war.[138] Suppression of opponents of the war proved Debs and Watson's point: commercial and special interests had overwhelmed the basic rights of Americans.

The relationship between these politics of opposition expressed by national figures and those on the ground across the nation can be observed in terms of induction statistics. By the fall of 1918 the Selective Service System reported that more than ninety-five thousand men had "deserted" in the Southern states alone. This number was likely skewed upward; however, it reveals that more reports of African American desertions were made than those for whites, and that the numbers of those not showing up for induction were quite high overall. At the state and local level this played out in surprising ways. Writing about the conditions of resistance to the draft in North Carolina, the APL leader in Lexington, R. D. Lusk, reported that "owing to the peculiar reaction of the mountaineer's philosophy to the draft laws, many of them 'stepped back' in the 'brush' to await the war's end." Claiming their reasons for desertion stemmed from apolitical ignorance, "isolated from inhabited centers," Lusk and Governor Thomas Bickett preferred to appeal to these recalcitrant men rather than to use force to track them down. When Bickett arrived to visit Jefferson, North Carolina, on June 30, 1918, newspaper reporter C. M. Waynick wrote that the Ashe County boys argued, "This is a Wilsonian war and waged to make the world safe for the Democratic party."[139]

Debs built on just these trends and sensibilities from the spring through the summer of 1918, knowing full well that he might incur the wrath of an increasingly repressive and punitive federal government. A sixty-three-year-old man with an increasingly weak immune system, prone to colds and exhaustion, Debs was still convalescing from another bout of being bedridden with what was likely a case of influenza early in 1918. Nonetheless, with many of his comrades jailed, indicted, and censored, and with much of the mainstream press representing his beliefs as "antipatriotic," Debs's letters reveal that he felt honor bound to remain in the political fray with all the vigor he could muster. He called for fair, impartial trials for all those facing sedition charges. Decrying the treatment of strikebreakers "in the cases of the union miners in West Virginia and the Southwestern states," Debs argued, "the war within the war and beyond the war in which I.W.W. is fighting—the war of the workers of all countries against the exploiters of all countries—is our war, the war of humanity against its oppressors and despoilers, the holiest war ever waged since the race began."[140]

Taking up this "war within and beyond the war" concept in February 1918, Debs shaped a new socialist antiwar argument. He planned a series of talks and speeches for June, once he was fully recovered from various depleting colds and debilitating pains in his joints. These were to be his opening salvos in an assault against the ongoing war, the oppressors of the working class, and toward a socialist revolution. His speeches over the next few months—most notably in Canton, Ohio, on June 16, 1918—in Indiana, Illinois, and neighboring states were a symbolic culmination of these aims. At the time, though, he had no idea the "war against war" motif would result in his indictment. Debs repeatedly highlighted the most overt injustices, such as the imprisonment of thousands of conscientious objectors and those who expressed reservations about the war or draft. On this subject Debs sounded more like a combination of Martin Luther and Thomas Jefferson than Karl Marx. He emphasized to his audience at Canton not to worry about treason against "masters," but to avoid treason against one's own core principles, to prevent at all costs any "trespassing" against the rights upon which the American tradition rests.[141]

With fewer sympathetic newspapers and journals to publish his writing, all heavily censored, Debs had many pressing concerns while out on bail in 1918 for his antiwar activism. He frantically tried to cobble together paid speaking engagements and articles to make enough money to support himself and his brother Theodore, and to keep their socialist offices in Indiana open. In parts of the Southwestern states where populism and socialism had held a strong appeal since the 1890s, the coercive power of wartime federal, state, and private patriotism severely undermined the ability of radicals to organize, gather, speak, or even send literature in the mail.

Put on trial for his beliefs, not only did Debs admit to his purported treasonous statements at Canton, but also he rejoiced in them. In his address to the jury he went so far as to connect his "cause" to that of the colonist revolutionaries. "Washington, Jefferson, Franklin, Paine and the compeers were the rebels of their day," Debs said. "They were opposed by the people and denounced by the press. . . . But they had the moral courage to be true to their convictions, to stand erect and defy all the forces of reaction and detraction; and that is why their names shine in history, and why the great respectable majority of their day sleep in forgotten graves."[142] This statement epitomized the essentially American form of liberalism underpinning Debs's values of revolutionary, socialist, humanist, and individualist protest.[143]

By March 1919, still out on bail under appeal and about to be ruled against by the Supreme Court, Debs wrote in the *Illinois Comrade* that it was time for "sound and efficient organization . . . to take advantage of the unprecedented opportunities created by the war." He argued that the Bolshevik Revolution in Russia was the example and that the "call comes to us all in this hour of supreme importance" to take action because the war had critically undermined capitalism in the United States and Europe.[144]

Writing in the *Appeal* in 1919, John Gunn agreed with Debs's assertions and also hoped to unite industrial and rural laborers under the banner of socialism. According to Gunn, the Non-Partisan League's rising popularity signaled an "awakening of farmers." In terms of the class struggle, he said it "represents a gratifying degree of class-conscious resistance to class rule," and as a form of democracy, it "represents a gratifying degree of alert and progressive citizenship." It seemed that there was cause for optimism. Looking at its Midwestern and Northwestern power, Gunn, like Debs, thought that the league might move across the nation. Citing a third-year membership of 150,000 and a new tally of roughly 210,000 in 1919, Gunn noted that small presses and personal solicitation were the powerful forces driving exposure to rural farmers.[145]

After the end of the war and during his almost three years in prison, from 1919 to 1921, Debs corresponded with a number of Southern farmers and constituents. During this period Debs continued to raise issues that bridged Southern Democratic dissent and democratic socialism. Letters came to him from Mississippi, Texas, Georgia, Louisiana, Virginia, and North Carolina. These citizens, along with greater numbers from the North and Midwest, supported Debs's cause. They also often expressed deep personal sympathy for his suffering.[146] Ranging from a clergyman who was also a leader of the socialist local in Washington, D.C., to nonpartisan residents of Atlanta, Debs's correspondents reveal a previously unexplored degree of contact with the South. But these efforts were of no avail.

While Debs received more aggregate votes in 1920 than in his landmark campaign of 1912, he did not gain the 6 percent of the vote that he had claimed eight years before. Still, these results illustrate the influence of his rhetoric despite heightened tension, imprisonment, and outright repression. They also show how obstructed Debs's ruralization and nationalization had been in wartime, though, as historian Nick Salvatore concluded, "Debs achieved a portion of what he desired. He was, once again, as in 1894, the preeminent symbol of American resistance to corporate capitalism."[147] Earning nearly one million total votes (901,255) is all the more remarkable because it came during the fragmentation of the SPA in the wake of wartime assaults and disputes over the meaning of the Russian Revolution. Political scientists have characterized these results as a classic example of a protest vote.[148]

In 1920, although Debs had no illusions of winning the race, he hoped to incite just such a "protest vote" from working people (albeit a socialist protest geared toward an eventual revolution) to awaken nationwide political opposition. In the South the percentage of the presidential vote for Debs in 1920 dropped slightly from 1912, yet he still carried an average of 1–2 percent of the vote per state despite new legal-mechanical impediments to a third party, and despite never campaigning in person that year (his strongest political asset).[149] This attempt to galvanize latent protest sentiments united Debs's opposition ideology with other populist-resistance arguments in spirit, if not in direct collaboration.

His influence spread far in another direction as well. Their harsh treatment of Debs and a small but vocal group of socialists and pacifists led to a severe backlash, particularly among the liberal progressive-minded intellectuals who had sided with Wilson in the war effort. Legal scholar Geoffrey Stone summarized this, noting that during the war the key question of the home front was "whether the United States could punish public opposition to the war because it might sap the nation's resolve and the war effort." In trying to reconcile the necessities of wartime with the constitutional promise not to abridge the freedom of speech, the Supreme Court for the first time had upheld legislation that limited speech and "established formal precedents that took the nation half a century to overcome." The extensive repression of vocal dissent and other civil liberties during the war led many supporters of the Wilson administration to backtrack after the conflict ended. This gave rise to the modern civil liberties movement and spurred a public movement to grant amnesty to all those still held in jail after the war on seditious-speech convictions. After the war John Dewey, for example, helped to found the American Civil Liberties Union in 1920, and he observed in the *New Republic* that he had been remiss to support such policies. In hindsight, he wrote that "the increase of intolerance of discussion to the point of religious bigotry" pushed the nation to deem as seditious "every opinion and belief which irritates the majority of loyal citizens."[150]

Isolation and Antiwar Rhetoric

Linking him to the vanishing tradition of Ralph Waldo Emerson and Henry David Thoreau—in terms of self-sacrifice and communitarian heroism—and at the same time invoking a producerist language in his populist yearning for lost community, Debs's antiwar ideology had a unique capacity to persuade people through personal pathos and fundamental ideals. His rhetorical power did not derive from the direct conversion of a constituent base to the socialist ideology, but from a highly adaptable antiwar belief system that tapped into deeply traditional and profoundly American views such as freedom of speech and freedom from corrupting foreign politics and destructive conflicts.[151]

Debs, like a number of dissenting conservative Southern Democrats, Midwestern socialists, liberals, pacifists, and nonconformist agrarians across these regions, built on this deeply personal sense of a common American liberal tradition to buttress assaults on what he considered injustice. Political differences, however, could not be overcome by proximate goals or ideological convergences. These facts have misled many scholars into the trap of highlighting the differences among these groups. To minimize cross-sectional and cross-ideological convergences is to underestimate the depth of antiwar radicalism, the role of isolationist ideas, and dissent in the South and across the nation, thereby overlooking shared isolationist antiwar rhetoric, activism, and the limited but significant cooperation between pacifists, socialists, populists, and conservatives.[152]

The development of Debs's antiwar protest ideology, viewed alongside the larger story of antiwar dissent, demonstrates the powerful connections between isolationist reasons for minimizing war and steering clear of foreign entanglements and the arguments of antiwar socialists, radicals, and pacifists. Debs's arguments had great appeal to those predisposed to distrust elites and any entrance into an unprovoked conflict. He did not just go to "every town and city," but also traveled into the countryside to pit localism against the big money, influence, and social and political corruption abetted by large corporate trusts. Debs opposed the capitalist loan-debt structure that had impoverished Southern and Midwestern farmers as well as the Green Corn rebels. He fought the Northern politicians and Anglophiles, for whom the South had a traditional antipathy. He articulated a populist assault on an interventionist federal government and built upon his humanist concern for the well-being and autonomy of farmers and industrial workers alike. Such ideals were as characteristically Southern as they were Midwestern, and as populist as they were politically radical. Debs's antiwar ideology, with its concomitant linkages to political protest and local draft evasion, found approving audiences widely throughout the South and the Midwest, and in urban bastions of socialism (e.g., New York, Milwaukee) precisely because of its breadth and elasticity.

The new research on the depth of draft resistance in the South coupled with new insights into Debs's antiwar arguments helps to demonstrate that ideology, action, and militarism did not correspond neatly in the World War I American South. The assertions of hyperpatriotic leaders, such as W. W. Larsen of Georgia, who depicted the "fires of patriotism" burning bright in every home, generally have been and perplexingly continue to be taken at face value. Yet even in the supposedly solid Southern states, antiwar socialism played a strong role in dissent.

Ironically, one of the most intriguing aspects of the regional analytical move in taking Debs outside of usual categories of analysis is that it shows parallels across regions—the varied isolationist arguments embedded in resistance to World War I being the most significant. There is a provocative connection here between the Midwest and the South and between elite politicians of conservative and radical persuasions, which linked farmers and industrial workers. Regionalism in isolationist public opinion also clearly played a role here, as numerous political scientists and historians have noted that isolationist sentiment from the 1910s through the 1930s tended to be located in the Midwest and across more rural portions of the middle of the nation.[153] For Debs, attempting to "sweep" across regions meant a renewed appeal to the common workingman, be he farmer or industrial laborer. Uniting opposition ideas in the Midwest and the South with an explicit "American" logic of sacrosanct individual rights were core isolationist ideas when Debs invoked revolutionary and patriotic icons.

Debs echoed a cross-regional class-based distrust of big government and business elites, a desire to avoid the corruptions of Old Europe and to minimize war, but he could not find real common ground with Southern Democrats and pacifists because of the divisive issues such as racial segregation, and the capitalist causes of war. Indeed, as James Weinstein concluded, popular favorable reactions "to Socialist and non-Socialist anti-war appeals demonstrates the considerable and continuing opposition to America's participation in the World War. The opposition, furthermore, was probably appreciably greater than the Socialist vote . . . would indicate."[154]

Accounts of the splintering of populism at the end of the nineteenth century illustrate how often events, themes, and geographic regions are compartmentalized. Although the Populist Party lost traction across the nation and their political fusion ticket was defeated in the election of

1896, it is clear that populist-style opposition—and the appeal of socialist and isolationist arguments—continued through World War I in the South and the nation.[155] Thus, Debs's changing rhetoric in the World War I period illuminates his adaptation of the traditional isolationist rhetoric to fit new circumstances and given his peculiarly American take on international socialism. Like the liberal intellectual and cultural critiques of Bourne, Debs's views invoked America's diversity and potential for exceptional pluralism, while seeking to tap populist sentiment to intervene internationally without recourse to military engagement (or buildup).

By the time of the debates over the ratification of the League of Nations covenant, Debs still had not been granted clemency. It was not until late 1921 that President Warren Harding released Debs from prison. With his advanced age and weakened physical condition, as well as with the Socialist Party of America in disarray after wartime censorship and splintering over the contentious issue of support for the USSR, Debs was no longer up to the task of leading American socialists and radicals. A new group of mainstream political opponents emerged to try to thwart Wilsonian internationalism and its claims for making the world safe for democracy through high-profile, binding alliances and global forms of government such as the League of Nations.

In 1918 a new bloc tapped into the populist pool of isolationist sentiment and resentment against entanglements of the Wilsonian type. In this case, however, they listened to different voices of the people and came to advance a conservative, hypernationalist "irreconcilable" form of isolationism, developed and implemented throughout the 1920s. The most staunchly isolationist of this group was its figurehead, William Borah, who was perhaps the man most identified as an isolationist in the American political tradition. A former populist, progressive-oriented Republican senator from Idaho, he was a man who as a prosecutor had pursued convictions against IWW socialists and labor leaders.

Borah had no love for socialism. And none for Eugene Debs, whom he saw as an anti-American troublemaker. But Borah did share quite a lot with Debs. They both aspired to be a genuine voice of the people, and they shared a critique of the excesses of big business, a profound love for individual rights and American principles, and a firm belief in nonentanglement in any alliances, leagues, or wars abroad.

6

THE IRRECONCILABLES

"What we want is what [Theodore] Roosevelt urged—a free, untrammeled nation, imbued anew and inspired again with the national spirit," Idaho's Republican senator William Borah bellowed to a packed Senate on February 21, 1919.[1] These evocative phrases came in a speech titled "Americanism," in which Borah positioned himself as a powerful voice against both the League of Nations as an organization and the Treaty of Versailles, of which it was an integral part. He became the foremost spokesman for a new nationalistic, populist, and unilateralist isolationism that became the archetype for opposition to the world order that President Wilson hoped to establish.

In his efforts from 1918 through 1922, Borah cogently described what he saw as the many flaws in the charter of the League of Nations and sought congressional rejection of the Treaty of Versailles as well as any entry into the League. He asserted that joining virtually any form of the proposed League would undermine American autonomy and tie the nation to the fractured systems of war-torn Europe through the treaty's vindictive reparations and guilt clauses. But he saved his greatest fury for railing against the controversial, binding Article X of the League covenant. That article, Borah said, compelled America to engage in multilateral actions against the national interest, forcing the commitment of U.S. forces abroad to aid League members without the constitutionally mandated domestic debate and mutual consent of the Congress and the executive. Borah's was no timid isolation, no mere manifestation of provincial thinking. His political visions largely stemmed from his desire for what he laid out as "freedom to do as our own people think wise and just; not isolation but simply the unembarrassed and unentangled freedom of a great Nation to determine for itself and in its own way where duty lies and where wisdom calls."[2]

Borah linked the nation's health to the vitality and sustenance of the system of checks and balances. He held close to his heart those beliefs of inalienable rights of individual freedom, local self-determination, and national autonomy articulated in the Declaration of Independence and reified by the Constitution. Like so many others who adhered to isolationist values, Borah claimed to follow the path conceived by the visionary leaders he greatly admired: Washington, Jefferson, and Monroe. Several of the most significant strands of isolationism came together within Borah's nationalist blending of old values for agrarian democracy and modern conditions. He saw binding political entanglements as undermining of American autonomy and anathema to the valuable precedent of isolation. He was consistent in an anti-imperialist stance against U.S. dominion abroad, or meddling in other nations' internal affairs; yet he was ambivalent in cases involving what he saw as obvious nationalist national interest and so, for example, he ardently defended the American farmer through tariff policy and asserted America's right to exempt its ships from tolls in the Panama Canal.[3] He also without fail argued that any open-ended military alliances were to be avoided at all costs, while arguing that to minimize war abroad as well as conflict at home should always be a top priority for American politicians. Borah found great merit in the principles of trust-busting. His populist-minded defense of state and individual rights made him suspicious of all large-scale uses of power. Against "bigness" in corporations, which he saw as undercutting the rights of both worker and consumer (à la William James), Borah also despised most forms of federal oversight of the states. Although he was attacked for negativism and naïveté with regard to international engagement, he keenly perceived the importance of promoting domestic prosperity through worldwide trade (and had no truck with most commercial reciprocity treaties). Given his acute exceptionalism, it is no wonder that he believed in deepening cultural exchanges abroad, which he believed would only serve to enhance American power and prestige.

In 1917 Borah had supported President Wilson's call for a war declaration as an "associate power" rather than an "ally." Borah's rationale was simple: he could "not vote against the resolution" for the war because American honor had to be protected. Still, he made clear that he would "accept no alliances."[4] The actual declaration of war did not prove particularly divisive for those of an isolationist proclivity. After all, as the United States entered the conflict, it did so of its own volition on the grounds of defense of national interests. Thus, an array of confirmed isolationist-minded politicians, from across the nation and transcending party lines, such as Democratic senators Charles Thomas of Colorado and Thomas Gore of Oklahoma, and Republican senators Borah, Hiram Johnson of California, and Joseph France of Maryland, voted for joining the conflict yet would soon turn against its Wilsonian internationalist ramifications. But we must make distinctions within this group and between the elements that made up their varied isolationist views about the war. While the majority of what was to become a stalwart isolationist bloc agreed on virtually all counts with Borah, and thus reluctantly voted for the war, a small group of six senators, led by Robert La Follette and George Norris, voted against authorizing American entry into the conflict. One year later, however, with the war drawing to a close, many of the Borah bloc sided with their more stalwart colleagues and began to publicly express second thoughts about the vote. Characteristically, Borah did not recant in public; however, in off-the-record conversations, he admitted to wishing he could turn back the clock and change his vote on the war.[5]

The issue that hardened their views, giving rise to a more consistent isolationist position, was possible entry into Wilson's proposed League of Nations. Such an organization quite obviously defied the injunctions of Washington and Jefferson. As early as winter 1917 Borah's speeches and writings reveal the gradual crystallizing of his stance against any postwar political league of equal nations, which he derided as foolhardy at best and national suicide at worst. Borah was shocked that Wilson would reject the precedents that had made the nation so strong to promote an "entirely new course of action." Further, Borah struggled to understand how Wilson could swallow what he saw as largely self-centered French and British rationales for a peace settlement based on harsh reparations and including the division of war spoils in the form of colonial assets (such as handing over the Shantung province in China to Japan), which were not merely disadvantageous to U.S. interests, but anathema to long-standing democratic ideals and anticolonial, isolationist principles.

Postwar debates on these issues were pivotal to the merging of several distinct isolationist positions with a non-Wilsonian progressive internationalism to create a new policy for the twentieth century. Historians have addressed the main political debates in this process—particularly the congressional rejection of membership in the League—but few have examined in much depth and over time the Irreconcilable senator's beliefs about both isolation and internationalism. Fewer still have examined the linkages between the domestic and foreign policy views that shaped these debates and transformed modern isolationism into a coherent political outlook.[6]

In looking at these subjects we can see that then, as now, there were deep connections between populist sentiment and foreign policy. Borah's political maneuvers represented a largely negative vision for most foreign affairs, in keeping with his opponents' assertion in the press that he was "the Great Opposer." Still, while foreign policy was (and still is) often relegated to elites, with the rise of Borah and others like him, we can see a bridge between populist sentiment and international relations on an ongoing basis—not just as produced by the drumbeat of war (as was largely the case with Theodore Roosevelt and to a far lesser extent with Wilson), but as a continual way of viewing the organic connection between domestic and foreign. That is, Borah sought to translate the will of the people as a means of adhering to his core isolationist beliefs.

As an agrarian populist in many ways, Borah and a bloc of largely Midwestern, Western, and Southern isolationists voted in 1917 for joining the war, which was widely if far from universally popular. His agrarian populism informed his increasingly vigorous opposition to the League, as the League concept gradually lost appeal for the American public. (This attempt to express a populist-popular will helps to explain why Borah later shifted to support the widely appealing effort to outlaw war, even though it entailed U.S. leadership in a major international agreement.) The key here is the argument that Borah's conception of federalism within the United States deeply informed his firm belief that a similar structure was the best framework for interaction between nations. The older values of isolationism and foundational political thought adapted by Borah animated his essentially populist stand against anything that might infringe on American autonomy. Thus, these points reinforced each other; after all, one of the most important arguments at the level of philosophy and practical politics for local governance in a republic has been that elected officials ought to be closer to their constituents and thus can better understand their needs. Borah believed this to his very core, and from his faith in the local he espoused a corollary belief in foreign policy, namely that nations should interact with a preference for nonintervention and local autonomy in virtually all instances.

Historians have spilled gallons of ink describing Borah as the archetypal "Irreconcilable" politician for his oppositional nature and his isolationist ideas. It has been exceedingly difficult to discern a consistent method behind Borah's perceived political "madness." Taken as a whole, in their attempts scholars appear more inconsistent than Borah himself. One biographer, LeRoy Ashby, termed him a "rugged individualist" whose agrarian-based reformism was handed down relatively unchanged from William Jennings Bryan.[7] Others, such as Arthur Schlesinger Jr., found Borah to be an outlier within the ranks of American liberals, calling him consistent mostly for his oppositional tendencies. He described the Idaho senator as a "lone wolf of American politics."[8]

The conundrum of trying to find coherence amid Borah's numerous political positions is illustrated by the historian William E. Leuchtenberg. In a brief biographical account of Borah, Leuchtenberg alternately characterized Borah as a "nationalist," a "civil libertarian," a "Progressive," a "particularist," and an "isolationist"; he even went on to call Borah "a constitutionalist with a nineteenth-century faith in the force of public opinion for good" (depending on the issue being discussed)[9]—quite a vast array of seemingly inconsistent classifications. Similarly, one of his most able biographers, Marian McKenna, concluded that character traits—and not ideas—explain Borah. She said his "vision might sometimes fail and his course might sometimes be erratic, but he could always be counted on for three of the rarest qualities of statesmanship: conscience, courage, and passion."[10]

In the first major biography sanctioned by Borah himself, Claudius O. Johnson summarized Borah as less political and more interested in the views of the public. "Borah of Idaho has always stood apart from the event," wrote Johnson. "He has initiated some movements, he has popularized more, he has given color to many; but he has seldom been in the inner circle of organizers and promoters. His part has been that of molding and expressing public opinion."[11]

Borah has eluded full characterization in part because of a missing conceptual link between his domestic philosophy and his international policy that developed most prominently from 1917 through 1928—from the fight against the League to his fight to outlaw war. During this time, concerned with economic and political reform within the United States, he pushed for greater checks on executive and legislative branches of government, insisting on deference to local autonomy ("states' rights") whenever possible. His belief in the need to protect and extend personal and national freedom led him to write, "There is only one thing sacred in all mundane affairs, and that is the individual, with his capabilities, possibilities, and his aspirations; and no government that does not found its right to exist upon this principle or this consideration is worth defending."[12] This was Borah's staunch guiding principle in the late 1910s; it hardened in the early 1920s, and deepened further late in the 1920s and into the Depression years of the 1930s as an "Americanism" that he cast against foreign wars and treaties as well as against big businesses, especially those in heavy industry and finance that profited from the war.[13]

The period from World War I through the 1920s was the crucible that caused Borah and the Irreconcilables to reshape their ideas and come together as a group. The Irreconcilables were a group of isolationist-oriented senators, led by Borah, who objected to American entry into the League of Nations under any circumstances. They shifted from hesitant critics of any international association to ruling-party statesmen who had to broker agreements and came to endorse an idealistic effort to outlaw war. Eventually they would ally themselves with an array of American and world activists and organizations for international peace, such as the Women's International League for Peace and Freedom, to pass international peace treaties that achieved internationalist and isolationist results simultaneously. After World War I and through the 1920s, the United States did not assume the full measure of global responsibilities that matched its emergent position as a preeminent power. Thinkers and politicians throughout the nation grappled with the meaning of this new position in the postwar world, and most came to realize that absolute isolation was neither desirable nor possible.

Borah was central to this process of forcing a nation—increasingly given to turning inward provincially after the war and wanting only to "return to normalcy"—to think in terms of the benefits and costs of global engagement. His reluctant vote for the war and the unexpected results of the conflict on domestic society propelled a conflict between his agrarian isolationist perspectives and the last elements of an ill-fitting Republican nationalism. He fought to update tradition and safeguard national autonomy given the new global realities. As Borah put it after the election of 1920, this was what the citizens wanted; it was "the judgment of the American people against any political alliance or combination. The United States had rededicated itself to the foreign policy of George Washington and James Monroe, undiluted and unemasculated."[14] As a result his sometimes extreme isolationist proposals pushed the national dialogue over how to engage abroad in new directions. The United States participated in various League of Nations conferences even after rejecting membership in the League, and later the World Court; the country assumed the initiative in naval disarmament and attempted to resolve the growing reparations issue; and all the while the United States engaged in global commercial expansion and cultural interchanges.

As we will see in this chapter and the next, from his reluctant vote for U.S. entry into the war in 1917 through the 1930s, Borah developed a strong opposition to all policies that he deemed "interventionist" and espoused traditional isolationist ideas as central to future prosperity and peace. His domestic views and his efforts to be a genuine voice of the people were pivotal in shaping his perspective on internationalism. In many ways Borah was the archetypal isolationist, and yet he called for and supported numerous international conferences, while also leading the fight to reject the League of Nations. He supported certain types of international arms reduction and propelled the effort to ratify the Kellogg-Briand Pact to outlaw war (1928). At home, Borah battled against "bigness," monopoly, and corruption, supported certain laws for labor organization, fought for immigration restriction, and staunchly advocated states' rights (even when states enacted laws of which he personally disapproved). He saw this set of policy positions as consistent and consonant with his overriding aim to protect the nation and maximize its autonomy, while enhancing rights and opportunities for American citizens.

Pro-Reform, Anti-League

A self-made man who grew up as one of ten children on a hardscrabble farm in Illinois, Borah held a lifelong interest in ensuring that "idle" wealth was properly taxed. He wanted those funds put to work for the best interests of the wider public. He also made it his mission to curtail corruption—across party lines—and to make democracy a more complete expression of the will of voters.

Borah vigorously opposed monopolies primarily at the state level, deeming them "un-American," but he also fought some of the most stringent federal legislative regulations because of his view that enforcement should be done locally. He opposed both of the dominant progressive arguments of the mid-1910s, the New Nationalism and the New Freedom. Instead, as Marian McKenna has shown, Borah solemnly believed that "a Republic is strong enough to destroy, but never could be strong enough to regulate monopoly." For this reason, he led the fight against two of Woodrow Wilson's major initiatives in 1914: the Federal Trade Commission and the

Clayton Antitrust Act. In fact, Borah considered them merely "political makeshift[s] to mislead the people into the belief that something tremendous has been done on the trust question." Only the Sherman Anti-Trust Act of 1890, which proposed abolishing "all combinations in restraint of trade," was powerful enough for Borah. Throughout his political career, fairness in business issues motivated Borah's political vision.[15] In foreign policy, the issues of the most direct bearing on his agrarian isolationist perspective arose during the Taft administration. Borah opposed the Canadian Reciprocity agreement as "discrimination against the American farmer," and he and a bloc of insurgent Republicans opposed loan conventions with Honduras and Nicaragua, and arbitration treaties with France and Great Britain. At home, however, Borah did not always reject federal regulation in state affairs. He saw strengthening the democratic rights and opportunities of citizens as paramount and strongly backed two important constitutional amendments, both ratified in 1913: the congressional power to lay and collect taxes (Sixteenth Amendment) and the direct election of senators by the citizens of each state (Seventeenth Amendment).

Throughout the 1910s Borah also favored women's suffrage on the same grounds yet with one major qualification. He conditioned his support of suffrage by seeking it at the state level, which represents a meaningful contradiction in his thought. Borah helped write the Republican Party platform at the Chicago convention in 1916, which asserted, "The Republican party, reaffirming its faith in government of the people, by the people and for the people favors the extension of the suffrage to women, but we recognize the right of each state to settle this question for itself."[16] Yet once women attained full suffrage after 1920, Borah declared that for him women had always been full citizens. Regardless of whether one could vote, Borah said, it was the American people as a whole who were ultimately "sovereign." Now that women could vote, he hoped that women would. Why? Because, Borah argued, bureaucracy and entrenched institutions were poor conveyors of the essential wisdom of the people. As he noted in 1918, "Shall men, shall the people, be governed by some remorseless and soulless entity softly called the 'State' or shall the instrumentalities of government yield alone and at all times to the wants and necessities, the hopes and aspirations of the masses?"[17] He urged his colleagues to "listen closely to the instructions of a well-formed and well-sustained public opinion"—both men and women—when writing laws.[18]

Borah's early activities as a corporate lawyer influenced his later politi-cal thought about the relationship between the state and private enter-prise. Interestingly, Borah's work defending corporations as a lawyer mis-led Rhode Island senator and Republican leader Nelson W. Aldrich, a friend of the Rockefellers and an unfaltering tariff advocate, who assumed Borah's legal work indicated how he would act as a senator. Aldrich as-sumed Borah would be pro-business and anti-labor. He was wrong and Borah took advantage of his misplaced patronage. Not long after he joined the Senate in 1907, he was assigned to select committee positions, includ-ing the chairmanship of the Committee on Education and Labor. In those roles Borah sponsored bills for the creation of the Department of Labor and a Children's Bureau, and lobbied for an eight-hour day for government-contracted labor. Again, citing nationalist reasons, Borah fa-vored mild protective economic tariffs that evened the international play-ing field for American producers; but he opposed large profit-oriented tariffs that artificially helped American corporate interests at the expense of the purchasing power of American consumers.

He had always supported trust-busting, which stemmed from an in-stinctive distrust of large corporate consolidations of power. He sought protection of the judiciary from politicization and struggled to develop a law to eliminate 5–4 rulings of the U.S. Supreme Court. Borah opposed most federal labor laws, although he had favored the creation of the Labor Department as a federal "honest broker" for individuals, corporations, and states. Instead, he favored enacting labor legislation at the local level; only in times of dire need, he believed, should the federal government be pro-active in regulating the economy. Citing "necessity" born of "poverty" and the needs of the vast majority of the people, late in his career Borah broke with numerous Republicans to support most of the major New Deal legislation (except the National Industrial Recovery Act, which he criti-cized for suspending antitrust laws).

Elemental to his channeling of the popular voice in efforts as diverse as restraining corporate excess and seeking the direct election of senators was Borah's proclaimed core value, which he expressed as an "unpurchas-able love of country," the "only security a republic can ever know." Borah argued that this was the very bedrock of his politics. "The faith of the citi-zen," he said, "is after all the sole source of power in a free government."[19] Blending populism, patriotism, and a deeply held value for America's unique national history and precedent, Borah wanted citizens to embrace the American past as their own, immigrants and native-born alike. In surprisingly similar language to that of Randolph Bourne on "true" patriotism, and to Eugene Debs's appeal to adhere faithfully to the Constitution, Borah expressed his hope that if Americans properly understood their past and their inalienable rights, then democracy would flourish. Borah stated his view of American values in these terms in 1911, but he could very well have said the same in his battle against the League in 1919 or in his support for New Deal policies in 1933: "A republic must have in it the element of respect and reverence, of devotion to its institutions and loyalty to its traditions. It, too, must have its altars, its memory of sacrifices—something for which men are willing to die. If the time ever comes when the fundamental principles of our Government . . . no longer hold the respect and fealty of a majority of our people popular government will, as a practical fact, not long survive that hour."[20] One fascinating implication of Borah's logic lies with the fact that in classical republicanism one paramount virtue was for citizens to fight and be willing to die for their polity. For Borah this held true absolutely. However, he was extremely wary of the ability of leaders to shape interpretations of national interest and thus send America's best citizens to die patriotically when there was no authentic case for doing so.

Civil liberties also were primary to Borah's understanding of American democracy. All Americans, Borah felt, should have the ability to object, to speak, to assemble freely, and to not be censored. Finding an audience and outlets for free speech was another matter altogether. For this reason Borah found the accusations of his being a "little American" vexing when he rejected joining the League of Nations on what he termed "patriotic" grounds of "Americanism." On free speech and group rights of assembly, Borah was convinced that a prerequisite for reform, in every case, was free discussion. He and his bloc of fellow senators vigorously opposed wartime censorship laws on the same democratic civil liberties grounds as figures such as Debs and Bourne. To that end, Borah consistently argued that in war just as in peace, for America to truly be a democracy its citizens must (paraphrasing the famous remark by Voltaire) "fight for the right to say anything at all."[21] In particular he battled the peacetime extension of the sedition acts, some of which were proposed in 1921. To counter, Borah proposed a "Bill to End Palmerism," and on February 24, 1921, he proposed a bill calling for a five-year imprisonment, a $10,000 fine, or both for "any federal employee who injures, threatens, or intimidates any person" exercising his constitutional freedoms.[22]

Borah allied himself with the newly formed American Civil Liberties Union (ACLU, 1920), even finding significant common ground with members of the far Left, such as pacifist socialists with whom he had not often seen eye-to-eye. Thus, in considering how those quintessentially American civil liberties could be destroyed by challenges to patriotism and by the hubris of politicians, Borah asserted that political imprisonment was abhorrent. He recoiled against Wilson's form of "Americanism" that had just produced George Creel's ingenious Committee on Public Information to disseminate wartime propaganda in 1917 and 1918, and which had pushed for the censorship of the mails. Throughout late 1920 and 1921 the ACLU lobbied Congress, Wilson, and incoming president Harding to pardon all of the political prisoners still being held after the war concluded. It advocated amnesty for all, not simply as an exception for high-profile individuals such as Debs, then running for office from his jail cell. Borah wrote, "I believe at all times in freedom of speech, in a free press, in the right for peaceful assemblage. . . . No government, no class of men, and no views are so sacred that they ought not to be subject to criticism."[23]

Borah's advocacy of the sacrosanct nature of civil liberties illuminated the connections between his nationalist isolationism in foreign policy and his populist, agrarian, individual-oriented federalist reform philosophy for domestic politics. In other words, his views about domestic rights and social change were critical to how he evaluated the nation's commitments abroad. The issue of political prisoners, jailed for their use of the right to assemble and speak, got at the very heart of this relationship. Borah called this issue of free speech "the vital issue" of the day. In an essay in the *Nation* in 1923, Borah argued, "Everybody believes in the right of peaceful assemblage—but the test comes when you are looking upon the gathering of those who hold a different point of view."[24] Freedom of speech regardless of race was paramount for Borah. Defending each American's right to participate in democracy, Borah opposed all African American disenfranchisement. He argued as early as 1908, "The Negroes have helped to build up this country. Their labors in slavery and out . . . have helped build it, and their valor has helped to preserve it. No man would take from the colored race of this country one iota of praise or honor for the heroic climb which it has made from slavery to its respectable position in the civilization of the world."[25]

He wanted to achieve greater education and assimilation for African Americans. Yet from 1907, when he entered the Senate, until he died in 1940, Borah opposed anti-lynching laws at the national level, saying, "If the states cannot enforce law, who can?" Though he was personally against lynching, he said that he knew of nothing constitutional and no federal statutes that gave the national government the ability to reach into the states to prosecute violations of the sort that a national anti-lynching bill (such as the Costigan-Wagner, 1935) would entail. Thus, he consistently maintained that each state should enact strong measures to prevent and harshly punish lynching within their boundaries.[26]

Borah's views on lynching and racism fit coherently, albeit imperfectly, with his outlooks on women's suffrage at home and imperialism and interventionism abroad. As with race, he saw suffrage as a federalist issue. In foreign affairs Borah disputed both particular and general arguments for intervention which posited that it was essential to "tutor" allegedly inferior people, especially those formerly under European colonial control. He did not believe in promoting democracy abroad. He could not countenance the Wilsonian mission to "teach" non-Americans how to govern their countries. Prizing local autonomy and many forms of self-determination, Borah similarly rejected Wilson's claim that Latin American leaders should be taught how to "elect good men."[27]

Americanism in Peace and War

To better understand Borah and the broader isolationist critique of the League of Nations, the developments of the wartime years need to be reviewed briefly. Before 1917, Borah's perspective on issues of international engagement vacillated between a general sympathy for the anti-imperialist, antimilitaristic outlook of agrarian Democrats and populists, and an attraction to the enthusiastic, aggressive nationalism shared by many of his fellow Rooseveltian Republicans. He had always been a party man and despite several opportunities to jump ship, he did vote for William Howard Taft in 1912.

Borah was uncertain at first about the impending war. In 1916 he supported preparation for entering the conflict. On December 26, 1916, his friend William Jennings Bryan wrote to him, saying that he had heard Borah was "opposed to the plan of the League to Enforce Peace. Am glad to hear it. It would require abandonment of Washington's doctrine— avoidance of entangling alliances—and of the Monroe doctrine. The people will not stand for either." Just three days later Borah responded favorably, saying, "Glad that we agree upon this."[28] He introduced Senate Resolution 329, reaffirming Washington's Farewell Address and the Monroe Doctrine on January 25, 1917, and challenged the assumptions behind Wilson's "Peace without Victory" speech. Senator Porter J. McCumber of North Dakota articulated the emerging populist, agrarian isolationist position at the time—and echoed the anti-imperialists—when he speculated that Wilson's abstractions were appealing but that the president likely did not reflect the views of the people "when he leaves the realm of generalities."[29] Joseph France, a progressive-minded Republican from Maryland, evolved from first reluctantly supporting American entry into World War I, like Borah, to staunchly opposing the League of Nations. France, too, came to regret his vote for the war resolution in April 1917.

Henry Cabot Lodge also changed his views. He briefly supported the League idea, but by late 1916—before the nation was formally in the war, and as the presidential campaign heated up—he came to oppose it. In a letter to Theodore Roosevelt on December 21, 1916, the day the peace note was published, Lodge wrote that he lamented being enticed by the League concept. He remarked that he was "perfectly dissatisfied with it."[30] In contrast, Borah cited broadly idealist and pacifist reasons when he voted to support Wilson's "peace note" asking merely for possible terms for peace. Most of the Senate approved this measure, to Lodge's chagrin, voting on January 5, 1917, with 48 in favor and 17 against, and including positive votes from such Borah friends and fellow progressive Republicans as George Norris, William Kenyon, Moses Clapp, and Wesley Jones. La Follette, who could not attend the session to cast his vote, stated publicly that he approved. In Lodge's last address on the president's plan for peace, given in February 1917, the personal animus between him and Wilson was becoming more public. Lodge rebuked Wilson on virtually every count in his "peace plan" speech. "I hear the clamor of those who have been shrieking for peace at any price," said Lodge. Dismissing this position as well as that of joining an unknown and powerful peace organization, he answered the critical question that he had already been asked countless times before: "Are you, then, unwilling to use the power and influence of the United States for the promotion of the permanent peace of the world?"

"Not at all," Lodge answered. "There is nothing that I have so much at heart, but I do not, in my eagerness to promote the permanent peace of the world, desire to involve this country in a scheme which may create a situation worse than that which now exists." Finally, Lodge revealed his core pessimism about peace organizations and human nature. He proclaimed, "I now see in this tortured and distracted world nothing but peril in abandoning our long and well-established policies, which have behind them not only the authority of Washington and Jefferson and Adams and Monroe, but a long acceptance by the American people. . . . The peace of the world, to be enduring, must be based on righteousness at any cost." He felt so strongly that these words must get out to the American people that Lodge decided to rapidly publish a compilation of these speeches in the Senate by May 1917.[31]

By the end of February 1917, Borah had moved closer to Lodge's position, then backpedaled once again and agreed in principle with Wilson's breaking of diplomatic relations with Germany and to his idealistic aims for world peace. In April, Borah solemnly voted for an American declaration of war, unlike his colleagues Norris and La Follette, who resolutely opposed entering the war. Lodge saw the war as an act of self-defense and sought to support the nation's natural ally, England. But he did not believe in any form of Wilson's vision for peace. Lodge voted for the war measure, and he distanced himself from the strict U.S.-led (Roosevelt-endorsed) League to Enforce Peace, which he believed had become associated in the American mind with Wilson's idealistic aims for a league of equals for collective security. In contrast, Borah and other Republicans who opposed Wilsonian internationalism were more reluctant about the peace or making alliances, even in war, and evidenced the fissures that would become chasms in thinking about the nature of the peace and unresolved ways in which they thought the nation should engage the world. We have been through the road to war in other chapters, and the point here is not to tread back over that ground but rather to illuminate the distinctions in Republican and agrarian politicians when most came to endorse the war. Borah concisely articulated the nationalist and populist elements of his prowar isolationist vote. As he put it, "I join no crusade. I seek or accept no alliances; I obligate this Government to no other power. I make war alone for my countrymen and their rights, for my country and its honor."[32]

Still, having cast his reluctant vote, Borah admired those who had stood against entering the war. He was aghast at how his colleagues and friends, particularly La Follette, were being excoriated in the press for voting against the war. The wave of homogenizing patriotism that swept the country after the war vote discouraged him even more. Borah wrote to the former Republican governor of Idaho, Frank Gooding, a fellow opponent of conscription laws, yet often a state-level party opponent of Borah's. Heralding La Follette's prescient and principled stand, Borah said that he "may yet prove the biggest man of the occasion."[33] Borah fought the subsequent legislation regarding Selective Service when it was being drafted, but the bill was overwhelmingly approved in Congress and supported by a broad base that included most nationalist Republicans, including Roosevelt, Lodge, and Elihu Root. Agreeing with Lodge along principled and partisan lines, Borah intensely doubted Wilson's idealistic vision for a progressive international peace without victory. Doubting himself and the results of casting a vote for entering the war, and unable to stanch the curtailment of civil liberties in wartime, Borah stated in a press release in April 1917 that he intended to step down from the Senate at the end of his term, in March 1919.

The New York Times implied that "financial" reasons had forced him to retire at age fifty-two, giving the distinct impression that there was more to the maneuver by noting Borah's excellent physical and mental shape. A personal letter, however, sheds light on his true motivations. Borah wanted to stand apart from the current policies of both parties in Washington and was deeply conflicted by the politics of wartime America. "Now I voted for a declaration of war," he conceded in the letter. "I did so because I felt that regardless of what had brought us . . . we had arrived at the point where action was . . . essential to protect the rights and honor of our country." Yet he believed that the subsequent war measures—restricting free speech, imposing conscription, and greatly heightening central regulation and federal oversight—conflicted with his most deeply held beliefs. "I am unwilling," he proclaimed, "to Prussianize this country in order to de-Prussianize Germany. I do not think it necessary."[34] Turning away from the position of more pro-British Republicans, such as Lodge and Roosevelt, Borah decried patriotic calls for widespread conscription and derided federal censorship of speech and the mail as antithetical to American values.

Notes from friends and constituents from Idaho, and various appeals on patriotic grounds from colleagues in Washington, poured into Borah's mailbox.[35] La Follette and Norris asked him to remain in office. This overwhelming support from constituents and allied politicians helped to convince him to remain in the Senate. On July 28, 1917, Borah began publicly countering Wilson's internationalist perspective. Borah primarily sounded the note of patriotism and tradition in making his case, but within his arguments we can discern the seeds of the isolationist views that would inform the rest of his career in the Senate.

The *New York Sun*'s editorial on Borah's war-vote speech is characteristic of how his message was received. The *Sun* approved Borah's interpretation of why the country had gone into the European conflict and opined, "Senator Borah is quite right. This is an American war. It ceased to be a European war for us when we entered upon it." On the other side of the nation, the *Seattle Times* echoed these sentiments and urged its readers to listen to his "appeal to patriotic America." Borah carefully orchestrated his language to hit the right popular notes. His files evidence a marked interest in how his rhetoric and rationale for entering the conflict were received across the nation. Borah's scrapbooks list numerous examples from Idaho, of course, as well as Boston, Chicago, San Francisco, and Dallas, where editors and citizens seem to have widely approved of Borah's assertion that this was "an American war" and not one for universal peace and democracy. Yet many of these news outlets and letter writers missed the essence of Borah's isolationist message and its implications for the postwar world. Yet at least one paper, the *Seattle Times*, hinted at Borah's deeper skepticism about Wilson's idealistic aims. The paper noted that Borah "left himself open to criticism when he declared the country's war aims have been stated in a 'nebulous manner,' but there is no question that he was right in declaring 'the hour of sacrifice has arrived.'"[36]

Borah opposed conscription and censorship, regardless of the wartime pressures. Still, popular demand in Idaho, as across the nation, was overwhelming and pressed heavily upon Borah and most of the isolationist-tending political leadership. He refused to abandon his convictions to conform to the popular doctrines of the hour but also found such a stand deeply troubling. He wrote privately of how his fight to oppose draft legislation and acts censoring the mails, and speech more broadly, was right; yet thwarting the will of his constituents was intensely difficult for him. "It is hard to get an idea of the pressure here to surrender conviction, conscience, and everything else to support a program which in many respects . . . will cost the people of the United States many hours of bitter regret," he wrote.[37] His letters reveal him struggling against a periodic spell of melancholia, which he attributed to the "blood" on his mother's side. At a deeper level, his letters demonstrate that the crux of his confusion was that his duty as a representative of the state of Idaho was diametrically opposed to his lifelong ideals of individual independence and his interpretation of the absolute sacrosanct nature of America's democratic foundational rights.

Domestic and Foreign Implications of Immigration

Borah's appeal to tradition and his effort to channel the popular will were crucial points of emphasis for most modern isolationists, even if he took the principles further than most. He also embraced the need for a Madisonian diversity of interests and factions in society. This particularist perspective aimed for an overarching Americanism, premised of course on a set of shared republican, American values that would unite particular groups and interests into what we now might term a more cohesive national whole. Members of society should work toward their own objectives, but he believed that they ought to have mutual respect, and that through elections and the impartial rule of law a shared patriotism could then be cultivated and refined.

Issues of immigration forced these beliefs into an odd, restrictionist shape. The expulsions and high-profile trials of "unfit" or "seditious" foreigners and radicals within the nation from the late 1910s through the 1920s forced the issue in postwar America. Borah did not favor free and unfettered immigration to the United States. However, earlier, when policies were far more open, he saw this as just fine so long as those entering the nation satisfied certain criteria as potentially productive members of society. In 1908, during his first term in the Senate, a bill to set immigration restrictions was under discussion. He stated that he had no "prejudice" against foreigners, but that he favored stringent tests to determine whether immigrants intended to remain in America and contribute to the national culture. If they simply wanted to compete for jobs and resources and then depart the country, then they were unwelcome, he reasoned. If immigrants genuinely wanted to embrace American values, join the labor market, and make a home, then they were welcome to enter the nation and eventually become Americans. This was in keeping with his overall philosophy of linking the health of the nation to the values and vitality of citizenry and those principles. Yet by 1916 (and more strongly after the war), he argued for rigorous restrictions on immigration. He worried about the inflow of seditious anti-American radicals and activists. But he was most concerned that a flood of wartime refugees might undercut jobs of American citizens or water down the natural capacities of the national racial stock.

Underlying these twin rationales for restriction, Borah made an additional argument that simultaneously played on nativist and scientific sentiments. He asserted that immigrant fitness was paramount. Borah evaluated the issue of immigration in light of two principles: first, the international refugee chaos likely to be generated by the war, giving rise to a need to protectively curtail the flow of immigrants into America; and second, the domestic need to produce and support the best possible American citizenship by allowing only those most useful or dedicated to immigrate. This echoed an older rationale for state-level immigration restriction that Borah first voiced during the waning days of the Taft administration. During that time he voted in 1912 to exclude immigration issues from international arbitration, and in 1914 he argued that the "Oriental exclusion" acts were just and that they represented a states' rights question.[38]

To support his assessments, Borah drew on data about numbers of adults who were working abroad and were likely to consider entering the nation. Hearkening to the same case he made against the Japanese in 1914, he also cited social scientific and popular literature noting the often-poor racial, mental, moral, and physical conditions of new immigrants. The least "fit," it seemed, were likely to emigrate from Europe or to come from the nations of the Pacific Slope. Borah's old friend, the progressive Hiram Johnson, one of the sixteen so-called Irreconcilable opponents of the League of Nations, also pushed for serious quotas throughout the 1920s. Both men concluded that the need for serious immigration restriction, with a precise and effective quota system, was the sort of dilemma that every generation of Americans faced and it would in time turn out to be a significant political feather in the cap of the isolationist bloc. As historian Mae Ngai aptly stated, "Although Congress legislated the first numerical restrictions in 1921, it would be nearly a decade before permanent immigration quotas were implemented. The intervening years were filled with contention and difficulty as Congress debated the design of a new system."[39]

Led by most of the Irreconcilables, who consistently voted to restrict immigration by a quota system, and in alliance with a bloc of race-nativists and other conservatives, these laws proceeded in fits and starts. Over eight hundred thousand immigrants poured into the country in 1921. In response came the increasingly restrictive Emergency Quota Act of 1921 and then the harsh Johnson-Reed Act of 1924, which included the National Origins Act and the Asian Exclusion Act. Americans like Borah were keenly aware of the stakes in making sure that "undesirables" did not immigrate. The national mood after the war pushed inward, seeking to limit disrupting new migration patterns as well as labor or racial tumult. It seemed that this "new order would codify certain values and judgments about the sources of immigration, the desired makeup of the nation, and the requirements of citizenship."[40] The law of 1924 thus can be seen as an isolationist achievement. It was the first congressional act to establish both numerical limits on immigration and a global quota system premised on a racial and national hierarchy of favoring certain immigrants and places of origin over others.[41]

Such policies made perfect sense to the inwardly focused Borah and like-minded Irreconcilables. Ultimately, they said, the people of the nation were the greatest source of the national wealth and thus required the highest levels of protection from destructive external influences. Though in historical perspective it was not traditional to restrict immigration, for Borah there had always been fitness tests for those newly arriving in the nation, and simply because it was easier for new immigrants to make their way into the United States did not mean that they did not need to be as fit, or more so, than his forebears. Therefore, just as he relied on the principles of long-standing isolation from foreign entanglements and corruptions, so too did he take his guidance from the philosophical precedents of past immigration policies. "There is a deeper and broader question involved," he remarked, "and that is obligatory upon every generation, and particularly upon this, in view of the tremendous conditions prevailing in Europe, to protect the citizenship of this country." Borah believed that primary importance should be given "to keep[ing] up the average standard of citizenship, that this great Republic of ours may rest in safety upon the shoulders not of the few, not of the public men alone, but upon the shoulders of the average man, for there and there alone is the foundation rock upon which the Republic must rest in every crisis."[42] Borah's main worry was reinforced by the wide popular support for testing immigrant worthiness and closing off the borders to undesirables. Further, we can see this as part of a broader evolution of isolationist positions on American values toward a more bounded understanding of the politics of citizenship and border policies after World War I.

Just as Borah's isolationism had a firm sense of idealistic hopes for avoiding wars yet permitted commercial and cultural international involvement, so too were his ideas about domestic freedoms, and even immigration, imbued with a touch of utopianism, although his idealism always seemed muted by his far more realistic calls for local determination in domestic politics and scientifically determined quotas for immigrants. An idealistic position on the makeup of American society actually was long-standing for Borah. When he had entered Boise politics in the early 1890s, he argued that the dynamic interplay of diverse groups was good for American society. Encouraging the existence and ability of such groups to achieve greater socio-democratic status, he asserted, was beneficial for the nation.[43] In reaction to the often-alienating, poor conditions produced by unrestrained capitalism and large corporations, Borah argued for the benefits of state-level action because "the law making power of the Government rests with us."[44] Essentially an assimilationist, then, Borah also argued for the inculcation of nationalistic feelings in citizens and for testing immigrants to ensure that they planned to stay in the country and to contribute to the nation's vitality. As such, Borah was a pioneer of a nationalistic form of what might be termed a tolerance-based assimilationism, yet it was also framed by his view that certain peoples as a whole, such as the Japanese, represented a different sort of "civilization" that did not mix well with Anglo-American democratic civilizations. He urged strict Americanization of all immigrants to bring them in line with America's values. Borah did not believe in the more expansive cultural pluralism espoused by Horace Kallen in 1915, although his thought was closer to that of Kallen than to the transnational cosmopolitan pluralism articulated by Randolph Bourne in 1916.[45]

Borah's worldview fused his conception of national isolation and domestic social changes with his beliefs about local autonomy and immigration restriction as "particularist." The particularity can be seen as how he understood the best ways to integrate each individual and group into society by providing a sense of multiple communities at the local, state, and national levels. Broadly defined as a philosophical term, particularism is a belief that groups pursue their own specific collective interests first and foremost.[46] This, in turn, led Borah to see the distinct limitations on specific race and skill types in immigration quotas as an advantageous legislative route, particularly at the state level, for keeping American society dynamic and prosperous. Walter Lippmann aptly termed this ill-seeming amalgam of conservative and liberal views as Borah's "western provincialism." Borah and many other Irreconcilable isolationists took a "western" political provincial perspective in that they aimed to be practical while being rhetorically idealistic, favoring local and states' rights whenever possible, assimilationist while sometimes seeing the strengths of immigrant groups, always nationalistic, often anti-imperial, and intensely suspicious of corporate and governmental "bigness" in virtually any form.[47]

Opposing the League

In most political matters Borah held consistently to these views, which he termed "Americanism" and which he differentiated starkly from the expansionist, interventionist Americanism associated with Theodore Roosevelt. In most cases of policy—foreign as well as domestic—Borah wanted the nation to rely on the citizenry, whom he referred to with the characteristically progressive moniker the "voters," rather than be obligated by foreign powers to take action. He often said that he could not be shaken even if coerced by misguided masses of popular support. Indeed, being resolute came naturally to Borah.

For the former frontier lawyer and state prosecutor, life experiences deeply informed his firm belief in strong laws, social order, and individual self-determination. He maintained that ultimately the nation ought to concentrate on itself—that is, by encouraging economic growth, fair corporate practices, and democratic processes. It should not be distracted, Borah said, from the essential "wisdom and justice" of Americans at home, which in part accounted for why he had voted in favor of the war resolution that so many of his constituents and fellow Americans had favored in 1917. These beliefs also help explain why, beginning with a speech and a resolution on December 5 and 6, 1918, Borah staked out his most famous stance against any binding international alliance system of the sort Wilson was completing.

Borah opposed the president's attendance at the Paris Peace Conference and rejected the team of sycophants that Wilson took with him. Still, casting himself as a good patriot, once the president departed, Borah wished him luck, though his letters reveal that Borah sensed a widening chasm between the two. "The President . . . is in favor of a League of Nations," said Borah. "If the Savior of mankind would revisit the earth and declare for a League . . . I would be opposed to it. That is my position and it is not a question of personality. It is a question of policy for my government."[48] Borah's reluctant vote for war and his strong position against the League were united by his rationale that it had been an "American war" to defend U.S. interests, not a mission to spread democracy, and certainly should not entail participating in binding global governance that might undermine the nation's autonomy.

In the hour and a half that Borah spoke to the galleries of the Senate in February 1919, he presented his case to reject the treaty and the League outright. He cited Washington's admonitions and heralded his injunctions not to enter into foolish entanglements with the Old World. Borah quoted Washington's critical question: "Why quit our own to stand upon foreign ground?" His response, of course, was a resounding "never!" Borah seized upon this classically isolationist perspective by articulating the principles of self-sufficiency, minimizing foreign conflicts, and maintaining a guiding view that nonentanglement was the best course of action in virtually all circumstances. The League, Borah declared, was a "first step in internationalism and the first distinct effort to sterilize nationalism." This strong language of "sterilizing" had much in common with the fiery words of other patriotic firebrands. It marked Borah as a fellow in the ultra-nationalist ranks, at least insofar as he stood up to those who would dilute American patriotism.[49]

To Borah, the world had changed in the modern age, and America had benefited greatly. But the Old World had largely remained the same since Washington's day. It was characterized by power politics and conflict. The words of Washington were no shibboleths to Borah—they went to the very deepest of his convictions as an irreconcilable isolationist.[50]

Who were these "Irreconcilables" whom Borah led in the fight against the League? A group of senators, they were a diverse lot, coming to so-called obstructionist positions for a variety of reasons. The exact number of senators who could be described as Irreconcilables is difficult to pin down; many gradually drifted from support to opposition over time and some were more vocal than others. The most accurate list includes sixteen senators who were central to the group by the time of the final vote.[51] Maverick progressive Republicans, by and large, in opposition to the Democratic president, made up fourteen of the members, but there were also two Bryanite Democrats:

William Borah (R, ID)

Frank Brandegee (R, CT)

Albert Fall (R, NM)

Bert Fernald (R, ME)

Joseph France (R, MD)

Asle Gronna (R, ND)

Hiram Johnson (R, CA)

Philander Knox (R, PA)

Robert La Follette (R, WI)

Joseph McCormick (R, IL)

George Moses (R, NH)

George Norris (R, NE)

Miles Poindexter (R, WA)

James Reed (D, MO)

Lawrence Sherman (R, IL)

Charles Thomas (D, CO)

Interestingly, out of these sixteen, five senators remained in office for the debates over the outlawry of war in 1928: Borah, Johnson, Moses, Norris, and Reed. While other senators also played pivotal roles, most notably Lodge as majority leader, the Irreconcilables were at the heart of the political and ideological confrontation.

If Congress voted for America to join the League, Borah opined, it would mark a radical break, a "surrender [of] the traditional foreign policy of this country, established for one hundred years." Times change, he acknowledged in his speech; but he hoped change would come in the form of reinforcing the concept of the Monroe Doctrine, which he called a "principle of self-defense" and which he argued was essential as a "distinct announcement that the European system could not be transferred to America." Repeatedly, Borah aligned himself with "Washington and Jefferson and Jackson and Lincoln and Roosevelt." "Let us be true to ourselves; and, whatever the obligations of the future, we can not then be false to others."[52] Borah reasoned that the nation was like an individual, whose central autonomy to make war, make peace, and send troops abroad at its own volition was not to be trifled with by others. Article X of the League covenant obligated the United States to enter Europe's affairs, he said. Because of that well-recognized fact, Americans should logically expect that other member nations would be forced to interfere in U.S. affairs. Further, Borah pointed out that each of the British dominions would have a vote in the proposed League and would outnumber the single vote of the United States.

Seven days after his "Americanism" speech, Borah made news by refusing a presidential invitation to come to the White House and discuss the new League plans with members of the Foreign Relations committees of both houses. He seethed that other anti-League Republicans agreed to attend the meeting with the president. In his private letter of explanation to Wilson's secretary, Borah stated his case diplomatically. "The differences between the President and myself on this question are fundamental." He noted, "I am sure no suggestions of mine would modify in the slightest the views of the President, and nothing could induce me to support the League. . . . I mean no personal disrespect." He felt that in good conscience he could not meet with the president and receive confidential information that he would not be "perfectly free" to transmit to his anti-League colleagues.[53] Nine months later, in November 1919, in another flourish of oratory directed against congressional ratification of the League charter, Borah said, "But your treaty does not mean peace—far, very far, from it. If we are to judge the future by the past it means war." He turned to the gallery and rhetorically questioned the audience in the Senate chambers. "Is there any guaranty of peace," he asked, "other than the guaranty which comes of the control of the war-making power by the people?"[54] For Borah this was not just about the past, or about precedent. This battle was about the future. To join the League, according to Borah, would constitute an inherent usurpation of the rights of Americans that would limit personal and national freedom to act in the world.

League Fight Is No Guarantee of Peace

Having entered the world war with a grand vision for global peace, Wilson emerged from the peace negotiations with a complex and thorough plan for establishing it. Embedded in the Treaty of Versailles, which officially halted hostilities, was the covenant for the League of Nations. Wilson presented the covenant on February 14, 1919, stating, "It is a definite guarantee of peace. . . . It is a definite guarantee against the things which have just come near bringing the whole structure of civilization into ruin."[55] He had high expectations for its success. Upon arriving in Boston after the Paris peace negotiations, Wilson declared that he would not allow "some narrow-minded minds that have no sweep beyond the day's horizon" to derail his plans.[56] The stubborn president could not have realized how much difficulty his proposal would meet in the Senate over the next year.

The reactions of the Irreconcilable senators to Wilson's proposal were immediate and stressed how it radically departed from traditional U.S. foreign policy. They emphasized diversions from the foreign policy precedents set by Washington and Monroe, the imperative that the United States retain control over where, when, and how it entered international disputes, the possibility of being controlled by foreign nations limiting U.S. autonomy in the future, and other specific aspects of the League and the treaty that they saw as incompatible with American values. Borah, the most eloquent of the group, stated unequivocally that the League constituted "the most radical departure from our policies hitherto obtaining that has been proposed at any time since our Government was established."[57]

As we have seen, modern isolationists tended to deploy precedent as a primary instrument of persuasion in their arguments. Citing Washington's Farewell Address was just such a ploy for Borah and it embodied the essence of his beliefs. To invoke Washington also revealed the Irreconcilable sense of the role the past had to play in the present. Namely, the nation should stick to foundational principles but update them. As Borah explained it, "[Washington's] idea was that we never could become a nation with a national mind, a national purpose, and national ideals until we divorce ourselves from the European system."[58] The Irreconcilables insisted upon retaining this policy, claiming that it had succeeded throughout the nineteenth century and should not be destroyed just because times had changed. For example, Poindexter declared, "This essential principle has done more to preserve peace for a hundred years than all the leagues of nations ever formed."[59] Monroe's doctrine of permanently separating the affairs of the Western Hemisphere from the affairs of Europe was what they pointed to, and it appears as the shared, critical element in tradition-based arguments that proved most effective in the debates over the League, uniting Lodge and Borah. While defending the Monroe Doctrine, Borah said simply, "It is personal; it is individual; it is the law of self defense."[60] It is fascinating that at least tacitly Lodge agreed to Borah's interpretation of the Monroe Doctrine for the purposes of the fight against the League. Both men came together with much wrangling to form a loose Republican bloc of mild, strict, and absolute "reservationists" to argue on the Senate floor throughout 1919 that maintaining Monroe *and* national autonomy was critical, no matter the status of the League. The precedents of the Washington-meets-Monroe model of foreign policy, Lodge and Borah said, that had successfully kept the peace between Europe and America for a century should not be scrapped and replaced with entangling alliances of dubious merit.

The League debates are well known by historians, so we will focus here on how isolationist ideas were woven into political arguments against the League and Wilsonian progressive internationalism. Many League provisions were intended to promote world peace, including plans for disarmament, colonial possessions, and labor rights. The most central and also the most contentious was Article X. This article stipulated, "The Members of the League undertake to respect and preserve as against external aggression the territorial integrity and existing political independence of all Members of the League."[61] The League's critics clung to autonomy-based, unilateralist isolationist arguments. They were outraged that the United States would be obligated to protect, with its own forces if necessary, the territory of another nation. Hiram Johnson explained, "Wilson is getting a paper league of nations without real power, and in return is pledging our country in various directions, which will require us to keep troops possibly in Togo land . . . and even the Dardanelles. . . . I never would vote for a treaty of peace requiring our boys to do anything of the sort."[62] In questioning Wilson, the Irreconcilable members of the Foreign Relations Committee attempted to ascertain whether this was a legal or a moral obligation. Wilson insisted that a moral obligation could carry as much force as a legal one, but the senators were not convinced. Senator Frank Brandegee rejected his interpretation, saying, "There is no doubt that that is an obligation in a contract, and I know of but one way to perform an obligation that you have contracted to perform, and that is to perform it." Article X received a plethora of criticism throughout the entirety of the League fight. Poindexter asked whether the United States would be obligated to send thousands of troops and a billion dollars to tiny Armenia.[63] Borah asked whether America must help protect every possession of the British Empire, which stretched to every corner of the globe.[64]

Similarly, the Irreconcilables objected that the League would put America's free will and sovereignty under the control of foreign nations. An often-repeated outcry was that the British Empire, with all of its global possessions, would have five votes. Borah asked, "You who are in favor of this league, are you willing to give to any nation five votes against our one?"[65] As for the League Council, it was designed so that there must be a unanimous vote for global agreements, such as disarmament. Poindexter commented, "So under the terms of this instrument . . . Japan can say to the United States, 'You can not increase your Army; we will not vote for it.' . . . I should like the President to discuss that question on the Pacific coast."[66] The question of other nations' having a direct say over U.S. armaments and the ability to outvote the United States on critical issues was of paramount importance, as the senators, particularly Borah and James Reed, repeatedly hammered home in their statements.

American sovereignty, Reed said, was being stripped away. "I want to burn it into the brain and heart of the American people, that every nation entering the league yields to its arbitrament [sic] and decision all controversies with other countries, even though they involve the national honor or the national life."[67] Direct control by Americans over American affairs always had been central to the country's peace. There was also a strong undercurrent of Monroe-style hemispherism in these anti-Wilsonian, anti-League arguments, even among those who were more hypernationalist than irreconcilable. As Roosevelt laid out in the *Kansas City Star*, the nation should not "completely withdraw into its shell" and international consultation might avert war, but there should be only a "spheres of influence"–type arrangement with Europe and Asia in which the United States would oversee the Western Hemisphere. Other nations in other regions could then "introduce some kind of police system in the weak and disorderly countries at their thresholds."[68] The modern isolationists like Borah saw Roosevelt's views as congruous with their role in safeguarding a nation that no longer needed to fear external threats as it once had, and they aimed to work with fellow Republican hypernationalists to defeat the League.

The senators moved from the Article X debate to other aspects of the covenant also seen as antithetical to traditional American values. In keeping with anti-imperialists' critiques in assessing Article X, most Irreconcilables broke with the Lodge-Roosevelt position of old as articulated in the "large policy." Borah and his colleagues perceived hypocrisy in the claim of protecting national sovereignty while the status quo of colonial possessions and minority subjugation was being upheld for other imperial powers. Most notable, Japan was essentially being rewarded with the absolute control of Shantung, a Chinese province. Johnson was incensed that the United States would be a signatory to such procolonialism after fighting a war ostensibly to support and spread liberal beliefs against Prussian militarism and oppression. "We made the Orient 'safe for democracy,'" said Johnson, "by dismembering its only democracy and handing the parts to the strongest autocracy on earth. The blackest page in all our history was written when our name was signed to the treaty delivering Shantung to Japan."[69] How could the United States pretend to uphold the value of popular sovereignty while handing over millions of Chinese to Japanese control? The integrity of the treaty was further undermined when Secretary of State Robert Lansing testified that Japan would have signed the treaty even without the Shantung stipulation.[70] Senator Norris, the Irreconcilable perhaps most inclined toward the League, claimed that Shantung was "the bribe to bring Japan into the war on the Allied side," and it was on these grounds that he was most troubled and primarily why he voted against ratification.[71]

In addition, Irish independence was a prominent point of contention. Many senators, particularly those with many Irish American constituents, claimed the League would force America to support the continued domination of Ireland by the English. A meeting with the president in January 1919 led to confusion over whether Wilson insinuated, "Ireland is to be left to the mercies of England!" Wilson denied it, but the rumor led to greater animosity between the two sides.[72] The senators' indignation continued, and Senator Borah proposed Senate Resolution 48, requesting that the American representatives at the peace commission demand a hearing on Irish independence, but ultimately no action was taken.[73] The Shantung and Ireland controversies demonstrated that the Irreconcilables would permit no leeway for policies they saw as fundamentally contrary to Wilson's own espousal of "popular" sovereignty. America, they said, had been founded on the principles of freedom and liberty, and the senators were not going to allow Wilson to get away with such hypocritical concessions.

Borah's Americanism

As his February 1919 speech showed, Borah considered his composite isolationist vision as a new "Americanism" for the new postwar era. He largely stuck to this framework for the next two decades, and these views reveal the contours of modern isolationist thought taken to the extreme. They are best understood as a unilateral, nationalist, and populist form of isolationism that he often called "Americanism." But the essence of this worldview was an "autonomism" of sorts, which prized American autonomy above virtually all else. Archetypal in the extreme, from 1918 through 1928 Borah developed and articulated his isolationist thought based on national autonomy first, cultural and commercial engagement with the world second, and he took a principally domestic orientation in working toward national economic and social progress reinforced by strategic, limited action (almost exclusively commercial) on the world stage.

Like his erstwhile ally in the League fight, Lodge, as well as a host of other Irreconcilables, Borah considered himself a nationalist. But his nationalistic Americanism represented a major shift in his thinking and in the organization of modern ideas about isolation as brought about by the experiences of his reluctant vote for the war, his battle against Wilson's progressive internationalism, and his perception of the patriotic excesses of the American people in wartime. Borah's postwar nationalist-isolationist beliefs sought to overturn the militaristic, expansionist, and interventionist Americanism of the turn-of-the-century imperialists and later pro–World War I hawks. Borah had not always held such views. In fact, though he briefly supported the Spanish-American War, he turned against the territorial expansion and the continued conflict that ensued. As a result of America's experiment with empire, Borah changed his mind about how the nation should contemplate going to war, in times of peace as well as times of impending conflict.

Invoking the rhetoric and many of the rationales of anti-imperialist arguments, once Borah was elected to the Senate in 1906 he sought the independence of the Philippines. He consistently argued against the use of American forces abroad unless absolutely necessary. His criteria for "necessity" varied over the years but generally were premised on a belief in self-defense as the primary rationale for war-making. In most instances from 1906 through his death in 1939 Borah opposed interventionist policies toward Latin America and Asia, as well as in Europe. In keeping with this consistent theme in his views on America's place in the world, he argued first against any threat of entanglement or loss of autonomy, but secondly, and even more significant into the 1920s and 1930s, Borah believed that the United States should deal on a level of equality, "honorably," with all nations and peoples regardless of their relative size or strength.

His opposition to the League, to the later Washington Conference on international disarmament, and the World Court was part and parcel of this fundamental worldview. It did not originate in a belief that working toward world peace was impossible or unnecessary—quite the opposite. As he often declared, the promotion of universal peace was a major goal, but it had to be accomplished in keeping with American tradition, while emphasizing domestic prosperity, freedom, and tranquility. This was no small qualification. As we will see in more detail in the next chapter, in the 1920s this came to fuse the inward-looking perspective of many reformers of progressive, populist, and even conservative stripes, with some of the idealistic internationalism of the peace activists and unilateralist internationalists. A moderate form of this modern isolationist internationalism came to predominate the American political discourse in the period. In many ways it became essential to how Americans evaluated how the nation might best operate in the world.

Borah, however, ratcheted this view up one more notch. He held to nationalist and individualist "autonomism." Essentially this meant that local autonomy was always best so long as it did not transgress criminally against other entities—this included people and businesses, as well as cities, states, and nations. In this way Borah was not simply "anti-treaty" or a mere "great opposer," as his opponents often claimed. He and his allied Irreconcilables, along with many in the ranks of the anti-League reservationists, wanted to maintain America's authority to take unilateral action as a major global economic and military power while not being bound to commit troops or matériel to other nations. Here too, Borah went a step further; he firmly opposed American expansion and imperial policies, yet he staunchly advocated strict American policing of the hemisphere in keeping with the tenets of the Monroe Doctrine, while rejecting interference in the governments of Latin America on behalf of U.S. commercial interests.

As the 1920s wore on, Borah became an even more formidable opponent of most forms of U.S. military or diplomatic engagement with other nations. Borah later pushed for conferences to limit naval armaments among the major powers while opposing international accords that bound U.S. autonomy; thus, he hoped to instantiate a legal internationalism while giving the nation as much freedom on the international stage as possible. Fundamentally, however, he saw the League question as essentially answered by what he perceived as the popular, which opposed any idealistic internationalism that trumped America's traditional hemispherism and autonomy as embodied in the Monroe Doctrine. On February 22, 1919, the front page of the *New York Times* carried the column headline "Borah Demands Vote on League." The subheadline continued: "Declares wisdom of the people alone can guide the nation on such an enterprise . . . Peril to Monroe Doctrine . . . Terms it a most radical departure from our ideals."[74]

Race, Religion, Rejecting the League

Appeals against the League did not wholly derive from deep-seated principles. Many opponents of the League based their critiques on more base reasoning or extreme ideological beliefs. For example, James Reed of Missouri sought to rouse racist feelings by telling his colleagues that it was a "colored league." He argued that joining as an equal member in the League would mean being dominated by the brown and yellow races, which he termed "so low in civilization that they constitute the very dregs of ignorance, superstition, and barbarism."[75] Conceding the nation's sovereignty to Europe was bad enough, but the involvement of all the "colored" nations of the world was appalling to Reed. Just as an array of both imperialist and anti-imperialist debaters played the political race card to their advantage, racial prejudice and xenophobia played roles on all sides in the League debates. So too did anti-Catholicism play a role. Senator Lawrence Sherman of Illinois, for example, claimed that the Catholic Church would dominate the League. Member nations, he said, were likely to be ordered to take action by the pope. Sherman noted that twenty-four of the forty Christian nations in the League were Catholic. "I believe it a matter of profound apprehension," he said, "that one man at the head of a great religious organization controls . . . or seeks to control the conduct of the delegates of the 24 member nations."[76] The nineteenth-century precedent of nonentangled foreign affairs was paired with this still-prevalent precedent of racial and religious insensitivity and ignorance, a potent combination.

Senator Johnson neatly summed up the ideological basis for their rejection of the League of Nations and the Treaty of Versailles, saying, "Our difficulty has been the past two years that we were Pro-Belgian, Pro-English, Pro-French—anything but Pro-American, and that it is time to be Pro-American now."[77] These senators who opposed the League were not about to tolerate a foreign policy that bowed to the demands of other nations at the expense of American priorities.

As a minority group of mostly Republicans facing a Democratic administration, the Irreconcilables' primary tactic was intense partisan politicization of the issue. The parties' wrangling over the direction of America's policy began well before the war ended. On October 25, 1918, Wilson, after previously calling for a halt to partisanship during the war, asked the nation to give him a Democratic Congress in the upcoming midterm elections; he claimed that it was "no time either for divided counsel or for divided leadership."[78] This caused an immediate uproar from the Republican caucus. Republican National Committee chairman Will H. Hays proclaimed, "A more ungracious, more unjust, more wanton, more mendacious accusation never was made by the most reckless stump orator, much less by a President of the United States."[79] After achieving a one-seat majority in the Senate, the Republicans prepared for direct, continuous conflict with the other side, particularly since the presidential election of 1920 was never far out of sight.[80]

The Republicans, nearing the end of the Sixty-Fifth Congress in March 1919, took a dramatic approach to ensure that they could gain control of the debate sooner than the start of the Sixty-Sixth Congress, which was not slated to begin for many months. La Follette, Sherman, Brandegee, and others, without official approval from majority leader Lodge, initiated an all-night filibuster on several end-of-session spending bills, including the Victory Bond Authorization bill. Johnson blamed the Democrats for forcing them to such drastic action: "They want the President to hold the stage, and have the only forum of expression . . . like all autocrats, he wants no opposition, nothing which will stir the slumbering spirit of freedom in the nation."[81] In forcing Wilson to call an emergency session of the Sixty-Sixth Congress in the spring, thus giving Republicans official control, Robert La Follette sounded Borah-like when he defended his actions as necessary for true democratic leadership. "Somebody has got to stand up," he declared. "Somebody has got to raise the flag. He may be shot, but it must be done."[82]

In addition to this huge embarrassment for Wilson, a number of Republican senators circulated a petition known as the "Round Robin," which rejected the League covenant as presently conceived. Thirty-nine senators signed it, many more than just the Irreconcilables, indicating that the treaty would not pass the two-thirds requirement without substantial change.[83] The filibuster infuriated Wilson. "A group of men in the Senate have deliberately chosen to embarrass the administration of the government," he stated emphatically. He continued that the core problem had nothing to do with his proposal or vision for internationalism. No, the issue was that these men "make arbitrary use of powers intended to be employed in the interest of the people."[84] Such a statement, though, was clearly inaccurate, as Irreconcilable Senator Miles Poindexter pointed out. As reported in the New York Times, he said, "The Republican party rendered a great service to the country in withholding approval until an effort could be given for consideration and amendment."[85] The Irreconcilables were gradually taking over the terms of the debate. They set the groundwork, and finally Lodge had to come to Borah to combine their numbers in the political maneuvers that were the first step in the full rejection process.

Wilson knew as much. Along with several of the most persuasive Democratic speakers, a pro-treaty/pro-League group traveled the nation to drum up support. Borah and Lodge, too, knew that this battle would be waged in the court of public opinion as much as in the halls of Congress. They put together a rival group and launched competing speaking tours of the country in the summer and fall of 1919. Borah's oratory was in full form during this period, but his good friend Hiram Johnson, according to the *New York Times,* was "the most smashing critic of the league and treaty before an audience." He stayed with the whole tour in the Midwest and across the West.[86]

This also was a moment of conspicuous personal animus. Well before the League battle heated up and the national barnstorming began, Lodge had written to Theodore Roosevelt, confiding that "I never expected to hate anyone in politics with the hatred I feel toward Wilson."[87] And the feeling was mutual, particularly once the League issue came to a head. Wilson privately rebuked Lodge as stubborn, called the Senate cohort of reservationists "bungalow-minded," and simply could not tolerate the critiques of the Irreconcilables.[88]

Several examples demonstrate the heightened rhetoric and help us better understand that even in these times of heated political debate, the crux of the matter pivoted around a politically isolationist vision with three major aims: keeping the nation isolated from foreign political-military entanglements; minimizing war and helping to arbitrate peace (on unilateral American terms); and adhering to national ideals, precedent, and internal improvements.

Wilson declared in Indianapolis, "There is in that covenant not one note of surrender of the independent judgment of the United States, but an expression of it."[89] Johnson responded to fire with fire, saying, "There never was a more specious or false plea made, but I presume like 'keeping us out of war' and the world vision of the League, he will put it over with the good church people of the land."[90] Joining Senators McCormick and Borah, Johnson stoked up a crowd of supporters in Chicago, asking, "Who was the quitter," abandoning American values in Paris? The crowd shouted back, "Wilson!" and "Impeach him!"[91] Democratic Senator Reed also braved unfriendly waters to spread the word against the League, being booed off the stage at one rally.[92] Johnson regarded his tours through New England and the West as extraordinary opportunities to spread the "doctrine of Americanism."[93]

The tours also served political ambitions beyond advancing an isolationist worldview. Speaking tours against the League were an opportunity to spread something else—name recognition and influence. Johnson, along with many leading Republicans, had strong presidential ambitions. He used his campaigning around the country as another outlet in his attempts to steer the nation in a more traditional direction. Johnson was quick to note all of the politicking in the caucus, observing that the "dominating personal characteristic with all is egotism and vanity."[94] While he did use the League fight as his presidential platform, Johnson came across as sincere, saying, "I feel so deeply upon the subject that I would sacrifice my political future (if I have any) in opposition. There are times when a man who loves his country must go his way, no matter what his people think. This time has come to me."[95]

Approaching the 1920 election, Lodge and Borah found more room to collaborate. Republicans tried to instill a sense that the country would get better care in their hands. Poindexter pronounced this message, saying, "The mission of the Republican Party in the immediate future is to save the Republic from the process of national disintegration in progress during the present administration."[96] Democratic Irreconcilable Charles Thomas of Colorado tried to retain a sense of nonpartisanship, explaining that the proposal's "stupendous importance to us, to posterity, and to the world lift it far above the limitations of party organisms." However, he was not able to stem the increasingly partisan tide of the debate.[97]

Joining Lodge was another former expansionist, former Indiana senator Albert Beveridge. He declared that Americans should oppose Wilson's "mongrel internationalism" and instead ought to concentrate on pressing domestic concerns. As he put it, the American global mission in the wake of the devastating war should be more exemplar than crusader. Beveridge wrote in a high-profile article on the "Pitfalls of the 'League of Nations'" that by rejecting the League and a punitive peace, policy-makers could focus on the "people and the development of a mighty continent."[98] He rejected the pursuit of greatness in the international arena if it came at the expense of progressive reform at home. Beveridge was particularly opposed to Wilson's chosen instrument of internationalism—the League—as it carried with it likely and unexpected consequences related to alliances that might lead to further conflicts abroad.

Others promulgated similar views but in more shrill terms. Illinois Senator Lawrence Sherman, a fellow Irreconcilable and a friend of Borah's, spoke to the Senate to explain his views. He staked out the modern vision of belligerent isolationism, shot through with the recognition of a need to engage the world as a commercial power, but to avoid being subjected to the whims of other nations or buying into the reparations-laced peace of Versailles. Sherman claimed that the "League is a Pandora's box of evil to empty upon the American people the aggregated calamities of the world." In more measured tones, Sherman, like the anti-imperialist opponents of expansion, asserted the nation's core beliefs when acting abroad. "We are not colonizers. We have not sought to sound our morning drumbeats around the world," argued Sherman. "The great labor-saving machines, the communication of thought, the secrets of nature's processes seized and adapted to human use, the greatest of world discoveries have been our contribution to mankind. While the nations fought for supremacy and territory around the globe, we labored with what we had to make the most of our blessings. . . . Now, having helped put the German where he belongs, and being willing in like circumstances to help do so again, we are asked to lend our lives and treasures to every feud that blazes out in three continents, whether it concerns or menaces our interest or safety or not. We are invited to become the knight-errant of the world." Sherman concluded forcefully that domestic focuses rather than world government were of paramount concern. "A nation's first duty is to its own people," he said. "Its government is for them."[99]

Hiram Johnson was more America-centered even than Sherman, Borah, or Lodge, for that matter. Like Borah, Johnson was a lawyer. Both men adopted legalistic mind-sets in approaching political issues. Johnson's assault against binding international treaties and organizations approached world problems not merely by prizing "America first"; in many ways he defined this as "American alone." Johnson may have been the most insular-thinking isolationist of the period, even among a group of staunch isolationists that included Borah and Reed. But when he focused on domestic issues he was passionate in advocating progressive solutions to internal problems of labor organizing, for promoting transparency and eliminating corruption in politics, as well as for a vigorous national defense, while manifesting an acute dislike for foreigners and other nations. Early on, as California governor from 1911 to 1917, Johnson had advanced direct non-partisan primaries, referendum initiatives, prison reform, workman's compensation legislation, and safe-workplace laws. Johnson opposed virtually all new immigration and advocated restrictive quotas. Indeed, his votes in the Senate were virtually all nays on any type of international involvement, from the war resolution to the League of Nations to the Washington Conferences on Naval Limitations in 1921–1922 (which Borah and Lodge supported) to even nonpolitical work with the League or World Court. He affirmed the ideals of the Kellogg-Briand Pact but not the policy itself, and much later voted against the United Nations. He evinced an ultranationalist xenophobia; Johnson championed the denial and seizure of land and landowning rights for all illegal aliens. He was tapped as the Progressive Party candidate for vice president as Theodore Roosevelt's running mate in 1912, and it was the only election loss of his career.

Though initially in favor of joining the European war while on the campaign trail for the Senate in 1916, Johnson became disillusioned even more rapidly than did Borah. Upon assuming his seat in March 1917, Johnson wrote in early April of what he had learned so far. "Everything here is war," he remarked. "That which has been so intimate a part of our lives in California during the past seven years, governmentally, could not get the slightest hearing."[100]

Partisanship and Ideological Unity

Lodge artfully orchestrated the Republican opposition to the League and its two major camps: Borah and Johnson's Irreconcilables and Lodge's own large group of stalwart Republican reservationists. On August 12, 1919, Lodge attempted to bring these groups together in rejecting the treaty. He addressed the Senate and expressed what we have seen as his somewhat different isolationist logic. He opposed the League but was more unilaterally aggressive, and therefore was not against intervention (like Johnson). Lodge also favored expansionism within the hemisphere and a league in the abstract (unlike Borah on those counts). Making an argument for internal improvement through the assimilation of immigrants, Lodge declared, "I object strongly to having the politics of the United States turn upon disputes where deep feeling is aroused but in which we have no direct interest. It will tend to delay the Americanization of our great population, and is more important not only to the United

States but to the peace of the world to make all these people good Americans than it is to determine that some piece of territory should belong to one European country rather than to another."[101] He continued by arguing for the nation's external, unilateralist realities, echoing his friend Roosevelt's positions made prominent by his editorial writing in the *Kansas City Star*.

"For this reason I wish to limit strictly our interference in the affairs of Europe and of Africa. We have interests of our own in Asia and in the Pacific which we must guard upon our own account, but the less we undertake to play the part of umpire and thrust ourselves into European conflicts the better for the United States and for the world." He called upon the Senate to reject the League. He derided the "murky covenant" and argued for the outward, international freedom to take action wherever the nation deemed fitting. He proclaimed, "Our first ideal is our country and we see her in the future, as in the past, giving service to all her people and to the world. Our ideal of the future is that she should continue to render that service of her own free will. She has great problems of her own to solve, very grim and perilous problems, and a right solution, if we can attain it, would largely benefit mankind."[102]

In his most famous speech, Borah built on the sentiments expressed by Sherman and many of the themes expressed by Lodge. The oratory succinctly encapsulates Borah's culminating argument. On the last day of debating the League of Nations treaty, November 19, 1919, Borah rose to categorically state, "I shall record my vote against this treaty [because] it imperils what I conceive to be the underlying, the very first principles of this Republic. It is in conflict with the right of our people to govern themselves free from all restraint, legal or moral, of foreign powers." Recalling Abraham Lincoln's advice, Borah suggested adhering to the wisdom of the "Great Emancipator": "Entertain no compromise; have none of it." Borah then informed the Senate that despite Lodge's efforts to find a compromise on certain reservations that would make the treaty palatable to all, "my objections to the league have not been met by the reservations." He reminded those in the gallery of "the great policy of 'no entangling alliances' upon which the strength of this Republic has been founded for one hundred and fifty years." And he argued that Washington's "great foreign policy . . . is today a vital, indispensable element in our entire plan, purpose, and mission as a nation." He then asked, "Where is the reservation which protects us against entangling alliances?"[103]

Beyond their national importance, these debates were personal to him. Borah took umbrage with the fact that nameless Democratic opponents impugned his patriotism when he had only the nation's best interests at heart. "Sir," he said, "since the debate opened months ago those of us who have stood against this proposition have been taunted many times with being little Americans." Rising to greater rhetorical and emotional power, Borah avowed, "Leave us the word American, keep that in your presumptuous impeachment, and no taunt can disturb us, no gibe discompose our purposes. . . . Call us little Americans if you will, but leave us the consolation and the pride which the term American, however modified, still imparts."[104] In short, Borah redefined the terms that Wilson and others tried to use to tar him and his position. He declared that to be Irreconcilable was the height of American patriotism.

A host of politicians and pundits weighed in on the issue. Lodge and Borah practiced a delaying tactic to ensure that the vote would not take place until at least late in 1919, when they felt sure public support for the League would have continued to plummet. Borah embarked on a series of speaking tours across the country. His persuasiveness was crucial to making the public case against the League. On Articles X and XXI, though, the jurist of most prominence in the debates was the venerated John Bassett Moore. A former member of the State Department and a leading international law expert at Columbia University for more than sixty years, Moore, like Root, worried that this language undermined at least two key principles of American foreign policy established early in America's formative period: Washingtonian nonentanglement and the Monroe Doctrine. Further, he asserted that if Article XXI protected the doctrine, it also undermined it by making America part of world politics and sacrificing America's unique and distinct meaning, and limiting America's geographic advantages by lumping it in with European powers with their own colonial projects, for example. Linking the abandonment of the Monroe Doctrine to the end of nonentanglement was a powerful threat to traditional understanding of the country's relationship to the world. More to the point, even some moderate internationalists who favored a league feared such an outcome, and this anxiety played right into the hands of Borah's Irreconcilables bloc and Lodge's strict reservationists.

Borah asserted that an outcome of eroding Monroe and Washingtonian nonentanglement had to be prevented at all costs. "No foreign flattery, no possible world glory and power have disturbed our poise or come between us and our devotion to the traditions which have made us a people or the policies which have made us a Nation, unselfish and commanding." Indeed, he continued by going further. "If we have erred," he said, "we have erred out of too much love for those things which from childhood you and we together have been taught to revere—yes, to defend even at the cost of limb and life. If we have erred it is because we have placed too high an estimate upon the wisdom of Washington and Jefferson, too exalted an opinion upon the patriotism of the sainted Lincoln."[105] Reportedly Lodge was so stirred by Borah's address that he was moved to tears. Borah's extemporaneous speech-making that day also impressed the former senator Albert Beveridge, himself a great orator, and even Democratic Vice President Thomas R. Marshall, along with scores of those in the press gallery, complimented Borah on his triumph not just of persuasion but of elocution and presentation.

Though other senators spoke after Borah, no one matched his emotion or eloquence. As the session closed, the Senate voted on the treaty. An odd alliance formed, as had been foreseen by astute political commentators of the day. The senators who were "irreconcilably" opposed to American entry into the League of Nations followed the lead of Borah, who himself generally agreed with Lodge, while urging him not to cut any deals to accept any modified treaty that might include Article X. Lodge, master politician that he was, orchestrated an up or down vote with his reservations included, knowing full well that there were not the votes to pass the treaty. The Irreconcilables would not vote even for the reservations, of course, and thus formed an effective opposition, just as Borah and Lodge calculated.

The tone of the League debate had been decidedly negative and personal throughout 1919. Extreme rhetoric marked the positions taken by Irreconcilables, Democrats, and even reservationist Republicans. After meeting for lunch with several senators, President Wilson berated them before the Democratic National Committee, saying, "They are going to have the most conspicuously contemptible names in history" and that they would be "utterly condemned by the whole spirit of humanity."[106] Frank Brandegee shot back, saying, "I feel as if I had been wandering with Alice in Wonderland and had tea with the Mad Hatter."[107] On one occasion, Johnson described Wilson as "a Czar" doing "absolutely as he pleases," exclaiming against a "base betrayal of the Republic."[108] Meanwhile, both Sherman and Norris intimated that Wilson belonged in an "insane patients ward."[109] The partisan opponents may have gone a bit too far in their impassioned attempts to control the political debate.

The main partisan battles occurred over whether to include reservations, statements of American interpretation, in the ratification of the treaty. The "Mild Reservationist" Republican senators did want to see the League approved, only with a few alterations, while the Democrats, for the most part, rejected calls for any changes. What was most significant here, however, was that the Irreconcilables were happy to play both sides. Sherman presented a sarcastic view on the issue, saying, "There could not be confusion worse confounded if every amendment offered were voted into the treaty. Nobody knows what it is. . . . So vote them in; and then, after every one of the amendments is voted into the treaty and the league, I will vote to reject it all."[110] Indeed, it seemed that Borah, too, played both sides and learned from Lodge's clever tactic of fighting the League as it was presently constructed, rather than *a* league in principle. In this way, we see the emerging isolationist position articulated and orchestrated by Borah and his fellow Irreconcilables as less obstructionism qua obstructionism but, rather, an attempt to articulate a constructive vision based on American values and for an autonomous, restricted role in the world.

Wilson advanced a diametrically opposite position. Had the president been willing to compromise his Fourteen Points idealism and the less ideal form those principles had assumed in the League and treaty, then the Senate might have been convinced to pass the appropriate treaties, with the reservations that Lodge argued were essential. This Wilsonian alternative should be seen, however, as a broader political theory that contrasted sharply with refined, modern isolationist positions on how the nation ought to operate at home and in the world. Having used the violation of neutral rights as a casus belli, Wilson moved far beyond such a rationale and tried to make sense of the war and his vision for the peace as a unique world-history moment. While the topic of Wilsonian internationalism has been well explored by historians, for our purposes it should be sufficient to note that it was idealistic in a philosophical sense and radical in a political sense because it marked a turn away from long-standing reluctance to join Europe's wars and enter binding alliances, and it promulgated an epoch-making effort to impose a supranational democratic form upon an otherwise chaotic and destructive modern world system of belligerent, interconnected nation-states.[111]

Wilson noted in 1919 that he saw the current geopolitical situation as fusing the domestic and global. As Thomas Knock has argued, Wilson envisioned his idealistic "progressive internationalism" as a response to a modern era in which domestic, national politics seemed to be increasingly democratic, particularly given the transatlantic progressive movement. American foreign affairs to that point had not matched such views. The war had proved that the modern world was more dangerous and seemed to teeter on the edge of cataclysm and chaos. As a solution Wilson took the opposite tact from Borah; he proposed that this mismatch based on power politics between nations and equalization of politics inside nations had to be rebalanced (of course, he had a poor record on civil liberties and racial equality, but that was not how he saw it). So, he argued in Congress and on the stump that the logical conclusion was to re-center liberalism at the very heart of global foreign policy. As Wilson put it in January 1919, "Liberalism must be more liberal than ever before, it must even be radical, if civilization is to escape the typhoon." He went on to warn that "I do not hesitate to say that the war we have just been through, though it was shot through with terror of every kind, is not to be compared with the war we would have to face the next time." But contrary to Wilson's assertions, the peace treaty was far from an extension of liberal values and an application of democratic principles. Even given Wilson's genuine negotiating efforts to moderate the terms of the peace, the treaty represented vindictive power politics at their most blatant. The flight of progressive internationalists like Walter Lippmann from the Wilsonian cause further undermined support for both the president and his internationalist vision. And after suffering a debilitating stroke on his 1919 tour to promote the treaty across America, Wilson maintained an uncompromising stance, which he summed up flatly: "It is this treaty or no treaty."[112]

Employing poor (if loyal) political judgment, most Democrats, urged by Wilson, refused to accept *any* reservations on the treaty. They combined with the Irreconcilables, who of course would not approve *any* League treaty. Together these two factions, diametrically opposed on the ends that they advocated, came to agree on means. They defeated the treaty with the "Lodge reservations" by an initial vote of 39 to 55. With a greatly amended treaty sent to the Senate floor for ratification, the sides stood their ground and in the subsequent vote, the treaty "without reservations" was defeated by a vote of 38 to 53. On March 19, 1920, the treaty once again failed to receive the two-thirds Senate vote needed for approval.[113]

From Local to Global . . . to Internationalism?

Borah had participated in the process of building a community ethos first-hand in America's burgeoning towns of Kansas and Idaho. To him the key components for building the nation from within were just like those for small frontier towns: enhancing social cohesion, encouraging a coopera-tive spirit, establishing law and order, maintaining local autonomy through elections and commission work, and producing prosperity through farm-ing, industry, entrepreneurship, and innovation. Tocquevillian awareness of mutual association and reciprocal interest were the foundational values of American labor and society, according to Borah. In turn, he extrapo-lated from this local model to draw conclusions for the nation's best inter-ests in the international arena. No matter how sympathetic he was to other nations, he stated that the United States had no need to intervene abroad unless the national interest was at stake. Each locality should take care of itself. This, he thought, was how individuals, localities, and na-tions could best develop. Or, as he put it, America need not become en-tangled abroad, because the country had enough on its domestic plate to "masticate and assimilate and digest what we have."[114]

Borah perceived that many of the most obvious negative aspects of mod-ern industrial society undermined the essential ties that bind communi-ties. Like William James, Borah was an unswerving opponent of monopoly and the "bigness" of corporate consolidation. Borah connected these ex-cesses of American capitalism with the improper claims of commercial and political elites urging the nation to commit to entanglement abroad. Domestic concerns were the prism through which he viewed the proper role of the nation in the world throughout virtually his entire political ca-reer. Writing in 1927, Borah declared, "The greatest domestic problem since the Civil War is: What shall the government do and how shall it exer-cise its purpose?"[115] His solution to his question was also his answer to the excesses of unrestrained capitalism and the failures of assimilation at home. It was straightforward and local: these conditions could be overcome by economic and domestic administrative decentralization and through the inculcation of nationalistic values in the broader citizenry.

As a nationalist with respect to foreign affairs, Borah opposed any inter-national agreements that would restrict the country's freedom of choice to act in the world. States were to the United States as nations were to the international system—or at least as Borah perceived America ought to participate in the international order. Greater harmony would be produced by greater autonomy for the pieces of the whole, not less. Borah blended new conceptions of a broader American national identity at home for a postwar world, with an emphasis on less political "entanglement" abroad, particularly evident in his central role as an Irreconcilable.

The successful fight against the treaty and the League propelled Borah into the national spotlight as he refined and articulated a new postwar vision for American isolation that became powerfully influential throughout the 1920s, when he was chairman of the Senate Foreign Affairs Committee, known as the "Lion of the Senate."

These anti-League actions seemingly ended any hope of a concerted and enduring international role for the United States. However, as we will see in the next chapter, less than ten years later, a similarly transformative world agreement presented these "isolationists" and their pacifist and internationalist colleagues with an opportunity to support international cooperation. The rejection of the treaty by the Senate and the overwhelming embrace of that action in the election results of 1920 can be seen as a triumph for the new values of modern isolationism. Even as Wilson's efforts were recognized on the world stage, with the Nobel Peace Prize for 1919 (awarded in 1920) for his peacemaking visions and initiatives, these American actions against internationalism in the form of the League and the treaty, though, did not represent, as has sometimes been argued, a return to an earlier isolationist policy, because such a paradigm had never really been abandoned. Rather than a return, this shift signified a reconfiguration of internationalism and isolationism.

The events of 1918 through 1922 represented what Borah and his cohort saw as a reassertion of traditional isolationism given the changed realities of the period and in the face of the second real challenge (since the imperialist debates of the late 1890s) that such a worldview had faced. Traditional isolationist views had always emphasized trade and commerce, while aiming to minimize political commitments and conflicts. By the early 1920s the tendency to embrace and enhance economic prosperity reinforced a need for greater social cohesion at home; it also recognized the modern need for complex international movements of capital, goods, and culture, and combined that modern commercial internationalism with an ambiguously isolationist desire for global power through "cooperation" but without commitment. This set the stage for a fascinating convergence of visions about America's best course of action in global politics. Borah's nationalist, isolationist worldview found surprising common ground with Emily Greene Balch's pacifist, new internationalist perspective.

7

NEW INTERNATIONALISM

Is peace best maintained by "friendly people on either side" of a national border, or is it best served by "preparedness . . . to protect against the dangers of war"?[1] This question, posed by Emily Balch in 1924, epitomizes the conundrum that plagued Americans grappling with how their nation ought to approach its relationship to the world in the years after World War I. In attempting to address this fundamental quandary, the isolationist nationalism associated with the Irreconcilables often overlapped with the pacifist internationalism common among the women's peace movements in the 1920s and into the 1930s.

These two strains of thought converged dynamically at one idealistic moment when the United States helped to lead the international effort to outlaw war. Initiatives pushed by two former progressives, William Borah and Emily Balch—the first a populist-oriented and powerful chairman of the Senate Foreign Relations Committee from Idaho, the latter, from Massachusetts, was a cofounder of a settlement house and of an international peace movement—laid the groundwork for unifying new ideas about isolation with fresh visions for international peace.

The ascendance and coherence of American isolationism dovetailed with the rise of a new internationalism during the 1920s and 1930s and the development of the "outlawry of war" movement. The unique convergence of nationalist isolationists and pacifist internationalists during this time and particularly in support of the symbolic Kellogg-Briand Pact has not received significant attention from historians. In trying to channel the popular will, Borah and Balch did not see eye to eye on America's proper role in the world. Yet they shared profound convictions. Both held anti-imperialist, anti-interventionist, largely anti–big business, pro-neutrality, and pro-peace perspectives on how to moderate state power. Both believed in treating all nations on equal terms, while seeking to encourage domestic democratic reform and enhance national prosperity. Like a host of other former progressives and populists after World War I, Borah and Balch—Irreconcilables and pacifists—rethought the state's role in bringing the nation into the war and in repressing free speech at home. While Borah initially supported the war effort, he came to regret his decision, finding common ground with Balch, who had opposed preparedness all along and felt that America should be a powerful force for change only as a mediator, definitely not as a combatant. They both placed faith in public opinion as a moral force and sought to mobilize that force through their speech-making, publications, and activities throughout the nation and around the world. Balch's fascinating and little-known alliance with William Borah reinforces how even what has often been cast as walled-and-bounded isolationism promulgated by Borah and fellow "Irreconcilable isolationists" was compatible with the pacifist internationalism of Balch, Addams, and the Women's International League for Peace and Freedom (WILPF) and in spearheading such efforts as the Washington Conferences for disarmament in the early 1920s and the Kellogg-Briand Pact to outlaw war in the late 1920s, and in terms of the efforts to disengage from interventions in Latin America while pushing for stricter American neutrality from the 1920s through the 1930s.[2]

Borah's strategy to maintain peace, at least in the period from 1918 to 1922, had been to prepare at home and to work against alliances abroad except for those narrowly defined to minimize the potential for future wars while remaining nonbinding. But Emily Balch and Jane Addams had a more comprehensive view of global interconnectedness. Balch and Addams observed that nationalists as well as militarists took too limited a view of the nation's place in the world in conceptual, geographical, and temporal terms. They did not explore what Balch believed was the essence of international peace, the shared "ground of morality, Christianity, and principle."[3] Balch and Addams thus aligned themselves with an emerging new internationalist vision and against the "fetish of force," a term William Borah used often.[4] Both Balch and Borah's opposition to belligerency was woven into arguments for maintaining national autonomy while supporting international peace. They diverged radically, however, on the scale and scope of institutional internationalism and they battled over American entry into the World Court and the League of Nations. Balch was no knee-jerk isolationist, but she and her internationalist allies shared a surprising number of values with Borah and his Irreconcilables. Organizations such as Addams and Balch's WILPF were part of a larger, related movement for global peace that heralded a new internationalism for the postwar era that became linked to newly refined modern isolationist concepts. As we shall see, Balch, Addams, and the wider activities of the WILPF represent a clear counterpoint to the sort of limited international engagement that is most often associated with the politics and ideas driving the U.S. role in the world during the interwar years.

The development of women's internationalist organizations with potent American leadership was vital to the new internationalism of the era. The developing internationalist associations and perspectives of the period assumed too many forms to be fully detailed here, but among the most prominent was that characterized by the efforts of Balch, who was an intellectual and organizer more than a high-profile figure, and Addams, who was the figurehead not just for the WILPF but for causes ranging from settlement work to suffrage and beyond. They exposed developing fissures in and played a role in shaping new configurations of post–World War I isolationism as it crystallized into a more coherent set of political positions. Toward the end of the 1920s Jane Addams summed up her vision of international interdependence, a view widely shared by internationalist and pacifist activists; she termed it an international "consciousness" that had matured into fullness only after the war. "There is a lively sense of the unexpected and yet inevitable action and reaction between ourselves and all the others who happen to be living upon the planet at the same moment," she wrote in her sequel to *Twenty Years at Hull-House*. Applying the lessons she learned in the settlement house movement to her international peace initiatives, Addams concluded that "the modern world is developing an almost mystic consciousness of the continuity and interdependence of mankind."[5]

If in the wake of a catastrophic war the modern world was developing a "consciousness" of global interdependence, as Addams supposed in the 1920s, then it followed that many Americans would regard this trend in terms of variations on the modern isolationist positions that had been staked out over the previous two decades. While the defeat of the League of Nations and the Treaty of Versailles did not bring about isolationism, it did solidify a coherent bloc of ideas within an isolationist framework. The period that followed was neither a retreat into isolation nor a march toward global community. The fresh perspectives and newfound power of the Irreconcilables in the 1920s heralded iconic isolationist tenets such as unilateralism and self-sufficiency, with a renewed emphasis on neutrality, retrenchment from global power politics, a focus on domestic economic progress, and for many a shared desire to return to what President Harding termed domestic "normalcy."[6]

Addams, Balch, Borah, and Robert La Follette, among others, scorned American military involvement. The alternative was not sheer avoidance of supranational organization and diplomacy, but rather the enthusiastic international cooperation of the countries of the world. At the same time, the rapid rise of the United States to world prominence raised many questions about resources and involvement in the economies and crises of other nations, while the American reform movement continued to diminish in the postwar era. So too the positions of a wide array of "peace progressives" ranging from Addams to La Follette show an inherent internationalism embedded in most isolationist arguments as these notions had matured in the intervening years since the 1890s. In the 1920s, however, isolationist and internationalist arguments merged in new ways and a new goal for U.S. internationalism emerged starkly: in spite of America's refusal to make binding military or political commitments to Europe, the disastrous events of the war had proven that the preservation of peace must be a central aim for the postwar world. The question became: how to fulfill that objective?

Building on the Senate's rejection of the League of Nations and later repeated defeats of legislation to join the World Court, there was a rising wariness among isolationist leaders in America about being bound to participate in the global community. These rejections, though, also increased popular discussion and a deepening sense of the urgency to ensure peace. It was not only internationalist peace activists who spoke out for this cause. Most of the foremost self-defined isolationists of the period strongly supported international antiwar efforts known broadly as the "outlawry of war movement." This was such a potent current of opinion that the antiwar cause crossed political lines and social classes. Liberals, conservatives, former progressives, and radicals found merit in antiwar work, broadly defined, and in specific proposals to eliminate war.

By recovering and chronicling the powerful influence of isolationist ideas within the multifaceted American peace movement, this chapter shows how Balch, the WILPF, Borah, and the Irreconcilables, and conservatives along with liberal peace activists found common ground. The new face of American nationalism in the postwar period was surprisingly international in nature. Unexpectedly, these developments created a new "isolationist internationalism" expressed most dramatically by Borah in the 1920s, which he then gradually backed away from in the 1930s. The vision for how America might lead other nations was cooperative enough to satisfy many internationalists, while it was nonentangled enough to placate many among the unilateralist-oriented isolationists. Because of the prominent role of women and former suffragists, and given the startling heterogeneity of the group and its allies, the community of peace advocates in which Balch was a major actor achieved a great symbolic triumph at the end of 1928. Alongside the remaining Irreconcilables, led by Borah, these groups galvanized support to realize the idealistic internationalism of the Kellogg-Briand Pact to outlaw war.

A Call to Pacifism

Emily Balch discovered her calling as an international peace advocate at the age of forty-seven when war broke out across Europe in 1914. Like Bourne, the experience of European nationalism precipitated Balch's most vigorous phase of antiwar political activism. Born in Boston in 1867, educated at excellent private schools and a member of the first class to graduate Bryn Mawr College (in 1889), Balch was an ambitious and talented student. Thin and vigorous, with keen, dark brown eyes and a thoroughly academic manner, she became a passionate and caring professor of political economy at Wellesley College, and she was well known for her lively lectures.[7]

From her earliest professional activity, Balch's research and publications reflected her global orientation and her firm commitment to the study of immigrants and migration patterns, and her concern for the poor. A founder of the Denison House settlement in Boston, Balch crusaded for the rights of immigrants and indigents, just as she made a persuasive case for broader democratic and progressive changes at home and for harmony and tolerance in foreign affairs. In an era when many Americans espoused nativist fears of immigration, particularly of perceived inferior peoples from Slavic countries, Balch lived with, studied, and traveled extensively among Slavs in Europe and in the United States to produce her pathbreaking study, *Our Slavic Fellow Citizens*, published in 1910.[8]

The book rejected the prevailing assumption that those of old English ancestry were the key to sustaining American democracy. Underscoring these insights, Balch made an empirical and philosophical case that new immigrants from places such as Russia, Poland, Italy, and the Balkans were assimilating and in fact becoming good citizens. Almost two decades before *Our Slavic Fellow Citizens* was published, Balch evidenced her passion as a pro-immigrant activist with a pluralist mind-set. In public writing and in taking to the streets to speak out and join other Denison House settlement workers and Women's Trade Union League activists in direct protest, Balch opposed the Boston-based Immigration Restriction League and later anti-immigrant activities (particularly in the 1910s). That league, formed in 1894 and headed by Henry Cabot Lodge and John Fiske, and including David Starr Jordan, A. Lawrence Lowell, John Commons, and other political and intellectual leading lights of the age, held significant power in Massachusetts and national policy centers.[9]

Sounding much like Bourne, and perhaps helping to plant the seed of his transnational concept (the two became friends on the antiwar People's Council), Balch's public writings and private letters reveal her deep concern with the perils of nativism and restrictions on immigration. She wrote that Slavic newcomers and other immigrants would bring "fresh vigorous blood to a rather sterile and inbred stock." These views were linked with a refutation of racial stereotypes.[10] Balch differed with the new cutting-edge science of racial difference. "There is no such person as a Slav," she asserted, "any more than there is such a person as a Teuton or a Celt."[11] Balch noted, "I feel a profound skepticism as to the value of generalizations in regard to the character of nations and races, more especially if it is assumed that such characters are inherited and unchangeable."[12] Remarkably for her time, she argued that "group types" most likely are produced by "social development and imitation, determined by historical causes economic and other," rather than by innate characteristics.[13] Teaching these beliefs at Wellesley, she continued her reform activities. She co-founded and led the Boston Women's Trade Union League just after the turn of the century, and wrote and organized to support striking workers. She became an avowed pacifist and socialist and spoke out for women's rights and against racial injustice and anti-immigrant prejudice throughout the first decade of the twentieth century. Unlike her colleague and friend Jane Addams, who was a public figure drawn to the limelight and comfortable in front of audiences, Balch's relatively shy nature, intellectual inclinations, and organizational talents led her to become a force behind the scenes in the settlement house and international peace movements.

But it was the outbreak of war across Europe that prompted the most significant transition in Balch's career. An absolute pacifist since the

Spanish-American War, Balch held views that were heightened in 1914 by what she regarded as a rapidly expanding ruinous world war, likely to involve her own nation if citizens did not stand up for peace. She immediately committed herself to the cause of American mediation and world peace. For the spring semester in 1915 Balch requested and received a formal leave of absence from teaching at Wellesley, never fully anticipating that because of her time away and her antiwar activism, she might well not return to teach there. In April 1915 she traveled to attend the first International Congress of Women (ICW) at The Hague. Balch served as an official American delegate to the ICW, where she was pivotal in a number of efforts, such as founding what became the WILPF and in writing proposals for peace. Preparing position papers and lists of possible compromises to be considered by the warring nations, Balch visited Russia and Northern Europe to urge a brokered peace. She worked against the Selective Service legislation and the draft process, defended the rights of conscientious objectors and the foreign-born, and campaigned vigorously for the United States to remain neutral.[14]

In these efforts Balch interacted with and influenced many of the foremost internationalist and pacifist thinkers. The Congress of Women was primarily composed of prominent women in the International Suffrage Alliance, many of whom perceived deep connections between their fight for equal rights and the global struggle for peace. European suffrage leaders Emmeline Pethick-Lawrence of Great Britain and Rosika Schwimmer of Austria-Hungary, representing both sides of the burgeoning war, worked with Addams, Balch, Carrie Chapman Catt, Lillian Wald, and other American suffrage and women's rights activists in the cause of world peace. Rejecting the dominant social Darwinian view that war was inevitable, and perhaps even productive, the ICW overcame the obstacles presented by wartime travel and gathered more than one thousand women from combatant and neutral nations to work out a plan to end World War I. Their pro-peace resolutions were bold but vague, endorsing international cooperation (e.g., a World Court and a "Society of Nations"), general disarmament, national self-determination, and so-called democratic control of foreign policy.[15]

These resolutions, adopted by acclamation on May 1, 1915, were printed in English, French, and German. The declaration documents then were disseminated widely to all the combatant heads of state and mailed to civic organizations, reformers, and scores of prominent citizens. Ultimately, their efforts at arbitration ran aground on the shoals of belligerent nationalism and patriarchy. Nevertheless, Balch and her colleagues from around the world found new allies across Europe and learned lessons in large-scale organization and diplomacy. They also formed the Woman's Peace Party (WPP) at home to lobby for peace; in 1919 the party became the U.S. section of the WILPF. Balch chronicled the experiences at the ICW as she assisted Jane Addams and Alice Hamilton in writing *Women at The Hague: The International Congress of Women and Its Results* (1916).[16]

Following the conference, in the *Survey* magazine Balch delineated the results from The Hague and in so doing distinguished the two great poles between which she believed the United States and many of the European nations vacillated. "In one sense the present war is a conflict between the two great sets of belligerent powers, but in a different and very real sense it is a conflict between two conceptions of national policy," she wrote. "The catchwords 'democracy' and 'imperialism' may be used briefly to indicate the opposing ideas. In every country both are represented, though in varying proportions, and in every country there is strife between them."[17] The battle then was between democracy and imperialism. She saw little room, and no need, for America to cut itself off from the world. Instead, her answer to the clash between empire and democracy was to create an organization to help manage global democracy. She aimed to advance that process first through building international dialogues and organizations to moderate imperialist conflict.

Balch repeatedly traveled to Washington, D.C., to lobby Congress and Woodrow Wilson in 1915. Along with Catt, Addams, Wald, and other prominent members of the WPP, she hoped that American leaders might accept the ICW's plan for mediation instead of committing the United States to war. Addams and Balch had numerous meetings with Wilson that summer but discovered that he was shifting to an official public position of American preparedness and a desire to act unilaterally, even if he privately confessed to sympathy for the ICW proposals and hoped for a result that might create an enduring peace. In her *Survey* article Balch observed, "There is a widespread feeling that this is not the moment to talk of a European peace." She laid out a bold position that international cooperation was her primary cause but that its corollary must be trying to outlaw war itself. She wrote, "There is reason to believe that the psychological moment may be very close upon us. If, in the wisdom that comes after the event, we see the United States was dilatory when it might have helped to end bloodshed and make a fair and lasting settlement, we shall have cause for deep self-reproach."[18] All of this lobbying, of course, came to naught.

Balch, like Addams, pursued her goals by taking a prominent public role. She joined Henry Ford's peace initiatives, and though she did not sail with his peace ship, she did serve as a member of his Neutral Conference for Continuous Mediation, also in 1915. In Balch's major position paper at that conference, she proposed a framework for creating a "global mediation organization," quite similar to what later became Wilson's proposed League of Nations. Part of the liberal antiwar intelligentsia, Balch also served as an editor and writer at the *Nation*, where she wrote for global peacemaking and U.S. mediation, rather than militancy.

In addition, she worked with antiwar intellectuals Paul Douglas, Randolph Bourne, and Emma Goldman as part of the leadership for the American Association for International Conciliation (AAIC). She also drafted the practical peace proposal *Approaches to the Great Settlement*, with an introduction by her friend Norman Angell, the future Nobel Peace Prize winner and an English peace activist. She defended the rights of conscientious objectors and the need for free speech in an exchange with Bishop Richard Cooke in the *Christian Advocate*. And she energetically crossed national boundaries with Addams, Catt, and others to oppose international aggression, to weaken male domination of political decision-making, and to expose oppression at home and abroad. But it was not until after the war ended that the WILPF could truly take flight. Wartime repression in American took its toll on the pacifist and liberal antiwar community, censoring their publications and activities in 1917 and 1918. Indeed, the battle over suffrage poured over into the global peace movement as leaders such as Massachusetts suffrage activist Lucia Ames Mead, who led the state cause in 1918, strongly supported the League concept and became increasingly active in the WILPF (she was the head of the U.S. WILPF division by 1922). This led to a major burst of activities in 1919 for Balch as suffragists shifted terrain to lobby for international peace, relying on transatlantic (particularly U.S.-British) ties in the movement and their belief in women's solidarity.[19]

Balch's heightened international political activism in 1919, however, was the result of unfortunate circumstances. By late 1917 her high-profile antiwar views had alienated her from Wellesley College's largely prowar administration and its board of trustees, though the president Ellen Pendleton and many colleagues remained her allies. Like numerous other antiwar and pacifist professors whose contracts were terminated or who were fired for their antiwar work, in 1918 Balch's reappointment was postponed; in 1919 she was released from her faculty position by dint of not having her tenure contract renewed. Wellesley's board of trustees ended her appointment, citing that she had not acted as an appropriate representative of the college and had been given several consecutive years of leave. Letters poured in to Balch from friends and family, urging her to "fight" and "sue," or otherwise "contest" the decision and bring a case against the college for violating her academic freedom. She refused. Balch's letters to family and friends reveal her honesty in the matter, saying that she had known there might be repercussions for her political actions, although she never suspected the consequences would be so vindictive as for her to lose her position at Wellesley.[20]

Then fifty-two years old and without a job, Balch's fellow peace activist and friend Oswald Garrison Villard offered her a position on the editorial staff of the *Nation*. She worked there through early 1919, when she traveled to Paris and then on to Switzerland for the next major International Congress of Women in Zurich, which in 1919 formally established a permanent organization, the WILPF. In Zurich Balch's organizational skills were put to the test and she orchestrated the majority of the conference—establishing the rules of order, making committee assignments, setting the program, and handling all sorts of conference logistics. As a result of her successful efforts, Balch became the league's first paid international secretary-treasurer, thus securing meaningful employment after the debacle at Wellesley and her enjoyable but temporary employment at the *Nation*. Jane Addams became the league's first international president. They held ambitious goals for world change and effective lobbying for reform by the institution. The official statement of the WILPF delineated "cooperation" and "compromise" as essential to the league's mission to "promote lasting peace" by attacking the underlying social, economic, and political conditions that gave rise to conflict in the first place.[21]

The organization was structured along the typical international association model: each member nation had an office, a president, and an administrative hierarchy, while the international headquarters were in Geneva. WILPF positions on the League varied. American Lucia Ames Mead of the Woman's Peace Party, for example, supported the League Covenant fully in 1919; while Brit Eleth Snowden objected to the League as a violation of the "principles upon which alone a just and lasting peace can be secured."[22] Chronically short on funding in these early years, WILPF had one great advantage: a highly experienced and motivated group of reform activists, largely from the ranks of the international suffrage movement. By the mid-1920s many Western nations had adopted women's suffrage and those that had not, including Spain, France, Italy, Switzerland, and Belgium, were staging grounds for international women's suffrage activism. In turn, this dynamism fed the WILPF reformers to pursue international peace as a "women's" cause with greater vigor. One of their basic tenets was "that peace is not rooted only in treaties between great powers or a turning away of weapons alone, but can only flourish when it is also planted in the soil of justice, freedom, non-violence, opportunity and equality for all."[23] The WILPF argued that the problems that precipitate domestic and international violence are interconnected and therefore need to be confronted and solved together to truly end war.

Balch and Addams presciently led the charge of the WILPF to criticize the harsh terms imposed on Germany by the Treaty of Versailles, predicting that the treaty would lead to "lingering hostility" between the victors and the vanquished.[24] As historians Akira Iriye and Thomas Knock have pointed out, this was a unique stage in the history of internationalism. The league may have been a spectacular example of postwar internationalism, but it embodied many of the deeper changes affecting cultural internationalism, owing much to prewar currents of pacifist internationalism in America and Great Britain. The WILPF emphasis on significant but not entirely undiluted pacifism and institutionalization reflected a potent postwar belief that the conflict had exposed the limits of good intentions and underscored the larger needs for and difficulties of translating cosmopolitan and peaceful intentions into workable organizations.[25] Interestingly, Balch's pacifist sensibilities did not limit her ability to embrace a realist perspective of sorts. Enforcement procedures would be critical, she argued, for international organization to be effective. Though she despised it, Balch and most of the WILPF leadership understood that the league would need to rely on force to prevent certain types of global evil and to reinforce the efforts of groups and nations attempting humanitarian projects.

Within the multifaceted American peace movement there was a striking diversity of people, groups, and opinions. Balch, Addams, the WILPF, and American isolationist leaders found common ground with Idaho Senator

William Borah, with his bloc of "Irreconcilables," and came to work shoulder-to-shoulder on international peace. Borah, too, saw limits to goodwill and to nationalism. Balch's loose alliance with Borah suggests that her vision resonated well beyond the backers of the WILPF; however, the two clearly diverged on the questions of binding enforcement mechanisms in international organization. More an intellectual coalition than a true political association, the convergence between isolationist nationalists and peace activists represented a landmark development for American political thought and policy-making in the postwar period.

This transition was surprisingly international in nature. Because of the prominent role of women and former suffragists, and because of the startling heterogeneity of the group and its allies, the community of peace advocates in which Balch was a major actor moved fluidly from the United States to Europe, through Latin America and Asia, to Africa. At the end of 1928 they achieved a great symbolic triumph. Alongside the remaining Irreconcilables, these groups galvanized support to ratify the idealistic internationalism of the Kellogg-Briand Pact to outlaw war as an instrument of national policy. The pact began as a bilateral treaty between the United States and France and ultimately was signed by most of the nations of the world.

Pacifist and Isolationist Anti-Interventionism

In most regards Balch and the leadership of the WILPF found common ground with prominent isolationists like Borah via the common ground of seeking to minimize war and maintain peace. Leading WILPF figures including Addams and Balch consistently championed international leagues and alliances to safeguard and spread peace and democratic practices. Far from seeking retrenchment from the League of Nations, they came to endorse the League, worked with it, and hoped to strengthen it, in sharp contrast to Borah's irreconcilable opposition to accepting U.S. involvement with the League. However, Addams, Balch, Mead, and others in the WILPF never accepted the League uncritically; throughout 1919 and into the early 1920s they decried the harsh peace terms set at Versailles. At the end of the Zurich Conference Addams succinctly summed up the critically pragmatic WILPF compromise view of the league, saying "If some of us who are looking at the terms of the Peace Treaty and the prospects for the future are not very happy, we must remember that the people who made the Peace Treaty are also far from happy." In turn, Addams and her

WILPF colleagues aimed to work with the League to reshape it through the efforts of their new organization, to be based in the same city as the League.[26]

One issue that united Balch and Borah was a consistent stand against American interventions throughout the Western Hemisphere. During the mid-1920s there was perhaps no greater advocate for this cause than Balch, who in 1926 waged a major political campaign to fulfill a long-promised congressional withdrawal of American soldiers from Haiti after more than eleven years of occupation. As we will see in more detail later in this chapter, Balch's zealous anti-imperialism pushed her to lead a WILPF delegation to Haiti, where she displayed significant investigative—and, later, political—acumen in diagnosing the troubled situation of continued insurgency on the island. This was a new internationalist ethic best seen as nongovernmental and voluntaristic in nature. Indeed, the international nongovernmental efforts of groups such as the WILPF and the American Red Cross embodied the practices of this new, soft-power approach of internationalism developing to shape a larger American presence in the world in the period after World War I.[27]

Balch wrote much of the resulting report and appeared in Congress to obtain acceptance of the recommendations for improving American reconstruction efforts and for removing U.S. soldiers. As a consequence, the troops were withdrawn. These Balch-Addams-type internationalist visions were anti-imperialist and pacifistic, favoring a militarily isolated, yet culturally engaged America that could act as mediator. In large part this vision came to define the changed paradigm of foreign policy for many former progressives during the late 1920s and 1930s. This was part of the infusion of isolationist ideas into U.S. foreign policy thought during the period.

As a leader in the Senate and one of the nation's principal articulators of foreign policy, William Borah—with his idealistic conception of a powerful, noble, isolated America, a concept not always based on a realistic appraisal of the actual circumstances—was greatly influential in the 1920s and 1930s. Like other populist-minded former progressives after World War I, both Balch and Borah rethought the state's role in bringing the nation into the war and in repressing free speech at home as a type of domestic quasi-colonial oppression, abrogating constitutional rights. However, in a trend that would continue, Borah and his remaining Irreconcilable colleagues frequently split with his Republican Party on major political issues and especially foreign policy, such as interventions across South and Central America and particularly in the Caribbean. But true to his overriding partisan loyalty in matters of sheer politics (rather than issues he believed turned on the pivot of principle), Borah refused to leave the party in 1924 to support his longtime political ally and friend, Robert La Follette, as the Progressive Party candidate for president.[28]

In the postwar period anti-imperialist ideas again emerged to support arguments against keeping troops on the ground for extended periods of time in Central and South America. Particularly important were Nicaragua and Mexico, the Caribbean, notably Haiti, and various Pacific regions, such as the Philippine Islands. So too, as in the early days after the Spanish-American War concluded, issues of limiting immigration to the United States, focusing inward on domestic economic progress with social cohesion, came to the fore. Of course, as an advocate for pluralism and the benefits of new immigrants and ethno-racial additions to American "stock," Balch rejected strict quotas in immigration policy.

Another factor was the more conservative peace groups of the period, among which were the Woodrow Wilson Foundation, the World Peace Foundation, the League of Nations Association, and the Carnegie Endowment for International Peace. Mostly located on the East Coast, these organizations tended to be well funded—Andrew Carnegie's $10 million gift started the Carnegie Endowment—and they tried to be realistic in adopting gradual approaches to generating world peace.[29] Their approach aimed to educate people in accordance with what historian Robert Johnson has found to be characteristic of peace progressives: the goal was "to achieve a more peaceful world order through an active American foreign policy along reformist lines. Their instrument for this reform," Johnson observed, "was a well-developed anti-imperialism that in the 1920s expanded considerably beyond domestic programs [and] . . . led the senators to oppose political commitments involving the Western European states."[30] Here again, Balch's anti-imperialism formed a perfect bridge to that of Borah, as both opposed American military interventions in Haiti and the Dominican Republic, and throughout the hemisphere. At the same time this bridge also permitted shared concern for global peacemaking to become a natural path to further common ground and collective action. Echoing the anti-imperialist warnings of the turn of the century, Borah and Balch perceived U.S. strong-arm tactics and financial interests, in particular, as the underlying causes of these engagements in the Caribbean. The combination of militarist passion and financial and corporate greed generated what they saw as un-American, antidemocratic colonialist efforts abroad.

Elements of this rhetoric, and strikingly similar arguments, can be found in the writings and speeches of Balch, Addams, and La Follette, as well as Borah. The collection of peace progressives leading the WILPF, in fact, began to develop what might best be understood as the core ideals of the "new internationalism" in and after 1919. They issued the first public condemnation of the plan for the League of Nations. These groups often differed, however, on how to work toward a shared end of world peace. Possible strategies included working toward international solutions through leagues and associations; finding agreeable terms for treaties to stem conflicts; minimizing colonial "scrambles" and related clashes—all aimed to moderate war and increase understanding across national boundaries. But these ideas were hotly contested in the harmonizing of isolationist internationalism. Pacifist internationalists, Irreconcilables, and peace progressives often disagreed. When a composite worldview emerged it did so fleetingly, just before new national and world crises—economic depression and the rise of aggressive, imperialistic totalitarian regimes—began to radically shift how Americans weighed present challenges and judged future threats, domestic and international. Nevertheless, they were able to converge and agree on important points about how to stave off future wars. Borah, Balch, Addams, and John Mott, among the others mentioned here, built new organizational methods and propounded crucial ideas for global cooperation to achieve peace. In many ways they succeeded in institutionalizing their approach even if they failed to stem another global maelstrom.[31]

Nationalism for a Changing Postwar World

Still, why did Borah join with the pacifist internationalists? After all, he wrote in late 1922, "The older I grow, the more I become a strong Nationalist." He believed resolutely that international affairs demanded American leadership. But he claimed this role must derive entirely from "a creed of international honor, morality, decency and justice," not from foreign alliances. Underlying his observations was his brand of powerful Americanism, and it is in terms of this Americanism that we can locate Borah's connection to limited pacifist sensibilities.[32]

Nationally chauvinistic and patriotically sentimental, Borah frequently revealed the intensity of his position on the nation's proper foreign policy when he discussed the American Revolution. But to be nationalistic in the age of "normalcy" also entailed taking a stand on the most contentious domestic issues of the day. It was not the simple matter of supporting soldiers while enthusiastically fighting for freedom by rejecting the League. Rather, some of the most divisive issues of the day became red-hot as class and racial antagonisms spread through the country during and after World War I in a series of high-profile race riots and in anti-labor, anti-socialist clashes known as the Red Scare. This trend toward suspicion and repression at home clearly had origins in the wartime effort to curtail dissent and alien ideologies. It also had roots in a longer-standing popular perception of a connection between domestic conflict and the revolutions in progress in Russia and Mexico. Persecution and deportation of American supporters for the Bolshevik Revolution were examples of the government's increasing antiradical tendencies in 1918–1919. The Red Scare, the tumultuous labor unrest and strikes of 1919, and the social upheaval caused by the extraordinary ravages of the influenza epidemic quieted the reform spirit.

By the early 1920s, one issue, one action for reform stood out as the most contentious and compelling for American citizens and politicians: prohibition. Positioning on the politics of the subject was no simple task for most politicians of the period. It was particularly problematic for those, like Borah, who wished to truly represent the wishes of their constituents. This political hot-button issue therefore represents a fascinating and complex test case of Borah's channeling of the public will and his own seemingly opposed views about protecting individual rights and not meddling at the federal level, yet also his explicit efforts to work to achieve a more ordered society through strict enforcement of the law.

His experience in prohibition reform in Idaho gave him the insight that local efforts to remain dry needed assistance at the federal level because of a vexing problem: wet-state entrepreneurs could cross borders with their products. Enforcement of the Eighteenth Amendment and the curtailing of criminal activities related to bootlegging were secondary legal issues, Borah argued. In a revealing debate sponsored by the Roosevelt Club of Boston in April 1927, Borah took on Columbia University President Nicholas Murray Butler on the topic "Should the Republican National Platform of 1928 Advocate the Repeal of the 18th Amendment?" Butler took the affirmative view, Borah the negative. Borah declared that just as the Republican Party had successfully tackled the social evil of slavery, so too should the party eradicate the evil of liquor and its destructive effects on society. He argued that the only proper way to repeal the amendment would be via a national referendum.[33]

Borah expressed serious concerns about many features of the American legal system throughout this period. For example, he had serious doubts about the prosecution of the Sacco and Vanzetti case, two Italian immigrant anarchists convicted and executed on minimal circumstantial evidence of robbery and murder. Borah asked the attorney general to provide him with detailed information about the case to review. Rejecting claims that a poor prosecution based on scant evidence (and heightened by xenophobic and antiradical public outrage) would have serious foreign policy implications, Borah declared in a letter to Jane Addams that "it would be a national humiliation, a shameless, cowardly compromise of national courage to pay the slightest attention to foreign protests or mob protests at home." Yet on the issue of their "innocence or unfair trial" he said, "I would gladly help insofar as I could."[34] He asked President Calvin Coolidge to make the files public before the execution of the two Italian immigrants; he also requested that Governor Alvan Fuller of Massachusetts stay the execution until all of the evidence of guilt was made plain. Eventually the executions were carried out, leading Borah to later write to Addams to reiterate that there should never be a moment when the public opinion of other nations should influence American jurisprudence. He argued, "If our courts are incompetent or corrupt, it is for us to deal with them."[35]

If America's vaunted legal system could operate so poorly at home, then—as Borah's isolationist ideas about America's national identity and international role expanded throughout the 1920s—he reasoned that such would likely be true abroad. He argued the classic isolationist nonentanglement position, yet not so much based on exceptionalism as on the local flaws of American jurisprudence. Thus Borah made his case against entrance into what would most likely be an even more unwieldy, mistake-prone, and less just World Court that could rule over American citizens or adjudicate national legislation. Still, his idealism also pressed upon him and he moved gradually into terrain that could be shared with internationalists like Balch.

If under Wilson the United States had practiced an interventionist form of liberal internationalism, most powerfully underscored by joining World War I and the ill-fated attempt to forge (and enter) the League of Nations, then with the influence of the Irreconcilable leaders like Borah, peace-time brought with it the ascendancy of an antiwar, anti-interventionist isolationism. This would proscribe any and all entangling alliances. Yet it also held out an idealistic hope for domestic ethno-racial and religious tolerance in a "New Era" and it seemed to create an opening for America to be a force for genuine good and peace in the world.[36]

International as well as personal concerns also affected Emily Balch's efforts. As the new League of Nations was taking shape without direct American participation, Balch and the WILPF looked abroad, seeking new peace advocates and increasing membership, put in place a democratic structure, and protected minority rights. Crushed by "exhaustion" in building the WILPF organization for almost three years, in 1922 Balch shifted to a voluntary role. Although Balch was a superb consensus builder and institutional force, and despite the group's pluralist rhetoric, the international environment in which the WILPF operated was also subject to the pressures and excesses of the nations from which its members originated. Thus, the WILPF continued onward in its mission but at times frustrated Balch because it was fractured by intense internal problems of race, class, and nationality in the 1920s.

The WILPF did not always live up to their lofty ideals in terms of racial inclusion. In *No Peace without Freedom: Race and the Women's International League for Peace and Freedom,* Joyce Blackwell critically examined the league's failure to integrate African American women as well as its lack of concern for race issues. At first Balch and other league leaders expended a "great deal of energy combating incidents of racial injustice within W.I.L.P.F." "After a rocky beginning, black and white women developed a relatively amicable working relationship" in the organization, due, in large measure, to the commitment and determination of the black women activists.[37] Nonetheless, as biographer Mercedes Randall noted, holding together the WILPF's mixed international constituency, which ranged from supporters of international socialist revolution to absolute pacifists from more than fifty nations, "was no easy feat."[38]

Internationalism in War, Isolationism in Peace?

In the decade after the defeat of the League, Republicans ruled the White House. Amid the domestic focus of the Roaring Twenties there were ever-present calls for American involvement in humanitarian missions to help maintain a safe, peaceful, and prosperous world system. The decade between the touchstones of Irreconcilable views relating the foreign and domestic (from the League debates to Kellogg-Briand) further clarifies how isolationists and internationalists were able to find so much common ground. President Warren Harding's announcement in 1921 that he had issued formal invitations to the major powers to attend an arms limitation conference in Washington predictably aroused Borah's concern. The 1921 Washington Conference had, in fact, been initiated in large part because of Borah's request for disarmament negotiations with Britain and Japan. Yet now he was concerned that in the hands of Harding and Secretary of State Charles Evans Hughes, it would become "a stepping stone to the formation of an association of nations."[39] Borah's aim was merely to preserve the status quo of politics and power in the Pacific.

He came to find the resulting conferences on the subject as a lesson that he ought to be vigilant in watching men like Harding and Hughes. Borah opposed those, Democrat or Republican, who undermined American autonomy in the name of world peace. He appreciated journalist Frank Cobb's disapproving opinion that the conference resulted from "nothing more serious than his [Harding's] personal vanity."[40] But the possibility that Harding was serious could not be overlooked. It could be a trap to return the national debate to the League issue, Borah believed. His correspondents flooded him with letters indicating similar opinions. Raymond Robbins cautioned, "You should not be forced into a position where you either lose disarmament or agree to an 'entangling alliance.'"[41] So Borah incited the Irreconcilables to gird themselves for a fight. The battle, however, would proceed on an improvised basis.

Harding, Hughes, and others saw the arms race not only as a symptom of conflicts among real and deeper national interests around the world, but also a possible threat to America. That danger: the ever-expanding Japanese imperial navy. Borah and his allies disagreed. Two days before the conference was scheduled to open, Borah wrote in the *Nation* that the "ghost of Versailles hangs over the conference." That treaty, he said, had "Balkanized" Europe. In a *Nation* editorial that appeared before Borah's article, the editors argued that the conference was "essentially another attempt to substitute an imperialist trust for competitive imperialism." They declared that both should be avoided.[42]

In opposition to Borah, Lodge found numerous congressional allies to support the process, and any fight to oppose arms limits found little traction in a peace-and-normalcy-oriented America. The so-called Four-Power

Treaty, which Lodge introduced in the Senate first, was the most controversial of the proposed limitations. The terms of the treaty agreed to the status quo in the Pacific, including affirmation of current colonial holdings by Japan and France as well as Great Britain and the United States.

Almost all of the Irreconcilables voted against the Four-Power Treaty, with Borah and Johnson leading the charge. They used claims of ambiguous language and potential entanglements to decry the treaty as just a regional League of Nations, but it passed the Senate easily as Harding and Lodge twisted arms to find unity on the issue.[43] Borah and the Irreconcilables were disappointed, but they could see one consolation, wondering "if individual conferences achieved such important results, did the need really exist for a permanent organization?"[44] On this subject Borah did not properly take the temperature of public opinion. Earlier in the year the *Literary Digest* polled its national papers and found an astonishing 723 of its 803 papers supported all of the treaties proposed for the Washington Conference.[45] Despite Borah's severe warnings, the treaty passed the Senate easily. With the exception of the Hearst press, and a few Irreconcilables, the issue was a nonstarter. The national press from California to Texas to New York almost universally commended the Republicans for winning a "battle for world peace."[46]

The Five-Power Naval Limitation Treaty, however, was a different case. It established "insular possession and insular dominions" in the Pacific, required "consultation" and "communication" between the powers if one was threatened, and set a battleship level of 5–5–3 for Great Britain, the United States, and Japan (with France and Italy on the outside looking in, with battleship levels at 1.67). The stated reason for why the United States and Britain required higher tonnage allowances was that both nations maintained two-ocean navies, something both Borah and Johnson supported as a necessary arm of American power abroad, yet one needed only in proportion to the navies of other major powers.[47]

A Refinement of Ideals

Further fleshing out his position—to the point of being attacked for inconsistency—Borah proposed a resolution in December 1922 that would convene a summit of nations to consider restoring international trade, developing sound fiscal policies, and disarming some land forces, naval craft, and all military aircraft. In principle he had always supported global peacemaking; his main concern had been in the arena of entanglement and permanence for alliances and treaties. His proposal seems to have won Borah wide popular acclaim, but Lodge, Harding, and others made it plain after three days of debate that Borah could not gather the votes.

What is significant in this event is that Borah explicitly argued and implicitly revealed he was no absolute isolationist. He backed that assertion with a precise proposal to bring nations together to combine economic internationalism with peaceful internationalism. He noted that the policy of the Republican Party had been to participate in foreign negotiations when American interests were involved and to settle disputes, seek arbitration, and ensure domestic prosperity. Borah summarized this perspective in an interview conducted by Theodore Knappen and published in the *Wall Street Magazine* January 6, 1923. He endorsed arms limitation pacts, particularly those led by America, as nonentangling alliances, and he firmly believed in the establishment and rule of international law.

Borah also made the case that economic interaction was essential for domestic, and global, prosperity. Hardly the obstructionist he has sometimes been made out to be, Borah subtly noted, "I have always favored international agreements concerning economic matters." He added, "To my mind there is a sharp distinction between political pacts or alliances and economic conferences. It is as proper for a government to promote the commercial well being of its citizens by foreign as by domestic arrangements." Yet when asked whether such efforts might constitute economic intervention in Europe and whether it could be done "without becoming involved politically," Borah responded, "I do not think that we shall have any difficultly in that respect if we stand pat on our economic objective." In short, he candidly clarified how he perceived this objective, saying, "I make no concealment of the judgment that nothing in the world is more important to the well-being of our internal affairs at this time than the economic stabilization of the world, particularly of Europe." He may have touted his non-obstructionism too much in his comments. Nevertheless, he embellished his comments by proclaiming that the United States should take the "bull by the horns" and push for a conference to end the vindictive reparations program that was part of the flawed Versailles agreement.[48]

Viewing economic interdependence as inevitable and perhaps even essential, Borah faced up to that obvious fact in ways that many anti-League isolationist arguments had not done explicitly in the recent past. Because of Midwestern farm proposals highlighting the need for larger markets for

American wheat and cotton, Borah made the uncharacteristic case that economic involvement with Europe through trade conferences would not necessarily entail political entanglement.[49]

The debates over possible American entrance into the World Court also illustrate the continuing evolution of Borah's foreign policy position. More broadly, they also reveal his expanding blend of isolationist nationalism with an idealized vision for peaceful legal internationalism. The Court debates additionally mark a deep division between Borah's isolationist stance and Balch's internationalist position. As we have seen, Borah prized justice but was suspicious of flaws in the application of the law at home, much less at the level of supranational leagues. The Geneva Protocol, drafted in 1924, provided a means for arbitrating disputes in still fragile Europe through a "Permanent Court of International Justice."[50]

Borah stridently opposed joining any World Court that bound the United States to what he thought might be flawed or otherwise obligatory international arbitration coupled with the passing of international judgment upon American citizens. He argued that the so-called Permanent Court would be just that, an enduring part of the League. And of course he had already staked out a strong position rejecting any binding League as a diminishment of American autonomy. Borah was so inflamed by the possibility of Republican leaders' moving forward with participating in the Court that he considered challenging Harding for renomination because of his support for membership in the Court.[51] However, Borah also claimed he could support some form of world court, as long as it was not tied to the League and, without a sense of the irony involved, he proposed that such a court permit nonbinding American leadership. Borah even proposed his own idea for a strong international judiciary "modeled on our Federal Supreme Court in its jurisdiction over controversies between our sovereign States."[52]

Borah, leading his Irreconcilable colleagues in the matter, attempted to deflect the label of "obstructionist" by putting forward a progressive, internationalist plan. As he put it, he would go along only if an international legal system "met his specifications, codified international law, and promoted Outlawry."[53] By January 1926, despite Borah's continued efforts and disapproval, the vote to have the United States "adhere" to the Permanent Court of International Justice passed the Senate with a two-thirds majority easily, though the United States would send only one formal representative to the meetings. Ultimately the ramifications of this effort were nowhere near the dire predictions that Borah put forward. Indeed, the United States never formally joined the World Court. Though Borah thought he had been defeated, the wording of the adherence document, with five major reservations articulated by Elihu Root, is significant in terms of its isolationist-internationalist positioning. "That adherence to the said protocol and statute hereby approved shall not be so construed as to require the United States to depart from its traditional policy of not intruding upon, interfering with, or entangling itself in the political questions of policy or internal administration of any foreign state; nor shall adherence to the said protocol and statute be construed to imply a relinquishment by the United States of its traditional attitude toward purely American questions."[54]

In the wake of the Washington Conference and the initial rounds of World Court battles from 1922 through 1924, Borah found solace. Reluctance to incur further senatorial debates impelled Harding and Hughes to limit discussion of the League or any other major associations of the nations of the world. A "Borah for President" movement sprang up in 1924, though it did not produce his nomination. He campaigned for Coolidge rather than support his friend Robert La Follette and the Progressive Party, a move that has perplexed many observers. Numerous biographers have speculated—and many of his friends seem to have believed—that Borah personally cast his ballot for La Follette. It seems that Borah could not bring himself to defy his party allegiance once Coolidge, rather than La Follette, received the GOP nomination.

Borah refrained from debating international issues in the election year. Instead he focused on American farmers and the domestic economy. In particular, he pushed for a Farm Loan Board. After a series of studies showed the poor state of the independent farmer, Borah made this a constant cause throughout his next fifteen years in office. He also continued to crusade for tax reduction and an end to tax-exempt securities.

Once again elected to serve Idaho, Borah ascended to the chair of the Senate Foreign Relations Committee, after Henry Cabot Lodge died. His elevation coincided with a period in which he was more actively concerned with domestic politics. He had virtually no major international battles to fight except for the vigorous campaign against America's joining the World Court, and he began to build on his work with Levinson in the cause of a nonbinding, multinational agreement to renounce war.

Internationalism to Achieve Greater Peace and Justice

Emily Balch's efforts against American militarism compelled her to take the offensive. Under her leadership the Women's International League for Peace and Freedom sent speakers and organizers around the world and sought to make supranational organizations and conferences principal methods of achieving greater peace and justice. In terms of the United States, the WILPF advocated an essentially isolationist argument against preparedness for war and for reducing naval and military capacity, although Balch argued that some binding elements to a robust international league were essential to sort out differences across nations.

The WILPF aim was basic and to the point: eliminate the instruments of war as well as to eradicate the conditions that caused conflicts to start. The Fourth Congress of the WILPF convened in Washington, D.C., in 1924 with the theme "A New International Order." As Balch commented in her report, the Western world had reached a "third stage" of "economic imperialism." She envisioned a new phase of development of economic independence that she termed "the phase of internationalism in business and finance." Many would think such internationalism of business might bring about peace, but she noted the tendencies for the opposite to occur. "What I believe to be the dangerous peculiarity in the situation," Balch wrote, "is the alliance between business in pursuit of profit, and the nationalist policies in pursuit of power."[55]

In the WILPF newspaper *Pax International*, Balch and other leading internationalists laid out this case. Balch, for instance, deployed her political economic expertise and frequently attacked the interdependence of big business and war, concerning the issue of poison gas introduced during the First World War. She asserted that the use of such technology would be ever more difficult to eliminate.[56] New war techniques involved financial interest on the part of companies, she claimed; unlike other forms of carrying out battle options, they "were never a means of self-defense and wholly a means of attack." She concluded that this combination of aggressive employment and an industry dependent on making them made it "harder to prevent war." Balch worried that such weapons, "for which there was no defense," would be used in the future upon the masses of helpless people who could be easily targeted by those who possessed them. Thus, the WILPF supported Washington Conference–style disarmament as a first step toward the sort of international cooperation needed to prevent such horrors as poison gas.[57]

In 1925 through 1926 Balch proceeded to a new fight closer to home: to fulfill the promised withdrawal of American soldiers from Haiti after ten years of occupation. The U.S. Marines had occupied Haiti since 1915, when Wilson sent them into the country after an attempted revolt against the pro-American government of President Guillaume Sam, who himself had been put into power by President Taft to protect American investments in Haiti under the policy of "dollar diplomacy."

Acting on a shared anti-imperialist sensibility, Balch and Borah, among other progressive-minded internationalists and isolationists, crusaded against ongoing American occupations in Latin America. Just after he had become a senator, in 1909 Borah declared his support for Philippine independence at the earliest date, although in 1900 he had derided Carl Schurz and the anti-imperialists as being un-American when they took that position. By 1930 he argued that by becoming a colonial power the nation had obviated an important element of self-rule as embodied in the Declaration of Independence.

So too did old progressive reformers and the new women's peace internationalists become vociferous in similar efforts as they redeployed anti-imperialist critiques to assert that Haitians, Nicaraguans, and Dominicans had as much right to self-determination as Belgians, Poles, and Czechs. Decrying the "drift toward imperialism" in places like Haiti, Balch also took a strong position against sending American troops abroad in any effort that smacked of political, economic, or cultural aggrandizement. Her view was reinforced by the proclamations of other peace activists and domestic progressive reformers, including Addams, as well as James Weldon Johnson and W. E. B. Du Bois of the NAACP, who came out publicly against the positioning of U.S. marines, or of American commercial and banking entities, in Haiti and elsewhere. Johnson's widely circulated series of articles in the Nation, titled "Self-Determining Haiti," were formative in this campaign to get American troops out. He attacked the continued occupation of the island for more than a decade, as delaying and diminishing democracy to support "the National City Bank." It was shameful, Johnson declared, this forcible "loss of [Haitian] political and economic freedom."[58]

The year 1925 marked a significant intersection of international anti-imperialist pacifist thought with the anticolonial impulses of Borah's isolationist nationalist bloc. In early 1925 several Haitian members of the WILPF formally requested that the International Executive Committee examine conditions in their country as part of the league's new major commitment to tackle issues of financial imperialism. Two WILPF representatives—Balch, representing the Foreign Service Committee of the Society of Friends, and a member of the Fellowship of Reconciliation—traveled as part of a group of six Americans to investigate the situation in Haiti, which at that time was under occupation by U.S. marines. The delegation also included Paul Douglas, a prominent professor of economics at the University of Chicago, dedicated anti-imperial internationalist, and soon-to-be senator from Illinois. Balch wrote much of the resulting report and appeared in Congress to obtain recommendations for improving American reconstruction efforts and removing U.S. soldiers. This work was a compilation of the committee's observations and recommendations regarding the current role of the marines in Haiti. While investigating the political, economic, financial, health, sanitation, education, public works, judiciary, and civil liberties, their assessment also attempted to explain the ulterior motives for the military occupation—American business dealings with Haiti. For example, Douglas argued in one chapter of the report, "The Political History of the Occupation," that economic friction between the American and Haitian governments precipitated the eventual occupation of Haiti. He observed that the roiling disputes between the Haitian government and the National Bank of Haiti and the National Railroad of Haiti were in large part the result of the latter two being largely financed and goaded on by American companies.[59]

The WILPF committee concluded its report on Haiti's occupation with the recommendation that it was "perfectly possible to be a good neighbor and help Haiti to attain health, education, public improvements and public order, by other less drastic, and ultimately more effective methods than military control."[60] *Occupied Haiti* cast the soldiers' pressure as un-American imperialism simply to prop up commercial and financial interests. They called the military occupation of Haiti "an unjustified use of power" and recommended a "restoration of independence and self-government."[61] Balch, though, remained optimistic. "It is going to take not only patience on our side but a willingness to have things done not in the American way," she wrote privately, "which we are always sure is best, but in their way, except as we can convince them that something else will serve them better."[62]

For progressives who had once been more interventionist-minded in humanitarian causes, the 1920s brought greater wariness and a skepticism that even beneficent intervention might possibly turn to imperialism. This caution was particularly evident in the writings and actions of former progressives who generally adhered to domestic-first, isolationist world-views rather than those like Balch, who conducted more international peace work as time went on.

Borah sided with Senators George Norris and Robert La Follette, pulling back as well. In the case of an intervention in Nicaragua, for example, Borah declared in 1922, "The people of Nicaragua are being exploited in shameless fashion by American corporations protected by United States Marines."[63] Taking the now-traditional progressive critique, they assaulted the role of greedy capital in these un-American imperialist actions. In another case in an article titled "The Fetish of Force" (he titled several pieces with modified versions of this title during the 1920s and 1930s), published in 1925, Borah opined:

> We have been impatient. We have not been just at all times. . . . Possessing great power, we have used it without adequate justification. . . . Who can contemplate without sorrow and humiliation a great and powerful nation, inexhaustible in wealth and unmeasured in manpower, imperiously invading a perfectly helpless country, seizing and holding for years her capital and directing her affairs, making a treaty with her. . . . The invasion of Nicaragua was unnecessary and therefore unmoral. . . . I think our conduct toward Santo Domingo and Haiti equally indefensible.[64]

He concluded by arguing from American democratic precedent and principle, his usual rhetorical fallback. Borah said the nation "ought to be ashamed to stand before the world . . . with all our professions of peace and against military power in the attitude of keeping a military heel upon a helpless people."[65] Most American politicians, however, were not quick to act. Four years after the WILPF investigation in Haiti, and three years after the findings were published, President Herbert Hoover's official commission returned from its own fact-finding mission and adopted recommendations similar to the WILPF's 1927 unofficial findings.

In 1930, after much agitation, Hoover finally ordered that U.S. troops be withdrawn from Haiti, but that did not come to fruition. It was not until

1934, under the Franklin D. Roosevelt administration, that the final American forces left Haiti. The lesson in the Haiti and Nicaragua examples, among others, was that pacifism and anti-imperialism bridged the chasm between internationalists and isolationists when they advanced a common political cause and kept the pressure on. Clearly theirs was more than a shared antiwar perspective. Together they were more effective, working from outside and inside government, yet only loosely allied, in pushing back against America's ongoing interventionist impulses, particularly those within the hemisphere. Nevertheless, the examples also illuminate a downside to their activism: its limited effectiveness. American military intervention in Haiti lasted far longer than Balch and Borah had supposed it would, and U.S. involvement proved far more intractable and resistant to their efforts than they assumed.

To Make War Nearly Impossible

The culmination of these attempts by Balch, Borah, and their allies to rein in American imperial efforts came in their collaboration to find a more lasting plan for peace. An odd alliance gathered behind the multilateral outlawing of war, without binding commitments, known as the Kellogg-Briand Pact.

As early as 1923 the so-called "father" of the outlawry of war movement, a prominent Chicago lawyer named Salmon O. Levinson, had convinced Borah to sign on to the basic principle of international law and a resolution for world peace. He had been a frequent donor to Hull House, to the education of the Chinese in China, outings for underprivileged children, and the WILPF.[66] In February 1923, seemingly in response to the prodding of Levinson, Borah first issued a Senate statement calling for a universal treaty to make war "a public crime under the law of nations."[67] Public sentiment had been driving toward such a policy, in many ways, since the wide approval of the arms limitations endorsed by the Washington Conference. But these efforts did not move forward with alacrity until 1927, when French Foreign Minister Aristide Briand and Columbia University historian James T. Shotwell drew up a proposal to consider a bilateral treaty to outlaw war. Borah worked closely with Secretary of State Frank B. Kellogg, who was lukewarm to the idea of an international agreement to eliminate war. So had Borah been at first.

Throughout 1927 Borah stayed on message. He blasted the neocolonial entanglement marked by the landing of an additional five thousand troops in Nicaragua in 1927 at the behest of Secretary of State Charles Evans Hughes, who later resigned in favor of Kellogg. Those troops, however, much to the consternation of Borah (and Balch), stayed on for three more years to protect American financial and commercial interests and uphold the regime there.[68]

Remnants of the populists and a number of progressive peace advocates, headed by Henry Ford, Jane Addams, and Emily Balch, and organizations such as the WILPF, the Carnegie Endowment for International Peace (led by Columbia University President Nicholas Murray Butler, and the domestic agrarian labor organization National Grange petitioned in support of the proposed peace agreement. These figures also opposed the interventions in Haiti and Nicaragua. Adding further gravitas to the cause, at first designed to be a diplomatic gesture between France and the United States, the pact rapidly opened up to include other nations, and Kellogg threw his support behind it as "an instrument of national policy," which Borah could certainly endorse.[69] Initially Borah noted that he favored international peace but there was too much pressing business for Congress to focus on a permanent peace plan. But the combination of public support, his own idealism, and pressures of outlawry advocates seems to have impressed Borah to take action more rapidly. The day after issuing that statement, on November 27, 1927, Borah came out in favor of outlawry as a move that did not take away any congressional authority. As the *New York Times* remarked, "It was gathered from what Mr. Borah said that he believed there was an opportunity for some one to come forward with a declaration that war was a crime and lead the crusade."[70] Borah himself stepped forward and began to expand on his nuanced foreign policy, becoming the most visible American supporter of an international pact to outlaw war.

The WILPF played its part in this process masterfully. As yet another sign of the alignment of values between Irreconcilables and internationalists, after much deliberation at the WILPF annual meeting in 1927, a resolution passed saying that the organization "desires to see the United States enter the League of Nations, providing only that it does so with the understanding that the United States is exempt from any obligation to supply military forces or to join in exerting military pressure in any case."[71] Building on those sentiments, Addams and a delegation called on President Coolidge on December 10 to seek his public adoption of the proposed treaty between France and America to outlaw war between the two nations. The delegation brought with them—as a measure of the support for the outlawry measure and movement—a petition for the treaty with thirty thousand signatures. According to Addams, Coolidge had agreed to have Ambassador Herrick place the Briand treaty on his agenda for discussions upon his return to France.[72] Interestingly, the Chicago branch of the WILPF also had taken matters into its own hands, as Addams had probably mentioned to Coolidge. The group had written directly to Aristide Briand about the petition and U.S. support for outlawry, and also to provide him with a copy of the petition to assist on his end of the negotiations.[73]

After rejecting an international system of cooperation for world peace less than ten years previously, the Senate approved the agreement nearly unanimously. Astonishing many observers at the time (and some scholars thereafter), those isolationist Irreconcilables still remaining in office—James Reed, George Norris, Hiram Johnson, George Moses, and Borah—enthusiastically voted for what might superficially have seemed like an international initiative akin to the League or World Court. Such a view is shortsighted because of the priority to keep American autonomy at the forefront, while also embracing the international community and seeking to establish a lasting peace if possible, lined up neatly with the precepts of the pact. Accordingly, they supported what most saw as an ambitious, idealistic, yet toothless worldwide effort to outlaw war. The Kellogg-Briand Pact, finalized and signed in Paris on August 27, 1928, and ratified in 1929, declared that the signatories would "condemn recourse to war for the solution of international controversies, and renounce it as an instrument of national policy."[74]

Behind the support for the outlawry of war was what seems to have been a strong conviction that the United States should play a legitimate role in helping create a safer world—but only if America's sovereign rights were upheld. Upon hearing about such a pact, George Norris said, "We should jump at the chance."[75] Norris had always been in favor of such a pact, spurred in part by the extreme injustice of the Japanese imperialist conquest of the Shantung provision, and hoped this initiative might "make war between civilized nations as nearly impossible as human ingenuity could devise."[76] Hiram Johnson also favored some sort of peace alliance before the actual details of Wilson's plan came out, saying, "If a League of Nations could be adopted which would prevent future wars, we'd all welcome it." He stipulated only that it not demand too high a price on our sovereignty.[77]

The ideological questions that undermined the ratification of the League, namely retaining American sovereignty and self-defense, not abrogating the injunctions of Washington, and maintaining the tradition for a limited U.S. diplomatic role in the world, were seen as essentially nullified by the nonbinding nature of this pact. So, let us look more closely at the isolationist and internationalist elements involved in the intellectual framework for the pact and in the outlawry movement. Borah explained the reasoning behind his support for a multilateral agreement in a February 1928 *New York Times Magazine* editorial. His main problem with the League covenant was that Article X forced member countries to go to war to defend another country. "It is safe to prophesy," he explained, "that the United States will never become identified or cooperate with a system for peace based upon 'pledges to wage war.' But the United States now stands ready to cooperate and identify itself with a system based upon pledges *not* to wage war."[78]

Equally significant, the hedge was that if a nation were to be attacked, it still had the right to defend itself. In that case the aggressor would have become the one to abandon the peace. Secretary Kellogg, questioned by the Foreign Relations Committee, assured the senators that it was "incomprehensible that anybody could say that any nation would sign a treaty which could be construed as taking away the right of self-defense."[79] Chairman Borah agreed, saying, "It is perfectly certain that every nation, when the time arrives, will construe this treaty in the way it regards as justifying self-defense."[80] The Irreconcilables had fought hard against the League because it did not protect America's inherent right to self-defense as embodied in the Monroe Doctrine, but Borah made sure that right was satisfactorily protected under the pact.

Borah was insistent, however, that the pact not obligate the deployment of coercive force against those nations that might violate it. It was, he thought, completely contradictory to answer illegal force with force. Therein lies the rub for the policy, because how could it operate without an ultimate resolve to the use of force? Lamenting current world policy and law, Borah explained, "We seem to have no faith in the power of public opinion or in an appeal to the moral sense of the people. When it comes to affairs between nations, we build all our schemes upon force."[81] Criticism of a nonbinding agreement often stated that "the refusal to enforce the law because enforcement resembles war, seems to . . . leave the 'outlawry' plan in the paradoxical condition of not outlawing anything."[82]

Nevertheless, the senator insisted that it could work. The great world powers had an opportunity to "determine international law, international morality and shape the course of peace to a controlling degree for many years."[83] If they could replace the "fetish of force" with a global commitment to peace, he argued, it was their duty to do so.

Some isolationist-minded senators still sensed that the Monroe Doctrine might be endangered by an agreement phrased in such a way. This in turn led to another debate over reservations and interpretations, while again underscoring the weaknesses of enforcement involved in the pact. Senators George Moses of New Hampshire and James Reed of Missouri insisted that the U.S. Senate add its own note to the pact specifying its own understanding. The resulting Reed-Moses Resolution laid out four necessary conditions for American involvement in the pact: (1) the United States was not obligated to coercive or punitive measures; (2) no limitations were imposed on the exercise of the Monroe Doctrine; (3) U.S. self-defense of territory or possessions was not impaired; and (4) the United States was not obligated to the League or any other treaties of which it was not a member.[84] Unlike in the League fight, however, these reservations did not pose much of an impediment to bipartisan cooperation.[85]

Building Support Abroad and at Home

In 1928 Emily Balch traveled extensively across Europe to build support for the pact, while the debates about it raged at home. The National Committee on the Cause and Cure of War sent a call for conventions in forty-eight states to support the pact, beginning with local peace meetings to lay the groundwork for state-level proceedings. The U.S. section of the WILPF, then headed by Balch as section president, set about arranging many of these local gatherings and affiliates behind the outlawry cause. According to the *New York Times*, the committee announced that more than twelve million American women had affiliated to study war's cause and cure.[86] In May 1928 the WILPF then adopted a resolution to commend Secretary Kellogg for his peace activities, and the next day Addams, along with WILPF representatives from ten states, met with President Coolidge at the White House to discuss the resolution and the possibilities for pushing the peace pact to rapid ratification.[87] In England at the time, Balch remained optimistic about the future of international peace through such efforts, although she was troubled that in the end the signatories reserved the right to self-defense.[88]

After Balch's organizing and speech-making trip, she returned to Geneva, where the WILPF was based. Her return coincided with the fiftieth meeting of the Council of the League of Nations, where she continued her outlawry efforts but on a scale far beyond that which Borah would have ever conceived. She asked to present to the council members the WILPF position on the importation of munitions to and through China, and the arms trade in general. Once she gave the WILPF policy positions, Balch scheduled meetings with Italian and Finnish delegates to discuss Kellogg-Briand. She reported, "They were more than merely courteous, and appeared cordially interested. I also spoke informally of the general situation as regards China, emphasizing the importance of respecting her integrity."[89]

In a speech in Geneva she summed up a remorseful evaluation of the League and how its ideals were becoming bureaucratic and stagnant. "There is little change [in Geneva], but one feels that with the passing of the first flush of early days, the League of Nations is entering a less enthusiastic era with traditions already much more fixed." Balch continued, "It is the period of Chamberlain and Poincaré and, except for the fact that Germany is now a member, one feels a certain let down in the tone of things. It is perhaps most of all the stalemate in regard to disarmament that causes a sense of bafflement and the Kellogg proposal meets too much skepticism in continental Europe to change this."[90]

Balch was well aware of the limitations of any such international pact or organization. Yet she threw herself and the WILPF behind Kellogg-Briand, even if she perceived some shortcomings in terms of enforcement mechanisms, as the first major international treaty to formally outlaw war. In Geneva in September 1928 Balch helped to arrange a speaker series with the themes of the "Kellogg Pact" and of disarmament broadly. Bringing in speakers headlined by Salvador de Madariaga, a prominent Spanish pacifist diplomat and a professor at Oxford, who was shortly to become ambassador to the United States (1931), and Professor William Rappard, a well-known internationalist, director of the Mandate Department of the League of Nations, founder of the Graduate Institute of International Studies in Geneva, and Swiss diplomatic delegate. Balch's conference was well attended. Her introductory remarks explain a great deal about her sense of history, national identity, internationalism, and the pact.

She stated boldly, "Science and technology opened immense vistas. The individual became again important as an active factor, however small, of a vast evolving cosmos. But the common future which history presents to us is uncertain. . . . For the first time in all history, our race faces the possibility of suicide." She turned to address "my own country, not because it is mine but because I believe it is in a degree a useful object of warning and of encouragement." Comparing America with Europe, she argued for more understanding and collaboration to build peace and prosperity from strengths. "If Europeans seem to Americans to find it too difficult to believe, too difficult to act, Americans seem to Europeans too uncritical, too naïve, impulsive and idealistic, not to say sentimental, exaggerated, unstable. . . . We are more or less aware of this. We turn with a rather pathetic wistfulness to Europeans with their wide human vision. . . . I wait as you wait to hear the ripest European thought has to offer us as we face this terrible, this wonderful alternative, a world of wars or a world of peace." The pact, said Balch, was symbolic of movement toward global disarmament and the peace that must come.[91]

But upon closer inspection of the terms of the pact, she aspired to combat skepticism about its idealism. At the same time, she hoped to embrace the utopian and pacifist values that it embodied as practical and genuinely wanted by American leaders while acknowledging some of the limitations. Balch made a series of speaking trips, in 1928 and through the summer of 1929, throughout England and Wales, and then through Northern Europe to urge its ratification. Ultimately she galvanized women's peace organizations, mostly local and national sections of the WILPF, across Europe to join in what eventually would be a vast international treaty, signed by virtually every major nation, as well as many smaller ones, to outlaw war. Balch was being constantly updated by mail about the progress of the pact in Congress and of various other issues of importance at the time, such as the plan not to remove U.S. marines from Nicaragua after their democratic election in 1928, by WILPF Executive Secretary Dorothy Detzer. In these letters Detzer emphasized much of what the WILPF wanted but did not have in the pact, and explained an interesting view of the future prospects for war and preventing conflict. "The Outlawry pact of Kellogg has sort of drowned out that idea [of all-inclusive arbitration with Great Britain], but it seems to me that it is as important a piece of work as we have to do. A treaty for so-called Compulsory Arbitration between Great Britain and ourselves, I am convinced would be the best security against war that we could have. We are not going to war with any other country except Great Britain."[92]

Balch did not agree that England represented the greatest threat of a future war with the United States, nor did she reply to Detzer with a proposal of what nation would be a more likely combatant. Ever focused on pushing peace first, Balch personally wrote to every member of the Senate Foreign Relations Committee, including corresponding with Borah in a limited but substantive manner. At home in the United States, the political tone of the debate over Kellogg-Briand was opposite from that of the League debates. There was no all-night filibuster, no competing speaking tours, and few impassioned political insults and instances of name-calling. In fact, apart from Borah, its idealism did not arouse much passion. Senators saw the pact as a well-intended international agreement, but there was no sense that the future of the Republic might be at stake.

The only question about the pact's passage concerned whether the four Reed-Moses reservations would be adopted. One senator said that they were simply doing what every other nation had done. "Is the Senate of the United States [the only entity] not to be accorded the right to place an interpretation upon it?"[93] Particularly at issue was the British note of interpretation, which specified that the empire retained its right to protect "certain regions of the world" over which it ruled.[94] Reed linked this stipulation to the insistence by Kellogg and Borah that further protection of the Monroe Doctrine was unnecessary, stating, "But suppose the Monroe doctrine was invaded, and we had said nothing about it. England has specifically reserved her rights over there, and we have said nothing. What would be our position before the world?"[95] Reed's argument proved so effective that Borah eventually conceded to include the reservations.[96]

Broad bipartisan support was clinched in the Senate after the Reed-Moses resolutions were added. Only Senator John Blaine of Wisconsin voted no, in objection to the British "certain regions" doctrine, saying that English protection of colonial possessions was an invitation for further war, thus violating the entire spirit of the compact. Despite certain qualms, the Republicans regarded passage as necessary because a presidential election was right around the corner, and the pact had overwhelming support among the American people. Herbert Hoover, the party's nominee for 1928, used the pact to refute the Democratic claim that "no accomplishment has been made by the Republican Administration in the advancement of world peace."[97] Hoover was quick to adopt the popular proposal as a part of his platform.

While senators widely supported the pact—and the press was enthralled by the message it was sending—most politicians and observers doubted its realistic effectiveness at outlawing war. Writing to his son Arch, Senator Johnson said, "I could not find myself getting excited over the Treaty. I think it is just a piece of bunk utilized by so-called statesmen the world over to fool their people."[98] Democrat Reed characterized the nonbinding expression of good feelings as exchanging a "sort of international kiss."[99] Minnesota's Farmer-Labor Party Senator Henrik Shipstead's questioning of Borah revealed an important matter regarding the pact's worth: "Is it not true that every government that took part in the last World War did so under the right of self-defense? . . . Under that construction how could this treaty have stopped the World War?" Borah had to concede that the treaty could not have stopped the horrific war that prompted these attempts at peace in the first place.[100] However, he did continue to believe that the weight of global, unified opinion—setting a new, widely respected public norm—was the best way to ensure peace in the future; it was certainly better than entangled alliances and obligations of force. Tennessee's Democratic Senator Kenneth McKellar summed up the sentiment of the Senate nicely when he declared, "It might deter some nation from making war . . . and I want to take no chances. At least it can do no great harm."[101] Since the Kellogg-Briand Pact did no harm to America's traditional isolationist stances, the Irreconcilables were able to support it, even recognizing that its effectiveness for ensuring world peace was debatable. If ineffective, it was still significant as an example of so-called isolationists reaching out to the world, attempting to create a safer and more prosperous global community.

The main formal provision of the pact was twofold when signed: to condemn war as "an instrument of national policy" or as "recourse to war for the solution of international controversies"; and to seek, instead, to solve disputes "by pacific means."[102] Triumphantly, Borah wrote to Kellogg. "The tremendous significance of your mission," he praised, "justified you in disregarding the petty bickering of those who have neither the intelligence to comprehend nor the moral conception to appreciate the worth or import of your achievement."[103]

Not a Party Issue

During the 1928 presidential campaign, Herbert Hoover endorsed the Republican foreign policy broadly and specifically singled out the pact as "a magnificent step toward world peace."[104] In contrast, Franklin Roosevelt discounted the treaty in his nomination speech for Al Smith in 1928, calling the probability low that peace could ever be achieved through the "platitudes of multilateral treaties piously deprecating armed conflict."[105] Yet this never became a campaign issue. Both Republicans and Democrats found the American public firmly behind it and assuaged the fears that Balch worried might undermine European and international support for this American-led initiative.

As Kellogg remarked, "I do not think the treaty for the renunciation of war should be made a party issue either in the campaign or the Senate, and I cannot conceive that it will be."[106] According to Borah, the pact "belonged to the nation." But as the U.S. Senate Foreign Relations Committee studied the treaty closely, led by Borah, some partisan distinctions did surface. He included a provision in their ensuing report that maintained that the pact did not impair the nation's ability to act to protect the Monroe Doctrine. In the ensuing Senate debates Borah made a powerful case, taking the floor again and again, to push the ratification forward and make it nearly unanimous. He emphasized in a forceful speech that no sanctions were implied expressly in the treaty.

Questions about the justifications for the use of force consumed much of his time and thinking. What made the pact and outlawry of war movement so appealing to him was that it relied on international law, order, and honor. But it also was the only conceivable recourse from what he called the "fetish of force" that hung like the sword of Damocles over international affairs. "The philosophy of the treaty," stated Borah, "is not that of preventing war, but that of organizing peace which is a wholly different thing."[107] This was the crux of a Borah-inspired nationalist and isolationist stance on the merits of a nonbinding agreement to outlaw international military conflict. "The treaty is not founded upon the theory of force or punitive measures at any place or at any time." What was most significant, Borah remarked in the Senate, was that the pact "does not rest upon the principles of alliances and a balance of power ordinarily rest—that of force behind the treaty to be applied in case anyone transgresses the treaty." "Under no circumstances or conditions," he continued forcefully, "do we recognize coercive measures as a method of enforcing the treaty."[108]

In contrast, though they were both behind the pact, Balch saw the rationale for outlawry and the specifics of what the United States was agreeing to somewhat differently. Writing to Borah when the pact was at the last stages of passage, she praised him for "all your work to make the renuncia-tion of war a political reality."[109] She reminded him that "this organiza-tion . . . is very eager for the prompt ratification of the Kellogg pact as it stands without any alterations."[110] Then, taking a global and comparative perspective based on her travels to drum up support for the pact and her duties with the WILPF, Balch explained that this was an issue both of global peacemaking and also of national interest. While the pact was not about coercion, Balch clearly saw it as having much to do with the inter-national community agreeing to act in concert to maintain peace without force but by dint of moral and legal suasion.

Now that the pact had raised international hopes, and some suspicion, she argued that the United States had to follow through with the pact and become a legitimate arm of the international peace movement. After re-turning from her mission in Haiti she had been speaking on the subject of the pact in 1928, "in more than twenty places in England and Wales last summer, as well as in France and Switzerland." Balch noted that in the UK she had "found people very much interested and ready to believe that the move was seriously meant. On the continent I found a tendency to profound skepticism and a belief that the proposal was a vote-catching device with reference to the presidential campaign."[111] Citing the fact that other nations and peoples were eagerly awaiting Senate ratification, Balch urged prompt passage in a letter to Borah. It was needed urgently for at least two reasons, she said. First, it would support American global pres-tige and consolidate American leadership on the peace initiative. Second, it fulfilled a global necessity to renounce war; others were looking to America on the issue, abroad and at home, she said, so the Senate must respond overwhelmingly and rapidly. Balch noted that in her experience the continental nations of Europe were closely scrutinizing American politics and the effort for peacemaking. It was a chance the nation could ill afford to relinquish by playing partisan games or debating excessively in Congress. Those nations are "waiting to see whether this country pro-poses to make the renunciation of war a reality or a farce and the impres-sion that any delay [will] be very unfortunate." Speaking to her recent ex-periences educating Europeans about the pact and her political activism, Balch remarked that "this is an aspect of the matter which must be most vividly in the mind of those who have felt the pulse of Europe this summer in however slight a degree." Speedy passage of the pact, she said, "would seem a matter of self regard as well as courtesy."[112]

Similarly the WILPF pressured U.S. and foreign politicians. Mary Sheepshanks, the international secretary of the WILPF, observed, "We find that the League of Nations Secretariat is very strongly in favor of accepting and developing the Kellogg proposals and thinks that it will be disastrous if they are not accepted."[113] The Kellogg proposals were sent to "all sections of the WILPF as we think public opinion ought to be answered in response to the position of the weaker and subject nations."[114] The pact took priority over other WILPF initiatives, such as an Eastern European peace conference to discuss the problems between Poland and Lithuania, which was scrapped so that organizers could focus on outlawry issues.[115] Another international group, the Committee on Educational Publicity in the Interests of World Peace, strongly supported the pact. As the committee noted to Addams, its immediate goals included "concentration of effort upon early Senate ratification of the Multilateral Treaty for the renunciation of war, making the prohibition of war a basic principle of international law, and further limitation of armaments."[116] Hoping to win Addams's support of these ideas, George Gordon Battle, secretary of the committee, sent these objectives to her before Kellogg arrived in Paris to complete negotiations with Premier Briand. Battle was also aware that it was "rather late now to have the form of the agreement to be entered into change in any way, but this does not affect future consideration of the proposal which we should all work for."[117]

These are but a few of the myriad examples of national and international lobbying that made the pact remarkably popular. Not long thereafter, in January 1929, with some minor quibbling and reservations, the Senate voted 85–1 to ratify what was also called the Pact of Paris.[118] Virtually all observers at the time credited Borah with shepherding the treaty to passage. "Never has the great ability of Senator Borah been displayed to finer advantage than in his winning battle for the Kellogg peace pact," wrote one editor in a widely shared appraisal.[119] Briand, Kellogg, Vice President Charles Dawes, and others also heralded Borah's leadership on the issue. With bilateral U.S.-French origins, the pact took on global scope as a flood of other nations followed the U.S. lead by ratifying the treaty, while reserving the right to act to protect their special interests. It was signed in August 1928 by the original fifteen nations: Australia, Belgium, Canada, Czechoslovakia, France, Germany, Great Britain, India, the Irish Free State, Italy, Japan, New Zealand, Poland, South Africa, and the United States. All agreed to adjudicate conflicts between signatory nations by "pacific" means. In the following months, the outlawry cause gained further momentum and more than sixty countries joined in this renunciation of war.[120] Indeed, in less than one year Borah had become a figurehead for the movement, although he never again spearheaded such an ambitious international pact. In 1929 S. O. Levinson established the William Edgar Borah Outlawry of War Foundation at the University of Iowa. According to its mission, "The name of the foundation reflects the desire of Mr. Levinson to honor Senator Borah for his efforts in behalf of peace, especially for his part in securing the ratification of the Kellogg-Briand pact by the United States Senate."[121]

According to Borah, Kellogg had accomplished the "most important step in the cause of peace that has ever been taken." Even if the ideals outmatched some of the nuances of the pact, Borah claimed that "I have seen it stated that the treaty does not amount to much because there is no force behind it. I regard this treaty as just as binding as any other treaty. There is nothing behind any treaty except the private word of the nations signing it."[122] On this there could be no dispute. Ultimately Borah's isolationist political philosophy lined up almost precisely with the broad contours of the pact: the autonomy, freedoms, and political traditions of the United States remained secure. Balch's WILPF philosophy was imperfectly served by the pact given the lack of mechanisms to enforce peace through at least compulsory arbitration.

"Opposing All Concentration of Power" at Home and Abroad

Walter Lippmann, who (like Balch and unlike Borah) advocated American entry into the World Court, described Borah as an irascible yet admirable "instinctive conscientious objector." While esteeming his resolve, Lippmann derided Borah's essentially negative politics, calling him "an individualist who opposes all concentration of power, who is against private privilege and private monopoly, against political bureaucracy and centralized government." Lippmann's Borah was a Jeffersonian Democrat, an advocate for agrarian values and believer in an ideal vision of the United States.[123]

Borah's positions often seemed contradictory, as evidenced by a 1923 cartoon in the *Idaho Daily Statesman*. It depicts a salesman selling a double-faced record of the "celebrated singer" Borah, saying, "On the front side is 'Get out and stay out,' on the back side is "Go in and do something.' He sings 'em both equally as well."[124] What the cartoon depicted as flip-flopping weakness, Borah saw as a strength. These positions can be reconciled in terms of what Borah considered the core of his political philosophy. Throughout his career, Borah held to a strong belief, developed first as a frontier lawyer, that large "remorseless and soulless" entities should be kept from domineering over a man's personal liberty.[125] This rhetoric had much in common with anti-imperialist, particularly Jamesian, suspicions of size in government, corporations, and other man-made institutions that wielded socioeconomic power. Borah applied this philosophy to large corporations, to federal intrusions on states' rights, and then, especially, to global governance through the League. He also applied it to other parts of the world; and this explains what may have been the greatest consistency in his political vision. He saw the outlawry of war as a means to ending the domination of powerful states, yet without the added dangers of a too-powerful bureaucracy or a binding large-scale alliance that might constrain American autonomy. For more than four years Borah had decried the permanence of U.S. military operations in Europe. It was not until January 1923 that the last sixteen thousand American soldiers "got out and stayed out," leaving their postwar peacekeeping duties in Europe to return to America.

A small minority of senators was able to halt American involvement in an international peace organization. But less than a decade later, several of the same group turned their passion toward creating an international pact to ensure peace. In so doing they worked closely with ardent pacifists and peace organizations. How can these ostensibly inconsistent Irreconcilable actions be explained?

The partisan political environment in the United States shaped the various groups struggling to win control and influence in determining how America should act in the world. Republican Party Chairman John T. Adams emphasized that the party "will continue to review and discuss political problems from the standpoint of 'America First.'"[126] This commitment was maintained over a decade of partisan maneuverings.

Balch's position also opposed most concentrations of power. She distrusted power politics and the patriarchal hierarchies that maintained the need for the sort of saber-rattling old-fashioned diplomacy that had been characteristic of European politics. Balch also was suspicious of the types of political and economic interests for whom wars and nationalist conflict might be profitable or otherwise advantageous. Unlike that of Borah, however, her remedy was internationalist and tended toward the binding: a strong concentration of power in a supranational association such as the League or in ad hoc conferences to adjudicate differences. Thus, it perplexed her that the League fight in Congress was based on principles that she, too, held dear. She believed in the traditional ideology of keeping America neutral and not meddling abroad. But she could see little merit in Borah's desire to make U.S. interests and sovereignty the forefront of policy, protecting the country's right to self-defense, and not letting anyone else dictate how its troops and its money were used around the world.

The Kellogg-Briand Pact was their middle ground. It seemed to be a way to help ensure peace, a noble cause eliciting little resistance, without giving up these key American values. Senator Philander Knox, an American statesmen and diplomat for more than thirty years, summarized how he saw this idealistic middle ground as a capacious worldview. "It is no strange policy that I propose, no heartless aloofness from world affairs," said Knox. "It was by being faithful exactly to the policy I now advocate that America had become great enough to bring victory. . . . Internationalism would destroy us at home. Nationalism will save us at home. If there is anything through which we can do good to the world it is our Americanism."[127] The senator felt that his ideals of popular sovereignty and democracy as lasting institutions, born in the United States, were worthy of being copied throughout the world—without the interference of bureaucratic associations or the threat of war.

America had a duty and responsibility, the proponents of the pact said, to show the world the wonders of democracy and freedom. But if it were to surrender the core of what made it the "greatest" nation on earth, it could not fulfill its mission. Borah expounded on this, saying, "We say to surrender her ancient policies or give up her great maxims of liberty means not service to mankind, but means the extinction of the last great hope of civilization. America can not be of service to the cause of humanity nor true to herself, she can not show her friendship to the world nor loyalty to her own," by accepting a union with the world that erases the very spirit of Americanism.[128] America's integrity had to be preserved so that it could remain an exemplar to the world.[129]

Woodrow Wilson's Republican successors in the 1920s enthusiastically restored a version of what can best be seen as a pre-Wilsonian isolationist view of internationalism. Under Harding, Coolidge, and Hoover the value of isolationism was firmly embedded in the politics that Borah and other prominent figures epitomized: a limited international engagement (mostly commercial), with few if any binding "entanglements," couched in terms of economic objectives and progress rather than the politico-military muscle or expansionist (sometimes billed as humanitarian) interventions that had been much more characteristic of the decade after the Spanish-American War and before World War I.

Yet visions of American foreign policy in the twenties tended to be neither Wilsonian nor unilateral. The United States took an active leadership role in promoting international cooperation in East Asia and Europe without entering the League. "By exercising leadership without responsibility," historian Frank Ninkovich argued, "American statesmen of the decade [1920s] attempted to construct a world without politics," a perspective that, compared with Wilson's, was "positively utopian."[130] In many ways this was the idealistic isolationist worldview held by Borah and his fellow Irreconcilables. They gave the highest priority to decentralized power, democratic representation and reform, and hoped to channel the will of the people to unite citizens as Americans, while prizing national autonomy in foreign affairs.

These ideas, in turn, drove Borah's ardent traditionalist belief that the nation had so much to do at home that it ought to be as free as possible from foreign entanglements. After all, as Charles Beard put it some years later, the main characteristics of interwar isolationism were "rejection of membership in the League of Nations; non-entanglement in the political controversies of Europe and Asia; non-intervention in the wars of these continents; neutrality, peace, and defense of the United States through measures appropriate to those purposes; and the pursuit of a foreign policy friendly to all nations disposed to reciprocate."[131] This cluster of ideas represented a set of interlocking principles that Borah, with his Irreconcilables, wholeheartedly endorsed. Balch and her pacifist internationalists were also idealistic. They largely embraced these same principles—except, of course, for seeking stronger organization through the League and Court and in supporting liberal immigration laws, their fundamental points of difference.

Still, this isolationist cast on the emerging "new" internationalism faced many obstacles as it transitioned into the 1930s. Fear of foreigners, suppression of competing political ideologies, and racial prejudice, exacerbated by economic collapse impeded arguments for closer ties with other countries. Upholding the tradition of Washington, Jefferson, and especially the Monroe Doctrine, those making isolationist arguments asserted the need to continue a "hemispheric" and anti-European (sometimes anticolonial) approach to national commitments abroad. But nationalism perhaps was the strongest force opposing the dynamic fusion of the cautiously modern principles of isolationism and a moderate form of internationalism.

The series of international crises beginning when Japan invaded Manchuria in 1931 and culminating in the events that led to World War II exposed the fallacies of so-called Republican internationalism without, however, reviving the idealistic internationalism of Wilsonianism. Within and between states, competing nationalisms made enemies of fellow citizens and allied countries alike, making genuine international comity difficult. In the scramble of the Depression each country did what it could to make socioeconomic progress, often by protecting domestic markets against foreign competition. Here protectionist isolationism took hold in certain American policies designed to address the Depression, building on the long-standing U.S. tradition of restrictive tariffs. The most notable such move was the Smoot-Hawley Act (1930), which increased tariffs on more than twenty thousand goods and exacerbated destructive international escalation and retaliatory protectionist legislation. Only Great Britain held fast to try to practice the free trade that many preached, and even they abandoned free-trade principles in 1932 in favor of a so-called imperial preference system.

As the world economy penetrated the farthest reaches of Africa, Asia, and beyond, America along with the other great powers competed for access to markets and in a militarized "scramble" for territorial expansion. Global trade and finance continued but was far more limited as the conditions of worldwide depression deepened. Still, the new internationalism remained a potent counterbalance to impulses toward greater inward focus. Jane Addams received the Bryn Mawr Award for Distinguished Service and the Pictorial Review Prize as the most famous woman in America. In December 1931 it was announced that the Nobel Peace Prize was to be awarded jointly to Addams and to Columbia University President and international peace activist Nicholas Murray Butler. In the presentation speech historian and Nobel committee member Halvdan Koht summarized the new world order, noting that the United States is "one of the great world powers and economically is now the greatest of all. By virtue of this position, she influences decisions on war and peace in all corners of the globe. We can say, in fact, that, because of this vast economic strength, she wields greater power over war and peace than any other country on earth. All who yearn for a lasting peace must therefore look to America for help." In "honoring Jane Addams," he argued that the award represented something more universal, "we also pay tribute to the work which women can do for peace and fraternity among nations."[132] Though Addams was too ill to attend the ceremony in Oslo, she declared that her share of the prize should go toward the Geneva office of the WILPF.

In proposing a moratorium on intergovernmental debts, Herbert Hoover, too, was keenly aware of international and not merely domestic concerns. He blended an effort to rejuvenate markets for American exports, while also aiming to restore financial order and economic stability in Europe. From a political standpoint, however, Hoover moved toward what he hoped would eradicate the vindictive reparations established at Versailles. The complicated moratorium process was designed to leave the Europeans free of debt, so that, as Hoover put it, they could "maintain courage and hope in the German nation" and support other European nations with the financial flexibility to "work out their problems."[133]

Still, a willingness to engage Europe, to reestablish the financial presence so crucial to America's transatlantic influence, never emerged in the years immediately after Hoover's action in June 1931. Evidencing a paradigm shift, the most vocal opponents of the moratorium were the longstanding isolationists. George Norris and William Borah criticized the move as one catering to the incompetence of Europe, depriving American citizens and banks of the proper repayment of war debts. Hoover's position as advanced by his secretary of state, Henry Stimson, was interventionist, according to Borah. While Hoover and Stimson won out on the issue, as events turned out the moratorium on intergovernmental debt payments and even the short-term European credits to German banks that Stimson and Hoover worked so hard to secure proved to be largely ineffective. Nevertheless, the moratorium and the response of its critics can be seen as part of a larger movement during the 1930s that eased the United States out of a position of significant influence abroad just at a moment when such an influence might have helped to stave off a future conflict.

While isolationists insisted on fair payment on all loans, they sought to limit future loans as a means of ensuring a lasting peace. A year after Hoover's initial announcement, an agreement at Lausanne, Switzerland, dramatically reduced war debts and postponed payment indefinitely, though American isolationists refused to accept the dissolution of all such debts.[134] Hailed by the League and internationalist groups such as the WILPF as finally presenting an end to the economically vindictive peace at Versailles, the moratorium had negligible effects for European and U.S. economic recovery. As Europe began to rearm in earnest in the wake of Adolf Hitler's ascent to power, the absent dollar could no longer work toward temperance and balance. The fiscal "activism" of Hoover's proposal to relinquish future debt payments led American policy-makers toward greater passivity in global financial oversight.[135]

In the face of the ongoing international crises of the early 1930s, Borah's views deepened in degree, rather than in kind. He favored a more protectionist form of isolationism. He argued for the restriction of American trade. He continued to oppose new immigration. He pushed for legislation to enshrine neutrality in foreign policy and thereby place constraints on the president's ability to pursue diplomatic involvement abroad. These efforts were encapsulated by a series of Neutrality Acts that Borah championed to passage in 1935, 1936, 1937, and 1939. These acts repudiated neutral rights as they were traditionally understood. The acts aimed to ensure that American businesses and citizens avoided virtually all commerce with belligerents and did not travel in war zones except at their own risk; thus, the acts sought to limit the risks of the United States' being involved in the sorts of imbroglios, such as the sinking of the *Lusitania* and the massive American loans and material trade with Great Britain and France, that helped precipitate U.S. entry into World War I. From 1931 to 1938 Balch supported neutrality and continued to oppose war, but increasingly parted ways with former isolationist allies such as Borah. She wrote and pushed proposals on such topics as disarmament, internationalization of aviation, economic reconstruction, reform of the League of Nations, mediation in Spain, and neutrality and collective security, all of which privileged supranational organizations and authorities and tried to promote a rethinking of old provisions and structures to come up with new solutions to achieve peace.[136] Though idealistic and nonbinding international engagement and the pursuit of peace were points of convergence for Borah with Balch, their common ground was sliding away by the mid-1930s.

Following his sixth consecutive election to the Senate, in 1936 Borah concentrated most of his energy on preventing U.S. activities in the sorts of leagues and initiatives that Balch hoped might stave off future conflicts and calamities. Borah sought stronger neutrality measures to bind the hands of the Roosevelt administration, which he feared would become more interventionist in light of developing turmoil in Europe. As it turned out, ignoring German, Italian, and Japanese global aggression in the mid-1930s and maneuvering the United States away from a position of aiding sympathetic groups who opposed the new fascist powers was a deeply flawed strategy. Borah, however, argued closer linkages to Europe via the League or in direct mediation would do no better and could do far worse by embroiling the United States in conflicts such as the Spanish Civil War. He did not live to recognize the dire limitations of such an approach. On January 16, 1940, Borah suffered a massive cerebral hemorrhage and died three days later.

There is good evidence in the popular press, ranging from articles and editorials to letters to the editor and poll data, that much of the nation had begun to think that the United States might well need to take global action for the best interests of mankind—in or after 1939. But what that action should be was hotly contested. Balch regarded American leadership as the best way to stave off a second world war, though her prescribed means to that end was through robust international organizations, a reorganized League of Nations, and a series of new alliances and binding antiwar treaties. But for Borah, America's first and foremost obligation was to act as a beacon of "righteousness." He argued persuasively that to do so the nation should embrace commercial and cultural international power and should remain neutral in deed and rhetoric to never unknowingly take a side through unequal trade with belligerent nations. In most situations until the late 1930s, he adhered to a view that the United States ought to achieve world economic and cultural supremacy—but always on the nation's own terms.[137]

Thus, in the 1920s and throughout the 1930s most Americans agreed with much of what Borah *and* Balch were trying to accomplish. Well into 1941 polls continued to find that more than half of all Americans wanted to remain out of the war in Europe, though they increasingly supported aid to the British. Still, American policy in the interwar era was not nearly as isolationist as many have characterized it.[138] Protecting American sovereignty and its inherent values was of the utmost importance. Working in tandem with the rest of the world for the common benefit of peace and economic prosperity, however, also was a powerful and widely shared priority of the consensus that gradually built the era's "new" internationalism.

The Japanese attack on Pearl Habor and American participation in a second and even more devastating world war irrevocably altered the isolationist calculus. Once attacked, the nation had to defend itself. But it was the peace that would mark a new direction in American internationalism and isolationism. In many ways this process culminated in late 1945. As the Nobel Prize committee met in Stockholm to decide who would earn the Peace Prize, they did so at a conspicuous moment of reassessment. Their decision would be scrutinized heavily as a symbol for the postwar era. The selection process was difficult, because global catastrophe had only barely been avoided, and recovering in the early months of peace was proving almost as problematic as surviving in wartime. The prize committee selected John Mott and Emily Balch to share the award in 1946. Balch followed in the footsteps of her friend Jane Addams (who had died a decade earlier, in 1935). Balch was the second American woman to receive the award and Mott was the first leader of a nongovernmental international ecumenical organization to receive the award.

The events of 1946 marked an apex in the new internationalism and heralded a shift in American political thought. Multilateral strength and ensuring peace seemed foremost given a world landscape forever altered by the war, the catastrophic evils of the Holocaust, and the unleashing of nuclear weapons. Global devastation, new technologies, increased interconnectedness, the looming rise of a bipolar geopolitics, and the Cold War created a new matrix that for many Americans—and nearly all of the nation's prominent politicians, thinkers, and activists—required the United States to be much more thoroughly involved abroad. Still, the terms of this engagement were under dispute. Americans continued to debate the questions that had arisen in the previous decades, but in the new environment of the postwar world. They asked how the nation should balance private initiatives and peace activities, unilateral actions, and international alliances and unions, even as it worked to demobilize and achieve continued economic and social progress at home.

CONCLUSION: THE INTRICATE BALANCE

The current reassessment of the nation's proper balance between engagement abroad and investment at home for the twenty-first century is just the latest reappraisal of this dilemma. Since the United States' rise to global power, its leaders and citizens have regularly scrutinized the costs and benefits of foreign ambition. In 1943, in the midst of the Second World War, Walter Lippmann explained the essential paradox involved in this delicate balancing act. He argued that foreign policy ends are inherently limited by their means. According to Lippmann, the relationship between means and ends is the critical question for policy-makers. "In foreign relations," he wrote, "as in all other relations, a policy has been formed only when commitments and power have been brought into balance. . . . The nation must maintain its objectives and its power in equilibrium, its purposes within its means and its means equal to its purposes."[1]

Historians have thoroughly analyzed America's global ascent and the debates over how to strike a Lippmannesque equilibrium in domestic and foreign affairs as well as between foreign policy means and ends. Yet the conventional wisdom that an isolationist tradition was neither serious nor effective is inadequate. What has been missing in many recent historical narratives has been a unified account of changing intellectual understandings of isolationism, as visions of isolation were adapted to the political debates about empire, international engagement, and domestic reform from the 1890s through the 1930s. Excellent, largely older histories of isolationism also miss elements of this intellectual transition because they almost exclusively emphasize diplomacy and political behavior with a focus on two periods. The first is the turbulent years from 1914 through 1920, culminating in the Senate rejection of the Treaty of Versailles and League of Nations. The second era—and the most well explored and well known— is the so-called battle against isolation and the neutrality debates centered on the period from the mid-1930s until the Japanese attack on Pearl Harbor.

The foremost histories of these periods were largely written and researched in the 1950s and 1960s. These works have tended to explore ideas about isolation using traditional methods of political history and the study of foreign relations, leaving the origins of the isolationist positions for these later periods underexamined. As we have seen, those views can be traced back to the 1880s and 1890s as intellectual and cultural phenomena. By doing so, and by juxtaposing their development with emerging visions of internationalism and domestic reform, we now better perceive just how pivotal ideas about isolation were to a wide range of new perspectives on the meaning of America in an age of rising global power from the late nineteenth century through World War II. And, just as importantly, these origins draw attention to the intensely international elements at work both in American foreign policy and in most American isolationist claims as they developed from the 1890s through the 1930s.[2]

Having come this far, let us return to ask: why is this important and how does this change our view of the history of the past 130 years?

This book presents at least four answers to that question. First, the seminal period for the growth of a modern, refined form of American isolationist thought came in the late nineteenth century during the debates over imperialism. New isolationist perspectives developed out of debates over American "empire." In turn, they became far more compatible with international engagement and were more influenced by domestic views—and in fact were often premised upon particular understandings of what domestic challenges meant for foreign commitments—than previous histories have emphasized.

Second, these new insights underscore the rationale for shifting the grounds for the historical analysis of isolationism and internationalism. Treating isolationist concepts as intellectual and cultural phenomena shows that they have been as much a part of domestic social and political thought as foreign policy. In turn, this has opened up new vistas on how isolationist principles could be—and often were—embedded in the arguments and actions of radical reformers and even some of the most internationalist-minded thinkers and activists from the 1890s through the 1930s. Further, treating isolation as an intellectual category more fully illuminates the wide uses and compelling appeal of varied isolationist rhetoric over time. The focus here generally has not been on how these arguments were received by "average" Americans. Rather, the aim has been to elucidate patterns in thought and action.

Third, this effort has revealed the personal and public ways that a diverse set of Americans grappled with the meaning of their nation's burgeoning global power and struggled to relate the nation's unique historical identity to its place in the rest of the world. The isolationist elements embedded in arguments for how the nation should or should not participate in global politics, commerce, and culture fueled dissent against expansionism and interventionism. So too this was a double-sided phenomenon. Unilateralist visions for expansion also came to be premised on interpretations of long-standing isolationist tenets. The resulting isolationist perspectives were intensely individualized in framing personal and group cases for and against imperialism, alliances, and collective security. The malleable new orientation of isolationist precepts thereby set the surprisingly broad parameters for post–World War I international engagements, most notably demonstrated by the rise of an isolationist bloc in Congress (and across society) that symbolically culminated their efforts in the nonbinding Kellogg-Briand Pact to outlaw war. Frequently imperial and anti-imperial, interventionist and anti-interventionist, reform and status quo arguments coexisted in the hearts and minds of the same person. Thus, fascinating hybrid beliefs linked isolation to a wide range of social, economic, philosophical, and political positions, which in turn resulted in odd configurations of strange political bedfellows, headlined by the anti-imperialists and the Irreconcilables.

Finally, fourth, the developing power, appeal, and widely varying influence of modern isolationism help explain why in both thought and action the United States traveled interventionist paths only in restricted ways—and why isolationist paths were not taken in the end. Isolationist ideas served to curb the impulses for audacious, usually unilateralist international action, supported a domestic focus, and reinforced a new rendering of the tradition for "nonentangled" commitments and informal or "soft" modes of international relations.

So, let us take a brief look back at the trajectory of isolationism and internationalism over the past century, bringing the narrative of this book up to the present to gain a sense of where the United States has been and where it may be headed.

From the 1890s to the 1920s

As we have seen, at no time were isolationist principles more potent than in the pivotal years when America rose to global power from the 1890s to the 1920s. Isolationist views never dominated how the United States interacted with the world in this period (or any other). They were influential, but they were far from the only prescriptions for how to engage internationally.

Yet isolationism was a crucial component first in the debates over empire, then in setting the terms for some domestic social reform, later in the dissent over entering World War I, and subsequently in the backlash against the war and the rise of a new internationalism. Isolation, nonintervention, anticolonialism, and avoidance of war are primordial American concepts; however, such values have been far from static. From Cleveland to Lodge to Balch, politicians and activists have built differing political philosophies on historical foundations that they interpreted as established by icons Washington, Jefferson, and Monroe. At base this broadly isolationist tradition, intensely subject to interpretation and to changing circumstances, continues to sway individuals and groups in powerful ways.

By locating the origins of modern isolationism in the 1890s, a generation earlier than most historians, this book has aimed to illuminate isolationist and internationalist ideas in such previously unexplored or underexplored areas as the rhetoric of imperialists and the actions of internationalists. This study demonstrates, too, the powerful conceptual linkages between isolationist perspectives and robust views of American nationalism, nationhood, and international order that were developed by turn-of-the-twentieth-century reformers, political leaders, and industrialists.

From the Civil War to just before the Second World War we saw three pivotal transitions during which Americans considered and disputed new modes of acting in the world. First, there were the initial convulsions of war and empire in the 1890s; second were the debates over eventual American entry into World War I in 1917; third were the attempts after World War I to create idealistic international organizations to make the world safe for democracy. As isolationist ideas were adapted, modernized, and sometimes rejected, they were central in determining tactics and outcomes, and in shaping the broader debates in which Americans conceived abstract visions of how their nation ought to act in the world.

The United States never became a major colonial power, nor did the nation establish an enduring peace after World War I. Increasing pressures and enticements to take action as a world power during the fifty years from the 1880s through the 1930s intensified conflicts between imperialist, interventionist, and internationalist impulses. During the 1890s and in the World War I era, neither these worldviews—nor Wilson's idealistic perspective—were able to resist the powerful pull of enduring, popular isolationist sentiments. The imperialist developments of the 1890s and the later internationalist impulses of the late 1910s failed to reconcile modernity and global involvement with the core democratic principles of the American isolationist "tradition." Nevertheless, the refined isolationist views developed in the 1890s came to buttress support for limited humanitarian intervention abroad and aimed to achieve a balance of domestic and foreign commitments.

Differing conceptions of isolation thus help to explain a conundrum of U.S. history in this period: why neither American "large policy" expansionist imperialism nor Woodrow Wilson's idealist internationalism reached its major conceptual or practical political aims. The failure to push either of these courses to logical ends must be understood in part as resulting from the fact that they both conflicted, on a deep level, with the long-standing tradition of isolationist tenets; thus, they could not surmount counterarguments that often employed or were couched in terms of modern adaptations of isolation. These newer iterations of isolationist thought evolved so that they were compatible with measured global involvement. And they achieved greater levels of hybridization between developing conceptions of how America could be engaged abroad and also isolated from wars, binding alliances, and power politics, while pursuing reform at home (à la Bourne's transnational America).

The resulting interrelated views about isolation and internationalism gained acceptance not as some unthinking sentimentalization of tradition, or as an abstract desire for "freedom of action" alone, but as a sophisticated framework for understanding and defining both national ideals and global imperatives. In part this composite development explains the many variations on isolationist thought, and why they have often been mistaken. The isolationist perspective was far from monolithic. Ideas about isolation, in light of the changing conditions of modern industrial society and ever-increasing global interconnections between nations and peoples, were located across a wide spectrum of political thought. Modern isolationist principles also were epistemological. That is, they structured beliefs not just about America's "proper" role in the world, but also provided a way to understand the nation and to envision its ideals, helping people to construct and articulate their visions of both nation and world, both self and society.

Shared values emerged as integral to the development of isolationist thought. Most prominent among these were an unyielding interpretation of America's democratic guiding principles (often stressing freedom of speech, action, dissent, and anticolonialism) and an updated view of the nation's vital interests. This view emphasized seeking peace, but also preserving freedom of action by combining economic and commercial international engagement with neutrality to avoid disadvantageous and permanent relationships with other nations and peoples. This concept of neutrality, as we have seen, was quite fungible indeed. Even today fierce debates rage about what "types" of international relationships are acceptable. Still, among those who held isolationist-oriented views there was wide agreement that the nation should prize neutrality as a general rule, especially given the nation's growing power to support proactively neutral declarations with force. As we have seen, there also was agreement that, at least in principle, the nation should avoid becoming entangled in costly modern conflicts or alliances abroad, and that it should seek international economic and cultural engagement.

These core focuses of modern, refined isolationism developed early on in anti-imperialist thought, notably in the psychologically and philosophically rich anticolonial thought of William James and the members of the Anti-Imperialist League. In turn these ideas quickly influenced the views of anti-imperial, anti-interventionist reformers, such as W. E. B. Du Bois, Jane Addams, and Randolph Bourne; similar notions surfaced to inform the anti-imperial, anti-intervention arguments of both William Borah and Emily Balch. Yet we must note that this cluster of modern isolationist tenets shared certain concerns with some predominantly nonisolationist, pro-neutrality arguments (such as the America-centric ideals of certain hyper-nationalists and, at another pole, with absolute pacifist internationalists).

At the same time, expansionists such as Henry Cabot Lodge adhered to some of these same long-standing principles of isolationist autonomy, reinterpreting them in terms of new American power and a robust sense of nationalism. Lodge's early politics were united with his later strident isolationist-nationalist position in the League of Nations debates by his updated interpretation of Washington and Monroe's perspectives on the need for national autonomy as critical to U.S. foreign policy. This position formed the core of his muscular "large policy" expansionism in the 1890s. A similar vision of isolationist national interest set within an exceptionalist framework also appeared in the arguments of Christian evangelizers and mission advocates such as John Mott, and also shaped the unilaterally nationalist positions advanced by William Borah and his fellow Irreconcilables.

Powerful new interpretations of the perceived advantages, disadvantages, and the value of isolation provide an analytical framework to understand the intellectual history of the period from the 1890s through the 1930s. The expansion of American empire in the late nineteenth century was followed by retrenchment from imperialism. This lull, marked by a predominant concern with domestic economic prosperity and social reform, was short-lived. New global changes spurred a reconsideration and further refinement of isolationist principles. A series of debates began, leading eventually to intervention, war, and then a significant backlash during World War I, making isolation far more appealing in the postwar period. Politicians, thinkers, and activists across a wide spectrum of personal beliefs and partisan views during this period reshaped and were shaped by ideas about changing policy outlooks, national goals, and personal visions for America's betterment.

World War I reshaped isolationist views of how, when, and where the nation might best engage abroad. The transformative effects of war on ideas and on society in America are well established; but the reconciliation of modern isolationism with the new internationalist and transnationalist positions during and particularly after the war adds further evidence to such an observation. Premised on hopes for peace, antiwar activists came together with an array of radical politicians and social critics during the crucial years of World War I. Though they were a small minority and did not prevent entry into the conflict, their criticism echoed in the interwar years, when opposing values against interventionism held significant sway, and a movement to outlaw war gained momentum.

After the war, Irreconcilable William Borah's rising vision of a "new isolationism" was actually a flexible quasi-populist and nationalist form of politics. He considered this view to be a genuine representation of the popular will. The growing appeal of the advantages of a new form of isolation appeared in the politics and advocacy of the Women's International League for Peace and Freedom, in Emily Balch's "new internationalism," and in the broader U.S. peace movement as well. This internationalist-isolationist framework—always in tension, never fully resolved—remains in the background of how Americans today evaluate and debate the "proper" role of the nation in the world.

It is a bold but accurate statement to say that isolation remains a national value, though it has been hotly contested. Often history reveals that the values that are most central are also those that are most debated. Specific interpretations of "isolation" remain subject to vigorous debate, and these interpretations have been as different as the people who have articulated them.

Proclaimed in its basic precepts by some of America's leading revolutionaries, ever since, isolation has been claimed or rejected by politicians when it suited them. But it has not remained unchanged. By tracking ideas for and against isolation over a period in which these notions have not received considerable attention by historians, we can better see the contours of modern isolationism and understand that it never conformed to the types of caricatures that have stripped isolationism of its real historical depth and analytical sophistication. Visions of the nation's proper role in the world often took isolationist ideas into account, albeit in implicit ways. Isolationism in the twentieth century was more complex than can be accounted for by the negativistic connotations of a walled-and-bounded, protectionist "isolationism."

In short, the historical case is clear: the aftermath of expansionism at the turn of the twentieth century never led to large-scale annexations, although it did permanently alter how Americans conceived the balance between assertive international action and the benefits of isolation and reform at home in two ways. First, the roiling debates over whether the United States should be a colonial, expansionist nation provoked significant backlash and reinvigorated traditional understanding of isolationist nonentanglement and deeper views of America as inherently democratic, anticolonial, and noninterventionist. Second, small annexations, new formal as well as informal commercial engagements, and various development projects provided the United States with new outposts in the Caribbean and the Pacific, and with an intercontinental canal to secure. This new territory provided fresh rationales for increased interaction abroad and heightened both connections and tensions with nations and peoples involved in those areas, making the United States simultaneously more global and more vulnerable.

Similarly this enlarged international role and even larger conception of America's power and place in the world fueled the fires of World War I interventionism. But by the late 1920s and certainly by the 1930s, the idealistic, seemingly impractical Wilsonian cast to American global engagement had already dimmed. While the era never lived up to a purported return or retreat to isolationism, it was marked by debating how to outlaw war, with vigorous attention and attraction to the view that America ought to act as a neutral democracy. As a time of significant global economic ties, the period represented a moment of unfulfilled direct American leadership in global politics and economics.

The 1920s through World War II

During the interwar years, isolation crystallized into a more coherent ideology and briefly assumed a positive cast in American politics. The Kellogg-Briand Pact in 1928 represented a rare moment of unity between isolationists and internationalists who sought to channel the public will to outlaw war. This also signaled the era's new possibilities for fusing isolation with international imperatives. Ultimately, Wilson's vision for a world order based upon a partial but genuine relinquishment of sovereignty by even the most powerful nations—including the United States—was more radical than any plan seriously pursued by policy-makers before or since. And it was rebuked precisely because it turned away from a long-standing and deeply held view that America should be free from foreign entanglement, not reshaping the world or tied to the corrupting influences of power politics, but always free to pursue its own course at home or abroad. Still, during the 1920s and 1930s the Wilsonian perspective was not entirely discarded. It inflected the idealistic rhetoric that served to combine fairly strict isolation in diplomacy (the new political isolationism) with largely open and private engagement in commerce and cultural arenas.

U.S. banks, industries, and American entrepreneurs of many stripes were active in global commerce, tying other nations into streams of cultural cross-connections. Hindsight reveals that the "interwar years" can be characterized best as a midway point between the prewar period—when a domestic focus had propelled a relative lack of international interest, particularly in terms of binding entanglements with Europe—and the wartime global, idealistic, even messianic position as championed by Woodrow Wilson–style internationalists. One scholar has aptly termed this compromise position for the 1920s as a "new isolationism," marked by economic, cultural, and limited political participation abroad.[3] Borah and other politicians, and Balch and other activists strived to make the United

States a leading force for outlawing war around the world. Even with all of this engagement, however, the dominant perspective of the era about the nation's global role was characterized by a local, nationalist, inward perspective that refused to make commitments abroad (or at home) that might impinge on a tradition of freedom of action, firmly entrenched within an isolationist framework. Well into the 1930s there was little sense that such perspectives and actions would in any way serve to precipitate another world war.

Late in his career, Borah famously remarked that not much had changed since the days of Washington, Jefferson, and Monroe. What had changed, he said, was with its rise to global power and its ties to other nations, America had to be more circumspect when employing that power, using authority rather than aggression. Circumstances altered radically, but for Borah principles required only modest reorientation in light of Depression-era domestic and foreign policy considerations. Speaking to the Council on Foreign Relations in New York in January 1934, Borah said, "In matters of trade and commerce we have never been isolationist and never will be. In matters of finance, unfortunately, we have not been isolationist and never will be. When earthquake and famine, or whatever brings human suffering, visit any part of the human race, we have not been isolationists, and never will be." He continued, "But in all matters political, in all commitments of any nature or kind, which encroach in the slightest upon the free and unembarrassed action of our people, or which circumscribe their discretion and judgment, we have been free, we have been independent, we have been isolationist."[4] This was a quintessential expression of the circumspect foreign policy position and underlying economic and cultural internationalism (fused with a domestic orientation) that characterized modern isolationism near its apex in the 1930s. From 1929 through 1934, long-standing undercurrents of protectionist isolationism came to the surface in the form of increased tariffs and often-shortsighted, inward-focused economic policies. After 1934, with the Reciprocal Trade Agreements Act, tariff policy finally moderated. Thereafter the United States moved gradually back toward free trade.

While not all of these developments and related views conformed to the main strains of modern isolationism developed during the debates about empire, the arguments of most isolationists and anti-imperialists formed the basis from which Borah and the Irreconcilables later built their diplomatic policy visions. Paramount to the modern isolationist switchboard of beliefs were unilateralism, but of a cautious rather than an aggressive sort; the desire to minimize war while recognizing and protecting America's ability to take military action abroad when needed; classic hemispherism, which in only a few cases could be used to justify (and generally denied) interventions in Latin America throughout the 1920s and 1930s; and safeguarding, adhering to, and enhancing democratic ideals through cultural and commercial engagement abroad.

Some scholars have argued that Borah supported the outlawry of war program as a means of preventing a resurgence of support for U.S. membership in the World Court. Others have asserted that it was more likely a tactic to pry votes from a 1929 bill to add naval cruisers. The point here, however, is that in whatever sense this was a political maneuver—surely public acts by politicians always entail a political calculus—it was also a genuine effort to enact change. As historian Robert Johnson has shown, virtually the entire peace bloc in Congress and the vast majority of the American population (so far as it could be ascertained accurately) strongly supported the peace pact despite having significant concerns about its effectiveness. Johnson found that isolationist antiwar thought was part of a broader effort to find an "alternative to corporatism," noting that "the peace progressives who favored Kellogg-Briand argued that the treaty embraced anti-imperialism."[5]

Seen in this light, the outlawry of war movement echoed William James and the anti-imperial isolationist views of several decades earlier. So too did Borah's assessment in the late 1920s that the pact, at least, might help to reconcile and equalize the problem of strong versus weak states; and it might shelter dependent regions from colonial excesses and conflicts, reminiscent of anti-imperialist arguments about the need to not replace one form of colonialism with another.[6] Those favoring the pact emphasized a unilateral and generally neutral form of nationalism to complement this anti-imperialism, pushed for moral and economic suasion abroad and once again emphasizing the commercial and agricultural base, and disarmament at home. These positions led Borah and allied isolationists in the 1920s and throughout the 1930s to aim for protection of domestic agrarian interests, even burgeoning agro-business, by raising the tariff; like Lodge and many imperialists of the 1890s, they also firmly supported immigration restriction. And they were unsuccessful in their attempts at serious disarmament or limitations on the U.S. Navy and Army.[7]

By the 1930s Borah's fusion of freedom and autonomy into an internationally engaged, belligerent type of isolationism, alongside his quixotic program for progressive reform at home, had gained wide influence. With regard to how domestic priorities might be linked to the need for certain international agreements and engagements, though, Borah deemed it perfectly appropriate to have multi- and unilateral economic and trade bills so long as they were not permanent and protected the average American worker. He differed with some fellow isolationists on this count and in his assertive approach to neutral rights. A distinction must be made between more aggressive isolationists, such as Borah and Hamilton Fish Jr., who called for full neutral trading rights, and more cautious noninterventionist oriented isolationists such as Senators Gerald Nye and Arthur Vandenberg, who were even willing to forgo traditional neutral trading rights in global commerce to prevent war.

Given limited resources, "why quit our own to stand upon foreign ground?" Borah asked rhetorically, paraphrasing Washington.[8] His "stand at home" political perspective, more than any other, found support across a vast swath of American society. It was particularly popular in the 1920s and 1930s, when an inward focus seemed essential to many Americans to ensure progress or at least security coming out of the war and then in mitigating conditions during the Depression. Such arguments also resonated across political lines, even finding such strange alliances with—and receiving sympathetic hearings from—socialist internationalists such as Norman Thomas. Thomas followed in the footsteps of Eugene Debs, concurring with Borah that the wisest course for America in the late 1920s (and especially during the economic cataclysm of the 1930s) was to reform at home, seek peaceful international engagement, and stay out of foreign treaties, political machinations, and wars. So too did progressive friends and fellow Irreconcilables like Johnson and La Follette agree with Borah. Later conservative isolationists, most notably Vandenberg and Robert Taft, joined Borah, helping to make internationally engaged isolationist principles a starting point for how many Americans viewed the world. Along similar grounds in the 1930s Senator Gerald Nye from North Dakota supported Borah's position against the overreach of business interests.

A commission chaired by Nye met from 1934 to 1936. In a series of hearings and reports the committee popularized and added official support to an anti-corporate/anti–special commercial interest interpretation of war causation. They issued a scathing final report attacking American prowar business interests, such as J. P. Morgan and the Du Pont Company. Adding new layers to the old critique of special interests (such as pushing the common or working man and the nation into war against the national interests, an argument we find in James, Bourne, Debs, Borah, Addams, and Balch), the commission's investigations over two years resulted in finding that the finance sector, heavy industry, and "merchants of death" (military-supply industries) helped steer the nation to war and thereby made immense profits before and during World War I.[9] The Nye Commission's well-publicized 1936 report summarized this point succinctly: "The committee finds, under the head of the effect of armament, on peace, that some of the munitions companies have occasionally had opportunities to intensify the fears of people for their neighbors and have used them to their own profit."[10] Updating the Jamesian anti-"bigness," anti-imperialist critique, they branded Du Pont, Morgan, and scores of Anglo-American banking interests as the critical factors, led by their own profit motives, that had purposefully tipped the nation—poised precariously on the fence of neutrality, the report made clear—into the conflict. The Neutrality Acts of 1935, 1936, and 1937 helped to solidify a solution to this problem and established the sacrosanct qualities of an isolationist economic neutralism. The time had come, many such as Nye and Borah argued, for America to concentrate its focus within and stop worrying about world events. The first of these acts, the 1935 Neutrality Act, represented a hallmark rejection of traditional neutral free trade. It forbade arms shipments to all belligerents involved in any war.

This newly emergent interpretation of neutrality was significant because it employed an innovative stratagem: to block future paths to war along the lines of World War I, reversing even the traditional Washingtonian view on neutral rights, by embargoing all arms and war material trade with belligerents. It also declared that Americans who traveled on combatant nations' ships did so at their own peril. Building on this legislative reasoning, it became important not to insist on neutral rights, but to resist them, as had not been done in 1914–1917, so as to minimize the risks of war, to turn toward domestic economic relief and reform as primary goals, and in commerce, to emphasize noncombatant markets. Global events seemed to trouble Depression-era Americans less than one might predict given the world-changing events that were to come.

In fact, regarding the Spanish Civil War, which served as a test case for the stringent neutrality position, a major Gallup Poll in 1937 found that 66 percent of Americans "had no opinion on events in Spain."[11] Debates over whether to wrest even more control of war-making power from the president and Congress fed this antiwar, anti-elite, and isolationist sentiment. The popularity of these views led to a renewed effort for a constitutional amendment, as proposed by Louis Ludlow and only narrowly defeated, to make the declaration of war a referendum to be put to a public vote. Intellectuals, such as historians Charles Beard and Charles Tansill, lent scholarly prestige and historical heft to pro-neutrality isolationist positioning—as did Nye's anti-corporate, antiwar stance more generally—all of which buttressed Borah's arguments during the 1930s.[12]

These developments made the period of the mid-1930s the so-called heyday or high-water mark of American isolationist thought.[13] Yet it is important to recognize that at root the oscillations of the two decades before World War II hearkened back to the parameters established in the anti-imperialist debates of the 1890s. Because the reputation of American business interests reached its nadir under depression conditions, the debates of the period centered on how to restrain the globally interconnected nature of modern commercial forces to make Washington and Jefferson's "commerce and honest friendship with all nations" compatible with "entangling alliances with none," not by increasing U.S. diplomatic or military involvement abroad but in a Jamesian sense by matching ideas with the conducts that they dictated. That is, the goal of the 1930s' neutrality and related acts was premised on distrust and circumspection. Isolationists like Borah aimed to manage and inhibit "bigness" in political leagues as well as in economic combinations to enhance American democracy at home and not become embroiled in costly alliances or imbroglios abroad.

Still, recall that these ideas had far-reaching consequences in the actions of Borah's isolationist Republican bloc and their allies who worked hard in Congress to keep the United States out of direct involvement in the Spanish Civil War, in Asia, and in Europe. Many Americans struggled to keep the nation out of all foreign conflicts, at all costs, including not fighting for or aiding (or even sympathizing with) those at war with Germany, Italy, and Japan. Briefly in 1940 the most powerful and most extreme form of antiwar isolationism (another permutation of the old hypernationalist isolationism also evident in the late 1890s and during World War I) rallied Gerald Nye and Norman Thomas with Charles Lindbergh into a group that was chaired by General Robert Wood under the banner of "America First" (AFC).

This utmost isolationist camp included a diverse set of intellectuals and such public figures such as Lindbergh, Walt Disney, Sinclair Lewis, E. E. Cummings, and Alice Roosevelt Longworth. One of the largest antiwar organizations ever formed in the United States, the AFC argued that America should remain entirely neutral in "words" as well as "deeds"; that aid to allies "short of war" only weakened America (Roosevelt's terms); and that no foreign nation would attack America if the nation pursued a robust preparedness plan of coastal defenses and air power. They made a powerful appeal to an insularly nationalistic type of exceptionalism and xenophobia. Many of these leading isolationists, usually conservative white Republicans, favored conscription only for "hemispheric" defense, though others preferred naval building as a policy prescription for preparedness, and most looked to air power as the best and most cost-effective direction for national defense, while opposing the building of a large standing army, even in light of the raging war. They cast the twin menaces of American globalism and interventionism as far worse than that posed by Nazism in Germany, fascism in Italy, or militarism in Japan. Large numbers of other American politicians and internationalist leaders, from President Franklin Delano Roosevelt to Emily Balch, disagreed. They fought tooth and nail against the hypernationalistic isolationist tide represented by the AFC.[14]

Polls as late as November 1941 indicated that most Americans did not support a declaration of war. The 1941 Atlantic Charter, which extended and formalized an Anglo-American set of "war and peace aims" in opposition to Nazism, well before the United States was officially in the war, represented an effort by Roosevelt, British Prime Minister Winston Churchill, and their foreign policy advisers to reject AFC-type isolation and to globalize for the postwar world an international corollary to the domestic New Deal. Buttressed by Roosevelt's powerful articulation of "Four Freedoms" and informed by the legacies of World War I, it was an effort, as one scholar put it, to "redefine human rights" as essential to America's vision of a "New Deal for the World."[15] Roosevelt slowly maneuvered the nation into tacit alliance with England by 1941 but it was not until the Japanese attack at Pearl Harbor that opposition to formally entering the war ended and the AFC was discredited. The obstinate and xenophobic isolationism espoused by the AFC, most memorably embodied in Lindbergh's anti-Semitism, laced with potent critiques of interventionism and unrestrained globalism, irrevocably tarnished the viability of a coherent isolationist politics and with it the term "isolationism." Balch's humanitarian internationalism naturally led her to support Roosevelt's Four Freedoms as a global policy. She eventually relinquished her heartfelt commitment to pacifism in the face of Axis atrocities and publicly came out in support of American entry into World War II to "save humanity," she said. For her willingness to engage with other countries in the search for peace, and for her efforts to stave off two world wars, she was accorded the signal honor of a Nobel Peace Prize.[16]

Isolation in the Wake of World War II

As a result of World War II, the United States embarked on a series of global initiatives that deeply influenced how Americans viewed their nation's international role and how global commitments relate to politics and society at home. Isolation as a national value remained a subject of debate but took on increasingly negative characteristics. It appeared severely outdated.

In many ways the attack on the "homeland" of Pearl Harbor sounded the death knell of isolationism for a globalized world. Yet it did not end the arguments for limited, temporary, and less entangled engagement abroad. The steps taken in these years would have been unthinkable a mere ten, much less fifty, years before. Rather than repeat the refusal to join the League of Nations, the United States helped to create the United Nations; its headquarters was located on American soil, at the hub of U.S. international commerce in New York City. Rather than insist on harsh postwar punishments, the United States asserted that the path to a permanent peace demanded U.S.-orchestrated economic integration, highlighted by reconstruction efforts such the Marshall Plan. Instead of eschewing permanent commitments, the United States established the first major peacetime alliance in its history, the North Atlantic Treaty Organization (NATO). At home, the army demobilized in part but never in full. The vaunted American military-industrial complex was born, and the varied educational, social, and political programs of the Cold War reshaped American society in terms of gender norms, family structures, and higher education, among a host of other important influences.[17]

Even as the postwar Republican Party of Dewey and Eisenhower embraced a new Cold War model of muscular internationalism, a few staunch isolationists remained and opposed most such moves. One of the most notable and powerful was the son of President William Howard Taft,

Senator Robert Taft from Ohio. He argued from 1948 through early 1953 (when he died) against joining NATO, and generally opposed the war in Korea. He accepted a policy of tacit support for European allies if attacked by Russia, rather than agreeing to a binding mutual defense alliance system. His view represented the modern isolationist formulation of weighing limited options always in favor of national autonomy, opposing long-term entanglements, and seeking heightened commercial interchange, a model seen fifty years before in the debates over empire. Taft, however, added a new level of defensive preparedness when he asserted, "In any war the result will not come from the battle put up by the western European countries. The outcome will finally depend on the armed forces of America. Let us keep our forces strong. Let us use the money we have for armament in building up the American Army, the American Air Forces, and the American Navy."[18]

While much changed about the viability of isolation in a bipolar Cold War world, the ideas did not dissipate. As U.S. commitments abroad transformed, in and out of hot and proxy wars, and through an array of overlapping treaties and alliance structures, American critics again returned to arguments for reducing international engagements. They noted the limits of U.S. power and the need for greater concentration of resources on domestic social, economic, and political, as well as civil rights reforms at home. Some among these critics—ranging from Walter Lippmann and George Kennan to George McGovern and even Martin Luther King Jr.—were labeled "neo-isolationist" at the time. Such a label is misleading, however, and virtually all resisted the term; indeed, many such critics had been "Europe-firsters" (those who favored a Europe-and-Germany first grand strategy during World War II). This meant that going forward as a whole they held little regard for the UN (though King and many in the civil rights movement had more optimism about the UN) and favored increased U.S. activities abroad, direct negotiations with the USSR, and retrenchment from costly foreign wars.[19]

In the early years of the Cold War the rise of a "new isolationism" was of pivotal concern to politicians, internationalists, and public intellectuals. Adlai Stevenson and Arthur Schlesinger Jr. wrote in the late 1940s and early 1950s about the challenge presented by a new isolationism. Singling out Robert Taft, who consistently opposed NATO and similarly binding or interventionist foreign policies, and worrying about his possible nomination for the presidency, Schlesinger warned of a "sinister pattern" in deeds rather than words related to the new isolationism. Schlesinger, in a fascinating turn of logic, claimed that McCarthyism served as an integral component and example of the inward-looking, reactionary nature of postwar isolationist thought. He hoped to dispense with dangerous internal ideological policing and repressive witch hunts as well as their external manifestations in the form of international "appeasement" efforts inspired by neo-isolationist values.[20]

Adlai Stevenson, in contrast, was more measured in his assessment. Still, he similarly worried that the nation needed to take up the mantle of world leadership more fully. His main fear was not repression at home or appeasement abroad, but what they were symptoms of: a gradual drawing away from globalism. Domestic prosperity and economic concerns, he observed, were beginning to assume overweening importance in American politics and leading toward geopolitical complacency. As he succinctly put his thesis, "There is no resurgence of blind, classical isolation in the Middle West, but there is a rapidly growing tax consciousness, and sooner or later we will have to face some stern issues. Can we, will we, pay the price of peace? Will we weary of the long ordeal? Will the disappointments, failures and frustrations light the fires of reaction?" As Stevenson concluded his answer to these questions he invoked those symbols that we began the book contemplating. "The eagle," he declared, "not the ostrich, is our national emblem."[21]

The heart of modern isolationism, a hybrid of international realities and isolationist traditions, clearly continued to throb long after its corpus had been declared dead following Pearl Harbor.[22] In 1952 Walter Lippmann wrote, "The traditional and fundamental themes of American foreign policy are now known as isolationism. . . . That is a term, however, which must be handled with the greatest care, or it can do nothing but confuse and mislead."[23] One aim of this study has been to treat "isolationism" and its attendant cluster of related ideas with just the sort of careful consideration for which Lippmann called. What may be most significant as we pause to reflect here in conclusion, tracing this history and themes through to the present, however, is that the very persistence of isolationist values may be evidence of another deep-rooted desire: the inclination to curb American democracy's aggressive and destructive impulses on the world stage.

Since the 1880s and 1890s initiated an era of increasing U.S. capacity to act internationally, leaders and citizens have advanced compelling economic, moral, racial, cultural, and strategic reasons to expand and intervene abroad. Yet these arguments repeatedly have generated countervailing forces, which in turn have been bolstered by a shifting constellation of isolationist positions. America, as Lippmann once observed, is rife with "contrary pushes which is to be too pacifist in time of peace and too bellicose in time of war. In this deadly cycle of pacifism and bellicosity we, and perhaps the other democracies as well, have wanted disarmament, neutrality, isolation, and if necessary appeasement."[24] In this reciprocal relationship the modern (often idealistic) form of isolationism developed and became essential as a counterbalance to urges for war and intervention.

By the late 1960s and through the 1970s this push and pull appeared again with renewed vigor. New warnings of yet another "new isolationism" dominated the headlines amid American involvement in Vietnam. But most potent were the calls for a "touch of new isolationism" in light of the perceived failings of a robustly interventionist worldview. Indeed, it seemed that the more the United States struggled in achieving the goals of intervention abroad, the greater the appeal of a return to—or updated invocation of—isolationist values. Isolation as a core value came roaring back, to be reoriented again and applied in limited form. As historian Robert Tucker put it in a 1972 essay, a more circumspect new isolationist outlook possessed significant advantages as well as a few considerable drawbacks. "The price of a new isolationism is that America would have to abandon its aspirations to an order that has become synonymous with the nation's vision of its role in history."[25] He called for a "touch" of isolationism. Still, while American withdrawal from Vietnam and a less directly interventionist path in fighting proxy wars abroad attenuated the intensity of debates over isolationism, many politicians and thinkers were unconvinced. American leaders of both parties continued to issue dire warnings of a retreat into isolation. Others, generally Left intellectuals, such as Noam Chomsky and Dwight MacDonald, however, looked to the example of Vietnam as they contemplated American global overreach and the merits or benefits of isolation as a means of achieving a more just domestic and international order.[26]

After the fall of the Berlin Wall and the demise of a significant Soviet threat in 1989–1990, the relative quiescence of geopolitics in the 1990s led to new calls for American global policing and countervailing cries for more caution and a more inward focus in the new world alignment. Almost forty years after warning of the rise of a "new isolationism," Arthur

Schlesinger Jr. again revivified his case. He argued that the new Republican Congress of the mid-1990s constituted an isolationism "risen yet again from the grave," taking on "the new form of unilateralism" to threaten "Wilson and F.D.R.[']s" "magnificent dream" of "multilateral diplomacy" and "collective security."[27] Or, as the *New York Times* assessed the situation in a 1999 editorial, "Isolationism—the notion that American interests arc best served by minimal involvement in foreign affairs and alliances—has been a recurrent issue in American political debate." In light of the 2000 presidential election and pulls of protectionist and nativist arguments for a new isolation (à la Pat Buchanan) as well as the impulse for a "smug and short-sighted isolationism" (à la Trent Lott and Dick Armey), the central problem appeared to be generational, according to the *Times*. "An entire generation, the one just below George W. Bush's, is growing up with no connection to World War II and only the dimmest memories of the cold war." Bill Clinton, Al Gore, and George W. Bush found this to be a rare point of agreement. Each derided what he saw as a generational inclination for the United States to be less active in a post–Cold War international system. Each in his own way argued for new avenues for American global commitment. Accordingly, the stakes seemed enormous. As the *Times* perceived it, the challenge for "internationalists in both parties will be to make the case for an expansive world view that defines broader diplomatic engagement and leadership by the United States as necessary components of national security and global stability."[28]

A decade later, the debates sound remarkably familiar. Isolationist ideas remain ever-present, off stage and often maligned. Yet isolationist-informed perspectives about limited engagement abroad in military and binding diplomatic forms, and in advancing national interest as a paramount domestic as well as foreign concern continue to have much to recommend them.[29] In the wake of the events of September 11, 2001, and in light of ongoing U.S. military involvement in numerous locations around the world, these sorts of views continue to operate as reflexive tests applied by Americans on both the Right and Left as they struggle to assess the nation's global relationships.

The debates during the period covered in this book represent the critical moment when Americans first fully confronted the nation's ability to create major international change by participating as a global power. Until the 1880s and 1890s this debate had been more or less academic. After that period disputes over the meaning and types of global engagement (and the potential positive and negative forms of isolation) developed to become intrinsic to broader conversations about what constitutes a "good society" and how such a society should operate at home, as well as abroad. This thinking still seems to structure our view of the nation's proper role in the world. For example, these ideas play a part in a domestic-foreign policy feedback loop of sorts, helping to evaluate and balance local, domestic concerns and global, international ones, such as in how we frame the issue at stake when someone asks whether or not the costs of the continuing operations in Afghanistan and Iraq are worth the relative lack of resources being devoted to such domestic concerns as economic growth, universal health care, or even tax cuts.

The international challenges that confront the United States today continue to make this topic timely. When President George W. Bush mentioned "isolationism" repeatedly in his 2006 State of the Union address, he was revisiting a century-old debate and recasting it given twenty-first-century concerns. Bush deployed the potent caricature of the scared, naive isolationist as his foil; he is just one of many politicians who have derided isolationism while paradoxically revivifying it as an option. A survey of newspapers, editorial pages, public policy journals, and cable news reveals a host of political commentators who, particularly in recent years (after the terrorist attacks on September 11, 2001, and in response to the interventions in Afghanistan and Iraq), hearkened back to the Washington-Jefferson-Monroe isolationist tradition and its unilateralist "go it alone" ideology.

In keeping with President Bush, recent thinkers and politicians again disparaged versions of a less or noninterventionist tradition, calling it obsolete, while employing variations on the nationalist "freedom to take action" arguments once deployed by both Henry Cabot Lodge and William Borah. Contemporary figures echo the old critiques. They tend to portray "isolationism" as atavistic, or something relegated to nonrealists with a "cut and run" mentality. Yet as they make that case, like their predecessors, these critics also tend to neglect attendant realities of today's "flattened" global world, a concept that would not have been lost on the peripatetic missionary John Mott, the transnationalist Randolph Bourne, or international pacifist organizers Jane Addams and Emily Balch.

In contrast, the isolationist tradition's inherent caution serves as a bulwark against hasty interventions and their likely unintended consequences. Some among the critics of the National Security Strategy's (2002) doctrine of

preemption, for example, took positions akin to the cultural internationalism and efforts for seeking domestic as well as global tolerance and peace
through pluralism as they developed from 1890 through the 1930s. Here
we are reminded of the thought and actions of Randolph Bourne, Emily
Balch and Jane Addams, Eugene Debs, and even William Borah.

And the beat goes on. In mid-summer 2007 the *Economist* examined
how some of these past precedents are reflected in the present and warned
that a U.S. isolationist turn was possible. The magazine argued that political debates over partial national isolation would be a pivot on which not
just the 2008 election might turn, but also on which internationalism itself revolves. "America is indispensable" for world betterment, stated the
Economist lead editorial. Yet it noted that "isolationism is also on the rise
[in the United States]" and wondered whether new alternatives or models
for engagement were even possible given America's recent geopolitical
setbacks and "new, rising sense [of isolationist retrenchment]."[30] Over the
past few years conservative politicians and pundits exclaimed that President Barack Obama's policies represent "neo-isolationism" or, as one author put it, his foreign policy marks a "throwback" to a "brand of isolationism that Americans haven't heard from a major presidential contender in
nearly a century."[31] In a *New York Review of Books* piece, Garry Wills
portrayed the recent developments in another light. He cited the aggregation of powers in the executive, particularly as related to the immense role
of the president in setting the contours of foreign affairs in wartime. Yet
Wills argued that President Obama's domestic and foreign policy challenges were shaped by the globalist problems of America's "National Security State." The United States, he maintained, is now an "entangled giant." The nation finds itself unable to retrench from global commitments
and its policies are functionally "self-entangling" in many ways. Nevertheless, Wills argued that the current situation requires a thorough rethinking and a less hubristic perspective on America's international role.[32]

The entanglements of the twenty-first century need not be intractable.
But the basis of any reliable change in course seems hard to fathom for
many Americans. Citizens clearly see pressing domestic economic challenges and are wary of a continued, muscular foreign policy. Citing recent
polls, one scholar opined that Americans seem to be moving in a direction best characterized as "neo-isolationism."[33] A Pew poll released in
December 2009—when President Obama was poised to add more troops

to the conflict in Afghanistan and sought commitments to a vigorous set of global environmental and other initiatives—reinforced this observation. The poll revealed the American public's isolationist and unilateralist sentiment at its highest level in forty years. Indeed, fully 49 percent of respondents stated that the United States ought to "mind its own business internationally" and leave other countries to their own devices. Closely related, 44 percent stated that because the United States "is the most powerful nation in the world, we should go our own way in international matters, not worrying about whether other countries agree with us or not." According to Pew, that expression of a unilateralist vision was the highest percentage since the question was first asked by Gallup in 1964.[34]

So what are the consequences of these current trends? Explicitly "isolationist" arguments are unlikely to become dominant. But it would be foolish to claim the early death of isolationist ideas. The historical record provides resilient intimations that core isolationist precepts—about limiting America's relationship to the world, about employing a cautiously realist approach to evaluating interventions abroad, and about balancing foreign and domestic policies—will be influential. Debating the degree and type of diplomatic, military, commercial, and cultural engagement will go on and on. Was or is America an "empire" of sorts? Are interventionist models for operating in the world essential for security? Such vital themes, timeless questions as circumstances unfold, criss-cross today's discussions about the U.S. role in the Middle East and in the "global war on terrorism."

The isolationist and internationalist views explored in this book traveled sinuous and at times subterranean routes to the present. Yet, in current considerations of America's role in the world, nationalist hawks as well as internationalist doves employ symbols, images, and tropes that would be familiar to those thinkers, politicians, and activists who considered the local as well as the global roles of the United States from the 1890s through the 1930s. Americans continue to invoke these scripts, and adapt them, in ways remarkably consistent with thinkers a century ago.

Before the United States embarked on the "American Century," passionate arguments raged over whether America's priorities should lie in domestic or in foreign fields. Largely forgotten by historians, political leaders, and citizens, the birth of turn-of-the-twentieth-century isolationism represented a critical development in American thought. Isolationist arguments inflected the language of many American politicians, thinkers, and activists. Their visions often inherently linked perspectives on foreign affairs with views of what could be done at home in terms of the trade-offs among resources dedicated to diverse objectives, short-term and long-term. It is very much the same today.

The old shift from debating empire to debating isolation was concerned with competing visions of the kernel of internationalism, embedded in innovative views about domestic reform. At stake throughout were essential definitions of the meaning of America and the stakes in the nation's global choices—both the promise and the peril.

STRAINS OF ISOLATIONISM

The following section elaborates on and seeks to define the major strains of isolationism as they developed historically in the American context. From the 1880s through the entry of the United States into World War I, growing globalization, interdependence, and an array of international economic factors divided isolationist thought into what can be best understood as two distinct strains and roughly eight points of emphasis. These strains and points of emphasis set the broad parameters for the isolationist positions and perspectives that then developed over the rest of the twentieth century.

The first strain, *political isolationism*, was often aligned with liberal market-oriented economic views. This concept stemmed from classical liberalism; it tended to consider free economic exchanges as independent of politics, arguing that economic ties, because they do not inherently seem to entail political entanglements or appear to erode American autonomy, are permissible, and are even essential to national progress. Indeed, one group of political isolationists, today commonly referred to as libertarians, aggressively advocated free trade. But a position of neutral free trade in an increasingly globalized economy has been and continues to be problematic. Shipping and trade make nations interconnected in profound ways that can be severely tested in times of war or crisis. The intrinsic politics of commerce and the related fractures to the possibility of neutral trade were amply demonstrated during the Spanish-American War, during World War I, and at various moments during the 1920s and 1930s.

The second strain has been equally long-standing. Critics of foreign economic ties, especially those involving processes and policies of globalization, have tended to cast this as an erosion of autonomy and self-sufficiency, which leads them to *protectionist isolationism*. While this viewpoint has been relatively muted in comparison to the "political" variety, the camp supporting it has been most heavily criticized because its intensely inward focus appears naive amid expanding and lucrative international commerce. One of the major focuses of protectionist arguments, isolationist and otherwise, has been the effort to secure higher import tariffs to protect American domestic production (in agricultural as well as heavy and light industry).

Within each of these two broad types of isolationist thought are at least eight distinct points of emphasis. Sometimes overlapping, these have been the main variations on isolationist arguments. Historically these variations are critical because they have appeared in cases for progressive and racial reform as well as for domestically organized missionary efforts abroad, not just in more narrowly defined diplomatic terms or specific foreign policy proposals.

All isolationist points of emphasis share one essential tenet. Located in interpretations of the injunctions laid out by Washington and Jefferson is a foundational aim to avoid "entangling alliances" and to pursue diplomatic and military *nonentanglement*. Why seek nonentanglement? For almost everyone espousing even mildly isolationist ideas—from Henry Cabot Lodge to Emily Balch—the purpose was to vouchsafe the nation from being drawn into other nations' wars.

Neutrality, a second major point of isolationist emphasis, continues to be critical to isolationist arguments through the present day. This isolationist position has much in common with other arguments opposing war. The cause of neutrality, combined with a broad application of nonentanglement and noninterventionist thought, often has been the central isolationist component of American pacifism. In many cases what differentiated such a position from being pacifist internationalism was the mixing of neutrality and nonentanglement as essential to America's "traditional" isolationist role in the world as a national value that permitted nationalism and war but prohibited binding international organizations or collective action to ensure peace.

Third, with respect to the practice of foreign policy, two isolationist possibilities emerged during the late nineteenth century. One would permit nonbinding international dialogues; the other would favor acting alone. In either case, such views of global diplomacy were essentially *unilateralist*. To preserve national autonomy, proponents of isolation, such as Senators William Borah and Robert Taft, with a few major exceptions, have proposed the unilateralist "going it alone" option. While the degree, type, and aggressiveness of unilateralism have often been fiercely debated, the unilateral impulse has undergirded much of modern isolationist thought since the 1890s. This form of isolationist politics, giving freedom to act alone, could and frequently did embrace unilateral military action. Thus, the interrelated elements of unilateralism and nonentanglement, emphasizing national autonomy as they do, have been two of the most prominent and widely shared isolationist points of emphasis.

Fourth, and related to unilateralism, is an objective most Americans would probably agree to in some form: a belief in maximizing *self-sufficiency*. The goal here was, and continues to be, to make the nation strong enough to protect core values (variously defined) and not be overly reliant on (or beholden to) other nations. Still, most Americans, as immigrants and descendants thereof, have tended to see some merits in eternal exchange and interdependence, generally avoiding the extreme of autarky.

Fifth, since the founding of the nation—and certainly after the Monroe Doctrine was issued in 1823—a central component of arguments about isolation was to keep foreign powers from gaining a foothold close to America. This is best understood as *hemispherism* or *continentalism* (the term historian and isolationist Charles Beard preferred). It occasionally has been defined as part of a wider effort to advance various forms of U.S. *hegemony*, with a strong focus on expansion and development within North America and the Caribbean (and appropriate distancing from Europe and Asia). In this way an isolationist seeking hemispheric or continentalist outcomes could support unilateral military action and preparedness.

The best examples of this continentalist idea appear in new expansionist-imperialist arguments at the dawn of twentieth century. Before that time, during the nineteenth century, most contemporary Americans saw U.S. westward expansion and continental territorial extension as goals or natural processes compatible with the Washingtonian-Jeffersonian isolationist injunction against entering into global (European) power politics. Thus, these expansions never cohered perfectly into any comprehensive view of "isolation" contrasted with "international engagement." By the early twentieth century, however, many unilateralists prized nationalistic priorities; some saw empire as in keeping with such an aim, while others could accept (or even desired) limits on expansion beyond the contiguous lands of North America or beyond the hemisphere.

Sixth, most isolationists asserted that although the nation must collaborate periodically with other countries, those instances of treaties, alliances, or other forms of collective action should be held to be *temporary*. Such a view of the temporary, nonbinding form of treaties and alliances was essential to ground opposition to binding and permanent internationalist initiatives—in the abstract, but also in specific cases such as the League of Nations, the World Court, and, later, the North Atlantic Treaty Organization (NATO).

Seventh, notions of nonentanglement and its corollary ideas were and are not ends in themselves. They represent means to a specific end. Many isolationist arguments proposed either an abstract (occasionally even a concrete) protective shell around American society so that the country could fulfill an inherently *exceptionalist* and *domestic* mission. According to this camp, to fulfill the goals of creating a "city on the hill" and the Republic's democratic mission, the Constitution provided a clear basis and prescription for domestic exceptionalism: to "establish justice, insure domestic tranquility, . . . promote the general welfare, and secure the blessings of liberty." This form of isolationist argument and the application of constitutional rights language overlapped with other compatible points of emphasis; it became popular among the anti-imperialists of the late nineteenth century and later antiwar progressive reformers because it relied on a shared republican mission that did not call for either committing troops or material abroad, or relate to pursuing an active foreign policy of territorial expansion. Rather, exceptionalist and domestic mission-oriented isolationist claims of the nation as "exemplar" can be easily distinguished from manifest destiny–type arguments for the nation as crusader state because they aimed to achieve national strength via adherence to—and enhancement of—core principles by focusing inward on (a dizzying array of) domestic goals to build a better American society. In turn, a more democratic, more prosperous, more moral nation, according to some following this line of thinking, would then be more likely to be a global force as an example to be emulated.

Finally, because wars and standing armies appear to endanger the Constitution's purposes, isolationists (at least rhetorically) have traditionally decried war. The kernel of emphasis for this camp was, quite simply, to *minimize war*. While not explicitly pacifistic, a politics premised on a positive view of isolation puts constraints on conflicts. In the era under study here, two wars—the Spanish-American War and World War I, along with the backlash against them—became the crucible for such arguments. An assertion that sometimes persuaded lukewarm isolationists was that wars ought to be entered into only as necessary to protect vital interests that were or soon could become threatened directly.

Another related argument many isolationist minimizers of war came to support was a national popular referendum to declare war, the most remarkable of which was a constitutional war referendum amendment proposed by Indiana Democratic Representative Louis Ludlow in the late 1930s. Other efforts at minimization often took the form of isolationist attacks on military and societal preparation for war; this spanned positions against the draft, against standing armies, against building larger, more modern navies, and reflexive opposition to any commitments that might require other preparations. In contrast, some isolationist-oriented thinkers, politicians, and activists vigorously supported building up the navy, and especially the air force, in order to create a "fortress America," a view that condemned interventions abroad but could be formulated in remarkably belligerent terms.

Aiming to minimize conflicts, however, leads to a strand of isolationist thought that remains to be examined further: its relationship to pacifism. The term "pacifist" has often been used to deride isolationist positions. Yet virtually none of those who espoused ideas of isolation were strict pacifists. A surprisingly large number of isolationist-oriented thinkers and politicians were quite confrontational and, in fact, considered themselves to be nationalist hawks. The evidence undercuts any facile analysis or simple dichotomization about isolation.

A distinction also must be drawn between two main types of pacifism: absolute and conditional. Political scientists rightly point out that each has much in common with ideas about isolation. Absolute pacifism dictates that no war between states or peoples is justifiable, even in cases of self-defense. However, many "absolute" pacifists and "absolute" isolationists moderated their views at some point. Even Emily Balch endorsed entering World War II because of the terrible global threat posed by Hitler and the Axis powers.

Conditional pacifists have been more common. In general, they are willing to endorse defensive but not offensive wars. Virtually everyone in this study takes such a view, at least at times. But herein lies the rub: when is a war "defensive"? It is a matter of interpretation. Recall the first principle of isolationist thought—nonentanglement expressed as noninterventionism.

In seeking "not to intervene or become entangled" particularly during instances of major conflicts and world-changing events, often significant numbers of conditional (and absolute) pacifists have tended to become more explicitly isolationist.

Finally, a wide array of models for *collective security* have been central to debates over the merits of an isolationist stance. The world wars and attacks on the American homeland were the watersheds for reorienting even the most staunch isolationist opposition to international collective security association and action. On this point we must revisit the comment of leading 1930s isolationist Michigan Senator Arthur Vandenberg, who wrote in his diary in December 1941, "My convictions regarding international cooperation and collective security for peace took firm form on the afternoon of the Pearl Harbor attack. That day ended isolationism for any realist."[1] Still, the remaining isolationists in the late 1940s and 1950s, such as Ohio Senator Robert Taft, continued to debate collective security organizations—usually opposing U.S. membership in NATO— and came to reject American leadership in the UN.

Out of these tangled elements emerged an identifiable characterization of an isolationist viewpoint as it became "modern" after the turn of the twentieth century. More of a constellation of ideas rather than a single principle or policy position, paradoxically *isolationism did not entail cultural, economic, or complete political separation from the rest of the world.* Yet such a separation from the world is the first reaction that comes to mind when we discuss those who favored isolationism as a foreign policy in American political and intellectual traditions. It also is the first conception that certainly must be dismissed. The inner logic of isolationist arguments frequently turned, in fact and in debate, on the inner life of the nation and tended to reinforce many carefully delineated limited forms of international engagement.

NOTES

Introduction

1. George W. Bush, January 31, 2006, "State of the Union Address of the President of the United States." See http://georgewbush-whitehouse.archives.gov/news/releases/2006/01/20060131-10.html (accessed September 1, 2010).
2. Political cartoons have portrayed this oppositional framework in terms of an ostrich and an eagle since the 1930s. Franklin Roosevelt talked about the need to escape the "illusion of isolationism" and rejected those who wanted the "American eagle to imitate the tactics of the ostrich." (Fireside chat 20, February 23, 1942; for full text, see www.mhric.org/fdr/chat20.html [accessed January 25, 2010].) Perhaps the most vivid such depiction accompanied Adlai Stevenson's "The Challenge of a New Isolationism," *New York Times*, November 6, 1949, SM9.
3. Grover Cleveland, March 4, 1885, in *A Compilation of the Messages and Papers of the Presidents, 1789–1902*, ed. James D. Richardson (Washington, DC: Published by authority of the Bureau of National Literature and Art, 1903), vol. 8, 301.
4. George Washington, *Farewell Address* (1796; New York: Bedford, 2002), 29–30.
5. Ibid., 30.
6. On Jefferson, see Peter Onuf, "Thomas Jefferson, Federalist," in *Essays in History* (Charlottesville, VA: Corcoran Department of History, 1993), vol. 35. On Bush's 2006 State of the Union address, see Andrew Bacevich, "What Isolationism?" *Los Angeles Times*, February 2, 2006.
7. Jefferson did not scorn all interventions abroad; he built up the American navy and battled the Barbary Coast pirates. It is significant that he saw this as a defense of American freedom of the seas and a national sovereignty issue. On this section I am thankful to conversations with Peter Onuf. On Jefferson's limited foreign policy perspective but expansive "continental" understanding of expansion and America's "republican empire," see Onuf, *Jefferson's Empire: The Language of American Nationhood* (Charlottesville: University of Virginia Press, 2000). See also Jefferson, *Writings: Autobiography / Notes on the State of Virginia / Public and Private Papers/Addresses / Letters* (New York: Library of

America, 1984). On Franklin, Benjamin Franklin to Lord Kames, January 3, 1760, in *The Papers of Benjamin Franklin*, ed. Leonard W. Labaree (New Haven, CT: Yale University Press, 1966), vol. 9, 7. On British debates about expansion and America's so-called empire, see Felix Gilbert, *To the Farewell Address: Ideas of Early American Foreign Policy* (Princeton, NJ: Princeton University Press, 1961), 33–35. Gerald Stourzh, *Benjamin Franklin and American Foreign Policy*, 2nd ed. (Chicago: University of Chicago Press, 1969), Franklin quote on 120.

8. James Monroe, "Monroe Doctrine," Annual Address to Congress on December 2, 1823. On the Monroe Doctrine's ideological development in later narratives of American empire, see Gretchen Murphy, *Hemispheric Imaginings: The Monroe Doctrine and Narratives of U.S. Empire* (Durham, NC, and London: Duke University Press, 2005).

9. Walter McDougall argues that this tradition is best understood as "unilateralism, or isolationism (so called)," in *Promised Land, Crusader State: The American Encounter with the World since 1776* (Boston: Houghton Mifflin Co., 1997); see 39–56. There is much to recommend such an interpretation; however, unilateralism does not fully account for the wide variety of isolationist perspectives that developed in the 1890s and deepened through the 1930s; nor does unilateralism have the literal historical roots in the American intellectual and political tradition that isolationism possesses to help account for historicist invocations of isolationist precedent or to explain the repeated use and contestation of the words and meanings of "isolation," "isolationist," and "isolationism." Nevertheless, McDougall is right to emphasize unilateralism as essential to these formative cautiously realist arguments.

10. Most histories of isolationism in America have examined isolationism as a political or diplomatic phenomenon and have centered on either the World War I era or the 1930s and the neutrality debates. The most notable examples of the former period include Ernest May's *The World War and American Isolation, 1914–1917* (Chicago: Quadrangle Books, 1966) and John Milton Cooper Jr.'s *The Vanity of Power: American Isolationism and the First World War, 1914–1917* (Westport, CT: Greenwood Press, 1969). See also Walter Millis, *Road to War: America, 1914–1917* (Boston: Houghton Mifflin Co., 1947), and Charles Seymour, *American Neutrality, 1914–1917* (Hamden, CT: Archon Books, 1967). For the later period see Selig Adler, *The Isolationist Impulse: Its Twentieth Century Reaction* (London: Abelard-Schuman Limited, 1957), Wayne S. Cole, *Roosevelt and the Isolationists, 1932–1945* (London: University of Nebraska Press, 1983), Manfred Jonas, *Isolationism in America, 1935–1941* (Ithaca, NY: Cornell University Press, 1966), William Langer and S. Everett Gleason, *The Challenge to Isolation, 1937–1940* (New York: Harper and Brothers, 1952), Walter Johnson, *The Battle against Isolation* (Chicago:

University of Chicago Press, 1944), Justus Doenecke and John Wilz, *From Isolation to War, 1931–1941* (1968; Arlington Heights, IL: Harlan Davidson, 1991), Leroy Rieselbach, *The Roots of Isolationism* (Indianapolis: Bobbs-Merrill, 1966), and Walter LaFeber, *The American Age: U.S. Foreign Policy at Home and Abroad since 1750* (New York: W. W. Norton, 1989).

11. These developments at the intersection of ideas, social change, and practical politics are best understood as an interconnected modernist "matrix." In particular I am thinking of this in terms of Olivier Zunz's useful theoretical concept of an institutional matrix. See Zunz, *Why the American Century?* (Chicago: University of Chicago Press, 1998), and Sanford Schwartz on literary modernism and philosophy, *The Matrix of Modernism: Pound, Eliot, and Early Twentieth-Century Thought* (Princeton, NJ: Princeton University Press, 1985). On the intersection of these ideas and the cultural underpinnings of U.S. foreign policy in the nineteenth century, see Frank Ninkovich, *Global Dawn* (Cambridge, MA: Harvard University Press, 2009).

12. On these points I draw upon the superb scholarship that explains the major intellectual and political transformations (and transnational connections) in this era. See George Cotkin, *Reluctant Modernism: American Thought and Culture, 1880–1900* (New York: Twayne Publishers, 1992), Eldon Eisenach, *The Lost Promise of Progressivism* (Lawrence: University Press of Kansas, 1994), James Kloppenberg, *Uncertain Victory* (New York: Oxford University Press, 1986), Bruce Kuklick, *The Rise of American Philosophy* (New Haven, CT: Yale University Press, 1977), T. J. Jackson Lears, *No Place of Grace* (Chicago: Pantheon Books, 1981), and Lears, *Rebirth of a Nation: The Making of Modern America, 1877–1920* (New York: HarperCollins, 2009), Dan Rodgers, *Atlantic Crossings* (Cambridge, MA: Harvard University Press, 1998), Robert Wiebe, *The Segmented Society: An Introduction to the Meaning of America* (New York: Oxford University Press, 1976), and Wiebe, *The Search for Order, 1877–1920* (New York: Hill & Wang, 1967), and Olivier Zunz, *Making America Corporate, 1870–1920* (Chicago: University of Chicago Press, 1992). On modernist ideas see also Schwartz, *The Matrix of Modernism*, Malcolm Bradbury and James McFarlane, eds., *Modernism, 1890–1930* (New York: Penguin Books, 1976), Stephen Kern, *The Culture of Space and Time, 1880–1918* (Cambridge, MA: Harvard University Press, 1983), and Daniel J. Singal, ed., *Modernist Culture in America* (Belmont, CA: Wadsworth Publishing Co., 1991).

13. On the rhetoric of nationalist exceptionalism in debates over empire, see Paul Kramer, "Empires, Exceptions, and Anglo-Saxons: Race and Rule between the British and United States Empires, 1880–1910," *Journal of American History* 88 (March 2002): 1315–1353; on empire and culture see Amy Kaplan, *The Anarchy of Empire in the Making of U.S. Culture* (Cambridge, MA: Harvard University Press, 2002).

14. The word "isolation" appears in a political–foreign policy sense in a great deal of political writing and numerous speeches, public documents, and personal letters during America's early Republic Era; however, the first recorded appearance of the word "isolationist" came in 1862 during the Civil War. Prominent and repeated uses of the term occurred during the Spanish-American War in 1898–1899. But it was not until 1921–1922 that a conceptually thick ideological form of the word—"isolationism"—came into widespread and accepted use on both sides of the Atlantic to describe the so-called irreconcilable isolationism espoused by those who rejected American ratification of the Treaty of Versailles, entry into the League of Nations, and most binding alliances. As a relatively coherent political ideology, "isolationism" then found prominent use and meaning as characterizing a foreign policy premised on avoiding politico-military commitments and alliances with foreign nations (particularly in Europe) with a number of domestic policy corollaries during the 1930s.

    The 1901 OED edition characterized an isolationist as "one who favors or advocates isolation. In U.S. politics one who thinks the Republic ought to pursue a policy of political isolation." *Oxford English Dictionary* (Oxford: Oxford University Press, 1901 and 1922); see also Ronald Powaski, *Toward an Entangling Alliance* (New York: Greenwood Press, 1991), ix; for a more overtly conservative contemporary (quasi)isolationist political view of the term and its historical meaning, see Patrick Buchanan, *A Republic, Not an Empire* (Washington, DC: Regnery Press, 1999), esp. 161. For more on the term, its etymology, and a brief overview, see Manfred Jonas's outstanding entry on "isolationism" in *Encyclopedia of American Foreign Policy: Studies of the Principal Movements and Ideas*, ed. Alexander DeConde (New York: Charles Scribner and Sons, 1978), vol. 2, 496–506.

15. John Mott, "Sam P. Jones Lecture" subtitled "Dwight Moody, the Greatest Evangelist of the 19th Century," given at Emory University (Atlanta, 1944), John R. Mott Papers, Yale Divinity School; also Mott, *The Evangelization of the World in This Generation* (New York: Published by the Student Volunteer Movement for Foreign Missions, 1900).

16. Cooper, *The Vanity of Power*, 1.

17. Walter LaFeber, *The New Empire: An Interpretation of American Expansion, 1860–1898* (1963; Ithaca, NY: Cornell University Press, rept. 1998); William Appleman Williams, *The Roots of the Modern American Empire: A Study of the Growth and Shaping of Social Consciousness in a Marketplace Society* (New York: Random House, 1969), and *The Tragedy of American Diplomacy* (New York: Delta, 1962); see also Ernest May, *Imperial Democracy: The Emergence of America as a Great Power* (New York: Harcourt, Brace and World, 1961).

18. I developed these subtypes but I owe the greatest debt to John Milton Cooper Jr.'s insights in *The Vanity of Power* for helping to elucidate the key elements of these distinctions within isolationist thought.

1. New World Power

1. On foreign policy and the economic preconditions for "phases of empire," Joseph A. Frye, "Phases of Empire: Late Nineteenth Century U.S. Foreign Relations," in *The Gilded Age: Essays on the Origins of Modern America*, ed. Charles W. Calhoun (Wilmington, DE: Scholarly Resources Inc., 1996), 261–288. Here I draw statistics from Frye's chapter and David M. Pletcher, "Economic Growth and Diplomatic Adjustment," in *Economics and World Power: An Assessment of American Diplomacy since 1789*, ed. William H. Becker Jr. and Samuel F. Wells Jr. (New York: Columbia University Press, 1984), esp. 120; from *The History of the American Economy*, ed. Gary M. Walton and Hugh Rockoff, 9th ed. (Toronto: Thomson Learning, 2002); and from *Historical Statistics* (Washington, DC: Government Printing Office, 2008). On the corporate transformation of American society, see Olivier Zunz, *Making America Corporate, 1870–1920* (Chicago: University of Chicago Press, 1992), and Walter Licht, *Industrializing America: The Nineteenth Century* (Baltimore: Johns Hopkins University Press, 1995). For an economic perspective, Claudia Goldin and Hugh Rockoff, eds., *Strategic Factors in Nineteenth Century American Economic History: A Volume to Honor Robert W. Fogel* (Chicago: University of Chicago Press, 1992), and Michael Hudson, *Super Imperialism: The Economic Strategy of American Empire* (New York: Holt, Rhinehart, and Winston, 1972). On the economy in relation to changing political and social philosophy, see James Kloppenberg, *Uncertain Victory: Social Democracy and Progressivism in European and American Thought, 1870–1920* (New York: Oxford University Press, 1986); the work of Alfred Chandler Jr. and Louis Galambos, "The American Economy and the Reorganization of the Sources of Knowledge," in *The Organization of Knowledge in Modern America, 1860-1920*, ed. Alexandra Oleson and John Voss (Baltimore: Johns Hopkins University Press, 1979), 269–282.
2. Henry Cabot Lodge, *The Life of George Washington* (1889; Boston and New York: Houghton Mifflin Co., 1920), 131.
3. Lodge to John T. Morse Jr., May 6, 1889. Lodge Papers.
4. Lodge, *The Life of George Washington*, esp. 131.
5. Theodore Roosevelt, *The Strenuous Life: Essays and Addresses* (New York: Century Co., 1901), 1–9, 16–21.
6. On Hay's thought and the related events of the Open Door and Boxer Rebellion, see Tyler Dennett, *John Hay, From Poetry to Politics* (New York: Dodd, Mead & Co., 1933).

7. Regarding the cultural underpinnings of this internationalist discourse, see Frank Ninkovich, *Global Dawn: The Cultural Foundation of American Internationalism, 1865–1890* (Cambridge, MA: Harvard University Press, 2009). On the transatlantic and Anglo-American context, see Robert Kelley, *The Transatlantic Persuasion: The Liberal-Democratic Mind in the Age of Gladstone* (New York: Knopf, 1969); John G. Sproat, *"The Best Men," Liberal Reformers in the Gilded Age* (New York: Oxford University Press, 1968); Leslie Butler, *Critical Americans: Victorian Intellectuals and Transatlantic Liberal Reform* (Chapel Hill: University of North Carolina Press, 2007); Kloppenberg, *Uncertain Victory*; Daniel T. Rodgers, *Atlantic Crossings: Social Politics in a Progressive Age* (Cambridge, MA: Harvard University Press, 1998).

8. Donald Marquad Dozier, "Anti-Imperialism in the U.S: 1865–1895" (PhD diss., Harvard University, 1936), 76.

9. First Inaugural Address, March 4, 1885, President Grover Cleveland. Cited in Richardson, *A Compilation*, vol. 6, 366.

10. Cited in Edward J. Renehan Jr., *The Lion's Pride: Theodore Roosevelt and His Family in Peace and War* (New York: Oxford University Press, 1999), 89. Renehan argues that by mid-1895, and perhaps earlier, Roosevelt was convinced of Mahan's position.

11. See Mahan, quoted in Foster Rhea Dulles, *America's Rise to World Power, 1898–1954* (New York: Harper, 1954), 33. For more on Mahan's life and thought, see W. D. Puleston, *The Life and Work of Captain Alfred Thayer Mahan* (New Haven, CT: Yale University Press, 1939). Mahan published *The Influence of Sea Power upon History* while he was president of the U.S. Naval War College. Mahan enclosed a copy of *The Influence of Sea Power upon History, 1660–1763* for Lodge and wrote to him, stating his hope that the book might "make the experience of the past influence the opinions and shape the policy of the future." Mahan to Lodge, May 19, 1890, Lodge Papers.

12. Alfred Thayer Mahan, *The Interest of America in Sea Power* (New York: Little, Brown & Co., 1897). For more on this naval strategy as foreign policy and Mahan as a "geopolitician," see Jon Sumida, "Alfred Thayer Mahan, Geopolitician," *Journal of Strategic Studies* 22, no. 2 and 3 (June 1999): 39–62.

13. Henry Cabot Lodge, *Daniel Webster* (Boston: Houghton Mifflin Co., 1883), 170.

14. William Widenor, *Henry Cabot Lodge and the Search for an American Foreign Policy* (Berkeley: University of California Press, 1980), 58.

15. Cited in James Lorence's excellent study of the AAA, "Organized Business and the Myth of the China Market: The American Asiatic Association, 1898–1937," *Transactions of the American Philosophical Society* 71, part 4 (1981): 10.

16. Matthew Frye Jacobson, *Barbarian Virtues: The United States Encounters Peoples at Home and Abroad, 1876–1917* (New York: Hill & Wang, 2000),

"export markets," 15–58; for another view, William H. Becker, "American Manufacturers and Foreign Markets, 1870–1900: Business Historians and the 'New Economic Determinists,'" *Business History Review* 47, no. 4 (Winter 1973): 466–481.

17. Festus P. Summers, *William L. Wilson and Tariff Reform* (New Brunswick, NJ: Rutgers University Press, 1953); for detail on the 1894 tariff in relation to the coal lobby, see John Alexander Williams, "The Bituminous Coal Lobby and the Wilson-Gorman Tariff of 1894," *Maryland Historical Magazine* 68, no. 3 (Fall 1973): 273–287. The Wilson-Gorman Tariff added a 40 percent duty to imported sugar at the point of consumption, hurting the Cuban economy, which depended significantly on exporting sugar to the United States. Contemporary anti-tariff pamphlets of the period fought such policies by emphasizing labor and populist concerns, and women's issues; see "Why They Suffer, Working Women and Working Men's Wives, How the Tariff Affects Them, Testimony of Women as Witnesses: The Wilson-Gorman Act Responsible for Hard Times, Protection, Not Free Silver, the True Remedy: Labor's Protest" (Chicago, 1894), microfiche pamphlet collection, University of Virginia Alderman Library Special Collections.

18. Robert Beisner, *From the Old Diplomacy to the New, 1865–1900* (New York: Harlan Davidson, 1986).

19. See Henry Cabot Lodge and Theodore Roosevelt, *Hero Tales from American History* (1917; New York: Century Co., 1895).

20. Widenor's *Lodge* contains a superb account of this aspect of Lodge's foreign policy.

21. *New York Advertiser*, November 28, 1895, clipping in Lodge Scrapbooks, Lodge Papers.

22. Lodge, *Speeches and Addresses* (Boston: Houghton Mifflin Co., 1909), 285–287.

23. Lodge, *Studies in History* (1884; Freeport, RI: Books for Libraries Press, 1972), 113; Lodge, *A Short History of the English Colonies in America* (1881; Ithaca, NY: Cornell University Libraries, 2009), 159.

24. See Robert Utley and Wilcomb Washburn, *Indian Wars* (New York: Mariner Books, 1985); Bill Yenne, *Indian Wars: The Campaign for the American West* (New York: Westholme Publishing, 2006); on ideas about race, expansion, and Native Americans, see Brian W. Dippie, *The Vanishing American: White Attitudes and U.S. Indian Policy* (Lawrence: University Press of Kansas, 1991); for the period at and after the end of the "Indian wars," see Frederick Hoxie, *Final Promise: The Campaign to Assimilate the Indians, 1880–1920* (Lincoln: University of Nebraska Press, 2001). Thanks to Peter Conn for his insights into these shifting trends.

25. On this, first see Gerald T. White, *The United States and the Problem of Recovery after 1893* (Tuscaloosa: University of Alabama Press, 1982); see also

Douglas Steeples and David Whitten, *Democracy in Desperation: The Depression of 1893* (Westport, CT: Greenwood Press, 1998); for an overview see Richard Timberlake, "Panic of 1893," in *Business Cycles and Depressions: An Encyclopedia*, ed. David Glasner (New York: Garland Publishers, 1997), and Charles Hoffmann, "The Depression of the Nineties," *Journal of Economic History* 16 (June 1956): 137–164.

26. There is an excellent account of this incident in Daniel B. Schirmer, *Republic or Empire, American Resistance to the Philippine War* (Cambridge, MA: Schenkman Publishing Co., 1972), "The Venezuela Crisis," 33–44, and Howard Jones, *Crucible of Power: A History of American Foreign Relations, to 1913* (Wilmington, DE: Scholarly Resources, 2002), 234–240; another view appears in Robert Kagan, *Dangerous Nation: America's Place in the World from Its Earliest Days to the Dawn of the Twentieth Century* (New York: Knopf, 2006), esp. 368–374.

27. Lodge, November 26, 1895, Address to Massachusetts Republicans, as quoted in the *Boston Evening Transcript*, November 27, 1895.

28. For a broad perspective, see George Herring, *From Colony to Superpower, U.S. Foreign Relations since 1776* (New York: Oxford University Press, 2008), 299–336.

29. Theodore Roosevelt, *The Strenuous Life: Essays and Addresses* (New York: Century Co., 1900), from chapter 1, "The Strenuous Life." For more, see chapter 2, "Expansion and Peace." Roosevelt's famous "strenuous life" address was originally a speech given in Chicago to the Hamilton Club on April 10, 1899.

30. The Lodge and Hoar papers at the MHS reveal the complexity of their relationship. On Lodge and the "large policy" in the context of his battles with the senior senator from Massachusetts George Hoar, see Richard E. Welch Jr., "Opponents and Colleagues: George Frisbie Hoar and Henry Cabot Lodge, 1898–1904," *New England Quarterly* 39, no. 2 (June 1966): 182–209.

31. Lodge, "England, Venezuela, and the Monroe Doctrine," *North American Review* 160, no. 463 (June 1895): 651.

32. Ibid.

33. Ibid.

34. Lodge, "The Results of Democratic Victory," *North American Review* 159 (September 1894): see 271–272, 277.

35. Lodge to the Senate, Congressional Record, 3rd sess., 1895: see 622, 630.

36. Ibid., quotes from 1211, 1213, 3108.

37. Secretary of State Richard Olney issued his "Venezuela Note" on July 20, 1895, to British Prime Minister and Foreign Secretary Lord Salisbury. William Eleroy Curtis, *Venezuela: A Land Where It Is Always Summer* (New York: Harper & Brothers, 1896), quote on 284. For more, see Gerald G. Eggert, *Richard Olney: The Evolution of a Statesman* (University Park: Pennsylvania

State University Press, 1972); Walter LaFeber, "The Background of Cleveland's Venezuelan Policy: A Reinterpretation," *American Historical Review* 66 (July 1961): 947–967.

38. Lodge to James Ford Rhodes, August 6, 1900, Lodge Papers.

39. Lodge to Roosevelt, May 24, 1898, Lodge Papers.

40. Roosevelt to Lodge, May 31, 1898, Lodge Papers.

41. Alfred Thayer Mahan to B. Clark, November 5, 1892, from *The Letters and Papers of Alfred Thayer Mahan,* ed. Robert Seager II and Doris D. Maguire (Annapolis, MD: Naval Institute Press, 1975). For more on these thoughts, see Mahan, *The Influence of Sea Power upon History,* 82–87.

42. Walter LaFeber astutely observed this in *The New Empire: An Interpretation of American Expansion, 1860–1898,* expanded 35th anniversary ed. (Ithaca, NY: Cornell University Press, rept. 1998), 62–101.

43. Ibid.; on "intellectual formation," see 91.

44. Brooks Adams, "Commercial Future: New Struggle for Life among Nations," *Fortnightly Review* 71 (New Series 65, February 1899): 274–283. Adams expanded these ideas into what would become the second chapter of his widely read expansionist economic tract, *America's Economic Supremacy* (New York: Macmillan, 1900).

45. Charles W. Calhoun, *Gilded Age Cato: The Life of Walter Q. Gresham* (Lexington: University Press of Kentucky, 1988), 143, 161.

46. William James to E. L. Godkin, December 24, 1895, William James Papers, Houghton Library, Harvard University. For published, transcribed versions of the vast majority of his correspondence, the best source is *The Correspondence of William James,* ed. Ignas K. Skrupskelis and Elizabeth M. Berkeley (Charlottesville: University of Virginia Press, 2001).

47. James to Honorable Samuel W. McCall, December 21, 1895, in William James, *Essays, Comments, and Reviews* (Cambridge, MA: Harvard University Press, 1987), 151–152.

48. James to McCall, December 21, 1895, cited in James, *Essays,* 151–152.

49. For the best scholarly treatment to date, see George Cotkin, *William James: Public Philosopher* (Champaign: University of Illinois Press, 1994), on the "imperial imperative."

50. James to E. L. Godkin, December 24, 1895, James Papers.

51. Lodge to Henry Higginson and Lodge to "Rawle" [unclear on original], January 20 and 21, 1896, Lodge Papers.

52. Lodge, *A Frontier Town and Other Essays* (New York: Scribner, 1906), 188.

53. Lodge, "Outlook and Duty of the Republican Party," *Forum* 12 (April 1893): 251–252.

54. For more on exceptionalism in American thought and foreign policy, see Michael Hunt, *Ideology and U.S. Foreign Policy* (New Haven, CT: Yale

University Press, 1988), and Seymour Lipset, *American Exceptionalism: A Double-Edged Sword* (New York: W. W. Norton, 1996).

55. Lodge, "Our Duty to Cuba," *Forum* 21 (May 1896): 278–287.

56. Lodge to Henry [Higginson], March 9, 1898, Lodge Papers.

57. Robert Friedenberg, *Theodore Roosevelt and the Rhetoric of Militant Decency* (Westport, CT: Greenwood Press, 1990).

58. Roosevelt, from *The Letters of Theodore Roosevelt*, ed. Elting E. Morrison (Cambridge, MA: Harvard University Press, 1954), vol. 1, quoted on 746.

59. Lodge, Congressional Record, 54th Cong., 1st sess., May 1 and 2, 1896, 4657 and 4713. Roosevelt consistently urged Lodge to fight for more torpedo boats in 1895. In particular, see Roosevelt to Lodge, February 28, 1895, Lodge Papers.

60. Lodge to Tom Reed, August [date unclear] 1897, Lodge Papers.

61. Reed to Lodge, Lodge to Reed, letters in August and September 1897, Lodge Papers. Lodge to Roosevelt re: Reed, 1898, see *Selections from the Correspondence of Theodore Roosevelt and Henry Cabot Lodge, 1884–1918* (New York: Scribner, 1925), vol. 1, 370.

62. Ibid., Reed to Lodge, Lodge Papers.

63. Ibid., Lodge to Reed, Lodge Papers.

64. Lodge to Roosevelt on Reed in *Roosevelt-Lodge Correspondence*, vol. 1, 370.

65. Lodge to James Ford Rhodes, August 6, 1900, Lodge Papers. See also Lodge's rapidly produced account of the conflict and its implications, *The War with Spain* (New York: Harper and Brothers, 1899). See Anders Stephanson's superb, concise account, *Manifest Destiny: American Expansion and the Empire of Right* (New York: Hill & Wang, 1996).

66. Warren Zimmermann, *First Great Triumph: How Five Americans Made Their Country a World Power* (New York: Farrar, Straus, and Giroux, 2002), 13.

67. Lodge and Roosevelt, *Hero Tales.*

68. Cited in John Offner, *An Unwanted War: The Diplomacy of the United States and Spain, 1895–1898* (Chapel Hill: University of North Carolina Press, 1992), 44–48.

69. I use the term "Spanish-American War" out of utility and with great reluctance, because though it is concise and reflects the most common understanding of the conflict, the term also obscures important places and peoples involved. A better albeit unwieldy phrase might be "Spanish-American-Cuban-Philippine Conflict."

70. John Fiske, "Manifest Destiny," *American Political Ideas: Viewed from the Standpoint of Universal History* (New York: Harper and Brothers, 1885), 103.

71. Fiske, "Manifest Destiny," 139, 151.

72. William Graham Sumner, *The Conquest of the United States by Spain: A Lecture before the Phi Beta Kappa Society of Yale University, January 16, 1899* (Boston: Dana Estes & Co., 1899), 32.

73. For a revealing analysis of Burgess and political scientific views of American imperialism, see Robert Vitalis, "The Noble American Science of Imperial Relations and Its Laws of Race Development," *Comparative Studies in Society and History* 52 (2010): 909–938; also available at www.allacademic.com/meta/p251266_index.html (accessed March 25, 2010).

74. William Allan Rogers's image was destined to become an iconic vision of the freed, feminized Cuba. The cartoon first appeared in *Harper's Weekly* on April 30, 1898, mere days after Spain declared war, and was widely reprinted and recirculated thereafter.

75. Charles Henry Brown, *The Correspondent's War: Journalists in the Spanish-American War* (New York: Charles Scribner's Sons, 1967).

76. David R. Spencer, *The Yellow Journalism: The Press and America's Emergence as a World Power* (Evanston, IL: Northwestern University Press, 2007); see also David Trask, *The War with Spain in 1898* (Lincoln: University of Nebraska Press, 1996), David Traxel, *1898: The Birth of the American Century* (New York: Knopf, 1998) and *Crusader Nation* (New York: Knopf, 2006), and David Silbey, *A War of Frontier and Empire* (New York: Hill & Wang, 2007); on McKinley and the war, see Lewis Gould, *The Spanish-American War and President McKinley* (Lawrence: University Press of Kansas, 1982).

77. Stanton quoted in Merle Curti, *Peace or War: The American Struggle, 1636–1936* (1936; New York: W. W. Norton, 1959), 171.

78. Roosevelt, February 16–28, 1898, from *Letters of Roosevelt*, vol. 1.

79. Roosevelt's thinking was logical, though it might not seem so to the modern reader. Germany was actively involved in the Pacific, seeking new Asian markets, and was expanding the nation's naval capabilities in direct competition with the United States.

80. Roosevelt to John D. Long, February 16, 1898, *Letters of Roosevelt*, vol. 1.

81. There are several examples in his private correspondence of Roosevelt jumping to this conclusion about the USS *Maine*; see *The Letters of Theodore Roosevelt*.

82. Karl Schriftgiesser, *The Gentleman from Massachusetts: Henry Cabot Lodge* (Boston: Little, Brown & Co., 1944), 175.

83. Lodge to Anna Cabot Lodge, April 23, 1898, Lodge Papers. This letter and incident are discussed in Garraty, *Lodge*, 190, footnote 5. Regarding Lodge as "cautious firebrand," see Widenor, *Lodge*, 66–120.

84. In 1976 Admiral H. G. Rickover published a definitive assessment, *How the Battleship Maine Was Destroyed* (1976; Annapolis, MD: Naval Institute Press, 1995). He revised previous conclusions and showed that the *Maine* likely sank due to "an accident which occurred inside the ship," in all probability an "internally initiated" spontaneous combustion of the coal supply due to poor

ventilation in the boiler system. Rickover's conclusions represent the consensus opinion on the cause of the sinking of the *Maine*.

85. Congressional Record, April 11, 1898.

86. *New York Journal*, April 14, 1898.

87. Walter McDougall, *Promised Land, Crusader State: The American Encounter with the World since 1776* (New York: Mariner Books, 1997), 172–198.

88. On the AALL see David A. Moss, *Socializing Security: Progressive-Era Economists and the Origins of American Social Policy* (Cambridge, MA: Harvard University Press, 1996); on reformers and empire see Jackson Lears, *Rebirth of a Nation: The Making of Modern America, 1877–1920* (New York: HarperCollins, 2009), 276–326.

89. See Matthew Frye Jacobsen, *Barbarian Virtues: United States Encounters Foreign Peoples at Home and Abroad, 1876–1917* (New York: Hill & Wang, 2001).

90. Roosevelt, *The Letters of Theodore Roosevelt*, vol. 1.

91. Lodge to Mr. Hayes (Elihu B. Hayes), May 18, 1898, Lodge Papers.

92. Lodge to Mr. Parker, May 31, 1898, Lodge Papers.

93. Lodge to Fred (most likely George "Fred" Williams), May 21, 1898, Lodge Papers.

94. Lodge to George Lyman, June 13, 1898, Lodge Papers.

95. For more in the Paris Peace conference and negotiations, see John Offner, "The United States and France: Ending the Spanish-American War," *Diplomatic History* 7 (1983): 1–21. For more on the Platt Amendment, see Lejeune Cummins, "The Formulation of the 'Platt' Amendment," *The Americas* 23, no. 4 (April 1967): 370–389.

96. From McKinley Papers as cited in Paulo E. Coletta, "McKinley, the Peace Negotiations, and the Acquisition of the Philippines," *Pacific Historical Review* 30, no. 4 (November 1961): 341–350; see also Coletta, "Bryan, McKinley, and the Treaty of Paris," *Pacific Historical Review* 26, no. 2 (May 1957): 131–146.

97. Treaty of Paris, signed December 10, 1898. Full document—as ratified and entered into the *Congressional Record*—located at Yale Law School Avalon Project website, http://avalon.law.yale.edu/19th_century/sp1898.asp (accessed June 24, 2010).

98. See Robert McGreevey, "Borderline Citizens: Puerto Ricans and the Politics of Migration, Race, and Empire, 1898–1950" (PhD diss., Brandeis University, 2008).

99. Albert Beveridge, Speech to the Senate, Congressional Record, 56th Cong., 1st sess., January 9, 1900, 711.

100. Roughly 130,000 Americans served in the Philippine campaign, which cost in excess of $160 million. For the Filipinos, estimates range but it seems that roughly twenty thousand armed combatants perished, and while historians

disagree over aggregate civilian losses, including those dying from famine and disease, conservative estimates of civilian casualties range from fifty thousand to two hundred thousand.

101. On the Philippine War, see Brian Linn's *Philippine War* (Lawrence: University Press of Kansas, 2000). On the continuing struggle and imperial impulse, Stanley Karnow, *In Our Image: America's Empire in the Philippines* (New York: Ballantine Books, 1990). Most of these relatively sparsely populated and remote islands deemed "unincorporated" were placed under the administration of American naval officers and accountable to the Department of the Navy. See also Linn, *The Philippine War, and the U.S. Army and Counterinsurgency in the Philippines, 1899–1902* (Chapel Hill: University of North Carolina Press, 2000), and Paul Kramer, *The Blood of Government: Race, Empire, the United States, and the Philippines* (Chapel Hill: University of North Carolina Press, 2006). Some representative recent works guiding new historiographical directions include Kristin Hoganson, *Fighting for American Manhood: How Gender Politics Provoked the Spanish-American and Philippine-American Wars* (New Haven, CT: Yale University Press, 2000); Matthew Frye Jacobson, *Barbarian Virtues*; Mary Renda, *Taking Haiti: Military Occupation and the Culture of U.S. Imperialism, 1915–1940* (Chapel Hill: University of North Carolina Press, 2001); Christopher Capozzola, "Empire as a Way of Life: Gender, Culture, and Power in New Histories of U.S. Imperialism," *Journal of the Gilded Age and Progressive Era* 1, no. 2 (October 2002): 364–374. See also Silbey, *A War of Frontier and Empire*.

102. See Hoganson, *Fighting for American Manhood*, and Kristin Hoganson, *Consumers' Imperium: The Global Production of American Domesticity, 1865–1920* (Chapel Hill: University of North Carolina Press, 2007); see also Gail Bederman, *Manliness and Civilization: A Cultural History of Gender and Race in the United States, 1880–1917* (Chicago: University of Chicago Press, 1995), 184–215.

103. Ibid., Bederman and Hoganson on the gendered language of empire.

104. Henry Cabot Lodge, *Studies in History* (1884; Freeport, RI: Books for Libraries Press, 1972), 365.

105. On U.S.-African missions, see Andrew Witmer, "God's Interpreters: African Missions, Transnational Protestantism, and Race in the United States, 1830–1910" (PhD diss., University of Virginia, 2008).

106. For more on Spencer, see Mark Francis, *Herbert Spencer and the Invention of Modern Life* (Ithaca, NY: Cornell University Press, 2007); on Spencer and evolutionary thought in America, see Barry Weth, *Banquet at Delmonico's: Great Minds, the Gilded Age, and the Triumph of Evolution in America* (New York: Random House, 2009).

107. Lodge and Roosevelt, *Hero Tales*, ix.

108. Ibid., preface.

109. Ibid., x.

110. Bederman, *Manliness and Civilization*, 184.

111. In *First Great Triumph*, Warren Zimmermann paints a strongly prejudicial picture of Lodge's racism, which he calls Lodge's "dauntless intolerance." Lodge's views about the inferiority of African Americans and non-Anglo-Saxons more broadly were grounded in his understanding of modern racial science and were moderated by his broadly abolitionist-Republican sensibilities.

112. As Carl Schurz put it in "American Imperialism: An Address Opposing Annexation of the Philippines, January 4, 1899." Pamphlets collection, MHS.

113. White as quoted in Walter Johnson, *William Allen White's America* (New York: Henry Holt & Co., 1947), 111. For more on how racial inferiority impacted expansionist-exceptionalist thinking, see Kramer, "Empire, Exceptions, and Anglo-Saxons." Kramer rightly observes that Mahan's arguments were "more antiexceptionalist" than those of his fellow expansionists, yet they were just as couched in racist discourse.

114. On the complicated racial justifications for expansion and incorporating colonials into the United States, see Kramer, *The Blood of Government*, 116–124. For a provocative but compelling account of how anti-imperialists were most explicit in wielding racism as a tool to oppose empire, see Eric T. Love, *Race over Empire: Racism and U.S. Imperialism, 1865–1900* (Chapel Hill: University of North Carolina Press, 2004). Lodge was an ardent supporter of immigration quotas and fitness tests for new immigrants. See Aristide Zolberg, *A Nation by Design: Immigration Policy in the Fashioning of America* (New York: Russell Sage Foundation with Harvard University Press, 2006).

115. Lodge, "The Date We Celebrate," on Forefathers' Day, Address to the New England Society of Brooklyn, December 21, 1888. Lodge Scrapbooks (1888), Lodge Papers.

116. Henry Cabot Lodge, *The War with Spain* (1899; New York: Arno Press, rept. 1970), 1.

117. Regarding Lodge's influence on Roosevelt, see John Garraty, *Henry Cabot Lodge: A Biography* (New York: Alfred A. Knopf, 1953); also on Lodge, Roosevelt, and Brooks Adams, see William Appleman Williams, "Brooks Adams and American Expansion," *New England Quarterly* 25, no. 2 (June 1952): 231.

118. Garraty, *Lodge*, 151.

119. Quoted in Schirmer, *Republic or Empire*, 44.

120. Zimmermann, *First Great Triumph*, 184. In addition to his work on behalf of Massachusetts fishermen, more examples of Lodge's serious efforts to uphold his party's promises to all Americans were his serial attempts to enforce

Lincoln's assurance to protect African American rights in the South. He consistently supported the extension of full citizenship rights to all black men.

121. John Hay to Theodore Roosevelt, July 27, 1898. Morrison, *Letters of Roosevelt.*

122. With roughly four hundred battle casualties, one can understand why Hay thought the conflict remained "little" in terms of combat losses. In scope, however, the war was vast; it covered two oceans and thousands of miles. In manpower, from a prewar army strength of roughly twenty-five thousand, more than two hundred thousand Americans in arms or otherwise serving roles in equipping, planning, transporting, and fighting the conflict by October 1, 1898.

123. Lodge, *War with Spain,* 234–235.

124. Examples of this dual understanding of Lodge appear in Schirmer, *Republic or Empire,* and Ronald Powaski, *Toward an Entangling Alliance* (New York: Greenwood Press, 1991); also, along the same lines but cast as a "war of choice" propelled by "special interests," see the characteristically "isolationist interwar" depiction of how the United States became involved in World War I in Walter Mills, *Road to War: 1914–1917* (Boston: Houghton Mifflin Co., 1935).

125. Lodge, "Our Blundering Foreign Policy," *Forum* 19 (March 1895): 16.

126. Congressional Record, 55th Cong., 3rd sess., 1899, 959.

127. Roosevelt, April 10, 1899, in *The Strenuous Life,* 6–7.

128. Henry Adams, cited in Bradford Perkins, *The Great Rapprochement: England and the United States, 1895–1914* (New York: Atheneum, 1968), 89.

129. London *Times,* lead editorial, December 12, 1898. On statistics, see Donald Dyal et al., eds., *Historical Dictionary of the Spanish American War* (Westport, CT: Greenwood Press, 1996), 67.

130. H. H. Powers, "The War as a Suggestion of Manifest Destiny," *Annals of the American Academy of Political and Social Science* (September 1898): 3.

131. Causal emphases vary. See James A. Field Jr. on how historians misconstrue imperialism and the "road to war," "American Imperialism: The Worst Chapter in Almost Any Book," *American Historical Review* 83, no. 3 (June 1978): 644–668. Thomas G. Patterson, "United States Intervention in Cuba, 1898: Interpretations of the Spanish-American-Cuban-Filipino War," *History Teacher* 29, no. 3 (May 1996): 341–361.

132. Michael Ignatieff, "Why Are We in Iraq? (And Liberia? And Afghanistan?)," *New York Times Magazine,* September 7, 2003, Section 6, 40.

133. Louis Perez Jr., *The War of 1898: The United States and Cuba in History and Historiography* (Chapel Hill: University of North Carolina Press, 1998).

134. Fareed Zakaria, *From Wealth to Power: The Unusual Origins of America's World Role* (Princeton, NJ: Princeton University Press, 1998), 128–180.

135. Congressional Record, 62nd Cong., 2nd sess., 1912, 5661. See also Thomas Bailey, "The Lodge Corollary to the Monroe Doctrine," *Political Science Quarterly* 48 (June 1933): 220–239.

136. *Speeches and Addresses of William McKinley from March 1, 1897, to May 30, 1900* (New York: Doubleday & McClure, 1900), 193.

137. Carl Schurz, *American Imperialism: The Convocation Address Delivered on the Occasion of the 27th Convocation of the University of Chicago, January 4th, 1899* (Boston: Dana Estes & Co., 1899), 30–32.

138. Charles J. Bonaparte to a Danish friend, quoted in Howard K. Beale, *Theodore Roosevelt and the Rise of America to World Power* (New York: Collier Books, 1956), 33.

139. John Bassett Moore in Edwin Borchard et al., eds., *The Collected Papers of John Bassett Moore*, vol. 2 (New Haven, CT: Yale University Press, 1944), 202; see Moore's own reflections in *The Principles of American Diplomacy* (New York: Harper and Brothers, 1918). On Moore and ideas about isolation in the 1940s, see Justus Doenecke, "Edwin Borchard, John Bassett Moore, and Opposition to American Intervention in World War II," *Journal of Libertarian Studies* 6, no. 1 (Winter 1982): 1–34.

140. Lodge, *The Story of the Revolution*, vol. 2 (New York: Charles Scribner's Sons, 1898), 247.

2. A Better Nation Morally

1. A rich body of literature exists on William James and his family. There is surprisingly little research on James's political philosophy. The one chapter on James in Robert Beisner's excellent book on the anti-imperialists, *Twelve against Empire: The Anti-Imperialists, 1898–1900* (New York: McGraw-Hill, 1968), ends in 1900. The best book on James's political thought is George Cotkin, *William James: Public Philosopher* (Champaign: University of Illinois Press, 1994).

2. *Reports of the Fifth, Sixth, and Seventh Annual Meetings of the Anti-Imperialist League*, Houghton Library, Harvard University (1903–1905). I have put much of this together from primary sources in the manuscript collections of Harvard University and the Massachusetts Historical Society.

3. James to François Pillon, June 15, 1898, James Papers, Houghton Library, Harvard University, hereafter "James Papers." Virtually all of James's writings now are transcribed and available in the multivolume *The Correspondence of William James*, ed. Ignas K. Skrupkelis and Elizabeth M. Berkeley (Charlottesville: University of Virginia Press, 2000).

4. Morton White explored philosophical discourses to explain the transformation of social thought in the era as a revolt against formalism, which he tried to define broadly as abstract and deductive methods of analysis in law, history,

philosophy, politics, economics, and across the social sciences. White, *Social Thought in America: The Revolt against Formalism* (New York: Viking Press, 1949), 6, 12.

5. Ibid., esp. 240–241.

6. Ibid., 241.

7. Originally James described truth this way in 1898. He then extended it as a measure for the pragmatic evaluation of ideas. See James, *Pragmatism: A New Name for Some Old Ways of Thinking* (New York: Longmans, Green, and Co., 1907); in brief, see introduction to Louis Menand, *Pragmatism: A Reader* (New York: Vintage Books, 1997). On James's intellectual milieu, see James T. Kloppenberg, *Uncertain Victory: Social Democracy and Progressivism in European and American Thought, 1870–1920* (New York: Oxford University Press, 1986).

8. William James to E. L. Godkin, December 24, 1895, James Papers.

9. William James, *Memories and Studies* (New York: Longmans, Green, and Co., 1911), 58.

10. See histories of the movement: E. Berkley Tompkins, *Anti-Imperialism in the United States: The Great Debate, 1890–1920* (Philadelphia: University of Pennsylvania Press, 1970); Beisner's *Twelve against Empire*; Fred Harrington, "The Anti-Imperialist Movement in the U.S., 1898–1900," *Mississippi Valley Historical Review* 22, no. 2 (September 1935): 211–230; and Richard E. Welch, *Response to Imperialism: The United States and the Philippine-American War, 1899–1902* (Chapel Hill: University of North Carolina Press, 1979), and Daniel B. Schirmer, *Republic or Empire, American Resistance to the Philippine War* (Cambridge, MA: Schenkman Publishing Co., 1972). Also, Christopher McKnight Nichols, "The Significance of Isolationism to the American Anti-Imperialist Movement" (AHA annual meeting, January 2009), and "Transnational Ideas and the Global Anti-Imperialist Movement" (AHA annual meeting, January 2010).

11. On James and the "choice of cause," see Gerald Myers, *William James: His Life and Thought* (New Haven, CT: Yale University Press, 1986), esp. "Attention and Will," 181–214, and "On Knowledge," 272–306.

12. James, "On a Certain Blindness in Human Beings," in *Talks to Teachers on Psychology and to Students on Some of Life's Ideals* (Cambridge, MA: Harvard University Press, 1983), esp. 149. Also James, *Principles of Psychology* (New York, 1890). On abstraction in American political philosophy and specifically on the emergence of the coherent concept "the state," Daniel T. Rodgers, *Contested Truths: Keywords in American Politics since Independence* (New York: Basic Books, 1987), 169–175. On James's attacks on Hegelian logic and critiques of the hubristic scientific commitments of Spencer, Tydnall, and Huxley, among others, see Robert Richardson, *William James in the Maelstrom of America Modernism* (Boston: Houghton Mifflin Co., 2006).

13. Four excellent studies of the rise of anti-imperialism in the United States are Tompkins, *Anti-Imperialism in the United States*; Beisner, *Twelve against Empire*; Harrington, "The Anti-Imperialist Movement"; and Welch, *Response to Imperialism.*

14. On patriotism and the "twinkling" rush to war, see William James, "To the Editors," *Harvard Crimson*, January 14, 1896.

15. Brooks Adams quoted in William Appleman Williams, "Brooks Adams and American Expansion," *New England Quarterly* 25 (June 1952): 217–232.

16. James, "On a Certain Blindness in Human Beings," *Talks to Teachers*, 132, 138, 149.

17. Edward Atkinson Papers, Massachusetts Historical Society. Atkinson's radical laissez-faire arguments dovetailed with his acute sense of fair play to underpin virtually all of his anti-imperialist writing. See, for example, Atkinson's three most sensational pamphlets from 1899: "The Cost of a National Crime," detailing both the U.S. military oppression of the newly subjugated Filipinos and directly linking it to the growing, excessive cost of the war and annexation upon American taxpayers; "The Hell of War and Its Penalties"; and "Criminal Aggression: By Whom Committed?" in the Atkinson Papers. See also David T. Beito and Linda Royster Beito, "Gold Democrats and the Decline of Classical Liberalism, 1896–1900," *Independent Review* 4 (Spring 2000): 555–575.

18. James, "On a Certain Blindness in Human Beings," 149.

19. James to Mrs. Henry Whitman, June 7, 1899, James Papers.

20. On Roosevelt and James, H. W. Brands, *T.R.: The Last Romantic* (New York: Basic Books, 1997); on their Americanism, Jonathan Hansen, *The Lost Promise of Patriotism: Debating American Identity, 1890–1920* (Chicago: University of Chicago Press, 2003), and Kim Townsend, *Manhood at Harvard: William James and Others* (New York: W. W. Norton, 1996).

21. Geoffrey Blodgett, "The Mugwump Reputation, 1870 to the Present," *Journal of American History* 66, no. 4 (March 1980): 867–887; Harrington, "The Anti-Imperialist Movement"; and Beisner, *Twelve against Empire*, introduction.

22. The highlights of the pamphlet came from the usual sources: Washington's Farewell Address, Jefferson's inaugural address, the Monroe Doctrine, and a set of comments by Albert Gallatin on "our destiny."

23. Anti-Imperialist League Broadside: *Arguments against the Adoption of a So-Called Imperial Policy* (Washington, DC: AIL Printing, 1898), Pamphlet Collection, MHS. *Report of the Executive Committee of the Anti-Imperialist League*, February 10, 1899, MHS; on foundational principles, see *Annual Meeting of the Anti-Imperialist League*, November 25, 1899, Pamphlet Collection, MHS. Charles Francis Adams Jr., *Imperialism and the Tracks of Our Forefathers* (Boston, 1899).

24. Speech on May 2, 1898, from David Starr Jordan, *The Days of a Man, Being Memories of a Naturalist, Teacher, and Minor Prophet of Democracy* (New York: World Book Co., 1922), vol. 1, 616.

25. *New York Times*, July 21, 1898.

26. William James, "To the Editors," *Harvard Crimson*, January 14, 1896. For more on the point-counterpoint with Roosevelt and their relationship, see Cotkin, *William James*, and the biographies by Perry and Myers. For more on the differences between Roosevelt and James, see Brands, Hansen, Townsend; see also Tom Lutz, *American Nervousness, 1903: An Anecdotal History* (Ithaca, NY: Cornell University Press, 1991), esp. chapter 2.

27. Carl Schurz to Bjornstjerne Bjornson, September 22, 1898, in *Speeches, Correspondence, and Political Papers of Carl Schurz*, ed. Frederic Bancroft (New York: G. P. Putnam and Sons, 1913), vol. 2, 514.

28. Andrew Carnegie, "The Venezuela Question," *North American Review* 162 (February 1896): esp. 131, 142.

29. Charles Eliot Norton to Leslie Stephen, January 3, 1896, in *Letters of Charles Eliot Norton*, ed. Sara Norton and M. A. DeWolfe Howe (Boston: Houghton Mifflin Co., 1913), vol. 2, 236–237; Norton to Godkin, December 22, 1895, E. L. Godkin Papers, MHS. On their relationship and this point, I am indebted to the observations in Beisner, *Twelve against Empire*, see esp. chapter 4.

30. Theodore Woolsey, "An Inquiry Concerning Our Foreign Relations," *Yale Review* 1 (August 1892): 174.

31. Ibid.

32. Carl Schurz, "Manifest Destiny," *Harper's New Monthly Magazine*, October 1893, 743.

33. W. E. B. Du Bois, *Souls of Black Folk* (Chicago: A. C. McClurg & Co., 1903), 78.

34. Ibid., 104. Peter Conn aptly termed this odd admixture of racial egalitarianism and animus as "myopic cosmopolitanism" for W. E. B. Du Bois. Conn, "Comments on Nichols's *From Empire to Isolation*," Penn Humanities Forum (January 19, 2010), in the author's possession. See also Conn, *The Divided Mind: Ideology and Imagination in America, 1898–1917* (Cambridge: Cambridge University Press, 1983).

35. William Leuchtenburg, "Progressivism and Imperialism: The Progressive Movement and American Foreign Policy, 1898–1916," *Mississippi Valley Historical Review* 39, no. 3 (December 1952): 483–490. On the relationship between the idea of "progress" and imperialism, see Alan Dawley, *Changing the Heart of the World* (Princeton, NJ: Princeton University Press, 2003), 76–83.

36. Reverend Charles G. Ames, "Address at the Meeting in Faneuil Hall, Boston, June 15, 1898," quoted in Eric Foner, *Voices of Freedom: A Documentary History* (New York: W. W. Norton, 2005), 60, 62.

37. See Timothy Yates, *Christian Mission in the Twentieth Century* (Cambridge: Cambridge University Press, 1994), chapter 1 on "mission as expansion." For the political side of the mission-expansion argument and Roosevelt's religious views of expansion, see Richard H. Collin, *Theodore Roosevelt, Culture, Diplomacy, and Expansion: A New View of American Imperialism* (Baton Rouge: Louisiana State University Press, 1985).

38. Josiah Strong, *Expansion, under New World-Conditions* (New York: Baker and Taylor Co., 1900), 269–270. Dorothea Muller, "Josiah Strong and American Nationalism: A Reevaluation," *Journal of American History* 53, no. 3 (1966): see 490–492, 495, 501.

39. Josiah Strong, *The New Era, or the Coming Kingdom* (New York: Baker and Taylor Co., 1893), 16.

40. See Ian Tyrrell, *Reforming the World: The Creation of America's Moral Empire* (Princeton, NJ: Princeton University Press, 2010), 49–73.

41. Washington Gladden, sermon on October 11, 1891, quoted in Jacob Henry Dorn, *Washington Gladden: Prophet of the Social Gospel* (Columbus: Ohio State University Press, 1968), 406.

42. Washington Gladden, *Recollections* (Boston: Houghton Mifflin Co., 1909), 386–387.

43. For more, see Ira V. Brown, *Lyman Abbott, Christian Evolutionist: A Study in Religious Liberalism* (Cambridge, MA: Harvard University Press, 1953), 161. See also Richard Gamble, *The War for Righteousness: Progressive Christians, the Great War, and the Rise of the Messianic Nation* (Wilmington, DE: ISI Books, 2003).

44. A similar pattern occurred in the business press. See Julius Pratt, *Expansionists of 1898: The Acquisition of Hawaii and the Spanish Islands* (Baltimore: Johns Hopkins University Press, 1936), 230–316.

45. Anti-Imperialist League Broadside: "Arguments against the Adoption of a So-Called Imperial Policy," Pamphlet Collection, MHS.

46. Ibid. *Report of the Executive Committee of the Anti-Imperialist League*, February 10, 1899, Pamphlet Collection, MHS; for more on the first rounds of discussion on how to return to foundation principles as expressed by Washington and Jefferson, and as embodied in the Monroe Doctrine, see Annual Meeting of the Anti-Imperialist League, November 25, 1899, Pamphlet Collection, MHS. "Pamphlet and Paper Read before the Lexington, Massachusetts, Historical Society," Tuesday, December 20, 1898, in Charles Francis Adams Jr., *Imperialism and the Tracks of Our Forefathers* (Boston: D. Estes and Co., 1899). For more on the conflict and timing, see the work of Augusto Spiritu, *The American Colonial State in the Philippines: Global Perspectives*, ed. Julian Go et al. (Durham, NC: Duke University Press, 2003); Angel Velasco Shaw and Luis H. Francia, eds., *Vestiges of War: The Philippine-American War*

and the Aftermath of an Imperial Dream, 1899–1999 (New York: New York University Press, 2002); Resil Mojares, *The War against the Americans: Resistance and Collaboration in Cebu, 1899–1906* (Quezon City, Philippines: Ateneo de Manila University Press, 1999).

47. Speech on May 2, 1898, from David Starr Jordan, *The Days of a Man*, vol. 1, 616.

48. *St. Louis Globe*, September 21, 1898, also printed as an excerpt in the *New York Times*, September 22, 1898.

49. On mugwumps, see Gerald McFarland, *Mugwumps, Morals, and Politics, 1884–1920* (Amherst: University of Massachusetts Press, 1975), and David Tucker, *Mugwumps: Public Moralists of the Gilded Age* (Columbia: University of Missouri Press, 1998).

50. Henry Steele Commager, *The American Mind: An Interpretation of American Thought and Character since the 1880s* (New Haven, CT: Yale University Press, 1950), 318.

51. Among other works on this subject, see Geoffrey T. Blodgett, *The Gentle Reformers: Massachusetts Democrats in the Cleveland Era* (Cambridge, MA: Harvard University Press, 1966), and his article "The Mind of the Boston Mugwump," *Mississippi Valley Historical Review* 48, no. 4 (March 1962): 614–634.

52. James to E. L. Godkin, April 15, 1889 (on his political education), James Papers.

53. James, "Letter to the Editor," *Boston Evening Transcript*, March 1, 1899, 16. Written on February 26, 1899, according to James's files.

54. Ibid. Also, Ignas K. Skrupskelis, ed., *Essays, Comments, and Reviews (The Works of William James)* (Cambridge, MA: Harvard University Press, 1987), 154–155.

55. James, "Letter to the Editor," in *Essays, Comments, and Reviews*, 154.

56. Ibid., 154–155.

57. Ibid., 155.

58. Ibid.

59. Ibid. Some scholars have taken this in connection with James's other writing to indicate that his anti-imperial and anti-institutional arguments of this period reveal him as moving toward "radicalization." See Deborah J. Coon, "'One Moment in the World's Salvation': Anarchism and the Radicalization of William James," *Journal of American History* 83, no. 1 (June 1996): 70–99.

60. James, "Letter to the Editor," in *Essays, Comments, and Reviews*, 154–155.

61. Ibid.

62. Ibid., 156.

63. Ibid., 157.

64. Ibid.

65. Ibid., 158.

66. Ibid.

67. James, "Letter on the Philippines," *New York Evening Post*, March 10, 1899; James, "On Governor Roosevelt's Oration," *Boston Evening Transcript*, April 15, 1899; for these and related writings see *Essays, Comments, and Reviews*, 154–166.

68. Atkinson to Andrew Carnegie, May 22, 1899, Atkinson Papers, MHS.

69. On how this incident gained national prominence, see Atkinson to Andrew Carnegie, May 22, 1899, Atkinson Papers; also Harrington, "The Anti-Imperialist Movement," 224–225, and Beisner, *Twelve against Empire*, 98–101. The Boston league, which changed its name to the New England Anti-Imperialist League in 1900, first was located in Atkinson's offices on November 19, 1898.

70. "Broadsides," *AntiImperialist*, August 29, 1899, Pamphlet Collection, Houghton Library, Harvard University; see also Maria C. Lanzar, "The Anti-Imperialist League," *Philippine Social Science Review* (Manila, 1929), 3 (1930), 21.

71. William Jennings Bryan, *Bryan on Imperialism* (New York: Arno Press, rept. 1970), 5–6; Kendrick Clements, *William Jennings Bryan: Missionary Isolationist* (Knoxville: University of Tennessee Press, 1982).

72. "The Real Issue" and "Isolation or Expansion," *Outlook*, June 9, 1900.

73. "Isolation Past, Says Davis," *New York Times*, July 16, 1898.

74. *Los Angeles Times*, October 1900, see compiled editorial section.

75. James, letter dated April 22, 1898; James, December 28, 1898; James, January 5, 1898, James Papers.

76. James, December 28, 1898, James Papers. Gustave le Bon, *The Crowd: A Study of the Popular Mind* (New York: Macmillan, 1897), was reviewed with modest praise by James in *Psychological Review* 4 (1897): 313–314, but found greater favor with Freud.

77. See William M. Gibson, "Mark Twain and Howells: Anti-Imperialists," *New England Quarterly* 20, no. 4 (December 1947): 435–470.

78. Mark Twain, "To the Person Sitting in Darkness," *North American Review* 182:531 (February 1901): 161–176.

79. John Mott, "Speech to the Cleveland, Ohio, Quadrennial Convention," 1898, John Mott Raleigh Papers, Yale Divinity School Archives, Yale University.

80. John Mott, *The Evangelization of the World in This Generation* (New York: Student Volunteers Movement for Foreign Missions, 1900), 2, 28.

81. *Savannah Tribune*, F. H. Crumbley quoted on March 7, 1900. For more detail see George Marks, *The Black Press Views American Imperialism, 1898–1900* (New York: Arno Press, 1971).

82. *Chicago Tribune*, October 10, 1900; *New York Herald*, December 30, 1900.

83. Beisner and Cotkin make similar assessments of James's views of his fellow anti-imperialists. I am drawing on the following letters: James to Alice James,

May 16, 1899 (see also, on the same lines but earlier, James to Alice, January 4, 1895); William James to Mrs. E. L. Godkin, March 14, 1902, James Papers.

84. James to Alice James, May 16, 1899 (also James to Alice, January 4, 1895); William James to Mrs. E. L. Godkin, March 14, 1902, James Papers.

85. James to Ernest Crosby, November 8, 1901, James Papers.

86. James, "The Moral Equivalent of War," 166–168, 171–172; also Julius S. Bixler, "Two Questions Raised by 'The Moral Equivalent of War,'" in *In Commemoration of William James, 1842–1942*, ed. Brand Blanshard (New York: Columbia University Press, 1942), 58–71; on James re: masculinity and gender, Jane Martin, "Martial Virtues or Capital Vices? William James's Moral Equivalent of War Revisited," *Journal of Thought* 22 (Fall 1987): 32–44.

87. Frank Ninkovich, *Global Dawn: The Cultural Foundations of American Internationalism, 1865–1890* (Cambridge, MA: Harvard University Press, 2009), on how elite writers of this period were intensely conflicted and not nearly as zero-sum in assessments of race, 137–166.

88. Samuel Gompers, "Imperialism, Its Dangers and Wrongs," *American Federation of Labor* 5 (November 1898), in *The Anti-Imperialist Reader: A Documentary History of Anti-Imperialism in the United States*, ed. Philip Foner and Richard Winchester (New York: Holmes and Meier), vol. 1, 207. Also, William George Whittaker, "Samuel Gompers, Anti-Imperialist," *Pacific Historical Review* 38, no. 4 (November 1969): 429–445.

89. *The Negro in Business: Report of a Social Study Made under the Direction of Atlanta University; Together with the Proceedings of the Fourth Conference for the Study of the Negro Problems, Held at Atlanta University, May 30–31, 1899*; W. E. B. Du Bois quoted, 5; *The College-Bred Negro American: Report of a Social Study Made by Atlanta University under the Patronage of the Trustees of the John F. Slater Fund; with the Proceedings of the 15th Annual Conference for the Study of the Negro Problems, Held at Atlanta University on May 30, 1911*, see reprint of 1901 common school study, quoted on 528. For more on this, see Richard K. Vedder and Lowell Gallaway, "Racial Differences in Unemployment in the United States, 1890–1990," *Journal of Economic History* 52, no. 3 (September 1992), 696–702.

90. *The Negro in Business*, W. E. B. Du Bois quoted on 5; *The College-Bred Negro American: May 30, 1911*, see reprint of 1901 common school study, quoted on 528.

91. On this point I am indebted to conversations with sociologist James Bryant. See Bryant, unpublished talk on "W. E. B. Du Bois and Human Flourishing in His Late Sociological Imagination," presented at the University of Virginia, January 25, 2008, in author's possession; see also Bryant, "Journeys along Damascus Road: Black Ministers, the Call, and the Modernization of Tradition" (PhD diss., Brown University, 2002). Du Bois's "sociological imagination"

has much in common with C. Wright Mills's concept in *The Sociological Imagination* (New York: Grove Press, 1961).

92. Du Bois, "Credo," *Independent*, October 6, 1904, 787, in *Writings by W. E. B. Du Bois in Periodicals Edited by Others*, ed. Herbert Aptheker (Amherst: University of Massachusetts, 1973), vol. 1, 229. Also cited in the W. E. B. Du Bois Papers, University of Massachusetts Archives, microfilm: Du Bois correspondence and unpublished papers. Quote on comradeship of races from Du Bois, "The Present Outlook for the Dark Races of Mankind" (delivered to the American Negro Academy in Washington, D.C., in 1900), in *Writings by W. E. B. Du Bois*, vol. 1, 78.

93. Paul Kramer, *Blood of Government: Race, Empire, the United States, and the Philippines* (Chapel Hill: University of North Carolina Press, 2006), 119.

94. See George P. Marks III, "Opposition of Negro Newspapers to American Philippine Policy, 1899–1900," *Midwest Journal*, 4 (Winter 1951–1952), see 8, 21. See also Welch, *Response to Imperialism*, chapter 7.

95. For a transnational perspective, see Ian Tyrrell, *Transnational Nation: United States History in Global Perspective since 1789* (New York: Palgrave, 2007). For more on how Du Bois applied a type of "imperial cartography" and elements of American exceptionalism (while opposing empire itself), see Amy Kaplan, *The Anarchy of Empire in the Making of U.S. Culture* (Cambridge, MA: Harvard University Press, 2002), 171–212.

96. *New York Evening Post*, October 1906. Clipped by Mott and located in his papers for October 1906. Mott Papers, Yale Divinity School Archives. For more on this period in Mott's life, see also Mott Papers, YMCA Archives, microfilm from Special Collections, University of Minnesota. The best account of Mott's life is C. Howard Hopkins, *John R. Mott, 1855–1955* (New York: Eerdmans, 1980).

97. On missionary thought, race, and U.S.-Africa relations, see Andrew Witmer, "God's Interpreters: African Missions, Transnational Protestantism, and Race in the United States, 1830–1910" (PhD diss., University of Virginia, 2008).

98. On "righteous" imperialism and its role in how Du Bois viewed the religious motivations and justifications for American and European imperial practices, see David Levering Lewis, *W. E. B. Du Bois: Biography of a Race, 1868–1919* (New York: Owl Books, 1994), esp. 504–505; also Richard Gamble, *The War for Righteousness: Progressive Christianity, the Great War, and the Rise of the Messianic Nation* (Wilmington, DE: ISI Books, 2003).

99. See Yates, *Christian Mission in the Twentieth Century* (Cambridge: Cambridge University Press, 1994); William R. Hutchison, *Errand to the World: American Protestant Thought and Foreign Missions* (Chicago: University of Chicago Press, 1987); Bruce Evensen, *God's Man for the Gilded Age: D. L. Moody and the Rise of Modern Mass Evangelism* (New York: Oxford University Press,

2003); on "beyond Orientalism," Ninkovich depicts this as part of a wider encounter among civilizations, *Global Dawn*, 199–231.

100. Cited in Hopkins, *John R. Mott*, 628.

101. This is my term; on mission, humanitarianism, and American power see Tyrrell, *Reforming the World*, esp. 98–120.

102. Du Bois, "The Color Line Belts the World," *Collier's Weekly*, October 20, 1906, 30, excerpted in *The Oxford W. E. B. Du Bois Reader*, ed. Eric J. Sundquist (New York: Oxford University Press, 1996), see 42–43.

103. Du Bois, "Declaration of Principles at Niagara" (1905); see Gilder-Lehrman Center for the Study of Slavery, Resistance, and Abolition, Archives Files, for the full-text original version at www.yale.edu/glc/archive/1152.htm; for more on Du Bois and the movement, see Lewis, *W. E. B. Du Bois*, chapter 12.

104. Lodge, "A Million Immigrants a Year," *Century*, January 1904, 469.

105. *Report of the Fifth Annual Meeting of the New England Anti-Imperialist League, November 28, 1903, and Its Adjournment November 30* (Boston: New England AIL, 1903), 21. From the "original printed wrappers," in the Library of William James, Pamphlet Collections and William James Papers, Houghton Library, Harvard University. The speech was given on November 30, 1903, at the Boston Twentieth Century Club. Cited from James, "Address on the Philippine Question," 1903, *Report of the Fifth Annual Meeting of the New England Anti-Imperialist League* (Boston, 1903), 21–26. See slightly different copy of the same address printed in the *New York Evening Post*, December 3, 1903, 8.

106. James, "Address on the Philippine Question," 21.

107. Ibid., 22; I draw here on Cotkin's insight in *William James: Public Philosopher*, see 145.

108. Jane Addams, *Newer Ideals of Peace* (New York: Macmillan, 1907); Addams, *Democracy and Social Ethics* (New York: Macmillan, 1902).

109. Linda Schott, "Jane Addams and William James on Alternatives to War," *Journal of the History of Ideas* 54, no. 2 (April 1993): 241–254.

110. *Report of the Fifth Annual Meeting of the New England AIL* (Boston: New England Anti-Imperialist League, 1903), 22; Cotkin makes a similar point, *William James*, see 145.

111. James, "Address on the Philippine Question," 21–26.

112. Ibid. "Deglutition," meaning to swallow down. The term was a favored piece of medical language often employed by James in the context of being forced to swallow something bad (medicine or worse).

113. James, "Address on the Philippine Question," 21–26.

114. Ibid.

115. Here I am thinking of Aristotle's arguments in *Nicomachean Ethics*; see translation by David Ross and Lesley Brown, eds. (Oxford: Oxford University

Press, 2009), and *Politics*, see J. Barnes, ed., *Complete Works of Aristotle* (Princeton, NJ: Princeton University Press, 1971).

116. James, "Address on the Philippine Question," 21–26.

117. Jon Roland's brief introduction to *The Moral Equivalent of War*, located at http://www.constitution.org/wj/meow_intro.htm.

118. Scholars have rightly made this point, including Alan Dawley and Michael McGerr recently, as well as Richard Leopold, Norman Graebner, Ernest May, and John Milton Cooper Jr. Jonathan Hansen's essay in *Americanism: New Perspectives on the History of an Ideal*, ed. Michael Kazin and Joseph A. Martin (Chapel Hill: University of North Carolina Press, 2006), deepens these insights about Jamesian and other patriotic dissent that appeared to limit further annexations.

119. Jonathan Hansen and Carrie Tirrado Bramen have each noted this regarding James and his generation.

120. Quotes from James, "The Moral Equivalent of War" (1910), and letters in 1902–1903 (E. L. Godkin and George Santayana); as this influenced Dewey and other major intellectuals and the democratic thought of the era, see Robert Westbrook's masterful *John Dewey and American Democracy* (Ithaca, NY: Cornell University Press, 1991).

3. *Toward a Transnational America*

1. Randolph Bourne, "Berlin in War Time," *Travel*, November 1914, 9–12, 58–59; see also Bourne's report to the Trustees of Columbia University evaluating his Gilder fellowship for thirteen months of European travel, "Impressions of Europe, 1913–1914: Report to the Trustees of Columbia University," in Randolph Bourne, *History of a Literary Radical and Other Papers* (New York: S. A. Russell, 1956), 75–101 (published in *Columbia University Quarterly* 17 [March 1915], quote on 100). This also is detailed in the Arthur Whittier Macmahon Papers, Rare Book and Manuscript Library, Columbia University.

2. Bourne, "Impressions of Europe, 1913–14," *History of a Literary Radical*, 75. For more on Bourne's time abroad see "Impressions of a European Tour," which he published in several installments in his hometown paper the *Citizen* (Bloomfield, NJ, 1913–1914); and Bourne, "Berlin in War Time," *Travel* (November 1914): 58–59

3. Bourne, "Impressions of Europe," *History of a Literary Radical*, 99.

4. Bourne to Sara Bourne, July 28, 1914, filed under "letters to his mother," Randolph Silliman Bourne Papers, Rare Book and Manuscript Library, Columbia University.

5. Macmahon, comments to Louis Filler, no date, Bourne Papers; for more on this incident, see Bourne, "Impressions of Europe," 100, and "Berlin in Wartime," 11–12.

6. Macmahon, comments to Filler, Bourne Papers.

7. Bourne, "Impressions of Europe," 100.

8. Bourne, "Trans-National America," *Atlantic Monthly* 118 (July 1916): 86–97, reprinted in *War and the Intellectuals: Essays by Randolph S. Bourne, 1915–1919*, ed. Carl Resek (New York: Harper and Row, 1964), 107–123.

9. Bourne, "The Jew and Trans-National America," *Menorah Journal* 2 (December 1915): 277–284, reprinted in *War and the Intellectuals*, 130.

10. On American pluralism, see David A. Hollinger, *Postethnic America: Beyond Multiculturalism*; John Higham, "Multiculturalism and Universalism: A History and Critique," *American Quarterly* 45 (June 1993): 195–219; Philip Gleason, *Speaking of Diversity: Language and Ethnicity in Twentieth-Century America* (Baltimore: Johns Hopkins University Press, 1992); Nathan Glazer, *We Are All Multiculturalists Now* (Cambridge, MA: Harvard University Press, 1997); Everett Helmut Akam, *Transnational America: Cultural Pluralist Thought in the Twentieth Century* (Lanham, MD: Rowman and Littlefield, 2002); for an excellent overview, see Philip Gleason's entry: "Americanization and American Identity," in *Harvard Encyclopedia of American Ethnic Groups* (Cambridge, MA: Harvard University Press, 1980).

12. James R. Vitelli, *Randolph Bourne* (Boston: Twayne Publishers, 1981), 155, 158.

13. A selection of the best historical scholarship on Bourne includes Casey Blake, *Beloved Community: The Cultural Criticism of Randolph Bourne, Van Wyck Brooks, Waldo Frank, and Lewis Mumford* (Chapel Hill: University of North Carolina Press, 1990); Bruce Clayton, *Forgotten Prophet: The Life of Randolph Bourne* (Baton Rouge: Louisiana State University Press, 1984); John Adam Moreau, *Randolph Bourne: Legend and Reality* (Washington, DC: Public Affairs Press, 1966); and Vitelli, *Randolph Bourne*. Also, Casey Blake, "Randolph Bourne," in *A Companion to American Thought*, ed. Richard Wightman Fox and James T. Kloppenberg (Oxford: Oxford University Press, 1998), 85–87; Leslie J. Vaughan, *Randolph Bourne and the Politics of Cultural Radicalism* (Lawrence: University Press of Kansas Press, 1997), 5–6.

14. See Bourne, *Youth and Life* (Boston: Houghton Mifflin Co., 1913), and Blake, *Beloved Community*, 114.

15. Bourne, "Trans-National America"; also Christopher Lasch, *The New Radicalism in America, 1889–1963: The Intellectual as Social Type* (New York: Knopf, 1965), 81.

16. On other categories of citizenship in Bourne's thought and the wider political discourse, see Christopher McKnight Nichols, "Citizenship and Transnationalism in Randolph Bourne's America," in "Citizenship and Social Justice," special issue, *The Peace Review: A Journal of Social Justice* 20, no. 3 (Fall 2008): 348–357.

17. I have elaborated this argument elsewhere; see Nichols, "Rethinking Randolph Bourne's Trans-National America: How World War I Created an Isolationist

Antiwar Pluralism," *Journal of the Gilded Age and Progressive Era* 8, no. 2 (April 2009): 217–257.

18. The trajectory of this argument as it is described here was deepened conceptually in light of a discussion with Columbia University professor Casey Blake at the UVa Miller Center for Public Affairs (Charlottesville, Virginia) in March 2005.

19. The three best compilations of his works are *Randolph Bourne: The Radical Will: Selected Writings, 1911–1918*, ed. Olaf Hansen (Berkeley: University of California Press, 1977), *The History of a Literary Radical*, and *War and the Intellectuals*.

20. Blake, *Beloved Community*, chapter 3, esp. 119.

21. Louis Filler, *Randolph Bourne* (Washington, DC: American Council on Public Affairs, 1943), 18.

22. In particular see Bourne's "Trans-National America," esp. on "hyphen stigma," in *The Radical Will*, 251.

23. Eric Sandeen, "Bourne Again: The Correspondence between Randolph Bourne and Elise Clews Parsons," *American Literary History* 1, no. 3 (Autumn 1989): 493.

24. Christine Stansell, *American Moderns: Bohemian New York and the Creation of a New Century* (New York: Metropolitan Books, 2000); Ann Douglas, *Terrible Honesty: Mongrel Manhattan in the 1920s* (New York: Noonday Press, 1996).

25. Bourne, "Trans-National America," in *War and the Intellectuals*, 122.

26. Alan Dawley, *Changing the World: American Progressives in War and Revolution* (Princeton, NJ: Princeton University Press, 2003), and Daniel Rodgers, *Atlantic Crossings: Social Politics in a Progressive Age* (Cambridge, MA: Harvard University Press, 1998).

27. Bourne to Alyse Gregory, August 25, 1914, Bourne Papers.

28. Bourne to Alyse Gregory, September 28, 1914, Bourne Papers. As a "double martyr," see A. F. Beringause, *Journal of the History of Ideas* 18, no. 4 (October 1957): 594–603.

29. Bourne wrote for a number of magazines and newspapers during this period, including the *New Republic*, *Atlantic Monthly*, *Masses*, *Seven Arts*, and *Dial*, among others.

30. John Dos Passos, writing in 1937, invoked the mythic image of Bourne as "This tiny sparrowlike man, tiny twisted bit of flesh in a black cape. . . . *War is the health of the state*." Dos Passos, "Randolph Bourne," *U.S.A.* (New York: Modern Library, 1937), 89–91.

31. Bourne to Alyse Gregory, July 14, 1915, Bourne Papers.

32. On these developments in Bourne's friendships and publishing career, I am indebted to his many able biographers; see Vitelli and Moreau in particular.

On Bourne's contentious relationship with the *New Republic*, see Paul F. Bourke, "The Status of Politics, 1909–1919: The New Republic, Randolph Bourne and Van Wyck Brooks," *Journal of American Studies* 8 (August 1974): 171–202. On the radical will, see Hansen's excellent introduction, "Affinity and Ambivalence," in *The Radical Will*, 17–62, drawing parallels to the romantic Marxism of the Frankfurt School.

33. Croly to Bourne, June 3, 1914, Bourne Papers.

34. Edward A. Stettner, *Shaping Modern Liberalism: Herbert Croly and Progressive Thought* (Lawrence: University Press of Kansas, 1993), 108–109.

35. For more on these referenced works, see Herbert Croly, *The Promise of American Life* (New York: Macmillan, 1909); Croly, *Progressive Democracy* (New York: Macmillan, 1914); Walter Lippmann, *Drift and Mastery, an Attempt to Diagnose the Current Unrest* (New York: Mitchell Kennerley, 1914); Walter Weyl. *The New Democracy: An Essay on Certain Political and Economic Tendencies in the United States* (New York: Macmillan, 1912).

36. Bourne to Alyse Gregory, September 28, 1914, Bourne Papers.

37. Bourne, "In a Schoolroom," *Radical Will*, 192.

38. Croly to Bourne, see August 27, 1914, and September 15, 1914, Bourne Papers. For the best brief overview of the history of the New Republic, see David Seideman, *The New Republic: A Voice of Modern Liberalism* (New York: Praeger Press, 1986), 19–46. Bourne later published an extended version entitled *The Gary Schools* (Boston: Houghton Mifflin Co., 1916).

39. Bobby Rogers to Mabel Dodge, November 12, 1914, quoted in Mabel Dodge Luhan, *Movers and Shakers* (New York: Harcourt, Brace, 1936), 302.

40. Woodrow Wilson, "Address of the President of the United States, Delivered at a Joint Session of the Two Houses of Congress, December 8, 1914" (Washington, DC, 1916).

41. Woodrow Wilson, *Selected Addresses and Public Papers of Woodrow Wilson* (New York: Boni and Liveright, 1918), 81.

42. "The End of American Isolation," *New Republic*, November 7, 1914, 9–10.

43. Charles Chatfield, "World War One and the Liberal Pacifist in the United States," *American Historical Review* 75, no. 7 (December 1970): 1920–1937; for debates over peace and war in the World War I period, see Merle Curti, *Peace or War*, and on the broader home-front context, David Kennedy, *Over Here: The First World War and American Society* (Oxford: Oxford University Press, 1980); for a contrast see Henry Cabot Lodge, *War Addresses, 1915–1917* (Boston: Houghton Mifflin Co., 1917), esp. "American Rights" (1915) and "National Defence" (1916).

44. Ray Stannard Baker and William E. Dodd, eds., *The Public Papers of Woodrow Wilson* (New York: Harper and Brothers, 1925–1927), vol. 3, 226; also 302–307, and vol. 4, 407–414.

45. For a brief overview see George Herring, *From Colony to Superpower: U.S. Foreign Relations since 1776* (New York: Oxford University Press, 2008), chapter 10.

46. John Milton Cooper Jr. makes this point in *The Vanity of Power: American Isolationism and the First World War, 1914–1917* (Westport, CT: Greenwood Press, 1969), see esp. 132 and 145–166.

47. Frank Trommler, "The *Lusitania* Effect: America's Mobilization against Germany in World War I," *German Studies* 32, no. 2 (2009): 241–266.

48. On the political economy of the war, see Kennedy, *Over Here*, 93–143; Cooper, *Vanity of Power*, 132–166; see also *Isolationism: Opposing Viewpoints*, ed. John C. Chalberg (San Diego, CA: Greenhaven Press, 1995), 42.

49. On framing this counterfactual point I am thankful to an OAH panel in San Jose (2005) chaired and with comments by James Kloppenberg, along with panelists Michael Rembis and Drew VandeCreek (OAH, San Jose, 2005).

50. Bourne to Alyse Gregory, July 14, 1915, Bourne Papers.

51. On how this changed over time in terms of the origins of cultural radicalism, see Edward Abrahams, *The Lyrical Left: Randolph Bourne, Alfred Stieglitz, and the Origins of Cultural Radicalism in America* (Charlottesville: University of Virginia Press, 1986); Casey Blake, "The Young Intellectuals and the Culture of Personality," *American Literary History* 1, no. 3 (Autumn 1989): 510–534.

52. Ellery Sedgwick, *The Happy Profession* (Boston: Little, Brown and Co., 1946), 223.

53. Bourne to Alyse Gregory, January 1915, Bourne Papers.

54. Quoted in Moreau, *Randolph Bourne: Legend and Reality*, 70.

55. Bourne to Elizabeth S. Sergeant, June 25, 1915, Bourne Papers.

56. Bourne to Simon Pelham Barr, December 14, 1913, Bourne Papers. Bourne mentions Angell's opinion that Columbia professor John Erskine's philosophies of education and intelligence tended toward superficiality; both Bourne and Angell contributed to *Towards an Enduring Peace* (New York: AAIC, 1916).

57. Norman Angell, *America and the New World State: A Plea for American Leadership in International Organization* (New York and London: G. P. Putnam's Sons, 1915), 41, 40.

58. Robert Tucker, *Woodrow Wilson and the Great War: Reconsidering America's Neutrality* (Charlottesville: University of Virginia Press, 2007).

59. Norman Angell, *America and the New World State*, 40.

60. Angell, *Europe's Optical Illusion* (London: Simpkin, Marshall, Hamilton, Kent & Co. Ltd., 1910).

61. Angell, *America and the New World State*, 18.

62. On Mott's wartime work, see Hopkins's extensive treatment in *John R. Mott, 1865–1955*.

63. John Mott, Speech at DePauw University, 1917. Unpublished speech, date uncertain (most likely before October 1917). Mott's notes for the speech, "At Its Close the War Will Present an Unparalleled Opportunity for Reconstruction," Mott Collection, Yale Divinity School Archives, see 19, 13.

64. Angell, *The Great Illusion* (1910; New York and London: G. P. Putnam's Sons, rev. rept. 1911).

65. Bourne, "A Moral Equivalent for Universal Military Service," *New Republic*, July 1, 1916, 217–229, reprinted in *War and the Intellectuals*, 145.

66. Bourne, "Twilight of the Idols," *Seven Arts* 2 (October 1917): 688–702; reprinted in *War and the Intellectuals*, 53.

67. "Timid Neutrality," *New Republic*, November 14, 1914, 7.

68. "'Preparedness' for What?" *New Republic*, June 26, 1915, 188; see also "Are We Militarists?" *New Republic*, March 20, 1915, 166–167; also, Crystal Eastman to *New Republic*, July 24, 1915, 313; Robert Herrick to *New Republic*, December 19, 1914, 22.

69. *King's Business*, 1917, cited in George Marsden, *Fundamentalism and American Culture: The Shaping of Twentieth Century Evangelism, 1870–1925* (New York: Oxford University Press, 1980), 149–151. See also Paul Boyer, *When Time Shall Be No More: Prophecy Belief in Modern American Culture* (Cambridge, MA: Harvard University Press, 1992), 96–100.

70. "Pro-German," *New Republic*, December 4, 1915, 108.

71. William Jennings Bryan to Woodrow Wilson, August 10, 1914, in *Robert Lansing Papers, 1914–1920* (Washington, DC, 1939), vol. 1, 131–132.

72. Michael Kazin, *A Godly Hero: The Life of William Jennings Bryan* (New York: Alfred A. Knopf, 2006), chapter 10, "Moralist at State."

73. Here I draw primarily upon Frank Ninkovich, *The Wilsonian Century* (Chicago: University of Chicago Press, 1999), Merle Curti, *Bryan and World Peace* (Northampton, MA: Smith College Studies in History, 1931), and Robert Lansing, *War Memoirs* (Indianapolis: Bobbs-Merrill Co., 1935).

74. David Traxel, *Crusader Nation: The United States in Peace and the Great War, 1898–1920* (New York: Alfred A. Knopf, 2006), chapter 11, "Henry Ford and the Peace Ship."

75. Bourne, "The Tradition of War," in *Towards an Enduring Peace*, 12–13, 9.

76. Bourne, *Towards an Enduring Peace*, xv.

77. Bourne, "Trans-National America," in *War and the Intellectuals*, esp. 117–123.

78. Bourne to Alyse Gregory, August 30, 1915, Bourne Papers.

79. Ibid.

80. Du Bois, "The Perpetual Dilemma," *Crisis* 13 (April 1917): 270–272, reprinted in *Selections from "The Crisis,"* ed. Herbert Aptheker (Amherst: University of Massachusetts Press, 1973), vol. 1, 134–135.

81. Ibid. See also "Officers," *Crisis* 14 (June 1917), reprinted in Aptheker, *Selections from "The Crisis,"* vol. 1, 137; "The Perpetual Dilemma," 134–135; and "Officers," *Crisis* 14 (June 1917), reprinted in Aptheker, *Selections from "The Crisis,"* vol. 1, 137. Du Bois's famous prowar essay titled "Close Ranks" appeared in the *Crisis* in July 1918, calling out to "forget our special grievances" in wartime; in *Selections from "The Crisis,"* 227. One of the best scholarly articles on the subject is Mark Ellis, " 'Closing Ranks' and 'Seeking Honors': W. E. B. Du Bois in World War I," *Journal of American History* 79, no. 1 (June 1992): 96–124. For more on Du Bois's developing pragmatic evaluation and view of patriotism, in the context of World War I, see Jonathan Hansen, *The Lost Promise of Patriotism: Debating American Identity, 1890–1920* (Chicago: University of Chicago Press, 2003).

82. Bourne's transnationalism fueled the antiwar pluralism and racial egalitarianism most prominently displayed in "Trans-National America." See also Jervis Anderson, A. *Philip Randolph: A Biographical Portrait* (Berkeley: University of California Press, rept. 1986).

4. The Powerful Mediating Neutral

1. Bourne, "Trans-National America," *Atlantic Monthly* 18 (July 1916): 86–97, reprinted in *War and the Intellectuals: Essays by Randolph S. Bourne, 1915–1919*, ed. Carl Resek (New York: Harper and Row, 1964), 107–123, quote on 121.
2. Ibid., 121.
3. Ibid., 122.
4. Ibid.
5. Ibid., 121.
6. George Creel, *The War, The World, and Wilson* (New York: Harper and Brothers, 1920), 39–41 on traditions; see also the conclusion of George Creel, *The War, the World, and Wilson* (New York: Harper and Brothers, 1920), esp. 359.
7. David Hollinger singles out Bourne as the first articulator of the concept of a cosmopolitan pluralism as part of an envisioned movement toward ethnic diversity and concomitant empowerment of the American liberal intelligentsia. See David Hollinger, "Ethnic Diversity, Cosmopolitanism, and the Emergence of the American Liberal Intelligentsia," in *In the American Province: Studies in the History and Historiography of Ideas*, ed. David Hollinger (Bloomington: Indiana University Press, 1985), 56–73.
8. Randolph Bourne, "Americanism," a review of Frances Kellor's *Straight America*, in *New Republic*, September 23, 1916, 197. On Bourne's thought about Americanism more broadly, see the introduction by Christopher Lasch in *Randolph Bourne: The Radical Will. Selected Writings, 1911–1918*, ed. Olaf Hansen (Berkeley: University of California Press, 1977); on other hyperpatriotic organizations, see the American Legion in Christopher Courtney Nehls,

"'A Grand and Glorious Feeling': The American Legion and American Nationalism between the World Wars" (PhD diss., University of Virginia, 2007).

9. Bourne, "Americanism," 197. For more on the changing Americanism over time, see *Americanism: New Perspectives on the History of an Ideal*, ed. Michael Kazin and Joseph A. McMartin (Chapel Hill: University of North Carolina Press, 2006).

10. Congressional Record, 64th Cong., 2nd sess., Senate Document No. 685, January 22, 1917, "A League for Peace."

11. His thought shifted significantly from July 1915 through July 1916. Useful comparisons are "The American Use for German Ideals," *New Republic*, July 1915; "A Moral Equivalent for Universal Military Service," *New Republic*, July 1916; and "Trans-National America," *Atlantic Monthly*, July 1916.

12. The Union was first organized in 1915 as the "anti-militarism committee," American Union against Militarism Records, 1915–1922, Swarthmore College Peace Collection.

13. "Do the American People Want War?" Full-page advertisement, display ad #16, *Chicago Daily Tribune*, March 5, 1917, p. 18.

14. This interpretive dissonance was particularly true among global colonials and nationalists around the world seeking to cast off the shackles of empire, as Erez Manela has documented in *The Wilsonian Moment: Self-Determination and the International Origins of Anticolonial Nationalism* (Oxford: Oxford University Press, 2007).

15. W. E. B. Du Bois, "Close Ranks," *Crisis*, July 1918. Also quoted and discussed in David Levering Lewis, *W. E. B. Du Bois: Biography of a Race, 1868–1919* (New York: Owl Books, 1994), 553–554.

16. Bourne, "The Jew and Trans-National America," *Menarah Journal* 2 (December 1916): 277–284.

17. For a concise overview, see Sacvan Bercovitch, "New England's Errand Reappraised," in *New Directions in American Intellectual History*, ed. John Higham and Paul Conkin (Baltimore: Johns Hopkins University Press, 1979), 85–104. Also Sacvan Bercovitch, *The American Jeremiad* (Madison: University of Wisconsin Press, 1980). Other Bourne scholars have observed this connection, such as Casey Blake, who cast it in comparative terms for Bourne and Van Wyck Brooks, *Beloved Community: The Cultural Criticism of Randolph Bourne, Van Wyck Brooks, Waldo Frank, and Lewis Mumford* (Chapel Hill: University of North Carolina Press, 1990), 113–119.

18. Randolph Bourne, "Below the Battle," *Seven Arts*, July 1917, 270–277, reprinted in *War and the Intellectuals*, 15–21.

19. Randolph Bourne, "The State," unfinished and unpublished manuscript in Bourne Papers; the best published version appears in *War and the Intellectuals*, 65–104.

20. Randolph Bourne, "The War and the Intellectuals," *Seven Arts*, June 1917: 133–146, in *War and the Intellectuals*, 13.

21. Ibid., 14.

22. Horace Kallen, "Democracy vs. the Melting Pot," *Nation*, February 25, 1915, 218–220.

23. Jane Addams, *The Second Twenty Years at Hull House: A Growing World Consciousness* (New York: Macmillan, 1930), 115; see also Balch's address on February 22, 1916, in *Beyond Nationalism: The Social Thought of Emily Greene Balch*, ed. Mercedes Randall (New York: Twayne Publishers, 1972), 39.

24. David Hollinger, "Ethnic Diversity, Cosmopolitanism, and the Emergence of the American Liberal Intelligentsia," in *In the American Province*, 57.

25. Hollinger, "Ethnic Diversity," 57. See also Hollinger's "Democracy and the Melting Pot Reconsidered," in the same volume; John Higham, "Ethnic Pluralism in Modern American Thought," in *Send These to Me: Jews and Other Immigrants in Urban America* (New York: Atheneum, 1975), 197–230; and Higham's "Multiculturalism and Universalism: A History and Critique," *American Quarterly* 45, no. 2 (June 1993): 195–219, as well as the work of Olivier Zunz on American pluralism and Rivka Lissak on pluralism and the progressives.

26. Bourne, "Trans-National America," in *War and the Intellectuals*, 114.

27. On cosmopolitan ideals and the role of ethnic diversity in the developing thought of the liberal intelligentsia, see Hollinger, "Ethnic Diversity," 56–73. On Kallen and pluralism, Werner Sollors, "A Critique of Pure Pluralism," in *Reconstructing American Literary History*, ed. Sacvan Bercovitch (Cambridge, MA: Harvard University Press, 1986), 250–279.

28. Bourne, "Doubts about Enforcing Peace," 6 pages, quotation on 1. The essay is undated, but judging from the references it was probably drafted in mid- to late 1916, Bourne Papers.

29. Ibid.

30. For an analysis suggesting that in fact Dewey may have been right in his assessment of American entry into World War I , see James Livingston, "War and the Intellectuals: Bourne, Dewey, and the Fate of Pragmatism," *Journal of the Gilded Age and Progressive Era* 2, no. 4 (October 2003); also, Livingston, *Pragmatism and the Political Economy of Cultural Revolution, 1850–1940* (Chapel Hill: University of North Carolina Press, 1994), chapter 9, "The Romantic Acquiescence: Pragmatism and the Young Intellectuals."

31. Bourne, "The Collapse of American Strategy," *Seven Arts*, August 1917, 409–424, reprinted in *War and the Intellectuals*, 22–35, quote on 22.

32. Bourne, "The Collapse of American Strategy," 34.

33. Ibid.

34. Ibid., 35.

35. Bourne to Benjamin Everett, November 26, 1917, Bourne Papers.

36. Woodrow Wilson, April 2, 1917, address to Congress seeking formal war declaration. *President Wilson's Great Speeches and Other History Making Documents* (Chicago: Stanton & Van Vliet Co., 1917), 11–22.

37. Congressional Record, 65th Cong., 1st sess., April 4, 1917, 252–253.

38. Ibid., 209.

39. Ibid., 210, 212–224, 228.

40. For more on how this camp fit into Bryan's broader views, see Michael Kazin, *A Godly Hero: The Life of William Jennings Bryan* (New York: Knopf, 2006).

41. See also Gary Gerstle, *American Crucible: Race and Nation in the Twentieth Century* (Princeton, NJ: Princeton University Press, 2001), 14–94; for more on the CPI and censorship, see Stephen Vaughan, *Holding Fast the Inner Lines: Democracy, Nationalism, and the Committee on Public Information* (Chapel Hill: University of North Carolina Press, 1980).

42. Bourne, "International Dubieties," *Dial*, May 3, 1917, 387–388.

43. Ibid.; quote on 388.

44. Bourne, "The Collapse of American Strategy," in *War and the Intellectuals*, 68–69.

45. *New York Times*, February 2, 1917.

46. See (Woman's Peace Party) New York Branch Records (1915–1920) and "Historical Introduction" by Eleanor Barr, Woman's Peace Party Papers, Swarthmore College Peace Collection.

47. Quoted by Randolph Bourne in "A Letter to the Editor of the *New Republic*," October 1917, in *History of a Literary Radical and Other Papers* (New York: S. A. Russell, 1956), 185–186.

48. Emily Balch, reminiscences, in "Working for Peace," *Bryn Mawr Alumnae Bulletin*, May 1933, 13–14, in Balch scrapbook files (1933), Balch Papers, Swarthmore College Peace Collection Archives. Henry Dana's papers in the Swarthmore Peace Collection contain a wealth of information. On academics and wartime dissent, see David Kennedy, *Over Here: The First World War and American Society* (Oxford: Oxford University Press, 1980), and William Summerscales, *Affirmation and Dissent: Columbia's Response to the Crisis of World War I* (New York: Teachers College Press, 1972).

49. Emily Balch to Jane Addams, June 1917 [exact day unclear], Balch Papers. The reference is to the Arabic term "djihn" (or "jinni," "djinn"). Balch is using the term here colloquially, meaning "to let the genie out of the bottle."

50. Mrs. Alice Balch Stone to Emily Balch, April 20, 1917, Balch Papers.

51. Jane Addams, *Peace and Bread in Time of War* (New York: Macmillan, 1922), 139.

52. Bourne, "A War Diary," *Seven Arts*, September 1917, 535–547, reprinted in *The War and the Intellectuals*, 45.

53. Ibid., 42.

54. Ibid., 45.

55. For a brief overview, see George Herring, *From Colony to Superpower: U.S. Foreign Relations since 1776* (New York: Oxford University Press, 2008), 378–435.

56. Bourne, "A War Diary," 46.

57. Bourne, "Trans-National America," 121. Here we also see hints of deeper parochial and American-centric sensibility in Bourne's cosmopolitanism. See Ian Tyrell, who touches on this in "American Exceptionalism in an Age of International History," *American Historical Review* 96, no. 4 (October 1991): 1052–1053.

58. Bourne's ideas on this subject are related to contemporary issues such as calls for civic renewal and volunteerism, along with the post–9/11/2001 dialogue about American national identity, the multiculturalist movement, and the role of intellectuals and patriotism in a time of war. See Higham, "Multiculturalism and Universalism: A History and Critique."

59. Robert Westbrook, "Randolph Bourne's America," Columbia University Conference, October 11, 2004, transcript, "Panel 1: Bourne the Historical View," 4–5; PDF accessed at www.randolphbourne.columbia.edu/video_archive.html.

60. Ibid., 5. Westbrook rightly terms Bourne's argument a "pragmatist's case against intervention." For more on Dewey's wartime thought, see Alan Cywar, "John Dewey in World War I: Patriotism and International Progressivism," *American Quarterly* 21, no. 3 (Autumn 1969): 578–594; see also Christopher Lasch, *The New Radicalism in America, 1889–1963* (New York: Alfred A. Knopf, 1965), 181–225, on the *New Republic* and liberal thought regarding the war.

61. Cywar, "John Dewey in World War I"; Lasch, *The New Radicalism*.

62. See John Dewey, "Conscience and Compulsion" (1917), in *John Dewey: The Middle Works*, ed. Jo Ann Boydston (Carbondale: Southern Illinois University Press, 1982), vol. 10, 264.

63. Bourne was most explicit about his critique of Dewey's philosophy and actions in the essays "The War and the Intellectuals" and "John Dewey's Philosophy."

64. Bourne, "Twilight of the Idols," in *War and the Intellectuals*, 53–54.

65. Ibid., 53, 56.

66. Robert Westbrook, *John Dewey and American Democracy* (Ithaca, NY: Cornell University Press, 1991), 197.

67. Bourne, "Collapse of American Strategy," 34.

68. For a contrasting view, see James Livingston, "War and the Intellectuals: Bourne, Dewey, and the Fate of Pragmatism," *Journal of the Gilded Age and Progressive Era* 1, no. 4 (October 2003): 431–450.

69. Westbrook, *John Dewey*, 197.

70. Bourne's "War and the Intellectuals" on "intellectual suicide," 13. On these developments in context, see C. Roland Marchand, *The American Peace Movement and Social Reform, 1898–1918* (Princeton, NJ: Princeton University Press, 1972), and Charles Chatfield, "World War I and the Liberal Pacifist in the United States," *American Historical Review* 75, no. 7 (December 1970): 1920–1937.

71. John Milton Cooper Jr., *The Vanity of Power: American Isolationism and the First World War, 1914–1917* (Westport, CT: Greenwood Press, 1969), 207–208. Pinchot and letter to Bourne, quoted on 207.

72. Ibid., 207–208.

73. Bourne on Nietzsche's "will to power" concept, see Bourne's "The Puritan's Will to Power," *Seven Arts*, April 1917, 631–637; on related ideas of Puritan and intellectual motivations, examine "H. L. Mencken," *New Republic*, November 24, 1917, 102–103. See also "Twilight of the Idols," *Seven Arts*, October 1917, 688–702.

74. I am indebted to Christopher Lasch for laying out the longer history and context of this "stance" as an intellectual social type in *The New Radicalism*. I am thinking here most about Bourne, "War and the Intellectuals" and "A War Diary."

75. For an overview on Bourne's belief that he had been marginalized, see James R. Vitelli, *Randolph Bourne* (Boston: Twayne Publishers, 1981), chapter 1, "The Forming of the Myth," 17–65, and chapter 6, "The Young Radical and War," 127–146.

76. On Herbert Croly and Walter Weyl, see Christopher Lasch, *The True and Only Heaven: Progress and Its Critics* (New York: W. W. Norton, 1991), 340–344.

77. Eldon Eisenach makes a useful distinction as to the definition and function of "para-state institutions" during the Progressive Era, see *The Lost Promise of Progressivism* (Lawrence: University Press of Kansas, 1994).

78. Bourne on the "herd" instinct; see his essay on "Below the Battle," in *War and the Intellectuals*, esp. 16–17.

79. Bourne held these beliefs at a unique moment when the leading African American intellectual of the period, Du Bois, had been persuaded on pragmatic and political grounds not to hold fast to such a belief. On the larger development of American pluralism, see Olivier Zunz in *Why the American Century?* (Chicago: University of Chicago Press, 1998), describing the transition from voluntarism to pluralism, 115–136; also Zunz, "Genèse du pluralisme américain" (The Genesis of American Pluralism), *Annales ESC* (Paris), no. 42 (March–April 1987): 429–444.

80. Jonathan Hansen, *The Lost Promise of Patriotism: Debating American Identity, 1890–1920* (Chicago: University of Chicago Press, 2003), 111.

81. In various forms this thought appears in most of the major biographical accounts of Bourne's life and work. See Blake, Clayton, Moreau, Vaughan, and Vitelli. Eric Sandeen, who edited Bourne's letters for publication, also makes this point.

82. Bourne, "The War and the Intellectuals," *Seven Arts*, July 1917, 270–277.

83. Walter Weyl, *The End of the War* (New York: Macmillan, 1918).

84. See Charles Forcey, *The Crossroads of Liberalism: Croly, Weyl, Lippmann, and the Progressive Era, 1900–1925* (New York: Oxford University Press, 1961), 273–316. On the role of the magazine in the culture of "smaller" political publications, see George A. Test, "The 'New Republic' as Little Magazine," *American Quarterly* 13, no. 2, Part 1 (Summer 1961),): 189–192. On Bourne's "Trans-National America" and Van Wyck Brooks's *America's Coming of Age*, see Blake, *Beloved Community*, 113, 119. Also, Van Wyck Brooks, *America's Coming-of-Age* (New York: B. W. Huebsch Inc., 1915).

85. Bourne, "The War and the Intellectuals," 14.

86. Bourne, "Twilight of the Idols," 64.

87. Bourne, "A War Diary," 47.

88. Bourne to Van Wyck Brooks, March 27, 1918, Bourne Papers.

89. I am drawing primarily upon twelve principal sources spanning the period 1916–1918. They are "Trans-National America" (1916); "The Jew and Trans-National America" (1916); "The Price of Radicalism," *New Republic*, March 11, 1916, 161; Bourne's edited volume, *Towards an Enduring Peace* (New York: AAIC, 1916); "What Is Exploitation?" *New Republic*, November 4, 1916, 12–14; "The Puritan's Will to Power," *Seven Arts*, April 1917, 631–637; "Below the Battle," *Seven Arts*, July 1917, 270–277; "The Collapse of American Strategy" (1917); "Twilight of the Idols" (1917); "A War Diary" (1917); "The War and the Intellectuals" (1917); "The State" (aka War Is the Health of the State), unpublished paper, Bourne Papers; "Traps for the Unwary," *Dial*, March 28, 1918, 277–279.

90. Bourne, "Trans-National America," 123.

91. Ibid.

92. Ibid.

93. Eric Sandeen, ed., *The Letters of Randolph Bourne: A Comprehensive Edition* (Troy, NY: Whitston Publishing Co., 1981), 357–358.

94. Ibid.

95. Bourne to Van Wyck Brooks, November, n.d., 1918, Bourne Papers.

96. Bourne to Sara Bourne, November 21, 1918, filed under "letters to his mother," Bourne Papers.

97. Bourne, "Review of a League to Enforce Peace by R. Goldsmith and American World Politics by W. Weyl," *Dial*, May 3, 1917, 388.

98. Bourne, "A War Diary," 43.

99. An excellent place to start on Bourne's modern legacy is the text of the symposium at Columbia University on *Randolph Bourne's America*, October 11, 2004. Many of the talks that day by Robert Westbrook, Jonathan Hansen, Chris Lehmann, Christopher Phelps, and others addressed the contemporary relevance and long history of Bourne's thought and the activities of those opposing American intervention abroad. For a text version of most of the speeches, see www.dkv.columbia.edu/w0410/. As cited before, most helpful are the minutes for Panel 1, "Bourne: The Historical View."

100. Merle Curti, *Peace or War: The American Struggle, 1636–1936* (1936; New York: W. W. Norton, rept. 1959), 230.

101. I also am thinking of Leon Wieseltier, Paul Berman, Todd Gitlin, George Packer, Sean Wilentz, and Cornel West, among the diverse camp of contemporary liberal critics of war in America who have invoked elements of a Bournian cosmopolitan isolationist antiwar logic. Tracking this intellectual genealogy is a worthy project beyond the scope of this book, but for a representative sample, see Michael Ignatieff, "A Mess of Intervention: Peacekeeping, Pre-Emption, Liberation, Revenge. When Should We Send in the Troops?" *New York Times Magazine*, September 7, 2003, and *The Lesser Evil: Political Ethics in an Age of Terror* (Princeton, NJ: Princeton University Press, 2004); Michael Walzer, *Just and Unjust Wars: A Moral Argument with Historical Illustrations*, 3rd ed. (New York: Basic Books, 2000); Walzer, *Arguing about War* (New Haven, CT: Yale University Press, 2004); Lasch on Bourne in *The New Radicalism*, 69–103; Chomsky recently, *Failed States: The Abuse of Power and the Assault on Democracy* (New York: Macmillan, 2006), *Hegemony and Survival: America's Quest for Global Dominance* (New York: Metropolitan Books, rept. 2004); this also goes back to his opposition to Vietnam-era interventionism; see Chomsky's *American Power and the New Mandarins* (New York: Penguin Books, 1969) with his provocative essay "The Responsibility of Intellectuals." Members of the New Left ridiculed the purported "pragmatic" rationale of those intellectuals originally supporting the war in Vietnam, while the Old Left seems to have been the first to have appropriated the Bourne legacy, an excellent example of which appears in the work of Alfred Kazin (see his memoir, *Starting Out in the Thirties* [Ithaca, NY: Cornell University Press, 1989], 136–137).

102. Randolph Bourne Institute mission statement, located at http://randolph-bourne.org (accessed September 12, 2005). Robert Westbrook's superb presentation, revised in light of recent events regarding the ongoing American presence in Iraq, appeared as "Bourne over Baghdad," *Raritan* 27 (Summer 2007): 104–117. On the Bournian legacy, see also Bruce Clayton, *Forgotten Prophet: The Life of Randolph Bourne* (Baton Rouge: Louisiana State University Press, 1984), 260–266. On understanding his legacy, I am particularly

indebted to conversations with Casey Blake, as well as his magisterial *Beloved Community.*

103. On the "flattening" effects of globalization and on the nature of human interaction, Thomas Friedman, *The World Is Flat: A Brief History of the Twentieth Century,* rev. ed. (New York: Farrar, Straus and Giroux, 2006).

5. Voices of the People

1. Carlo Tresca to Eugene Debs, ca. September 18, 1916, from Duluth, Minnesota, Debs Papers, Special Collections, Indiana State University.

2. For more on socialism, see David Shannon, *The Socialist Party of America* (Chicago: Quadrangle Books, 1967), and James Weinstein, *The Decline of Socialism in America, 1912–1925* (New York: Monthly Review Press, 1967).

3. This overview of Debs's ideological transition has been compiled from his correspondence, speeches, and published work. For a representative sample see "Industrial Unionism," *International Socialist Review,* December 1909; "Sound Socialist Tactics," *International Socialist Review,* February 1912; "A Plea for Solidarity," *International Socialist Review,* March 1914; "The Prospect for Peace," *American Socialist,* February 19, 1916; "Ruling Class Robbers," *American Socialist,* July 1, 1916; "The Class War and Its Outlook," *International Socialist Review,* September 1916; "Tom Mooney Sentenced to Death," *International Socialist Review,* April 1917; "The I.W.W. Bogey," *International Socialist Review,* February 1918; "John Swinton: Radical Editor and Leader," *Pearson's Magazine,* February 1918; his famous Canton speech (1918); and "The Day of the People," *Class Struggle,* February 1919. After his release from prison, see also "Serving the Labor Movement," *New York Call Magazine,* October 1, 1922, and his book *Walls and Bars* (Chicago: Charles H. Kerr & Co., 1973).

4. Recent scholarship has begun to reverse this position by revealing antiwar dissent. On the cultural tensions about race, class, and organizing in the New South vis-à-vis issues of national reunion and the role of elite white Southern political and social leaders, see Edward L. Ayers, *The Promise of the New South: Life after Reconstruction* (New York: Oxford University Press, 1992), see vi–x, 249–282; on sectional reconciliation and war, chapter 12, "Reunion and Reaction." For some of the best new studies of the South and foreign policy, see Joseph A. Fry, *Dixie Looks Abroad: The South and U.S. Foreign Relations, 1789–1973* (Baton Rouge: Louisiana State University Press, 2002), esp. 159–164; Tennant S. McWilliams, *The New South Faces the World: Foreign Affairs and the Southern Sense of Self, 1877–1950* (Baton Rouge: Louisiana State University Press, 1988); and Anthony Gaughan, "Woodrow Wilson and the Rise of Militant Interventionism in the South," *Journal of Southern History* 65, no. 4 (November 1999): 771–808. The new literature on the prevalence of Southern

draft resistance includes *Journal of American History* 87, no. 4 (March 2001), in which Jeanette Keith, Jacqueline Jones, and K. Walter Hickel discuss draft resistance, federal policy, and aid during this period. In particular, see Keith, "The Politics of Southern Draft Resistance, 1917–1918: Class, Race, and Conscription in the Rural South," 1335–1361. K. Walter Hickel, " 'Justice and the Highest Kind of Equality Require Discrimination': Citizenship, Dependency, and Conscription in the South, 1917–1919," *Journal of Southern History*, 66, no. 4 (November 2000): 749–780. Keith's pioneering treatment of draft resistance in the South deeply informs my work, and I draw heavily from it here. See Keith, *Rich Man's War, Poor Man's Fight: Race, Class, and Power in the Rural South during the First World War* (Chapel Hill: University of North Carolina Press, 2004).

5. "Antiwar" is broadly defined here as opposition to Wilson's policies leading up to and after the war's resolution on April 6, 1917. Debs's best biographers have noted this transition; see Nick Salvatore, *Eugene V. Debs: Citizen and Socialist* (Urbana: University of Illinois Press, 1982), and Ray Ginger, *The Bending Cross* (New Brunswick, NJ: Rutgers University Press, 1949); also Marguerite Young, *Harp Song for a Radical: The Life and Times of Eugene Victor Debs* (New York: Knopf, 1999), Bernard Brommel, *Eugene V. Debs: Spokesman for Labor and Socialism* (Chicago: University of Chicago Press, 1978), and McAllister Coleman, *Eugene V. Debs: A Man Unafraid* (New York: Greenberg, 1930). Much of this historiography overlooks Debs's thinking about the South. The indices and selection of letters for the three-volume *Letters of Eugene Debs*, ed. J. Robert Constantine (Urbana: University of Illinois Press, 1990), bears this out.

6. On Jefferson and the democratic language of statehood see Peter Onuf, *Jefferson's Empire: The Language of American Statehood* (Charlottesville: University of Virginia Press, 2000), chapter 1.

7. Nick Salvatore and Ray Ginger observed this subtle linguistic turn. Arthur Schlesinger Jr. also noted this discursive change in his introduction to *The Writings and Speeches of Eugene V. Debs*, ed. Joseph M. Bernstein (New York: Hermitage, 1948).

8. Nigel Sellers, "With Folded Arms? Or with Squirrel Guns? The IWW and the Green Corn Rebellion," *Chronicles of Oklahoma* 77 (Summer 1999): 150–169; see also Garin Burbank, *When Farmers Voted Red: The Gospel of Socialism in the Oklahoma Countryside, 1910–1924* (Westport, CT: Greenwood Press, 1976).

9. Debs, "Sweeping the South," *Rebel*, July 6, 1912, front page, clippings file, Debs Papers.

10. Ibid. A superb brief study of Debsian socialism is Stephen Burwood, "Debsian Socialism through a Transnational Lens," *Journal of the Gilded Age and Progressive Era* (July 2003): 253–282; see also Shannon, *The Socialist Party*, 27. On race, ethnicity, land, and the Socialist Party, see Sally Miller, "For White

Men Only: The Socialist Party of America and Issues of Gender, Ethnicity, and Race," *Journal of the Gilded Age and Progressive Era* 2, no. 3 (July 2003), and other essays in that issue, "New Perspectives on Socialism"; Miller, "The Socialist Party and the Negro, 1901–20," *Journal of Negro History* 56, no. 3 (July 1971): 220–229; Anthony Esposito, *The Ideology of the Socialist Party of America, 1901–1917* (New York: Garland, 1997).

11. On socialism leading up to and during World War I, see David A. Shannon, "The Socialist Party before the First World War: An Analysis," *Mississippi Valley Historical Review* 38, no. 2 (September 1951): 279–288; James Weinstein, "Anti-War Sentiment and the Socialist Party, 1917–1918," *Political Science Quarterly* 74, no. 2 (June 1959): 215–239. Another useful account is provided by Ira Kipnis, *The American Socialist Movement, 1897–1912* (Westport, CT: Greenwood Press, 1968).

12. Debs, "Sweeping the South," Debs Papers.

13. Ibid.; also, Janis P. Stout, "'Something of a Reputation as a Radical': Katherine Anne Porter's Shifting Politics," *South Central Review* 10, no. 1 (Spring 1993): 49–66; Arthur Schlesinger Jr., introduction to *The Writings and Speeches of Eugene V. Debs*, x; see Jim Bissett, *Agrarian Socialism in America: Marx, Jefferson, and Jesus in the American Countryside* (Norman: University of Oklahoma Press, 1999). See Coleman, *Eugene V. Debs*, who also noted that estimates for circulation are difficult to discern precisely. Coleman on *Appeal* readership, 271. Other estimates are in the same range. Stephen Burwood states that as of 1913 the national circulation figures were as follows: *Appeal to Reason*, 761,747; *National Rip-Saw*, 150,000; the *Rebel*, 23,750; see Burwood, "Debsian Socialism," note 26.

14. Burwood, "Debsian Socialism," 279. Ira Kipnis termed this a "consolidation" stage for the Social Democratic Party in 1900; Kipnis, *The American Socialist Movement, 1897–1912*, 79.

15. Debs, "Revolutionary Encampments," *National Rip-Saw*, September 1914, 12, Debs Papers.

16. Ibid.

17. Here the South is defined as composed only of the original eleven Confederate states.

18. Definitive evidence for this lies with election results for 1912 and 1920, which demonstrate the remarkable SPA poll pattern. On the appeal of democratic socialism, see Robert Fitrakis, *The Idea of Democratic Socialism in America and the Decline of the Socialist Party* (New York: Garland Publishers, 1993). On Debs and the genesis of American democratic socialism, Fitrakis, *The Idea of Democratic Socialism*, 37–72; democratic socialism during World War I, 105–132. See W. E. Farmer, president of the Texas Socialist Party, in the *Social Democratic Herald* (Texas), June 11, 1899. Also, see Donald T. Critchlow, ed.,

Socialism in the Heartland: The Midwestern Experience, 1900–1925 (Notre Dame, IN: Notre Dame University Press, 1986).

19. Debs to an unidentified "Comrad," undated correspondence files (most likely 1913–1916), Debs Papers. On the language of populism and opponents of World War I, Michael Kazin, *The Populist Persuasion: An American History* (Ithaca, NY: Cornell University Press, 1995), 69–72.

20. James R. Green, *Grass-Roots Socialism: Radical Movements in the Southwest, 1895–1943* (Baton Rouge: Louisiana State University Press, 1978), xi.

21. Debs, "Sweeping the South," Debs Papers.

22. Ibid.

23. Howard H. Quint, "Julius A. Wayland, Pioneer Socialist Propagandist," *Mississippi Valley Historical Review* 35, no. 4 (March 1949): 585–606; see also A. M. Simmons, "J. A. Wayland, Propagandist," *Metropolitan Magazine* (New York), January 1913; for more on Wayland, see Elliott Shore, *Talkin' Socialism: J. A. Wayland and the Role of the Press in American Radicalism, 1890–1912* (Lawrence: University Press of Kansas, 1988).

24. For more on the rustic tradition of Louisiana socialists, see Grady McWhitney, "Louisiana Socialists in the Early Twentieth Century: A Study of Rustic Radicalism," *Journal of Southern History* 20, no. 3 (August 1954): 315–336; see also David Roediger, *Covington Hall's Labor Struggles in the Deep South* (Chicago: University of Chicago Press, 1999), and Roediger's *The Wages of Whiteness: Race and the Making of the American Working Class* (London and New York: Verso Press, 1991). On Tennessee, for example, see Jeanette Keith, *Country People in the New South: Tennessee's Upper Cumberland Country* (Chapel Hill: University of North Carolina Press, 1995).

25. Debs, "A Plea for Solidarity," *International Socialist Review*, March 1914.

26. Ibid.

27. "Who's Who at the *Appeal*," *Appeal to Reason*, 1914; summary minutes of SPA NEC and delegates in 1914, Socialist Party of America Papers, 1897–1976, Duke University Archives.

28. Debs, "A Plea for Solidarity."

29. *National Rip-Saw*, July 1914, 9; see also Debs, "Revolutionary Encampments," *National Rip-Saw*, September 1914, 12.

30. Debs summarized this in an article, "On the Barricades," *Rebellion Magazine* (New Orleans), December 1915, 37, from clippings and articles section for 1915, Debs Papers. On health, Eugene Debs to Max Warren, May 18, 1915, Debs Papers. See also Theodore Debs's letters on Eugene's poor health at the time, esp. June 1915.

31. Debs, "The Prospect for Peace," *American Socialist*, February 19, 1916; Debs, "Ruling Class Robbers," *American Socialist*, July 1, 1916, Debs Papers.

32. See Merle Curti on this in more detail, *Peace or War: The American Struggle, 1636–1936* (1936; New York: W. W. Norton, rept. 1959), 238–261; for additional detail see Alan Dawley, *Changing the World: American Progressives in War and Revolution* (Princeton, NJ: Princeton University Press, 2003), and Robert Johnson, *The Peace Progressives and American Foreign Relations* (Cambridge, MA: Harvard University Press, 1995).

33. Richard Franklin Pettigrew to Eugene Debs, August 24, 1916, Debs Papers.

34. Ibid.

35. Debs to Adolph Germer, April 1917, Debs Papers.

36. *Dayton* (Ohio) *News*, August 18, 1917.

37. Eugene Debs to Daniel Hoan, August 11, 1916, Debs Papers.

38. Daniel Hoan to Eugene Debs, August 15, 1916, Debs Papers. For the prowar nationalist counterpoint to Hoan's and Debs's argument of that year, see Theodore Roosevelt, *National Strength and International Duty* (Princeton, NJ: Princeton University Press, 1917).

39. Debs to Daniel Hoan, August 17, 1916, Debs Papers.

40. Ibid. This amounts to a shared critique of what they deemed America's nationalist oligopoly.

41. For example, Debs's "The Class War and Its Outlook," *International Socialist Review* (September 1916) was widely reprinted and distributed.

42. Ibid.; other quotations here from "Canton, Ohio Speech" and "Day of the People," in *Writings and Speeches of Debs*, 417, 441. For more on his activities at this time, see Salvatore, *Eugene V. Debs*, chapter 9.

43. C. Vann Woodward, *Origins of the New South, 1877–1913* (Baton Rouge: Louisiana State University Press, 1951), 75–106.

44. All of the quotes in this paragraph come from the same letter, Debs to an unidentified "Comrad," undated correspondence files (most likely 1913–1916), Debs Papers.

45. H. C. Peterson and Gilbert Fite, *Opponents of War, 1917–1918* (Madison: University of Wisconsin Press, 1957), 30–42.

46. *Literary Digest* (New York), November 14, 1914, 939, 974–978.

47. Quoted in Coleman, *Eugene V. Debs*, 268–269.

48. Debs to Editors, *New York Sun*, November 29, 1915, 1, 2m, Debs Papers.

49. From "The President's Plan for World Peace" (February 1, 1917), in Henry Cabot Lodge, *War Addresses, 1915–1917* (Boston: Houghton Mifflin Co., 1917), 273.

50. Drawn from foreign policy scrapbooks for 1914, Lodge Papers.

51. Roosevelt to Lodge, December 8, 1914. *Roosevelt-Lodge Correspondence*, vol. 2, 449.

52. Lodge to Roosevelt, January 15, 1915. *Roosevelt-Lodge Correspondence*, vol. 2, 451–452.

53. Ibid.

54. Drawn from foreign policy scrapbooks for 1915, Lodge Papers.

55. Lodge, "Address on Flag Day," Lynn Common, Lynn, Massachusetts, 1915, scrapbooks on foreign policy, Lodge Papers; also in full text on microfilm reel 179, Lodge Papers.

56. John Sharp Williams to Woodrow Wilson, June 29, 1915. Quoted in Arthur Link, "The Cotton Crisis, the South, and Anglo-American Diplomacy, 1914–1915," in *Studies in Southern History*, ed. J. Carlyle Sitterson (Chapel Hill: University of North Carolina Press, 1957), 135. For more on these connections, see Alexander DeConde, "The South and Isolation," *Journal of Southern History* 24, no. 3 (August 1958): 337–338.

57. Richard Abrams, "Woodrow Wilson and the Southern Congressmen, 1913–1916," *Journal of Southern History* 22, no. 4 (November 1956): 432. Quoted from Congressional Record, 63rd Cong., 2nd sess., 44, 16204.

58. Three of the most influential of those pushing for the initial farm subsidy bill were Heflin, Vardaman, and Asbury F. Lever of South Carolina. Abrams, "Woodrow Wilson and the Southern Congressmen, 1913–1916," 432–433.

59. DeConde, "The South and Isolation," 336n–337n. DeConde quoted from Claude Kitchin to Reverend C. H. Nash, February 29, 1916. Claude Kitchin Papers, Chapel Hill, University of North Carolina.

60. *The Writings and Speeches of Eugene V. Debs*, 203.

61. Debs, "The Class War and Its Outlook," *International Socialist Review*, September 1916; see also the *National Rip-Saw* and the *Appeal to Reason*, October–December 1916.

62. Ibid.

63. Dewey Grantham Jr., "Southern Congressional Leaders and the New Freedom," *Journal of Southern History* 13, no. 4 (November 1947): 456.

64. George Tindall, *Emergence of the New South: 1913–1945* (Baton Rouge: Louisiana State University Press, 1967), 46.

65. Debs to Frank O'Hare letter, quoted in Ginger, *Bending Cross*, 332–333; Salvatore, *Eugene V. Debs*, 280–281.

66. Though George Tindall emphasized political accommodation and the abandonment of states' rights issues in war negotiation by Southern politicians in his *Emergence of the New South*, one can persuasively turn his argument on its head to reveal an astounding level of dissent.

67. Southerners voting against the war resolution in April 1917 were Senator James Vardaman (Mississippi) and Representatives Claude Kitchin (North Carolina), A. Jeff McLemore (Texas), Edward Almon (Alabama), John Burnett (Alabama), and Frederick Dominick (South Carolina). Dominick was Cole Blease's law partner at the time.

68. Lodge Papers, foreign policy scrapbooks for 1917. Quote here from *Boston Evening Transcript*, April 2, 1917.

69. Ibid.

70. *New York Evening World*, April 3, 1917, Lodge Papers, foreign policy scrapbook files.

71. See Lodge Papers, foreign policy scrapbook for newspaper clippings regarding this event. Cited here in order: *Boston Evening Transcript*, April 2, 1917; *Evening Bulletin* (Philadelphia), April 3, 1917; *New York Evening World*, April 2, 1917; *Charlottesville* (Virginia) *Daily Progress*, April 4, 1917. See also *New York Times* and *Washington Post* (reporting on April 2 and 3, 1917).

72. O. B. Eaton to Claude Kitchin, April 6, 1917. Kitchin Papers, University of North Carolina Archives; Reverend A. R. Beck to Claude Kitchin, April 6, 1917. Kitchin Papers.

73. H. B. Hammeter to Claude Kitchin, April 6, 1917. Kitchin Papers.

74. Robert Block, "Southern Opinion of Woodrow Wilson's Foreign Policies, 1913–1917" (PhD diss., Duke University, 1968), 310–314.

75. Bernard J. Brommel, "The Pacifist Speechmaking of Eugene V. Debs," *Quarterly Journal of Speech* 52 (April 1966): 145, 146–160.

76. On farmers' alliances and this ideological milieu, see Ayers, *Promise of the New South*, 214–248.

77. On Kitchin, see Richard L. Watson Jr., "A Testing Time for Southern Congressional Leadership: The War Crisis of 1917–1918," *Journal of Southern History* 44, no. 1 (February 1978): 6–7; also, footnote 15 for further references on this dispute.

78. Murray E. King to Eugene Debs, July 2, 1916, Debs Papers.

79. Speech quoted in *Cincinnati Commercial Tribune*, October 15, 1914.

80. H. Q. Alexander to Claude Kitchin, April 6, 1917, Kitchin Papers.

81. Debs, *The Canton Speech* (New York: Oriole Editions, rept. 1970), see especially the language on 4–5, 10–11. Speech issued Canton, Ohio, on Sunday, June 16, 1918.

82. Quoted in Howard Zinn, *A People's History of the United States* (New York: HarperCollins, 1995), 355.

83. Ibid.

84. David Montgomery, *The Fall of the House of Labor: The Workplace, the State, and American Labor Activism, 1865–1925* (Cambridge: Cambridge University Press, 1987), 375–385.

85. "Proceeding of Emergency Convention of the Socialist Party of America. At St. Louis, 1917," quoted in Salvatore, *Eugene V. Debs*, 287.

86. "Replies of the National Committee of the SPA to the Proposed Emergency National Convention of 1917," as published in the *Socialist Party Bulletin* 1, no. 2 (March 1917): 12, SPA Papers, Duke University Archives.

87. Tindall, *Emergence of the New South*, 46.

88. Quoted in Zinn, *A People's History*, 361.

89. Charles Bush, "The Green Corn Rebellion" (Master's thesis, University of Oklahoma, 1932), 27.

90. Most of this event has been compiled from three sources: Bush, "The Green Corn Rebellion," 18–68; Peterson and Fite, *Opponents of War*, 40–41; and Nigel Sellars "With Folded Arms? Or with Squirrel Guns? The IWW and the Green Corn Rebellion," *Chronicles of Oklahoma* 77 (Summer 1999): 150–169.

91. Nigel Sellars, *Oil, Wheat and Wobblies: The Industrial Workers of the World in Oklahoma, 1905–1930* (Norman: University of Oklahoma Press, 1998), 77–92.

92. *Draftees or Volunteers*, ed. John Whiteclay Chambers II (New York: Garland Publishing, 1975), 296.

93. *New York Times*, July 9, 1917.

94. *New York Times*, July 2, 1917; see also Peterson and Fite, *Opponents of War*, 45–46; Weinstein, *The Decline of Socialism*, 141.

95. Max Eastman, *Love and Revolution: My Journey through an Epoch* (New York: Random House, 1964), 34.

96. *Minneapolis Journal* reported this on August 8, 1917. Author's best rendering, microfilm blurry via Inter-Library Loan, University of Virginia.

97. Keith, "The Politics of Southern Draft Resistance, 1917–1918," 1346. I thank Jeanette Keith for conversations that helped me conceptualize the ideological issues at work in World War I and Southern draft resistance. I am indebted to insights based on her superb research on this topic.

98. Ibid., 1345. One also might argue that had elites been drafted more readily and not been exempted due to salary considerations, then this might have led to far higher levels of national draft resistance. For more detail see National Archives, Records of the Selective Service System (World War I), 163.1 Administrative History.

99. Many Americans of German heritage found themselves mistreated by burgeoning patriotic organizations. Thus, an ethnic rationale merged with the populist critique for German Americans and Irish Americans, Joseph Edward Cuddy, *Irish-Americans and National Isolationism, 1914–1920* (New York: Arno Press, 1976), chapter 9, "Irish-Americans and the Coming of War," 129–157.

100. Keith, "The Politics of Southern Draft Resistance, 1917–1918," 1359.

101. Quoted in Zinn, *A People's History*, 355.

102. Jacqueline Jones, "Federal Power, Southern Power: A Long View, 1860–1940," *Journal of American History* 87, no. 4 (March 2001): 1392–1393.

103. Alex Arnett, *Claude Kitchin and the Wilson War Policies* (Boston: Russell and Russell, 1937), 219. *Greensboro Daily News* quoted in Arnett, 219.

104. Congressional Record, 65th Cong., 1st sess., April 5, 1917, 374.

105. Peterson and Fite, *Opponents of War*, 9.

106. National Office of the Socialist Party of America, Chicago: Member's Individual Ballot and Anti-War Proclamation and Program, adopted by the

National Emergency Convention, in St. Louis, Missouri, April 7–14, 1917, Socialist Party of America Papers, see NEC Convention (1917), Duke Archives.

107. Keith, *Rich Man's War*, 198.

108. The Provost Marshall's statistics declare 337,649 "deserters" either not attending induction or leaving training facilities unannounced. In all, more than twenty-four million men were registered with three million called into arms by 1919. Thus, it is significant that national draft dodgers represented roughly 11 percent of the total mustered into the armed service. However, they were only 1.4 percent of those registered for Selective Service by the end of the war. Some scholars, such as John Whiteclay Chambers II and Gilbert Fite, dismiss these percentages as "sporadic, not a threat to the enforcement or legitimacy of Selective Service." See Chambers, *To Raise an Army: The Draft Comes to Modern America* (New York: Free Press, 1987), 211–213. I disagree with Chambers's categorization, which seems to me to be premised on an ex post facto logic that an effective army was raised. See also Alan Lichtman and Ken DeCell, *The Thirteen Keys to the Presidency* (Lanham, MD: Madison Books, 1990), 220; Zinn, *A People's History*, 361; Ayers et al., *American Passages* (Fort Worth, TX: Wadsworth, 2000), vol. 2, 766.

109. Michael Sistrom, "North Carolinians and the Great War: The Impact of World War I on the Tar Heel State," *Documenting the American South*, University of North Carolina at Chapel Hill, http://docSouth.unc.edu/wwi/homeintro.html#resources (accessed 2005).

110. Chambers, *Draftees or Volunteers*; see introduction to "World War I: The Modern Draft," 203.

111. Ibid., 211–212.

112. Ibid., 212.

113. Keith, "The Politics of Southern Draft Resistance, 1917–1918," 1337, 1359–1360; compare Debs, "The Class War and Its Outlook," *International Socialist Review*, September 1916 to his view of the class aspects of the war in the Canton Speech, June 1918.

114. Keith, *Rich Man's War*, 85; on agrarian opposition, see 84–110.

115. Lichtman and DeCell, *The Thirteen Keys to the Presidency*, 220–223. On the inaction of the police in East St. Louis, see *Biennial Report and Opinions of the Attorney General of the State of Illinois* (Springfield, IL: Illinois State Journal Co. Printers, 1918).

116. Debs to Bruce Rodgers, April 9, 1917; Debs to Germer, April 11, 1917, Debs Papers.

117. Charles Chatfield, "World War I and the Liberal Pacifist in the United States," *American Historical Review* 75, no. 7 (December 1970): 1929.

118. Salvatore, *Eugene V. Debs*, 280.

119. Roland Marchand, *The American Peace Movement and Social Reform, 1898–1918* (Princeton, NJ: Princeton University Press, 1972), 356–363; see also Covington Hall, *Labor Struggles in the Deep South and Other Writings*, ed. David R. Roediger (Chicago: Charles H. Kerr, 2000).

120. C. Howard Hopkins, *John R. Mott, 1865–1955* (Grand Rapids, MI: Eerdmans, 1979), 528. As the war came to a close, Norman Thomas wrote to Mott on behalf of the Fellowship of Reconciliation in America, accusing him of not heeding the mistreatment of conscientious objectors. Norman Thomas to Mott, July 16, 1918. Mott Papers, Yale Divinity School.

121. Brief history of the YMCA and biography of John R. Mott in the catalogue of YMCA Armed Services Department, Kautz Family YMCA Papers, Anderson Library, University of Minnesota.

122. Hopkins, *Mott*, 45–56; well before his wartime service, in 1914 Wilson praised Mott as "one of the most nobly useful men in the world," cited in *Mott*, 435.

123. *The Papers of Woodrow Wilson*, ed. Arthur Link (Princeton, NJ: Princeton University Press, 1994), vol. 49, 236.

124. Zinn, *A People's History*, 355–356.

125. Seward Livermore, "The Sectional Issue in the 1918 Congressional Elections," *Mississippi Valley Historical Review* 35, no. 1 (June 1948): 29.

126. Dawley, *Changing the World*, chapter 5.

127. Debs to Comrade Lehane, November 30, 1918, Debs Papers.

128. Covington Hall to Eugene Debs, November 6, 1919, from Dallas, Texas, Debs Papers.

129. Murray Kaufman, "The Image of Eugene V. Debs in the American Popular Mind, 1894–1926" (PhD diss., Carnegie Mellon University, 1981), 126.

130. On this "feverish patriotism" and the "ostentatious silence" of Debs's neighbors in Terre Haute, and wartime images of Debs in the press, Kaufman, "The Image of Eugene V. Debs in the American Popular Mind," 126–127.

131. Geoffrey Stone, *Perilous Times: Free Speech in Wartime, from the Sedition Act of 1798 to the War on Terrorism* (New York: W. W. Norton, 2004), 138.

132. Wilson, "Need of a Censorship Law," in *Selected Addresses and Public Papers of Woodrow Wilson*, ed. Albert Bushnell Hart (New York: Modern Library, 1918), 206; see also Zechariah Chaffee Jr., *Free Speech in the United States* (Cambridge, MA: Harvard University Press, 1954), 42–51; Donald Johnson, "Wilson, Burleson, and Censorship in the First World War," *Journal of Southern History* 28, no. 1 (February 1962): 46–58; and Stephen Vaughn, "The First Amendment and the Committee on Public Information," *American Journal of Legal History* 23, no. 2 (April 1979): 95–119.

133. On free speech during World War I, Justice Holmes, and the concept of "clear and present danger," Geoffrey Stone, *Perilous Times*, 135–234.

134. Gilbert Roe to Roger Baldwin, June 30, 1917, in American Civil Liberties Union Papers, at Princeton University Archives, ACLU microfilm collection.

135. Donald Johnson, "Wilson, Burleson, and Censorship in the First World War"; Stephen Vaughn, "First Amendment Liberties and the Committee on Public Information," *American Journal of Legal History* 23, no. 2 (April 1979): 95–119.

136. Shannon, *Socialist Party of America*, chapter 5, on how the SPA fragmented during the war.

137. Debs, *The Canton Speech: With Statements to the Jury and the Court*, 10–11.

138. C. Vann Woodward, *Tom Watson, Agrarian Rebel* (New York: Macmillan, 1938), 360–410; Watson's editorial in the *Jeffersonian*, July 19, 1917.

139. Cited in Keith, *Rich Man's War*, 179, 182–183.

140. Debs, "The I.W.W. Bogey," *International Socialist Review*, February 1918.

141. Salvatore, *Eugene V. Debs*, 294.

142. Address to the Jury, in *The Writings and Speeches of Eugene V. Debs*, 435.

143. The best recent study is Ernest Freeberg, *Democracy's Prisoner: Eugene V. Debs, the Great War, and the Right to Dissent* (Cambridge, MA: Harvard University Press, 2008).

144. Debs, "Our Opportunity," *Illinois Comrade*, March 1, 1919.

145. John W. Gunn, "Awakening Farmers Is Shown in Growth of Nonpartisan League," *Appeal to Reason*, September 6, 1919.

146. While the archives do not demonstrate a significantly large body of correspondence addressed to Debs by detractors, this is particularly true of the South. I have singled out the most representative letters from 1919 to 1921. Specific references from correspondence with Father O'Donoghue, A. W. York, Estie Bowers, Mary Meeks, David Clark, and John Avirette, among others, Debs Papers.

147. Salvatore, *Eugene V. Debs*, 301.

148. Lichtman and DeCell, *The Thirteen Keys to the Presidency*, on election of 1920, 218–226.

149. After he campaigned in Louisiana in 1912, for instance, a constituency formed and one in fourteen voters voted for him. In 1912, 2–3 percent of the vote was for Debs on average in the Southern states, and much more in areas that had been politically divided after the birth of the Bull Moose Party: 8.27 percent in Texas, for instance; Florida, 9.45 percent; Louisiana, 6.64 percent; West Virginia, 5.67 percent. By 1920 Mississippi carried a surprising 1.99 percent; Maryland, 2.07 percent; and Florida, 3.56 percent. South Carolina, North Carolina, Georgia, and Virginia all factored in the lowest range, roughly 0.25–1 percent of the vote for Debs in 1912 and 1920 largely due to voting procedures that made third parties write-ins or favored incumbents. For socialism's role see Weinstein, *The Decline of Socialism in America*, and Shannon, *The Socialist Party of America*. For national elections, see Lichtman and DeCell, *The Thirteen Keys*

to the Presidency, 203–210, and Walter Dean Burnham, *Critical Elections and the Mainsprings of American Politics* (New York: W. W. Norton, 1970).

150. Stone, *Perilous Times*, 138, 229–233; Ernest Freeberg, *Democracy's Prisoner: Eugene V. Debs, The Great War, and the "Right" to Dissent* (Cambridge, MA: Harvard University Press, 2008).

151. On Debs and tradition see Salvatore, *Eugene V. Debs*, esp. 186–187.

152. In *The Mind of the South* (New York: Vintage Books, 1941), W. J. Cash posited that region makes a clear and observable difference in how individuals and groups conceive of America's place in the world.

153. On isolationism in more rural and often Republican districts from Ohio through Idaho, see Ralph Smuckler, "The Region of Isolationism," *American Political Science Review* 47 (June 1953): 386–401. For a contrast, see William Carleton, "Isolationism and the Middle West," *Mississippi Valley Historical Review* 33 (1946): 377–390. For the South, Wayne Cole argued that the America Firsters found fewer inroads in the region in 1940–1941 than in the World War I era, and Alexander DeConde confirmed in finding the South to be more isolationist throughout the World War I period. See Cole, "America First and the South, 1940–1941," *Journal of Southern History* 22 (1956): 36–47, and DeConde, "The South and Isolationism," *Journal of Southern History* 24 (1958): 332–346.

154. James Weinstein, "Anti-War Sentiment and the Socialist Party, 1917–1918," *Political Science Quarterly* 74, no. 2 (June 1959): 238–239.

155. These conclusions provide new insights into Werner Sombart's famous question from 1906: "why is there no socialism in the United States?" Sombart, *Why Is There No Socialism in the United States?* (White Plains, NY: International Arts and Sciences Press, rept. 1976).

6. The Irreconcilables

1. Congressional Record, 64th Cong., 2nd sess., February 21, 1919. William E. Borah, "Americanism," February 21, 1919, quoted here from William Borah, *American Problems*, ed. Horace Green (New York: Duffield & Company, 1924), 67–104; see 102.

2. Borah, "Americanism," 102.

3. Borah believed firmly that the Panama Canal and tolls issue was a question of domestic policy. Congressional Record, 62nd Cong., 2nd sess., July 29, 1912, on the Panama Canal: 10456–10463. See Wayne Cole on links between domestic and foreign policy in isolationist thought into the 1930s, *Roosevelt and the Isolationists, 1932–1945* (Lincoln: University of Nebraska Press, 1983), and *Senator Gerald Nye and American Foreign Relations* (Minneapolis: University of Minnesota Press, 1962).

4. Congressional Record, 65th Cong., 1st sess., April 4, 1917, 253.

5. Multiple scholarly and primary sources confirm his private recantation, including his letters to Hiram Johnson and Robert La Follette for June and July 1917, Borah Papers, Manuscripts Division, Library of Congress. Also cited in an interview by biographer Marian C. McKenna in *Borah* (Ann Arbor: University of Michigan Press, 1961).

6. See Thomas Knock's magisterial *To End All Wars: Woodrow Wilson and the Quest for a New World Order* (Princeton, NJ: Princeton University Press, 1992).

7. LeRoy Ashby, *The Spearless Leader: Senator Borah and the Progressive Movement in the 1920s* (Urbana: University of Illinois Press, 1972), 286–287.

8. Arthur Schlesinger Jr., *The Politics of Upheaval: The Age of Roosevelt* (Boston: Houghton Mifflin Co., 1960), 528.

9. William E. Leuchtenberg, "William Edgar Borah," in *Dictionary of American Biography* (New York: Charles Scribner, 1958), vol. 2, 49–53. Numerous scholars have pointed out this historiographical inconsistency, yet it remains a perplexing challenge. On scholarship regarding Borah's thought and Midwestern liberalism, see Kevin Murphy's excellent senior thesis, "A Lion among the Liberals: Senator William Edgar Borah and the Rise of New Deal Liberalism" (Harvard University, 1997).

10. McKenna, *Borah*, 379.

11. Claudius O. Johnson, *Borah of Idaho* (1936; Seattle: University of Washington Press, 1967), preface, ix–x.

12. William Borah, "Democracy Has Not Failed," in *Challenging Essays in Modern Thought*, 2nd Series, ed. J. M. Bachelor and R. L. Henry (New York: Century Co., 1933).

13. On Borah, see Ashby, *The Spearless Leader*; Johnson, *Borah of Idaho*; Robert James Maddox, *William E. Borah and American Foreign Policy* (Baton Rouge: Louisiana State University Press, 1969); McKenna, *Borah*; Charles W. Toth, "Isolationism and the Emergence of Borah: An Appeal to American Tradition," *Western Political Quarterly* 14, no. 2 (June 1961): 555–568; John Chalmers Vinson, *William E. Borah and the Outlawry of War* (Athens: University of Georgia Press, 1957). On Borah and the Republican ascendancy, see John D. Hicks, *Republican Ascendancy, 1921–1933* (New York: Harper and Brothers, 1960); Samuel Adams, *The Incredible Era: The Life and Times of Warren Gamaliel Harding* (Boston: Houghton Mifflin Co., 1939); Fred Greenbaum, *Men against Myths: The Progressive Response* (Westport, CT: Praeger, 2000).

14. Quoted in Thomas Guinsburg, *The Pursuit of Isolationism in the United States Senate from Versailles to Pearl Harbor* (New York: Garland, 1982), 52.

15. McKenna, *Borah*, 132–133.

16. Republican Party Platform, Women's Suffrage Plank, Chicago Convention, June 1916. See www.presidency.ucsb.edu/ws/index.php?pid=29634 (accessed July 2010).

17. Borah, "On the Issue of the War," March 18, 1918, in *American Problems*, 152.

18. Borah, "Recall of Judges," August 7, 1911, in *American Problems*, 166–180.

19. These quotes come from his comments on providing a bonus to veterans; see Borah, "Taxation for the Bonus," July 6, 1922, in *American Problems*, 26, 29.

20. Borah, Senate Address, on the "Recall of Judges," see August 7, 1911, in *American Problems*, 177–178. For an alternative view, see Peter Onuf, *Jefferson's Empire: The Language of American Nationhood* (Charlottesville: University of Virginia Press, 2001), in which Onuf observes that Jefferson's vision of nationalism was not sectional in nature.

21. Lincoln Colcord to Oswald Garrison Villard, December 16, 1919, Villard Papers, Folder 655. Quoted in Ashby, *Spearless Leader*, 27.

22. Borah, "Bill to End Palmerism," February 24, 1921; Borah worked closely with the National Popular Government League on the bill; see Ashby, *Spearless Leader*, 28.

23. Borah to Dan L. Lindsley, January 17, 1922, Borah Papers.

24. Borah, "Free Speech: The Vital Issue," *Nation*, June 4, 1923, 8.

25. Quoted in McKenna, *Borah*, 101.

26. Ibid., 325.

27. Despite his own belief in Anglo-Saxon superiority, he considered what was widely seen as the minimal educational attainment and poor governments of other races as largely produced by environment, and compounded by imperial meddling, rather than being the direct results of innate inferiority. Borah to Bishop Philip M. Rhinelander, March 26, 1927 (on Chinese settling their own affairs), Borah Papers; for the debates on Haiti, see Select Committee on Haiti and Santo Domingo, "Hearings, Inquiry into the Occupation and Administration of Haiti and Santo Domingo," Congressional Record, 67th Cong., 1st and 2nd sess., esp. March 1922, 1198–2000, and July 1922, 9739; on "white" imperialism, see Borah's typed statement dated October 19, 1925, Borah Papers.

28. Bryan to Borah, December 26, 1916, Borah Papers. Borah to Bryan, December 29, 1916, Borah Papers.

29. Congressional Record, 64th Cong., 2nd sess., February 1, 1917, 2361–2364.

30. There are numerous examples in the Lodge papers from September through December 1916 and in January and February 1917. Quote from Lodge to Roosevelt, December 21, 1916, Lodge Papers.

31. See Lodge's *War Addresses, 1915–1917* (Boston: Houghton Mifflin Co., 1917), concluding comments from "The President and a World Peace," 245–280; also in *War Addresses*, see "Armed Merchantmen," 109; "On Washington's Neutrality," 121; "Force and Peace," 27.

32. Quotes in Ralph Stone, *The Irreconcilables: The Fight against the League of Nations* (Lexington: University Press of Kentucky, 1970), 14.

33. Borah to Frank R. Gooding, April 16, 1917, Borah Papers.

34. See Borah Papers for more on this transition from February through July 1917. Cited here: Borah to Ed Dewey, May 9, June 28, 1917, Borah Papers.

35. Borah, general correspondence, 1916–1918, Borah Papers.
36. Borah Scrapbooks for 1917, Borah Papers. Borah's collected files indicate that he cared more than usual about how people across the nation responded to this statement on "why we fight" and why he voted for the war. (*Boston Post*, July 28, 1917, underlined in his scrapbooks.)
37. Borah to W. L. Penny, May 21, 1917, Borah Papers.
38. Congressional Record, 63rd Cong., 2nd sess., March 17, 1914, 4961.
39. Mae Ngai, *Impossible Subjects: Illegal Aliens and the Making of Modern America* (Princeton, NJ: Princeton University Press, 2004), 21.
40. Ibid.
41. For a comparative perspective, see Martin A. Shain, *The Politcs of Immigration in France, Britain, and the United States* (New York: Palgrave Macmillan, 2008).
42. Borah, "The Need for Immigration Restriction," adapted from a speech in the Senate, 1916, in *American Problems*, 49.
43. On this point, see McKenna, *Borah*, chapters 5 and 6.
44. Borah made this remark during his first term in the Senate in opposing the federal administration of public lands. Congressional Record, 60th Cong., 1st sess., May 4, 1908, 5983–5984.
45. For a useful comparison, examine Kallen's "Democracy vs. the Melting Pot" vis-à-vis Bourne's "Trans-National America." Horace Kallen, "Democracy vs. the Melting Pot," *Nation*, February 25, 1915, 218–220. Randolph Bourne, "Trans-National America," *Atlantic Monthly*, July 1916. Borah's mildly pluralistic ideas about the particularism of groups within the United States are reminiscent of the intellectual path traveled by Frances Kellor leading up to and after World War I. See Kellor, *Straight America* (1916) and *Immigration and the Future* (1920). See also David Hollinger, "Ethnic Diversity, Cosmopolitanism, and the Emergence of the American Liberal Intelligentsia," in *In the American Province: Studies in the History and Historiography of Ideas*, ed. David Hollinger (Bloomington: Indiana University Press, 1985), 56–73; and Hollinger's "Democracy and the Melting Pot Reconsidered" in the same volume. As I put it elsewhere, see Christopher McKnight Nichols, "Rethinking Randolph Bourne's 'Trans-National America': How WWI Created Isolationist Antiwar Pluralism," *Journal of the Gilded Age and Progressive Era* 8, no. 2 (April 2009): 217–257.
46. Diane Ravitch has made a useful distinction between particularism and pluralism in her analysis of multiculturalism. Ravitch, "Multiculturalism: E Pluribus Plures," *American Scholar* 59, no. 3 (1990): 337–354; see also Simon Upton's review essay, "Isaiah Berlin as Anti-Rationalist," *Philosophy and Literature* 21, no. 2 (1997): 426–432. On the philosophical concern with particularism and its resistance to theory, David Bakhurst, "Ethical Particularism in Context," and Roger Crisp, "Particularizing Particularism," in *Moral*

Particularism, ed. Brad Hooker and Margaret Olivia Little (Oxford: Clarendon Press, 2000).

47. Walter Lippmann, "Concerning Senator Borah," *Foreign Affairs*, January 1926, 211–222.

48. Quoted in the *New York Times*, February 1, 1919. Borah retracted this statement almost immediately thereafter. See also Borah to J. Hamilton Lewis, February 1919, Borah Papers.

49. Borah, "Americanism," in *American Problems*, 102.

50. Congressional Record, 65th Cong., 3rd sess., 3911–3912.

51. Stone, *The Irreconcilables*, 4.

52. Borah, "Americanism," 97, 78, 104.

53. Borah to Secretary Joseph Tumulty, February 18, 1919, Borah Papers. News of Borah's rejection of the invitation met wide public disapproval. See *Nation*, February 22, 1919, 273; one example of approval is "Borah Can Be Spared," *Indianapolis Times-Star*, February 19, 1919.

54. Congressional Record, 66th Cong., 1st sess., November 19, 1919, 8782. Borah, "On the League of Nations." For full text see also in *American Problems*, 105–130.

55. *New York Times*, February 15, 1919.

56. *Chicago Daily Tribune*, February 25, 1919.

57. Congressional Record, 65th Cong., 3rd sess., February 21, 1919, 3911.

58. Ibid.

59. Miles Poindexter, "American Independence," speech at Rochester, New York, July 4, 1919. Poindexter pamphlet no. 10, University of Virginia, Special Collections Library.

60. *New York Times*, February 22, 1919, 1.

61. *Official Report of the Senate Foreign Relations Committee*, "Covenant of the League of Nations," August 11, 1919, and "Treaty of Peace with Germany," August 19, 1919, 66th Cong., 1st sess., Senate, Docs. 72 and 76.

62. See Hiram Johnson to Jack Johnson (his son), February 8, 1919, in *The Diary Letters of Hiram Johnson*, ed. Robert Burke (New York: Garland Publishing, 1983) (hereafter Johnson Papers).

63. Miles Poindexter, "League of Nations—The President's Addresses," speech in the Senate, September 8, 1919. Poindexter pamphlet no. 15, University of Virginia, Special Collections Library.

64. Congressional Record, 65th Cong., 3rd sess., February 21, 1919, 3913.

65. Ibid., 3914.

66. Poindexter, "League of Nations."

67. Congressional Record, 65th Cong., 3rd sess., February 22, 1919, 4028.

68. Quoted in John Milton Cooper Jr., *The Warrior and the Priest: Woodrow Wilson and Theodore Roosevelt* (Cambridge, MA: Harvard University Press, 1983), 334. See also Serge Ricard, "Anti-Wilsonian Internationalism: Theodore

Roosevelt in the *Kansas City Star*," in *From Theodore Roosevelt to FDR*, ed. Daniela Rossini (Bodmin, UK: Keele University Press, 1995), 25–44.

69. Congressional Record, 66th Cong., 1st sess., June 2, 1919, 508.

70. *New York Tribune*, August 7, 1919.

71. George W. Norris, *Fighting Liberal: The Autobiography of George W. Norris* (Lincoln: University of Nebraska Press, 1945), 208.

72. *New York Times*, March 1, 1919, 1.

73. Congressional Record, 66th Cong., 1st sess., May 29, 1919, 393.

74. *New York Times*, February 22, 1919.

75. James Reed, "Racial Equality and the League of Nations," speech to the Senate, May 26, 1919. Pamphlet located at University of Virginia, Special Collections Library.

76. Congressional Record, 66th Cong., 1st sess., June 20, 1919, 1437.

77. Johnson to his son Jack, January 24, 1919, Johnson Papers.

78. *New York Times*, October 26, 1918.

79. Will H. Hays, *The Memoirs of Will H. Hays* (Garden City, NY: Doubleday & Company, 1955), 176.

80. For more on Wilson's mind-set, see John Milton Cooper Jr.'s magisterial *Woodrow Wilson: A Biography* (New York: Knopf, 2009), esp. 506–560.

81. Johnson, February 16, 1919, Johnson Papers.

82. *New York Times*, March 2, 1919.

83. Congressional Record, 65th Cong., 3rd sess., March 4, 1919, 4974.

84. *New York Tribune*, March 5, 1919.

85. Ibid.

86. Ibid., August 31, 1919.

87. Lodge to Theodore Roosevelt, March 1, 1915, Lodge Papers.

88. For more on this wrangling see Cooper Jr., *Woodrow Wilson*, 513–550.

89. Woodrow Wilson, *The Hope of the World* (New York: Harper and Brothers, 1920), 87.

90. Johnson, August 23, 1919, Johnson Papers.

91. *Chicago Daily Tribune*, September 11, 1919.

92. *New York Times*, March 19, 1919, and September 12, 1919.

93. Johnson, July 2, 1919, Johnson Papers.

94. Ibid., February 16, 1919.

95. Ibid., April 29, 1919.

96. Miles Poindexter, "The Future of the Republican Party," speech before the 15th District Republican Club, New York City, June 24, 1919. Pamphlet in University of Virginia Special Collections Library.

97. Congressional Record, 66th Cong., 1st sess., September 22, 1919, 5674.

98. Albert Beveridge, "The Pitfalls of the 'League of Nations,'" *North American Review*, March 1919, esp. 314.

99. Congressional Record, 66th Cong., 1st sess., March 3, 1919, 4865–4867.

100. Johnson to Chester Rockwell, April 10, 1917, Chester Rockwell Papers, cited in John Milton Cooper Jr., *The Vanity of Power: American Isolationism and the First World War, 1914–1917* (Westport, CT: Greenwood Press, 1969), 206.

101. Henry Cabot Lodge, address to the Senate, August 12, 1919. Congressional Record, 66th Cong., 1st sess., August 12, 1919, cited in *Reform, War, and Reaction, 1912–1932*, ed. Stanley Coben (Columbia: University of South Carolina Press, 1972), quotations from 136–137.

102. Ibid., 136–137, 139.

103. Borah, "On the League," in *American Problems*, 105–130.

104. Ibid.

105. Ibid.

106. Joseph Tumulty, *Woodrow Wilson as I Know Him* (New York: Doubleday, Page & Co., 1921), 378.

107. *New York Sun*, February 28, 1919.

108. Johnson, March 16, 1919, Johnson Papers.

109. Sherman, Congressional Record, 65th Cong., 3rd sess., March 3, 1919, 4867. On Norris, see *New York Times*, February 15, 1920.

110. Congressional Record, 66th Cong., 1st sess., October 16, 1919, 7000.

111. For more on Wilsonian internationalism, see Frank Ninkovich, *The Wilsonian Century: U.S. Foreign Policy since 1900* (Chicago: University of Chicago Press, 1999), 48–77; on Wilson's geopolitics, N. Gordon Levin Jr., *Woodrow Wilson and World Politics: America's Response to War and Revolution* (New York: Oxford University Press, 1968); Gardner, *Safe for Democracy*, see 1 on liberalism as Wilson's internationalist vision; in global terms, Erez Manela, *The Wilsonian Moment; Self-Determination and the International Origins of Anti-colonial Nationalism* (New York: Oxford University Press, 2007); for a different take, see Walter Russell Mead, *Special Providence: American Foreign Policy and How It Changed the World* (New York: Routledge, 2002), esp. 166–173.

112. On liberalism, quoted in January 1919, cited in Ninkovich, *Wilsonian Century*, 72; Ninkovich rightly observes that Wilson's rhetoric should be seen less as utopian and can more accurately be described as an "internationalism of fear"; see "Treaty or No Treaty," *New York Tribune*, September 12, 1919; see also Knock, *To End All Wars*, 246–270.

113. Congressional Record, 66th Cong., 1st sess., March 19, 1920, 8786.

114. Borah to F. J. Hagenbarth, April 29, 1914, Borah Papers.

115. Typed copy of Borah's "Address at Denver, Colorado," June 18, 1927, Borah Papers.

7. New Internationalism

1. Emily Greene Balch to Kaskia Chapter of the Daughters of the American Revolution, July 10, 1924, Addams Papers, Swarthmore College Peace Collection.

2. Regarding Balch's activities at this time, see Mercedes Randall, *Improper Bostonian: Emily Greene Balch* (New York: Twayne Publishers, 1964), 290–320. Long overdue, the first scholarly biography of Balch in almost fifty years has just been published and sheds new light on Balch's internationalism; see Kristen Gwinn, *Emily Greene Balch: The Long Road to Internationalism* (Urbana: University of Illinois Press, 2010). On the wider context, see Harriet Hyman Alonso, *Peace as a Women's Issue: A History of the U.S. Movement for World Peace and Women's Rights* (Syracuse, NY: Syracuse University Press, 1993).

3. Balch to Kaskia Chapter of the DAR, Addams Papers.

4. This phrase was notably used in the title of an article by Borah, "The Fetish of Force, a New Pan-American Policy," *Forum*, August 1925, 240–246.

5. Jane Addams, *The Second Twenty Years at Hull House* (New York: Macmillan, 1930), 7.

6. For more on this see Alan Dawley, *Changing the World*, 312; see also Robert A. Divine, *The Illusion of Neutrality* (Chicago: University of Chicago Press, 1962).

7. On Wellesley and the exceptional women there, see Patricia A. Palmieri, "Here Was Fellowship: A Social Portrait of Academic Women at Wellesley, 1895–1920," *History of Education Quarterly* 23, no. 2 (Summer 1983): 195–214.

8. Emily Balch, *Our Slavic Fellow Citizens* (Boston: Charities Publication Committee, 1910); on her scholarship and peace advocacy, see Mercedes Randall, ed., *Beyond Nationalism: The Social Thought of Emily Greene Balch* (New York: Twayne Publishers, 1972).

9. For more see Mae Ngai, *Impossible Subjects Impossible Subjects: Illegal Aliens and the Making of Modern America* (Princeton, NJ: Princeton University Press, 2004), and John Higham, *Strangers in the Land*.

10. Balch, *Our Slavic Fellow Citizens*, 3–9.

11. Ibid., 6.

12. Ibid., 20.

13. Ibid.

14. The Hague members were working hard on these drafts and proposals, listed in Balch Papers for 1915, Swarthmore College Peace Collection. For more on international organization in terms of the "emotion culture" of this association, see Verta Taylor and Leila J. Rupp, "Loving Internationalism: The Emotion Culture of Transnational Women's Organizations, 1888–1945," *Mobilization: An International Journal* 7, no. 2 (2002): 141–158.

15. "Resolutions Adopted at the Hague Congress," in *Women at The Hague: The International Congress of Women and Its Results*, ed. Jane Addams, Emily Greene Balch, and Alice Hamilton (New York: Macmillan, 1916), 150–159.

16. On the ICW and the wartime peace movement, see Addams, Balch, and Hamilton, *Women at The Hague*. In terms of the fit of women's internationalism and modern feminism, see Nancy Cott, *The Grounding of Modern Feminism* (New Haven, CT: Yale University Press, 1987), esp. 113–124, 246–257.

17. Emily Balch, "The Time to Make Peace," *Survey*, October 2, 1915, 24.

18. Ibid., 24–25.

19. Cott, *Grounding of Modern Feminism*, 243–267, Alonso, *Peace as a Women's Issue*, 85–124.

20. Balch; numerous letters from colleagues and from the departments at the college during the spring and summer of 1918 attest to this point. See, for example, Department of Economics to the Wellesley College Board of Trustees, April 29, 1918, Balch Papers.

21. WILPF, *Report of the International Congress of Women: Zurich, May 12–17, 1919*, preface (written by Balch), WILPF Files, Swarthmore College Peace Collection.

22. WILPF, *Zurich Report*, 60.

23. WILPF Charter (1919), Balch Papers. See also files of the U.S. Section of WILPF Archives; and WILPF website (www.wilpf.org) for a limited number of transcriptions.

24. WILPF, "Statement on the Treaty Made at Versailles" (1918), Balch Papers (also duplicated in the WILPF Archival Collection).

25. Akira Iriye, *Cultural Internationalism and World Order* (Baltimore: Johns Hopkins University Press, 1997), esp. chapter 2 on the origins of cultural internationalism; also Thomas J. Knock, *To End All Wars: Woodrow Wilson and the Quest for a New World Order* (Princeton, NJ: Princeton University Press, 1992).

26. WILPF, *Zurich Report*, 237.

27. Randall, *Improper Bostonian*, regarding Balch's activities at this time; for more detail of the movement as a whole at this time, see Alonso, *Peace as a Women's Issue*.

28. On new visions of "soft power" internationalism, see Julia F. Irwin, "Humanitarian Occupations: International Civilian Relief, Voluntary Diplomacy, and the American Red Cross, 1898–1928" (PhD diss., Yale University, 2009).

29. For an overview of these trends for the earlier period through World War I, see Roland Marchand's excellent study, *The American Peace Movement and Social Reform, 1898–1918* (Princeton, NJ: Princeton University Press, 1972); for the 1920s, see David Patterson, *Toward a Warless World* (Bloomington: Indiana University Press, 1976), and Dawley, *Changing the World*; for a broader

perspective, Merle Curti, *Peace or War: The American Struggle, 1636–1936* (1936; New York: W. W. Norton, rept. 1959); on women and the peace movement, Leila J. Rupp, *Worlds of Women* (Princeton, NJ: Princeton University Press, 1997).

30. Robert Johnson, *The Peace Progressives and American Foreign Relations* (Cambridge, MA: Harvard University Press, 1995), 3.

31. The conferral of the Nobel Peace Prize on Balch and Mott in 1946 signaled the importance of their pioneering "new internationalist" initiatives.

32. Quotes from Borah to Lyman Abbott, November 25, 1922, Borah Papers.

33. Borah Papers, scrapbook clippings from 1926 and 1927; Marian McKenna, *Borah* (Ann Arbor: University of Michigan Press, 1961), on prohibition and the political campaigns of 1928 and 1932, 253–258, 277–282.

34. Borah to Jane Addams, August 18, 1927, Borah Papers.

35. Ibid., September 3, 1927, Borah Papers.

36. Globally Wilsonian idealism radiated outward. Erez Manela, *Wilsonian Moment: Self-Determination and the International Origins of Anticolonial Nationalism* (New York: Oxford University Press, 2007), 7.

37. Joyce Blackwell, *No Peace without Freedom: Race and the Women's International League for Peace and Freedom* (Carbondale: Southern Illinois University Press, 2004), 8–9. See also Judy D. Whipps, "The Feminist Pacifism of Emily Greene Balch, Nobel Peace Laureate," *NWSA Journal* 18, no. 3 (2006): 122–132.

38. Randall, *Improper Bostonian*, details Balch's masterful organizational abilities.

39. Robert J. Maddox, *William E. Borah and American Foreign Policy* (Baton Rouge: Louisiana State University Press, 1969), 98.

40. Frank Cobb to Borah, July 12, 1921, Borah Papers.

41. Raymond Robbins to Borah, July 19, 1921, Borah Papers.

42. Borah, "The Ghost of Versailles at the Conference," *Nation*, November 9, 1921, 525–526, and September 21, 1921, 310.

43. Lodge and Johnson cited in *New York Times*, March 14, 1922.

44. Maddox, *William E. Borah and American Foreign Policy*, 119.

45. *Literary Digest* 77 (April 8, 1922).

46. See John Chalmers Vinson, *Parchment Peace: The United States Senate and the Washington Conference, 1921–1922* (Athens: University of Georgia Press, 1955), 191–192, also Maddox, *William E. Borah and American Foreign Policy*, on Borah and this issue in foreign policy, 117.

47. For more on the nuances of Irreconcilable opposition to the Four-Power Treaty, see Karen Miller, *Populist Nationalism: Republican Insurgency and American Foreign Policy Making, 1918–1925* (Westport, CT: Greenwood Press, 1999), 119–158.

48. *Wall Street Magazine,* January 6, 1923, in Borah Scrapbooks, Borah Papers. See also John Chalmers Vinson, *William E. Borah and the Outlawry of War* (Athens: University of Georgia Press, 1957), chapter 4.

49. *Wall Street Magazine,* January 6, 1923; also Vinson, *William E. Borah and the Outlawry of War,* chapter 4.

50. Regarding Borah's view see Maddox, *Borah and Foreign Policy,* 147.

51. *Literary Digest* 76, no. 10 (March 10, 1923), 7.

52. Congressional Record, 64th Cong., 4th sess., February 14, 1923, 3605.

53. Cited in Maddox, *Borah and Foreign Policy,* 169.

54. Senate Resolution to Adhere to World Court, issued January 27, 1926. For more see Manley O. Hudson, "The United States Senate and the World Court," *American Journal of International Law* 29, no. 2 (April 1935): 301–307.

55. Balch, *Beyond Nationalism: The Social Thought of Emily Greene Balch,* ed. Mercedes Randall (New York: Twayne Publishers, 1972), 112.

56. Balch, *Pax International,* March 1927, *Pax International* clippings, Balch Papers.

57. Ibid. See also Tara Lambert, "Emily Greene Balch: Crusader for Peace and Justice" (Master's thesis, Marshall University, 2002).

58. See the excellent account in Mary Renda's *Taking Haiti: Military Occupation and the Culture of U.S. Imperialism, 1915–1960* (Chapel Hill: University of North Carolina Press, 2001), citations from 191, 265–267.

59. Emily Greene Balch, Paul H. Douglas, Addie Hunton, Charlotte Atwood, Zonia Baber, and Grace D. Watson, eds., *Occupied Haiti; Being the Report of a Committee of Six Disinterested Americans Representing Organizations Exclusively American, Who, Having Personally Studied Conditions in Haiti in 1926, Favor the Restoration of the Independence of the Negro Republic* (New York: Negro Universities Press, rept. 1969). For more on Balch's thought on U.S. interventionism, see *Beyond Nationalism,* 140–157.

60. Balch et al., *Occupied Haiti,* 151.

61. Ibid.

62. Balch, 1927, Balch Papers. Author could not find original in Swarthmore College Peace Collection; text here as quoted in Randall, *Improper Bostonian,* 306.

63. Report in *New York Call,* December 8, 1922.

64. Borah, "The Fetish of Force." See Claudius Johnson, *Borah of Idaho* (1936; Seattle: University of Washington Press, 1967), chapter 17, "Anti-Imperialist," 336–353.

65. *New York Times,* January 9, 1930, not long before American forces left Haiti.

66. John E. Stoner, *S. O. Levinson and the Treaty of Paris* (Chicago: University of Chicago Press, 1942), 9.

67. Ibid.

68. For an excellent account of U.S. troop activities in the region and American foreign policy, see Renda, *Taking Haiti.*

69. Kellogg on the pact, letter, as quoted in Powaski; for more on their relationship and Kellogg's role, see Vinson's treatment in *William E. Borah and the Outlawry of War.*

70. *New York Times*, November 27, 1927.

71. WILPF, "Historical Introduction, 1919–1959," written by Archivist Eleanor Barr in 1987, in the WILPF historical files, U.S. Section, 1927 Annual Meeting, Swarthmore College Peace Collection.

72. Interview with Addams as reported in the *New York Times*, December 11, 1927.

73. WILPF files, December 1927, Swarthmore Peace Collection. As part of their efforts the WILPF requested that Harvard Law Professor Francis B. Sayre draft a model arbitration treaty that was subsequently widely circulated. WILPF, "Historical Introduction, 1919–1959."

74. The full text of the "General Pact for the Renunciation of War" was entered into the *Report of the Senate Foreign Relations Committee*, December 7, 1928, 2.

75. *New York Times*, April 26, 1927, 8.

76. Congressional Record, 66th Cong., 1st sess., July 15, 1919, 2592.

77. Hiram Johnson, letter dated February 24, 1919, Johnson Papers.

78. *New York Times*, February 5, 1928.

79. *Official Senate Foreign Relations Committee Report*, December 7, 1928, 4.

80. Ibid., 16.

81. William E. Borah, "The Fetish of Force," 240.

82. James T. Shotwell, *War as an Instrument of National Policy and Its Renunciation in the Pact of Paris* (New York: Harcourt, Brace, and Company, 1929), 112.

83. *New York Times*, February 5, 1928, 127.

84. Congressional Record, 70th Cong., 2nd sess., December 14, 1928, 599.

85. This account is derived from the pact and related articles. See *Selected Articles on the Pact of Paris: Officially the General Pact for the Renunciation of War*, compiled by James Thayer Gerould (New York: H. W. Wilson Co., 1929).

86. *New York Times*, April 8, 1928.

87. Reported in the *New York Times*, May 6, 1928.

88. Balch as quoted by Randall, *Improper Bostonian*, 307–308.

89. Balch, speech in Geneva, printed as Balch, "Back in Geneva," *Pax International*, July 1928, Balch Papers.

90. Ibid. Only one account does justice to the powerful support that the WILPF put behind the outlawry movement and Kellogg-Briand: Harriet Hyman Alonso, *The Women's Peace Union and the Outlawry of War, 1921–1942* (Syracuse, NY: Syracuse University Press, 1997).

91. Balch, speech in Geneva, typescript introduction, September 14, 1928, Balch Papers.

92. Dorothy Detzer to Balch, October 29, 1928, Balch Papers.

93. Congressional Record, 70th Cong., 2nd sess., January 24, 1929, 1658.

94. *Senate Foreign Relations Committee Report*, December 7, 1928, 5.

95. Ibid., 15.

96. *New York Times*, January 16, 1929.

97. Ibid., September 8, 1928.

98. Hiram Johnson letters, dated January 19, 1929, Johnson Papers.

99. Congressional Record, 70th Cong., 2nd sess., January 5, 1929, 1186.

100. Ibid., January 4, 1929, 1134.

101. Ibid., January 9, 1929, 1414.

102. Borah to Kellogg, August 14, 1928, Borah Papers.

103. Ibid.

104. *New York Times*, September 8, 1928.

105. Franklin Delano Roosevelt, Democratic Party nomination speech for Al Smith, as quoted in *New York Times*, June 28, 1928.

106. Cited in Drew Pearson and Constantine Brown, *The American Diplomatic Game* (Garden City, NJ: Doubleday, Doran & Company, 1935), 40–42; for more context, Kellogg is also quoted in Robert Ferrell, *Peace in Their Time: The Origins of the Kellogg-Briand Pact* (New Haven, CT: Yale University Press, 1952), 228.

107. Borah to the Senate, Congressional Record, 70th Cong., 2nd sess., January 30, 1929, 1067–1068.

108. Ibid.

109. Balch to Borah, December 3, 1928, Balch Papers.

110. Ibid., December 3, 1928.

111. Ibid.

112. Ibid.

113. Mary Sheepshanks to Addams, from Geneva, March 28, 1928, Addams Papers.

114. Louie Bennett to Addams, from Dublin, June 4, 1928, Addams Papers.

115. See Gertrud Baer to Addams, from Munich, June 10, 1928, Addams Papers.

116. George Gordon Battle to Addams, October 17, 1928, WILPF Correspondence Files.

117. Ibid.

118. Wisconsin Senator John J. Blaine cast the only vote against the pact. See John J. Blaine Papers, Wisconsin State Historical Society. For more on the issues involved, see Robert H. Ferrell, *Peace in Their Time: The Origins of the Kellogg-Briand Pact* (New Haven, CT: Yale University Press, 1952).

119. *Chicago Evening Post*, January 17, 1929. See also *New York Times, Wall Street Journal,* and the *Nation*, editorial pages spanning January 16–20, 1929.

120. Some objected, of course. It is particularly interesting that the former secretary of state under Wilson, Robert Lansing, saw some merit in the ideals but, as with the League treaty, he believed in adding teeth to such pacts. Even then, he thought, war was inevitable. See Norman Graebner, ed., *Ideas and Diplomacy: Readings in the Intellectual Tradition of American Foreign Policy* (New York: Oxford University Press, 1964), 519. For more on this narrative, see Stephen Kneeshaw, *In Pursuit of Peace: The American Reaction to the Kellogg-Briand Pact, 1928–1929* (New York: Garland Publishing, 1991).

121. *Borah Foundation Lectures: 1954—Addresses Delivered at the Seventh Annual Conference of the W. E. Borah Outlawry of War Foundation on the Causes of War and the Conditions of Peace,* University of Idaho–Moscow, March 18–19, 1954, preface. University of Virginia Ivy Stacks, Special Collections pamphlet.

122. Quoted in the *Washington Daily Times,* September 5, 1928.

123. Ronald Steel, *Walter Lippmann and the American Century* (New York: Vintage Books, 1980), 253–254. H. L. Mencken, also an opponent of Borah's on many issues, made similar statements about the "Lion of the Senate," see Mencken, *On Politics: A Carnival of Buncombe,* ed. Malcolm Moos (Baltimore: Johns Hopkins University Press, 1956).

124. *Idaho Daily Statesman,* April 22, 1923, front page.

125. Claudius O. Johnson, *Borah of Idaho* (New York: Longmans, Green, and Co., 1936), 208.

126. *Literary Digest* 76, no. 10 (March 10, 1923): 11.

127. Philander C. Knox, "The True Relation of the United States to the League of Nations," speech in the Senate, November 6, 1919 (Washington, DC: Government Printing Office, 1919), held by Alderman Library, University of Virginia.

128. William Borah, *American Problems: A Selection of Speeches and Prophesies* (New York: AMS Press, 1970), 137. (Speech on the Senate floor, September 26, 1921.)

129. Frank Ninkovich makes this point in *Wilsonian Century,* 76; regarding these broader tendencies in peace progressivism, I draw primarily on Johnson, *The Peace Progressives,* and Dawley, *Changing the World.*

130. For more on this point, see Ninkovich, *Wilsonian Century,* 81.

131. Charles Beard, *American Foreign Policy in the Making, 1932–1940* (New Haven, CT: Yale University Press, 1946), 17.

132. Nobel Peace Prize Award Ceremony Speech, 1931, Presentation Speech by Halvdan Koht, http://nobelprize.org/nobel_prizes/peace/laureates/1931/press.html (accessed August 30, 2010). On Addams, the Nobel, and her activism in the 1930s, see Lucy Knight, *Jane Addams: Spirit in Action* (New York: W. W. Norton, 2010), 224–269.

133. See Herbert Hoover, *Memoirs: The Great Depression* (New York: Macmillan, 1952), 61–80. Quote in William S. Myers, *The State Papers and Other Public Writings of Herbert Hoover* (Garden City, NY: Doubleday, 1934), vol. 2, 96.

134. Elliot A. Rosen, *Hoover, Roosevelt and the Brains Trust: From Depression to New Deal* (New York: Columbia University Press, 1977), 92–94.

135. Thomas Sherman, "Balancing Payments, Not Powers" (University of Pennsylvania seminar on Isolationism in American Culture and Politics, 2009), argues that Hoover's fiscal policy of moratorium in 1931 was an activist and ultimately isolationist act (forthcoming in *Penn History Review*, AY 2010–2011). See Patricia Clavin, *The Failure of Economic Diplomacy: Britain, Germany, France, and the United States, 1931–1936* (New York: St. Martin's Press, 1996); Emily Rosenberg, *Financial Missionaries: The Politics and Culture of the Dollar, 1900–1930* (Durham, NC: Duke University Press, 2003); Jordan Schwarz, *The Interregnum of Despair* (Champaign: University of Illinois Press, 1970), 87–88.

136. Balch proposals on Disarmament (1932), Internationalization of Aviation (1932), Reform of the League of Nations (1936), Economic Reconstruction (1936), A Mediated Spain (1937), Neutrality and Collective Security (1938), Balch Papers. See also Randall, *Improper Bostonian*, 312–338.

137. On these sides and their gradual parting of the ways, see Manfred Jonas, *Isolationism in America, 1935–1941* (Ithaca, NY: Cornell University Press, 1966), and Alonso, *The Women's Peace Union and the Outlawry of War.*

138. For a succinct and convincing account of global interconnections and American involvement even in an era of purported isolationism from the 1920s through the 1930s, see Bear F. Braumoeller, "The Myth of Isolationism," Harvard University Department of Government paper, November 2002. In the author's possession; accessible at www.wcfia.harvard.edu/sites/default/files/579 _MythOfUSIsol.pdf.

Conclusion

1. Walter Lippmann, *U.S. Foreign Policy: Shield of the Republic* (New York: Little, Brown and Company, 1943), 7.

2. There is much excellent political and diplomatic scholarship on isolationism in America for the period 1914–1917, most notably Ernest May's *The World War and American Isolation, 1914–1917* (Chicago: Quadrangle Books, 1966), and John Milton Cooper Jr.'s *The Vanity of Power: American Isolationism and the First World War, 1914–1917* (Westport, CT: Greenwood Press, 1969); for the better-known later period from 1930 to 1945, representative exemplary work includes Selig Adler, *The Isolationist Impulse: Its Twentieth Century Reaction* (London: Abelard-Schuman Limited, 1957), Wayne S. Cole, *Roosevelt and the Isolationists, 1932–1945* (Lincoln: University of Nebraska Press, 1983), Manfred

Jonas, *Isolationism in America, 1935–1941* (Ithaca, NY: Cornell University Press, 1966), and Justus Doenecke and John Wilz, *From Isolation to War, 1931–1941* (1968; Arlington Heights: Harlan Davidson, rept. 1991),

3. On the "new isolationism" see Adler, *The Isolationist Impulse*, chapters 10 and 11; see also Adler, *The Uncertain Giant, 1921–1941* (New York: Macmillan, 1965).

4. William Borah, speech to Council on Foreign Relations, New York, January 8, 1934, in Borah Papers; also Borah, *Bedrock: Views on National Problems* (Washington, DC: National Home Library Foundation, 1936), 58. For another view see Ross A. Kennedy, "The Ideology of American Isolationism: 1931–1939," *Cercles* 5 (2002): 57–76.

5. Robert Johnson, *The Peace Progressives and American Foreign Relations* (Cambridge, MA: Harvard University Press, 1995), 178.

6. For more on this as "peace progressivism" see Johnson, *The Peace Progressives*, esp. 178.

7. See, for example, Congressional Record, 69th Cong., 1st sess., April 14, 1924, 6304; 70th Cong., 1st sess., November 1928, 2011; 70th Cong., 2nd sess., January 3, 1929, 1064–1066; 74th Cong., 2nd sess., February 20, 1936, 2428; and David Horowitz, *Beyond Left and Right: Insurgency and the Establishment* (Champaign: University of Illinois Press, 1997), 143–150.

8. William Borah, *American Problems*, ed. Horace Green (New York: Duffield & Company, 1924), 102.

9. *Report of the Special Committee on Investigation of the Munitions Industry* (Nye Report), U.S. Congress, Senate, 74th Cong., 2nd sess., February 24, 1936, 3–13.

10. Ibid.

11. George H. Gallup, Public Opinion Poll (February 1937), George H. Gallup, *The Gallup Poll: Public Opinion, 1935–1971* (New York: Random House, 1972), vol. 1, 49; on this poll in near-contemporary perspective, Philip E. Jacob, "Influences of World Events on U.S. 'Neutrality' Opinion," *Public Opinion Quarterly* 4, no. 1 (March 1940): 48–65. See also as referenced in David Kennedy, *Freedom from Fear: The American People in Depression and War* (New York: Oxford University Press, 1999), 398–399.

12. On Nye's anti–big business views and neutral rights orientation in foreign policy, see Wayne Cole, *Senator Gerald Nye and American Foreign Relations* (Minneapolis: University of Minnesota Press, 1962); regarding the crystallizing isolationist political positions of the 1930s, see Manfred Jonas, *Isolationism in America, 1935–1941*, chapter 1, "The Isolationism of the Thirties." On the "calm before the storm" and the "isolationist tornado" of the 1930s, see also Adler, *The Isolationist Impulse*, 218–274.

13. For examples, see Manfred Jonas, Wayne Cole, and Selig Adler, to name a few.

14. On the America First Committee see Wayne Cole, *America First: The Battle against Intervention, 1940–1941* (Madison: University of Wisconsin Press, 1953);

see also Justus Doenecke, "American Isolationism, 1939–1941," *Journal of Libertarian Studies* 6, no. 3 (Summer/Fall 1982): 201–216; and Doenecke, *Storm on the Horizon: The Challenge to American Intervention, 1939–1941* (New York: Rowman & Littlefield, 2003).

15. Elizabeth Borgwardt, *A New Deal for the World: America's Vision for Human Rights* (Cambridge, MA: Harvard University Press, 2005), on the Atlantic charter, see introduction, on the legacy of Wilson, see chapter 1.

16. It is insightful to compare the AFC "battle against intervention" with Balch's battle against her own pacifist inclinations in her book *Beyond Nationalism*.

17. An exemplary brief debate on isolationism from 1944 is Raymond Dennett, "Isolationism Is Dead," *Far Eastern Survey* 13, no. 15 (July 26, 1944): 135–137, while the pro was expressed by Benjamin H. Kizer, "Isolationism Is Not Dead," *Far Eastern Survey* 13, no. 17 (August 23, 1944): 155–156. Postwar progressives often invoked international human rights language to push for domestic social justice rather than engagement abroad, see Hugh H. Smythe, "The N.A.A.C.P. Protest to UN," *Phylon* 8, no. 4 (4th Quarter, 1947): 355–358. In the debates over the UN "neo"/"new" isolationism came to be seen as a threat. See Cabell Phillips, "New Isolationism Endangers 'Marshall Plan,'" *New York Times*, July 20, 1947; Adlai Stevenson, "The Challenge of a New Isolationism," *New York Times*, November 6, 1949; Arthur Schlesinger Jr., "The New Isolationism," *Atlantic Monthly*, May 1952; Paul H. Douglas, "A New Isolationism—Ripples or Tide?" *New York Times*, August 18, 1957. Norman Graebner, *The New Isolationism: A Study in Politics and Foreign Policy since 1950* (New York: Ronald Press, 1956).

18. Robert Taft, speech to Senate, Congressional Record, 81st Cong., 1st sess., July 11, 1949, 9205; for more detail see James T. Patterson, *Mr. Republican: A Biography of Robert A. Taft* (Boston: Houghton Mifflin, 1972), and Russell Kirk and James McClellan, *The Political Principles of Robert A. Taft* (New York: Fleet Press Co., 1967).

19. Justus Doenecke, *Not to the Swift: The Old Isolationists in the Cold War Era* (Lewisburg, PA: Bucknell University Press, 1979), 113–130; on the domestic politics see Julian Zelizer, *Arsenal of Democracy: The Politics of National Security from World War II to the War on Terrorism* (New York: Basic Books, 2009), chapter 4.

20. On "old" isolationist arguments and anti-communism see Doenecke, *Not to the Swift*, 211–230.

21. Adlai Stevenson, "The Challenge of a New Isolationism," *New York Times*, November 6, 1949; Arthur Schlesinger Jr., "The New Isolationism," *Atlantic Monthly* 189, no. 5 (May 1952): 34–38.

22. I paraphrase Selig Adler's splendid expression at the outset of *The Isolationist Impulse*, 9.

23. Walter Lippmann, *Isolation and Alliances: An American Speaks to the British* (New York: Little, Brown and Company, 1952), 8.

24. Ibid., 8.

25. Quote from Robert W. Tucker, "What This Country Needs Is a Touch of New Isolationism," *New York Times*, June 21, 1972. Many of the most potent expressions of "neo-isolationism" appeared in the mid-1960s and gained further traction into the 1970s in lockstep with opposition to the war in Vietnam. For the best representations of such views in the period, as they developed over time, see "The New Isolationism," *Time* magazine, January 8, 1965; Henry F. Graff, "Isolationism Again—With a Difference," *New York Times*, May 16, 1965; Hans J. Morgenthau, "To Intervene or Not to Intervene," *Foreign Affairs*, April 1967, excerpted in James F. Hoge Jr. and Fareed Zakaria, eds., *The American Encounter: The United States and the Making of the Modern World: Essays from 75 Years of "Foreign Affairs"* (New York: Basic Books, 1998), 265–273; "Harris Poll Finds New Isolationism," *New York Times*, February 6, 1970; Hamilton Fish Armstrong, "Isolated America," *Foreign Affairs*, October 1972, excerpted in *The American Encounter*, 329–335.

26. See for example Noam Chomsky, *American Power and the New Mandarins* (New York: Penguin Books, 1969); for insights into Dwight Macdonald's thought see *A Moral Temper: The Letters of Dwight Macdonald* (Chicago: Ivan R. Dee, 2001).

27. Arthur Schlesinger Jr., "Back to the Womb? Isolationism's Renewed Threat," *Foreign Affairs*, July/August 1995, 5, 6, 8.

28. "Isolationism's Return," *New York Times*, October 31, 1999.

29. For an outstanding example see Andrew Bacevich, *The Limits of Power: The End of American Exceptionalism* (New York: Metropolitan Books, 2008).

30. "American Power: Still #1," *Economist*, June 28, 2007; also "The Isolationist Temptation," *Economist*, February 11, 2006.

31. For a modest sample of references that deal with isolationism in foreign policy vis-à-vis Iraq, Afghanistan, the "war on terrorism," international institutions, and free trade in a global context , see Douglas Stone, "Obama's Neo-Isolationism," *American Thinker*, August 11, 2008; Eric Trager, "Barack's Throwback," *New York Post*, June 4, 2008; James Kirchuck, "Barack Obama, Isolationist," *Standpoint Magazine*, July 2008; Andrew Sullivan, "The Isolationist Beast Stirs in America Again," *Sunday Times/TimesOnline*, July 29, 2007; see also Ron Paul's statements summer–fall 2009 on the Obama administration's "protectionist" isolationism and trade policy.

32. Garry Wills, "Entangled Giant," *New York Review of Books*, September 10, 2009.

33. Amy Chua, "Crossroads: Where Is U.S. Foreign Policy Headed?" *New York Times*, October 25, 2009.

34. Pew Research Center for the People and Press, "America's Place in the World," poll undertaken with the Council on Foreign Relations, full report located at http://people-press.org/report/569/americas-place-in-the-world. Released and accessed December 3, 2009.

Strains of Isolationism

1. Arthur Vandenberg, *Private Papers of Senator Vandenberg* (Boston: Houghton Mifflin Co., 1952), 1.

A bibliographic selection of the major primary and secondary works that informed this book is available on the author's faculty website.

ACKNOWLEDGMENTS

Many people at many institutions have helped me to develop this book. In doing research, living all over the country, presenting papers, and receiving insights from scholars near and far, I accumulated intellectual debts far greater than mere words of thanks can repay. Nevertheless, it is my honor and pleasure to thank here in print these many supportive friends, colleagues, and organizations. Apologies in advance to any people or institutions that I might have left out inadvertently.

At the outset I would like to note that I am keenly aware of the impressive historiography relevant to this volume. In the American intellectual, cultural, political, and foreign policy scholarship that touches on the book's themes and arguments, a number of extraordinary scholars have paved the way for my research. I thank John Milton Cooper Jr., Justus Doenecke, Norman Graebner, Manfred Jonas, Walter LaFeber, Ernest May, and William Appleman Williams, along with Alan Dawley, James Kloppenberg, and Daniel Rodgers, to name just a few who cleared the way for this study. I humbly stand on the shoulders of these giants.

In the course of the many years that I have researched, written, and revised this book, I have benefited greatly from extended exchanges with Olivier Zunz, Brian Balogh, Ed Ayers, and James Hunter. In particular, I single out the important personal and professional support of Olivier Zunz and Brian Balogh at the University of Virginia. They have been genuine mentors not only about research and writing, but also about the flexible thinking necessary to conceptualize the past and to construct historical scholarship. I am deeply informed by Olivier's robust model of historical inquiry. I have enjoyed the intellectual life of working closely with Olivier over many years and the rare pleasures of excellent meals and wide-ranging conversations with Olivier and Christine Zunz at their home in Charlottesville.

I also have shared history and family with Brian Balogh while working on a slew of community service and public history projects together, and participating in scores of forums and discussions at the University of Virginia's Miller Center of Public Affairs. His spectacular knowledge of historiography is a special gift. He is a friend and trusted adviser, and I have relied on him time and again. Thank you. Having moved from Virginia, I miss him, Kathy, and their family.

Conversations and courses with Ed Ayers during my time in graduate school were unique in their capacity to inspire, invigorate, and provide insight. Help from Ronald

Dimberg and Chuck McCurdy, early support from Michael Holt, and discussions with Mel Leffler and Gary Gallagher also contributed to building the foundation for my career as a historian. Allan Megill has been a superb sounding board and I thank him for walking the second mile with me, both in my time at Virginia and thereafter. While I was a graduate student I benefited greatly from reading and discussing Latin American history and theory with Brian Owensby, whom I thank for opening up his seminars, home, and office to an Americanist with an abiding interest in Latin America.

At crucial junctures in my research and career I have turned to James Hunter for guidance. An extraordinary leader in intellectual and institutional life, he has been unfailingly supportive of me and my scholarship. The Institute for Advanced Studies in Culture, founded and directed by Hunter, was a lively home for me as I researched and wrote portions of this book. In addition, I have benefited from generous and critical readings of my work by a range of scholars, notably Glenda Gilmore, Michael Kazin, James Kloppenberg, Jacqueline Jones, Alan Lessoff, and Eric Rauchway. I thank them all. In particular, I offer special thanks to Glenda Gilmore. She was a perceptive guide early on as I put this project together, prompting me to explore new angles on progressivism and race as well as on region and political ideas. At various times she has been an employer, a mentor, a recommender, and a friend.

I thank the anonymous readers of this book's manuscript for Harvard University Press as well as those readers who reviewed portions of the scholarship later published in the *Journal of the Gilded Age and Progressive Era*, the *Peace Review*, and the *Long Term View*. The many readers of my work provided thoughtful analyses that have been immeasurably helpful and for which I am deeply appreciative. I also am obliged to those three journals and their editors for encouraging me early in my career and permitting me to use sections of my articles for this book. Portions reworked from chapters 3 and 4 were published as "Rethinking Randolph Bourne's Trans-national America" in the *Journal of the Gilded Age and Progressive Era* (April 2009).

I have been honored to present my work at the annual meetings of the American Historical Association, the Organization of American Historians, the Southern Historical Association, and the Society for Historians of American Foreign Relations. I thank the many commentators, panelists, and audiences at those and other conferences for their perspectives and for pushing my investigations in new directions.

At Penn I have been delighted with the history department's warm responses to my work. I thank the faculty for being so giving with their time and comments. Kathy Peiss has been a superb mentor. Bruce Kuklick welcomed me kindly. Brief discussions with Bruce and Walter McDougall have been energizing. The comments of the faculty involved in the interdisciplinary Race and Empire Working Group, to which I was invited by Amy Kaplan, and the History Department's Annenberg Seminar, magnificently orchestrated by Antonio Feros, yielded useful insights at a late stage in my revisions. I also thank the Penn Humanities Forum, and Peter Conn in particular, for the vigor of intellectual discourse and quality of interdisciplinary critique that helped hone my introduction to this book.

At the University of Virginia I had the enduring pleasure of knowing phenomenal young scholars: Wayne Hsieh, Derek Hoff, Chris Loss, Johann Neem, Kevin Schultz, and David Ciepley, to name just a few. I thank you all for making my work better and for making my time at UVa more fun.

Among the nonhistorians I thank, one stands out: Charles Mathewes. Chuck and I share a fascination with trying to understand patterns of thought and how they have changed over time. When we worked together on *Prophesies of Godlessness*, he continually asked searching questions about my interpretations of the historical development of ideas, on details of American thought, and on the role of ideas in democratic politics.

Claire Potter and Richard Slotkin have been exceptionally supportive since I first approached them with my passion for U.S. history and American studies, and my embryonic interest in going to graduate school. Thank you. One thinker and teacher was pivotal in my earliest development as a historian: Maxine McClintock. I thank her for her inspiration and for her passion for history, which was contagious. Thank you, Doc, for helping to chart my path to becoming a professional historian.

Institutions, too, have been important for my study. To the Corcoran Department of History and the Graduate School of Arts and Sciences at the University of Virginia, I present my heartfelt acknowledgment. They generously funded my graduate studies, supported research trips and conference presentations, and provided an exceedingly dynamic place to investigate America's past.

The research and writing of this book have been underwritten by fellowships and grants. I thank the Center on Religion and Democracy and the Institute for Advanced Studies in Culture, both at the University of Virginia, for supporting my work on this project. I also happily recognize a research associateship on a study of American philanthropy investigated by Olivier Zunz and funded by the Ford, Mott, and Kellogg foundations. The Institute for Advanced Studies in Culture at UVa, the Andrew W. Mellon Foundation, and the University of Pennsylvania supported my postdoctoral work, and I will be forever grateful to them.

As I have traveled coast to coast, archivists and librarians have been invaluable. The Alderman Library staff at UVa secured scores of obscure primary and secondary sources, and somehow were able to procure copies, microfilm, and even originals, of documents from the late nineteenth and early twentieth centuries. I thank Gary Treadway for his efforts on my behalf and the whole Inter-Library Loan department (I know a few of my requests were demanding!). At the University of Pennsylvania, the resources of the Van Pelt Library have been essential; librarian Nick Okrent always has been forthcoming and gone above and beyond the call of duty in assisting me with research and teaching.

Thanks to David Vancil at Indiana State University in Terre Haute. He was crucial to success in my far-ranging forays into Eugene Debs's writings. I also offer my warmest thanks to the Massachusetts Historical Society, where I was in residence as a Fellow and where Carrie Supple and other reference librarians did outstanding work.

Many other institutions were supportive of my research and writing: the Houghton and Widener Libraries at Harvard University, the Swarthmore College Library—

particularly Wendy Chmielewski—and the curators of the Swarthmore College Peace Collection, the Columbia University Special Collections and Butler Library, the Library of Congress and National Archives and Manuscripts Division, the New-York Historical Society, the University of Wisconsin–Madison Archives and the Wisconsin State Historical Society, the University of North Carolina–Chapel Hill Special Collections, and the Sterling, Beinecke, and Divinity School libraries at Yale University.

During the final stages of revisions of this book, Ian Nash, a former student and recent Penn graduate, provided diligent, smart, and cheerfully efficient research assistance. Thank you, Ian. I am indebted to John Paine for all of his editorial work on various stages of this manuscript. I also am grateful to Wendy Strothman and Dan O'Connell for their unstinting support and efforts on my behalf. I look forward to a long and productive relationship with Wendy and her team.

At Harvard University Press Kathleen McDermott championed this book and valued its central insights from our very first conversations. During the revisions to the manuscript, Kathleen did superb work to improve the volume. Other Harvard Press staff members, notably Kathi Drummy, Sophia Khan, and Molly Atlas, also have been friendly, attentive, and expert in handling illustrations, copyediting, marketing, and so much else. I cannot thank you all enough for all of your hard work on this book. In terms of production, I must thank Barbara Goodhouse and the staff at Westchester Book Group for helping with the final push to the finish line on the manuscript.

Three people come last. Yet these are my most important personal acknowledgments and I dedicate this book to them. I thank my mother, Carolyn Nichols; and I thank my father, Rodney Nichols. I am grateful to them for their loving support and for sharing their love of ideas. Both deeply value the written and spoken word, the life of the mind, and history. They have showed steady faith in me and in my scholarship over the many years this project has stretched on. What may be even more incredible than their deep reserves of kindness, their intense loyalty, and their ability to listen to me opine about obscure nuances of debates over America's role in the world is that they still seem interested in the subject of this book! I am honored to count them as friends, as advisers, as editors, and as beloved parents. Thank you both so much.

Finally, Lily Sheehan has been the absolute best reader, editor, thinker, and supporter I could possibly imagine. An exceptional scholar in her own right, Lily's presence has made my life a joy, even during the seemingly endless process of completing the many stages of this book. My study of America's past took shape as we began to share and shape our lives together for the future. Publication arrives as we are partners in life. Thank you, Lily.

My acknowledgments mark not only gratitude but also comradeship. The shared nature of historical inquiry is infrequently noted, but it sustains the spirit of historical search and creates a sense of community. Moreover, I think it is this inherently communal aspect of historical scholarship—only superficially a solitary endeavor—that undergirds our collective project as historians and enhances the power and significance of our results. Or so I hope. As for any shortcomings of this book, they are mine alone.

INDEX

Abbott, Lyman, 83, 140

Abstractions, 72, 75–77, 97, 99, 106, 118, 241

Accommodationist liberals, 137–138, 141

Acquisitions, U.S., 46, 50–52, 53, 54, 61, 62, 111–112. *See also* Annexation; Anti-imperialists/anti-imperialism; Colonialism

Activism. *See also* Antiwar activism; Peace activism; Reform

Adams, Brooks, 24, 28, 74

Adams, Henry, 61

Adams, John, 5

Addams, Jane, 8–9, 16, 48, 70, 76, 80, 97, 104–106, 110, 123, 142, 160, 162, 168, 170, 182, 197, 274–276, 279–281, 283, 287, 289, 297, 311, 320, 326, 342, *fig1*; James and, 106–107; World War I dissent of, 142; cosmopolitanism of Bourne and, 153; Balch personality compared to, 278; Balch-Addams internationalist visions, 284–285; Kellogg-Briand Pact and, 301–302; honors awarded, 316–317

Afghanistan, 63, 341, 342–343

Africa, 6, 101, 265, 284, 316

African Americans, 104–105; Christianization of, 94; anti-imperialists on reform and, 96–100; Philippine people and, 99–100; press and war, 99–100, 142–143; migration North of, 215; World War I deserters as, 221–222; assimilation and education of, 239–240; WILPF women, 290

Agrarianism, 242; anti-, 184; Borah's populist, 232, 327, 331

Agricultural policy, Wilson's, 203

Aguinaldo, Emilio, 87–89

Alexander, High Q., 208

Alliances, 25–26, 60, 139; expansionists on European, 46; U.S. support of, 139, 150; Bourne's wartime, 168, 169–170; farm-labor, 183, 185–191; socialist, 183. *See also* Nonentanglement

America, as associate power, 230

America, as rising world power (1890s–1920s), 22–67; isolationist and internationalist debates critical to definition of, 2; colonialism debates in, 6, 13–14, 20–21, unilateralist isolationism and, 23–24, 50–52, 61; expansionism-isolation tradition reconciliation, 25–31; Monroe Doctrine test and, 32–36; foreign policy partisanship and party politics, 41–44; distant dependencies and expansion in, 48–50; imperialist backlash, 65–67; "ancient soul" of, 69, 71, 90, 110. *See also* "Large policy," Lodge's; Transnational America, Bourne's; United States; *specific topics*

America First Committee (AFC), 334–335

American Association for International Conciliation (AAIC), 140–141, 281

American Expeditionary Force (AEF), 159–160

Americanism, 238, 239, 249, 251, 256–258, 287; in peace and war, 240–245. *See also* Melting pot concept; Nationalism

Americanization, 114, 145–146, 162–163, 248, 264–265

American Patriotic League (APL), 209, 210, 215, 222

American promise, 155–167; conservation of, 155–164

American Union Against Militarism (AUAM), 16, 150, 160, 168